John

WISDEN

*PUBLISHED EVERY
YEAR SINCE 1864*

www.wisden.com

137TH YEAR

WISDEN
CRICKETERS' ALMANACK

2000

THE MILLENNIUM EDITION

EDITED BY MATTHEW ENGEL

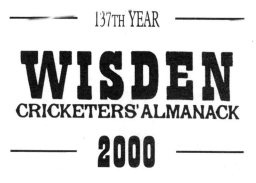

PUBLISHED BY JOHN WISDEN & CO LTD
25 DOWN ROAD, MERROW
GUILDFOR

Cased edition ISBN 0 947766 57 X   £29.99

Soft cover edition ISBN 0 947766 58 8   £29.99

Leatherbound edition ISBN 0 947766 59 6   £225.00

© John Wisden & Co Ltd 2000

Published in 2000 by
JOHN WISDEN & CO LTD
25 Down Road, Merrow, Guildford, Surrey GU1 2PY
Tel: 01483 570358 Fax: 01485 533153
E-mail: wisden@ndirect.co.uk
Website: www.wisden.com

WISDEN CRICKETERS' ALMANACK

Editor: Matthew Engel, Fair Oak, Nr Bacton, Herefordshire HR2 0AT.
Editor, *Wisden* 2001: Graeme Wright, 14 Field End Road, Eastcote, Middlesex HA5 2QL.

Deputy editor: Harriet Monkhouse.
Managing editor: Hugh Chevallier.
Editorial assistant: Matthew Hancock.
Production co-ordinator: Peter Bather.
Chief typesetter: Mike Smith.
Advertisement sales by Colin Ackehurst and by London and Edinburgh plc.
Managing director: Christopher Lane.

Computer typeset by LazerType, Colchester.

Printed and bound in Great Britain by Clays Ltd, St Ives plc.
Distributed by The Penguin Group.
Distributed in Australia by Hardie Grant Books, Melbourne.

PREFACE

This preface is written (as always) in the depths of an English winter and (as nearly always) at a time when the gloom encircling English cricket seems impenetrably dark. It would have been easy for this year's *Wisden* to have turned into an extension of all that: "Whither the County Championship? A 48-page Special Report" or something.

But cricket-lovers know better than most that when it's bitter-cold in England the sun is beating down somewhere else. I hope we have covered the game's traumas dutifully enough. However, it seemed right that this *Wisden* should be, above all, a celebration. It is, after all, the first edition of the 21st century.

Or the last of the 20th. The school of thought that the millennium does not end until December 31, 2000, appears to be better-represented among our readers than anywhere else. I think pedantry on this point presumes there is precise knowledge about the chronology of ancient events in Judea, whereas most Biblical scholars agree that (as an old county scorer used to put it) "Everything's approximate."

So this is *Wisden's* millennium edition, once again the largest ever. It focuses both on the past year, which has produced not merely the World Cup but some of the most astonishing Test matches of all time, and on the 20th century in all its glory. We have chosen our Five Cricketers of the Century, plus Ten Images, 100 Great Matches, and a good deal else besides. The aim is for an Almanack fit to rank alongside the wonderful 1963 edition in readers' affections.

But the bad news takes its toll. This is the eighth edition of *Wisden* I have edited (only three of the 12 other editors in 137 years have lasted longer) and the moment has come when everyone needs a break, including the readership. I hope to return. In the meantime, the editor of *Wisden* 2001 will be my predecessor, Graeme Wright – refreshed, I trust, since he contemplated the game's future rather glumly in the 1992 edition. I am delighted Graeme has agreed to make a comeback.

Since his departure, two stalwart staff members have stayed throughout, and sustained and tolerated my erratic editorship: Harriet Monkhouse, the deputy editor, and Christopher Lane, the managing director. As they sigh with relief, I would like to extend them special thanks for their support and staying power. Both have been crucial to the Almanack's survival and continuing success.

My thanks too to our excellent managing editor, Hugh Chevallier; to Sir Paul Getty and the board and management committee of John Wisden and Co; to Simon Briggs, Lawrence Booth, Matthew Hancock, Gordon Burling, Gordon Vince; Philip Bailey; Andrew Radd and Robert Brooke; to Peter Bather, Mike Smith and everyone at LazerType; and to my colleagues at *Wisden Cricket Monthly* and *The Guardian*. My most profound thanks, again, go to my family: Hilary, Laurie and Victoria. Over the next year I hope to see them more often.

MATTHEW ENGEL

Newton St Margarets, Herefordshire
February 2000

CONTRIBUTORS

Tanya Aldred
Andy Arlidge
Chris Aspin
Philip Bailey
Jack Bannister
Colin Bateman
Peter Bather
Greg Baum
Richard Becht
Marcus Berkmann
Mike Berry
Scyld Berry
Edward Bevan
J. Watson Blair
Lawrence Booth
Simon Briggs
Robert Brooke
Colin Bryden
Don Cameron
Patrick Collins
Mike Coward
Lord Cowdrey
Tony Cozier
Robert Craddock
John Curtis

Debasish Datta
Geoffrey Dean
Peter Deeley
Tim de Lisle
Ralph Dellor
Norman de Mesquita
Mike Dickson
Patrick Eagar
Philip Eden
John Etheridge
Colin Evans
Stephen Fay
David Foot
Nigel Fuller
Pat Gibson
Andrew Gidley
Chris Goddard
Gideon Haigh
David Hallett
David Hardy
Peter S. Hargreaves
Norman Harris
Les Hatton
Murray Hedgecock
Jim Holden

Grenville Holland
Gerald Howat
Peter Johnson
Abid Ali Kazi
Frank Keating
Malcolm Knox
Kate Laven
Alan Lee
David Llewellyn
Nick Lucy
Steven Lynch
John MacKinnon
Alastair McLellan
Vic Marks
Mohandas Menon
R. Mohan
Gerald Mortimer
Stephen Moss
Mark Nicholas
Francis Payne
Gordon Phillips
Qamar Ahmed
Andrew Radd
Mark Ray
Sir Tim Rice

Graham Russell
Dicky Rutnagur
Carol Salmon
Andrew Samson
Derek Scott
Utpal Shuvro
Jasmer Singh
Anirban Sircar
John Stern
E. W. Swanton
Pat Symes
Sa'adi Thawfeeq
Peter Tinniswood
Andrew Tong
Gerry Vaidyasekera
Gordon Vince
Waheed Khan
John Ward
David Warner
Tim Wellock
Simon Wilde
John Woodcock
Ian Wooldridge
Graeme Wright

Photographers: Shaun Botterill, Russell Boyle, Gordon Brooks, Graham Chadwick, Arko Datta, Patrick Eagar, Darren England, Laurence Griffiths, Fayaz Kabli, Ross Kinnaird, Kamal Kishore, Alain Lockyer, Anuruddh Lokuhapuarachchi, Sunil Malhotra, David Marsden, Clive Mason, Graham Morris, Mueen ud din Hameed, Adrian Murrell, Stuart Outterside, Craig Prentis, Adam Pretty, Ben Radford, Bill Smith, Jan Traylen and William West.

Round the World: Alum Bati, Trevor Bayley, John Cribbin, Olivier de Braekeleer, Geoff Edwards, Brian Fell, T. J. Finlayson, Simone Gambino, Bob Gibb, Michael Glasford, Chris Hartley, Syed Azmat Hassan, Simon Hewitt, Mike Holmes, Francis King, John McKillop, Pierre Naudi, Guy Parker, Stanley Perlman, Laurie Pieters, Atul Rai, Venkatesh Ramaswami, Ken Sainsbury, Karu Selvaratnam, Jai Kumar Shah, Mark Stafford, Derek Thursby, Colin Wolfe and Adrian Wykes.

Thanks are accorded to the following for checking the scorecards of county and tourist matches: John Blondel, Keith Booth, Len Chandler, Byron Denning, Jack Foley, Keith Gerrish, Sam Hale, Neil Harris, Brian Hewes, Brian Hunt, Vic Isaacs, David Kendix, Tony Kingston, Reg May, David Norris, Gerry Stickley, Gordon Stringfellow, Stan Tacey, David Wainwright, Tony Weld, Alan West, Roy Wilkinson and Graham York.

The editor also acknowledges with gratitude assistance from the following: David Armstrong, Brian Austin, Dick Brittenden, Andrew Burgess-Tupling, Gerry Byrne, Richard Colbey, Nick Cole, Marion Collin, Brian Croudy, Prakash Dahatonde, Nigel Davies, Christopher Douglas, E. E. Drake, Frank Duckworth, Robert Eastaway, Ron Ellis, Jack Endacott, Ric Finlay, Amanda Finnis, Professor James L. Ford, Christine Forrest, Cris Freddi, Sujoy Ghosh, Ghulam Mustafa Khan, Ray Goble, Col. Malcolm Havergal, Keith Hayhurst, Andrew Hignell, Paul Holden, Robin Isherwood, Mohammad Ali Jafri, Jo King, John Kitchin, Rajesh Kumar, Stephanie Lawrence, Neil Leitch, Edward Liddle, Malcolm Lorimer, David Luxton, Mahendra Mapagunaratne, John May, Pamela Monkhouse, Diana Morris, Don Moyes, Barry Nott, Michael O'Neil, D. B. L. Podmore, S. Pervez Qaiser, John Rogers, Major R. W. K. Ross-Hurst, Christopher Sandford, Richard Streeton, Ken Thomas, Mike Turner, Mike Vimpany, Charlie Wat, Barrie Watkins, Dr David Webb, Wendy Wimbush and Peter Wynne-Thomas.

The production of *Wisden* would not be possible without the support and co-operation of many other cricket officials, writers and lovers of the game. To them all, many thanks.

CONTENTS

Part Five: English Cricket in 1999

Part Six: Overseas Cricket in 1998-99

Part Seven: Administration and Laws

Part Eight: Miscellaneous

The Index of Fillers and Inserts can be found on pages 1599–1600.

PART ONE: THE 20TH CENTURY

FIVE CRICKETERS OF THE CENTURY

SIR DONALD BRADMAN

"HE'S OUT." To the thousands who read them, whether they were interested in cricket or not, the two words blazoned across the London evening newspaper placards could have meant only one thing: somewhere, someone had managed to dismiss Don Bradman, of itself a lifelong claim to fame.

Sir DONALD GEORGE BRADMAN was, without any question, the greatest phenomenon in the history of cricket, indeed in the history of all ball games. To start with, he had a deep and undying love of cricket, as well, of course, as exceptional natural ability. It was always said he could have become a champion at squash or tennis or golf or billiards, had he preferred them to cricket. The fact that, as a boy, he sharpened his reflexes and developed his strokes by hitting a golf ball with a cricket stump as it rebounded off a water tank attests to his eye, fleetness of foot and, even when young, his rare powers of concentration.

Bradman himself was of the opinion that there were other batsmen, contemporaries of his, who had the talent to be just as prolific as he was but lacked the concentration. Stan McCabe, who needed a particular challenge to bring the best out of him, was no doubt one of them. "I wish I could bat like that," Bradman's assessment of McCabe's 232 in the Trent Bridge Test of 1938, must stand with W.G.'s "Give me Arthur [Shrewsbury]!", when asked to name the best batsman he had played with, as the grandest tribute ever paid by one great cricketer to another.

So, with the concentration and the commitment and the calculation and the certainty that were synonymous with Bradman, went a less obvious but no less telling humility. He sought privacy and attracted adulation.

How did anyone ever get him out? The two bowlers to do it most often, if sometimes at horrendous cost, were both spinners – Clarrie Grimmett, who had ten such coups to his credit with leg-breaks and googlies, and Hedley Verity, who also had ten, eight of them for England. Is there anything, I wonder, to be deduced from this? Both, for example, had a flattish trajectory, which may have deterred Bradman from jumping out to drive, something he was always looking to do.

Grimmett was not, in fact, the only wrist-spinner to make the great man seem, at times, almost mortal. Bill O'Reilly was another – Bradman called him the finest and therefore, presumably, the most testing bowler he played against – as were Ian Peebles and Walter Robins; and it was with a googly that Eric Hollies bowled him for a duck in his last Test innings, at The Oval in 1948, when he was within four runs of averaging 100 in Test cricket. Perhaps, very occasionally, he did have trouble reading wrist-spin; but that, after all, is its devious purpose.

By his own unique standards, Bradman was discomfited by Bodyline, the shameless method of attack which Douglas Jardine employed to depose him in Australia in 1932-33. Discomfited, yes – but he still averaged 56.57 in the Test series. If there really is a blemish on his amazing record it is, I suppose, the absence of a significant innings on one of those "sticky dogs" of old, when the ball was hissing and cavorting under a hot sun following heavy rain. This is not to say he couldn't have played one, but that on the big occasion, when the chance arose, he never did.

His dominance on all other occasions was absolute. R. C. Robertson-Glasgow called the Don "that rarest of Nature's creatures, a genius with an eye for business". He could be 250 not out and yet still scampering the first run to third man or long leg with a view to inducing a fielding error. Batsmen of today would be amazed had they seen it, and better cricketers for having done so. It may be apocryphal, but if, to a well-wisher, he did describe his 309 not out on the first day of the Headingley Test of 1930 as "a nice bit of practice for tomorrow", he could easily have meant it.

He knows as well as anyone, though, that with so much more emphasis being placed on containment and so many fewer overs being bowled, his 309 of 70 years ago would be nearer 209 today. Which makes it all the more fortuitous that he played when he did, and, by doing so, had the chance to renew a nation and reinvent a game. His fame, like W.G.'s, will never fade. – JOHN WOODCOCK.

SIR GARFIELD SOBERS

Born to frugality and early tragedy in a one-storey wooden house on July 28, 1936, Garfield Sobers seemed an unlikely candidate to become an icon at anything outside the parish of St Michael in Barbados. He was one of seven children, one of whom died in an accident with a kerosene lamp. Then, when he was five, a telegram arrived saying his father, a merchant seaman, had drowned with all hands when his ship was torpedoed by a U-Boat in the Atlantic. His mother, a strong Christian woman, heroically kept the family intact. Her pension was insulting. At 14, hardly an academic, he was a gopher in a furniture factory.

In February 1975, already celebrated as a face on Barbadian postage stamps, Sir GARFIELD St AUBRUN SOBERS was knighted by the Queen at the Barbados Garrison Racecourse, barely a mile down the road from where he was born in Walcott Avenue. It was not quite the ultimate accolade. In 1988, Sir Donald Bradman conferred on Sobers the title of the greatest all-round cricketer he had ever seen. Bradman's judgment in these matters is regarded as Holy Writ.

None would contest it. Across two decades Sobers brought to a cricket world as diverse as the Caribbean, the Test arena, English county cricket with Nottinghamshire, Sheffield Shield cricket with South Australia, and even North Staffs and South Cheshire League cricket with Norton, plus hundreds of charity games, a vibrancy, nobility of spirit and versatility of accomplishment that transcended all statistics.

These were remarkable enough: 8,032 runs, 235 wickets and 109 catches in 93 Test matches for West Indies. More significantly, he could turn the tide of a Test within an hour, and it was on these occasions that partisanship was suspended. You simply sat back and marvelled at the occasion. From the direst situation his only thought was to attack. He was physically fearless. He never wore a thigh-pad, never mind a helmet, and, from his boyhood days with the Barbados Police team until his retirement, he was only seriously hit twice. Such was his adaptability that he could bowl left-arm very fast, swinging it both ways, left-arm finger-spin and left-arm wrist-spin. By his own recollection, he was no-balled fewer than half a dozen times during his entire career.

Perhaps the most fundamental argument against the modern idiom of cricket is that Sobers was never coached. He mistrusted coaches. He learned the game playing all spare hours in the street with his brothers and friends and then, after the early Barbados sunset, playing on with miniature implements, much to the detriment of the furniture, in his despairing mother's house.

His real apprenticeship started at the age of 12 when, as the kid next door, he started bowling in the nets to members of the fashionable Wanderers Club, earning a 50-cent piece every time he knocked it off the centre stump. It made him more money than he earned at the furniture factory down the road. At 16, he was playing for Barbados against the touring Indians and taking seven wickets. At 17, he played his first Test for West Indies. At 21, against Pakistan in Jamaica, he broke Len Hutton's Test record with 365 not out.

By now the world was acquainted with the kid from Walcott Avenue. He was an instinctive back-foot player, attacking with the lightest of bats (2lb 4oz) which frequently slapped his buttocks on the follow-through. Then he would bowl, crouched for wrist-spin, back arched for finger-spin, lithe as a panther when bowling fast. There was never a moment on a cricket field when you could take your eyes off him.

In 1971-72, Sobers led a World XI to Australia. Watching him in Melbourne, Bradman saw him play a straight drive against Dennis Lillee which smashed into the sightscreen almost before Lillee had straightened up from his follow-through. Sobers scored 254 (after a first-innings duck). Bradman, no soft touch when it came to criticism, rated it the greatest innings he had ever seen on Australian soil.

There was a fourth dimension to Sobers. In fact there were several others, since he was not averse to a drink or a gamble, and had a pretty complicated domestic life. But on the Test cricket field, when he succeeded Frank Worrell as captain, he was the last Corinthian of a dying breed. He walked when he had nicked a catch to slip, without even bothering the umpire. He would not abide sledging. And, once to his own detriment, he would risk the result to entertain a crowd.

In Trinidad in 1967-68, against Colin Cowdrey's England team, he became so frustrated by their go-slow tactics that he declared, setting England 215 to win at 78 an hour. His bowlers sent down 19 overs an hour. England won. I met him that evening in a bar down by the port. He was all alone, and next day the Caribbean press rated him alongside a war criminal. It was never war to him, which was part of his greatness. – IAN WOOLDRIDGE.

SIR JACK HOBBS

Every December 16, a special club meets at The Oval for a lunch party to celebrate the anniversary of the birth of one man. The menu, by tradition, is that man's favourite meal – tomato soup, roast lamb, apple pie – though it is now nearly 40 years since he himself was able to attend. At this lunch, there is just one toast. It is, quite simply, to "The Master". This is the Master's Club. Note the position of the apostrophe. There is only one Master: Jack Hobbs.

The vast majority of the guests now never even saw him play. But the tradition thrives. It is a telling tribute, not simply to Hobbs the cricketer, but to Hobbs the human being.

Jack Hobbs scored more runs than anyone else in the history of first-class cricket: 61,237. He scored more centuries than anyone else, 197. Most astonishingly from a modern perspective, the last 98 came after his 40th birthday. However, his career batting average is 50.65, which does not even put him in *Wisden's* top fifty.

Only 16 of those hundreds were double-hundreds. One says "only" with trepidation, because just four men have surpassed that. But the figure does not remotely compare with Bradman's 37 or Walter Hammond's 36. Hobbs was not primarily interested in scoring runs for their own sake. For much of his career he would go in at the top of a strong Surrey batting order on good Oval pitches. His job was to get the innings started. He would frequently be out for a-hundred-and-few, and was content enough himself with 60 or 70, though he liked to please his friends who took such things more seriously. But there were other times, when wickets had fallen and the ball was flying: "That was the time you had to earn your living," he said.

More than that, it was when he earned his undying reputation, his knighthood and his place as a Cricketer of the Century. He was never as dominant as Bradman; he never wanted to be. But his contemporaries were in awe of his ability to play supremely and at whim, whatever the conditions.

Hobbs set the standard for 20th-century batsmanship. As he attained his peak in the years before the First World War, he switched the emphasis away from gentlemanly Victorian off-side play to a more pragmatic approach, with an emphasis on the businesslike pull, plus an acute judgment of length, footwork and, where necessary, pad play to counter the googly bowlers of his youth. He was not an artist, like some of his predecessors, nor yet a scientist, like some of the moderns; he was perhaps the supreme craftsman.

Sir JOHN BERRY HOBBS was born in 1882 in Cambridge, then a place of strict hierarchies. His father was a net bowler at Fenner's and later a college groundsman. Jack was the oldest of 12 children and the family teetered on the brink of outright poverty. Nothing came easy except the art of batting. When his father began to bowl to him, he said later, "I could sense the spin."

But there was another aspect to his mastery. There seems no record of any unkindness in his make-up. Perhaps the least creditable episode in his life was his failure to condemn Bodyline when, with the help of a ghost writer, he was covering the 1932-33 Australian tour as a journalist. But the

England captain, Douglas Jardine, was his county captain, and there were loyalties that could not be breached. In old age, he was never even heard to utter a word deprecating modern cricketers. He would always say, if the subject were broached, that he made his runs when the lbw law was framed more kindly to the batsman.

This graceful modesty characterised everything in his life. He was deferential but quietly determined, on the field and off it; unlike his contemporary Sydney Barnes, he shied away from confronting authority, not because it was wrong but because his way worked better. He was neat and correct and moral, yet never humourless (indeed, he was a renowned dressing-room joker). He shied away from the limelight without ever resenting it. Into old age, he could be sought out by all-comers at his sports shop in Fleet Street.

More than anyone else, he lifted the status and dignity of the English professional cricketer. If some of that has vanished in an age of chancers and graspers and slackers and hustlers, the enduring glow of Hobbs's life gives us hope that the golden flame could yet be rekindled. – MATTHEW ENGEL.

SHANE WARNE

There are three elements to Shane Warne's greatness – skill, novelty and drama – and all were manifest in the one great delivery that made his name, at Old Trafford in 1993.

The delivery was exceptionally skilful. It began its flight innocently so as to lull Mike Gatting, drifted to leg, pitched in the batsman's blind spot, then rounded on him fiercely and bent back off stump. It was at once pinpoint in its accuracy and prodigious in its spin, qualities that had always been thought to be irreconcilable. Later that summer, John Woodcock would write that it was doubtful if there had ever been a bowler who could aim the ball as precisely and turn it as far as Warne. This is a sentiment that has echoed down the seasons.

The delivery was something different. West Indies and their battery of pace bowlers had set the agenda for 20 years; spin, particularly wrist-spin, had become nearly defunct, but suddenly here it was again in more irresistible form than ever before.

Most of all, the Gatting ball was not just early in his spell, but his very first delivery – in the match, in the series, in Ashes cricket. That gave the ball a sense of theatre, and Warne a name for showmanship, that has grown at each new threshold of his startling career, and at its peak made him nearly mystical. In the modern era, only Ian Botham could compare.

The triumph of SHANE KEITH WARNE is of the rarest kind, of both substance and style together. At his best, he has the ruthlessness of a clinician and the flourish of a performer, and his bowling is simultaneously a technical and dramatic masterpiece. It was not enough for him to take a hat-trick; it had to be in an Ashes Test on the MCG. It was not enough for him to take 300 wickets; the 300th had to be accompanied by lightning and apocalyptic thunderclaps at the climax of another consummate and match-winning performance against South Africa at the SCG.

Thus in 1993 a theme was established for Warne's career: extraordinary performances, extraordinary production values. He was the cricketer of and for his times. Australia's finest moments, but also their worst, their most controversial, most splendid, most dramatic, most sordid, have all revolved around Warne. From the wretchedness of the bookmakers' scandal to the glory of the World Cup triumph, from the agony of a one-wicket defeat in Pakistan in 1994-95 to the ecstasy of a come-from-behind Ashes win in 1997, he was always the central character.

By cold statistics, Warne has not had such a profound influence on Australian cricket in his time as Dennis Lillee in his. Australia were already on the rise when Warne joined the team and, when they had their crowning moment, in the Caribbean in 1994-95, he was good, but not dominant. He takes fewer wickets per match than Lillee at a more profligate average. Moreover, Australia can and do win matches without him. But Warne's impact can never be understated. When he was first picked, cricket was under the tyranny of fast bowling and aching for another dimension. Soon enough, the world came to know that a man could take Test wickets by seduction as well as extortion.

And the legend grew, moment by moment, coup by coup, performance by performance. He made fools of good players, short work of fools. Australia's method was indestructibly simple: bat first, bowl last, win quickly. Always, it was the stage that invigorated him as much as the challenge. For Victoria, who play in empty stadia, he averages more than 40. But for Australia, he has taken more than 350 wickets and, although projections for him to take 600 now seem fanciful, he is already by some margin the most successful spinner in Test history.

At length, intimations came of Warne's mortality. Wear, tear and public glare took a toll. Variously, the fitness of his finger, shoulder, stomach, ethics and manners for Test cricket were called into question, but not until recently, when he returned too hastily from shoulder surgery, was his capability doubted.

Physically, undoubtedly, his powers have declined, but not his hold on opponents. So it was that on the biggest stage of all, at the climax of the World Cup, at a moment when Australia looked impossibly behind, he came again. The only caveat on making him one of the cricketers of the 20th century is that he may yet figure in deliberations for the 21st. – GREG BAUM.

SIR VIVIAN RICHARDS

Fast bowlers, usually West Indian, have caused countless sleepless nights and/or some nasty nightmares over the years, but Vivian Richards was the one *batsman* I've encountered who could intimidate his opponents – even before he had received a ball.

His journey to the crease was a clear declaration of intent. It was usually delayed a fraction to enable the outgoing batsman to disappear from view. Richards did not want any distractions from his entry. He glided slowly to the crease in his own time, checking the light on the way; there was a hint of a swagger, which became more marked as the years rolled by. And there was the cap, the most obvious symbol of his superiority. In a decade when the fast bowler's stock ball whizzed past the batsman's nostrils, Richards was the last hold-out who shunned the helmet. The cap was the reminder that no bowler, however fast, would threaten his domination.

For Richards was never content with mere survival. Bowlers had to be subjugated, to recognise that he was the master. There were occasions when he might sleepily tap back some medium-pacers from a novice who had just graduated from the second team – for Richards was not primarily an avaricious gleaner of runs. But he would always launch a fearsome assault upon anyone with an international reputation. In England, this meant that Derek Underwood and Bob Willis, England's two world-class bowlers of the 1970s, had to be destroyed rather than blunted. Richards's pride demanded nothing less. In fact, it was a compliment to be on the receiving end of an onslaught from him, though the bowlers in question rarely appreciated it at the time.

Richards was capable of technical excellence. His forward defensive stroke, which he sometimes played with exaggerated, ironic care, just to inform the bowler that he could have smashed a boundary but had chosen not to, could be as impenetrable as Boycott's. But he didn't use it that often. More frequently, he ignored the coaching manuals and, relying on the keenest pair of eyes and phenomenal reflexes, just trusted his instincts.

He reckoned that, if he played an on-drive in classical style, the ball would simply speed into the hands of mid-on. So instead he continued to turn the wrists and play the ball squarer – through the gaps. His front foot was planted down the wicket and his bat swung across his pad. All wrong, yet Richards made it seem the safest shot in the world. We tried to copy him and were plumb lbw. Despite the lunge of that front foot, his hook shot was the one that astounded his new county colleagues in 1974. No one hooked his fellow Antiguan Andy Roberts, who was terrorising county batsmen for Hampshire, except Richards. We couldn't work out how he did that.

Sir ISAAC VIVIAN ALEXANDER RICHARDS (he was knighted by the Antiguan Government in 1999) separated himself from his rivals by his ability to perform at his peak on the grand occasion. He adored Lord's in a way that is peculiar to overseas players, who first pictured the ground while listening to crackling radios in the old colonies. He played in eight Lord's finals, five for Somerset and three for West Indies, and failed – by normal standards – only once. Even that day, the inaugural World Cup final against Australia in 1975, his fielding altered the course of the match. "When I was batting at Lord's," he said, "I wanted to make sure that no one else was going to come in. It was my stage."

When it really mattered, he might proceed a little more cautiously at the start of his innings; he would sweat even more profusely, and then he would set about tinkering with fate as only the great players can. Take two innings at another of his favourite spots, the Recreation Ground at St John's, Antigua. West Indies played their first Test there in 1981 – mostly thanks to the prominence Richards himself had given the island. He willed himself to a hundred, edgy by his standards. Five years later, against England again, his mission was to entertain those who had seen him grow up. One hundred came from 56 balls, the swiftest Test century recorded. Sixes disappeared down the high street. Richards could destroy both clinically and ferociously, provided he had a cause to play for. He usually did. – VIC MARKS.

HOW THEY WERE CHOSEN

By MATTHEW ENGEL

The selection of *Wisden's* Five Cricketers of the Year has always been the perquisite of the Almanack's editor of the day. Perhaps he gets a little help from his friends. But the process has always been rather secretive, even mystical, and the choice personal, sometimes downright eccentric.

The system works and, over the years, has come up with more interesting and less predictable names than a committee might have done. But once the decision was taken for *Wisden* to choose Five Cricketers of the 20th Century, it seemed inadequate. There was a precedent. When the centenary Almanack was published in 1963, Sir Neville Cardus was asked to name "Six [not, interestingly, five] Giants of the Wisden Century." He went for Sydney Barnes, Sir Donald Bradman, W. G. Grace, Sir Jack Hobbs, Tom Richardson and Victor Trumper.

But the cricketing 20th century was a much more global one than *Wisden's* first century. No list to cover the years 1900 to 1999 could reasonably include only white males: four Englishman and two Australians. And no one person's perception could properly cover the entire sweep of the game as it is now played. So it seemed right that, for the age of democracy, the choice should be made differently.

To reflect the pattern of cricket history, we established an electorate of 100, from all nine Test-playing countries but weighted to reflect each country's role in international cricket over the century, judged – very roughly – on the number of Tests played. So there were 28 English voters, 20 from Australia and so on down the line to just one from Zimbabwe.

The electorate comprised 97 men and three women (the doyenne of English women's cricket, Netta Rheinberg, the Pakistani journalist Fareshteh Gati and the Barbadian commentator Donna Symmonds). They were a mixture of cricketers, journalists (indeed many count as both), historians or even just expert observers of the game like Sir Carlisle Burton of Barbados. More than half had played Test cricket; all of them had watched copious amounts of it. There were many people whose broad knowledge and expertise would have added further lustre but who could not be squeezed in; to all of them my apologies.

Those who were asked faced a task that was essentially impossible. The major problem with this exercise is, of course, that no one watched all the cricket of the century. Some, however, came close, led by E. W. Swanton, whose first-hand knowledge of all cricket since the First World War was unsurpassable. We were fortunate that he was able to take part before he died in January 2000. We were also privileged to have three electors who played Test matches before the Second World War: Norman Gordon, Alf Gover and Lindsay Weir. It would be wrong, though, to have had this decision entirely filtered through the perhaps rheumy eyes of age. The current generation of cricketers, not all of whom have much feel for the game's history, was represented by the Australian captain Steve Waugh, who does.

THE VOTING

1. **Sir Donald Bradman**	**100**	16. I. T. Botham	9
2. **Sir Garfield Sobers**	**90**	17. H. Larwood	6
3. **Sir Jack Hobbs**	**30**	R. R. Lindwall	6
4. **S. K. Warne**	**27**	S. R. Tendulkar	6
5. **Sir Vivian Richards**	**25**	20. R. Benaud	5
		G. A. Headley	5
		Kapil Dev	5
6. D. K. Lillee	19	23. R. G. Pollock	4
Sir Frank Worrell	19	W. Rhodes	4
8. W. R. Hammond	18	V. T. Trumper	4
9. D. C. S. Compton	14	26. T. G. Evans	3
10. Sir Richard Hadlee	13	M. D. Marshall	3
Imran Khan	13	Wasim Akram	3
12. S. M. Gavaskar	12	29. Sir Alec Bedser	2
13. S. F. Barnes	11	C. V. Grimmett	2
Sir Leonard Hutton	11	F. S. Trueman	2
15. W. J. O'Reilly	10	F. E. Woolley	2

33. C. E. L. Ambrose	1
K. C. Bland	1
A. R. Border	1
B. J. T. Bosanquet	1
B. S. Chandrasekhar	1
I. M. Chappell	1
Lord Constantine	1
A. A. Donald	1
A. P. Freeman	1
L. R. Gibbs	1
M. A. Holding	1
C. H. Lloyd	1
S. J. McCabe	1
B. Mitchell	1
K. S. Ranjitsinhji	1
M. W. Tate	1
Sir Pelham Warner	1

THE ELECTORATE

England (28)
Jonathan Agnew
Trevor Bailey
Alex Bannister
Jack Bannister
Sir Alec Bedser
Scyld Berry
Dickie Bird
Brian Close
Lord Cowdrey
Ted Dexter
Matthew Engel
Alf Gover
Tom Graveney
Frank Keating
Tony Lewis
George Mann
Vic Marks
Christopher Martin-Jenkins
Derek Pringle
Netta Rheinberg
Mike Selvey
E. W. Swanton
Bob Taylor
Fred Trueman
Crawford White
John Woodcock
Ian Wooldridge

Peter Wynne-Thomas

Australia (20)
Greg Baum
Percy Beames
Richie Benaud
Bill Brown
Richard Cashman
Ian Chappell
Mike Coward
Alan Davidson
Gideon Haigh
Murray Hedgcock
John Inverarity
Bill Lawry
Peter McFarline
Jim Maxwell
Arthur Morris
Jack Pollard
Paul Sheahan
Bob Simpson
Cec Starr
Steve Waugh

South Africa (11)
Ali Bacher
Eddie Barlow
Colin Bryden
Russell Endean
Trevor Goddard

Norman Gordon
Michael Owen-Smith
Peter Pollock
Krish Reddy
Peter van der Merwe
John Waite

West Indies (11)
Gerry Alexander
Tony Becca
Sir Carlisle Burton
Tony Cozier
Esmond Kentish
Clive Lloyd
Reds Pereira
Allan Rae
Donna Symmonds
Sir Clyde Walcott
Sir Everton Weekes

India (10)
Mihir Bose
Dilip Doshi
Sunil Gavaskar
Ayaz Memon
R. Mohan
K. N. Prabhu
Raj Singh
Kris Srikkanth

Polly Umrigar
S. Venkataraghavan

New Zealand (8)
Dick Brittenden
Don Cameron
Walter Hadlee
Don Neely
John R. Reid
Bert Sutcliffe
Lindsay Weir
Graeme Wright

Pakistan (8)
Arif Abbasi
Fareshteh Gati
Hanif Mohammad
Intikhab Alam
Javed Burki
Mushtaq Mohammad
Omar Kureishi
Qamar Ahmed

Sri Lanka (3)
Stanley Jayasinghe
Ranjan Madugalle
Gerry Vaidyasekera

Zimbabwe (1)
Dave Houghton

To avoid embarrassment, it was decided not to ask any of the most obvious candidates for the accolade to be voters themselves, even though this meant losing, most obviously, the unparalleled judgment of Sir Donald Bradman. Even so, there was some overlap, and half a dozen of those asked to cast votes also received them. No one voted for himself, though there was one near-miss, which we will come to.

During the World Cup and just afterwards, the 100 voters were asked "to set aside any bias towards your own country and your own era, and name the five whose excellence at cricket during the 20th century you think has made the greatest contribution to the game".

They were told not to put the players in any order of merit, just to name the five, and given only two pieces of advice. One was a general point that has always driven the selection of Cricketers of the Year. "Excellence can be interpreted broadly," we said. "It is legitimate to take into account leadership qualities, personality, character and impact on the public." The second was more specific: "Please don't vote for W. G. Grace. We consider him a Cricketer of the 19th Century." They were given the option of explaining their choices if they wanted; some of the most telling remarks are quoted below.

There were no problems with the guidelines. A few (mostly journalists, of course) had problems with the deadlines. The terror on my part was that there might be a tie for fifth place, forcing us to find some kind of tiebreak mechanism. But it was not a problem: the final verdict was unexpectedly decisive, and there was a substantial gap between fifth and sixth.

It was not, of course, as great as the gap between second and third. The endorsement of Bradman was every bit as ringing as expected (I did wonder if someone, somewhere, might be contrarian, but no one dared). Steve Waugh summed up the consensus as eloquently as anyone: "Sir Donald really speaks for himself." "Only one Don," said Alan Davidson. No one can doubt, no one does doubt, that here was the greatest cricketer of the 20th century.

But Sir Garfield Sobers was not far behind. He was on 90 of the 100 ballot papers and those who left him out must have wrestled with their consciences first. "If there's been a better all-rounder," as Dickie Bird put it, "I'd love to have seen him play." Thus the overwhelming majority of those who voted felt, frustratingly, that they did not really have five votes but three – because the top two were certainties.

Indeed, many felt the same applied to Sir Jack Hobbs. But here there was a complication. Most people wanted to include someone to represent the pinnacle of English batsmanship, and there were alternatives. Walter Hammond's statistics are overwhelming. Then consider "impact on the public"; on that basis it is hard to argue against Denis Compton. And what about Sir Leonard? Many exceptional judges did not vote for Hobbs. John Woodcock chose Compton "for enchantment". Swanton made the case for Frank Woolley: "He scored more runs than anyone bar Hobbs and scored at around 50 an hour, giving more pleasure and for longer than any other English cricketer." And he took 2,000 wickets and 1,000 catches.

Enough, however, opted for Hobbs's quiet but devastating impact on the game. "He challenged the key assumption that no professional could bat as well as a thoroughbred amateur," said Gideon Haigh, editor of *Wisden*

Australia. And he was, as our long-standing Sri Lankan correspondent Gerry Vaidyasekera put it, "a batsman with a charming smile and a kind heart".

Perhaps the biggest surprise is the identity of the player in fourth place. There were people among our hundred frightened to make a judgment on players they had not seen, which might have given present-day players an advantage. With perfect knowledge, maybe there would have been more votes for some of the early players, for Barnes, say, or Victor Trumper. But there are always former players who scorn the moderns, and perhaps an equal number of ballot papers reflected this factor. In any case, the votes for Shane Warne came from across the globe and across the generations. If anyone doubts his status, listen to Crawford White, 88 last year and the former cricket correspondent of the *Daily Express*, who watched both Warne and Bill O'Reilly. "O'Reilly didn't rip the ball through like Warne does," said White. "And I don't think he caught the imagination quite as much as this lad."

The fifth selection turned out to be a third specialist batsman, Viv Richards, "a master of both versions of the game," in the words of the Pakistani journalist Omar Kureishi. No one better epitomises the ferocious nature of cricket in the 1970s and 1980s – except perhaps Dennis Lillee. No specialist fast bowler made the final cut, arguably the one flaw in our selection. But Lillee was by far the nearest, with a particularly high poll from those who saw him at closest quarters – "To me, the greatest fast bowler in history," said Dickie Bird – as well as votes from such luminaries as Sir Everton Weekes and Peter Pollock.

Others preferred Harold Larwood or Ray Lindwall ("the greatest quickie of all in pace, control and movement" – Tom Graveney). In the end, Lillee was not even outright sixth, but finished equal with Sir Frank Worrell, whose position perhaps bore testament to the concept of interpreting excellence broadly, and the near-reverence in which he is still held as a leader whose impact resounded far beyond cricket. "A great man," said Richie Benaud, his most worthy opponent, putting Worrell in his five.

Some voters – quite legitimately – used at least one of their picks to include their personal heroes. Fred Trueman chose Wilfred Rhodes; one South African sheet anchor, Russell Endean, voted for another, Bruce Mitchell; Bob Taylor struck a blow for wicket-keepers, not easy to do in a list of just five, by choosing Godfrey Evans.

Others honoured their contemporaries. Vic Marks had the chance to name two of his Somerset team-mates – Richards and Ian Botham – and took it, though he resisted including Peter Denning, Peter Roebuck and Colin Dredge as well. Peter van der Merwe, the former South African captain, picked out Colin Bland: "He revolutionised the attitude to fielding, and set a standard not yet equalled." Alf Gover named Maurice Tate. Brian Close went for Trueman.

But there were also some touching, and unexpected, tributes across the generations. The great New Zealand batsman John Reid voted for Malcolm Marshall, before Marshall's tragically early death: "He seems to have had everything: pace, movement, accuracy, and the right attitude, which is hard to say of some other fast bowlers." Ian Chappell, that bonny fighter for cricketers' rights, went for Barnes: "Statistically a great bowler and stamped

his character on the game by demanding that he always be paid his worth."
Jonathan Agnew went for A. P. Freeman: "His statistics blow my mind
whenever I read them."

One member of the panel, however, went very close to home indeed.
Walter Hadlee confronted the issue squarely as he cast his ballot for his son,
Sir Richard. "This has to be embarrassing for me," he wrote. "But there's a
job to be done. I will cite the bare facts." And he did: 431 Test wickets and
the transformation of New Zealand's Test record. "I consider him to be
marginally ahead of Dennis Lillee," he concluded. And a dozen other people
– all unrelated – came to a similar conclusion.

Not one of our hundred voted for all the final five. Yet I don't believe
anyone will argue that we have got it terribly wrong. At least one of the five
played in every decade of the century. We have two Australians, two West
Indians and an Englishman, which seems geographically right (though one
suspects an Asian or three will be up there for the 21st century). A total of
49 players received at least one vote. And the difficulty of the choice can
be gauged by the quality of some of those who failed to get on the scoresheet
at all: Keith Miller (who received many mentions in despatches), Barry
Richards, Greg Chappell, Gooch, Laker, Lara, Hanif, C. B. Fry. . .

It was enormous fun just counting the votes; I think almost everyone
enjoyed the exquisite torment of making a decision. If there is a sadness, it
is only that none of us can expect to be around to have a second bite in
2100. But I hope our successors will make the attempt, and (with more video
to guide them) will have just as many great cricketers from whom to choose.

*In choosing and contacting the electorate, I was given special help by Mike
Coward, Colin Bryden, Tony Cozier, R. Mohan, Qamar Ahmed and Don
Cameron. To these, and everyone else who took part, I would like to express
my gratitude.*

FIVE CRICKETERS OF THE CENTURY – COMPETITION RESULTS

A year ago, on page 21 of *Wisden 1999*, readers were invited to predict the selection panel's
choice of the five Cricketers of the Century. The competition attracted well over a thousand entries
and, though many guessed three or four correctly, very few could complete a full set. The first
five all-correct entries drawn at random were: D. C. Dodd from Marshfield, Gloucestershire;
Lorraine Heal, Leigh-on-Sea; Richard James, Norwich; Robert Robinson, Nottingham; and
P. Wildsmith, Hull. Each wins a leather-bound copy of this Almanack.

The ten runners-up, who receive a copy of the limited edition *Wisden Millennium Calendar
of Cricket*, were: Colin Blake from Aylesbury; Peter James, Worthing; Alan King, Brighton;
B. Pickering, Otley; Iorwerth Prothero, Manchester; D. Robinson, Retford; J. Stamard, Sevenoaks;
S. Taylor, Huddersfield; R. J. West, Gainsborough; and A. P. Williams, Sanderstead.

SUMMERS OF THE CENTURY (1)

PHILIP EDEN on the weather

The wettest summers in living memory, according to various *Wisdens*, were 1903, 1946, 1956 and 1958. Indeed, Norman Preston tried to disarm any possible accusation of repetitiousness or amnesia when reviewing the last of those summers by writing, "Cricket in England suffered cruelly from rain in 1958. Two years ago I recorded that 1956 was the wettest season in memory and now I have to state that last summer was even worse."

Curiously, he had forgotten 1954, which he had accurately described at the time as the wettest since 1903, and which was significantly worse than either 1956 or 1958. His predecessor (and father), Hubert Preston, celebrating the successful return of first-class cricket in 1946, added that "all this satisfaction was enjoyed in spite of conditions described as the worst ever experienced". He went on to make a comparison both with 1888, when the then editor Charles Pardon wrote, "June was detestable, July indescribable", and with 1912, when August was "lamentable". (There is much to be said for these laconic dismissals of such meteorological unpleasantnesses, which I might recommend to some of my radio and television colleagues.)

In the 1960s, arguably the poorest decade of the 20th century for weather, a stoic acceptance of gloom and dampness seemed to develop, as season after season passed without a single lengthy spell of sunshine and warmth. In fact, there was no warm and sunny summer from 1960 to 1974 inclusive. The 1965 season produced the coldest-ever Test match day in England (and almost certainly worldwide): the second day of the First Test against New Zealand at Edgbaston saw the mercury standing at eight degrees Centigrade (46 degrees Fahrenheit) at lunchtime, the cold accentuated by a nasty, nagging nor'easterly.

Nevertheless, there was some pithy editorial comment about the "wretched" May of 1967, when 13 of the 51 scheduled Championship matches ending that month reached a conclusion, while five were abandoned without a ball being bowled. And, following the rain-spoilt 1968 Ashes, Jack Fingleton penned a vivid piece entitled "Watery Reflections from Australia". Charles Pardon would, no doubt, have had a choice word for that summer – execrable, perhaps. Helping other England supporters to clear the water from the outfield at The Oval following a final-day lunchtime deluge is a particularly fond memory of mine, for it set the scene for Derek Underwood to bowl England to victory at the last gasp.

On the other side of the coin, there have been some seasons of truly outstanding weather. The summers of 1911, 1976, 1989 and 1995 were in a class of their own. But 1901, 1921, 1933, 1947, 1949, 1959, 1975 and 1990 were almost as fine. The last 11 years have been as consistently good as the 1960s were bad.

In 1947, the extraordinary performances of Denis Compton and Bill Edrich could only have been sustained against a backdrop of blue skies, brilliant sunshine and soaring temperatures, culminating in a record-breaking August. Norman Preston described 1959, a year of prolific run-scoring, as "a wonderful summer with days on end of glorious sunshine and one in deep contrast to the miserable wet days of several preceding years". In 1975, the warmth and sunshine arrived just in time for the beginning of the first World Cup after surely the most inauspicious of starts that June could ever have had: snow showers fell across the entire country on the morning of June 2, and the second day of the Championship match between Derbyshire and Lancashire at Buxton was abandoned because an inch of snow lay on the ground.

England's hottest Test match weather prevailed at Lord's that year, when 34 degrees Centigrade (93 degrees Fahrenheit) was logged on the fourth day, an appropriate temperature for cricket's first-ever streaker. The following summer, 1976, was one of legendary heat and drought, and the West Indians played several matches, including the Leeds Test, in temperatures higher than prevail in Barbados or Jamaica.

Even if we could recall every single summer of the century, the human memory is a fallible instrument, and comparisons are very subjective. Some cricket seasons have been notably dry, but also cool (such as 1961 and 1972); others have been hot, but spoilt by frequent thunderstorms (like 1997). Several damp summers have been preceded by a brilliant May or June (1992), while cold and wet Mays are often forgotten when the rest of the season is fine and warm (1983). The following table shows the best and worst for each meteorological element, averaged from May 1 to August 31.

Warmest (degrees Centigrade)	Sunniest (hours of sunshine)	Most dry days (out of 123)	Driest (millimetres of rain)
23.2 (1976)	1,040 (1989)	96 (1949)	68 (1921)
22.3 (1911)	957 (1976)	92 (1911)	68 (1995)
22.2 (1995)	924 (1959)	92 (1976)	91 (1990)
22.1 (1989)	919 (1911)	90 (1959)	94 (1929)
21.9 (1947)	918 (1949)	90 (1989)	96 (1976)
21.7 (1990)	913 (1901)	90 (1990)	123 (1975)
21.5 (1933)	911 (1929)	90 (1995)	131 (1911)
21.2 (1997)	902 (1995)	88 (1961)	137 (1989)
21.2 (1959)	898 (1933)	87 (1921)	138 (1913)
21.1 (1983)	863 (1906)	87 (1955)	140 (1934)

Coldest (degrees Centigrade)	Gloomiest (hours of sunshine)	Fewest dry days (out of 123)	Wettest (millimetres of rain)
17.7 (1954)	503 (1954)	39 (1912)	449 (1903)
17.7 (1907)	528 (1968)	51 (1902)	434 (1917)
17.8 (1902)	575 (1987)	51 (1902)	365 (1954)
17.9 (1962)	577 (1927)	53 (1907)	366 (1924)
17.9 (1972)	590 (1972)	54 (1927)	358 (1992)
18.0 (1968)	593 (1912)	54 (1945)	357 (1936)
18.1 (1903)	595 (1958)	54 (1965)	356 (1931)
18.1 (1977)	602 (1965)	55 (1985)	340 (1966)
18.2 (1956)	612 (1956)	56 (1931)	331 (1932)
18.2 (1965)	614 (1981)	58 (1987)	330 (1909)

All figures are averages for England and Wales or for Central England.

The summer weather index, introduced in last year's *Wisden* and explained in this volume on pages 1528–1529, enables us to make an objective comparison using meteorological statistics. The index combines rainfall,

[*County Press, Wigan*

A change in the weather: snow (*above*) stops play between Derbyshire and Lancashire at Buxton,
June 2, 1975; streaker (*below*) stops play between England and Australia at Lord's, August 2, 1975.

[*Patrick Eagar*

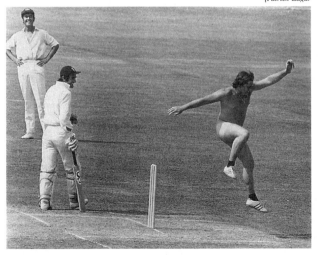

temperature and sunshine, averaged across England and Wales, and the figure obtained ranges from zero for the theoretical worst possible summer to 1,000 for the theoretical best. We can now see where those worst summers in living memory fit (incidentally, Pardon's detestable, indescribable 1888 scores an abysmal 389, although 1879 with 309 was even worse) and whether 1976 truly was the best of the century.

1900	620	1910	510	1920	547	1930	587	1940	690
1901	707	1911	770	1921	737	1931	439	1941	538
1902	454	1912	429	1922	559	1932	495	1942	581
1903	445	1913	621	1923	590	1933	710	1943	620
1904	614	1914	620	1924	450	1934	683	1944	587
1905	594	1915	626	1925	631	1935	650	1945	546
1906	665	1916	535	1926	539	1936	501	1946	503
1907	465	1917	528	1927	452	1937	566	1947	718
1908	602	1918	627	1928	601	1938	533	1948	530
1909	528	1919	636	1929	697	1939	535	1949	741
1950	599	1960	566	1970	637	1980	542	1990	746
1951	568	1961	650	1971	544	1981	541	1991	538
1952	646	1962	549	1972	512	1982	564	1992	556
1953	551	1963	547	1973	615	1983	634	1993	573
1954	394	1964	620	1974	543	1984	602	1994	651
1955	619	1965	460	1975	712	1985	493	1995	777
1956	479	1966	517	1976	812	1986	568	1996	663
1957	584	1967	568	1977	506	1987	444	1997	601
1958	485	1968	431	1978	535	1988	507	1998	565
1959	726	1969	585	1979	546	1989	799	1999	637

(*Note: adjustments have been made to the figures for 1985 and 1989 published in last year's* Wisden. *The war years have been included for the sake of completeness.*)

The best and worst individual cricket seasons were:

Best	Worst
812 (1976)	394 (1954)
799 (1989)	429 (1912)
777 (1995)	431 (1968)
770 (1911)	439 (1931)
746 (1990)	444 (1987)
741 (1949)	445 (1903)
737 (1921)	450 (1924)
726 (1959)	452 (1927)
718 (1947)	454 (1902)
712 (1975)	460 (1965)
710 (1933)	465 (1907)
707 (1901)	479 (1956)

The worst decade was clearly the 1960s, averaging 549, and the best was the 1990s, averaging 631. The individual summer of the century was 1976. You think that summers aren't what they used to be? You're right. They're better.

Philip Eden is weather expert for BBC Radio Five Live, and the Daily *and* Sunday Telegraph. *His review of the weather in 1999 is on pages 1528–1529.*

SUMMERS OF THE CENTURY (2)

FRANK KEATING on the cricket

Here are some of the century's cricket seasons, vintage in their different ways and for various reasons: 1912... 1913... 1934... 1938... 1948... 1953... 1956... 1966... 1977... 1999. As the man said, eternal summer gilds them and they shall not fade. (We talk here of English summers, of course, which are more precious than anyone else's.)

Then, having listed them, in turn we eliminate them, tweezer them out one by one as though it were an ongoing knockout cup or, to be sure, like the first long and long-legged chorus line of an old Miss World competition: "Sorry, darlin', not tonight." If we are talking about summers of the 20th century, not a single one of those evocative years makes the bag for the final shake-up – not one is in the top dozen.

Only 90 years qualify for this lark. Ten were lost to war, and the utter poignancy fore and aft of the guns demands that a romantic at least genuflects to those anguished seasons – 1914, 1919, 1939, 1946 – in a list like this. On September 3, 1914, the German Army were camped scarcely 100 miles from Kilner and Hirst batting out time for a draw against Sussex. But, no, even that end of an era cannot make the shortlist.

Begin almost at the beginning. On the morning of January 1, 1902, in the first-ever heavyweight "clash of the century", the Australian champ Victor Trumper was dismissed by Sydney Barnes's second ball for a duck – to signal precisely the start of a cricketing twelvemonth which was to set the standard for quality, the yardstick for the lore, by which all other years would be measured. By March, Australia had won that series 4–1. By May 29, a serene English summer already in the bud, Joe Darling's same Australians were in Birmingham for a new Test rubber against Archie MacLaren's men. Edgbaston's first Test is still said to have hosted the finest XI ever to be put out by England – MacLaren, Fry, Ranji, Jackson, J. Tyldesley, Lilley, Hirst, Jessop, Braund, Lockwood, Rhodes. The series, a thrilling one, pinned back the ears of the nation – Fleet Street's burgeoning popular press had "discovered" sport, and Gilbert Jessop's ravishing match-winning century in the final Test at The Oval remains hymned and hurrahed to this day. Like Jessop's 104, that 1902 summer was going to take some beating.

In one of those minor classics which were his introductory essays to the *Wisden* anthologies, that quirky Autolycus, Benny Green, lights on the seemingly nondescript year of 1911. Although there were no Test matches in England, there was "All India's rigorous introduction to the implications of western pragmatism in the shape of Sydney Barnes" (14 for 29 in one day for Staffordshire at Stoke); F. R. Foster's 105 at No. 7 for Warwickshire against Yorkshire, followed at once with nine for 118; Leicestershire's C. J. B. Wood carrying his bat (107 and 117) through both innings against Hirst and Rhodes at Bradford; and, crowning glory, Ted Alletson's almightiest of one-offs "down at Hove, where in an hour or two he fashioned a monument to himself that will stand as long as the game is played".

There was a heck of a year in 1926. Arnold Bennett was there for the Test when England regained the Ashes: "Monday, August 16. At 11 a.m., suddenly decide on The Oval. Crowd very quick to take up every point. Every maiden over cheered. Women fainting here and there. Attendants to look after them. Cricket cautious and slow. Great roar when Woodfull's wicket went. Heat of crowd, and great difficulty seeing anything at all." Woodfull had been bowled by Rhodes, recalled aged 48 to play alongside 21-year-old Harold Larwood. They shared 12 wickets.

The most rewarding interview of my life was with Larwood, in 1994 in his 90th year. He was sparrow-tiny and stone-blind, but chuckled merrily at each recall. Rhodes was a one, he said. "He fetched me up, closer and closer till I was all but standing on Ponsford's toes. 'What's going on, boy?' said Ponsford. 'We'll both soon find out, sir,' I said, nervous-like. Two balls later, a fraction more quick and lifting, and I catch Ponsford, easy, for 12, don't I?" At the end of 1926, far away from England, a small-print one-paragraph abridged cricket score from a one-day match appeared in the *Sydney Morning Herald* – "SCG – 1-day Boys' Trial: Probables 302 for nine (A. F. Kippax 58, A. A. Jackson 53 retd). Possibles 237 (D. Mullarkey 64 retd, D. G. Bradman 37 not out)".

Bradman was just 18. It was the first time the country boy had trodden the Sydney Cricket Ground. For 22 years, Bradman was the earth and the sun, ensuring that England's summers of 1930, 1934, 1938 and 1948 remain ripe and bounteous in a wincing but everlasting memory. But it is the first one that makes the shortlist – that was when good, misguided Maurice Tate taunted "You're my bunny, boy!" when he bowled him for eight, first innings at Trent Bridge, to which nerveless young Bradman vengefully answered with 131, 254, 1, 334, 14 and 232.

If his 99.94 remains the most lustrously garlanded four digits in cricket, the three Ws are the most esteemed collection of capitals. The century's very middle summer unquestionably makes the list. It provided a vivid prophecy for almost the whole of the next half-century. The unconsidered West Indians heavily lost the First Test at Manchester against Norman Yardley's unconcerned English. Then, at Lord's, Hutton and Washbrook reached 62 with imperious and threatening calm before visiting captain John Goddard made a double bowling change. At once, the little printing-press in the scorecard office began to clank and chunter:

L. Hutton st Walcott b Valentine 35
C. Washbrook st Walcott b Ramadhin . . 36

Things would never be quite the same for England's cricketers and, though the Ashes were imminently to be regained and then retained, from 1950 on they would be permanently looking over their shoulders.

Frank Worrell's side played a glistening series in 1963, a year which had history's permanent asterisk thrust upon it with the inauguration of the one-day Gillette Cup competition. In 1970, England lost a "Test" series to a thrilling Rest of the World team hastily recruited on the banishment of South Africa. Even if Lord's had to be dragged, kicking and apoplectic, into compliance, the cause and effect – the ban and the substitute series – made for a refreshingly glorious summer.

[*Fox Photos/Hulton Getty*

Summer of summers: at the 1947 Cheltenham Festival, patients at the nearby General Hospital were included too.

The sun was as happily high as the shirtsleeves in 1975, when a compelling first World Cup was held. For the same sort of reasons, but in their different ways, 1981, 1993 and 1994 also irresistibly clamour for inclusion here. It was under the bright suns of those three summers – laud and log them permanently – that Ian Botham, Shane Warne and Brian Lara each leapt with such heart and heartening hooraymanship to their meridian.

So: 1994... 1993... 1981... 1975... 1970... 1963... 1950... 1930... 1926... 1911... 1902... Eleven summers for the century in reverse order. Make 1902, 1926, and 1950 – nicely, exactly 24 years between each – place-money runners-up. Now, roll those drums and clash those cymbals, and stop rabbiting on and open the ruddy envelope...

It just has to be, doesn't it? 1947. The sun shone, the pitches were uncovered, it was the innocent year before the beastly new and faraway government of those nice chaps in green caps espoused apartheid, and from May to September, it seemed, Compton and Edrich were batting.

I was nine in 1947. I went to the Cheltenham Festival for the first time and, at lunch and tea, our hundred or so tennis-ball cricket games criss-crossed the sun-blessed field. Plums cost 3d a pound, and glorious Glorse came second to mighty Middlesex in the Championship. And a bloke called John Arlott was word-painting wondrous stuff on the wireless. In 1947. Summer of the Century. Summer of Summers.

Frank Keating is sports columnist on The Guardian *and author of* Frank Keating's Sporting Century *(Robson Books).*

A CENTURY OF CRICKET WRITING

By STEPHEN MOSS

It is a pity that Samuel Beckett, first-class cricketer and lifelong fan, never wrote about the game. *Waiting for Goddard* would have greatly enhanced cricket's literature. Shame too about James Joyce, a useful bat according to his brother, but whose only contribution was a coded list in *Finnegans Wake* ("…as he studd and stoddard and trutted and trumpered, to see had lordherry's blackham's red bobby abbels…").

Harold Pinter has written well on the game ("Hutton was never dull. His bat was part of his nervous system. His play was sculptured. His forward defensive stroke was a complete statement."). But, for the most part, the truly great writers have not graced cricket.

It is often said that cricket has a great literature, but the contention is arguable. Certainly, it has a large literature; in his essay on cricket writing in the 100th *Wisden*, John Arlott noted that there were some 8,000 titles, far more than on any other game. In the 37 years since then, the ephemera of the late 20th century may well have ensured that the figure has doubled.

Arlott argued that this number emphasised "the unique quality of cricket in stimulating art, imagination and study". He was, rightly, less sanguine about the results. Throughout the 20th century, the arch-enemies of cricket writing have been wistfulness, artifice and silliness. There were too many books, too few real subjects: shelf-fulls of dim biographies, tedious tour books, unrevealing memoirs, jokey reminiscences.

Publishers for too long took their market for granted, assumed that book-buyers' loyalty to the game was limitless, that they would buy any old tosh. In recent years, their opportunistic optimism has proved ill-founded: chickens have come home to roost, golden geese have been laid off, only Dickie Bird (and Ian Botham) seem to have survived the slaughter.

A trawl through the cricket section of the London bookshop, Sportspages, is dispiritingly predictable. When the store opened in 1987, cricket took up more space than any other sport. Football has now leapfrogged into a big lead and the quality of the books that remain is not encouraging. One word sums up the output: nostalgia. With the exception of a few thin how-to guides, the shelves at Sportspages are an invitation to wallow.

Cricket literature is largely characterised by reverence for the game – its traditions, character and ethos – and has been dominated by Englishmen, often using cricket to memorialise a better, truer past. Since the 1830s, cricket writers have hymned a golden age, usually a generation or two before the period in which they were writing.

This genre was in full command a century ago. Take the example of Sydney Goodman, eulogising the village game in an anthology called *The Light Side of Cricket*, published in 1898: "Under the blue sky, field after field stretches far away to the wooded hills, while from hedge and copse alike comes the music of birds and streams, and the mingled fragrance of summer flowers. This primeval grace and rural poetry of the game is in great measure lost in routine-like dullness in vast and crowded amphitheatres surrounded by ugly pavilions, smoky houses and evil-smelling gasometers. Cricket on the village green... is more like the cricket in the days of those heroes of renown, Alfred Mynn and Caesar, Felix and Fuller Pilch, and round it still lingers that halo of glory which many minds love to associate with most things of a far-off and forgotten time."

This end-of-century anthology sums up an approach to cricket that we have never quite shaken off: dewy-eyed reminiscence, limp fiction, condescending reports of cricket at the edge of empire, lamentable poetry, the unfaltering belief that cricket is the best of England. Take the final contribution, by A. N. Other: "What do I think of cricket? Why, I think it's the noblest of sport – bar none – of all those noble sports which have done so much to make Englishmen the fine stalwart fellows they are, and Old England the grand country she is." I keep looking for irony in this piece, and find none, while the report of an Ethiopian cricket match can simply not be quoted, so offensive is it to modern ears. A different age and different sensibilities, of course, yet with an enduring legacy for our attitude to the game.

The 1890s were still in thrall to W.G., who dominates in poetry ("Grace's praise demands my song, / Grace the swift and Grace the strong, / Fairest flower of Cricket's stem / Gloucester's shield and England's gem" – E. B. V. Christian) and prose. The prose writing does show a growing interest in comparing and contextualising players, using that very 1890s weapon: averages. The era was notable for the proliferation of statistical works.

Thus, a hundred years ago, most of the elements of 20th-century cricket writing were in place: the pastoralism; the belief in the rootedness and essential Englishness of the game; the obsession with figures; the co-opting of famous players in commercial enterprises, as with Ranji's *Jubilee Book of Cricket* (1897); and the defence of past against present – this even in the most gilded of golden ages.

The memorable practitioners did not emerge until the 1920s, yet they were refining the themes of their less illustrious predecessors, rather than attempting to rewrite the script. The orthodoxy established in 1900 was later given literary form by a generation which saw the years before the First World War as Arcadia: they had a lyrical, elegiac view of a game inseparable from the fields and villages of England. That was its strength – and its great limitation.

There is a contradiction at the heart of cricket: it is a game with great continuity, but also a sense of closure; it is both immanent and evanescent, preoccupied at once with changelessness and decay. Take Sir Neville Cardus. In *Cricket All the Year*, he wrote: "Cricket has no past and no present. The seasons mingle in one another as with no other game." Yet in *Cricket*, he bids farewell to a season with such regret that you can see the sinking sun, feel the chill of the approaching autumn: "One late August afternoon, I said goodbye to a cricket season on a field which lay silent in the evening sunshine; the match, the last of the year, was over and the players gone. I stayed for a while in the falling light and saw birds run over the grass as the mists began to spread. That day we had watched Woolley in all his glory, batting his way through a hundred felicitous runs... It was all over and gone now, as I stood on the little field alone in the glow of the declining day."

All this romanticism is easily parodied, as Peter Sellers and Peter Munro Smith demonstrated in *The Boundary Book*: "Broiling afternoon... deck-chairs under the spreading... the muted coo of pigeons in the immemorial... cucumber sandwiches... distant tinkle of ice in lemonade jug... satisfying clunk of pad against willow... warp and woof of very fabric... shadow of church spire imperceptibly... white figures moving like ghosts in ancient... where else but in England would you..."

The – for want of a better phrase – tweedy English view has dominated the literary representation of cricket in the past: romantic, lyrical, infused with a sense of love and loss. It has produced works of passion, elegance and beauty, yet at the beginning of a new century the tradition appears played out. The convoluted, self-conscious style of the Cardus school is unwieldy for modern readers; we want our prose in black and white, not purple. Its anglocentricity is absurd for a game where the balance of power now lies on the Indian subcontinent and in Australia. The commemoration of the past is dangerous for a sport which must quickly find a role for the future. Cricket writing, like cricket as a whole, must remake itself.

In doing so, the model should perhaps not be the elegance and erudition of Cardus or Alan Ross, but the astringency of R. C. Robertson-Glasgow, the cultural breadth of C. L. R. James, the honesty and simplicity of style of Arlott, the perceptive qualities of David Foot, the coolness of Mike Brearley, the bloody-mindedness of Simon Hughes. Wit, vision, a close reading of the game, a sense of its languor and lunacies, rather than unremitting reverence, should henceforth dictate the play, dominate the field.

Michael Davie and Simon Davie's excellent anthology, *The Faber Book of Cricket*, did unearth one piece of cricket prose by an unquestionably great writer, Evelyn Waugh, though he was only 20 when he wrote it It was published in the Oxford student magazine *Cherwell* and recounts a disastrous day when his cricket-mad brother Alec drafted him into a college side to play a village team in Hertfordshire. It is everything that the traditional, lyrical view of village cricket is not. "When I returned home, I reasoned thus with myself," wrote Waugh. "Today I have wearied myself utterly; I have seen nothing and no one of any interest; I have suffered discomfort of every sense and in every limb; I have suffered acute pain in my great toe; I have walked several miles; I have stood about for several hours; I have drunken several pints of indifferently good beer; I have spent nearly two pounds... But my brother maintained that it had been a great day. Village cricket, he said, was always like that."

The rosy-eyed romantics should declare and let the revisionists in to bat. Subvert the stereotypes of cricketing parsons and public schools, hymn the joys of global cricket, let writing play its part in re-energising the game for a new age, a generation less devoted to a dreamy past. The pen may yet prove mightier than the sward.

Stephen Moss is a writer on The Guardian. *He was the paper's literary editor from 1995 to 1998.*

FIVE CRICKETERS OF THE CENTURY

[*Fox Photos/Hulton Getty*

SIR DONALD BRADMAN

FIVE CRICKETERS OF THE CENTURY

[*Both Patrick Eagar*

SIR GARRY SOBERS

FIVE CRICKETERS OF THE CENTURY

[*PA News*

SIR JACK HOBBS

FIVE CRICKETERS OF THE CENTURY

[*Patrick Eagar*

SHANE WARNE

[*Patrick Eagar*

SIR VIVIAN RICHARDS

THE RUNNERS-UP

[*Patrick Eagar*

Dennis Lillee

[*Hulton Getty*

Sir Frank Worrell

[*Central Press/Hulton Getty*

Walter Hammond

[*Central Press/Hulton Getty*

Denis Compton

[*Patrick Eagar*

Sir Richard Hadlee

[*Patrick Eagar*

Imran Khan

IMAGES OF THE CENTURY: 1900s

[*The George Beldam Collection*

London, an Edwardian summer's day. George Beldam, cricket's photographic pioneer, captures the essence of Victor
Trumper in a picture that has become an Australian icon.

IMAGES OF THE CENTURY: 1910s

[PA News]

Lord's, July 11, 1919. In that relieved yet forlorn summer, an anonymous agency photographer saw King George V being introduced to the captains of Eton and Harrow in their first post-war fixture. The King is with the President of MCC, H. W. Forster (later Lord Forster, Governor-General of Australia), and the team captains, W. A. R. Collins (later Sir William Collins the publisher) of Harrow and C. H. "Clem" Gibson of Eton, who is hidden by Collins. Everything has changed since then except the background.

[*Herbert Fishwick, Sydney Morning Herald*

Sydney, November 9 or 10, 1928. Using one of the new telephoto lenses, Fishwick ensures that future generations can glimpse the majesty of Walter Hammond's batting. The wicket-keeper is Bert Oldfield.

IMAGES OF THE CENTURY: 1930s

[*Central Press/Hulton Getty*]

Brisbane, February 10, 1933. The photographer is unknown. But the picture has become famous: perhaps the most graphic of all illustrations of the menace of Bodyline. Harold Larwood bowling to Bill Woodfull.

IMAGES OF THE CENTURY: 1940s

[*Central Press/Hulton Getty*]

The Oval, August 14, 1948. An unknown Central Press photographer was there for the bathetic end to Don Bradman's Test career: he faced two balls from Eric Hollies, then "the wistful backward glance, the crucial broken wicket".

IMAGES OF THE CENTURY: 1950s

[*Central Press/Hulton Getty*]

The Oval, August 19, 1953. Yet another forgotten hero from Central Press helped ensure that this moment would be remembered: Denis Compton and Bill Edrich come off the field in triumph as England regain the Ashes in Coronation Year.

IMAGES OF THE CENTURY: 1960s

[*Ron Lovitt*, The Age

Brisbane, December 14, 1960. Most of the photographers had already drifted away from Australia v West Indies. Lovitt was left behind with his colleague Harry Martin when the game suddenly turned nerve-tingling. They agreed that Martin should concentrate on the stroke, and Lovitt on whatever happened next. And he had the luck and skill to get the moment when Test cricket produced its first tie.

[*Patrick Eagar*

Lord's, June 1, 1975. The power and glory of fast bowling embodied by Jeff Thomson in his prime.

[*Graham Morris*

Faisalabad, December 8, 1987. In football or baseball, such a moment would hardly be worth photographing. In cricket, it produced a shot seen around the world. England captain Mike Gatting and Pakistani umpire Shakoor Rana square up to each other.

[*Adrian Murrell, Allsport*

Edgbaston, August 18, 1998: Robert Croft caught by Jonty Rhodes. Jonty Rhodes caught by one of modern cricket's most skilful photographers.

IMAGES OF THE CENTURY

By PATRICK EAGAR

By happy accident, the dawn of the 20th century coincided almost exactly with the beginnings of cricket photography as a serious proposition. Until about 1900, photographers were still limited by the technology to the inert subjects of the Victorian age. But things were changing fast.

It had suddenly become possible to freeze a fast-moving subject. And an inquisitive young-man-about-London called George Beldam – who was an amateur all-rounder for Middlesex and a scratch golfer as well as a photographic pioneer – began to experiment with the cricketing possibilities.

Beldam was fascinated by the new highly sensitive plates available to him, and revelled in the use of fast shutter speeds that could capture sportsmen in action. In 1905, he published, with C. B. Fry, *Great Batsmen: Their Methods at a Glance*. Beldam still did not have equipment that was of much use from the boundary edge; everything would probably have been done before play (which is why so many old photographs were taken on the Lord's Nursery). During the project he became so frustrated at the inaccuracy of the net bowlers that he took to bowling himself, firing the camera by use of a long shutter release held in his left hand.

The second major technical breakthrough of the century came after the First World War. One of the spin-offs of the conflict was the development of telephoto lenses, which had been widely used for photo-reconnaissance from aeroplanes and airships. At last, it was feasible to show a match in progress.

But for the next 50 years there was remarkably little change. As late as 1970, some photographers were using cameras their forefathers might have recognised, often very beautiful mahogany and brass contraptions – but dreadful things to lug up staircases. It was in the next decade that high-quality long lenses and motor-driven cameras came into general usage, and Fleet Street's cricket photographers were able to move from plates to 35mm film.

There was another difficulty that was not resolved until 1972. Until that time, English Test grounds were closed shops. One photographic agency, Sport and General, had the contracts at Lord's and Headingley; another, Central Press, did the other four venues. In the case of Lord's and The Oval, no other photographer was allowed in, even for minor matches. The *quid pro quo* for Sport and General – who paid a remarkably small fee – was that they had to be represented at every Lord's game, even Cheltenham v Haileybury. This system clearly became untenable and, these days, seems unimaginable. At the 1999 World Cup final, there were probably 80 professional photographers at Lord's, perched in every nook and cranny.

The ten photographs I have chosen as the Images of the Century reflect all these developments. There is one representing each of the ten decades, which is obviously not quite the same as picking the best ten of the century. Some decades are richer in content than others, and there are many runners-up from the great decades that might challenge some of those chosen. None

the less, I hope they are all, in their way, great pictures. The first comes
from Beldam: much of his work would qualify, but I have picked the famous
shot of Victor Trumper leaping out to drive, the image now used on the
green cover of *Wisden Australia*.

The second decade of the century included the First World War and there
is little to find in the archives after 1914. I have chosen a moment of social
history – George V meeting the captains of Eton and Harrow at Lord's in
1919. A final glimpse of an age that had already all but disappeared.

Herbert Fishwick of the Sydney *Mail* used one of the new telephoto lenses
in Australia in the 1920s. Probably his best-known photograph of that era
is of Walter Hammond cover-driving during his 225 for MCC against New
South Wales at Sydney in November 1928. One of the saddest aspects of
this famous shot is that no negative appears to exist and thus its reproduction
suffers. The original negative would have been on a fragile glass plate, and
it would have taken only a moment's carelessness in the dark room to lose
it for ever.

For the 1930s, I have chosen the sight of six short legs set to Larwood's
bowling in the Brisbane Test of 1932-33. And would "Bradman b Hollies 0"
be the most famous scoreline of the century? This photographic record of
that moment, at The Oval 1948, is almost as famous: the slightly bent knee,
the wistful backward glance, the crucial broken wicket.

Also at The Oval, and my choice from the 1950s, is the magnificent picture
of Compton and Edrich storming through the crowd following the regaining
of the Ashes in 1953. If the movie footage of Compton's winning boundary
lingers in the memory, this still image wonderfully sums up the euphoria.
In the same decade, mention would have to be made of Jim Laker's 19
wickets at Old Trafford in 1956, but somehow none of the pictures taken
conveys the majesty of the achievement itself.

In those more reticent days, the names of the photographers themselves
were often unrecorded. From the 1960s, we can give credit where it is due.
One of the most unusual Test match pictures was by Dennis Oulds of Central
Press at the 1968 Ashes Test at The Oval, showing all 11 England fielders
as they surrounded the last Australian batsman. However, Ron Lovitt's
superbly timed shot of Meckiff being run out to tie the Test at Brisbane in
1960-61 just gets my vote.

Technical advances in film, cameras and lenses made the job a lot easier
from the 1970s onwards. I was lucky enough to be able to take advantage
of these changes and, at the editor's insistence, have included an example
of my own work: Jeff Thomson in full cry at Lord's in 1975.

For the 1980s, I have chosen an icon of the modern game. Graham Morris
will have to forgive me: he has taken many better cricket photographs, but
this will probably remain his most famous. Although there were other
photographers present, they had already packed up their cameras in the failing
light towards the end of a long and tedious day in Faisalabad in December
1987.

I had two possibles on the shortlist for the final decade and, coincidentally,
both were of Jonty Rhodes fielding, highlighting one of the most fascinating
aspects of the modern game. One, taken during the 1992 World Cup by the

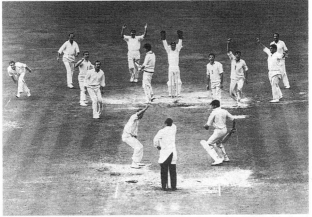

[*Dennis Oulds, Central Press/Hulton Getty*]

England get there! Unfortunately, the picture was squeezed out of our top ten: victory over Australia at The Oval, 1968.

Indian photographer V. V. Krishnan, is simply stunning: Jonty running out Inzamam in South Africa's match against Pakistan at Brisbane. Unfortunately, *The Hindu*, the newspaper which owns the copyright, has exceptionally strict rules regarding the publication of its work elsewhere; so I can only commend this photo to anyone who is lucky enough to have the relevant back issue of *The Hindu*. The alternative is the wonderful photo of Rhodes catching, taken by Adrian Murrell.

This was the only one of the ten shot in colour, and certainly the only one in which the player was wearing coloured clothes. It was published in its full glory in *Wisden* 1999; this time it is black-and-white, reflecting the stark brilliance of the old ways.

Since Fleet Street papers were slow to switch to colour, most pictures were in monochrome until the mid-1990s. In the 21st century, black-and-white will be an extreme rarity. There has been another dramatic development, within the past 12 months: the arrival of digital cameras, which do away even with the need for film, is transforming our trade once again.

Choosing these few pictures to represent the century has been a tough job; and I feel guilty that I have been obliged to leave out the work of people as gifted as Ken Kelly and Hugh Routledge, as well as the talented younger generation who have made such an impact over the past few years. But, all being well, whoever makes this choice in 2100 will have an even tougher time.

Patrick Eagar is chief photographer of Wisden. *He has been photographing cricket around the world since 1965.*

A HUNDRED MATCHES OF THE CENTURY

Selected by STEVEN LYNCH

No list of this kind can possibly be definitive, and the one that follows is as subjective, biased and open to argument as anyone else's. It is based on the fantasy that every cricket match reported in *Wisden* might somehow be available on some kind of celestial videotape; if so, these are the hundred that might be the most fascinating to borrow from St Peter's library.

Record-breaking matches have not been chosen for their own sake, and some of the most famous occasions in cricket have been excluded. Many agonising decisions had to be taken, and some of those games that have made the final list might not be worth watching all the way through; we assume that the video machine will have a fast-forward facility.

But this selection offers a range of the best that cricket has to offer: great batting, great bowling, great drama, great excitement, great achievements... A handful of the games represented nothing more than county cricket at its most beguiling and idyllic. Others showed cricket at its most thrilling and intense. Every one was undeniably very special.

	Year		*Venue*	*See* Wisden
1.	1900	Gentlemen (297 and 339) lost to Players (136 and 502-8) by two wickets.............	Lord's	1901 *p. 343*

The professionals won after being set 501.

2.	1901	Somerset (87 and 630) beat Yorkshire (325 and 113) by 279 runs	Leeds	1902 *p. 17*

"Sensational" – Wisden. Yorkshire lost in 1901 and 1902 to lowly Somerset but to no other county.

3.	1902	Australia (299 and 86) beat England (262 and 120) by three runs	Manchester	1903 *p. 275*

Fred Tate's match – he dropped a vital catch and was last out in his only Test.

4.	1902	Australia (324 and 121) lost to England (183 and 263-9) by one wicket	The Oval	1903 *p. 282*

The next Test – 104 in 75 minutes by Jessop, then Hirst and Rhodes supposedly "got 'em in singles".

5.	1903	Somerset (253 and 371) lost to Middlesex (312 and 316-8) by two wickets...........	Taunton	1904 *p. 163*

Set 313 in 3½ hours, Middlesex got home with 15 minutes to spare.

6.	1904	Essex (597 and 97) lost to Derbyshire (548 and 149-1) by nine wickets	Chesterfield	1905 *p. 168*

Percy Perrin made 343 not out and finished on the losing side.

7.	1907	Middlesex (286 and 213) beat Somerset (236 and 97) by 166 runs	Lord's	1908 *p. 134*

Albert Trott took two hat-tricks (one a four-in-four) in his benefit match.

8.	1907-08	Australia (266 and 397) lost to England (382 and 282-9) by one wicket	Melbourne	1909 *p. 503*

A wild last-ball throw gave England victory and prevented the first Test tie.

9.	1907-08	South Australia (349 and 519) beat New South Wales (276 and 572) by 20 runs...............	Sydney	1909 *p. 522*

New South Wales were set 593.

10.	1908-09	Western Province (126 and 232) beat Transvaal (170 and 182) by six runs................	Cape Town	1910 *p. 504*

Fred Le Roux, batting one-handed, just failed to secure Transvaal's fifth successive Currie Cup.

	Year		*Venue*	*See* Wisden

11. 1909-10   South Africa (208 and 345) beat England
        (310 and 224) by 19 runs. . . . .   Johannesburg   1911 *p. 493*
Twenty-eight wickets fell to leg-spin, googlies and lobs.

12. 1910   Harrow (232 and 45) lost to Eton
        (67 and 219) by nine runs . . . .   Lord's   1911 *p. 299*
"Fowler's match": he hit 64 when Eton, following on, were 169-9 – then took 8-23.

13. 1910   Nottinghamshire (376 and 185) lost to Lancashire
        (162 and 403-8) by two wickets . . . .   Manchester   1911 *p. 74*
The first score of 400 to win a Championship match – Lancashire did it again six weeks later.

14. 1910-11   South Africa (482 and 360) beat Australia
        (465 and 339) by 38 runs. . . . .   Adelaide   1912 *p. 514*
South Africa beat Australia for the first time, despite 214 not out from Victor Trumper.

15. 1911   Nottinghamshire (238 and 412) drew with Sussex
        (414 and 213-8) . . . .   Hove   1912 *p. 225*
"Alletson's innings" for Nottinghamshire: 189 in 90 minutes batting No. 9.

16. 1919   Somerset (243 and 103) tied with Sussex
        (242 and 104) . . . .   Taunton   1920 *p. 103*
Declared a tie when Sussex's sickly last man, H. J. Heygate, took too long getting to the crease.

17. 1920   Middlesex (268 and 316-7 dec.) beat Surrey
        (341-9 dec. and 188) by 55 runs . . . .   Lord's   1921 *p. 50*
A crucial Championship match ("never to be forgotten" – Wisden), watched by huge crowds.

18. 1921   Surrey (269 and 184) lost to Middlesex
        (132 and 322-4) by six wickets . . . .   Lord's   1922 *p. 104*
Another last-match Championship decider.

19. 1921   An England XI (43 and 326) beat Australians
        (174 and 167) by 28 runs. . . . .   Eastbourne   1922 *p. 47*
Archie MacLaren promised his amateurs could beat the all-conquering Aussies – and they did.

20. 1922   Warwickshire (223 and 158) lost to Hampshire
        (15 and 521) by 155 runs. . . . .   Birmingham   1923 *p. 271*
Hampshire were 186-6 following on – but walked it. Frank Keating's County Match of the Century.

21. 1925   Somerset (167 and 374) lost to Surrey
        (359 and 183-0) by ten wickets. . . . .   Taunton   1926 *p. 351*
Jack Hobbs equalled W.G.'s record 126 hundreds in first innings – and passed it in the second.

22. 1926   Lancashire (336 and 243-5 dec.) beat Kent
        (154 and 392) by 33 runs. . . . .   Dover   1927 *p. 156*
"Fascinating... and everything done in a beautiful cricket field" – Cardus.

23. 1927-28   New South Wales (519 and 150) lost to South
        Australia (481 and 189-9) by one wicket . . . . .   Adelaide   1929 *p. 670*
Don Bradman made 118 on his first-class debut, but finished on the losing side.

24. 1928-29   South Australia (185 and 183) lost to Queensland
        (188 and 181-9) by one wicket . . . .   Brisbane   1930 *p. 713*
Clarrie Grimmett took a hat-trick, dropped a catch, and gave away the winning overthrow.

	Year		Venue	See Wisden

25. 1930 England (425 and 375) lost to Australia
(729-6 dec. and 72-3) by seven wickets . . . . . . Lord's 1931 *p. 28*
Bradman regarded his 254 as his greatest innings.

26. 1930 Australia (566) drew with England (391 and 95-3). Leeds 1931 *p. 33*
Bradman scored 334, including 309 in a day.

27. 1932-33 England (341 and 412) beat Australia
(222 and 193) by 338 runs . . . . Adelaide 1934 *p. 652*
"A disgrace to cricket" – Wisden, *but the fiercest match of the fiercest-ever series.*

28. 1934 England (440) beat Australia (284 and 118)
by an innings and 38 runs . . . . Lord's 1935 *p. 28*
England's only Ashes win at Lord's in the 20th century.

29. 1934-35 West Indies (102 and 51-6 dec.) lost to England
(81-7 dec. and 75-6) by four wickets . . . . Bridgetown 1936 *p. 621*
A thrilling match on a spiteful, rain-affected pitch.

30. 1935 Somerset (337) beat Essex (141 and 147)
by an innings and 49 runs . . . . Frome 1936 *p. 379*
Harold Gimblett made 123 in 80 minutes: the most remarkable debut of all.

31. 1937-38 Western Province (474 and 120-2) beat
Eastern Province (221 and 369) by eight wickets Cape Town 1939 *p. 816†*
Western Province needed 26 with one (eight-ball) over left. Pieter van der Bijl hit 446644.

32. 1938 England (658-8 dec.) drew with Australia
(411 and 427-6 dec.) . . . . Nottingham 1939 *p. 218*
Stan McCabe's 232: "the greatest innings ever played" – Sir Donald Bradman.

33. 1939 Derbyshire (193 and 148) beat Gloucestershire
(81 and 259) by one run . . . . Cheltenham 1940 *p. 317*
Chasing 261, Gloucestershire were 246-5.

34. 1944-45 Bombay (462 and 764) beat Holkar (360 and 492)
by 374 runs . . . . Bombay 1946 *p. 242§*
Denis Compton (in India due to the war) scored 249 not out as Holkar valiantly chased 867.

35. 1945 The Dominions (307 and 336) beat England
(287 and 311) by 45 runs . . . . Lord's 1946 *p. 151*
Joyous end-of-war run-feast. "The perfect game." – Denzil Batchelor.

36. 1945-46 Barbados (246 and 619-3 dec.) drew with Trinidad
(194 and 576-8) . . . . Port-of-Spain 1947 *p. 632†*
Walcott 314, Worrell 255, Gomez 213, all not out. "Merciless hitting" – Wisden.

37. 1947 England (554-8 dec. and 26-0) beat South Africa
(327 and 252) by ten wickets . . . . Lord's 1948 *p. 206*
Compton and Bill Edrich put on 370: the apogee of 1940s cricket.

38. 1947 Middlesex (180 and 141) beat Gloucestershire
(153 and 100) by 68 runs . . . . Cheltenham 1948 *p. 325*
Tom Goddard took 15 wickets, but still Gloucestershire could not be champions.

	Year		Venue	*See* Wisden

39. 1948   Australians (721) beat Essex (83 and 187) by an
innings and 451 runs . . . . Southend 1949 *p. 221*
The Australians scored 721 in a day (Bradman 187), and hardly seemed to hurry.

40. 1948   England (496 and 365-8 dec.) lost to Australia
(458 and 404-3) by seven wickets . . . . Leeds 1949 *p. 244*
Bradman's "Invincibles" made light of a final-day target of 404.

41. 1948-49 South Africa (161 and 219) lost to England
(253 and 128-8) by two wickets . . . . Durban 1950 *p. 773*
England won with a last-ball leg-bye.

42. 1950   West Indies (326 and 425-6 dec.) beat England
(151 and 274) by 326 runs . . . . Lord's 1951 *p. 231*
The Calypso Test: Caribbean cricket came of age.

43. 1950   Gentlemen (325 and 235-4 dec.) drew with Players
(308-9 dec. and 242-9) . . . . Lord's 1951 *p. 276*
Freddie Brown scored 122 out of 131 in 110 minutes – and was promptly made England captain.

44. 1951-52 West Indies (272 and 203) lost to Australia
(216 and 260-9) by one wicket . . . . Melbourne 1953 *p. 829*
Last pair Doug Ring and Bill Johnston added 38 for an unlikely win.

45. 1953   Warwickshire (45 and 52) lost to Surrey
(146) by an innings and 49 runs . . . . The Oval 1954 *p. 541*
All over in a day: Surrey on the march to the second of seven successive titles.

46. 1955   Surrey (268 and 75) lost to Yorkshire
(166 and 178-4) by six wickets . . . . Leeds 1956 *p. 640*
"The atmosphere resembled that of a Test match" – Wisden. Yorkshire won with 11 minutes left.

47. 1956   England (459) beat Australia (84 and 205)
by an innings and 170 runs . . . . Manchester 1957 *p. 259*
Laker's Test.

48. 1956-57 Victoria (244 and 197) tied with New South Wales
(281 and 160) . . . . St Kilda 1958 *p. 875*
A Christmas Shield classic; heroic batting from Ian Craig (sick) and Jimmy Burke (broken finger).

49. 1959   Sussex (210 and 311) lost to Yorkshire
(307 and 218-5) by five wickets . . . . Hove 1960 *p. 591*
Yorkshire clinched the Championship by reaching target of 215 in 105 minutes with seven to spare.

50. 1960   Yorkshire (154 and 149) lost to Lancashire
(226 and 81-8) by two wickets . . . . Manchester 1961 *p. 459*
An edged four off the last ball gave Lancashire a famous Roses win.

51. 1960-61 West Indies (453 and 284) tied with Australia
(505 and 232) . . . . Brisbane 1962 *p. 842*
A deadeye direct-hit run-out by Joe Solomon in the last over created Test cricket's first tie.

52. 1960-61 West Indies (393 and 432-6 dec.) drew with
Australia (366 and 273-9) . . . . Adelaide 1962 *p. 850*
Last pair Ken Mackay and Lindsay Kline survived for 110 minutes to draw the Fourth Test.

	Year		Venue	See Wisden

53. 1961   Australia (190 and 432) beat England
(367 and 201) by 54 runs . . . .   Manchester   1962 *p. 306*
Set 256, England were 150-1 – then Richie Benaud went around the wicket.

54. 1961-62   South Australia (190 and 459-8 dec.) beat New
South Wales (249 and 270) by 130 runs . . . . .   Adelaide   1963 *p. 944*
Garry Sobers scored 251 and took nine wickets, first with swing, then with spin.

55. 1963   West Indies (301 and 229) drew with England
(297 and 228-9) . . . .   Lord's   1964 *p. 290*
Broken-armed Colin Cowdrey went out to bat in the final over, with all four results possible.

56. 1964-65   Railways (910-6 dec.) beat Dera Ismail Khan
(32 and 27) by an innings and 851 runs. . . . . .   Lahore   1966 *p. 891*†
The largest margin of victory in first-class cricket – and DIK's only first-class game.

57. 1968   England (494 and 181) beat Australia
(324 and 125) by 226 runs . . . .   The Oval   1969 *p. 316*
The crowd mopped up the pitch, and England won with six minutes to spare.

58. 1968-69   Western Australia (615-5 dec.) beat Queensland
(282 and 258) by an innings and 75 runs . . . . .   Brisbane   1970 *p. 929*
Six months before his car accident, Colin Milburn scored 243, 181 of them in a session.

59. 1968-69   West Indies (276 and 616) drew with Australia
(533 and 339-9) . . . .   Adelaide   1970 *p. 898*
Set 360, Australia were 304-3, then hung on to draw against the new ball.

60. 1969   Glamorgan (241 and 284-8 dec.) beat Essex
(336-7 dec. and 188) by one run . . . .   Swansea   1970 *p. 402*
Last-ball run-out sealed victory – and Glamorgan clinched the Championship three days later.

61. 1969-70   South Africa (622-9 dec.) beat Australia
(157 and 336) by an innings and 129 runs . . . .   Durban   1971 *p. 894*
A taste of what the world missed: Graeme Pollock 274, Barry Richards 140.

62. 1970   England (222 and 376) lost to Rest of World
(376-9 dec. and 226-8) by two wickets . . . . . .   Leeds   1971 *p. 301*
Closest encounter of a star-studded series.

63. 1971   Gloucestershire (229-6) lost to Lancashire
(230-7) by three wickets . . . .   Manchester   1972 *p. 758*
The moonlit Gillette Cup semi-final, ending at 8.50, causing havoc with BBC schedules.

64. 1972   England (272 and 116) lost to Australia
(308 and 81-2) by eight wickets . . . .   Lord's   1973 *p. 317*
England undone by 16 wickets from debutant swing bowler Bob Massie.

65. 1972   Surrey (300-4 dec. and 130-5 dec.) drew with
Sussex (226-5 dec. and 202-9) . . . .   Eastbourne   1973 *p. 554*
Set 205, Sussex were 187-1 before Pat Pocock took seven wickets in 11 balls.

66. 1974-75   Australia (309 and 288-5 dec.) beat England
(265 and 166) by 166 runs . . . .   Brisbane   1976 *p. 934*
Jeff Thomson's ferocious arrival.

	Year		Venue	See Wisden
67.	1975	West Indies (291-8) beat Australia (274) by 17 runs	Lord's	1976 *p. 318*

The epic first World Cup final, which finished at 8.43 p.m.

68.	1976	West Indies (687-8 dec. and 182-0 dec.) beat England (435 and 203) by 231 runs	The Oval	1977 *p. 339*

Michael Holding bowled sensationally on an unhelpful pitch.

69.	1976-77	Australia (138 and 419-9 dec.) beat England (95 and 417) by 45 runs..............	Melbourne	1978 *p. 130*

The showpiece Centenary Test, which produced exactly the same result as the first one.

70.	1977	England (436) beat Australia (103 and 248) by an innings and 85 runs.................	Leeds	1978 *p. 338*

England regained the Ashes – and Geoff Boycott made his 100th hundred on his home ground.

71.	1977-78	World XI (625) beat Australian XI (393 and 159) by an innings and 73 runs.............	Perth	1979 *p. 1007*

The best of World Series Cricket: Barry and Viv Richards batting brilliantly together.

72.	1981	Australia (401-9 dec. and 111) lost to England (174 and 356) by 18 runs.............	Leeds	1982 *p. 326*

A century by Ian Botham and bowling by Bob Willis gave England victory – at 500 to 1.

73.	1981	England (189 and 219) beat Australia (258 and 121) by 29 runs........................	Birmingham	1982 *p. 330*

This time Botham took 5-1 for another turnaround win, England's greatest for a fortnight.

74.	1981	Sussex (208 and 144) drew with Nottinghamshire (102 and 223-9)....................	Nottingham	1982 *p. 536*

Nottinghamshire held on in a crucial Championship fixture.

75.	1982	Warwickshire (523-4 dec. and 111) lost to Lancashire (414-6 dec. and 226-0) by ten wickets......	Southport	1983 *p. 483*

Warwickshire made 523 in a day – and lost. Graeme Fowler hit two hundreds with a runner.

76.	1982-83	England (284 and 294) beat Australia (287 and 288) by three runs	Melbourne	1984 *p. 897*

Allan Border and Jeff Thomson, the last pair, needed 74 – and made 70 of them.

77.	1983	India (266-8) beat Zimbabwe (235) by 31 runs. .	Tunbridge Wells	1984 *p. 308*

Kapil Dev (175 not out) rescued India from 17-5 – and they went on to win the third World Cup.

78.	1983	Yorkshire (239 and 184-9 dec.) lost to Warwickshire (125 and 302-9) by one wicket	Birmingham	1984 *p. 574*

Last pair Geoff Humpage and Bob Willis added 64 for victory.

79.	1984	West Indies (272-9) beat England (168) by 104 runs	Manchester	1985 *p. 287*

Viv Richards scored phenomenal 189 not out to rescue West Indies from 102-7 and 166-9.

80.	1985-86	India (245-7) lost to Pakistan (248-9) by one wicket........................	Sharjah	1987 *p. 1029*

Javed Miandad hit the last ball of the match for six.

| | *Year* | | *Venue* | *See* Wisden |

81. 1986　　Sussex (283-9 dec. and 173-3 dec.) lost to
　　　　　　　Northamptonshire (136 and 321-9) by one
　　　　　　　wicket . . . . Hastings　1987 *p. 575*
"Cricket somewhere near to perfection with sun and sea breezes" – Matthew Engel.

82. 1986-87　Australia (574-7 dec. and 170-5 dec.) tied
　　　　　　　with India (397 and 347) . . . . Madras　1988 *p. 937*
Test cricket's second tie.

83. 1986-87　Pakistan (116 and 249) beat India (145 and 204)
　　　　　　　by 16 runs . . . . Bangalore　1988 *p. 995*
Pakistan's first series win in India, in doubt until Gavaskar, in his last Test innings, fell for 96.

84. 1987-88　Pakistan (309 and 262) lost to West Indies
　　　　　　　(306 and 268-8) by two wickets . . . . Bridgetown　1989 *p. 990*
Ninth-wicket pair added 61 as West Indies squared an exciting series.

85. 1990　　England (653-4 dec. and 272-4 dec.) beat India
　　　　　　　(454 and 224) by 247 runs. . . . . Lord's　1991 *p. 333*
Gooch's 333, Kapil Dev's four successive sixes – but Azharuddin's 121 was perhaps best of all.

86. 1991　　Kent (381 and 408-7 dec.) tied with Sussex
　　　　　　　(353 and 436) . . . . Hove　1992 *p. 594*
Sussex scored 402 on the final day.

87. 1992-93　Australia (256 and 471) beat Sri Lanka
　　　　　　　(547-8 dec. and 164) by 16 runs. . . . . Colombo　1994 *p. 1000*
Shane Warne's first hint of greatness – 3-11 as the last eight wickets tumbled for 37.

88. 1992-93　West Indies (252 and 146) beat Australia
　　　　　　　(213 and 184) by one run . . . . Adelaide　1994 *p. 1057*
Set 186, Australia were 102-8, recovered, then fell.

89. 1993　　Sussex (321-6) lost to Warwickshire (322-5)
　　　　　　　by five wickets . . . . Lord's　1994 *p. 661*
This NatWest final produced the highest aggregate – and a pulsating last-ball finish.

90. 1993-94　South Africa (169 and 239) beat Australia
　　　　　　　(292 and 111) by five runs. . . . . Sydney　1995 *p. 1084*
Another Australian collapse in the face of a simple target.

91. 1994-95　Australia (337 and 232) lost to Pakistan
　　　　　　　(256 and 315-9) by one wicket . . . . Karachi　1996 *p. 1030*
Inzamam-ul-Haq and Mushtaq Ahmed put on 57, the best by a last pair to win a Test.

92. 1995　　Northamptonshire (152 and 346) beat Warwickshire
　　　　　　　(224 and 267) by seven runs . . . . Birmingham　1996 *p. 632*
"Nerve-shredding"　Wisden. "The way county cricket should be played"　Allan Lamb.

93. 1995-96　Kenya (166) beat West Indies (93) by 73 runs . . Pune　1997 *p. 1024*
The World Cup's greatest upset.

94. 1995-96　India (271-3) lost to Sri Lanka (272-4)
　　　　　　　by six wickets. . . . . Delhi　1997 *p. 1026*
The Sri Lankans woke up world cricket with 42 in the first three overs.

Year		Venue	*See* Wisden
95. 1996-97	Zimbabwe (376 and 234) drew with England (406 and 204-6)	Bulawayo	1998 *p. 1003*

The only Test to finish as a draw with the scores level.

96. 1997   France (267-9) beat Germany (266) by one run . . Zuoz,
. . . .   Switzerland 1998 *p. 1320*§

European Nations Cup final: David Bordes staggered the vital leg-bye with a fractured skull.

97. 1997-98   West Indies (159 and 210) lost to England
(145 and 225-7) by three wickets. . . . .   Port-of-Spain 1999 *p. 1036*

Second of two Trinidad nail-biters in successive weeks.

98. 1998-99   Australia (490 and 146) lost to West Indies
(329 and 311-9) by one wicket . . . .   Bridgetown   2000 *p. 1227*

Brian Lara's magnificent 153 not out swept his side to an unlikely victory.

99. 1999   Australia (213) tied with South Africa (213) . . . .   Birmingham   2000 *p. 486*

The greatest World Cup match. Australia went through to the final on a tiebreak.

100. 1999-2000 Pakistan (222 and 392) lost to Australia
(246 and 369-6) by four wickets . . . .   Hobart   2000 *p. 1573*‡

Justin Langer and Adam Gilchrist led Australia from 126-5 to a stunning win.

† *potted scorecard only.*
‡ *potted scorecard only; full report in* Wisden *2001.*
§ *mentioned; full scores not reported.*

Note: from match No. 7 to No. 30, the page numbers refer to Part II of *Wisden.*

A CENTURY OF NOTES

By TIM RICE

This edition of *Wisden* is the 100th since Sydney H. Pardon, the Almanack's fourth and longest-serving editor, initiated "Notes By The Editor". Ninety-nine years and nine editors later, this has become the most important disinterested pontification of the cricket calendar. The inaugural 1901 article occupied a mere two and a half pages; in 1999, it was 11.

Pardon had already used *Wisden* in the 1890s to attack throwing and, by 1901, his campaign was close to success. He was still using powerful language on the subject – "admitted evil", "scandals", "flagrantly disregarded". But perhaps he was emboldened by the influence *Wisden* had evidently wielded to turn what had started as a simple "Note" on throwing into the more general "Notes" on every imaginable cricketing subject.

Indeed he moved rapidly to the very particular, railing against "the MCC" (not simply "MCC") for an "ungracious and uncalled for act" in moving the press out of the Grand Stand. "I cannot see why the MCC should be so reluctant to build a proper Press-box – commanding an end-on view of the game – as a continuation of the new Mound stand". Just 98 years later, his vision, as it turned out an award-winning one, became fact. A sideswipe at the appalling number of dropped catches in 1900 completed Pardon's first sermon. He must have enjoyed his blast against the monstrous regiments of the day: his broadside at once became an annual event (save for a wartime edition or two).

The Notes gradually lengthened and widened in scope as Pardon's seasons passed. Many of his concerns strike a chord today, if not perhaps his lack of enthusiasm for liquid manure as an agent of wicket preparation. But in the first decade of the 20th century, he also expressed concern that the attractions of cricket should match those of football, and that the relentless demands of the fixture list on first-class players should be curtailed lest staleness take hold. The thought of two divisions in the County Championship was anathema – "the idea of a county with the traditions of Surrey or Notts being relegated to the second-class as the result of one bad season could not be entertained for a moment" (1905). It will have to be entertained at Trent Bridge in 2000. *Wisden* is still against it now.

Sydney Pardon had quite a few radical ideas but, paradoxically, they were usually conservative in the extreme. He even suggested in 1909 abolishing all statistical or points methods of deciding the Championship in favour of letting the order of merit be determined by an MCC committee, based on their observations throughout the season, an idea he resurrected in his 1923 Notes. This was especially surprising since he had no exaggerated faith in the thinking of Lord's committees. The selection for the 1909 Oval Test, he said the following year in perhaps *Wisden's* most famous phrase, "touched the confines of lunacy".

His reign, from 1891 to 1925, was of course scarred viciously by the Great War. By 1914, the Notes had become an outspoken but reasoned review of the year past, attempting to cover all aspects of the season (and close season) rather than just two or three personal hobby-horses. However, these were still ridden with verve, and the financial struggles and structure of county clubs, the need for maximum amateur representation in the England team, and the wisdom of Lord Harris all received plenty of repeat airings. The *Wisdens* of the First World War were thin, mournful volumes: in 1916 and 1917 there were no Notes at all, obituaries dominating. In 1919 Pardon wrote perhaps the most powerful Notes of his editorship, a passionate defence of the status quo. "By some evil chance, cricket, alone among our games and pastimes, has since the signing of the Armistice been signalled out for adverse criticism… the resumption of first-class matches was no sooner announced than all the faddists in Great Britain began to fill the newspapers with their ideas of what they were pleased to call reform or reconstruction." Pardon was proved right; notably as far as the mistaken move to two-day first-class cricket in 1919 was concerned.

He died suddenly, in November 1925, having not written his Notes for the year, and C. Stewart Caine took over. Caine preferred a modestly gifted amateur as captain to a professional, and argued his case intriguingly in 1928: "The professional may have difficulty in enforcing discipline. He would naturally hesitate to suggest to his committee that this player or that should be dropped, and so be instrumental in depriving the man in question of some part of his livelihood. Further, feeling that an error of judgment would prejudice his standing with the committee, he might well hesitate to take risks."

Caine's final Notes were written with the Bodyline tour actually in progress; the contentious Adelaide Test had just concluded. Writing with the benefit of no hindsight whatsoever, he stated firmly that if the bowlers' intention is to hit the batsman "the practice is altogether against the spirit of cricket… that Jardine would acquiesce in such a course is inconceivable."

His successor, Sydney J. Southerton, was in a far better position to comment on what he called "fast leg-theory bowling". This he did in a separate, memorable, article, having dealt with matters of lesser import in his first Notes. After measuring his run-up, he damned the Bodyline strategy: "Mainly because it makes cricket a battle instead of a game I deplore its introduction and pray for its abolition."

The Notes dwindled for a while afterwards and disappeared altogether in the war, being replaced in three of the years by a seasonal review from R. C. Robertson-Glasgow. When Hubert Preston took over in 1944, they were restored. The Preston era, father Hubert and son Norman, lasted until 1980. Preston senior's first Notes, in the reduced 1944 Almanack, headed "Cricket's Place In War-Time", emphasised the role of the game as an antidote to gloom. Both *Wisden* and cricket quickly returned to full health in 1947, and Hubert's peacetime Notes were written against a background of great optimism, not to mention the glamour of Denis Compton.

However, his son Norman had to see *Wisden* through almost three decades of the game's most traumatic changes, including the abolition of the amateur, the arrival of one-day cricket, the end of MCC's control, the D'Oliveira and Packer affairs, the casting of South Africa into the wilderness, the World Cups, the covering of wickets, the arrival of helmets and floodlights, the return of coloured clothing, and – last but not least – the realisation that England would never again have an easy path to Test match success. The world of cricket when Norman died in 1980 was more distant from that of 1946 than 1946 was from 1880.

Nevertheless, Norman Preston's Notes in his 29 Almanacks were generally up to the mark, tinged with an appropriate flavouring of reaction. His first Notes in 1952 astutely listed the burgeoning numbers of rival attractions to cricket – such as 5.2 million private cars licensed in 1951 compared with 4,300 in 1900, and 5,700 cinemas in the country compared with 12 in 1900. He maintained the tradition of unwavering condemnation of throwing. And many of his forecasts found their mark: in 1956 Preston noted that "Laker, in his benefit year, should be at the top of his form." He singled out the 17-year-old Colin Milburn in 1960, and in 1975 he first mentioned Ian Botham, "a 19-year-old opening bowler and splendid batsman... I would particularly like to see Botham given a chance while he is young and enthusiastic."

Preston's unhurried, measured comments ensured that *Wisden* opinions in general were never in danger of being considered antediluvian. For all that, he regretted the demise of the amateur and feared that "cricket is in danger of losing the spirit of freedom and gaiety which the best amateur players brought to the game" (1963). If at times his overviews careered wildly from sunny optimism one season to overcast pessimism the next, this only reflected the entertainment value of Test cricket in general and the erratic performances of England in particular.

The pronouncements of his successor, John Woodcock, were awaited with special interest since he had written the equivalent of *War and Peace* several times over during his lifetime in journalism, but had always refused to slip between hard covers. "Wooders" did not disappoint. He began in *plus ça change* mode by quoting, rather gloomily, from Notes of the past, and his first sub-heading read "Unbridled Dissent".

Woodcock's "graceless age" continued to be a subject for his 1982 survey, but he was able to begin the Notes with the story of 1981 when "English cricket emerged from a period of much gloom to a well-being that was reflected even in the enthusiasm with which ordinary men and women set about their labours" – a wonderfully accurate description of the lift Botham and Willis gave the nation in 1981, in language that might have graced the Notes of S. H. Pardon.

When his successor, the New Zealander Graeme Wright, took over, he was able to include a section in his first Notes entitled "The parlous state of Australian cricket". Another line catches the eye: "There are those, of course, who would like to see the marketing men run even before they cut their loooooo!"

Time and time again the concerns that dominated the Editor's Notes throughout the century resurface in those of the two most recent occupants of the crease, Wright and Matthew Engel: umpiring, dissent, throwing, the ups and downs of the England side (which always seem respectively more glorious and less disastrous from a distance), the endless tinkering with lbw and the fixture lists, money, MCC, and the effects of wider society on the game – all these are rehearsed over and over. But modern Editors are more involved with society as a whole and cricket's relevance to it than their distant seniors. Wright's parting shot in 1992 tells of the ever-increasing illiteracy and numerical incompetence displayed by schools returning their season's records to *Wisden*. One suspects this brief observation tells us more than many a government survey of national examination results.

This year marks Engel's eighth set of Notes. Probably the most politically liberal writer to have edited the Almanack, Engel nobly attacked (and refused to implement) the ICC decision to rule certain South African rebel tour matches non-first-class, even though "I have never wavered in my view that the rebel tours were immoral." His leanings have perhaps affected the balance of his paragraphs on women and MCC, and on the extent of racism in English cricket, but – as with each predecessor – his concern and love for the game shine through.

His other editorial reflections, whether on the good old standbys like umpiring ("I have never been an enthusiast for the third umpire, but I know when I'm licked") or an original concept such as the Wisden World Championship for Test matches, are perfectly in line with the permanently anxious, happy, innovative, conservative, serious, flippant, morose and triumphant Notes By The Editor that have been the heartbeat of *Wisden* since they started.

Sir Tim Rice has written the lyrics for several internationally known musicals. He has won three Oscars (one of which he dedicated to Denis Compton) but regards his brief membership of the BBC commentary team during the 1987 World Cup in India and Pakistan as a greater honour.

EDITORS OF WISDEN, 1864–2000

W. H. Crockford* and W. H. Knight*	1864–1869	Wilfrid H. Brookes	1936–1939
		Haddon Whitaker	1940–1943
W. H. Knight*	1870–1879	Hubert Preston	1944–1951
George H. West*	1880–1886	Norman Preston	1952–1980
Charles F. Pardon	1887–1890	John Woodcock	1981–1986
Sydney H. Pardon	1891–1925	Graeme Wright	1987–1992
C. Stewart Caine	1926–1933	Matthew Engel	1993–2000
Sydney J. Southerton	1934–1935		

* Exact dates and roles unconfirmed.

A CENTURY OF EDITORS

By E. W. SWANTON

There have been 13 official editors of *Wisden* since the first unpretentious appearance of the Almanack in 1864. The early years of struggle culminated in the 1886 edition coming out a year late. At this critical juncture, however, occurs for the first time the magic name of Pardon, not the famous Sydney, but his elder brother Charles. He and his helpers gave authority and substance for the next four years but, aged 40, Charles then died, and Sydney Pardon's editorship began. It lasted from 1891 until 1925.

The 1890s saw a considerable expansion of the game in all directions. When Sydney took over there were eight first-class counties. Yet by 1895 there were 14. Tests spread themselves from Lord's, Old Trafford and The Oval to take in Headingley, Trent Bridge and Edgbaston. Clubs of all sorts multiplied. Cricket was on the march and happily the editorship of the Almanack was in ideal hands for the new century.

No evidence has survived with regard to Sydney Pardon as a player. He wrote with distinction in *The Times* on music, on drama, and on racing. He was a talented, civilised man who, luckily, gave the best of himself to cricket. The Almanack under him became not only the faithful chronicle of events but also the accepted authority on the important issues of the day.

The most serious threat to the game came from suspect bowling actions, and his continued crusade against throwing was not merely strongly worded but enormously influential. That the county captains and MCC stamped out illegal actions so resolutely in 1901 that the game was free of throwers for 50 years was Pardon's triumph.

Pardon's Notes by the Editor became required reading for players, administrators and followers generally. His stance was traditionalist, but always independent. He was more in touch with the game than some members of MCC, and his opinions were greatly respected at Lord's. On hearing of his death, Lord Harris said: "He knew how the game should be played, and was a staunch advocate of the classical style and a fearless critic of the reverse." His influence by no means ended with his sudden death aged 70 in November 1925, for his successors were brought up reporting the game for what had become Pardon's Cricket Agency.

I was merely introduced to Pardon outside the Oval press box in 1925. From his successor, C. Stewart Caine (1926–33), however, I had much kindness and encouragement in the old Press Club. He was a big, broad-shouldered man, a dedicated journalist and editor, and much engaged with charitable work for the Newspaper Press Fund. Caine had been associated with *Wisden* since the time Charles Pardon took over, and was implicitly trusted at Lord's.

So also was his successor, Sydney Southerton, son of James Southerton, who played in the first of all Tests in 1877. Southerton was a small man who always wore what seemed like half a garden in his buttonhole. He edited for only two years (1934–35) before he died after speaking at a club dinner. But he wrote one of the most important articles in the history of the Almanack,

[*Patrick Eagar*

The two men who edited 55 of the last 100 *Wisdens*: Sydney Pardon (*left*) and Norman Preston (*right*).

the damning but full and fair summing-up of the Bodyline crisis of 1932–33. The late Reg Hayter used to tell how Southerton dictated his Bodyline piece to him on to a typewriter, after which it went straight to the printer with no amendments.

To Wilfrid H. Brookes (1936–39) went the credit of modernising the make-up of *Wisden* and, in some respects, clarifying the contents. However, he left abruptly. His successor, Haddon Whitaker (1940–43), was a member of the Whitaker family which then published the Almanack and regarded himself as no more than a wartime caretaker. Next came Hubert Preston (1944–51) whose association with Pardon's Agency went back to 1895.

Hubert was known to everyone in cricket as "Deafy". Cricket affairs got across to him pretty well considering that he wielded a largeish ear-trumpet. The agency tradition was maintained by his son, Norman, who edited 29 editions (1952–1980), second only to Sydney Pardon's 35. Even Pardon would have been hard-put to see in perspective the many changes of Norman's years. Nevertheless, no one could have guarded more faithfully the integrity and dignity of the Almanack.

The succession of agency men came to an end when John Woodcock assumed the editorship in 1981. For six years he brought to the Almanack the great prestige and experience which came from 26 years as cricket correspondent of *The Times*. He introduced a new, more literary, tradition to *Wisden*, which has been continued by his successors Graeme Wright (1987–1992) and Matthew Engel (1993–2000). It is a tradition which, let it be hoped, will continue for years to come.

E. W. Swanton, the distinguished cricket writer and broadcaster, knew all ten of Wisden's *20th-century editors. He died, aged 92, in January 2000.*

COUNTY OF THE CENTURY

By PHILIP BAILEY

To prove that the methods of the hare occasionally prevail, Yorkshire have clearly emerged as the county side of the 20th century. They dominated the first seven decades, winning 26 Championships out of 60, and shared one of the others. Then they went to sleep, but still clearly emerged as the most successful county throughout.

Yorkshire achieved their 1,000th victory since 1900 at Trent Bridge in August 1999. No one else came close to reaching that target. They also lost almost 100 fewer matches than any of their rivals (excluding Durham). In many seasons, especially before the war, there were considerable disparities between the number of fixtures played by different counties. And since the points system has changed frequently, the percentage of wins was the fairest method to determine the century's champion county. But whichever criterion is used, the answer is the same.

Surrey had the second-highest number of wins overall and, on percentages, were just ahead of Kent and Middlesex. Further to the table of post-war success, published in *Wisden* 1996 (pages 25–30), Surrey have now climbed ahead of Middlesex as the most successful post-war team. Kent's record before then was exceptional. They and Yorkshire were the top two teams in each of the first four decades, even though Kent were not champions at all between the wars.

Over the course of the century, Somerset lost by far the most matches both numerically and (again excluding Durham) by percentage. On draws, the facts support the weather lore: Lancashire were the only county to draw more than 1,000 games. Their nearest rivals in percentage terms were Nottinghamshire (Trent Bridge pitches were once famously flat) and Glamorgan. Five of the top nine in the table will be in the second division in 2000.

COUNTY CHAMPIONSHIP, 1900–1999

		P	W	L	D	T	%W	%L	%D	Titles*
1	Yorkshire	2,331	1,001	351	977	2	42.94	15.05	41.91	26
2	Surrey	2,263	833	450	979	1	36.80	19.88	43.26	10
3	Kent	2,235	819	603	808	5	36.64	26.97	36.15	6
4	Middlesex.	2,091	765	491	832	3	36.58	23.48	39.78	10
5	Lancashire . . .	2,315	789	451	1,073	2	34.08	19.48	46.34	6
6	Gloucestershire .	2,179	635	783	759	2	29.14	35.93	34.83	0
7	Essex.	2,169	613	631	920	5	28.26	29.09	42.41	6
8	Sussex	2,303	646	715	936	6	28.05	31.04	40.64	0
9	Nottinghamshire.	2,151	593	585	972	1	27.56	27.19	45.18	4
10	Warwickshire. . .	2,141	589	618	933	1	27.51	28.86	43.57	5
11	Hampshire	2,211	576	722	909	4	26.05	32.65	41.11	2
12	Derbyshire	2,105	528	726	850	1	25.08	34.48	40.38	1
13	Worcestershire . .	2,157	539	742	874	2	24.98	34.39	40.51	5
14	Northamptonshire	1,983	484	688	808	3	24.40	34.69	40.74	0
15	Somerset	2,091	492	812	784	3	23.52	38.83	37.49	0
16	Leicestershire . .	2,143	493	755	894	1	23.00	35.23	41.71	3
17	Glamorgan	1,781	388	604	789	0	21.78	33.91	44.30	3
18	Durham	141	23	79	39	0	16.31	56.02	27.65	0

* Outright titles only.

COUNTY CHAMPIONS, DECADE BY DECADE

		% W			% W
1900–1909	Yorkshire	53.28	1950–1959	Surrey	56.07
1910–1919	Kent	62.16	1960–1969	Yorkshire	42.36
1920–1929	Yorkshire	51.68	1970–1979	Kent	34.11
1930–1939	Yorkshire	56.16	1980–1989	Essex	35.65
1946–1949	Middlesex	59.62	1990–1999	Warwickshire	42.70

Note: full tables for each of these decades can be found on the Wisden website, www.wisden.com.

COUNTY CHAMPIONSHIP, 1990–1999

		P	W	L	D	T	%W	%L	%D	Titles
1	Warwickshire . . .	185	79	51	55	0	42.70	27.56	29.72	2
2	Surrey	185	70	49	66	0	37.83	26.48	35.67	1
3	Essex	185	69	62	54	0	37.29	33.51	29.18	2
4	Middlesex	185	68	43	74	0	36.75	23.24	40.00	2
5	Leicestershire . . .	185	67	47	71	0	36.21	25.40	38.37	2
6	Lancashire	185	64	53	68	0	34.59	28.64	36.75	0
7	Kent	185	61	48	75	1	32.97	25.94	40.54	0
8	Yorkshire	185	60	56	69	0	32.43	30.27	37.29	0
9	Northamptonshire .	185	59	54	72	0	31.89	29.18	38.91	0
10	Derbyshire	185	58	71	56	0	31.35	38.37	30.27	0
11	Worcestershire. . .	185	55	45	84	1	29.72	24.32	45.40	0
	Gloucestershire . .	185	55	72	58	0	29.72	38.91	31.35	0
13	Somerset	185	52	52	81	0	28.10	28.10	43.78	0
	Glamorgan	185	52	56	77	0	28.10	30.27	41.62	1
15	Nottinghamshire .	185	49	70	65	1	26.48	37.83	35.13	0
16	Sussex	185	48	69	67	1	25.94	37.29	36.21	0
17	Hampshire	185	47	59	79	0	25.40	31.89	42.70	0
18	Durham	141	23	79	39	0	16.31	56.02	27.65	0

Notes: in all decades, draws include all abandoned matches, including those abandoned because of war (1914 and 1939), the King's death and funeral (1910), matches not counted originally because less than six hours' play took place (1927 and 1928), and matches regarded as abandoned because there was no decision on first innings (1938 and 1939). This column also includes the Yorkshire v Kent fixture at Harrogate in 1904, which was void because someone tampered with the pitch.

LEADING TEST PLAYERS, DECADE BY DECADE

The following scored most Test match runs and took most wickets in each decade of the 20th century.

	Batting	Tests	Runs	*Bowling*	Tests	Wickets
1900–1909	V. T. Trumper	33	1,953	M. A. Noble	33	89
1910–1919	J. B. Hobbs	21	2,031	S. F. Barnes	15	122
1920–1929	H. Sutcliffe	32	2,960	M. W. Tate	26	118
1930–1939	W. R. Hammond	60	5,194	C. V. Grimmett	28	169
1940–1949	D. C. S. Compton	28	2,664	A. V. Bedser	23	89
1950–1959	R. N. Harvey	57*	4,719	R. Benaud	42	165
1960–1969	K. F. Barrington	75	6,397	G. D. McKenzie	54	238
1970–1979	S. M. Gavaskar	60	5,647	D. L. Underwood	59	202
1980–1989	A. R. Border	98	7,386	M. D. Marshall	63	323
1990–1999	A. J. Stewart	93	6,407	S. K. Warne	80	351

* At Cape Town, in an innings straddling New Year 1950, Harvey hit 178, including 55 on New Year's Eve. His 1950s total excludes these 55 runs.

A fuller version of this table can be found at the Wisden website, www.wisden.com, during 2000.

PART TWO: COMMENT

NOTES BY THE EDITOR

On May 30, 1999, *The Observer* newspaper carried an advert offering readers the chance to win tickets for "all England's Super Six games" in the World Cup. "It is unclear who England will be playing," said the blurb innocently. "However, we know they have qualified." At the time the words were written, that was, if not a mathematical fact, then a reasonable assumption. It's just that reasonable assumptions have no place in discussion of the prospects for the England cricket team. A few hours later, they were out of the World Cup.

The script for English cricket now seems to be more like the Book of Job than anything else: the Sabeans have stolen the oxen; the Chaldeans have stolen the camels; and the fire of God has burned up the sheep. Something like that. Anyway, a tournament officially regarded as the English game's make-or-break opportunity to re-establish itself in the public's affection had produced the worst case imaginable: a fall at the first fence.

And so it went on to the end of that millennium and beyond. England contrived to lose a Test series to New Zealand in almost equally improbable circumstances. In the winter, they effectively lost the series against South Africa in the first half-hour. The Under-19 team performed pretty hopelessly in their World Cup. And the women's team lost to Australia by margins that could terrify anyone who thought the men's team could now get no worse (a sampler: Australia 299 for two; England 79 all out).

With the match-fixing scandal temporarily swept under various carpets, the English crisis is now the greatest crisis in world cricket. It is currently difficult to imagine any circumstances in which England (male version) could face Australia over at least the next three series and have a cat in hell's chance of the Ashes. That's not even good for Australian cricket. It is particularly bad for the future of traditional Test cricket, which depends greatly on English influence wherever it is played.

The miracle, so far as the World Cup was concerned, was that the tournament survived. Local interest remained high. It was as though the British public were able to appreciate everything much better once released from the anguish of following England; and the team's absence enabled the England and Wales Cricket Board (ECB) to notice the enthusiasm for cricket of Britain's Asians, something which until then had largely escaped them. True, the final was a miserable disappointment, but it was not quite as dreadful as the opening ceremony. And these two let-downs framed much excellent cricket, culminating in the wonderful Edgbaston semi-final and, indeed, the final result: no one could argue with the notion of Australia as world champions.

The format was still not quite right. South Africa, the hosts in 2003, like the Super Six concept that was used for the closing stages but are thinking of extending it to a Super Eight (if they expand it far enough, England are bound to qualify some day). They may also change the random nature of the points system, so that the qualifying teams count all their points from the early stages. I would get rid of net run-rate as a tie-breaker myself, and replace it with something more transparent. Overall, you can sense the tournament gaining strength as an institution, and taking its place among the planet's great sporting events.

Biennial is the answer

Yet England could stage an Olympics and a football World Cup before the cricket version returns. It probably will not be back until 2019; it will not even be staged in Asia until 2011 or 2015. Why on earth not? There is no good reason why cricket remains committed to the self-denying ordinance of holding a World Cup only every four years. It should be every two years.

Cricket is bedevilled by wrong-headed analogies with football. A football World Cup actually *lasts* two years because almost everyone has to qualify. For the major teams, the cricket World Cup lasts only a few weeks. And the game's unique spread – global but scattered – means that all the World Cups outside one's own home country are very distant and quite likely to be played through the night. A change would not overwhelm public demand, and it would help justify the investment in stadia that is going to be vital, especially before the West Indies tournament of 2007.

The alternative is a continuation and expansion of all the other one-day tournaments that have little meaning and are tainted by the suspicion of betting-related corruption. The World Cup is cricket's most glittering show-case. It needs to be on display. The International Cricket Council (ICC) should decide at the first opportunity to hold a 2005 tournament – in Asia or Australasia, if that's too soon for the Caribbean to cope – and then rejig future schedules appropriately.

Imbalance of power

Australia began 2000, indisputably, as the world's leading cricket team, with South Africa their closest rivals, New Zealand the fastest risers and England the basket case. In their 1999-2000 home season, Australia played 16 Tests and one-day internationals, and won 15 of them, which is breathtaking. Steve Waugh's leadership had improved to the point where – especially as a motivator – he could be ranked close to his predecessor, Mark Taylor. The new coach, John Buchanan, was impressive too. Buchanan's brief tenure as Middlesex coach has to be viewed with a renewed sense that his failure said far more about county cricket than it did about him.

England, meanwhile, spent 108 days in the second half of 1999 lying ninth out of nine in the Wisden World Championship, a position they only escaped when Zimbabwe again fell beneath them. England hit bottom after a series in which they played the wrong opposition on the wrong grounds under the wrong management who picked the wrong team who performed in the wrong way.

Two years ago, these Notes said the England set-up was better-run than it had been for a generation. Well, it emphatically was not in 1999. To begin at the beginning: New Zealand should never have been asked to tour. This is not because of any inadequacy in the team – far better-equipped than England's – but because the post-World Cup series desperately needed a sexy match-up that would have enthused the British public. Sri Lanka, who have still never had more than one Test at a time against England, would have been a better choice. So would West Indies, who were due on the traditional four-year cycle.

The provincial Tests were assigned to Old Trafford, where the ground authority would have preferred to miss a year, and Edgbaston, where the pitch was yet again palpably substandard. Trent Bridge and Headingley, which offered the marketing bonuses of a centenary of Test cricket, were ignored. Attendances at the non-London Tests were the worst in years. David Lloyd, the coach, was allowed to pack up after the World Cup, leaving a glaring dressing-room vacuum. Some people at the ECB appeared to imagine that they could hire Bob Woolmer, the former South African coach, though Woolmer had stated publicly that he wanted a break from travelling, above anything.

Selection was bizarre. It became clear during the World Cup that combining captaincy, batting and wicket-keeping was over-taxing even a man as enthusiastic as Alec Stewart. He was then relieved not of one job, but of two, and played as a specialist batsman in the first three Tests. Stewart was replaced as keeper by 20-year-old Chris Read who, despite his promise, had no qualifications whatever for the vital job of being England's No. 7. There is a lot of sentimental bunk talked about specialist wicket-keepers. In the late 1990s, England had one – and only one – advantage over all the other Test teams: possession of a world-class batsman who could none the less keep wicket at least as well as anyone else available. It touched the confines of lunacy (to borrow Sydney Pardon's phrase about the 1909 selectors) to toss this away. It was not as though England were operating a consistent youth policy – they recalled yet again the 33-year-old perennial under-achiever, Graeme Hick. Eventually, two selectors, Mike Gatting and Graham Gooch, were scapegoated for this. But only a few months later Hick's phone was ringing with an enquiry if he might be available as a replacement on the South African tour.

Of England's performances, there is quite enough elsewhere in *Wisden*. What one suspects, but cannot prove, is that the internal politics involving the various power clusters who have a say in England matters was even more horrific than anything happening on the field. What we do know is that the most determined and successful rearguard action of the year was the one mounted by Lord's officials to ensure that the chairman of the England Management Advisory Committee, Brian Bolus, never spoke in public.

In South Africa in the winter, there were some signs that the new regime, coach Duncan Fletcher and captain Nasser Hussain, were righting the situation. But though there were sessions, days, sometimes consecutive days, when England were competitive or even dominant, these were punctuated by periods of utter hopelessness. England gained respectability in the series, losing 2–1 to a strong team, through the (technically illegal) generosity of Hansie Cronje, normally the most conservative captain in cricket, who enticed

Hussain into the run-chase at Centurion. England were always a good bet that day: they were allowed to chase a target under first-class rather than one-day rules, one of the few skills that the county circuit teaches better than any other cricketing academy.

The never-ending story

We will try and keep the "Why, oh why?" section brief this year. To reprise: I believe England will be at a disadvantage for generations because children in all the other Test-playing countries grow up either playing freely or going to schools with superior facilities or both. English children are barred from the street cricket which is the norm in Asia or the West Indies by the weight of modern traffic and their parents' terror of paedophiles. Only the tiniest minority go to schools which offer the high-quality organised cricket that is the norm in Australasia and white South Africa.

In comparison, the County Championship is a lesser problem. None the less, it is now sunk in wretchedness. Although the Championship's detractors (like Mike Atherton) always sound a great deal more convincing than its defenders (especially when the ECB's response is merely to tell Atherton to shut up), neither side seems capable of analysing the problems properly, never mind starting to put them right.

The Championship's prime trouble is not that it is unwatched. In that respect, it is little different from domestic first-class cricket anywhere else. It is, however, largely unwatchable: played indifferently by uninteresting and under-motivated cricketers on terrible pitches. In 1990, the counties were playing three-day games on what were essentially four-day pitches, hence all the third-morning declarations. Ten years on, the situation is reversed: four-day games without either players or pitches capable of lasting that long.

Neither administrators nor the so-called radicals can decide what it is they want or why. In effect, England cricketers are being removed from the Championship, through a combination of central contracts and the new international fixture list. Yet a logical county structure of playing Championship fixtures in midweek (Tuesday starts) and one-day games at weekends has been vetoed, partly because it would make it harder for Test players to appear for their counties.

In the early 1980s, it would be quite possible to have, say, a Somerset–Hampshire three-day match with Botham, Richards and Garner on one side and Marshall and Greenidge on the other. Hardly anyone watched, even then. Now it is a rarity to have any current Test players, English or otherwise, let alone a box-office name (there will be a few more genuine overseas stars in 2000 but the pressure of schedules means this will be a short-lived boom). Some people imagine they can somehow replicate Premiership football by having an elite of big-city teams and junking the smaller counties. It is fantasy.

Tests and one-day cricket are the spectator branches of the sport. The domestic first-class game is essential to nurture those. It should be made as enjoyable as possible, spread as widely as possible, taken to as many outposts as possible, and made comprehensible by being granted a sane fixture list, but it is not and cannot be a mass entertainment. The urgent need is to build a culture of greater *individual* competitiveness from which great players can emerge. That, for what it's worth, is the Australian way – not promotion and relegation.

The new word of the Law

The Laws of Cricket, as published in the first *Wisden* in 1864, ran to three pages – which left the printers plenty of space to chuck in the rules of bowls, quoits, and knur and spell. At that stage, Law 42 said simply "No Umpire shall be allowed to bet." This year, the Laws are again undergoing a major revision, the first in 20 years. The new Law 42 takes up about as much space as the entire document did then, which rather damages the belief that the Victorians were more verbose than we are.

Normally, *Wisden* publishes the Laws as they exist. This year is an exception. The 1980 Laws have been published every year since then (excepting 1987, when they were omitted); the changeover is due to come six months before the next Almanack is published; and we reckon that the vast majority of our readers would rather read something fresh and relevant. So we are publishing the 2000 code. Once again, however, the Laws have expanded: 44 pages rather than 28 last year. And that's without various appendices.

They come plastered with health warnings. Firstly, we are publishing – with kind permission of the copyright holders, MCC – a draft. It is possible that the final version will be changed, though we are assured that any changes will be fine and legalistic ones. Secondly, the whole thing is subject to approval by the MCC membership at a special general meeting in May, and they could vote to throw it all out.

Equally, the House of Lords – the other one, down the road at Westminster – can vote to have the elected Prime Minister boiled in oil. The members' powers are somewhat notional here, rather like possession of a blunderbuss that would blow the user's own head off. In any case, MCC members tend to get excited only about their own privileges, rather than about something as trivial as cricket. The fact that the Laws remain in Marylebone's keeping, rather than in the hands of their upstart tenants, ICC, is a tribute to cricket's genius for gradual evolution and to MCC's continuing expertise and integrity. John Jameson, the club's assistant secretary (cricket), has worked long and hard. But he has merely been at the centre of an international panel, involving such figures as Bob Simpson, Sir Clyde Walcott, Tony Crafter, Steve Bucknor and Venkat. MCC does not really lay down the Laws in quite the old way.

"Oi, umpire! That's a penalty!"

Many of the changes are clarifications, to deal with the little curiosities that simultaneously confuse and delight our readers. In two different Tests in New Zealand in 1996-97, similar incidents occurred in which the ball got trapped amid the batsman's equipment and was then caught before hitting the ground. Andrew Caddick was given not out at Christchurch; Romesh Kaluwitharana was out at Dunedin. The Caddick ruling will apply.

Last summer Daryll Cullinan was out in the World Cup at Northampton, caught by Chaminda Vaas, who released the ball a split second before he tumbled over the boundary rope. In future, fielders will have to have control over themselves (as it were) as well as the ball. The forfeiture in the recent Centurion Test – implicitly illegal under old Law 14 – would become lawful.

There are regulations governing the design of wicket-keeping gloves, which have been edging closer to baseball mitts; and fielders will now formally be banned from wearing any gloves at all (thus proving the panel's international credentials – some of these people have never played at Fenner's in April). No-balls will henceforth count one run in addition to anything else scored, ending the absurdity of the meaningless single; this, amazingly, is precisely as advocated in these Notes last year.

The major change to the game itself is the introduction of penalty runs, covering a variety of infringements. This answers the call from umpires, especially at the highest level, for some kind of power to regulate players' behaviour within the game itself. They will now be able to donate runs to either side, which is absolutely right. To take a legitimate footballing analogy: a penalty kick is a much more effective deterrent than a yellow card.

Whether this system ever gets used remains to be seen; even members of the drafting panel think not. My concern is that it should not bring about any principle of retrospection. An innings once closed must be just that. The only score affected should be the innings in progress. Scores can be added or subtracted, but tinkering with previous innings would be chaotic.

In the hope of preventing penalty runs ever being imposed, the Laws will henceforth be preceded by the sonorous cadences of a new preamble: The Spirit of Cricket. This is expected to sell well as a poster and a tea towel, and to be repeated by teachers at the more genteel prep schools. It will probably not, however, be displayed on the walls of professional cricketers' dressing-rooms.

John Jameson says – only half-joking, I think – that he would like a new Law 43 as well: "In all cases not mentioned above, common sense applies." I regret this did not happen because the Laws have now grown long and unwieldy. For the game as played on midden and maidan, in the bush and the backyard, they could probably be half the length. I fail to see why case and statute law governing obscure possibilities, mainly in the professional game, cannot be kept separate, leaving the Laws as a more straightforward guide to cricket. Distinguished lawyers were involved in the drafting; they should have asked some old-fashioned sub-editors from, say, the *Daily Mail* – men traditionally capable of boiling the Ten Commandments down to four and a half.

The last throw?

Sydney Pardon who, as related by Tim Rice on pages 45–48, initiated these Notes in 1901, died 75 years ago. If he were able to read this *Wisden*, he would probably be baffled by some of the contents, depressed by much of them, and would greet the fact that we are still wrestling with the problem of throwing with a sigh of intense weariness.

The new Law 24 attempts to clarify what a throw is, or is not: A ball is fair if "once the bowler's arm has reached the level of the shoulder in the delivery swing, the elbow joint is not straightened partially or completely from that point until the ball has left the hand". This does pin down the moment of truth more precisely than the previous wording, but I am not sure that it will have much practical effect in dealing with the players now under most scrutiny. It is certainly irrelevant to the Muralitharan question.

What matters most is an effective mechanism to deal with suspected throwers. The suspension of Shoaib Akhtar, who was banned from Test cricket on New Year's Eve, was handled in the usual clumsy ICC fashion – especially from the point of view of maintaining Shoaib's career, which is vital, because he is a huge asset to the game. It ended in a humiliating climbdown. But the principle employed was the right one: these decisions must in future be made rationally, using all the super slo-mo technology now available, not on an umpire's whim.

It is extremely rare these days to find a bowler in top-level cricket whose action is blatantly and consistently illegal. The problem, as it has been for the last 40 years, stems from those bowlers who throw the occasional ball, usually a faster ball or a bouncer, to gain the advantage of surprise. Such bowlers are *never* called by umpires. It is up to ICC to put a stop to them.

The pain barrier

I remember, when I was young, being told about a little boy who had some physical defect which meant he felt no pain. But I was enjoined not to be jealous of him. He was constantly cut and bruised because he was deprived of the early-warning system pain provides. I know very little about sports medicine, but I think of that boy every time I read that someone has passed a fitness test and will play in a match, having had a "pain-killing injection".

As one doctor put it to me recently: "Pain is a signal that something isn't right. You ignore it at your peril." Captains are entitled to expect players to go through the pain barrier on the team's behalf once in a while. But when that barrier is being artificially lowered by the constant use of injections and anti-inflammatory tablets, there is cause for concern. There is growing evidence that fast bowlers, in particular, are pill-popping every day in order to cope with their workload. Nothing in cricket justifies endangering the long-term health and welfare of players. I suspect future generations may consider our complacency on this subject barbaric.

Overkill

In 1927, there were no Test matches in England, and the highlight of the summer was the centenary Oxford v Cambridge match. In 1949, there were still only 12 days of Test cricket in the season: four three-day games. In the 1950s and 1960s there was a nice rhythm of five five-day Tests: 25 days in all. As one-day internationals came in, there were generally 33 days – six Tests, three one-dayers – and the number remained there until 1997. In 2000, there will be at least 45 scheduled days, probably rising to 48 if negotiations succeed to stage some India–Pakistan one-day internationals. Either 41 or 42 of these will involve England, depending on whether they reach the triangular tournament final. One of the problems with recent England teams has been getting them to regard representing their country as special rather than another day at the office. At this level – seven weeks of international cricket – it is not going to feel special for anyone at all.

Three one-day internationals was not enough. There may be an occasional need to slot in the extra Test match now and again to accommodate Zimbabwe and, maybe, Bangladesh – especially if an official World Championship ever starts. Floodlit international cricket is a worthwhile development (though not an especially urgent one, since England's one-day games have been full for years).

But this is too much. It beggars belief that a Test match has had to be scheduled for Lord's on May 18. This may be one method of maximising short-term TV revenue. It also looks like a promising way of making English cricket look even more pitiful: we could have the first Test ever with more sweaters than spectators. The greatest success of English cricket administration for most of the 1990s was to maintain the momentum of Test cricket as a big occasion, even if the home team was rotten. All that is being jeopardised.

Impure milk

With the 1999-2000 competition already under way, the Sheffield Shield, Australian cricket's inter-state Championship for the last 107 years, suddenly ceased to exist. The competition had acquired a sponsor and, as part of the deal, the trophy itself was immediately retired, as were both parts of the name. Inter-state first-class cricket is henceforth to be contested for – one can hardly bring oneself to write it – the Pura Milk Cup. The very phrases that have been part of the fabric of the Australian language for generations were effectively banned: Shield cricket, Shield records, Shield player.

This is not sponsorship. It is an act of vandalism against both cricket's past and its future: an attempt to blank out future generations from any understanding of the game's history. Tradition is harder to come by in Australia than in England, and therefore more highly valued. *The Age* in Melbourne rightly called the decision "abhorrent".

Domestic first-class cricket is hard to sell and the game has to make a living. But this time cricket has sold its dignity as well as its advertising space. Tim Lamb, chief executive of the ECB, once said, in perhaps his happiest piece of phrase-making, that professional cricket was "a business inside a game" not "a game inside a business". He should have that drawn up as a motto in appliqué work and distributed at the next ICC meeting to be stuck up in every chief executive's office around the globe.

Ground rules

New Zealand's remarkable Test win over West Indies (who were 276 for nought on the first day) in Hamilton took place, apparently, at Westpac Trust Park. Other recent Tests in Hamilton were held at Trust Bank Park. Before that they were at Seddon Park. Trust is hardly the word here: the unwary might imagine that Hamilton is unusually well-served with cricket grounds, like Colombo.

This is, of course, a single ground changing its name at sponsors' whims. It is a spreading phenomenon: Lancaster Park in Christchurch is now the Jade Stadium. In South Africa, brand-new Springbok Park, Bloemfontein, has become Goodyear Park, and Centurion Park is now, hideously, SuperSport Park. This is particularly sad: the town of Centurion (which originally had the apartheid-tainted name of Verwoerdburg) was, rather charmingly, renamed after the cricket ground.

Such changes pose unique difficulties for *Wisden*. We have an obligation to try and ensure that, long after these contracts end and the names have changed again, future readers can learn where cricket matches were played. And thus we have to be as unhelpful as possible to the deal-makers in this regard. We will stick with cricket grounds' traditional and original names wherever possible. It will be a battle. In England, Hampshire are hoping their new stadium will have a name-sponsor from the start. But how long can such a deal last? We will do our utmost to work round ground-sponsorship as best we can in the interest of our readers. I understand cricket administrators' problems. I hope they understand ours.

Five for the future

Wisden's Five Cricketers of the Year for 2000 may be a little overshadowed by the Five Cricketers of the Century but they are a group worthy of the honour. For the fifth time (after 1949, 1962, 1982 and 1997) there is no England-qualified player among them. Even on our traditional criterion – "influence on the English season" – it was impossible to get one in, though it is fair to say Caddick was an unlucky loser. The peculiar combination of a World Cup summer and England's general hopelessness, however, were the determining factors.

The situation has given us cause to look again at how we choose Cricketers of the Year. As I said, even a few years ago most of the world's star players were active in the County Championship. Now they are outnumbered by Aussies who lord it at this level but can't make their own Test team. On current form, not many of the world's leading players will be taking part in England's two Test series this summer either. The turn of the century seems like a good moment to recognise this reality and tweak our own traditions. Graeme Wright, who is editing *Wisden* 2001, and I have agreed that, in future, Cricketers of the Year should reflect a more global view of cricket, not just the English season.

I hope this does not mean that our choice will lose its personal – and occasionally idiosyncratic – nature. I hope players will still be chosen from the County Championship. But, the way things are going, don't bank on it.

Radio waves

Over the past year, English cricket followers have had to get used to being separated from the BBC, which lost the rights to televise home Tests until 2002 and, for one winter at any rate, the radio rights as well. Their increasingly half-hearted TV coverage was not much missed, and Channel 4 brought a welcome sense of adventure to proceedings, though overall, I thought, the newcomers were a touch over-praised. Aside from the iconic figure of Richie Benaud, they were short on commentators with real authority and bite.

Talk Radio, aka Talk Sport, who covered the series in South Africa, solved that last problem by hiring Geoff Boycott. They offered far more commitment than has been possible for years on the BBC, with no breaks for shipping forecasts and the like (the BBC are hampered because so many of their spare wavelengths were lost to outfits like Talk Radio). And I didn't even mind the adverts. Unfortunately, Talk fell down on the basics. You couldn't trust their commentators to read out the score or fill you in on developments. Often, one felt like an eavesdropper, trying to piece together the scraps of information they occasionally let slip. Some thought the coverage improved as the series went on, but by then the bond of trust had snapped as far as I was concerned.

Talk insisted that their commentators had to be ex-cricketers. This is now the norm; anyone who wants to commentate on the game probably has to play for England first (though maybe only a few times). This has had two disadvantages. Firstly, we have lost the lovely balance between professional broadcaster and professional cricketer – the one subtly deferring to the other – that made a combination like John Arlott or Brian Johnston with Freddie Brown or Trevor Bailey so right. Secondly, the essential journalistic skills of covering the cricket have been lost. Talk was fine on technicalities but failed to convey the mood – and, very often, the facts.

Behind the glass

Another point Tim Rice spotted is that the 1901 *Wisden* Notes included a whinge by Sydney Pardon about press facilities at Lord's – although even then, conditions had moved on since the time of one of Pardon's predecessors, W. H. Knight, who had to report games from a shrubbery.

Now we have a media centre, built at vast expense in pole position behind the bowler's arm. It has won a major architectural award, though not everyone shares the enthusiasm. The building has been compared to an alien spaceship, a barcode reader, Wallace's teeth (from Wallace and Gromit), Tony Blair's smile, Mrs Blair's smile, a digital alarm clock and a pickled gherkin. Those of us allowed inside don't have to worry about how it looks, however. We ought to be eternally grateful to MCC, and promise never to write horrid things about them ever again.

There is a problem, though. None of the windows (except in the *Test Match Special* box) opens at all. We watch from behind plate glass as though in a cataleptic fit: able to see what goes on but wholly removed from it. If Lord's is full, we have nowhere else to go. It confirms my view of architects:

they win awards for grand conceptions, not concern with the comfort of a building's users. The new media centres at Taunton, Nottingham and Leicester are enclosed in the same wretched way. It is said that health and safety officers are worried that, if a window opens, one of us might throw himself out. (The *Evening News* did once hurl the *Sunday Times* typewriter off the balcony at Leyton, but that's as near as we've got.) I became a cricket writer partly because I wanted to spend my summer days in the fresh air, rather than cooped up in an office. These new arrangements are deeply depressing. End of this whinge. Could someone direct me to the shrubbery, please?

On the road

On the morning of the Lord's Test last July, Angus Fraser had to leave a county match between Somerset and Middlesex to join the England squad because of a last-minute injury scare. He drove as far as the end of the M4 (130-odd miles), then got a call telling him to turn round because he was not required. He would have travelled the previous night but his kit was locked in the ground at Taunton. In fact, Fraser would not have been called at all, except that the preferred alternative, Chris Silverwood, was playing at Scarborough, and that was thought to be too long a car journey.

Some questions. 1. Why couldn't a key-holder be summoned to the Taunton ground? I am assured some were available. 2. In any case, why couldn't Fraser have taken a taxi? There are taxi-firms in Taunton. They charge £160 to go to London. Wouldn't that have been a worthwhile investment to ensure that an England fast bowler arrived reasonably rested? 3. Come to that, did it occur to anyone that they have taxis in Scarborough too? Sometimes, English cricket looks shambolic and amateurish. But sometimes it looks far worse than that.

Before I nod off...

In his autobiography, *Tiger by the Tail*, Lord MacLaurin, the chairman of the ECB, has the following passage: "It is no longer possible to capture the somnolence of John Arlott's poem 'Cricket at Worcester, 1938', when 'Drowsing in deck-chair's gentle curve, through half closed eyes, I watched the cricket.' Those times are long gone."

I am not entirely sure what Lord MacLaurin is on about. He is right in the sense that there are no deck-chairs at Worcester these days, rather those plastic tip-up thingies, which are less conducive to drowsing. I still don't find it impossible. I half-dozed very happily on a sunny September afternoon last year; there was even someone called Hutton batting. Does he think county cricket isn't somnolent any more? Has he *been* to Worcester lately?

Heaven knows, I am not against reforming cricket where it is desirable and essential. I have been banging on about it in this space for the past eight years, and Lord MacLaurin can go on tinkering with the game in his way if he insists. But he really ought to leave us snoozers alone. They have done away with the deck-chairs. There are those whose future plans for cricket would include doing away with Worcester. Do away with somnolence, and you will do away with cricket once and for all. And England with it, probably.

THE WISDEN WORLD CHAMPIONSHIP

The Wisden World Championship moved into its fifth calendar year of operation at the start of 2000 while the cricketing community still waited for the International Cricket Council to come up with an official alternative.

In the meantime, the relevance of a Championship was spectacularly demonstrated in 1999 when New Zealand won the Oval Test and thus took their series in England 2–1. This sent England to the bottom of the Championship, and a tremor round the cricketing world. It was a simple and graphic illustration of their plight. Headlines proclaimed England "The Worst Team in the World", which was somewhat overstating the case: even we would not claim that their position proved anything other than that they were the least successful of the nine Test-playing nations.

There was rather less fanfare when, four months later, Zimbabwe lost to Sri Lanka, fell behind England and inherited the wooden spoon. Zimbabwe, as the newest Test team, are expected to be bottom and, for Fleet Street papers, "The Second-Worst Team in the World" was a less compelling notion. Meanwhile, New Zealand, who had been bottom, were close to mid-table respectability after beating West Indies in 1999-2000.

Australia completed their third year unchallenged at the top of the table early in 2000. However, South Africa had closed the gap, the Australians having lost ground when they were held to a draw in the Caribbean and then beaten in Sri Lanka. The epic battle for the Worrell Trophy ensured that West Indies did not fall as fast as their general air of crisis might suggest. They were helped in this by Pakistan's inconsistency and India's away form, which was almost as bad as their own.

The Championship works by counting the most recent series, both home and away, between each pair of countries. Teams receive two points for winning a series, and one for drawing. A one-off Test counts as a series. Because not everyone has played everyone else, percentages are used. Series not renewed after seven years are excluded from the table, recalculation taking place each September.

THE WISDEN WORLD CHAMPIONSHIP TABLE

(as at February 24, 2000)

		Series played	Won	Lost	Drawn	Points	Average
1.	Australia	15	11	2	2	24	1.60
2.	South Africa	15	10	4	1	21	1.40
3.	West Indies	13	5	4	4	14	1.08
4.	Pakistan	14	6	5	3	15	1.07
5.	Sri Lanka	16	6	6	4	16	1.00
6.	India	15	5	7	3	13	0.87
7.	New Zealand	16	5	8	3	13	0.81
8.	England	14	3	9	2	8	0.57
9.	Zimbabwe	12	2	8	2	6	0.50

Previous leaders: October 13–December 12, 1996 South Africa; December 12–January 28, 1997 Australia, South Africa and West Indies (joint); Australia have led since January 28, 1997.

Matches between the Asian countries in 1998-99, including the Asian Championship final in Dhaka, are treated as three series: India v Pakistan; Sri Lanka v India; Pakistan v Sri Lanka.

The table is updated regularly in *Wisden Cricket Monthly* and on the Wisden website, www.wisden.com.

WITH A VENGEANCE

[Patrick Eagar

Allan Donald bowls Mike Atherton with the sixth ball of the 1999-2000 series between England and South Africa. This superb delivery provided a dramatic turnaround from Atherton's victory in their personal confrontation in England 18 months earlier. It also set the tone for the match – and the series.

THE GRAND SEMI-FINALE

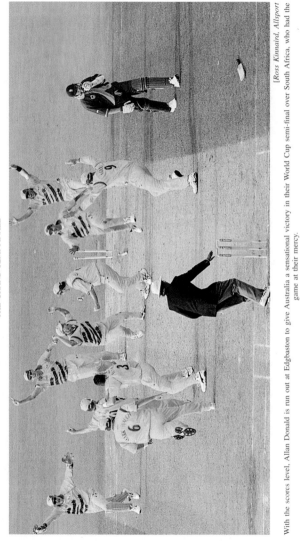

[*Ross Kinnaird, Allsport*

With the scores level, Allan Donald is run out at Edgbaston to give Australia a sensational victory in their World Cup semi-final over South Africa, who had the game at their mercy.

WAR AND PEACE

[Fayaz Kabli, Reuters/Popperfoto

Above: An Indian soldier in Kashmir listens to commentary on the India–Pakistan World Cup tie. Fierce fighting had broken out yet again between the two countries in the disputed territory two weeks earlier. *Below:* Indian spectators delight in their team's success against England in the vital fixture at Edgbaston.

[Patrick Eagar

WITH FRIENDS LIKE THESE . . .

[*Anuruddh Lokuhapuarachchi, Reuters/Popperfoto*

One of the few setbacks for Australia in 1999: Jason Gillespie and Steve Waugh collide trying to take a catch in the outfield during their Test at Kandy. Gillespie broke his leg, Waugh broke his nose – and Sri Lanka went on to win.

MANY A SLIP

[Popperfoto/Reuters]

Steve Waugh set the ultimate in attacking fields for Damien Fleming as he bowled to tailender David Mutendera at Harare in October 1999. Australia were going in for the kill in their second one-day international against Zimbabwe. From the left, the fielders are: Adam Dale, Michael Bevan, Andrew Symonds, Steve Waugh, Ricky Ponting, Damien Martyn, Tom Moody, Mark Waugh, Shane Warne and wicket-keeper Adam Gilchrist.

[*Stuart Outterside, North News*]

David Boon, the Durham captain, poses on the opening day of the 1999 county season when more than normally severe weather hit the match against Worcestershire at Chester-le-Street. It was a good omen: Durham went on to enjoy their best season ever – a happy ending to Boon's career.

SURREY SIDE UP

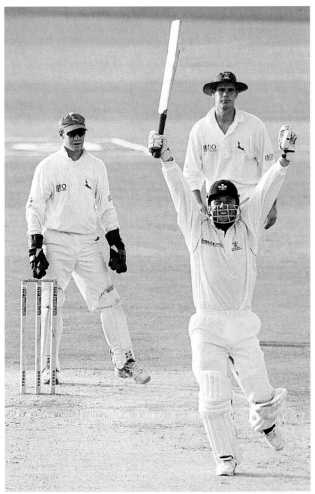

[*Graham Chadwick, Allsport*

Ian Ward celebrates at The Oval after hitting the run against Nottinghamshire that made Surrey
the 1999 county champions after 27 blank seasons.

FIVE CRICKETERS OF THE YEAR

[*Patrick Eagar*

CHRIS CAIRNS

FIVE CRICKETERS OF THE YEAR

[*Graham Morris*

RAHUL DRAVID

[*Graham Morris*

LANCE KLUSENER

[*Patrick Eagar*

TOM MOODY

FIVE CRICKETERS OF THE YEAR

[*Patrick Eagar*

SAQLAIN MUSHTAQ

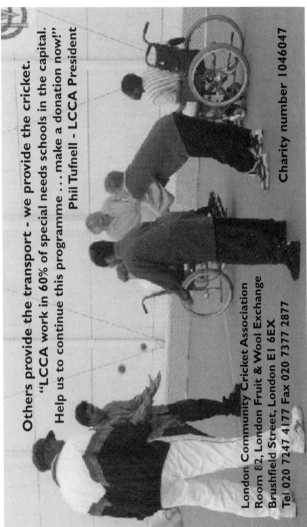

FIVE CRICKETERS OF THE YEAR

CHRIS CAIRNS

Chris Cairns might be expected to nominate Lord's or The Oval as his places of the heart after a summer of cricketing content. Yet, for all his glorious feats there in 1999, one of the world's less appealing venues provided a snapshot that meant just as much – Kanpur's Green Park, the dusty ground where he experienced, celebrated and then demonstratively revelled in one of the biggest moments in his cricketing life.

New Zealand were facing Sachin Tendulkar's Indians in the second of three Tests. India had the untaxing task of scoring 82 to win, an uneventful end to an unmemorable match for New Zealand. But Chris Cairns wanted to seize a moment. Sitting on 130 Test wickets, he was desperate to lift that total to 131 to go ahead of his father, national folk hero Lance, on New Zealand's roll of honour. And, in the throes of defeat, came the triumph he craved, as he castled opener Sadagoppan Ramesh for five. He didn't just savour it, but made a grand statement with his next delivery. This was no rhythmical thing of cricketing beauty, rather an uncoordinated flurry of arms, the ball unmistakably delivered off the wrong foot – the way Bernard Lance Cairns did. As the "son of" said, it was his tribute to "the old man".

That moment meant much to the man himself, but it was his string of wondrous deeds earlier in the year that really had the cricketing world paying attention. Back home, Cairns's batting was critical against India, a half-century contributing to victory in Wellington and a restrained 126, only his second Test hundred, batting the tourists out of contention in Hamilton to secure a series win. It was also Cairns the batsman, rather than the bowler, who excited in the one-day games against India, and at Christchurch he made a hundred off just 75 deliveries, New Zealand's fastest in limited-overs internationals, with seven sixes.

In such mood, he seemed destined to prosper in England, both at the World Cup, then on the tour to follow. Excel he did, boosting New Zealand's run to the World Cup semi-finals with his all-round contributions, including a blistering 60 in the famous five-wicket win over eventual champions Australia. For all that, the Test series against England was Cairns's *tour de force*. His six-wicket haul was a key ingredient in New Zealand's nine-wicket win at Lord's and, in the series decider at The Oval, he was matchless. He began with five wickets, but the jewel was his last innings of the tour. New Zealand were 39 for six and leading by just 122 when he took guard – and instantly applied the blowtorch to England's attack. When it was all over, he had 80 beside his name from only 94 deliveries, a priceless and daring innings which effectively won the series: England folded in the run-chase and lost by 83 runs. With series returns of 183 runs at 30.50 and 19 wickets at 21.26, Cairns was unquestionably New Zealand's outstanding performer.

That CHRISTOPHER LANCE CAIRNS should be able to deliver all-round performances of such substance and panache is no surprise. It was in the genes. He was born in Picton (like his father) on June 13, 1970, and cricket was an inescapable part of his upbringing. By the time he was five, he was already showing prodigious ability. He could play rugby too, and was a reserve for the New Zealand Under-17 side against Australia in 1987. Cricket, though, was the constant in his life, a passion developed in Dunedin when Lance switched from Central Districts to Otago in 1976.

Throughout these times, Chris's goal was to play for New Zealand, and almost everyone wondered when rather than if. By 1988, he was treading in Richard Hadlee's footsteps at Nottinghamshire, where he made his first-class debut. He was still only 18 when he scored his maiden century for Northern Districts. But, though his career was headed in just one direction, it would also prove to be studded with setbacks. In his Test debut against Australia in November 1989, he suffered a back injury. He had a kidney operation, various injuries and conflicts with officialdom (he quit mid-tour in the West Indies in 1995-96). But all those paled beside the devastation he felt when his sister Louise was killed in a train crash in 1993.

Trying to cope with such events, Cairns would tantalise one moment only to regress just as quickly. The good would be very good, like his first Test hundred, 120 in 96 balls against Zimbabwe in 1995-96. But there were many periods of mediocrity. He is far more pure, in the technical sense, than his father, who worked on instinct and effect, and to hell with the style. Yet, after ten years in elite company, the younger Cairns had played only 42 Tests by the end of the 1999-2000 tour of India, with his batting average still below the 30-mark, his bowling average above it. His one-day output mirrored those figures.

But in the short home series against West Indies that followed, he truly began to do justice to his luminous talent: 17 wickets in two Tests, including a devastating seven for 27 at Hamilton, figures surpassed in New Zealand Test history only by Hadlee. At the start of 2000, Cairns had a claim to be considered the game's pre-eminent all-rounder. Even Hadlee struggled to say that. – RICHARD BECHT.

RAHUL DRAVID

Think of modern Indian batsmen and the Englishman thinks of Tendulkar. Even regular cricket followers find it hard to recognise the other members of India's top order. This may be a comment on enduring gulfs in culture or, more simply, gaps in fixtures; but after the summer of 1999 it is an unsustainable position. India supplied two of the outstanding batsmen in the World Cup, and neither of them was Tendulkar.

Sourav Ganguly and Rahul Dravid had introduced themselves three years earlier. They made their Test debuts together at Lord's, Ganguly scoring 131 and Dravid 95 from No. 7. David Lloyd, then the England coach, had been told by his observers that Ganguly would open the face of his bat outside off stump, while Dravid's weakness was working the straight balls to leg. This dossier was quickly consigned to the out-tray.

Three years on, and the scene changes to Taunton, its bucolic traditions given over for a day to Asian exuberance. India are playing Sri Lanka in a World Cup group match. India lose a wicket in the opening over but they will not lose another until the total has reached 324. Ganguly and Dravid's stand of 318 is, by a distance, a record for any wicket in international one-day cricket (until November, when Dravid and Tendulkar raise it to 331). For Dravid, the day brings his second century in four days. Despite India's failure to qualify for the semi-finals, he would complete the tournament as its leading run-scorer, and return home fêted as a hero among perceived failures. To his embarrassment, Dravid fan clubs have sprung up, their membership loaded with teenage girls, and though his features may still be shamefully unfamiliar in England, they have attracted advertisers and film-makers in the land where star cricketers are national property.

RAHUL DRAVID was born in Indore on January 11, 1973. The son of a food scientist, he was firmly encouraged to complete his studies before branching into sport, and obtained a degree in commerce at Bangalore University. But he made his first-class debut at 18, for Karnataka, and scored 134 in his second match. He was soon identified as one of the meteors of Indian cricket. Shy and introspective, he did not seek attention, but it was to come his way naturally, through weight of runs and an impression of quiet authority that led to him captaining most of the teams he represented.

At first, his method was a painstaking one, his fierce determination to preserve his wicket matched by a desire to learn. In Toronto one year, he button-holed Ian Chappell at a party and put searching questions to him for an hour. At Lord's, he learned how to succeed and how to fail, all in the same innings. Had he made five more runs, it would have been the first time in the history of Test cricket that two debutants in the same team had made centuries. "It hurt," he recalls. "But I realised it would not do me any good to keep thinking about it." He went out in the next Test and made 84.

At the start of 1999, India, a team that had spent too long confining its talents to one-day cricket, played a sudden raft of Test matches. They were beaten 1–0 in New Zealand, but the third game of that series, at Hamilton, belonged to Dravid, who made an elegant, eight-hour 190 in the first innings and followed it with 103 not out in the second. In Colombo seven weeks later, he made his fifth Test century, against Sri Lanka. By now, he had a Test average of 54 and had cemented his preferred place at No. 3.

Next, though, came the World Cup and further evidence that this pleasing player is far more capable than most of his countrymen on alien pitches, reason enough for Kent to engage Dravid as their overseas player for 2000. He was also to demonstrate that his game had moved on and that he was resourceful enough to dominate.

In late November, as he waited in a Mumbai hotel for the flight to Australia and another challenging chapter in his development, Dravid reflected on his golden year. "I have improved a lot since 1996," he said earnestly, "but my game can still progress further." Taunton, he said, had been "great fun, fantastic" but the World Cup, overall, had left him with mixed emotions. "There are such expectations of us at home. We are followed very closely and people were disappointed. We had no excuses, although I thought we played well enough to reach the semi-finals."

Dravid certainly did. His total of 461 runs, 63 more than his closest challenger, Steve Waugh (Ganguly was third with 379), contained not only two successive centuries but also fifties under pressure against England and

Pakistan. His batting was as undemonstrative as his personality, but as eloquent, too. It spoke of a man who has the time, both in technique and age, to graduate into the very highest company, and to do it with an understated, old-fashioned grace. – ALAN LEE.

LANCE KLUSENER

It was Gary Player who once said, in response to claims that he enjoyed remarkable fortune extricating himself from bunkers: "You know, the funny thing is, the more I practise, the luckier I get." These words might have been echoed by another South African, Lance Klusener, at the 1999 World Cup. He stalked out to bat, carrying a three-pound weapon, with all the menace of the soldier he once was, crew-cut under helmet, muscular frame hidden beneath baggy shirt. Klusener already had a reputation as an exceptionally effective tail-end slogger – but prepared by smiting up to 100 balls every day from a bowling machine.

"Of course cricket is about luck," he says. "Balls go in the air and fall in gaps, but hitting does not just happen. You have to learn to improvise and swipe – and be at peace with what you do."

Thus chance turns into science. He swung match after match South Africa's way: 52 off 45 balls turned the tables on Sri Lanka at Northampton; 48 off 40 sealed England's fate at The Oval; 46 off 41 pulled the game with Pakistan at Trent Bridge from the fire. It was hardly his fault Zimbabwe won at Chelmsford. Arguments will continue for ever about his role at the very last gasp when South Africa went out at Edgbaston, but remember *he* had already almost transformed desperation into delight.

In nine matches, the left-handed Klusener smashed 281 runs off 230 balls, only two of which cost him his wicket. When he was finally out, to Gavin Larsen on the 28th day, it brought to an end a one-day international record dating back to February of 400 runs without dismissal. Almost two-thirds of his World Cup runs came in front of square on the on side.

His main skill was supposedly his aggressive, intelligent fast-medium bowling. He claimed 17 wickets (18 had not Herschelle Gibbs dropped Steve Waugh, disastrously, at Headingley), and his fielding was excellent – Klusener stood out as the player of the tournament.

LANCE KLUSENER was born in Durban on September 4, 1971. He grew up on his parents' sugar-cane farm, and would retain the independence and shyness of a country boy. His companions were largely the children of black farm workers, with whom he talked in Zulu and played garden games of football and cricket. His team-mates still call him "Zulu".

Though his father played polo, sport did not feature large in the family. As a boarder at Durban High School, he made the first team, as a batsman, only in his final year. It was not until his military service – which he extended from one to three years for want of anything else to do – that he attracted attention.

Denis Carlstein, the manager of Natal, saw potential in his bowling, and recommended that Klusener attend provincial nets. There, he was spotted by the late Malcolm Marshall, Natal's Barbadian overseas player, and in 1993-94 was drafted into the first eleven, where he flourished under Marshall's guidance. "Malcolm did not believe in interfering with the way you played," Klusener recalls. "He liked to hit the ball and so did I. He told me not to stop – and to never stop attacking as a bowler."

His development was now swift. Three years later, he made his Test debut and immediately established a reputation as a man for a crisis. In his first match, he took eight second-innings wickets on a flat pitch in Calcutta after Allan Donald broke down, and in his fourth he swept to what was then the fastest Test hundred in South Africa's history – 102 off 100 balls – against India in Cape Town. Only ten Test cricketers had previously scored a hundred and taken eight wickets in an innings; Klusener had achieved the double in five weeks. He saved the next game with cool batting.

A brilliant Test career beckoned, but by the World Cup he had not come near to repeating these performances. As a lower-order batsman and reluctant stock bowler, he was struggling for a meaningful role, calling himself "a fill-in bowler who can bat a bit". That description had to be revised after he scored 174 against England in the Port Elizabeth Test in December 1999.

In one-day cricket, though, his fearlessness in tight corners was already considered essential. His six off the last ball, an attempted yorker by Dion Nash, to settle a match in Napier in March 1999 gave warning of the pyrotechnics to come. Klusener believes that the turning point for him as a batsman was the ankle injury that cut short his tour of England in 1998. After surgery, he was told not to bowl for several months and focused on fine-tuning his batting.

For all the World Cup games he won, Klusener will probably be best remembered for his part in the game that saw his side eliminated – his two blunderbuss boundaries off the first two balls of Damien Fleming's last over and Donald missing his call in the mêlée moments later, when one run would have put them in the final.

"In hindsight, there were ten other ways we could have done it, but when you are out there it's not easy," he says. "You forget that you haven't quite finished the job. We thought we had won it. Maybe we should have communicated more." Maybe Chance was simply reasserting its hold over one of the most calculating hitters the game has seen. – SIMON WILDE.

TOM MOODY

Many factors contributed to Australia's triumph in the 1999 World Cup. But the major difference between the team's early edginess and their supremacy at Lord's came from a selection decision. In Tests, Australia for years have had enough quality specialists not to worry about having a class all-rounder. But in English one-day conditions, where the need for five front-line bowlers was paramount, this nearly proved disastrous.

Australia changed both their personnel and their attitude. But perhaps the most crucial switch was the inclusion of a player who gave them balance – and perhaps in a psychological sense as well as a cricketing one: Tom Moody.

On the face of it, Moody's contribution was not all that compelling: in seven games, he scored 117 runs and took seven wickets – two of them in the final. But the killer stat is that he scored his runs at 1.3 a ball, faster even than Lance Klusener. In tight games – and, boy, did Australia have some tight games – this was vital.

It was fairly freakish that Moody was in the World Cup at all. He had been injured for much of the Australian summer and had not made the original 19-man preliminary list, so Australia needed special permission to add him to the final 15. In a country that worships cricketing youth, 33-year-old fringe players don't get much respect.

But Moody is a special case. He had been part of the squad – though not the team – that won the Calcutta World Cup final almost 12 years earlier. Now he was on the field for a reprise that gave pleasure well beyond Australia. Like many Aussies who had not quite hacked it in Test cricket, Moody had gone to England, settled at one of the quieter county grounds and become a local hero, not just because of numbers and trophies, but because of his personal qualities. He is one of those courtly Australians with beautiful manners: not merely a practitioner of the game but an ambassador for it.

THOMAS MASSON MOODY was born in Adelaide on October 2, 1965. When he was 13, his father, a headmaster, took over at Guildford Grammar School in Perth (his old job went to the Test cricketer John Inverarity), and Tom went there too. Having a father as headmaster can be a doubtful blessing for a child, but sporting skill conquers all sorts of prejudice. "Physical presence helped a bit too," he says – he was heading for 6ft 6in.

Tom was the youngest of four children, and had two older brothers, both good cricketers (Richard made it into the Western Australia state squad), so Tom had to work hard to compete in their driveway games. But the hard schooling paid off. As an 18-year-old, he travelled to England to spend a season with Hetton Lyons in the Durham Coast League, a responsibility which helped him think of himself as someone going into professional cricket, rather than playing a bit *en route* to something else.

By 1985-86, he was in the Western Australia Shield team and, two years later – aged just 22 – he was in the World Cup squad. "I'd had a good season," Moody recalls, "but they weren't spoiled for choice." He was picked in three early games but then tore a side muscle and lost his place.

At that stage, he was almost wholly a batsman. But when he came to England for the Ashes tour of 1989, he again had to spend most of the time as a reserve. So he took the chance to learn from the seam bowlers on that trip. "I reckoned I knew how bowlers thought. I didn't. So I learned to think as a bowler."

That was to pay rich dividends, especially in one-day cricket: he was an ever-present in Australia's ill-fated 1992 World Cup campaign. But he never had the pace to be a real Test bowler, so he had to succeed as a batsman. And when he did get into the Test team later in 1989, he started with 61 on debut against New Zealand, and 106 against Sri Lanka at the Gabba a fortnight later. By now, competition for places was getting intense, and he drifted in and out. Two years later he made another century, against India at the WACA, and finally got a clear run in the side on the 1992-93 Sri Lanka tour. The coach, Bob Simpson, wanted him to open. It was never right: he scored 71 in six innings, and that was the end of his Test career.

He had already put a toe or two in county cricket, first with Warwickshire then with Worcestershire. After 1994, he settled at New Road. Indeed, there were days when he – even more than Graeme Hick – seemed to *be* Worcestershire, with both bat and ball. Moody was largely responsible for both their trophies in the 1990s: the 1991 Benson and Hedges and the 1994 NatWest, when he won the match award in both semi-final and final, batting magnificently and bowling unhittably. He scored a century to lead Western Australia to victory in the 1998 Shield final and they won again a year later. His figures have been consistently impressive – 64 first-class centuries, an average around 47 with the bat, only just above 30 with the ball. His captaincy of both state and county has been understated, but effective.

By 1999, he was thinking of retirement: "I've always wanted to go out with the fire still roaring." But he also wanted to play in this World Cup. And beneath that placid exterior, as every opponent knows, there is a cricketer of steely determination. – MATTHEW ENGEL.

SAQLAIN MUSHTAQ

When politics and ethnic and religious differences mix with the exuberance and passion of Indian crowds, there is every chance the resulting volatility will damage cricket as a spectacle. But, though Pakistan's first Test tour of India for 12 years in early 1999 had potential for trouble across the subcontinent, it proved more memorable for the right things. In Delhi, Anil Kumble became only the second player in Test history to take ten wickets in an innings – yet he was not the man of the series. The award went to another spinner, of whom Kumble himself graciously remarked: "He bowled so well that the credit must be his."

Saqlain Mushtaq took five wickets in each innings of the Chennai and Delhi Tests, using such variety and control that India's formidable array of batsmen were rarely able to exert any authority over him. Most telling was his superiority over Sachin Tendulkar, who fell to Saqlain in three successive innings. On the second day in Chennai, when he dismissed Tendulkar for nought, Saqlain bowled 34 overs in the scorching heat. He was often unreadable, interspersing orthodox off-spin with what has come to be called his mystery ball", delivered with the same action but turning the other way.

It was in the second innings, however, that Saqlain drew on hitherto untapped reservoirs of stamina at the crucial moment. In an atmosphere of near-hysteria in the Chidambaram stadium, a century by Tendulkar carried India to within 17 runs of victory. Saqlain, who was by then suffering from heat fatigue, was punished for four boundaries in an over, and admits that "I thought I had had it and India were going to win." His captain, Wasim Akram, came across to urge him on: "You can do it, you're No. 1." When he tried again to force Saqlain away, Tendulkar was caught by Wasim in the deep. Saqlain took the final wicket for an astonishing triumph.

SAQLAIN MUSHTAQ was born in Lahore on December 29, 1976, the son of a government clerk. Two elder brothers taught him the game's rudiments. One, Sibtain, played at first-class level for Lahore and instructed his younger brother in off-spin, while Zulqarnain helped with his batting. The nine-year-old Saqlain was sometimes allowed to bowl in the nets at his brothers' club. He never got a chance to play at school, but by 13 was an all-rounder in the Zariff Memorial Club Second Eleven. It was always off-spin for Saqlain. "I never wanted to be a quick bowler. I was very skinny and never had too much strength in the body. I just played for enjoyment, never thinking I would be a pro. But my brothers and the club coach Ahmed Hassan thought I had a future. No one ever told me, though. It was only discussed with my brothers. The big step which turned my life was when I was 14 and went to the MAO (Mohammedan Anglo-Oriental) College. I got a new coach there, Mumtaz Akhtar Butt. I played for the college for three years and we won the championship three years."

However, he ascribes the secret of his wrong'un to the yard and street cricket he played as a teenager, at his home in Lahore, with relatives and neighbourhood boys. "We would get up at 4.30 a.m., go to the mosque and then play a Test match. We drew lines in chalk on the walls for the wickets. We would bet soft drinks or a dinner on the result. I used a tennis ball bound with electric tape. Then it goes a bit quicker, swings and dips. You can make it go both ways."

Saqlain made his first-class debut in 1994-95, aged 17. He took 52 wickets in his first season and was picked to represent Pakistan A in a one-day tournament in Dhaka. Full international recognition came quickly in September 1995, after Saqlain got seven wickets for the PCB Patron's Eleven against the touring Sri Lankans. His Test debut came three days later, at Peshawar: he took four wickets in that game and five in the next. By the end of 1999, his total had reached 107 in 24 Tests and 210 in 111 one-day internationals; he was the quickest bowler in history to reach 100 one-day international wickets. Wasim believes he is the greatest off-spinner he has seen. "He is as aggressive as a fast bowler, not afraid of getting hit, and has this total belief in himself."

Saqlain joined Surrey in 1997, a step which he considers to have been wholly beneficial. "Before that I had never really bowled very much. In England, you play every day, sometimes ten days continuous. I've learned so much from different weather, pitches, conditions, different players, stances, techniques." Last summer he played seven games after the World Cup, taking 58 wickets at an extraordinary 11.37. A knee injury in August prevented him playing the final games, but Surrey were already assured of the title by then.

During the World Cup, Saqlain claimed 17 wickets, including a hat-trick against Zimbabwe, but time has not lessened the pain he felt when Pakistan lost the final to Australia. "I left the team hotel and went back to my London flat and cried. For two days I didn't speak to anyone apart from my wife. She helped pull me through." Helping Surrey to the County Championship assisted in the healing process. And he is only 23; there could be several more World Cups to come for Saqlain. – PETER DEELEY.

TAYLOR: HIS PLACE IN THE PANTHEON

By SCYLD BERRY

When Mark Taylor came off the field for the final time in Test cricket, on January 5, 1999, he was wearing his baggy green cap, not his normal white hat, to signal that retirement was at hand. It was the end of an era not just for Australian cricket, but for the game worldwide, because he had no challenger as the finest captain of modern times.

It would be fruitless to compare "Tubby" with the leaders of other ages. Warwick Armstrong, who was tubbier still, never had to address TV viewers ten minutes after the breathless finish of a day/night international, as Taylor did with unfailing articulacy. Sir Donald Bradman did not have to calculate net run-rate and work to keep the media on side: newspapers then were deferential. When Richie Benaud was captain, he knew the workings of the media all right, but he did not have to speak to them about players taking money from an Indian bookmaker, as Taylor did, with the diplomacy of an elder statesman.

Taylor can only be compared with other captains of the post-Packer era. And – bearing in mind that Mike Brearley led in just eight Tests in this period – among them he was unquestionably supreme. His only possible rivals, Clive Lloyd and Viv Richards, had a single game-plan in the field: they did not need more with the West Indian fast bowling.

But while he had to play a more complicated game than any of these, Taylor was, like them, an autocratic captain. The wicket-keeper Ian Healy, at times Australia's vice-captain and always in a position to know what was going on, testifies that he was never consulted on any major decision. A French or Italian stranger to cricket, introduced to a ground where Australia were in the field, would surely have been able to point out who was in charge: the one who strode down the pitch between overs, carrying a helmet under his left arm, directing with his right arm here or there, and chewing gum, his very jaw the focus of Australian cricket in the field. Even in the World Cup semi-final at Mohali in 1996, when Australia were on the verge of elimination by West Indies, Taylor's jaw and eyes never wavered. The impression that he always had something left up his sleeve – if only Stuart Law's leg-breaks – was never punctured. It was as well he never accepted the opportunity of captaining Northamptonshire.

An alternative style of captaincy has been tried in English county cricket – a less autocratic, more collegiate way in which every player is expected to offer his opinion so that all the ideas and energies of the team are pooled. It was pioneered by Brearley at Middlesex, and worked very well for them and, more recently, for Warwickshire under Dermot Reeve and Leicestershire under James Whitaker. But this collective style is suited to the long haul of the county game. In the heat of Test cricket, decisions need to be taken immediately, not after consultations in the dressing-room at tea. In Taylor's penultimate Test, a low-scoring match at Melbourne, Warren Hegg upper-cut the new fast bowler Matthew Nicholson to the boundary. Before the next ball, without consultation, Taylor moved Stuart MacGill back to deep fly-slip and, the next time Nicholson pitched short, Hegg upper-cut a catch straight to him. The idea of him agreeing to an earpiece – as Hansie Cronje did in the World Cup – so a coach could prompt him, would have been total anathema.

To this end, of being his own captain, Taylor's first act upon his appointment in 1994 was a political one. With his predecessor, Allan Border, Bobby Simpson had worked hand-in-hand, planning ahead the bowling strategies and field-placings of each session. Taylor caused Simpson to revert to being coach again, the organiser of nets and conductor of fielding practices, and determined to do all the captaincy himself – so much so that he omitted to think about his own batting and made a pair in his first Test as Australia's captain in Karachi. Soon he learned how to compartmentalise.

He had the essential attribute of being lucky. His record of tosses – 26 wins out of 50 – was in keeping with statistical norms, but he seemed to win the ones that mattered, for instance Adelaide and Sydney in his last Ashes series. And he had two great bowlers so that he could always keep control at one end. The Australian system helped him in protecting Glenn McGrath from being overbowled: during Taylor's captaincy, McGrath played only ten Shield matches for his state, New South Wales. Shane Warne, though, needed more than the system to protect him. On Border's last tour, to South Africa, Warne had exploded in the face of Andrew Hudson and the growing pressures of superstardom. Taylor was less of a friend to Warne than Border had been, more of a counsellor. He brought Warne under his wing, into the slips between Mark Waugh at second and Steve Waugh at gully, and relieved the pressure by explaining that as long as Australia won it didn't matter if Warne failed to take bundles of wickets.

When Taylor's batting form deserted him, as it did through the first half of 1997, he was still able to hang on to his catches at first slip (Mike Atherton still regrets that he did not captain England from that prime position) and therefore his position of authority. His batting could never live up to his first full series, when he scored 839 runs against England in 1989, but it recovered to the point when he scored 334 not out against Pakistan in Peshawar in 1998-99 to equal the highest innings for Australia. For declaring then, he received Bradman's thanks – and some recompense from a lucrative venture of jointly signed bats. Taylor did not believe much in technique; scoring runs and taking wickets were simply the means to getting on top of the opposition and staying there.

Yet he was perhaps the least conservative captain of his era as well. In contrast to Border, his declarations were not designed to kill all hope in the opposition, and interest in the match: he set New Zealand 288 at less than five an over at Hobart in 1997-98, albeit when Australia were 2–0 up in a three-Test series. If his record has a weakness, it is the minor one of losing Tests after a series had been decided, the mission accomplished. Whereas he learned from his Northern District club captain Ross Turner about backing himself and his players in tight situations, his New South Wales captain Geoff Lawson showed him how to take the risk of losing in the pursuit of winning.

He also upheld the dignity of the game. If he did not abolish Australian sledging, he oversaw a reduction of the racism in it. When Dickie Bird

And then there was no tomorrow: Mark Taylor in the home dressing-room of the Sydney Cricket Ground on his last day in first-class cricket before retiring.

umpired in the Tests in Australia after Salim Malik's return to the Pakistan side, he noticed that Taylor did not permit any verbals about match-fixing. In his press conferences and TV interviews, Taylor talked so well that he raised the standard of debate in Australia – and perhaps of cricket itself – in a way which was an example to all professional cricketers (except for an irritating phase when he kept referring to himself in the third person). His deeds mattered more than his words, however. His teams played such good and entertaining cricket that he strengthened its potentially vulnerable position as the No. 1 sport in Australia.

When Steve Waugh took over for the 1998-99 Test series in the West Indies, he made the error at Kingston of having two part-time bowlers on together, which Tubby would never have done. His difficulties there turned out to be mere teething troubles before leading Australia to the World Cup and a clean sweep of the following season's home Tests. Waugh won golden opinions, but it is too early to assess his place in the history of captaincy.

Taylor had disagreed with the decision to make Waugh one-day captain while he was still in charge of the Test side. But it was sensible selection policy which helped the team to keep on evolving until they won the World Cup, and Taylor to keep on going as Test captain until his last Ashes series was won and another tour of the West Indies loomed. He had been there and done that, his greatest Test triumph the 2–1 win in the West Indies in 1994-95, something which his predecessor so dearly wanted to achieve and never did. Border stopped Australia losing. Taylor made them into winners, the acknowledged if not official world champions of Test cricket.

Scyld Berry is cricket correspondent of the Sunday Telegraph.

MOST SUCCESSFUL TEST CAPTAINS

(Qualification: completed reigns of at least 20 Tests as captain)

	P	W	L	D	% won	% lost	% drawn
D. G. Bradman (*Australia*)	24	15	3	6	62.5	12.5	25.0
A. L. Hassett (*Australia*).	24	14	4	6	58.3	16.7	25.0
J. M. Brearley (*England*)	31	18	4	9	58.1	12.9	29.0
W. M. Woodfull (*Australia*). . . .	25	14	7	4	56.0	28.0	16.0
I. V. A. Richards (*West Indies*). .	50	27	8	15	54.0	16.0	30.0
M. A. Taylor (*Australia*)	**50**	**26**	**13**	**11**	**52.0**	**26.0**	**22.0**
I. M. Chappell (*Australia*).	30	15	5	10	50.0	16.7	33.3
P. B. H. May (*England*)	41	20	10	11	48.8	24.4	26.8
C. H. Lloyd (*West Indies*)	74	36	12	26	48.6	16.2	35.1
L. Hutton (*England*)	23	11	4	8	47.8	17.4	34.8
R. B. Richardson (*West Indies*) .	24	11	6	7	45.8	25.0	29.2
G. S. Chappell (*Australia*).	48	21	13	14	43.8	27.1	29.2
R. Benaud (*Australia*)	28	12	4	12*	42.9	14.3	42.9
Javed Miandad (*Pakistan*)	34	14	6	14	41.2	17.6	41.2

*Taylor suffered four of his 13 defeats in series Australia had already won. * Includes one tie. W. J. Cronje (South Africa) had won 25 of his 51 Tests, Wasim Akram (Pakistan) 12 of his 25 and S. P. Fleming (New Zealand) 10 of his 24 by February 24, 2000.*

Research: Gordon Vince

THE GREAT FAST BOWLER

By MARK NICHOLAS

From the address given at the funeral of Malcolm Marshall at the Sir Garfield Sobers Sports Complex, Barbados, on November 13, 1999:

Many years ago my mother suggested to me, in reference to a splendid schoolteacher who had died, that in life one came across only a few truly special people. Lots of good'uns, she said, plenty of fabulous folk, but only a few who are special.

Malcolm Marshall, conclusively, was one of those – one of those special people. Not so much because he was so extraordinarily good at cricket, but because of the way in which he applied the various gifts, cricket amongst them, which were given to him. Malcolm was no waster – not of time, not of talent – nor a shirker of any situation or challenge which confronted him.

He maintained excellence without arrogance, earned respect without ever assuming it, and displayed confidence and self-assurance within his immense humility.

For as long as perhaps the last two months – maybe more, maybe less – he knew deep down, I think, that the game was up. But he was damned if he would let us know. He was such a stubborn fellow. It was as if he was more concerned about the suffering of those around him, those few intensely close friends kept by this very private man, than about the suffering he was going through himself. The qualities of thoughtfulness and caring, of courage and bravery – and didn't he so often show that in his play? – were among his finest. For all the flamboyance and bravado as a sportsman, Malcolm was not one to over-dramatise off the field. He said things as they were, and he resolved that his dreadful illness would be his own problem and, as it escalated, he would not panic others with its potential end.

For everyone who lives here, on this magical island, the name of Malcolm Marshall is synonymous with the style of the place: with the game of cricket in its purest calypso form, but also in its more modern professional form; with fun and sun; with the good and simple living that is typical here; and with the honesty and generosity of spirit that characterises the people of Barbados. It is clear to a visitor his loss has stunned his nation.

And yet, most fascinatingly, amazingly really, his loss has echoed all around the world, volley upon volley of shock stabbing at friends and fans wherever the game is treasured. The internet, for example, is jammed with messages and memories, and telephone lines have been on heat. Among the first calls I received were from Shaun Pollock, in Natal, South Africa, who attributes so much of his success to Malcolm; from Barry Richards, the great South African batsman, living now in Australia; from Martin Crowe, who called him "the finest opponent of them all – furious but fair, and fantastic value in the bar"; and from Ian Botham, busy on his final walk raising millions of pounds for Leukaemia Research, who for once found himself virtually unable to speak, so sad was he not to say goodbye to "the skinny wimp from the Windies", as he loved to call him.

Richards said how sorry he was not to have played with Marshall at Hampshire; he had the privilege of Gordon Greenidge and Andy Roberts but not of him. It was Captain Peter Short who brought Marshall to Hampshire, continuing the line of Barbadians who played for the county, the first of whom was another Marshall, that wonderful batsman Roy, who Malcolm used to follow in the papers.

It was funny to watch opponents greet Macko. The greats, his peers, relished the moment with hand-slapping glee and then they all tore the life out of each other on the pitch. The less good used to whisper among themselves if he was late, as he often was, incidentally, saying "no sign of Macko today? Phew!" Then, when he arrived, wrapped in gold chains and fancy clothes – and boy did he dress snappy or what? – their faces would fall. Ray East and David Acfield, the Essex spinners and terrified tail-enders, used to wait by his car and offer to carry his bags to the dressing-room. "Why?" asked Malcolm, when it first happened. "Well, Mr Marshall, we thought you might consider a couple of half-volleys and, if they're nice and straight, we promise to miss them!"

It is an amazing phenomenon of his short life that opponents everywhere, from Barbados to Bombay, from Sydney to Southampton, loved him so. Let's face it, he was a lethal bowler – that skidding bouncer homed in on its target like a Scud missile – and a brilliantly skilful bowler capable of all kinds of swing and cut and subtle changes of pace. But, of course, he was revered after play when he drank his beloved brandies, when his sharp mind chewed the cud of the game and when he boasted of his batting exploits. How he rejoiced in batting!

He loved talking cricket: he knew it so well, and people listened to his strong opinion, his deep insight and his remarkable ability to explore the game's present and future with uncanny foresight. He had time for everyone after play; in the mornings before play too, when he would share the secrets of his success equally with anyone, friend or foe. Pollock, Lance Klusener, Dominic Cork and Chris Cairns are among those who lapped up his advice. Imran Khan, who calls Malcolm the greatest of all fast bowlers, learned the leg-cutter from him. Malcolm, in turn, had learnt it from Dennis Lillee. Theirs was the Fast Bowlers Union, and how he loved to share the nuances and stories of the spoils with all-comers.

So far then, we have a universally loved and respected character who is unselfish and warm, and a man of supreme skill. But we mustn't forget his sense of humour, the extravagant plans for each batsman and those often hysterical, detailed field settings. And then he would turn up his collar and swagger away, job done clinically yet with such flair. That swagger, the swaying of the hips, the brim of the sunhat tilted forwards, the collar pointing to the sky, were all a result of his adoration of Sir Garfield Sobers, whose hundred against New Zealand at the Kensington Oval in 1972 was the definitive moment in the 13-year-old Malcolm's dream to reach the top. He wanted to *be* Sobers. And of course he was closer to being him than most. "Come on Sobey, come and have a bowl," Clive Lloyd would sometimes say years later, and in would stroll this languid, almost liquid cricketer, immaculate every inch of the way even when dripping with the sweat of his efforts.

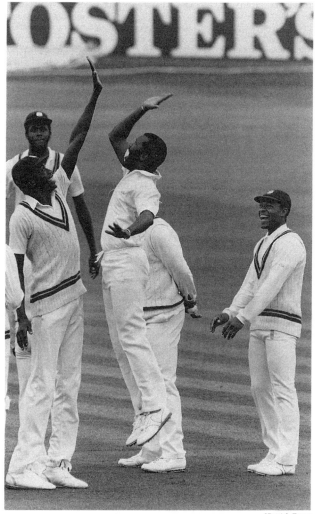

[*Patrick Eagar*

"A man of joy and delight in all he did": Malcolm Marshall celebrates another West Indian success.

Not much got the old boy's back up, though you didn't dare meddle with his cricket case or nick a T-shirt from his wardrobe – blimey, you would have thought an atomic bomb had gone off if he found anything out of place, so neat and tidy were clothes and kit. And he didn't like sloppiness from cricketers, or from people in general – and certainly didn't suffer indifference from anyone. And he couldn't stand bad manners. Oh, and he liked to get his own way, but then don't we all? And you know why these things frustrated him?

Because he cared. He cared about standards, about commitment to the chosen cause, about quality in all things. Joel Garner once said that "Malcolm's real strength is that he never gives less than 100 per cent for any team in which he plays or is involved." Even to the end, before his operation, he would be bowling in the nets, in-swing and out-swing, appeals and exasperation, smiles and scowls and so much joy.

That's Macko for me. A man of joy and delight in all he did and in others around him. The endless chatter, that laughter with his head thrown skywards, those dancing, happy eyes and that welcoming ripper of a smile. And the unbridled enthusiasm for a determined march on all the challenges of life – it didn't matter what they were, simple things even such as a round of golf, a hand of backgammon, a night on the town – all met with relish and hope.

He is gone now, and of course we're sad. We're heartbroken. But he is a man we *must* celebrate, for he gave life all that he had, and from him came an unforgettable warmth and always a sense of direction. The Hampshire captain of the 1960s, Colin Ingleby-Mackenzie, said last week, "We can only assume the great Maestro in the sky was short of a class all-rounder." Not only does the Maestro in the sky have with him a great all-rounder, but, in Malcolm, has the greatest enthusiast for the game I have known. They will probably be having a party together right now, as we must in time, in his honour. Let's be honest, he'd hate us not to smile from within each time we think of him – the Marshall memory really is one to treasure.

Malcolm always referred to himself as "a lucky man". Well, we're the lucky ones to have known him. What a privilege it has been.

Malcolm Marshall died on November 4, 1999, aged 41. His obituary is on pages 1553–1555. Mark Nicholas, now a broadcaster and journalist, was captain of Hampshire from 1984 to 1995.

THE GREAT WICKET-KEEPER

By LORD COWDREY

From the address given at the memorial service for Godfrey Evans CBE at Canterbury Cathedral on September 20, 1999:

Behind the stumps, Godfrey Evans was a genius – no doubt about that. In a sense, he was something of a genius off the field, too, for being such enormous fun and for his eternal optimism. So on no account should there be any glum faces here today. He loved the big occasion. He is loving every minute of this, a huge crowd and a Test match venue…

Godfrey went on four tours of Australia. First under Wally Hammond, second under Freddie Brown in 1950, where *Wisden* records that Evans played in all five Test matches and never missed a chance. Then, Len Hutton's Ashes-winning tour, which was my first, and I was able to see at first hand, often from gully or short leg, the most irrepressible cricketer and truest sportsman that I was ever to play alongside.

Yet he was even better in England, whether it be handling the fast, looping, waspish leg-breaks and googlies of Doug Wright, another genius, or keeping to Jim Laker and Tony Lock on rain-affected pitches, not forgetting his mastery standing up to Alec Bedser.

Only last week, Doug Insole, with us here today, received a hand-written letter from Don Bradman, a personal friend, lamenting the passing of two great Men of Kent, saying: "Douglas Wright, surely England's finest attacking leg-spinner – and, as for Godfrey, probably the greatest wicket-keeper of them all". Sir Donald is not given to extravagant praise. Surely this is the ultimate tribute.

Why was he so good? Godfrey had the eye of a hawk, exceptional agility, instinctive footwork, wonderful timing in his taking of a ball, and extraordinary speed of hand, each hand just as strong as the other. He was the fittest and strongest of cricketers, with endless courage. He used to take some fearful knocks on the arms and shoulder when the ball bounced unpredictably, but he would never show pain. He would laugh it off, saying out of the corner of his mouth: "Just nothing – nothing that a large glass or two and a pretty face won't put right tonight." No day was too long or sun too hot. He saw it as part of his daily run to be at his keenest in the last half-hour of the day, supporting his captain and urging everyone on.

It was his power of concentration that ensured his success. As the bowler turned to start his run up, Godfrey would tap his gloves together before bending – the signal for all other thoughts to be put out of his mind. Once the ball had been bowled and he was sure that it was dead, he would, however briefly, try to switch off again. Application, relaxation, vitality, loyalty, humour and total integrity were all there in abundance. He made his presence felt by his flair and brilliance, no time for the endless and mindless chatter that spoils today's fun.

Surprisingly, for one who so enjoyed living life to the full, calculated rest was one of his disciplines. The daily ritual: coming off the field at lunchtime,

[*Alpha*

(*Above*) Godfrey Evans in his pomp: the confident appeal, the despairing batsman – Burke st Evans b Laker at Lord's, 1956. (*Below*) Evans poses for the camera in 1967 as he prepares to make his comeback with Kent, aged 46.

[Daily Express/*Hulton Getty*

the twelfth man would be primed to have ready in his place in the dressing-room a sandwich and a mug of tea, with specific instructions to be on hand to take all his wet clothes as he peeled off – for he would be soaked through. As fast as he could, he would towel himself down, re-dress in dry clothes, swallow his sandwich, swig his tea and, in a flash, he would be fast asleep. On the bench, under the bench, even on the shower-room floor, for 15 minutes he would be dead to the world. The twelfth man would waken him with a few minutes to go. Then, head in a basin of cold water. A dry cap and inner gloves, and he would be off down the pavilion steps to entertain his adoring public, looking the youngest and perkiest of the team: "the one and only Godders".

Like many here today, I enjoyed many hours being driven by him, not as you might expect, in a Porsche roaring around the countryside on two wheels, but a comfortable, very old, second-hand Bentley. On the road he was the original old fogey, never exceeding the speed limit, however long the journey, pottering up the old A1 at 65 mph, Godfrey at peace with his pipe, enjoying the countryside, long silences, the occasional sage comment – we could have been with the Dean of Christ Church.

Next evening, fielding-stint over, he was bound to sniff out a party which would need enlivening. He would be there, over-robust maybe, certainly too *risqué* for most hosts. His friends would melt away, consoling themselves that the sun would come up again tomorrow, a new day, and Godfrey would be back to normal again.

On board ship, with Godfrey as Master of Ceremonies, the MCC team would carry away every prize on fancy-dress night. He was always Carmen Miranda, beautifully made up, carrying a basket of fruit precariously balanced on his head. He would steal the show, and would lead our inevitable victory parade in a never-ending dance through every corner of the ship.

He was the most generous of men. When he moved into the jewellery business, and knew quite a lot about it, he surprised everyone, including himself, I suspect, by winning £1,000 on a live televised quiz – tough questions on jewellery. He needed the money (he always needed the money), but straight away he announced that the first £500 would go to his cricketing friend, the Rev. David Sheppard, who needed it to build a play area for his youngsters in Islington.

So, today, we salute him – as a great cricketer, a simple soul, with a heart of gold. He loved the game, always courteous to opponents, trusted by umpires. He made people smile all around the cricket world, first as a player and, later on, with his white, bewhiskered, cheery face, the caring courier of touring parties. Godfrey may have left us, but all of us here today, and countless others, warm to his memory.

He was a rare, sparkling bird – dear Godfrey. You might say, quite unique.

Godfrey Evans died on May 3, 1999, aged 78. His obituary is on pages 1543–1544. Lord Cowdrey of Tonbridge was captain of Kent and England.

THE GREAT SAGE

By JOHN WOODCOCK

E. W. Swanton died on January 22, 2000, aged 92. He was the cricket correspondent of the Daily Telegraph *from 1946 to 1975, but continued working until a few days before his death, and remained for generations the game's most influential writer. His obituary will appear in* Wisden 2001. *Here, one of his closest friends pays tribute.*

For the whole of the second half of the 20th century E. W. (Jim) Swanton was, as it were, the conscience of cricket; and because he lived to a great age, and retained his wits and enthusiasm right to the end, he became an ever-rarer, ever-more precious source of reference and enlightenment.

He died of a heart attack on a Saturday afternoon, three weeks short of his 93rd birthday. He had been in hospital for a few days after being taken ill quite suddenly. On the Thursday evening, we had been talking somewhat idly, over the phone, as we often did: a little harmless gossip, the occasional reminiscence. For no particular reason, the last day of the Headingley Test match of 1948 came up – that ill-fated day, if you were an Englishman, on which Australia were left to score 404 in 345 minutes on a turning pitch and made them for the loss of three wickets with a quarter of an hour to spare (Arthur Morris 182; Don Bradman 173 not out; Jim Laker nought for 93).

"I remember some time later 'Fergie' [Bill Ferguson, that is, the baggage master for most touring sides in those days] saying how The Don had told him he had better have the team's coach at the ground by four o'clock, so dire was the outlook for Australia. Don, though, told his side that they would far better try to win the match than draw it; if they played for a draw, he said, they'd be more likely to lose." That was Jim, extemporising. He was an inexhaustible, irreplaceable, unstinting fund of cricketing intelligence.

Affecting everything he did was a strong and forceful personality, and a love of cricket that withstood, sometimes painfully but always objectively, the constant and countless changes that come with evolution. With the passing years came benevolence, and a standing in the game, worldwide, that very few, if any, have enjoyed who have not themselves, at some time or other, been famous players. I suppose the only other sporting journalist to have commanded such attention and had so influential a following was Bernard Darwin, who wrote about golf, mostly for *The Times,* for 46 years, ending in 1953.

It would be as wrong to give the impression that Jim was an absolute paragon as it was for one of his obituarists to say that he was a man of little humour. I am one of many who were introduced into the world of sports journalism as his amanuensis, a job which was underwritten by the *Daily Telegraph* when he was their cricket correspondent, and entailed being typist, chauffeur, chronicler, batman and butt. Among others whom he helped to bring forward were Christopher Martin-Jenkins (now a household

Jim Swanton in 1971.

name), Brian Moore (of TV footballing fame) and, briefly, the erudite Scyld Berry (who found secretarial work not to be his strongest suit). The chances are, too, that only by breaking the male line and filling the post herself did Daphne Surfleet become Mrs Richie Benaud back in the 1960s.

We all came to know what drove Jim to become the towering figure he was: attention to detail; discretion; the strength of his convictions (not least spiritually); a potentially daunting presence (not least physically); an eye for the main chance (not least socially); goodwill towards cricketers in the making; not the longest of fuses; great kindness and generosity; a wonderful memory; unwavering loyalty, both to the game and his friends; a proper knowledge of the technique of cricket; a prolific output; and a thinly disguised preference for getting his own way.

In the 1930s, E. M. Wellings, then a recent Oxford blue, felt obliged to give up playing the game upon becoming cricket correspondent of the London *Evening News* in order to concentrate on his work. Swanton, his opposite number on the rival paper, the *Evening Standard*, made sure he had the time to score 1,000 runs most seasons and take plenty of wickets with gentle leg-breaks ("holy rollers" they were sometimes called) in a good class of cricket. Even then, still in his twenties, Jim was setting his own agenda. In so far as it was at all possible, I dare say he did so as a prisoner of the Japanese in the Second World War, when the 1939 *Wisden*, which he had with him, did the rounds among his fellow prisoners. Lovingly rebound several times, marked "non-subversive" – and now no doubt a collector's item – it helped remind them of what the fighting was for. Back in England by the end of 1945, he very soon acquired, in the *Daily Telegraph*, the platform from which he spent the next 54 years upholding the best principles of cricket – always lucidly, at times pontifically, and invariably fairly. And what he wrote counted; it formed opinion.

Because he did rather lay down the law, there were, inevitably, clashes of opinion and personality. Had he gone to Australia on the Bodyline tour of 1932-33, as he very nearly did, I doubt whether it would have suited Douglas Jardine at all: history, too, would be better informed. In South Africa in 1956-57, Peter May, the England captain, gave him a distinctly cold shoulder as a result of his pronounced aversion, partly aesthetic, to Doug Insole's unorthodox batting method, which Swanton thought could never be successful on South African pitches. In the event, Insole, who was May's vice-captain, continued to play as he always had and headed the England Test batting averages. "Wonders never cease," said Swanton, with a wry smile. And now, with Jim's passing, Insole becomes the leading authority on what has happened, when and where and how and why, in the world of cricket in the last 50 years.

Those who opposed Swanton, perhaps through jealousy or perceived exclusion, were inclined to see him either as a reactionary or as being too high and mighty. In fact, though honouring the past, he was always looking to the future. He abhorred Kerry Packer – not personally (they never met) but for the vulgarity and militancy with which, in the late 1970s, he hijacked the game. On the other hand, he loved with a passion to see cricket hard, skilfully and sportingly played and, if it was at Lord's or during the Canterbury Week or in Barbados, so much the better. So far as the highness and the mightiness goes, that may not entirely be a myth – but neither did it affect in any way what he wrote.

Many people meeting Jim for the first time were surprised to discover what fun and what riveting company he was. Never was that more evident than at the Cricket Writers' Club Golden Jubilee Dinner in the Long Room at Lord's in 1996: a majestic speech, brimming with cadence, wit and wisdom, brought him a standing ovation from by no means the least cynical of audiences. He was 89 at the time. His writing, like his broadcasting, had clarity and resonance, and was never forced. His reports were informative, his commentaries judicial. "Have you read what Swanton said today?" was a question posed by a majority of cricketers from the time he joined the *Daily Telegraph* until he wrote his last piece for them, a full page of recollections, shortly before he died. The game will miss him badly, his sense of perspective perhaps most of all.

John Woodcock was cricket correspondent of The Times *from 1954 to 1987 and editor of* Wisden *1981 to 1986. He first met E. W. Swanton in 1946, toured Australia in 1950-51 as his assistant and was his friend for the next 50 years.*

A LOVELY DAY, EVERYTHING RIGHT

By PATRICK COLLINS

The early mist had persisted into mid-morning, and a few thick grey clouds still clung to the rooftops of Taunton. But the lady at the newsagent's counter smiled at my concern. "Don't you worry yourself, m'dear," she said. "You'll have a right lovely day at the cricket. You'll see." An hour later, a Glamorgan fielder leaned on the boundary fence and mopped his brow with a large white handkerchief. "'S'ot, ain't it?" muttered a Somerset member. "Bloody 'ot," said the cricketer, as the sun stared down from a flawless September sky.

You reminded yourself that this was 1999: English cricket's *annus horribilis*, a year which had seen the national team thrashed in Australia, brusquely dismissed from the World Cup, then comprehensively beaten at home by the might of New Zealand. Soon we were sending our brave lads off to South Africa, where they were expected to win nothing but widespread sympathy and the occasional toss.

A thousand reasons have been suggested for this state of affairs, ranging from the perversity of the English climate to the absurdity of English administrators. But the one thing upon which everybody seemed agreed was that the County Championship was a discredited anachronism; a friendless, pointless, worthless competition despised by the players and disregarded by the public. The Championship, we are told, is the sporting equivalent of Monty Python's Norwegian Blue. It may well be nailed to its perch and dreaming of the fjords, but it is, beyond doubt or question, a dead parrot. All I can say is that the sombre message has yet to reach Taunton.

And so, on a Thursday morning, they trooped into the County Ground to watch their beloved Somerset play Glamorgan. In fairness, there wasn't a lot of trooping involved, since the crowd never rose much above 2,000. But the ground was rather more than a quarter full and the atmosphere was splendidly animated.

Naturally, the stereotypes were out in force. There were old gentlemen, leaning on their sticks and dozing in the shade. And there were elderly ladies, knitting and gossiping and gently fanning themselves with scorecards. One *grande dame*, striding through the members' stand in sensible shoes and superfluous cardigan, was briefly challenged by a steward. She incinerated him with a glare which could have quelled a colonial mutiny.

You remembered that the game has been played on this entrancing ground since 1882. They were playing cricket here, by the River Tone, in the summer of 1914 when the great guns began to boom at Mons. And they played here the very week 25 years later when a second war was declared on Germany. To be sure, some of those on the ground had memories of that terrible week. Yet they formed only a part of the picture, for the young had turned out in pleasing numbers. A few children studied scorebooks, others yelled approval of every Somerset boundary. Down at the third-man fence, half a dozen lads played cricket with a bat and tennis ball, joining in shrill argument as one fair-haired kid bolted a short single. "You were out!" "I was in!" "Out!" "In!" And you smiled as you listened to the sounds of your childhood.

Across the sunlit ground stood a thoroughly modern grandstand: a touch short on charm, but sharp-edged and palpably confident. The Ian Botham Stand. They still speak of Botham down here; of the pranks he pulled and the runs he scored and of the time he turned up for one match in a helicopter. "*A helicopter*," said one dowager, Lady Bracknell to the life.

They speak too, of the other great men of Somerset. Of Vivian Richards, who scored a triple-hundred on a single summer's day in 1985. Of Brian Close, who came from Yorkshire and inspired them with his uncompromising courage. And of the gifted farmer's son named Harold Gimblett, who was called up at the last moment for his debut in 1935, went in with Somerset at 107 for six against Essex, and scored the fastest century of the summer in 63 minutes. With a borrowed bat.

The day grows hotter, so you take shelter in the indoor school: a superb facility with nets, bowling machines and coaching videos to aid the development of the next generation of Somerset cricketers. Vic Marks, the old England off-spinner who is one of the county's favourite sons as well as chairman of cricket, shows you around with justifiable pride. On one wall is a statement of "Values and Targets" for the youth teams: "Constant Improvement, Discipline, Team Comes First, Will to Win – No Fear, Challenge the Game". Marks played his cricket in a rather more cynical age. "Hmmm," he mutters. "Not sure if Closey knew about all that stuff." Somerset are dismissed for 203 and the ground is buzzing with worried mumbles. Then Glamorgan collapse quite dramatically. At tea, they are 20 for four. The Somerset players wear enormous smiles. Andrew Caddick signs autographs with the cheery solicitude of a man in his benefit season.

The Somerset groundsman sets about his wicket with a broom of twigs. He is accosted by a small, irate Glamorgan supporter. "You don't want to brush it, mate," says the Welshman. "You want to blow the bugger up." The groundsman is indignant. "It's a bit quick, that's all," he says. "Not my fault they can't handle it." Over in the members' bar, a local historian recalls that this was the ground upon which Archie MacLaren hit 424 for Lancashire in 1895, and Dr Grace himself scored his final century for Gloucestershire as recently as 1898. "So don't try telling me there's something wrong with the wicket," he says. Everybody nods their agreement. It is a wonderful moment.

Now you may dismiss the foregoing as so much romantic tosh. You may argue that the Championship has failed English cricket by offering a comfortable home to the hopelessly mediocre. You may further argue that the benefit system, in all its feudal idiocy, represents an active enticement to mundane cricketers to hang around the county scene long after their usefulness is over.

You may contend that the grind of daily combat, allied to the endless journeys up and down the nation's motorways, has blunted the competitive edge of English cricketers – although not, it would seem, of imports such as Surrey's Saqlain Mushtaq or Jacques Kallis of Glamorgan. Finally, you may cite the almost unwaveringly abysmal record of English Test teams across the past decade and conclude that international success and the County Championship are mutually exclusive.

[*Alain Lockyer, Somerset News*

"…that idyllic cricket ground": Taunton on a timeless summer's day.

These are respectable arguments, relentlessly advocated by those who believe that the health of English cricket must exclusively be measured by international performance and that the domestic game should be reduced to the status it occupies in Australia, where the Sheffield Shield has been played for decades before rows of empty seats but whose Test team is the envy of the cricketing world.

There was a time when those arguments carried conviction, but now they seem to miss the point. What, pray, is wrong with playing the game as widely as possible, and on as many homespun stages as the public can support? Why are we misguided in observing a ritual which has endured throughout the sporting century, bringing pride, pleasure and a genuine sense of identity to communities which value such virtues? And why should we apologise for finding joy in such dramatic beauty; for sitting in that idyllic cricket ground, with the handsome Victorian bulk of St James's Church at our back and the blue remembered hills of the Quantocks away in the hazy distance?

The pragmatists tell us we can have one or the other, but not both. We can set ourselves to design a Test team which takes most matches into the fifth day and even wins the occasional series. Or we can continue to support an institution which offers a great deal of pleasure to a significant number of people, young and old.

Personally, I believe the county game is one of this nation's happier and worthier institutions. I believe that this simple sporting contest has contributed much to the serene and civilised quality of life in England. And, given the choice, I know where my loyalties lie. For I have enjoyed "a right lovely day at the cricket". It was a memorable experience. We should destroy it at our peril.

Patrick Collins is chief sports writer of the Mail on Sunday, *where this piece first appeared. It is reproduced by kind permission of the newspaper.*

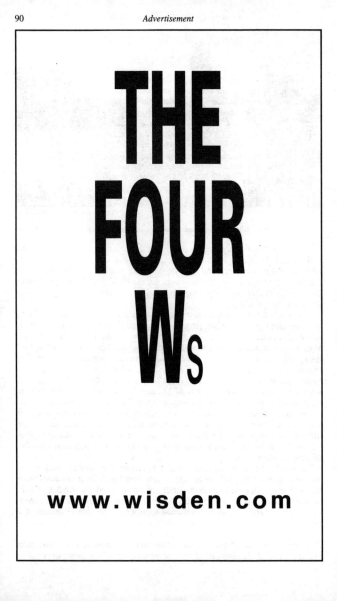

RICH GAME, POOR GAME

By STEPHEN FAY

English cricket's balance sheet was finally published in 1999 in the first-ever annual report of the England and Wales Cricket Board (ECB); its predecessor, the Test and County Cricket Board, always kept its figures secret. Unlike a normal company report, however, this 52-page glossy does not focus on profit and loss.

The concentration is not on traditional concerns either: more prominence is given to women's cricket, the disabled, racism and child protection than to the England Test team, which is dealt with in a single paragraph. Perhaps there was no more to say, but detail, judgment and analysis have also been edited out of the section devoted to the balance sheet.

The report does show that, in the year ending December 31, 1998, the ECB made a surplus of £7,928,000 on a turnover of £50,733,000. Turnover was up 16 per cent and profits were up by 12.7 per cent. The report also recorded the best news of 1999 – the £103 million four-year deal with Channel 4 and BSkyB for the rights to televise cricket. Apart from a 28 per cent rise in administration expenses (now above £5 million) to pay a staff of 135, the balance sheet would satisfy the shareholders of most public companies.

The 18 first-class counties, MCC and the Minor Counties received £28,177,000 from the ECB in 1998, which was an increase of 15 per cent for the third year in a row. This money kept weak counties solvent, and enabled county cricketers to earn a decent wage.

Cricket's finances appear to be sound, but the outline figures in the annual report mask many tensions. Relations between the five counties with Test match grounds (Middlesex are a special case since MCC owns Lord's) and the other first-class counties have become bitter and mistrustful. In the background, there is an edgy power struggle between those at the centre, who believe in a powerful executive, and the first-class counties.

Nobody seems to reflect on the fundamental question about finance, and ask whether the way cricket spends its money affects the performance of the Test team. The question matters because Tests are cricket's shop window, and the county game survives only because of the revenue raised from Test matches. In 1998, 40 per cent of the ECB's revenue came from broadcasting; ticket income provided 26 per cent, and sponsorship 21 per cent; other income (13 per cent) included revenue from advertising boards. Annual turnover from all first-class cricket – MCC and the counties as well as the ECB – is £88 million – much the same as that of Manchester United.

And, after three years of steadily rising income, there was a drop in 1999. The first-class counties had been told that World Cup year would bring them another 15 per cent increase in 1999, but the agency hired by the ECB to sign up eight principal World Cup sponsors at £2 million each came up with only four. At the start of the year, the ECB informed the counties that they could expect an increase of only five per cent.

This was dire news for several of the smaller counties. But eventually, excellent World Cup ticket sales and the respectable television deal meant that the figures were much better than feared. The increase in the share-out rose to ten per cent rather than five. The uncertainty had, however, aggravated the tensions between the Test match grounds and the other counties.

Until 1999, the share-out had been distributed fairly equally among all first-class counties. However, the Test match grounds are required to spend millions on improvements to make the grounds fit for occupation by spectators who are impatient at having to pay £35 to sit in squalor in sections of Headingley and Old Trafford. They wanted a bigger share of the money.

Negotiations started badly, and lasted for months before the Test match grounds accepted a new deal that gives each of them 12.5 per cent of ticket sales rather than 7.5 per cent at present, and a daily rental fee of £110,000 in 2000, rising to £145,000 in 2002, to cover the extra costs of staging a Test. At the insistence of the other 13 counties, this substantial extra revenue must be spent on capital improvements to the ground, rather than on expensive baubles like cricketers from overseas, or, indeed, from other counties. At the outset of a two-division Championship, most non-Test counties are acutely aware of their financial insecurity. Forget that three of the Test-match counties are in the second division in 2000; the trend is for the rich to get richer and the poor poorer.

There are opportunities at the Test grounds for money-making that would be impossible elsewhere. Boxes in the new Radcliffe Road Stand at Trent Bridge can be turned into bedrooms, and hospitality suites into conference centres. Half Warwickshire's income is from conferences, exhibitions and banquets. At Lancashire, catering is a principal source of income. The purpose is to become financially independent of cricket.

Gate receipts for county cricket are risible. At Edgbaston, ticket sales for a season's nine county games amount to £8,000; hiring stewards and manning the scoreboards costs £1,000 a day. Members provide more revenue, of course, but the £610,000 raised that way does not amount to more than one-third of the cricket budget, never mind the costs of the ground.

But cricket clubs are still controlled by their members, and run by committees, whether they are members' clubs or industrial and provident societies; only Durham is a limited company. Members take a proprietorial interest in something they do not really own. "I pay your wages," shouted a disgruntled member at Chelmsford at Derek Pringle. ("I'll take a tuppenny-ha'penny cut if you'll stay home," Pringle replied.)

Membership fees have ceased to be a significant source of revenue, however. Take the case of Nottinghamshire. In 1960, 30 per cent of the club's income came from subscriptions. By 1995, it had slipped below 10 per cent. Among all the counties, average income from subs in 1998 was 11 per cent.

This figure does not come from the ECB, which does not appear to analyse the financial statistics in the annual reports of the counties. Like others in this article, it comes from a survey of English cricket in 1998 done by a Nottingham accountant-turned-agent named Robert Matusiewicz, who runs a company called Ambition Management.

The survey shows that the average ECB share-out in 1998 was £1,188,000; for ten counties, the ECB provided more than half their income. The big spenders were the big earners. The average total income for the Test ground clubs was £4,397,000; for the rest, it was £2,210,000. But when it came to wages, the differential narrowed sharply: payrolls at Warwickshire, Lancashire, Yorkshire, Surrey and Nottinghamshire averaged £937,000 compared to £701,000 in the other 13 counties.

My own random survey of wages in the Midland counties confirms the Matusiewicz survey's general figures. At Warwickshire, the average wage was £40,000, plus bonuses for capped players in a good year. Imports like Nick Knight and Ed Giddins got nearly double that. Use of a sponsored car is worth another £4,000. At Nottinghamshire, all 24 professional players got a Daewoo. At Derbyshire only capped players got a car, and there were not many of those; a journeyman's income was £25,000. But these rankings are upset when an apparently poor club like Sussex pays a new captain £70,000 a year; or Hampshire hires Shane Warne before it knows where his salary is coming from; or, at Worcestershire, a benefactor agrees to pay Glenn McGrath's salary. The effect of central contracts remains to be seen, but over the last few years differentials between Test players and the best-paid county players have actually been narrowing.

The principal beneficiaries of the share-out in recent years have been the players. Wages at Nottinghamshire are four times higher over a decade, at a time of relatively low inflation. At Leicestershire, champions in 1996 and 1998, they have doubled in the last three years – but they still could not hold on to Alan Mullally and Paul Nixon.

The England players were acutely conscious of their wages in the build-up to the World Cup. Although they denied the suggestion that the dispute about wages and bonuses affected their performance, they did fall out with the ECB. Eventually, signing-on fees were raised and so were the bonuses for getting to the semi-final and beyond. (The ECB pays the win-bonus by the ingenious expedient of insuring against an England victory, and it was reluctant to raise the premium.)

Soon after the players grudgingly agreed to the revised formula, England failed to qualify even for the intermediate stages, and the players trundled home with less than £15,000 for six weeks' work. But they remained offended by the payment to the counties of £30,000 for each player in the squad to compensate for his absence – far more than they were ever offered: "It wasn't the money, it was the attitude," said Angus Fraser. The priorities were emblematic: they showed cricket was still run by the ECB on behalf of 18 first-class counties, not the players or the Test audience.

Counties do not question this. "We own the rights to cricket," says David Collier, formerly Leicestershire chief executive, now next door with Nottinghamshire. These rights derive from the fact that England players learn the game in county cricket. But, while they do appreciate the importance of good Test performances to cricket's finances, no county chairman or chief executive I have spoken to considers that poor England performances can be attributed to the organisation of county cricket, or the way it is financed. But they wouldn't, would they?

Stephen Fay writes about cricket for the Independent on Sunday. *He was formerly editor of* Business *and is the author of several books on banking.*

FIFTY YEARS OF THE LORD'S TAVERNERS

By PAT GIBSON

It sounded as though the England team had finally reached rock bottom during the fateful Test series against New Zealand last summer when Graham Gooch, hitherto player, captain, manager and selector, was described as the "acting coach". The implication was that if they could not play like Test cricketers they could at least be taught to act like them, in which case the authorities might have done better to turn to the Lord's Taverners to do the job properly.

The Taverners has been full of cricketing actors and acting cricketers ever since the opera singer and actor Martin Boddey (Lord's Taverner No. 1) first dreamed up the idea of starting a formal fraternity of cricket-lovers from the informal group who used to watch the game, pint in hand, from the late and still lamented Tavern at Lord's.

The idea was to have fun and raise a few quid to encourage youngsters to share their passion. They recruited some like-minded souls, most of them actors and broadcasters, persuaded the Duke of Edinburgh to join with the unforgettable title of "patron and twelfth man", and installed John Mills as their president. In the process, they founded what turned into a unique club and charity which in 2000 celebrates its 50th anniversary. A few friends turned into nearly 4,000 members; a few quid turned, in 1999, to around £1.5 million.

Groucho Marx may not have wanted to belong to any club that would accept him as a member, but there were few others who could not be persuaded to join an organisation in which the stars of show business rubbed shoulders with the great cricketers of the day, and vice versa. Nor was there any shortage of people from outside both kinds of dressing-rooms who wanted to be part of it too.

These days there are as many businessmen as there are showbiz and sports people; it is easy to be sceptical about the motives of some when you see them at a Taverners' lunch or dinner competing with each other to pay hundreds, sometimes thousands, of pounds for an autographed bat or, for heaven's sake, a signed print of Sir Alex Ferguson.

All scepticism disappears, however, when you realise how much money the Taverners make. In 1950, they collected £15,000. In 2000, they hope to celebrate the half-century by doubling the recent average and raising £3 million, making a grand total of around £25 million over 50 years.

Then look where the money goes. The founders simply intended to put money into cricket through the National Playing Fields Association. Today's aims are more wide-ranging. "Giving young people, particularly those with special needs, a sporting chance," says the mission statement.

In line with that, about half the Taverners' money goes directly into the game, where the Cricket Foundation channels it to where it is needed among the young. It is a vital contribution when the decline of cricket in schools has been a root cause of England's troubles.

Another 40 per cent goes on the special minibuses which help the physically and mentally handicapped get around – the Taverners put 25 on the road annually but hope to make it 75 in 2000 – and the final ten per cent goes towards helping disabled youngsters in other sports, like providing wheelchairs for them to play basketball.

So where does all the money come from? Cricket itself is still the driving force, with the Taverners playing about 16 matches every year and going on tour all over the world. There is never any shortage of players – or stories about them. Prince Charles once turned up on horseback, wearing his pads, for a match at RAF Cranwell, while Kevin Keegan went out to bat with a football at his feet at Arundel. They say that, when one disgruntled Taverner complained that he and his mates were not in the side, he was told: "Sorry old boy, we've got Len Hutton, Denis Compton and Jim Laker instead."

It is not all about cricket, though. Other Taverners' events have run from golf to tiddlywinks. Like the lunches, dinners and balls, they are now run

PRESIDENTS OF THE LORD'S TAVERNERS

1950-51 Sir John Mills; 1952 John Snagge; 1953 Martin Boddey; 1954 Jack Hawkins; 1955 Major A. Huskisson; 1956 Tommy Trinder; 1957 Stephen Mitchell; 1958 Sir John Barbirolli; 1959 Sir Ian Jacob; 1960-61 HRH The Duke of Edinburgh; 1962 Sir Robert Menzies; 1963 Richard Hearne; 1964 John Snagge; 1965 Sir Edward Lewis; 1966 Ronald Waldman; 1967-68 Harry Secombe; 1969 Lord Luke; 1970 Sir Brian Rix; 1971 Martin Boddey; 1972 Victor Silvester; 1973 Jimmy Edwards; 1974 Alf Gover; 1975-76 HRH The Prince of Wales; 1977-79 Eric Morecambe; 1980-81 Sir Harry Secombe; 1982 Ronnie Corbett; 1983-84 Terry Wogan; 1985-86 Sir David Frost; 1987 Ronnie Corbett; 1988-90 Sir Tim Rice; 1991-92 Leslie Crowther; 1993-94 HRH Prince Edward; 1995-97 Lord Cowdrey; 1998-99 Nicholas Parsons; 2000 Sir Tim Rice.

not only by the original organisation but also by the Lady Taverners, the Young Lord's Taverners and 25 separate regions. Tony Swainson, the director from 1972 to 1992, fought against the idea of the Taverners remaining a relatively exclusive celebrity club and helped turn it into a major charity. He was followed by Patrick Shervington and (briefly) David Stickels. Even such a happy organisation has been unable to escape internal politics. The new chief executive, Mark Williams, came from the Foreign Office, after being chosen from 411 applicants; his powers of diplomacy will be useful in directing the fund-raising efforts of so many big names and their matching egos.

The object remains the same: to have a lot of fun, to raise a lot of money. As Richard Groom, the chairman of the commercial committee, put it: "I think the strength of the Taverners is that it is a club as well as a charity." The Tavern may be long gone; its spirit lives on.

Pat Gibson (Lord's Taverner No. 2744) was formerly cricket correspondent of the Daily Express *and* Sunday Express, *and now writes for* The Times. *Details of the Taverners are on page 1525.*

JOHN WISDEN – 150 YEARS ON

By MURRAY HEDGCOCK

How difficult it would be for cricket to regard its great volume of record with proper appreciation if the man who gave it his name had been not John Wisden, but John Smith, Jones, or Robinson. There have been splendid Smiths, judicious Joneses, and reliable Robinsons – but it is impossible to imagine a cricketing world in which you looked up *Smith* to check a score; hunted down early editions to augment your run of cherished *Joneses*; or waited eagerly for the spring appearance of the daffodil-hued *Robinson*.

The company which spawned the Almanack and its other good works was under the direction of its founder for 34 of its 150 years. Wisden was only 57 when he died of cancer at his London business base, 21 Cranbourn Street, on April 5, 1884. There was no family, and control passed to his business manager, the hardworking Henry Luff, who retained it until his own even earlier death, aged 54, in 1910. Since then, despite the outward calm exuded by the unbroken run of 137 Almanacks, the company has survived bombings, bankruptcy and some very improbable owners, none of them called Wisden.

John Wisden himself was fairly improbable. He was 5ft 4in tall and weighed just seven stone when he first played for Sussex. But he soon became known as "The Little Wonder". He went on to spin his fast off-breaks for the All-England XI and, at Lord's on July 15, 1850, playing for the North against the South, he took all ten second-innings wickets, every one of them bowled. There was no *Wisden* around yet to record the feat, and his analysis was not kept, but *Scores and Biographies* noted that, though ten wickets in an innings had been done before, "never in a *great* match or against such good players. Without exaggeration, his balls turned in a yard from the off…"

By then, he already had his own ground, with George Parr, in Leamington, and it is believed that he began selling cricket equipment there in 1850. Five years later, he opened his "cricket and cigar depot" in London, at 2 Coventry Street. This was in partnership with Fred Lillywhite, who had established the first major cricket annual in 1849 – *Lillywhite's Guide*.

But the Wisden–Lillywhite partnership was dissolved in 1858. Fred Lillywhite went into bat-making with his brother John. Later, their older brother James joined them and the company trading as James Lillywhite opened the sports shop whose modern successor still stands in Piccadilly Circus. Wisden launched his Almanack on his own in 1864 and, by 1877, John Lillywhite was bitterly criticising *Wisden*'s claim to be the biggest-selling cricket annual.

In 1897, Wisden set up a factory to make its own branded gear for the first time, at Tonbridge. And even after Luff's death it continued to expand. A London works was added at West Ham before the First World War, and the spread of sport among a more leisure-minded population led to the decision in 1925 to lease bigger premises at Fitzgerald Avenue, Mortlake.

By then, Wisden had acquired Duke & Son, who in those days made bats as well as balls, and also a controlling interest in Taylor–Rolph, whose founder, Gordon Taylor, had devised a machine to ensure absolute accuracy in building bias into a lawn bowl; the handful of craftsmen involved had to sign a secrecy document. The Fitzgerald Works were also the office of Denby's, who built hard tennis courts. The Wisden range covered 23 different sports, including bandy and stool ball. The company proclaimed itself "Athletic Outfitters to the King" and, in 1931, it was able to announce grandly: "We do not pay commission or pecuniary consideration of any kind to famous players whose names appear in connection with a brand of article marketed by us."

In 1930, Wisden considered opening a factory in Australia, but then the depression struck. Two years later, the company was reporting difficulties in export markets, with almost no orders from Australia, which now had its own sports-goods industry – boosted by the Bradman factor. By 1937, suppliers were imposing restrictions on credit and, on February 6, 1939, the company went into liquidation. Chief creditor was the Westminster Bank, which appointed an accountant, P. J. Chaplin of Singleton Fabian & Co, as receiver and manager, with the aim of keeping the business afloat. He took full advantage of the special demands of wartime, and the company pulled through. Sports goods played second fiddle to camouflage netting.

Wisden's Mortlake years ended in the early hours of February 19, 1944, when a number of bombs fell in the area, killing eight people and wrecking the Fitzgerald Works. Some staff were reported to have died, but it is unclear how many. All records kept at Mortlake were lost, and the only item salvaged was a large circular saw.

The Co-Operative Wholesale Society acquired John Wisden & Co later that year but, in 1961, decided sports goods did not fit its future: John Wisden amalgamated with the cricket-ball departments of Surridge and Ives at Tonbridge, and Gray-Nicolls at nearby Hildenborough, under the name Tonbridge Sports Industries. Nine years later, the family-owned Grays of Cambridge, itself established in 1855, bought the whole group. For a few years, the Wisden name flourished as sports continued to revive and expand, sales holding up well for cricket bats and, to a lesser extent, tennis rackets. But increasing competition from Asia took its toll.

The publication of *Wisden Cricketers' Almanack* itself had passed out of the company's hands to Whitakers – publishers of another famous almanack – in 1938, at which point the book received its only complete makeover. Six years later, the name on the spine changed to Sporting Handbooks (a division of Whitakers). In 1979, the task was transferred to Macdonald where, more or less by accident, effective control passed to the egregious Robert Maxwell. He startled an annual launch dinner by announcing that the book should henceforth be published in the quite different format of the Rothmans sports annuals, which he also published. And he warned the cricket writers present, who were accustomed to getting free copies, that they had better write about the book, or they would have to buy their own.

Those connected with *Wisden* now began to manoeuvre to wrest control from Maxwell. His attention span being very limited, this was achieved. A series of complex deals eventually brought the printers McCorquodales into

[*Jan Traylen at Patrick Eagar*

From bats to batter: the exterior of Wisden's old HQ in Cranbourn Street.

partnership with Grays. John Wisden and Co was revived as a publishing company, with its imprint back on the Almanack; later, it also acquired *Wisden Cricket Monthly*, which had been using the company's name under licence. But as part of the same process, the Wisden name finally disappeared from sporting equipment, and that part of a proud history came to an abrupt if, by now, hardly unexpected end.

In 1993, John Wisden and Co was acquired by the cricket-absorbed Paul Getty, a move widely welcomed by those involved in the game. It thus acquired an identity and an independence it had not known since 1939. The bats, the basketballs, the boxing gloves and the bandy sticks have all gone. The final, remote, link was severed in the late 1990s with the closure of the Brighton sports shop founded by John's brother William. But the name Wisden goes proudly on, after 150 years (we believe), into the new millennium.

Murray Hedgcock was posted to London by The Australian *in 1966, and has been reporting on English cricket and other mysteries of British life to readers in Australia ever since. For 15 years he was the London bureau chief.*

PART THREE: THE PLAYERS

TEST CRICKETERS

Full list from 1877 to August 22, 1999

These lists have been compiled on a home and abroad basis, appearances abroad being printed in *italics*.

Abbreviations. E: England. A: Australia. SA: South Africa. WI: West Indies. NZ: New Zealand. In: India. P: Pakistan. SL: Sri Lanka. Z: Zimbabwe.

All appearances are placed in this order of seniority. Hence, any England cricketer playing against Australia in England has that achievement recorded first and the remainder of his appearances at home (if any) set down before passing to matches abroad. The figures immediately following each name represent the total number of appearances in *all* Tests.

Where the season embraces two different years, the first year is given; i.e. 1876 indicates 1876-77.

ENGLAND

Number of Test cricketers: 597

Abel, R. 13: v A 1888 (3) 1896 (3) 1902 (2); *v A 1891 (3); v SA 1888 (2)*

Absolom, C. A. 1: *v A 1878*

Agnew, J. P. 3: v A 1985 (1); v WI 1984 (1); v SL 1984 (1)

Allen, D. A. 39: v A 1961 (4) 1964 (1); v SA 1960 (2); v WI 1963 (2) 1966 (1); v P 1962 (4); *v A 1962 (1) 1965 (4); v SA 1964 (4); v WI 1959 (5); v NZ 1965 (3); v In 1961 (5); v P 1961 (3)*

Allen, G. O. B. 25: v A 1930 (1) 1934 (2); v WI 1933 (1); v NZ 1931 (3); v In 1936 (3); *v A 1932 (5) 1936 (5); v WI 1947 (3); v NZ 1932 (2)*

Allom, M. J. C. 5: *v SA 1930 (1); v NZ 1929 (4)*

Allott, P. J. W. 13: v A 1981 (1) 1985 (4); v WI 1984 (3); v In 1982 (2); v SL 1984 (1); *v In 1981 (1); v SL 1981 (1)*

Ames, L. E. G. 47: v A 1934 (5) 1938 (2); v SA 1929 (1) 1935 (4); v WI 1933 (3); v NZ 1931 (3) 1937 (3); v In 1932 (1); *v A 1932 (5) 1936 (5); v SA 1938 (5); v WI 1929 (4) 1934 (4); v NZ 1932 (2)*

Amiss, D. L. 50: v A 1968 (1) 1975 (2) 1977 (2); v WI 1966 (1) 1973 (3) 1976 (1); v NZ 1973 (3); v In 1967 (2) 1971 (1) 1974 (3); v P 1967 (1) 1971 (3) 1974 (3); *v A 1974 (5) 1976 (1); v WI 1973 (5); v NZ 1974 (2); v In 1972 (3) 1976 (5); v P 1972 (3)*

Andrew, K. V. 2: v WI 1963 (1); *v A 1954 (1)*

Appleyard, R. 9: v A 1956 (1); v SA 1955 (1); v P 1954 (1); *v A 1954 (4); v NZ 1954 (2)*

Archer, A. G. 1: *v SA 1898*

Armitage, T. 2: *v A 1876 (2)*

Arnold, E. G. 10: v A 1905 (4); v SA 1907 (2); *v A 1903 (4)*

Arnold, G. G. 34: v A 1972 (3) 1975 (1); v WI 1973 (3); v NZ 1969 (1) 1973 (3); v In 1974 (2); v P 1967 (2) 1974 (3); *v A 1974 (4); v WI 1973 (3); v NZ 1974 (2); v In 1972 (1); v P 1972 (3)*

Arnold, J. 1: v NZ 1931

Astill, W. E. 9: *v SA 1927 (5); v WI 1929 (4)*

Atherton, M. A. 90: v A 1989 (2) 1993 (6) 1997 (6); v SA 1994 (3) 1998 (5); v WI 1991 (5) 1995 (6); v NZ 1990 (3) 1994 (3) 1999 (2); v In 1990 (3) 1996 (3); v P 1992 (3) 1996 (3); *v A 1990 (5) 1994 (5) 1998 (4); v SA 1995 (5); v WI 1993 (5) 1997 (6); v NZ 1996 (3); v In 1992 (1); v SL 1992 (1); v Z 1996 (2)*

Athey, C. W. J. 23: v A 1980 (1); v WI 1988 (1); v NZ 1986 (3); v In 1986 (2); v P 1987 (4); *v A 1986 (5) 1987 (1); v WI 1980 (2); v NZ 1987 (1); v P 1987 (3)*

Attewell, W. 10: v A 1890 (1); *v A 1884 (5) 1887 (1) 1891 (3)*

Bailey, R. J. 4: v WI 1988 (1); *v WI 1989 (3)*

Bailey, T. E. 61: v A 1953 (5) 1956 (4); v WI 1950 (2) 1957 (4); v NZ 1949 (4) 1958 (4); v P 1954 (3); *v A 1950 (4) 1954 (5) 1958 (5); v SA 1956 (5); v WI 1953 (5); v NZ 1950 (2) 1954 (2)*

Bairstow, D. L. 4: v A 1980 (1); v WI 1980 (1); v In 1979 (1); *v WI 1980 (1)*

Bakewell, A. H. 6: v SA 1935 (2); v WI 1933 (1); v NZ 1931 (2); *v In 1933 (1)*

Balderstone, J. C. 2: v WI 1976 (2)

Barber, R. W. 28: v A 1964 (1) 1968 (1); v SA 1960 (1) 1965 (3); v WI 1966 (2); v NZ 1965 (3); *v A 1965 (5); v SA 1964 (4); v In 1961 (5); v P 1961 (3)*

Barber, W. 2: v SA 1935 (2)

Barlow, G. D. 3: v A 1977 (1); *v In 1976 (2)*

Barlow, R. G. 17: v A 1882 (1) 1884 (3) 1886 (3); *v A 1881 (4) 1882 (4) 1886 (2)*

Barnes, S. F. 27: v A 1902 (3) 1909 (3) 1912 (3); v SA 1912 (3); *v A 1901 (3) 1907 (5) 1911 (5); v SA 1913 (4)*

Barnes, W. 21: v A 1880 (1) 1882 (1) 1884 (2) 1886 (2) 1888 (3) 1890 (2); *v A 1882 (4) 1884 (5) 1886 (1)*

Barnett, C. J. 20: v A 1938 (3) 1948 (1); v SA 1947 (3); v WI 1933 (1); v NZ 1937 (3); v In 1936 (1); *v A 1936 (5); v In 1933 (3)*

Barnett, K. J. 4: v A 1989 (3); v SL 1988 (1)

Barratt, F. 5: v SA 1929 (1); *v NZ 1929 (4)*

Barrington, K. F. 82: v A 1961 (5) 1964 (5) 1968 (3); v SA 1955 (3) 1960 (3) 1965 (3); v WI 1963 (5) 1966 (2); v NZ 1965 (2); v In 1959 (5) 1967 (3); v P 1962 (4) 1967 (3); *v A 1962 (5) 1965 (5); v SA 1964 (5); v WI 1959 (5) 1967 (5); v NZ 1962 (3); v In 1961 (5) 1963 (1); v P 1961 (2)*

Barton, V. A. 1: *v SA 1891*

Bates, W. 15: v A 1881 (4) 1882 (4) 1884 (5) 1886 (2)

Bean, G. 3: *v A 1891 (3)*

Bedser, A. V. 51: v A 1948 (5) 1953 (5); v SA 1947 (2) 1951 (5) 1955 (1); v WI 1950 (3); v NZ 1949 (2); v In 1946 (3) 1952 (4); v P 1954 (2); *v A 1946 (5) 1950 (5) 1954 (1); v SA 1948 (5); v NZ 1946 (1) 1950 (2)*

Benjamin, J. E. 1: v SA 1994

Benson, M. R. 1: v In 1986

Berry, R. 2: v WI 1950 (2)

Bicknell, M. P. 2: v A 1993 (2)

Binks, J. G. 2: *v In 1963 (2)*

Bird, M. C. 10: *v SA 1909 (5) 1913 (5)*

Birkenshaw, J. 5: *v WI 1973 (2); v In 1972 (2); v P 1972 (1)*

Blakey, R. J. 2: *v In 1992 (2)*

Bligh, Hon. I. F. W. 4: *v A 1882 (4)*

Blythe, C. 19: v A 1905 (1) 1909 (2); v SA 1907 (3); *v A 1901 (5) 1907 (1); v SA 1905 (5) 1909 (2)*

Board, J. H. 6: *v SA 1898 (2) 1905 (4)*

Bolus, J. B. 7: v WI 1963 (2); *v In 1963 (5)*

Booth, M. W. 2: v SA 1913 (2)

Bosanquet, B. J. T. 7: v A 1905 (3); *v A 1903 (4)*

Botham, I. T. 102: v A 1977 (2) 1980 (1) 1981 (6) 1985 (6) 1989 (3); v WI 1980 (5) 1984 (5) 1991 (1); v NZ 1978 (3) 1983 (4) 1986 (1); v In 1979 (4) 1982 (3); v P 1978 (3) 1982 (3) 1987 (5) 1992 (2); v SL 1984 (1) 1991 (1); *v A 1978 (6) 1979 (3) 1982 (5) 1986 (4); v WI 1980 (4) 1985 (5); v NZ 1977 (3) 1983 (3) 1991 (1); v In 1979 (1) 1981 (6); v P 1983 (1); v SL 1981 (1)*

Bowden, M. P. 2: *v SA 1888 (2)*

Bowes, W. E. 15: v A 1934 (3) 1938 (2); v SA 1935 (4); v WI 1939 (1); v In 1932 (1) 1946 (1); *v A 1932 (1); v NZ 1932 (1)*

Bowley, E. H. 5: v SA 1929 (2); *v NZ 1929 (3)*

Boycott, G. 108: v A 1964 (1) 1968 (3) 1972 (2) 1977 (3) 1980 (1) 1981 (6); v SA 1965 (2); v WI 1966 (4) 1969 (3) 1973 (3) 1980 (5); v NZ 1965 (2) 1969 (3) 1973 (3) 1978 (2); v In 1967 (2) 1971 (1) 1974 (1) 1979 (4); v P 1967 (1) 1971 (2); *v A 1965 (5) 1970 (5) 1978 (6) 1979 (3); v SA 1964 (5); v WI 1967 (5) 1973 (5) 1980 (4); v NZ 1965 (2) 1977 (3); v In 1979 (1) 1981 (4); v P 1977 (3)*

Bradley, W. M. 2: v A 1899 (2)

Braund, L. C. 23: v A 1902 (5); v SA 1907 (3); *v A 1901 (5) 1903 (5) 1907 (5)*

Brearley, J. M. 39: v A 1977 (5) 1981 (4); v WI 1976 (2); v NZ 1978 (3); v In 1979 (4); v P 1978 (3); *v A 1976 (1) 1978 (6) 1979 (3); v In 1976 (5) 1979 (1); v P 1977 (2)*

Brearley, W. 4: v A 1905 (2) 1909 (1); v SA 1912 (1)

Brennan, D. V. 2: v SA 1951 (2)

Briggs, John 33: v A 1886 (3) 1888 (3) 1893 (2) 1896 (1) 1899 (1); *v A 1884 (5) 1886 (2) 1887 (1) 1891 (3) 1894 (5) 1897 (5); v SA 1888 (2)*

Broad, B. C. 25: v A 1989 (2); v WI 1984 (4) 1988 (2); v P 1987 (4); v SL 1984 (1); *v A 1986 (5) 1987 (1); v NZ 1987 (3); v P 1987 (3)*

Brockwell, W. 7: v A 1893 (1) 1899 (1); *v A 1894 (5)*

Bromley-Davenport, H. R. 4: *v SA 1895 (3) 1898 (1)*

Brookes, D. 1: *v WI 1947*

Brown, A. 2: *v In 1961 (1); v P 1961 (1)*

Brown, D. J. 26: v A 1968 (4); v SA 1965 (2); v WI 1966 (1) 1969 (3); v NZ 1969 (1); v In 1967 (2): *v A 1965 (4); v WI 1967 (4); v NZ 1965 (2); v P 1968 (3)*

Brown, F. R. 22: v A 1953 (1); v SA 1951 (5); v WI 1950 (1); v NZ 1931 (2) 1937 (1) 1949 (2); v In 1932 (1); *v A 1950 (5); v NZ 1932 (2) 1950 (2)*

Brown, G. 7: v A 1921 (3); *v SA 1922 (4)*

Brown, J. T. 8: v A 1896 (2) 1899 (1); *v A 1894 (5)*

Brown, S. J. E. 1: v P 1996

Buckenham, C. P. 4: *v SA 1909 (4)*

Butcher, A. R. 1: v In 1979

Butcher, M. A. 22: v A 1997 (5); v SA 1998 (3); v NZ 1999 (3); v SL 1998 (1); *v A 1998 (5); v WI 1997 (5)*

Butcher, R. O. 3: *v WI 1980 (3)*

Butler, H. J. 2: v SA 1947 (1); *v WI 1947 (1)*

Butt, H. R. 3: *v SA 1895 (3)*

Caddick, A. R. 25: v A 1993 (4) 1997 (5); v NZ 1999 (4); v P 1996 (1); *v WI 1993 (4) 1997 (5); v NZ 1996 (2)*

Calthorpe, Hon. F. S. G. 4: *v WI 1929 (4)*

Capel, D. J. 15: v A 1989 (1); v WI 1988 (2); v P 1987 (1); *v A 1987 (1); v WI 1989 (4); v NZ 1987 (3); v P 1987 (3)*

Carr, A. W. 11: v A 1926 (4); v SA 1929 (2); *v SA 1922 (5)*

Carr, D. B. 2: *v In 1951 (2)*

Carr, D. W. 1: v A 1909

Cartwright, T. W. 5: v A 1964 (2); v SA 1965 (1); v NZ 1965 (1); *v SA 1964 (1)*

Chapman, A. P. F. 26: v A 1926 (4) 1930 (4); v SA 1924 (2); v WI 1928 (3); *v A 1924 (4) 1928 (4); v SA 1930 (5)*

Charlwood, H. R. J. 2: *v A 1876 (2)*

Chatterton, W. 1: *v SA 1891*

Childs, J. H. 2: v WI 1988 (2)

Christopherson, S. 1: v A 1884

Clark, E. W. 8: v A 1934 (2); v SA 1929 (1); v WI 1933 (2); *v In 1933 (3)*

Clay, J. C. 1: v SA 1935

Close, D. B. 22: v A 1961 (1); v SA 1955 (1); v WI 1957 (2) 1963 (5) 1966 (1) 1976 (3); v NZ 1949 (1); v In 1959 (1) 1967 (3); v P 1967 (3); *v A 1950 (1)*

Coldwell, L. J. 7: v A 1964 (2); v P 1962 (2); *v A 1962 (2); v NZ 1962 (1)*

Compton, D. C. S. 78: v A 1938 (4) 1948 (5) 1953 (5) 1956 (1); v SA 1947 (5) 1951 (5) 1955 (5); v WI 1939 (3) 1950 (1); v NZ 1937 (1) 1949 (4); v In 1946 (3) 1952 (2); v P 1954 (4); *v A 1946 (5) 1950 (4) 1954 (4); v SA 1948 (5) 1956 (5); v WI 1953 (5); v NZ 1946 (1) 1950 (2)*

Cook, C. 1: v SA 1947

Cook, G. 7: v In 1982 (3); *v A 1982 (3); v SL 1981 (1)*

Cook, N. G. B. 15: v A 1989 (3); v WI 1984 (3); v NZ 1983 (2); *v NZ 1983 (1); v P 1983 (3) 1987 (3)*

Cope, G. A. 3: *v P 1977 (3)*

Copson, W. H. 3: v SA 1947 (1); v WI 1939 (2)

Cork, D. G. 27: v SA 1998 (5); v WI 1995 (5); v In 1996 (3); v P 1996 (3); v SL 1998 (1); *v A 1998 (2); v SA 1995 (5); v NZ 1996 (3)*

Cornford, W. L. 4: *v NZ 1929 (4)*

Cottam, R. M. H. 4: *v In 1972 (2); v P 1968 (2)*

Coventry, Hon. C. J. 2: *v SA 1888 (2)*

Cowans, N. G. 19: v A 1985 (1); v WI 1984 (1); v NZ 1983 (4); *v A 1982 (4); v NZ 1983 (2); v In 1984 (5); v P 1983 (2)*

Cowdrey, C. S. 6: v WI 1988 (1); *v In 1984 (5)*

Cowdrey, M. C. 114: v A 1956 (5) 1961 (4) 1964 (3) 1968 (4); v SA 1955 (1) 1960 (5) 1965 (3); v WI 1957 (5) 1963 (2) 1966 (4); v NZ 1958 (4) 1965 (3); v In 1959 (5); v P 1962 (4) 1967 (2) 1971 (1); *v A 1954 (5) 1958 (5) 1962 (5) 1965 (4) 1970 (3) 1974 (5); v SA 1956 (5); v WI 1959 (5) 1967 (5); v NZ 1954 (2) 1958 (2) 1962 (3) 1965 (3) 1970 (1); v In 1963 (3); v P 1968 (3)*
Coxon, A. 1: v A 1948
Cranston, J. 1: v A 1890
Cranston, K. 8: v A 1948 (1); v SA 1947 (3); *v WI 1947 (4)*
Crapp, J. F. 7: v A 1948 (3); *v SA 1948 (4)*
Crawford, J. N. 12: v SA 1907 (2); *v A 1907 (5); v SA 1905 (5)*
Crawley, J. P. 29: v A 1997 (5); v SA 1994 (3); v WI 1995 (3); v P 1996 (2); v SL 1998 (1); *v A 1994 (3) 1998 (3); v SA 1995 (1); v WI 1997 (3); v NZ 1996 (3); v Z 1996 (2)*
Croft, R. D. B. 15: v A 1997 (5); v SA 1998 (3); v P 1996 (1); *v A 1998 (1); v WI 1997 (1); v NZ 1996 (2); v Z 1996 (2)*
Curtis, T. S. 5: v A 1989 (3); v WI 1988 (2)
Cuttell, W. R. 2: *v SA 1898 (2)*

Dawson, E. W. 5: *v SA 1927 (1); v NZ 1929 (4)*
Dean, H. 3: v A 1912 (2); v SA 1912 (1)
DeFreitas, P. A. J. 44: v A 1989 (1) 1993 (1); v SA 1994 (3); v WI 1988 (3) 1991 (5) 1995 (1); v NZ 1990 (2) 1994 (3); v P 1987 (1) 1992 (2); v SL 1991 (1); *v A 1986 (4) 1990 (3) 1994 (4); v WI 1989 (2); v NZ 1987 (2) 1991 (3); v In 1992 (1); v P 1987 (2)*
Denness, M. H. 28: v A 1975 (1); v NZ 1969 (1); v In 1974 (3); v P 1974 (3); *v A 1974 (5); v WI 1973 (5); v NZ 1974 (2); v In 1972 (5); v P 1972 (3)*
Denton, D. 11: v A 1905 (1); *v SA 1905 (5) 1909 (5)*
Dewes, J. G. 5: v A 1948 (1); v WI 1950 (2); *v A 1950 (2)*
Dexter, E. R. 62: v A 1961 (5) 1964 (5) 1968 (2); v SA 1960 (5); v WI 1963 (5); v NZ 1958 (1) 1965 (2); v In 1959 (2); v P 1962 (5); *v A 1958 (2) 1962 (5); v SA 1964 (5); v WI 1959 (5); v NZ 1958 (2) 1962 (3); v In 1961 (5); v P 1961 (3)*
Dilley, G. R. 41: v A 1981 (3) 1989 (2); v WI 1980 (3) 1988 (4); v NZ 1983 (1) 1986 (2); v In 1986 (2); v P 1987 (4); *v A 1979 (2) 1986 (4) 1987 (1); v WI 1980 (4); v NZ 1987 (3); v In 1981 (4); v P 1983 (1) 1987 (1)*
Dipper, A. E. 1: v A 1921
Doggart, G. H. G. 2: v WI 1950 (2)
D'Oliveira, B. L. 44: v A 1968 (2) 1972 (5); v WI 1966 (4) 1969 (3); v NZ 1969 (3); v In 1967 (2) 1971 (3); v P 1967 (3) 1971 (3); *v A 1970 (6); v WI 1967 (5); v NZ 1970 (2); v P 1968 (3)*
Dollery, H. E. 4: v A 1948 (2); v SA 1947 (1); v WI 1950 (1)
Dolphin, A. 1: *v A 1920*
Douglas, J. W. H. T. 23: v A 1912 (1) 1921 (5); v SA 1924 (1); *v A 1911 (5) 1920 (5) 1924 (1); v SA 1913 (5)*
Downton, P. R. 30: v A 1981 (1) 1985 (6); v WI 1984 (5) 1988 (3); v In 1986 (1); v SL 1984 (1); *v WI 1980 (3) 1985 (5); v In 1984 (5)*
Druce, N. F. 5: *v A 1897 (5)*
Ducat, A. 1: v A 1921
Duckworth, G. 24: v A 1930 (5); v SA 1924 (1) 1929 (4) 1935 (4); v WI 1928 (1); v In 1936 (3); *v A 1928 (5); v SA 1930 (3); v NZ 1932 (1)*
Duleepsinhji, K. S. 12: v A 1930 (4); v SA 1929 (1); v NZ 1931 (3); *v NZ 1929 (4)*
Durston, F. J. 1: v A 1921

Ealham, M. A. 8: v A 1997 (4); v SA 1998 (2); v NZ 1996 (1); v P 1996 (1)
Edmonds, P. H. 51: v A 1975 (2) 1985 (5); v NZ 1978 (3) 1983 (2) 1986 (3); v In 1979 (4) 1982 (3) 1986 (2); v P 1978 (3) 1987 (5); *v A 1978 (1) 1986 (5); v WI 1985 (3); v NZ 1977 (3); v In 1984 (5); v P 1977 (2)*
Edrich, J. H. 77: v A 1964 (3) 1968 (5) 1972 (5) 1975 (4); v SA 1965 (1); v WI 1963 (5) 1966 (1) 1969 (3) 1976 (2); v NZ 1965 (1) 1969 (3); v In 1967 (2) 1971 (3) 1974 (3); v P 1971 (3) 1974 (3); *v A 1965 (5) 1970 (6) 1974 (4); v WI 1967 (5); v NZ 1965 (3) 1970 (2) 1974 (2); v In 1963 (2); v P 1968 (3)*
Edrich, W. J. 39: v A 1938 (4) 1948 (5) 1953 (3); v SA 1947 (4); v WI 1950 (2); v NZ 1949 (4); v In 1946 (1); v P 1954 (1); *v A 1946 (5) 1954 (4); v SA 1938 (5); v NZ 1946 (1)*
Elliott, H. 4: v WI 1928 (1); *v SA 1927 (1); v In 1933 (2)*

Ellison, R. M. 11: v A 1985 (2); v WI 1984 (1); v In 1986 (1); v SL 1984 (1); *v WI 1985 (3); v In 1984 (3)*

Emburey, J. E. 64: v A 1980 (1) 1981 (4) 1985 (6) 1989 (3) 1993 (1); v WI 1980 (3) 1988 (3) 1995 (1); v NZ 1978 (1) 1986 (2); v In 1986 (3); v P 1987 (4); v SL 1988 (1); *v A 1978 (4) 1986 (5) 1987 (1); v WI 1980 (4) 1985 (4); v NZ 1987 (3); v In 1979 (1) 1981 (3) 1992 (1); v P 1987 (3); v SL 1981 (1) 1992 (1)*

Emmett, G. M. 1: v A 1948

Emmett, T. 7: *v A 1876 (2) 1878 (1) 1881 (4)*

Evans, A. J. 1: v A 1921

Evans, T. G. 91: v A 1948 (5) 1953 (5) 1956 (5); v SA 1947 (5) 1951 (3) 1955 (3); v WI 1950 (3) 1957 (5); v NZ 1949 (4) 1958 (5); v In 1946 (1) 1952 (4) 1959 (2); v P 1954 (4); *v A 1946 (1) 1950 (5) 1954 (4) 1958 (3); v SA 1948 (3) 1956 (5); v WI 1947 (4) 1953 (4); v NZ 1946 (1) 1950 (2) 1954 (2)*

Fagg, A. E. 5: v WI 1939 (1); v In 1936 (2); *v A 1936 (2)*

Fairbrother, N. H. 10: v NZ 1990 (3); v P 1987 (1); *v NZ 1987 (2); v In 1992 (2); v P 1987 (1); v SL 1992 (1)*

Fane, F. L. 14: *v A 1907 (4); v SA 1905 (5) 1909 (5)*

Farnes, K. 15: v A 1934 (2) 1938 (4); v A 1936 (2); *v SA 1938 (5); v WI 1934 (2)*

Farrimond, W. 4: v SA 1935 (1); *v SA 1930 (2); v WI 1934 (1)*

Fender, P. G. H. 13: v A 1921 (2); v SA 1924 (2) 1929 (1); *v A 1920 (3); v SA 1922 (5)*

Ferris, J. J. 1: *v SA 1891*

Fielder, A. 6: *v A 1903 (2) 1907 (4)*

Fishlock, L. B. 4: v In 1936 (1) 1946 (1); *v A 1946 (1)*

Flavell, J. A. 4: v A 1961 (2) 1964 (2)

Fletcher, K. W. R. 59: v A 1968 (1) 1972 (1) 1975 (2); v WI 1973 (3); v NZ 1969 (2) 1973 (3); v In 1971 (2) 1974 (3); v P 1974 (3); *v A 1970 (5) 1974 (5) 1976 (1); v WI 1973 (4); v NZ 1970 (1) 1974 (2); v In 1972 (5) 1976 (3) 1981 (6); v P 1968 (2) 1972 (3); v SL 1981 (1)*

Flintoff, A. 2: v WI 1998 (2)

Flowers, W. 8: v A 1893 (1); *v A 1884 (5) 1886 (2)*

Ford, F. G. J. 5: *v A 1894 (5)*

Foster, F. R. 11: v A 1912 (3); v SA 1912 (3); *v A 1911 (5)*

Foster, N. A. 29: v A 1985 (1) 1989 (3) 1993 (1); v WI 1984 (1) 1988 (2); v NZ 1983 (1) 1986 (1); v In 1986 (1); v P 1987 (5); v SL 1988 (1); *v A 1987 (1); v WI 1985 (3); v NZ 1983 (2); v In 1984 (2); v P 1983 (2) 1987 (2)*

Foster, R. E. 8: v SA 1907 (3); *v A 1903 (5)*

Fothergill, A. J. 2: *v SA 1888 (2)*

Fowler, G. 21: v WI 1984 (5); v NZ 1983 (2); v P 1982 (1); v SL 1984 (1); *v A 1982 (3); v NZ 1983 (2); v In 1984 (5); v P 1983 (2)*

Fraser, A. R. C. 46: v A 1989 (3) 1993 (1); v SA 1994 (2) 1998 (5); v WI 1995 (5); v NZ 1994 (3); v In 1990 (3); v SL 1998 (1); *v A 1990 (3) 1994 (3) 1998 (2); v SA 1995 (3); v WI 1989 (2) 1993 (4) 1997 (6)*

Freeman, A. P. 12: v SA 1929 (3); v WI 1928 (3); *v A 1924 (2); v SA 1927 (4)*

French, B. N. 16: v NZ 1986 (3); v In 1986 (2); v P 1987 (4); *v A 1987 (1); v NZ 1987 (3); v P 1987 (3)*

Fry, C. B. 26: v A 1899 (5) 1902 (3) 1905 (4) 1909 (3) 1912 (3); v SA 1907 (3) 1912 (3); *v SA 1895 (2)*

Gallian, J. E. R. 3: v WI 1995 (2); *v SA 1995 (1)*

Gatting, M. W. 79: v A 1980 (1) 1981 (6) 1985 (6) 1989 (1) 1993 (2); v WI 1980 (4) 1984 (1) 1988 (2); v NZ 1983 (2) 1986 (3); v In 1986 (3); v P 1982 (3) 1987 (5); *v A 1986 (5) 1987 (1) 1994 (5); v WI 1980 (1) 1985 (1); v NZ 1977 (1) 1983 (2) 1987 (3); v In 1981 (5) 1984 (5) 1992 (3); v P 1977 (1) 1983 (3) 1987 (3); v SL 1992 (1)*

Gay, L. H. 1: *v A 1894*

Geary, G. 14: v A 1926 (2) 1930 (1) 1934 (2); v SA 1924 (1) 1929 (2); *v A 1928 (4); v SA 1927 (2)*

Gibb, P. A. 8: v In 1946 (2); *v A 1946 (1); v SA 1938 (5)*

Giddins, E. S. H. 1: v NZ 1999

Gifford, N. 15: v A 1964 (2) 1972 (3); v NZ 1973 (2); v In 1971 (2); v P 1971 (2); *v In 1972 (2); v P 1972 (5)*

Giles, A. F. 1: v SA 1998

Gilligan, A. E. R. 11: v SA 1924 (4); *v A 1924 (5); v SA 1922 (2)*

Gilligan, A. H. H. 4: *v NZ 1929 (4)*

Gimblett, H. 3: v WI 1939 (1); v In 1936 (2)

Gladwin, C. 8: v SA 1947 (2); v NZ 1949 (1); *v SA 1948 (5)*

Goddard, T. W. 8: v A 1930 (1); v WI 1939 (2); v NZ 1937 (2); *v SA 1938 (3)*

Gooch, G. A. 118: v A 1975 (2) 1980 (1) 1981 (5) 1985 (6) 1989 (5) 1993 (6); v SA 1994 (3); v WI 1980 (5) 1988 (5) 1991 (5); v NZ 1978 (3) 1986 (3) 1990 (3) 1994 (3); v In 1979 (4) 1986 (3) 1990 (3); v P 1978 (3) 1992 (5); v SL 1988 (1) 1991 (1); *v A 1978 (6) 1979 (2) 1990 (4) 1994 (5); v WI 1980 (4) 1985 (5) 1989 (2); v NZ 1991 (3); v In 1979 (1) 1981 (6) 1992 (2); v P 1987 (3); v SL 1981 (1)*

Gough, D. 31: v A 1997 (4); v SA 1994 (3) 1998 (4); v WI 1995 (3); v NZ 1994 (1); v̇ SL 1998 (1); *v A 1994 (3) 1998 (5); v SA 1995 (2); v NZ 1996 (3); v Z 1996 (2)*

Gover, A. R. 4: v NZ 1937 (2); v In 1936 (1) 1946 (1)

Gower, D. I. 117: v A 1980 (1) 1981 (5) 1985 (6) 1989 (6); v WI 1980 (1) 1984 (5) 1988 (4); v NZ 1978 (3) 1983 (4) 1986 (3); v In 1979 (4) 1982 (3) 1986 (2) 1990 (3); v P 1978 (3) 1982 (3) 1987 (5) 1992 (5); v SL 1984 (1); *v A 1978 (6) 1979 (2) 1982 (3) 1986 (5) 1990 (5); v WI 1980 (4) 1985 (5); v NZ 1983 (3); v In 1979 (1) 1981 (6) 1984 (5); v P 1983 (3); v SL 1981 (1)*

Greenhough, T. 4: v SA 1960 (1); v In 1959 (3)

Greenwood, A. 2: *v A 1876 (2)*

Greig, A. W. 58: v A 1972 (5) 1975 (4) 1977 (5); v WI 1973 (3) 1976 (5); v NZ 1973 (3); v In 1974 (3); v P 1974 (3); *v A 1974 (6) 1976 (1); v WI 1973 (5); v NZ 1974 (2); v In 1972 (5) 1976 (5); v P 1972 (3)*

Greig, I. A. 2: v P 1982 (2)

Grieve, B. A. F. 2: *v SA 1888 (2)*

Griffith, S. C. 3: *v SA 1948 (2); v WI 1947 (1)*

Gunn, G. 15: v A 1909 (1); *v A 1907 (5) 1911 (5); v WI 1929 (4)*

Gunn, J. 6: v A 1905 (1); *v A 1901 (5)*

Gunn, W. 11: v A 1888 (2) 1890 (2) 1893 (3) 1896 (1) 1899 (1); *v A 1886 (2)*

Habib, A. 2: v NZ 1999 (2)

Haig, N. E. 5: v A 1921 (1); *v WI 1929 (4)*

Haigh, S. 11: v A 1905 (2) 1909 (1) 1912 (1); *v SA 1898 (2) 1905 (5)*

Hallows, C. 2: v A 1921 (1); v WI 1928 (1)

Hammond, W. R. 85: v A 1930 (5) 1934 (5) 1938 (4); v SA 1929 (4) 1935 (5); v WI 1928 (3) 1933 (3) 1939 (3); v NZ 1931 (3) 1937 (3); v In 1932 (1) 1936 (2) 1946 (3); *v A 1928 (5) 1932 (5) 1936 (5) 1946 (4); v SA 1927 (5) 1930 (5) 1938 (5); v WI 1934 (4); v NZ 1932 (2) 1946 (1)*

Hampshire, J. H. 8: v A 1972 (1) 1975 (1); v WI 1969 (2); *v A 1970 (2); v NZ 1970 (2)*

Hardinge, H. T. W. 1: v A 1921

Hardstaff, J. 5: *v A 1907 (5)*

Hardstaff, J. jun. 23: v A 1938 (2) 1948 (1); v SA 1935 (1); v WI 1939 (3); v NZ 1937 (3); v In 1936 (2) 1946 (2); *v A 1936 (5) 1946 (1); v WI 1947 (3)*

Harris, Lord 4: v A 1880 (1) 1884 (2); *v A 1878 (1)*

Hartley, J. C. 2: *v SA 1905 (2)*

Hawke, Lord 5: *v SA 1895 (3) 1898 (2)*

Hayes, E. G. 5: v A 1909 (1); v SA 1912 (1); *v SA 1905 (3)*

Hayes, F. C. 9: v WI 1973 (3) 1976 (2); *v WI 1973 (4)*

Hayward, T. W. 35: v A 1896 (2) 1899 (5) 1902 (5) 1905 (5) 1909 (1); v SA 1907 (3); *v A 1897 (5) 1901 (5) 1903 (5); v SA 1895 (3)*

Headley, D. W. 15: v A 1997 (3); v SA 1998 (1); v NZ 1999 (2); *v A 1998 (3); v WI 1997 (6)*

Hearne, A. 1: *v SA 1891*

Hearne, F. 2: *v SA 1888 (2)*

Hearne, G. G. 1: *v SA 1891*

Hearne, J. T. 12: v A 1896 (3) 1899 (3); *v A 1897 (5); v SA 1891 (1)*

Hearne, J. W. 24: v A 1912 (3) 1921 (1) 1926 (1); v SA 1912 (2) 1924 (3); *v A 1911 (5) 1920 (2) 1924 (4); v SA 1913 (3)*

Hegg, W. K. 2: *v A 1998 (2)*

Hemmings, E. E. 16: v A 1989 (1); v NZ 1990 (3); v In 1990 (3); v P 1982 (2); *v A 1982 (3) 1987 (1) 1990 (1); v NZ 1987 (1); v P 1987 (1)*

Hendren, E. H. 51: v A 1921 (2) 1926 (5) 1930 (2) 1934 (4); v SA 1924 (5) 1929 (5); v WI 1928 (1); *v A 1920 (5) 1924 (5) 1928 (5); v SA 1930 (5); v WI 1929 (4) 1934 (4)*

Hendrick, M. 30: v A 1977 (3) 1980 (1) 1981 (2); v WI 1976 (2) 1980 (2); v NZ 1978 (2); v In 1974 (3) 1979 (4); v P 1974 (2); *v A 1974 (2) 1978 (5); v NZ 1974 (1) 1977 (1)*

Heseltine, C. 2: *v SA 1895 (2)*

Hick, G. A. 54: v A 1993 (3); v SA 1994 (3) 1998 (2); v WI 1991 (4) 1995 (5); v NZ 1994 (3) 1999 (1); v In 1996 (3); v P 1992 (4) 1996 (1); v SL 1998 (1); *v A 1994 (3) 1998 (4); v SA 1995 (5); v WI 1993 (5); v NZ 1991 (3); v In 1992 (3); v SL 1992 (1)*

Higgs, K. 15: v A 1968 (1); v WI 1966 (5); v SA 1965 (1); v In 1967 (1); v P 1967 (3); *v A 1965 (1); v NZ 1965 (3)*

Hill, A. 2: *v A 1876 (2)*

Hill, A. J. L. 3: *v SA 1895 (3)*

Hilton, M. J. 4: v SA 1951 (1); v WI 1950 (1); *v In 1951 (2)*

Hirst, G. H. 24: v A 1899 (1) 1902 (4) 1905 (3) 1909 (4); v SA 1907 (3); *v A 1897 (4) 1903 (5)*

Hitch, J. W. 7: v A 1912 (1) 1921 (1); v SA 1912 (1); *v A 1911 (3) 1920 (1)*

Hobbs, J. B. 61: v A 1909 (3) 1912 (3) 1921 (1) 1926 (5) 1930 (5); v SA 1912 (3) 1924 (4) 1929 (1); v WI 1928 (2); *v A 1907 (4) 1911 (5) 1920 (5) 1924 (5) 1928 (5); v SA 1909 (5) 1913 (5)*

Hobbs, R. N. S. 7: v In 1967 (3); v P 1967 (1) 1971 (1); *v WI 1967 (1); v P 1968 (1)*

Hollies, W. E. 13: v A 1948 (1); v SA 1947 (3); v WI 1950 (2); v NZ 1949 (1); *v WI 1934 (3)*

Hollioake, A. J. 4: v A 1997 (2); *v WI 1997 (2)*

Hollioake, B. C. 2: v A 1997 (1); v SL 1998 (1)

Holmes, E. R. T. 5: v SA 1935 (1); *v WI 1934 (4)*

Holmes, P. 7: v A 1921 (1); v In 1932 (1); *v SA 1927 (5)*

Hone, L. 1: *v A 1878*

Hopwood, J. L. 2: v A 1934 (2)

Hornby, A. N. 3: v A 1882 (1) 1884 (1); *v A 1878 (1)*

Horton, M. J. 2: *v In 1959 (2)*

Howard, N. D. 4: *v In 1951 (4)*

Howell, H. 5: v A 1921 (1); v SA 1924 (1); *v A 1920 (3)*

Howorth, R. 5: v SA 1947 (1); *v WI 1947 (4)*

Humphries, J. 3: *v A 1907 (3)*

Hunter, J. 5: *v A 1884 (5)*

Hussain, N. 42: v A 1993 (4) 1997 (6); v SA 1998 (5); v NZ 1999 (3); v In 1996 (3); v P 1996 (2); *v A 1998 (5); v WI 1989 (3) 1997 (6); v NZ 1996 (3); v Z 1996 (2)*

Hutchings, K. L. 7: v A 1909 (2); *v A 1907 (5)*

Hutton, L. 79: v A 1938 (3) 1948 (4) 1953 (5); v SA 1947 (5) 1951 (5); v WI 1939 (3) 1950 (3); v NZ 1937 (3) 1949 (4); v In 1946 (3) 1952 (4); v P 1954 (2); *v A 1946 (5) 1950 (5) 1954 (5); v SA 1938 (4) 1948 (5); v WI 1947 (2) 1953 (5); v NZ 1950 (2) 1954 (2)*

Hutton, R. A. 5: v In 1971 (3); v P 1971 (2)

Iddon, J. 5: v SA 1935 (1); *v WI 1934 (4)*

Igglesden, A. P. 3: v A 1989 (1); *v WI 1993 (2)*

Ikin, J. T. 18: v SA 1951 (1) 1955 (1); v In 1946 (2) 1952 (2); *v A 1946 (5); v NZ 1946 (1); v WI 1947 (4)*

Illingworth, R. 61: v A 1961 (2) 1968 (3) 1972 (5); v SA 1960 (4); v WI 1966 (2) 1969 (3) 1973 (3); v NZ 1958 (1) 1965 (1) 1969 (3) 1973 (3); v In 1959 (2) 1967 (3) 1971 (3); v P 1962 (1) 1967 (1) 1971 (3); *v A 1962 (2) 1970 (6); v WI 1959 (5); v NZ 1962 (3) 1970 (2)*

Illingworth, R. K. 9: v WI 1991 (2) 1995 (4); *v SA 1995 (3)*

Ilott, M. C. 5: v A 1993 (3); *v SA 1995 (2)*

Insole, D. J. 9: v A 1956 (1); v SA 1955 (1); v WI 1950 (1) 1957 (1); *v SA 1956 (5)*

Irani, R. C. 3: v NZ 1999 (1); v In 1996 (2)

Jackman, R. D. 4: v P 1982 (2); *v WI 1980 (2)*

Jackson, F. S. 20: v A 1893 (2) 1896 (3) 1899 (5) 1902 (5) 1905 (5)

Jackson, H. L. 2: v A 1961 (1); v NZ 1949 (1)

James, S. P. 2: v SA 1998 (1); v SL 1998 (1)

Jameson, J. A. 4: v In 1971 (2); *v WI 1973 (2)*

Jardine, D. R. 22: v WI 1928 (2) 1933 (2); v NZ 1931 (3); v In 1932 (1); *v A 1928 (5) 1932 (5); v NZ 1932 (1); v In 1933 (3)*

Jarvis, P. W. 9: v A 1989 (2); v WI 1988 (2); *v NZ 1987 (2); v In 1992 (2); v SL 1992 (1)*

Jenkins, R. O. 9: v WI 1950 (2); v In 1952 (2); *v SA 1948 (5)*

Jessop, G. L. 18: v A 1899 (1) 1902 (4) 1905 (1) 1909 (2); v SA 1907 (3) 1912 (2); *v A 1901 (5)*

Jones, A. O. 12: v A 1899 (1) 1905 (2) 1909 (2); *v A 1901 (5) 1907 (2)*

Jones, I. J. 15: v WI 1966 (1); *v A 1965 (4); v WI 1967 (5); v NZ 1965 (3); v In 1963 (1)*

Jupp, H. 2: *v A 1876 (2)*

Jupp, V. W. C. 8: v A 1921 (2); v WI 1928 (2); *v SA 1922 (4)*

Keeton, W. W. 2: v A 1934 (1); v WI 1939 (1)

Kennedy, A. S. 5: *v SA 1922 (5)*

Kenyon, D. 8: v A 1953 (2); v SA 1955 (3); *v In 1951 (3)*

Killick, E. T. 2: v SA 1929 (2)

Kilner, R. 9: v A 1926 (4); v SA 1924 (2); *v A 1924 (3)*

King, J. H. 1: v A 1909

Kinneir, S. P. 1: *v A 1911*

Knight, A. E. 3: *v A 1903 (3)*

Knight, B. R. 29: v A 1968 (2); v WI 1966 (1) 1969 (3); v NZ 1969 (2); v P 1962 (2); *v A 1962 (1) 1965 (2); v NZ 1962 (3) 1965 (2); v In 1961 (4) 1963 (5); v P 1961 (2)*

Knight, D. J. 2: v A 1921 (2)

Knight, N. V. 12: v SA 1998 (1); v WI 1995 (2); v In 1996 (1); v P 1996 (3); *v NZ 1996 (3); v Z 1996 (2)*

Knott, A. P. E. 95: v A 1968 (5) 1972 (5) 1975 (4) 1977 (5) 1981 (2); v WI 1969 (3) 1973 (3) 1976 (5) 1980 (4); v NZ 1969 (3) 1973 (3); v In 1971 (3) 1974 (3); v P 1967 (2) 1971 (3) 1974 (3); *v A 1970 (6) 1974 (6) 1976 (1); v WI 1967 (2) 1973 (5); v NZ 1970 (1) 1974 (2); v In 1972 (5) 1976 (5); v P 1968 (3) 1972 (3)*

Knox, N. A. 2: v SA 1907 (2)

Laker, J. C. 46: v A 1948 (3) 1953 (3) 1956 (5); v SA 1951 (2) 1955 (1); v WI 1950 (1) 1957 (4); v NZ 1949 (1) 1958 (4); v In 1952 (4); v P 1954 (1); *v A 1958 (4); v SA 1956 (5); v WI 1947 (4) 1953 (4)*

Lamb, A. J. 79: v A 1985 (6) 1989 (1); v WI 1984 (5) 1988 (4) 1991 (4); v NZ 1983 (4) 1986 (1) 1990 (3); v In 1982 (3) 1986 (2) 1990 (3); v P 1982 (3) 1992 (2); v SL 1984 (1) 1988 (1); *v A 1982 (3) 1986 (5) 1990 (3); v WI 1985 (5) 1989 (4); v NZ 1983 (3) 1991 (3); v In 1984 (5); v P 1983 (3)*

Langridge, James 8: v SA 1935 (1); v WI 1933 (2); v In 1936 (1) 1946 (1); *v In 1933 (3)*

Larkins, W. 13: v A 1981 (1); v WI 1980 (3); *v A 1979 (1) 1990 (3); v WI 1989 (4); v In 1979 (1)*

Larter, J. D. F. 10: v SA 1965 (2); v NZ 1965 (1); v P 1962 (1); *v NZ 1962 (3); v In 1963 (3)*

Larwood, H. 21: v A 1926 (2) 1930 (3); v SA 1929 (3); v WI 1928 (2); v NZ 1931 (1); *v A 1928 (5) 1932 (5)*

Lathwell, M. N. 2: v A 1993 (2)

Lawrence, D. V. 5: v WI 1991 (2); v SL 1988 (1) 1991 (1); *v NZ 1991 (1)*

Leadbeater, E. 2: *v In 1951 (2)*

Lee, H. W. 1: *v SA 1930*

Lees, W. S. 5: *v SA 1905 (5)*

Legge, G. B. 5: *v SA 1927 (1); v NZ 1929 (4)*

Leslie, C. F. H. 4: *v A 1882 (4)*

Lever, J. K. 21: v A 1977 (3); v WI 1980 (1); v In 1979 (1) 1986 (1); *v A 1976 (1) 1978 (1) 1979 (1); v NZ 1977 (1); v In 1976 (5) 1979 (1) 1981 (2); v P 1977 (3)*

Lever, P. 17: v A 1972 (1) 1975 (1); v In 1971 (1); v P 1971 (3); *v A 1970 (5) 1974 (2); v NZ 1970 (2) 1974 (2)*

Leveson Gower, H. D. G. 3: *v SA 1909 (3)*

Levett, W. H. V. 1: *v In 1933*

Lewis, A. R. 9: v NZ 1973 (1); *v In 1972 (5); v P 1972 (3)*

Lewis, C. C. 32: v A 1990 (1); v WI 1991 (2); v NZ 1990 (1); v In 1990 (2) 1996 (3); v P 1992 (5) 1996 (2); v SL 1991 (1); *v A 1990 (1) 1994 (2); v WI 1993 (5); v NZ 1991 (2); v In 1992 (3); v SL 1992 (1)*

Leyland, M. 41: v A 1930 (3) 1934 (5) 1938 (1); v SA 1929 (5) 1935 (4); v WI 1928 (1) 1933 (1); v In 1936 (2); *v A 1928 (1) 1932 (5) 1936 (5); v SA 1930 (3); v WI 1934 (3)*

Lilley, A. A. 35: v A 1896 (3) 1899 (4) 1902 (5) 1905 (5) 1909 (5); v SA 1907 (3); *v A 1901 (5) 1903 (5)*

Lillywhite, James jun. 2: *v A 1876 (2)*

Lloyd, D. 9: v In 1974 (2); v P 1974 (3); *v A 1974 (4)*

Lloyd, T. A. 1: v WI 1984

Loader, P. J. 13: v SA 1955 (1); v WI 1957 (2); v NZ 1958 (3); v P 1954 (1); *v A 1958 (2); v SA 1956 (4)*

Lock, G. A. R. 49: v A 1953 (2) 1956 (4) 1961 (3); v SA 1955 (3); v WI 1957 (3) 1963 (3); v NZ 1958 (5); v In 1952 (2); v P 1962 (3); *v A 1958 (4); v SA 1956 (1); v WI 1953 (5) 1967 (2); v NZ 1958 (2); v In 1961 (5); v P 1961 (2)*

Lockwood, W. H. 12: v A 1893 (2) 1899 (1) 1902 (4); *v A 1894 (5)*

Lohmann, G. A. 18: v A 1886 (3) 1888 (3) 1890 (2) 1896 (1); *v A 1886 (2) 1887 (1) 1891 (3); v SA 1895 (3)*

Lowson, F. A. 7: v SA 1951 (2) 1955 (1); *v In 1951 (4)*

Lucas, A. P. 5: v A 1880 (1) 1882 (1) 1884 (2); *v A 1878 (1)*

Luckhurst, B. W. 21: v A 1972 (4); v WI 1973 (3); v In 1971 (3); v P 1971 (3); *v A 1970 (5) 1974 (2); v NZ 1970 (2)*

Lyttelton, Hon. A. 4: v A 1880 (1) 1882 (1) 1884 (2)

Macaulay, G. G. 8: v A 1926 (1); v SA 1924 (1); v WI 1933 (2); *v SA 1922 (4)*

MacBryan, J. C. W. 1: v SA 1924

McCague, M. J. 3: v A 1993 (2); *v A 1994 (1)*

McConnon, J. E. 2: v P 1954 (2)

McGahey, C. P. 2: *v A 1901 (2)*

MacGregor, G. 8: v A 1890 (2) 1893 (3); *v A 1891 (3)*

McIntyre, A. J. W. 3: v SA 1955 (1); v WI 1950 (1); *v A 1950 (1)*

MacKinnon, F. A. 1: *v A 1878*

MacLaren, A. C. 35: v A 1896 (2) 1899 (4) 1902 (5) 1905 (5) 1909 (5); *v A 1894 (5) 1897 (5) 1901 (5)*

McMaster, J. E. P. 1: *v SA 1888*

Maddy, D. L. 1: v NZ 1999

Makepeace, J. W. H. 4: *v A 1920 (4)*

Malcolm, D. E. 40: v A 1989 (1) 1993 (1) 1997 (4); v SA 1994 (1); v WI 1991 (2) 1995 (2); v NZ 1990 (3) 1994 (1); v In 1990 (3); v P 1992 (3); *v A 1990 (5) 1994 (4); v SA 1995 (2); v WI 1989 (4) 1993 (1); v In 1992 (2); v SL 1992 (1)*

Mallender, N. A. 2: v P 1992 (2)

Mann, F. G. 7: v NZ 1949 (2); *v SA 1948 (5)*

Mann, F. T. 5: *v SA 1922 (5)*

Marks, V. J. 6: v NZ 1983 (1); v P 1982 (1); *v NZ 1983 (1); v P 1983 (3)*

Marriott, C. S. 1: v WI 1933

Martin, F. 2: v A 1890 (1); *v SA 1891 (1)*

Martin, J. W. 1: v SA 1947

Martin, P. J. 8: v A 1997 (1); v WI 1995 (3); v In 1996 (1); *v SA 1995 (3)*

Mason, J. R. 5: *v A 1897 (5)*

Matthews, A. D. G. 1: v NZ 1937

May, P. B. H. 66: v A 1953 (2) 1956 (5) 1961 (4); v SA 1951 (2) 1955 (5); v WI 1957 (5); v NZ 1958 (5); v In 1952 (4) 1959 (3); v P 1954 (4); *v A 1954 (5) 1958 (5); v SA 1956 (5); v WI 1953 (5) 1959 (3); v NZ 1954 (2) 1958 (2)*

Maynard, C. P. 4: v WI 1988 (1); *v WI 1993 (1)*

Mead, C. P. 17: v A 1921 (2); *v A 1911 (4) 1928 (1); v SA 1913 (5) 1922 (5)*

Mead, W. 1: v A 1899

Midwinter, W. E. 4: *v A 1881 (4)*

Milburn, C. 9: v A 1968 (2); v WI 1966 (4); v In 1967 (1); v P 1967 (1); *v P 1968 (1)*

Miller, A. M. 1: *v SA 1895*

Miller, G. 34: v A 1977 (2); v WI 1976 (1) 1984 (2); v NZ 1978 (2); v In 1979 (3) 1982 (1); v P 1978 (3) 1982 (1); *v A 1978 (6) 1979 (1) 1982 (5); v WI 1980 (1); v NZ 1977 (3); v P 1977 (3)*

Milligan, F. W. 2: *v SA 1898 (2)*

Millman, G. 6: v P 1962 (2); *v In 1961 (2); v P 1961 (2)*

Milton, C. A. 6: v NZ 1958 (2); v In 1959 (2); *v A 1958 (2)*

Mitchell, A. 6: v SA 1935 (2); v In 1936 (1); *v In 1933 (3)*

Mitchell, F. 2: *v SA 1898 (2)*

Mitchell, T. B. 5: v A 1934 (2); v SA 1935 (1); *v A 1932 (1); v NZ 1932 (1)*
Mitchell-Innes, N. S. 1: v SA 1935
Mold, A. W. 3: v A 1893 (3)
Moon, L. J. 4: *v SA 1905 (4)*
Morley, F. 4: v A 1880 (1); *v A 1882 (3)*
Morris, H. 3: v WI 1991 (2); v SL 1991 (1)
Morris, J. E. 3: v In 1990 (3)
Mortimore, J. B. 9: v A 1964 (1); v In 1959 (2); *v A 1958 (1); v NZ 1958 (2); v In 1963 (3)*
Moss, A. E. 9: v A 1956 (1); v SA 1960 (2); v In 1959 (3); *v WI 1953 (1) 1959 (2)*
Moxon, M. D. 10: v A 1989 (1); v WI 1988 (2); v NZ 1986 (2); v P 1987 (1); *v A 1987 (1); v NZ 1987 (3)*
Mullally, A. D. 16: v NZ 1999 (3); v In 1996 (3); v P 1996 (3); *v A 1998 (4); v NZ 1996 (1); v Z 1996 (2)*
Munton, T. A. 2: v P 1992 (2)
Murdoch, W. L. 1: *v SA 1891*
Murray, J. T. 21: v A 1961 (5); v WI 1966 (1); v In 1967 (3); v P 1962 (3) 1967 (1); *v A 1962 (1); v SA 1964 (1); v NZ 1962 (1) 1965 (1); v In 1961 (3); v P 1961 (1)*

Newham, W. 1: *v A 1887*
Newport, P. J. 3: v A 1989 (1); v SL 1988 (1); *v A 1990 (1)*
Nichols, M. S. 14: v A 1930 (1); v SA 1935 (4); v WI 1933 (1) 1939 (1); *v NZ 1929 (4); v In 1933 (3)*

Oakman, A. S. M. 2: v A 1956 (2)
O'Brien, Sir T. C. 5: v A 1884 (1) 1888 (1); *v SA 1895 (3)*
O'Connor, J. 4: v A 1929 (1); *v WI 1929 (3)*
Old, C. M. 46: v A 1975 (2) 1977 (2) 1980 (1) 1981 (2); v WI 1973 (1) 1976 (2) 1980 (1); v NZ 1973 (2) 1978 (1); v In 1974 (3); v P 1974 (3) 1978 (3); *v A 1974 (2) 1976 (1) 1978 (1); v WI 1973 (4) 1980 (1); v NZ 1974 (1) 1977 (2); v In 1972 (4) 1976 (4); v P 1972 (1) 1977 (1)*
Oldfield, N. 1: v WI 1939

Padgett, D. E. V. 2: v SA 1960 (2)
Paine, G. A. E. 4: *v WI 1934 (4)*
Palairet, L. C. H. 2: v A 1902 (2)
Palmer, C. H. 1: *v WI 1953*
Palmer, K. E. 1: *v SA 1964*
Parfitt, P. H. 37: v A 1964 (4) 1972 (3); v SA 1965 (2); v WI 1969 (1); v NZ 1965 (2); v P 1962 (5); *v A 1962 (2); v SA 1964 (5); v NZ 1962 (3) 1965 (3); v In 1961 (2) 1963 (3); v P 1961 (2)*
Parker, C. W. L. 1: v A 1921
Parker, P. W. G. 1: v A 1981
Parkhouse, W. G. A. 7: v WI 1950 (2); v In 1959 (2); *v A 1950 (2); v NZ 1950 (1)*
Parkin, C. H. 10: v A 1921 (4); v SA 1924 (1); *v A 1920 (5)*
Parks, J. H. 1: v NZ 1937
Parks, J. M. 46: v A 1964 (5); v SA 1960 (5) 1965 (3); v WI 1963 (4) 1966 (4); v NZ 1965 (3); v P 1954 (1); *v A 1965 (5); v SA 1964 (5); v WI 1959 (1) 1967 (3); v NZ 1965 (2); v In 1963 (5)*
Pataudi sen., Nawab of, 3: v A 1934 (1); *v A 1932 (2)*
Patel, M. M. 2: v In 1996 (2)
Paynter, E. 20: v A 1938 (4); v WI 1939 (2); v NZ 1931 (1) 1937 (2); v In 1932 (1); *v A 1932 (3); v SA 1938 (5); v NZ 1932 (2)*
Peate, E. 9: v A 1882 (1) 1884 (3) 1886 (1); *v A 1881 (4)*
Peebles, I. A. R. 13: v A 1930 (2); v NZ 1931 (3); *v SA 1927 (4) 1930 (4)*
Peel, R. 20: v A 1888 (3) 1890 (1) 1893 (1) 1896 (1); *v A 1884 (5) 1887 (1) 1891 (3) 1894 (5)*
Penn, F. 1: v A 1880
Perks, R. T. D. 2: v WI 1939 (1); *v SA 1938 (1)*
Philipson, H. 5: *v A 1891 (1) 1894 (4)*
Pigott, A. C. S. 1: *v NZ 1983*
Pilling, R. 8: v A 1884 (1) 1886 (1) 1888 (1); *v A 1881 (4) 1887 (1)*
Place, W. 3: *v WI 1947 (3)*
Pocock, P. I. 25: v A 1968 (1); v WI 1976 (2) 1984 (2); v SL 1984 (1); *v WI 1967 (2) 1973 (4); v In 1972 (4) 1984 (5); v P 1968 (1) 1972 (3)*

Pollard, R. 4: v A 1948 (2); v In 1946 (1); *v NZ 1946 (1)*
Poole, C. J. 3: *v In 1951 (3)*
Pope, G. H. 1: v SA 1947
Pougher, A. D. 1: *v SA 1891*
Price, J. S. E. 15: v A 1964 (2) 1972 (1); v In 1971 (3); v P 1971 (1); *v SA 1964 (4); v In 1963 (4)*
Price, W. F. F. 1: v A 1938
Prideaux, R. M. 3: v A 1968 (1); *v P 1968 (2)*
Pringle, D. R. 30: v A 1989 (2); v WI 1984 (3) 1988 (4) 1991 (4); v NZ 1986 (1); v In 1982 (3) 1986 (3); v P 1982 (1) 1992 (3); v SL 1988 (1); *v A 1982 (3); v NZ 1991 (2)*
Pullar, G. 28: v A 1961 (5); v SA 1960 (3); v In 1959 (3); v P 1962 (2); *v A 1962 (4); v WI 1959 (5); v In 1961 (3); v P 1961 (3)*

Quaife, W. G. 7: v A 1899 (2); *v A 1901 (5)*

Radford, N. V. 3: v NZ 1986 (1); v In 1986 (1); *v NZ 1987 (1)*
Radley, C. T. 8: v NZ 1978 (3); v P 1978 (3); *v NZ 1977 (2)*
Ramprakash, M. R. 38: v A 1993 (1) 1997 (1); v SA 1998 (5); v WI 1991 (5) 1995 (2); v NZ 1999 (4); v P 1992 (3); v SL 1991 (1) 1998 (1); *v A 1994 (1) 1998 (5); v WI 1993 (4) 1997 (3); v SA 1995 (2)*
Randall, D. W. 47: v A 1977 (5); v WI 1984 (1); v NZ 1983 (3); v In 1979 (3) 1982 (3); v P 1982 (3); *v A 1976 (1) 1978 (6) 1979 (2) 1982 (4); v NZ 1977 (3) 1983 (3); v In 1976 (4); v P 1977 (3) 1983 (3)*
Ranjitsinhji, K. S. 15: v A 1896 (2) 1899 (5) 1902 (3); *v A 1897 (5)*
Read, C. M. W. 3: v NZ 1999 (3)
Read, H. D. 1: v SA 1935
Read, J. M. 17: v A 1882 (1) 1890 (2) 1893 (1); *v A 1884 (5) 1886 (2) 1887 (1) 1891 (3); v SA 1888 (1)*
Read, W. W. 18: v A 1884 (2) 1886 (3) 1888 (3) 1890 (3) 1893 (2); *v A 1882 (4) 1887 (1); v SA 1891 (1)*
Reeve, D. A. 3: *v NZ 1991 (3)*
Relf, A. E. 13: v A 1909 (1); *v A 1903 (2); v SA 1905 (5) 1913 (5)*
Rhodes, H. J. 2: v In 1959 (2)
Rhodes, S. J. 11: v SA 1994 (3); v NZ 1994 (3); *v A 1994 (5)*
Rhodes, W. 58: v A 1899 (3) 1902 (5) 1905 (4) 1909 (4) 1912 (3) 1921 (1) 1926 (1); v SA 1912 (3); *v A 1903 (5) 1907 (5) 1911 (5) 1920 (5); v SA 1909 (5) 1913 (5); v WI 1929 (4)*
Richards, C. J. 8: v WI 1988 (2); v P 1987 (1); *v A 1986 (5)*
Richardson, D. W. 1: v WI 1957
Richardson, P. E. 34: v A 1956 (5); v WI 1957 (5) 1963 (1); v NZ 1958 (2); *v A 1958 (4); v SA 1956 (5); v WI 1957 (5); v In 1961 (5); v P 1961 (3)*
Richardson, T. 14: v A 1893 (1) 1896 (3); *v A 1894 (5) 1897 (5)*
Richmond, T. L. 1: v A 1921
Ridgway, F. 5: *v In 1951 (5)*
Robertson, J. D. 11: v SA 1947 (1); v NZ 1949 (1); *v WI 1947 (4); v In 1951 (5)*
Robins, R. W. V. 19: v A 1930 (2); v SA 1929 (1) 1935 (3); v WI 1933 (2); v NZ 1931 (1) 1937 (3); v In 1932 (1) 1936 (2); *v A 1936 (4)*
Robinson, R. T. 29: v A 1985 (6) 1989 (1); v In 1986 (1); v P 1987 (5); v SL 1988 (1); *v A 1987 (1); v WI 1985 (4); v NZ 1987 (3); v In 1984 (5); v P 1987 (2)*
Roope, G. R. J. 21: v A 1975 (1) 1977 (2); v WI 1973 (1); v NZ 1973 (3) 1978 (1); v P 1978 (3); *v NZ 1977 (3); v In 1972 (2); v P 1972 (2) 1977 (3)*
Root, C. F. 3: v A 1926 (3)
Rose, B. C. 9: v WI 1980 (3); *v WI 1980 (1); v NZ 1977 (2); v P 1977 (3)*
Royle, V. P. F. A. 1: *v A 1878*
Rumsey, F. E. 5: v A 1964 (1); v SA 1965 (1); v NZ 1965 (3)
Russell, A. C. 10: v A 1921 (2); *v A 1920 (4); v SA 1922 (4)*
Russell, R. C. 54: v A 1989 (6); v WI 1991 (4) 1995 (3); v NZ 1990 (3); v In 1990 (3) 1996 (3); v P 1992 (3) 1996 (2); v SL 1988 (1) 1991 (1); *v A 1990 (3); v SA 1995 (5); v WI 1989 (4) 1993 (5) 1997 (5); v NZ 1991 (3)*
Russell, W. E. 10: v SA 1965 (1); v WI 1966 (2); v P 1967 (1); *v A 1965 (1); v NZ 1965 (3); v In 1961 (1); v P 1961 (1)*

Salisbury, I. D. K. 12: v SA 1994 (1) 1998 (2); v P 1992 (2) 1996 (2); v SL 1998 (1); *v WI 1993 (2); v In 1992 (2)*

Sandham, A. 14: v A 1921 (1); v SA 1924 (2); *v A 1924 (2); v SA 1922 (5); v WI 1929 (4)*

Schultz, S. S. 1: *v A 1878*

Scotton, W. H. 15: v A 1884 (1) 1886 (3); *v A 1881 (4) 1884 (5) 1886 (2)*

Selby, J. 6: *v A 1876 (2) 1881 (4)*

Selvey, M. W. W. 3: v WI 1976 (2); *v In 1976 (1)*

Shackleton, D. 7: v SA 1951 (1); v WI 1950 (1) 1963 (4); *v In 1951 (1)*

Sharp, J. 3: v A 1909 (3)

Sharpe, J. W. 3: v A 1890 (1); *v A 1891 (2)*

Sharpe, P. J. 12: v A 1964 (2); v WI 1963 (3) 1969 (3); v NZ 1969 (3); *v In 1963 (1)*

Shaw, A. 7: v A 1880 (1); *v A 1876 (2) 1881 (4)*

Sheppard, Rev. D. S. 22: v A 1956 (2); v WI 1950 (1) 1957 (2); v In 1952 (2); v P 1954 (2) 1962 (2); *v A 1950 (2) 1962 (5); v NZ 1950 (1) 1963 (3)*

Sherwin, M. 3: v A 1888 (1); *v A 1886 (2)*

Shrewsbury, A. 23: v A 1884 (3) 1886 (3) 1890 (2) 1893 (3); *v A 1881 (4) 1884 (5) 1886 (2) 1887 (1)*

Shuter, J. 1: v A 1888

Shuttleworth, K. 5: v P 1971 (1); *v A 1970 (2); v NZ 1970 (2)*

Sidebottom, A. 1: v A 1985

Silverwood, C. E. W. 1: *v Z 1996*

Simpson, R. T. 27: v A 1953 (3); v WI 1950 (3); v NZ 1949 (2); v In 1952 (2); v P 1954 (2); *v A 1950 (5) 1954 (1); v SA 1948 (1); v NZ 1950 (2) 1954 (2)*

Simpson-Hayward, G. H. 5: *v SA 1909 (5)*

Sims, J. M. 4: v SA 1935 (1); v In 1936 (1); *v A 1936 (2)*

Sinfield, R. A. 1: v A 1938

Slack, W. N. 3: v In 1986 (1); *v WI 1985 (2)*

Smailes, T. F. 1: v In 1946

Small, G. C. 17: v A 1989 (1); v WI 1988 (1); v NZ 1986 (2) 1990 (3); *v A 1986 (2) 1990 (4); v WI 1989 (4)*

Smith, A. C. 6: *v A 1962 (4); v NZ 1962 (2)*

Smith, A. M. 1: v A 1997

Smith, C. A. 1: *v SA 1888*

Smith, C. I. J. 5: v NZ 1937 (1); *v WI 1934 (4)*

Smith, C. L. 8: v NZ 1983 (2); v In 1986 (1); *v NZ 1983 (2); v P 1983 (3)*

Smith, D. 2: v SA 1935 (2)

Smith, D. M. 2: *v WI 1985 (2)*

Smith, D. R. 5: *v In 1961 (5)*

Smith, D. V. 3: v WI 1957 (3)

Smith, E. J. 11: v A 1912 (3); v SA 1912 (3); *v A 1911 (4); v SA 1913 (1)*

Smith, H. 1: v WI 1928

Smith, M. J. K. 50: v A 1961 (1) 1972 (3); v SA 1960 (4) 1965 (3); v WI 1966 (1); v NZ 1958 (3) 1965 (3); v In 1959 (2); *v A 1965 (5); v SA 1964 (5); v WI 1959 (5); v NZ 1965 (3); v In 1961 (4) 1963 (5); v P 1961 (3)*

Smith, R. A. 62: v A 1989 (5) 1993 (5); v WI 1988 (2) 1991 (4) 1995 (4); v NZ 1990 (3) 1994 (3); v In 1990 (3); v P 1992 (5); v SL 1988 (1) 1991 (1); *v A 1990 (5); v SA 1995 (5); v WI 1989 (4) 1993 (5); v NZ 1991 (3); v In 1992 (3); v SL 1992 (1)*

Smith, T. P. B. 4: v In 1946 (1); *v A 1946 (2); v NZ 1946 (1)*

Smithson, G. A. 2: *v WI 1947 (2)*

Snow, J. A. 49: v A 1968 (5) 1972 (5) 1975 (4); v SA 1965 (1); v WI 1966 (3) 1969 (3) 1973 (1) 1976 (3); v NZ 1965 (1) 1969 (2) 1973 (3); v In 1967 (3) 1971 (2); v P 1967 (1); *v A 1970 (6); v WI 1967 (4); v P 1968 (2)*

Southerton, J. 2: *v A 1876 (2)*

Spooner, R. H. 10: v A 1905 (2) 1909 (2) 1912 (3); v SA 1912 (3)

Spooner, R. T. 7: v SA 1955 (1); *v In 1951 (5); v WI 1953 (1)*

Stanyforth, R. T. 4: *v SA 1927 (4)*

Staples, S. J. 3: *v SA 1927 (3)*

Statham, J. B. 70: v A 1953 (1) 1956 (3) 1961 (4); v SA 1951 (2) 1955 (4) 1960 (5) 1965 (1); v WI 1957 (3) 1963 (2); v NZ 1958 (2); v In 1959 (3); v P 1954 (4) 1962 (3); *v A 1954 (5) 1958 (4) 1962 (5); v SA 1956 (4); v WI 1953 (4) 1959 (3); v NZ 1950 (1) 1954 (2); v In 1951 (5)*

Steel, A. G. 13: v A 1880 (1) 1882 (1) 1884 (3) 1886 (3) 1888 (1); *v A 1882 (4)*

Steele, D. S. 8: v A 1975 (3); v WI 1976 (5)

Stephenson, J. P. 1: v A 1989

Stevens, G. T. S. 10: v A 1926 (2); *v SA 1922 (1) 1927 (5); v WI 1929 (2)*

Stevenson, G. B. 2: *v WI 1980 (1); v In 1979 (1)*

Stewart, A. J. 90: v A 1993 (6) 1997 (6); v SA 1994 (3) 1998 (5); v WI 1991 (1) 1995 (3); v NZ 1990 (3) 1994 (3) 1999 (4); v In 1996 (2); v P 1992 (5) 1996 (3); v SL 1991 (1) 1998 (1); *v A 1990 (5) 1994 (2) 1998 (5); v SA 1995 (5); v WI 1989 (4) 1993 (5) 1997 (6); v NZ 1991 (3) 1996 (3); v In 1992 (3); v SL 1992 (1); v Z 1996 (2)*

Stewart, M. J. 8: v WI 1963 (4); v P 1962 (2); *v In 1963 (2)*

Stoddart, A. E. 16: v A 1893 (3) 1896 (2); *v A 1887 (1) 1891 (3) 1894 (5) 1897 (2)*

Storer, W. 6: v A 1899 (1); *v A 1897 (5)*

Street, G. B. 1: *v SA 1922*

Strudwick, H. 28: v A 1921 (2) 1926 (5); v SA 1924 (1); *v A 1911 (1) 1920 (4) 1924 (5); v SA 1909 (5) 1913 (5)*

Studd, C. T. 5: v A 1882 (1); *v A 1882 (4)*

Studd, G. B. 4: *v A 1882 (4)*

Subba Row, R. 13: v A 1961 (5); v SA 1960 (4); v NZ 1958 (1); v In 1959 (1); *v WI 1959 (2)*

Such, P. M. 11: v A 1993 (5); v NZ 1994 (3) 1999 (1); *v A 1998 (2)*

Sugg, F. H. 2: v A 1888 (2)

Sutcliffe, H. 54: v A 1926 (5) 1930 (4) 1934 (4); v SA 1924 (5) 1929 (5) 1935 (2); v WI 1928 (3) 1933 (2); v NZ 1931 (2); v In 1932 (1); *v A 1924 (5) 1928 (4) 1932 (5); v SA 1927 (5); v NZ 1932 (2)*

Swetman, R. 11: v In 1959 (3); *v A 1958 (2); v WI 1959 (4); v NZ 1958 (2)*

Tate, F. W. 1: v A 1902

Tate, M. W. 39: v A 1926 (5) 1930 (5); v SA 1924 (5) 1929 (3) 1935 (1); v WI 1928 (3); v NZ 1931 (1); *v A 1924 (5) 1928 (5); v SA 1930 (5); v NZ 1932 (1)*

Tattersall, R. 16: v A 1953 (1); v SA 1951 (5); v P 1954 (1); *v A 1950 (2); v NZ 1950 (2); v In 1951 (5)*

Tavaré, C. J. 31: v A 1981 (2) 1989 (1); v WI 1980 (2) 1984 (1); v NZ 1983 (4); v In 1982 (3); v P 1982 (3); v SL 1984 (1); *v A 1982 (5); v NZ 1983 (2); v In 1981 (6); v SL 1981 (1)*

Taylor, J. P. 2: v NZ 1994 (1); *v In 1992 (1)*

Taylor, K. 3: v A 1964 (1); v In 1959 (2)

Taylor, L. B. 2: v A 1985 (2)

Taylor, R. W. 57: v A 1981 (3); v NZ 1978 (3) 1983 (4); v In 1979 (3) 1982 (3); v P 1978 (3) 1982 (3); *v A 1978 (6) 1979 (3) 1982 (5); v NZ 1970 (1) 1977 (3) 1983 (3); v In 1979 (1) 1981 (6); v P 1977 (3) 1983 (3); v SL 1981 (1)*

Tennyson, Hon. L. H. 9: v A 1921 (4); *v SA 1913 (5)*

Terry, V. P. 2: v WI 1984 (2)

Thomas, J. G. 5: v NZ 1986 (1); *v WI 1985 (4)*

Thompson, G. J. 6: v A 1909 (1); *v SA 1909 (5)*

Thomson, N. I. 5: *v SA 1964 (5)*

Thorpe, G. P. 57: v A 1993 (3) 1997 (6); v SA 1994 (2) 1998 (3); v WI 1995 (6); v NZ 1999 (4); v In 1996 (3); v P 1996 (3); *v A 1994 (5) 1998 (1); v SA 1995 (5); v WI 1993 (5) 1997 (6); v NZ 1996 (3); v Z 1996 (2)*

Titmus, F. J. 53: v A 1964 (5); v SA 1955 (2) 1965 (3); v WI 1963 (4) 1966 (3); v NZ 1965 (3); v P 1962 (2) 1967 (2); *v A 1962 (5) 1965 (5) 1974 (4); v SA 1964 (5); v WI 1967 (2); v NZ 1962 (3); v In 1963 (5)*

Tolchard, R. W. 4: *v In 1976 (4)*

Townsend, C. L. 2: v A 1899 (2)

Townsend, D. C. H. 3: *v WI 1934 (3)*

Townsend, L. F. 4: *v WI 1929 (1); v In 1933 (3)*

Tremlett, M. F. 3: *v WI 1947 (3)*

Trott, A. E. 2: *v SA 1898 (2)*

Trueman, F. S. 67: v A 1953 (1) 1956 (2) 1961 (4) 1964 (4); v SA 1955 (1) 1960 (5); v WI 1957 (5) 1963 (5); v NZ 1958 (5) 1965 (2); v In 1952 (4) 1959 (5); v P 1962 (4); *v A 1958 (3) 1962 (5); v WI 1953 (3) 1959 (5); v NZ 1958 (2) 1962 (2)*

Tudor, A. J. 3: v NZ 1999 (1); *v A 1998 (2)*

Tufnell, N. C. 1: *v SA 1909*

Tufnell, P. C. R. 38: v A 1993 (2) 1997 (1); v SA 1994 (1); v WI 1991 (1); v NZ 1999 (4); v P
	1992 (1); v SL 1991 (1); *v A 1990 (4) 1994 (4); v WI 1993 (2) 1997 (6); v NZ 1991 (3) 1996 (3);
	v In 1992 (2); v SL 1992 (1); v Z 1996 (2)*

Turnbull, M. J. 9: v WI 1933 (2); v In 1936 (1); *v SA 1930 (5); v NZ 1929 (1)*

Tyldesley, E. 14: v A 1921 (3) 1926 (1); v SA 1924 (1); v WI 1928 (3); *v A 1928 (1): v SA 1927 (5)*

Tyldesley, J. T. 31: v A 1899 (2) 1902 (5) 1905 (5) 1909 (4); v SA 1907 (3); *v A 1901 (5) 1903 (5);
	v SA 1898 (2)*

Tyldesley, R. K. 7: v A 1930 (2); v SA 1924 (4); *v A 1924 (1)*

Tylecote, E. F. S. 6: v A 1886 (2); *v A 1882 (4)*

Tyler, E. J. 1: *v SA 1895*

Tyson, F. H. 17: v A 1956 (1); v SA 1955 (2); v P 1954 (1); *v A 1954 (5) 1958 (2); v SA 1956 (2);
	v NZ 1954 (2) 1958 (2)*

Ulyett, G. 25: v A 1882 (1) 1884 (3) 1886 (3) 1888 (2) 1890 (1); *v A 1876 (2) 1878 (1) 1881 (4)
	1884 (5) 1887 (1); v SA 1888 (2)*

Underwood, D. L. 86: v A 1968 (4) 1972 (2) 1975 (4) 1977 (5); v WI 1966 (2) 1969 (2) 1973 (3)
	1976 (5) 1980 (1); v NZ 1969 (3) 1973 (1); v In 1971 (1) 1974 (3); v P 1967 (2) 1971 (1)
	1974 (3); *v A 1970 (5) 1974 (5) 1976 (1) 1979 (3); v WI 1973 (4); v NZ 1970 (2) 1974 (2); v In
	1972 (4) 1976 (5) 1979 (1) 1981 (6); v P 1968 (3) 1972 (2); v SL 1981 (1)*

Valentine, B. H. 7: *v SA 1938 (5); v In 1933 (2)*

Verity, H. 40: v A 1934 (5) 1938 (4); v WI 1933 (2) 1939 (1); v NZ 1931 (2)
	1937 (1); v In 1936 (3); *v A 1932 (4) 1936 (5); v SA 1938 (5); v NZ 1932 (1); v In 1933 (3)*

Vernon, G. F. 1: *v A 1882*

Vine, J. 2: *v A 1911 (2)*

Voce, W. 27: v NZ 1931 (1) 1937 (1); v In 1932 (1) 1936 (1) 1946 (1); *v A 1932 (4) 1936 (5)
	1946 (2); v SA 1930 (5); v WI 1929 (4); v NZ 1932 (2)*

Waddington, A. 2: *v A 1920 (2)*

Wainwright, E. 5: v A 1893 (1); *v A 1897 (4)*

Walker, P. M. 3: v SA 1960 (3)

Walters, C. F. 11: v A 1934 (5); v WI 1933 (3); *v In 1933 (3)*

Ward, A. 5: v WI 1976 (1); v NZ 1969 (3); v P 1971 (1)

Ward, A. 7: v A 1893 (2); *v A 1894 (5)*

Wardle, J. H. 28: v A 1953 (3) 1956 (1); v SA 1951 (2) 1955 (3); v WI 1950 (1) 1957 (1); *v P
	1954 (1); v A 1954 (4); v SA 1956 (4); v WI 1947 (1) 1953 (2); v NZ 1954 (2)*

Warner, P. F. 15: v A 1909 (1) 1912 (3); v SA 1912 (1); *v A 1903 (5); v SA 1898 (2) 1905 (5)*

Warr, J. J. 2: *v A 1950 (2)*

Warren, A. R. 1: v A 1905

Washbrook, C. 37: v A 1948 (4) 1956 (3); v SA 1947 (5); v WI 1950 (2); v NZ 1937 (1) 1949 (2);
	v In 1946 (3); *v A 1946 (5) 1950 (5); v SA 1948 (5); v NZ 1946 (1) 1950 (1)*

Watkin, S. L. 3: v A 1993 (1); v WI 1991 (1)

Watkins, A. J. 15: v A 1948 (1); v NZ 1949 (1); v In 1952 (3); *v SA 1948 (5); v In 1951 (5)*

Watkinson, M. 4: v WI 1995 (3); v SA 1995 (1)

Watson, W. 23: v A 1953 (3) 1956 (2); v SA 1951 (5) 1955 (1); v NZ 1958 (2); v In 1952 (1);
	v A 1958 (2); v WI 1953 (5); v NZ 1958 (2)

Webbe, A. J. 1: *v A 1878*

Wellard, A. W. 2: v A 1938 (1); v NZ 1937 (1)

Wells, A. P. 1: v WI 1995

Wharton, A. 1: v NZ 1949

Whitaker, J. J. 1: *v A 1986*

White, C. 8: v A 1994 (1); v WI 1995 (2); v NZ 1994 (3); *v NZ 1996 (1); v Z 1996 (1)*

White, D. W. 2: *v P 1961 (2)*

White, J. C. 15: v A 1921 (1) 1930 (1); v SA 1929 (3); v WI 1928 (1); *v A 1928 (5); v SA 1930 (4)*

Whysall, W. W. 4: v A 1930 (1); *v A 1924 (3)*

Wilkinson, L. L. 3: *v SA 1938 (3)*

Willey, P. 26: v A 1980 (1) 1981 (4) 1985 (1); v WI 1976 (2) 1980 (5); v NZ 1986 (1); v In 1979 (1); *v A 1979 (3); v WI 1980 (4) 1985 (4)*

Williams, N. F. 1: v In 1990

Willis, R. G. D. 90: v A 1977 (5) 1981 (6); v WI 1973 (1) 1976 (2) 1980 (4) 1984 (3); v NZ 1978 (3) 1983 (4); v In 1974 (1) 1979 (3) 1982 (3); v P 1974 (1) 1978 (3) 1982 (2); *v A 1970 (4) 1974 (5) 1976 (1) 1978 (6) 1979 (3) 1982 (5); v WI 1973 (3); v NZ 1970 (1) 1977 (3) 1983 (3); v In 1976 (5) 1981 (5); v P 1977 (3) 1983 (1); v SL 1981 (1)*

Wilson, C. E. M. 2: *v SA 1898 (2)*

Wilson, D. 6: *v NZ 1970 (1); v In 1963 (5)*

Wilson, E. R. 1: *v A 1920*

Wood, A. 4: v A 1938 (1); v WI 1939 (3)

Wood, B. 12: v A 1972 (1) 1975 (3); v WI 1976 (1); v P 1978 (1); *v NZ 1974 (2); v In 1972 (3); v P 1972 (1)*

Wood, G. E. C. 3: v SA 1924 (3)

Wood, H. 4: v A 1888 (1); *v SA 1888 (2) 1891 (1)*

Wood, R. 1: *v A 1886*

Woods S. M. J. 3: *v SA 1895 (3)*

Woolley, F. E. 64: v A 1909 (1) 1912 (3) 1921 (5) 1926 (5) 1930 (2) 1934 (1); v SA 1912 (3) 1924 (5) 1929 (3); v NZ 1931 (1); v In 1932 (1); *v A 1911 (5) 1920 (5) 1924 (5); v SA 1909 (5) 1913 (5) 1922 (5); v NZ 1929 (4)*

Woolmer, R. A. 19: v A 1975 (2) 1977 (5) 1981 (2); v WI 1976 (5) 1980 (2); *v A 1976 (1); v In 1976 (2)*

Worthington, T. S. 9: v In 1936 (2); *v A 1936 (3); v NZ 1929 (4)*

Wright, C. W. 3: *v SA 1895 (3)*

Wright, D. V. P. 34: v A 1938 (3) 1948 (1); v SA 1947 (4); v WI 1939 (3) 1950 (1); v NZ 1949 (1); v In 1946 (2); *v A 1946 (5) 1950 (5); v SA 1938 (3) 1948 (3); v NZ 1946 (1) 1950 (2)*

Wyatt, R. E. S. 40: v A 1930 (1) 1934 (4); v SA 1929 (2) 1935 (5); v WI 1933 (2); v In 1936 (1); *v A 1932 (5) 1936 (2); v SA 1927 (5) 1930 (5); v WI 1929 (2) 1934 (4); v NZ 1932 (2)*

Wynyard, E. G. 3: v A 1896 (1); *v SA 1905 (2)*

Yardley, N. W. D. 20: v A 1948 (5); v SA 1947 (5); v WI 1950 (3); *v A 1946 (5); v SA 1938 (1); v NZ 1946 (1)*

Young, H. I. 2: v A 1899 (2)

Young, J. A. 8: v A 1948 (3); v SA 1947 (1); v NZ 1949 (2); *v SA 1948 (2)*

Young, R. A. 2: *v A 1907 (2)*

AUSTRALIA

Number of Test cricketers: 380

a'Beckett, E. L. 4: v E 1928 (2); v SA 1931 (1); *v E 1930 (1)*

Alderman, T. M. 41: v E 1982 (1) 1990 (4); v WI 1981 (2) 1984 (3) 1988 (2); v NZ 1989 (1); v P 1981 (3) 1989 (2); v E 1981 (6) 1989 (6); *v WI 1983 (3) 1990 (1); v NZ 1981 (3) 1989 (1); v P 1982 (1)*

Alexander, G. 2: v E 1884 (1); *v E 1880 (1)*

Alexander, H. H. 1: v E 1932

Allan, F. E. 1: v E 1878

Allan, P. J. 1: v E 1965

Allen, R. C. 1: v E 1886

Andrews, T. J. E. 16: v E 1924 (1); *v E 1921 (5) 1926 (5); v SA 1921 (3)*

Angel, J. 4: v E 1994 (1); v WI 1992 (1); *v P 1994 (2)*

Archer, K. A. 5: v E 1950 (3); v WI 1951 (2)

Archer, R. G. 19: v E 1954 (4); v SA 1952 (1); *v E 1953 (3) 1956 (5); v WI 1954 (5); v P 1956 (1)*

Armstrong, W. W. 50: v E 1901 (4) 1903 (5) 1907 (5) 1911 (5) 1920 (5); v SA 1910 (5); *v E 1902 (5) 1905 (5) 1909 (5) 1921 (5); v SA 1902 (3)*

Badcock, C. L. 7: v E 1936 (3); *v E 1938 (4)*

Bannerman, A. C. 28: v E 1878 (1) 1881 (3) 1882 (4) 1884 (4) 1886 (1) 1887 (1) 1891 (3); *v E 1880 (1) 1882 (1) 1884 (3) 1888 (3) 1893 (3)*

Bannerman, C. 3: v E 1876 (2) 1878 (1)

Bardsley, W. .41: v E 1911 (4) 1920 (5) 1924 (3); v SA 1910 (5); *v E 1909 (5) 1912 (3) 1921 (5) 1926 (5); v SA 1912 (3) 1921 (3)*

Barnes, S. G. 13: v E 1946 (4); v In 1947 (3); *v E 1938 (1) 1948 (4); v NZ 1945 (1)*

Barnett, B. A. 4: *v E 1938 (4)*

Barrett, J. E. 2: *v E 1890 (2)*

Beard, G. R. 3: *v P 1979 (3)*

Benaud, J. 3: v P 1972 (2); *v WI 1972 (1)*

Benaud, R. 63: v E 1954 (5) 1958 (5) 1962 (5); v SA 1952 (4) 1963 (4); v WI 1951 (1) 1960 (5); *v E 1953 (3) 1956 (5) 1961 (4); v SA 1957 (5); v WI 1954 (5); v In 1956 (3) 1959 (5); v P 1956 (1) 1959 (3)*

Bennett, M. J. 3: v WI 1984 (2); *v E 1985 (1)*

Bevan, M. G. 18: v E 1994 (3); v SA 1997 (1); v WI 1996 (4); *v E 1997 (3); v SA 1996 (3); v In 1996 (1); v P 1994 (3)*

Bichel, A. J. 3: v SA 1997 (1); v WI 1996 (2)

Blackham, J. McC. 35: v E 1876 (2) 1878 (1) 1881 (4) 1882 (4) 1884 (2) 1886 (1) 1887 (1) 1891 (3) 1894 (1); *v E 1880 (1) 1882 (1) 1884 (3) 1886 (3) 1888 (3) 1890 (2) 1893 (3)*

Blackie, D. D. 3: v E 1928 (3)

Blewett, G. S. 34: v E 1994 (3); v SA 1997 (3); v WI 1996 (4); v NZ 1997 (3); v P 1995 (3); *v E 1997 (6); v SA 1996 (3); v WI 1994 (3) 1998 (3); v In 1997 (3)*

Bonnor, G. J. 17: v E 1882 (4) 1884 (3); *v E 1880 (1) 1882 (1) 1884 (3) 1886 (2) 1888 (3)*

Boon, D. C. 107: v E 1986 (4) 1987 (1) 1990 (5) 1994 (5); v SA 1993 (3); v WI 1984 (3) 1988 (5) 1992 (5); v NZ 1985 (3) 1987 (3) 1989 (1) 1993 (3); v In 1985 (3) 1991 (5); v P 1989 (2) 1995 (3); v SL 1987 (1) 1989 (2) 1995 (3); *v E 1985 (4) 1989 (6) 1993 (6); v SA 1993 (3); v WI 1990 (5) 1994 (4); v NZ 1985 (3) 1989 (1) 1992 (3); v In 1986 (3); v P 1988 (3) 1994 (3); v SL 1992 (3)*

Booth, B. C. 29: v E 1962 (5) 1965 (3); v SA 1963 (4); v P 1964 (1); *v E 1961 (2) 1964 (5); v WI 1964 (5); v In 1964 (3); v P 1964 (1)*

Border, A. R. 156: v E 1978 (3) 1979 (3) 1982 (5) 1986 (5) 1987 (1) 1990 (5); v SA 1993 (3); v WI 1979 (3) 1981 (3) 1984 (5) 1988 (5) 1992 (5); v NZ 1980 (3) 1985 (3) 1987 (3) 1989 (1) 1993 (3); v In 1980 (3) 1985 (3) 1991 (5); v P 1978 (2) 1981 (3) 1983 (5) 1989 (3); v SL 1987 (1) 1989 (2); *v E 1980 (1) 1981 (6) 1985 (6) 1989 (6) 1993 (6); v SA 1993 (3); v WI 1983 (5) 1990 (5); v NZ 1981 (3) 1985 (3) 1989 (1) 1992 (3); v In 1979 (6) 1986 (3); v P 1979 (3) 1982 (3) 1988 (3); v SL 1982 (1) 1992 (3)*

Boyle, H. F. 12: v E 1878 (1) 1881 (4) 1882 (1) 1884 (1); *v E 1880 (1) 1882 (1) 1884 (3)*

Bradman, D. G. 52: v E 1928 (4) 1932 (4) 1936 (5) 1946 (5); v SA 1931 (5); v WI 1930 (5); v In 1947 (5); *v E 1930 (5) 1934 (5) 1938 (4) 1948 (5)*

Bright, R. J. 25: v E 1979 (1); v WI 1979 (1); v NZ 1985 (1); v In 1985 (3); *v E 1977 (3) 1980 (1) 1981 (5); v NZ 1985 (2); v In 1986 (3); v P 1979 (3) 1982 (2)*

Bromley, E. H. 2: v E 1932 (1); *v E 1934 (1)*

Brown, W. A. 22: v E 1936 (2); v In 1947 (3); *v E 1934 (5) 1938 (4) 1948 (2); v SA 1935 (5); v NZ 1945 (1)*

Bruce, W. 14: v E 1884 (2) 1891 (3) 1894 (4); *v E 1886 (2) 1893 (3)*

Burge, P. J. 42: v E 1954 (1) 1958 (1) 1962 (3) 1965 (4); v SA 1963 (5); v WI 1960 (2); *v E 1956 (3) 1961 (5) 1964 (5); v SA 1957 (1); v WI 1954 (1); v In 1956 (3) 1959 (2) 1964 (3); v P 1959 (2) 1964 (1)*

Burke, J. W. 24: v E 1950 (2) 1954 (2) 1958 (5); v WI 1951 (1); *v E 1956 (5); v SA 1957 (5); v In 1956 (3); v P 1956 (1)*

Burn, K. E. 2: *v E 1890 (2)*

Burton, F. J. 2: v E 1886 (1) 1887 (1)

Callaway, S. T. 3: v E 1891 (2) 1894 (1)

Callen, I. W. 1: v In 1977

Campbell, G. D. 4: v P 1989 (1); v SL 1989 (1); *v E 1989 (1); v NZ 1989 (1)*

Carkeek, W. 6: *v E 1912 (3); v SA 1912 (3)*

Carlson, P. H. 2: v E 1978 (2)

Carter, H. 28: v E 1907 (5) 1911 (5) 1920 (2); v SA 1910 (5); *v E 1909 (5) 1921 (4); v SA 1921 (2)*

Chappell, G. S. 87: v E 1970 (5) 1974 (6) 1976 (1) 1979 (3) 1982 (5); v WI 1975 (6) 1979 (3) 1981 (3); v NZ 1973 (3) 1980 (3); v In 1980 (3); v P 1972 (3) 1976 (3) 1981 (3) 1983 (5);

v E 1972 (5) 1975 (4) 1977 (5) 1980 (1); v WI 1972 (5); v NZ 1973 (3) 1976 (2) 1981 (3); v P 1979 (3); v SL 1982 (1)

Chappell, I. M. 75: v E 1965 (2) 1970 (6) 1974 (6) 1979 (2); v WI 1968 (5) 1975 (6) 1979 (1); v NZ 1973 (3); v In 1967 (4); v P 1964 (1) 1972 (3); *v E 1968 (5) 1972 (5) 1975 (4); v SA 1966 (5) 1969 (4); v WI 1972 (5); v NZ 1973 (3); v In 1969 (5)*

Chappell, T. M. 3: *v E 1981 (3)*

Charlton, P. C. 2: *v E 1890 (2)*

Chipperfield, A. G. 14: v E 1936 (3); *v E 1934 (5) 1938 (1); v SA 1935 (5)*

Clark, W. M. 10: v In 1977 (5); v P 1978 (1); *v WI 1977 (4)*

Colley, D. J. 3: *v E 1972 (3)*

Collins, H. L. 19: v E 1920 (5) 1924 (5); *v E 1921 (3) 1926 (3); v SA 1921 (3)*

Coningham, A. 1: v E 1894

Connolly, A. N. 29: v E 1965 (1) 1970 (1); v SA 1963 (3); v WI 1968 (5); v In 1967 (3); *v E 1968 (5); v SA 1969 (4); v In 1964 (2) 1969 (5)*

Cook, S. H. 2: v NZ 1997 (2)

Cooper, B. B. 1: v E 1876

Cooper, W. H. 2: v E 1881 (1) 1884 (1)

Corling, G. E. 5: *v E 1964 (5)*

Cosier, G. J. 18: v E 1976 (1) 1978 (2); v WI 1975 (3); v In 1977 (4); v P 1976 (3); *v WI 1977 (3); v NZ 1976 (2)*

Cottam, J. T. 1: v E 1886

Cotter, A. 21: v E 1903 (2) 1907 (2) 1911 (4); v SA 1910 (5); *v E 1905 (3) 1909 (5)*

Coulthard, G. 1: v E 1881

Cowper, R. M. 27: v E 1965 (4); v In 1967 (4); v P 1964 (1); *v E 1964 (1) 1968 (4); v SA 1966 (5); v WI 1964 (5); v In 1964 (2); v P 1964 (1)*

Craig, I. D. 11: v SA 1952 (1); *v E 1956 (2); v SA 1957 (5); v In 1956 (2); v P 1956 (1)*

Crawford, P. 4: *v E 1956 (1); v In 1956 (3)*

Dale, A. C. 2: *v WI 1998 (1); v In 1997 (1)*

Darling, J. 34: v E 1894 (5) 1897 (5) 1901 (3); *v E 1896 (3) 1899 (5) 1902 (5) 1905 (5); v SA 1902 (3)*

Darling, L. S. 12: v E 1932 (2) 1936 (1); *v E 1934 (4); v SA 1935 (5)*

Darling, W. M. 14: v E 1978 (4); v In 1977 (1); v P 1978 (1); *v WI 1977 (3); v In 1979 (5)*

Davidson, A. K. 44: v E 1954 (3) 1958 (5) 1962 (5); v WI 1960 (4); *v E 1953 (5) 1956 (2) 1961 (5); v SA 1957 (5); v In 1956 (1) 1959 (5); v P 1956 (1) 1959 (3)*

Davis, I. C. 15: v E 1976 (1); v NZ 1973 (3); v P 1976 (3); *v E 1977 (3); v NZ 1973 (3) 1976 (2)*

Davis, S. P. 1: *v NZ 1985*

De Courcy, J. H. 3: *v E 1953 (3)*

Dell, A. R. 2: v E 1970 (1); v NZ 1973 (1)

Dodemaide, A. I. C. 10: v E 1987 (1); v WI 1988 (2); v NZ 1987 (1); v SL 1987 (1); *v P 1988 (3); v SL 1992 (2)*

Donnan, H. 5: v E 1891 (2); *v E 1896 (3)*

Dooland, B. 3: v E 1946 (2); v In 1947 (1)

Duff, R. A. 22: v E 1901 (4) 1903 (5); *v E 1902 (5) 1905 (5); v SA 1902 (3)*

Duncan, J. R. F. 1: v E 1970

Dyer, G. C. 6: v E 1986 (1) 1987 (1); v NZ 1987 (3); v SL 1987 (1)

Dymock, G. 21: v E 1974 (1) 1978 (3) 1979 (3); v WI 1979 (2); v NZ 1973 (1); v P 1978 (1); *v NZ 1973 (2); v In 1979 (5); v P 1979 (3)*

Dyson, J. 30: v E 1982 (5); v WI 1981 (2) 1984 (3); v NZ 1980 (3); v In 1977 (3) 1980 (3); *v E 1981 (5); v NZ 1981 (3); v P 1982 (3)*

Eady, C. J. 2: v E 1901 (1); *v E 1896 (1)*

Eastwood, K. H. 1: v E 1970

Ebeling, H. I. 1: *v E 1934*

Edwards, J. D. 3: *v E 1888 (3)*

Edwards, R. 20: v E 1974 (5); v P 1972 (2); *v E 1972 (4) 1975 (4); v WI 1972 (5)*

Edwards, W. J. 3: v E 1974 (3)

Elliott, M. T. G. 20: v SA 1997 (3); v WI 1996 (2); v NZ 1997 (3); *v E 1997 (6); v SA 1996 (3); v WI 1998 (3)*

Emery, P. A. 1: *v P 1994*

Emery, S. H. 4: *v E 1912 (2); v SA 1912 (2)*
Evans, E. 6: *v E 1881 (2) 1882 (1) 1884 (1); v E 1886 (2)*

Fairfax, A. G. 10: *v E 1928 (1); v WI 1930 (5); v E 1930 (4)*
Favell, L. E. 19: *v E 1954 (4) 1958 (2); v WI 1960 (4); v WI 1954 (2); v In 1959 (4); v P 1959 (3)*
Ferris, J. J. 8: *v E 1886 (2) 1887 (1); v E 1888 (3) 1890 (2)*
Fingleton, J. H. 18: *v E 1932 (3) 1936 (5); v SA 1931 (1); v E 1938 (4); v SA 1935 (5)*
Fleetwood-Smith, L. O'B. 10: *v E 1936 (3); v E 1938 (4); v SA 1935 (3)*
Fleming, D. W. 10: *v E 1994 (3) 1998 (4); v P 1994 (1) 1998 (2)*
Francis, B. C. 3: *v E 1972 (3)*
Freeman, E. W. 11: *v WI 1968 (4); v In 1967 (2); v E 1968 (2); v SA 1969 (2); v In 1969 (1)*
Freer, F. W. 1: *v E 1946*

Gannon, J. B. 3: *v In 1977 (3)*
Garrett, T. W. 19: *v E 1876 (2) 1878 (1) 1881 (3) 1882 (3) 1884 (3) 1886 (2) 1887 (1); v E 1882 (1) 1886 (3)*
Gaunt, R. A. 3: *v SA 1963 (1); v E 1961 (1); v SA 1957 (1)*
Gehrs, D. R. A. 6: *v E 1903 (1); v E 1903 (1) 1910 (4); v E 1905 (1)*
Giffen, G. 31: *v E 1881 (3) 1882 (4) 1884 (3) 1891 (3) 1894 (5); v E 1882 (1) 1884 (3) 1886 (3) 1893 (3) 1896 (3)*
Giffen, W. F. 3: *v E 1886 (1) 1891 (2)*
Gilbert, D. R. 9: *v NZ 1985 (3); v In 1985 (2); v E 1985 (1); v NZ 1985 (1); v In 1986 (2)*
Gillespie, J. N. 13: *v E 1998 (1); v WI 1996 (2); v E 1997 (4); v SA 1996 (3); v WI 1998 (3)*
Gilmour, G. J. 15: *v E 1976 (1); v WI 1975 (5); v NZ 1973 (2); v P 1976 (3); v E 1975 (1); v NZ 1973 (1) 1976 (2)*
Gleeson, J. W. 29: *v E 1970 (5); v WI 1968 (5); v In 1967 (4); v E 1968 (5) 1972 (3); v SA 1969 (4); v In 1969 (3)*
Graham, H. 6: *v E 1894 (2); v E 1893 (3) 1896 (1)*
Gregory, D. W. 3: *v E 1876 (2) 1878 (1)*
Gregory, E. J. 1: *v E 1876*
Gregory, J. M. 24: *v E 1920 (5) 1924 (5) 1928 (1); v E 1921 (5) 1926 (5); v SA 1921 (3)*
Gregory, R. G. 2: *v E 1936 (2)*
Gregory, S. E. 58: *v E 1891 (1) 1894 (5) 1897 (5) 1901 (5) 1903 (4) 1907 (2) 1911 (1); v E 1890 (2) 1893 (3) 1896 (3) 1899 (5) 1902 (5) 1905 (3) 1909 (5) 1912 (3); v SA 1902 (3) 1912 (3)*
Grimmett, C. V. 37: *v E 1924 (1) 1928 (5) 1932 (3); v SA 1931 (5); v WI 1930 (5); v E 1926 (3) 1930 (5) 1934 (5); v SA 1935 (5)*
Groube, T. U. 1: *v E 1880*
Grout, A. T. W. 51: *v E 1958 (5) 1962 (2) 1965 (5); v SA 1963 (5); v WI 1960 (5); v E 1961 (5) 1964 (5); v SA 1957 (5); v WI 1964 (5); v In 1959 (4) 1964 (1); v P 1959 (3) 1964 (1)*
Guest, C. E. J. 1: *v E 1962*

Hamence, R. A. 3: *v E 1946 (1); v In 1947 (2)*
Hammond, J. R. 5: *v WI 1972 (5)*
Harry, J. 1: *v E 1894*
Hartigan, R. J. 2: *v E 1907 (2)*
Hartkopf, A. E. V. 1: *v E 1924*
Harvey, M. R. 1: *v E 1946*
Harvey, R. N. 79: *v E 1950 (5) 1954 (5) 1958 (5) 1962 (5); v SA 1952 (5); v WI 1951 (5) 1960 (4); v In 1947 (2); v E 1948 (2) 1953 (5) 1956 (5) 1961 (5); v SA 1949 (5) 1957 (4); v WI 1954 (5); v In 1956 (3) 1959 (5); v P 1956 (1) 1959 (3)*
Hassett, A. L. 43: *v E 1946 (5) 1950 (5); v SA 1952 (5); v WI 1951 (4); v In 1947 (4); v E 1938 (4) 1948 (5) 1953 (5); v SA 1949 (5); v NZ 1945 (1)*
Hawke, N. J. N. 27: *v E 1962 (1) 1965 (4); v SA 1963 (4); v In 1967 (1); v P 1964 (1); v E 1964 (5) 1968 (2); v SA 1966 (2); v WI 1964 (5); v In 1964 (1); v P 1964 (1)*
Hayden, M. L. 7: *v WI 1996 (3); v SA 1993 (1) 1996 (3)*
Hazlitt, G. R. 9: *v E 1907 (2) 1911 (1); v E 1912 (3); v SA 1912 (3)*
Healy, I. A. 115: *v E 1990 (5) 1994 (5) 1998 (5); v SA 1993 (3) 1997 (3); v WI 1988 (5) 1992 (5) 1996 (5); v NZ 1989 (1) 1993 (3) 1997 (3); v In 1991 (5); v P 1989 (3) 1995 (3); v SL 1989 (2) 1995 (3); v E 1989 (6) 1993 (6) 1997 (6); v SA 1993 (3) 1996 (3); v WI 1990 (5) 1994 (4) 1998 (4); v NZ 1989 (1) 1992 (3); v In 1996 (1) 1997 (3); v P 1988 (3) 1994 (2) 1998 (3); v SL 1992 (3)*

Hendry, H. L. 11: v E 1924 (1) 1928 (4); *v E 1921 (4); v SA 1921 (2)*

Hibbert, P. A. 1: v In 1977

Higgs, J. D. 22: v E 1978 (5) 1979 (1); v WI 1979 (1); v NZ 1980 (3); v In 1980 (2); *v WI 1977 (4); v In 1979 (6)*

Hilditch, A. M. J. 18: v E 1978 (1); v WI 1984 (2); v NZ 1985 (1); v P 1978 (2); *v E 1985 (6); v In 1979 (6)*

Hill, C. 49: v E 1897 (5) 1901 (5) 1903 (5) 1907 (5) 1911 (5); v SA 1910 (5); *v E 1896 (3) 1899 (3) 1902 (5) 1905 (5); v SA 1902 (3)*

Hill, J. C. 3: *v E 1953 (2); v WI 1954 (1)*

Hoare, D. E. 1: v WI 1960

Hodges, J. 2: v E 1876 (2)

Hogan, T. G. 7: v P 1983 (1); *v WI 1983 (5); v SL 1982 (1)*

Hogg, G. B. 1: *v In 1996*

Hogg, R. M. 38: v E 1978 (6) 1982 (3); v WI 1979 (2) 1984 (4); v NZ 1980 (2); v In 1980 (2); v P 1978 (2) 1983 (4); *v E 1981 (2); v WI 1983 (4); v In 1979 (6); v SL 1982 (1)*

Hohns, T. V. 7: v WI 1988 (2); *v E 1989 (5)*

Hole, G. B. 18: v E 1950 (1) 1954 (3); v SA 1952 (4); v WI 1951 (5); *v E 1953 (5)*

Holland, R. G. 11: v WI 1984 (3); v NZ 1985 (1); v In 1985 (1); *v E 1985 (4)*

Hookes, D. W. 23: v E 1976 (1) 1982 (5); v WI 1979 (1); v NZ 1985 (2); v In 1985 (2); *v E 1977 (5); v WI 1983 (2); v P 1979 (1); v SL 1982 (1)*

Hopkins, A. J. 20: v E 1901 (2) 1903 (5); *v E 1902 (5) 1905 (3) 1909 (2); v SA 1902 (3)*

Horan, T. P. 15: v E 1876 (1) 1878 (1) 1881 (4) 1882 (4) 1884 (4); *v E 1882 (1)*

Hordern, H. V. 7: v E·1911 (5); v SA 1910 (2)

Hornibrook, P. M. 6: v E 1928 (1); *v E 1930 (5)*

Howell, W. P. 18: v E 1897 (3) 1901 (4) 1903 (3); *v E 1899 (5) 1902 (1); v SA 1902 (3)*

Hughes, K. J. 70: v E 1978 (6) 1979 (3) 1982 (5); v WI 1979 (3) 1981 (3) 1984 (4); v NZ 1980 (3); v In 1977 (2) 1980 (3); v P 1978 (2) 1981 (3) 1983 (5); *v E 1977 (1) 1980 (1) 1981 (6); v WI 1983 (5); v NZ 1981 (3); v In 1979 (6); v P 1979 (3) 1982 (3)*

Hughes, M. G. 53: v E 1986 (4) 1990 (4); v WI 1988 (4) 1992 (5); v NZ 1987 (1) 1989 (1); v In 1985 (1) 1991 (5); v P 1989 (3); v SL 1987 (1) 1989 (2); *v E 1989 (6) 1993 (6); v SA 1993 (2); v WI 1990 (5); v NZ 1992 (3)*

Hunt, W. A. 1: v SA 1931

Hurst, A. G. 12: v E 1978 (6); v NZ 1973 (1); v In 1977 (1); v P 1978 (2); *v In 1979 (2)*

Hurwood, A. 2: v WI 1930 (2)

Inverarity, R. J. 6: v WI 1968 (1); *v E 1968 (2) 1972 (3)*

Iredale, F. A. 14: v E 1894 (5) 1897 (4); *v E 1896 (2) 1899 (3)*

Ironmonger, H. 14: v E 1928 (2) 1932 (4); v SA 1931 (4); v WI 1930 (4)

Iverson, J. B. 5: v E 1950 (5)

Jackson, A. A. 8: v E 1928 (2); v WI 1930 (4); *v E 1930 (2)*

Jarman, B. N. 19: v E 1962 (3); v WI 1968 (4); v In 1967 (4); v P 1964 (1); *v E 1968 (4); v In 1959 (1) 1964 (2)*

Jarvis, A. H. 11: v E 1884 (3) 1894 (4); *v E 1886 (2) 1888 (2)*

Jenner, T. J. 9: v E 1970 (2) 1974 (2); v WI 1975 (1); *v WI 1972 (4)*

Jennings, C. B. 6: *v E 1912 (3); v SA 1912 (3)*

Johnson I. W. 45: v E 1946 (4) 1950 (5) 1954 (4); v SA 1952 (1); v WI 1951 (4); v In 1947 (4); *v E 1948 (4) 1956 (5); v SA 1949 (5); v WI 1954 (5); v NZ 1945 (1); v In 1956 (2); v P 1956 (1)*

Johnson, L. J. 1: v In 1947

Johnston W. A. 40: v E 1950 (5) 1954 (4); v SA 1952 (5); v WI 1951 (5); v In 1947 (4); *v E 1948 (5) 1953 (3); v SA 1949 (5); v WI 1954 (4)*

Jones, D. M. 52: v E 1986 (5) 1987 (1) 1990 (5); v WI 1988 (3); v NZ 1987 (3) 1989 (1); v In 1991 (5); v P 1989 (3); v SL 1987 (1) 1989 (2); *v E 1989 (6); v WI 1983 (2) 1990 (5); v NZ 1989 (1); v In 1986 (3); v P 1988 (3); v SL 1992 (3)*

Jones, E. 19: v E 1894 (1) 1897 (5) 1901 (2); *v E 1896 (3) 1899 (5) 1902 (2); v SA 1902 (1)*

Jones, S. P. 12: v E 1881 (2) 1884 (4) 1886 (1) 1887 (1); *v E 1882 (1) 1886 (3)*

Joslin, L. R. 1: v In 1967

Julian, B. P. 7: v SL 1995 (1); *v E 1993 (2); v WI 1994 (4)*

Kasprowicz, M. S. 14: v E 1998 (1); v SA 1997 (2); v WI 1996 (2); v NZ 1997 (3); *v E 1997 (3); v In 1997 (3)*

Test Cricketers – Australia

Kelleway, C. 26: v E 1911 (4) 1920 (5) 1924 (5) 1928 (1); v SA 1910 (5); *v E 1912 (3); v SA 1912 (3)*

Kelly, J. J. 36: v E 1897 (5) 1901 (5) 1903 (5); *v E 1896 (3) 1899 (5) 1902 (5) 1905 (5); v SA 1902 (3)*

Kelly, T. J. D. 2: v E 1876 (1) 1878 (1)

Kendall, T. 2: v E 1876 (2)

Kent, M. F. 3: *v E 1981 (3)*

Kerr, R. B. 2: v NZ 1985 (2)

Kippax, A. F. 22: v E 1924 (1) 1928 (5) 1932 (1); v SA 1931 (4); v WI 1930 (5); *v E 1930 (5) 1934 (1)*

Kline L. F. 13: v E 1958 (2); v WI 1960 (1); *v SA 1957 (5); v In 1959 (3); v P 1959 (1)*

Laird, B. M. 21: v E 1979 (2); v WI 1979 (3) 1981 (3); v P 1981 (3); *v E 1980 (1); v NZ 1981 (3); v P 1979 (3) 1982 (3)*

Langer, J. L. 20: v E 1998 (5); v WI 1992 (2) 1996 (2); *v WI 1998 (4); v NZ 1992 (3); v P 1994 (1) 1998 (3)*

Langley, G. R. A. 26: v E 1954 (2); v SA 1952 (5); v WI 1951 (5); *v E 1953 (4) 1956 (3); v WI 1954 (4); v In 1956 (2); v P 1956 (1)*

Laughlin, T. J. 3: v E 1978 (1); *v WI 1977 (2)*

Laver, F. 15: v E 1901 (1) 1903 (1); *v E 1899 (4) 1905 (5) 1909 (4)*

Law, S. G. 1: v SL 1995

Lawry, W. M. 67: v E 1962 (5) 1965 (5) 1970 (5); v SA 1963 (5); v WI 1968 (5); v In 1967 (4); v P 1964 (1); *v E 1961 (5) 1964 (5) 1968 (4); v SA 1966 (5) 1969 (4); v WI 1964 (5); v In 1964 (3) 1969 (5); v P 1964 (1)*

Lawson, G. F. 46: v E 1982 (5) 1986 (1); v WI 1981 (1) 1984 (5) 1988 (1); v NZ 1980 (1) 1985 (2) 1989 (1); v P 1983 (5); v SL 1989 (1); *v E 1981 (3) 1985 (6) 1989 (6); v WI 1983 (5); v P 1982 (3)*

Lee, P. K. 2: v E 1932 (1); v SA 1931 (1)

Lehmann, D. S. 5: v E 1998 (2); *v In 1997 (1); v P 1998 (2)*

Lillee, D. K. 70: v E 1970 (2) 1974 (6) 1976 (1) 1979 (3) 1982 (1); v WI 1975 (5) 1979 (3) 1981 (3); v NZ 1980 (3); v In 1980 (3); v P 1972 (3) 1976 (3) 1981 (3) 1983 (5); *v E 1972 (5) 1975 (4) 1980 (1) 1981 (6); v WI 1972 (1); v NZ 1976 (2) 1981 (3); v P 1979 (3); v SL 1982 (1)*

Lindwall, R. R. 61: v E 1946 (4) 1950 (5) 1954 (4) 1958 (2); v SA 1952 (4); v WI 1951 (5); v In 1947 (5); *v E 1948 (5) 1953 (5) 1956 (4); v SA 1949 (4); v WI 1954 (5); v NZ 1945 (1); v In 1956 (3) 1959 (2); v P 1956 (1) 1959 (2)*

Love, H. S. B. 1: v E 1932

Loxton, S. J. E. 12: v E 1950 (3); v In 1947 (1); *v E 1948 (3); v SA 1949 (5)*

Lyons, J. J. 14: v E 1886 (1) 1891 (3) 1894 (3) 1897 (1); *v E 1888 (1) 1890 (2) 1893 (3)*

McAlister, P. A. 8: v E 1903 (2) 1907 (4); *v E 1909 (2)*

Macartney, C. G. 35: v E 1907 (5) 1911 (1) 1920 (2); v SA 1910 (4); *v E 1909 (5) 1912 (3) 1921 (5) 1926 (5); v SA 1912 (3) 1921 (2)*

McCabe, S. J. 39: v E 1932 (5) 1936 (5); v SA 1931 (5); v WI 1930 (5); *v E 1930 (5) 1934 (5) 1938 (4); v SA 1935 (5)*

McCool, C. L. 14: v E 1946 (5); v In 1947 (3); *v SA 1949 (5); v NZ 1945 (1)*

McCormick, E. L. 12: v E 1936 (4); *v E 1938 (3); v SA 1935 (5)*

McCosker, R. B. 25: v E 1974 (3) 1976 (1) 1979 (2); v WI 1975 (4) 1979 (1); v P 1976 (3); *v E 1975 (4) 1977 (5); v NZ 1976 (2)*

McDermott, C. J. 71: v E 1986 (1) 1987 (1) 1990 (2) 1994 (5); v SA 1993 (3); v WI 1984 (2) 1988 (2) 1992 (5); v NZ 1985 (2) 1987 (3) 1993 (3); v In 1985 (2) 1991 (5); v P 1995 (3); v SL 1987 (1) 1995 (3); *v E 1985 (6) 1993 (2); v SA 1993 (3); v WI 1990 (5); v NZ 1985 (2) 1992 (3); v In 1986 (2); v P 1994 (2); v SL 1992 (3)*

McDonald, C. C. 47: v E 1954 (2) 1958 (5); v SA 1952 (5); v WI 1951 (1) 1960 (5); *v E 1956 (5) 1961 (3); v SA 1957 (5); v WI 1954 (5); v In 1956 (2) 1959 (5); v P 1956 (1) 1959 (3)*

McDonald, E. A. 11: v E 1920 (3); *v E 1921 (5); v SA 1921 (3)*

McDonnell, P. S. 19: v E 1881 (4) 1882 (3) 1884 (2) 1886 (2) 1887 (1); *v E 1880 (1) 1884 (3) 1888 (3)*

MacGill, S. C. G. 12: v E 1998 (4); v SA 1997 (1); *v WI 1998 (4); v P 1998 (3)*

McGrath, G. D. 49: v E 1994 (2) 1998 (5); v SA 1993 (1) 1997 (2); v WI 1996 (5); v NZ 1993 (2) 1997 (1); v P 1995 (3); v SL 1995 (3); *v E 1997 (6); v SA 1993 (2) 1996 (3); v WI 1994 (4) 1998 (4); v In 1996 (1); v P 1994 (2) 1998 (3)*

McIlwraith, J. 1: *v E 1886*

McIntyre, P. E. 2: v E 1994 (1); *v In 1996 (1)*

Mackay, K. D. 37: v E 1958 (5) 1962 (3); v WI 1960 (5); *v E 1956 (3) 1961 (5); v SA 1957 (5); v In 1956 (3) 1959 (5); v P 1959 (3)*

McKenzie, G. D. 60: v E 1962 (5) 1965 (4) 1970 (3); v SA 1963 (5); v WI 1968 (5); v In 1967 (2); v P 1964 (1); *v E 1961 (3) 1964 (5) 1968 (5); v SA 1966 (5) 1969 (3); v WI 1964 (5); v In 1964 (3) 1969 (5); v P 1964 (1)*

McKibbin, T. R. 5: v E 1894 (1) 1897 (2); *v E 1896 (2)*

McLaren, J. W. 1: v E 1911

Maclean, J. A. 4: v E 1978 (4)

McLeod, C. E. 17: v E 1894 (1) 1897 (5) 1901 (2) 1903 (3); *v E 1899 (1) 1905 (5)*

McLeod, R. W. 6: v E 1891 (3); *v E 1893 (3)*

McShane, P. G. 3: v E 1884 (1) 1886 (1) 1887 (1)

Maddocks, L. V. 7: v E 1954 (3); *v E 1956 (2); v WI 1954 (1); v In 1956 (1)*

Maguire, J. N. 3: v P 1983 (1); *v WI 1983 (2)*

Mailey, A. A. 21: v E 1920 (5) 1924 (5); *v E 1921 (3) 1926 (5); v SA 1921 (3)*

Mallett, A. A. 38: v E 1970 (2) 1974 (5) 1979 (1); v WI 1968 (1) 1975 (6) 1979 (1); v NZ 1973 (3); v P 1972 (2); *v E 1968 (1) 1972 (2) 1975 (4) 1980 (1); v SA 1969 (1); v NZ 1973 (3); v In 1969 (5)*

Malone, M. F. 1: *v E 1977*

Mann, A. L. 4: v In 1977 (4)

Marr, A. P. 1: v E 1884

Marsh, G. R. 50: v E 1986 (5) 1987 (1) 1990 (5); v WI 1988 (5); v NZ 1987 (3); v In 1985 (3) 1991 (4); v P 1989 (2); v SL 1987 (1); *v E 1989 (6); v WI 1990 (5); v NZ 1985 (3) 1989 (1); v In 1986 (3); v P 1988 (3)*

Marsh, R. W. 96: v E 1970 (6) 1974 (6) 1976 (1) 1979 (3) 1982 (5); v WI 1975 (6) 1979 (3) 1981 (3); v NZ 1973 (3) 1980 (3); v In 1980 (3); v P 1972 (3) 1976 (3) 1981 (3) 1983 (5); *v E 1972 (5) 1975 (4) 1977 (5) 1980 (1) 1981 (6); v WI 1972 (5); v NZ 1973 (3) 1976 (2) 1981 (3); v P 1979 (3) 1982 (3)*

Martin, J. W. 8: v SA 1963 (1); v WI 1960 (3); *v SA 1966 (1); v In 1964 (2); v P 1964 (1)*

Martyn, D. R. 7: v SA 1993 (2); v WI 1992 (4); *v NZ 1992 (1)*

Massie, H. H. 9: v E 1881 (4) 1882 (3) 1884 (1); *v E 1882 (1)*

Massie, R. A. L. 6: v P 1972 (2); *v E 1972 (4)*

Matthews, C. D. 3: v E 1986 (2); v WI 1988 (1)

Matthews, G. R. J. 33: v E 1986 (4) 1990 (5); v WI 1984 (1) 1992 (2); v NZ 1985 (3); v In 1985 (3); v P 1983 (2); *v E 1985 (1); v WI 1983 (1) 1990 (2); v NZ 1985 (3); v In 1986 (3); v SL 1992 (3)*

Matthews, T. J. 8: v E 1911 (2); *v E 1912 (3); v SA 1912 (3)*

May, T. B. A. 24: v E 1994 (3); v SA 1993 (3); v WI 1988 (3) 1992 (1); v NZ 1987 (1) 1993 (2); *v E 1993 (5); v SA 1993 (1); v P 1988 (3) 1994 (2)*

Mayne, E. R. 4: *v E 1912 (1); v SA 1912 (1) 1921 (2)*

Mayne, L. C. 6: v SA 1969 (2); v WI 1964 (3); v In 1969 (1)

Meckiff, I. 18: v E 1958 (4); v SA 1963 (1); v WI 1960 (2); *v SA 1957 (4); v In 1959 (5); v P 1959 (2)*

Meuleman, K. D. 1: *v NZ 1945*

Midwinter, W. E. 8: v E 1876 (2) 1882 (1) 1886 (2); *v E 1884 (3)*

Miller, C. R. 7: v E 1998 (3); *v WI 1998 (1); v P 1998 (3)*

Miller, K. R. 55: v E 1946 (5) 1950 (5) 1954 (4); v SA 1952 (4); v WI 1951 (5); v In 1947 (5); *v E 1948 (5) 1953 (5) 1956 (5); v SA 1949 (5); v WI 1954 (5); v NZ 1945 (1); v P 1956 (1)*

Minnett, R. B. 9: v E 1911 (5); *v E 1912 (1); v SA 1912 (3)*

Misson, F. M. 5: v WI 1960 (3); *v E 1961 (2)*

Moody, T. M. 8: v NZ 1989 (1); v P 1989 (1); v SL 1989 (2); *v SL 1992 (3)*

Moroney, J. 7: v E 1950 (1); v WI 1951 (1); *v SA 1949 (5)*

Morris, A. R. 46: v E 1946 (5) 1950 (5) 1954 (4); v SA 1952 (4); v WI 1951 (4); v In 1947 (5); *v E 1948 (5) 1953 (5); v SA 1949 (5); v WI 1954 (4)*

Morris, S. 1: v E 1884

Moses, H. 6: v E 1886 (2) 1887 (1) 1891 (2) 1894 (1)

Moss, J. K. 1: v P 1978

Moule, W. H. 1: *v E 1880*

Murdoch, W. L. 18: v E 1876 (1) 1878 (1) 1881 (4) 1882 (4) 1884 (1); *v E 1880 (1) 1882 (1) 1884 (3) 1890 (2)*

Musgrove, H. 1: v E 1884

Nagel, L. E. 1: v E 1932

Nash, L. J. 2: v E 1936 (1); v SA 1931 (1)
Nicholson, M. J. 1: v E 1998
Nitschke, H. C. 2: v SA 1931 (2)
Noble, M. A. 42: v E 1897 (4) 1901 (5) 1903 (5) 1907 (5); *v E 1899 (5) 1902 (5) 1905 (5) 1909 (5); v SA 1902 (3)*
Noblet, G. 3: v SA 1952 (1); v WI 1951 (1); *v SA 1949 (1)*
Nothling, O. E. 1: v E 1928

O'Brien, L. P. J. 5: v E 1932 (2) 1936 (1); *v SA 1935 (2)*
O'Connor, J. D. A. 4: v E 1907 (3); *v E 1909 (1)*
O'Donnell, S. P. 6: v NZ 1985 (1); *v E 1985 (5)*
Ogilvie, A. D. 5: v In 1977 (3); *v WI 1977 (2)*
O'Keeffe, K. J. 24: v E 1970 (2) 1976 (1); v NZ 1973 (3); v P 1972 (2) 1976 (3); *v E 1977 (3); v WI 1972 (5); v NZ 1973 (3) 1976 (2)*
Oldfield, W. A. 54: v E 1920 (3) 1924 (5) 1928 (5) 1932 (4) 1936 (5); v SA 1931 (5); v WI 1930 (5); *v E 1921 (1) 1926 (5) 1930 (5) 1934 (5); v SA 1921 (1) 1935 (5)*
O'Neill, N. C. 42: v E 1958 (5) 1962 (5); v SA 1963 (4); v WI 1960 (5); *v E 1961 (5) 1964 (4); v WI 1964 (4); v In 1959 (5) 1964 (2); v P 1959 (3)*
O'Reilly, W. J. 27: v E 1932 (5) 1936 (5); v SA 1931 (2); *v E 1934 (5) 1938 (4); v SA 1935 (5); v NZ 1945 (1)*
Oxenham, R. K. 7: v E 1928 (3); v SA 1931 (1); v WI 1930 (3)

Palmer, G. E. 17: v E 1881 (4) 1882 (4) 1884 (2); *v E 1880 (1) 1884 (3) 1886 (3)*
Park, R. L. 1: v E 1920
Pascoe, L. S. 14: v E 1979 (2); v WI 1979 (1) 1981 (1); v NZ 1980 (3); v In 1980 (3); *v E 1977 (3) 1980 (1)*
Pellew, C. E. 10: v E 1920 (4); *v E 1921 (5); v SA 1921 (1)*
Phillips, W. B. 27: v WI 1984 (2); v NZ 1985 (3); v In 1985 (3); v P 1983 (5); *v E 1985 (6); v WI 1983 (5); v NZ 1985 (3)*
Phillips, W. N. 1: v In 1991
Philpott, P. I. 8: v E 1965 (5); *v WI 1964 (5)*
Ponsford, W. H. 29: v E 1924 (5) 1928 (2) 1932 (3); v SA 1931 (3); v WI 1930 (5); *v E 1926 (2) 1930 (4) 1934 (4)*
Ponting, R. T. 24: v E 1998 (3); v SA 1997 (3); v WI 1996 (2); v NZ 1997 (3); v SL 1995 (3); *v E 1997 (3); v WI 1998 (2); v In 1996 (1) 1997 (3); v P 1998 (1)*
Pope, R. J. 1: v E 1884

Rackemann, C. G. 12: v E 1982 (1) 1990 (1); v WI 1984 (1); v NZ 1989 (1); v P 1983 (2) 1989 (3); v SL 1989 (1); *v WI 1983 (1); v NZ 1989 (1)*
Ransford, V. S. 20: v E 1907 (5) 1911 (5); v SA 1910 (5); *v E 1909 (5)*
Redpath, I. R. 66: v E 1965 (1) 1970 (6) 1974 (6); v SA 1963 (1); v WI 1968 (5) 1975 (6); v In 1967 (3); v P 1972 (3); *v E 1964 (5) 1968 (5); v SA 1966 (5) 1969 (4); v WI 1972 (5); v NZ 1973 (3); v In 1964 (2) 1969 (5); v P 1964 (1)*
Reedman, J. C. 1: v E 1894
Reid, B. A. 27: v E 1986 (5) 1990 (4); v WI 1992 (1); v NZ 1987 (3); v In 1985 (3) 1991 (2); *v WI 1990 (1); v NZ 1985 (3); v In 1986 (2); v P 1988 (3)*
Reiffel, P. R. 35: v SA 1993 (2) 1997 (2); v WI 1996 (3); v NZ 1993 (2) 1997 (3); v In 1991 (1); v P 1995 (3); v SL 1995 (2); *v E 1993 (3) 1997 (4); v SA 1993 (1); v WI 1995 (4); v NZ 1992 (3); v In 1996 (1) 1997 (1)*
Renneberg, D. A. 8: v In 1967 (3); *v SA 1966 (5)*
Richardson, A. J. 9: v E 1924 (4); *v E 1926 (5)*
Richardson, V. Y. 19: v E 1924 (3) 1928 (2) 1932 (5); *v E 1930 (4); v SA 1935 (5)*
Rigg, K. E. 8: v E 1936 (3); v SA 1931 (4); v WI 1930 (1)
Ring, D. T. 13: v SA 1952 (5); v WI 1951 (5); v In 1947 (1); *v E 1948 (1) 1953 (1)*
Ritchie, G. M. 30: v E 1986 (4); v WI 1984 (1); v NZ 1985 (3); v In 1985 (2); *v E 1985 (6); v WI 1983 (5); v NZ 1985 (3); v In 1986 (3); v P 1982 (3)*
Rixon, S. J. 13: v WI 1984 (3); v In 1977 (5); *v WI 1977 (5)*
Robertson, G. R. 4: *v In 1997 (3); v P 1998 (1)*
Robertson, W. R. 1: v E 1884
Robinson, R. D. 3: *v E 1977 (3)*

Robinson, R. H. 1: v E 1936
Rorke, G. F. 4: v E 1958 (2); *v In 1959 (2)*
Rutherford, J. W. 1: *v In 1956*
Ryder, J. 20: v E 1920 (5) 1924 (3) 1928 (5); *v E 1926 (4); v SA 1921 (3)*

Saggers, R. A. 6: *v E 1948 (1); v SA 1949 (5)*
Saunders, J. V. 14: v E 1901 (1) 1903 (2) 1907 (5); *v E 1902 (4); v SA 1902 (2)*
Scott, H. J. H. 8: v E 1884 (2); *v E 1884 (3) 1886 (3)*
Sellers, R. H. D. 1: *v In 1964*
Serjeant, C. S. 12: v In 1977 (4); *v E 1977 (3); v WI 1977 (5)*
Sheahan, A. P. 31: v E 1970 (2); v WI 1968 (5); v NZ 1973 (2); v In 1967 (4); v P 1972 (2); *v E 1968 (5) 1972 (2); v SA 1969 (4); v In 1969 (5)*
Shepherd, B. K. 9: v E 1962 (2); v SA 1963 (4); v P 1964 (1); *v WI 1964 (2)*
Sievers, M. W. 3: v E 1936 (3)
Simpson, R. B. 62: v E 1958 (1) 1962 (5) 1965 (3); v SA 1963 (5); v WI 1960 (5); v In 1967 (5) 1977 (5); v P 1964 (1); *v E 1961 (5) 1964 (5); v SA 1957 (5) 1966 (5); v WI 1964 (5) 1977 (5); v In 1964 (3); v P 1964 (1)*
Sincock, D. J. 3: v E 1965 (1); v P 1964 (1); *v WI 1964 (1)*
Slater, K. N. 1: v E 1958
Slater, M. J. 49: v E 1994 (5) 1998 (5); v SA 1993 (3); v NZ 1993 (3); v P 1995 (3); v SL 1995 (3); *v E 1993 (6); v SA 1993 (3); v WI 1994 (4) 1998 (4); v In 1996 (1) 1997 (3); v P 1994 (3) 1998 (3)*
Sleep, P. R. 14: v E 1986 (3) 1987 (1); v NZ 1987 (3); v P 1978 (1) 1989 (1); v SL 1989 (1); *v In 1979 (2); v P 1982 (1) 1988 (1)*
Slight, J. 1: *v E 1880*
Smith, D. B. M. 2: *v E 1912 (2)*
Smith, S. B. 3: *v WI 1983 (3)*
Spofforth, F. R. 18: v E 1876 (1) 1878 (1) 1881 (1) 1882 (4) 1884 (3) 1886 (1); *v E 1882 (1) 1884 (3) 1886 (3)*
Stackpole, K. R. 43: v E 1965 (2) 1970 (6); v WI 1968 (5); v NZ 1973 (3); v P 1972 (1); *v E 1972 (5); v SA 1966 (5) 1969 (4); v WI 1972 (4); v NZ 1973 (3); v In 1969 (5)*
Stevens, G. B. 4: *v In 1959 (2); v P 1959 (2)*

Taber, H. B. 16: v WI 1968 (1); *v E 1968 (1); v SA 1966 (5) 1969 (4); v In 1969 (5)*
Tallon, D. 21: v E 1946 (5) 1950 (5); v In 1947 (5); *v E 1948 (4) 1953 (1); v NZ 1945 (1)*
Taylor, J. M. 20: v E 1920 (5) 1924 (5); *v E 1921 (5) 1926 (3); v SA 1921 (2)*
Taylor, M. A. 104: v E 1990 (5) 1994 (5) 1998 (5); v SA 1993 (3) 1997 (3); v WI 1988 (2) 1992 (4) 1996 (5); v NZ 1989 (1) 1993 (3) 1997 (3); v In 1991 (5); v P 1989 (3) 1995 (3); v SL 1989 (2) 1995 (3); *v E 1989 (6) 1993 (6) 1997 (6); v SA 1993 (2) 1996 (3); v WI 1990 (5) 1994 (4); v NZ 1989 (1) 1992 (3); v In 1996 (1) 1997 (3); v P 1994 (3) 1998 (3); v SL 1992 (3)*
Taylor, P. L. 13: v E 1986 (1) 1987 (1); v WI 1988 (2); v In 1991 (2); v P 1989 (2); v SL 1987 (1); *v WI 1990 (1); v NZ 1989 (1); v P 1988 (2)*
Thomas, G. 8: v E 1965 (3); *v WI 1964 (5)*
Thoms, G. R. 1: v E 1951
Thomson, A. L. 4: v E 1970 (4)
Thomson, J. R. 51: v E 1974 (5) 1979 (1) 1982 (4); v WI 1975 (6) 1979 (1) 1981 (2); v In 1977 (5); v P 1972 (1) 1976 (1) 1981 (3); *v E 1975 (4) 1977 (5) 1985 (2); v WI 1977 (5); v NZ 1981 (3); v P 1982 (3)*
Thomson, N. F. D. 2: v E 1876 (2)
Thurlow, H. M. 1: v SA 1931
Toohey, P. M. 15: v E 1978 (5) 1979 (1); v WI 1979 (1); v In 1977 (5); *v WI 1977 (3)*
Toshack, E. R. H. 12: v E 1946 (5); v In 1947 (2); *v E 1948 (4); v NZ 1945 (1)*
Travers, J. P. F. 1: v E 1901
Tribe, G. E. 3: v E 1946 (3)
Trott, A. E. 3: v E 1894 (3)
Trott, G. H. S. 24: v E 1891 (3) 1894 (5) 1897 (5); *v E 1888 (3) 1890 (2) 1893 (3) 1896 (3)*
Trumble, H. 32: v E 1894 (1) 1897 (5) 1901 (5) 1903 (4); *v E 1890 (2) 1893 (3) 1896 (3) 1899 (5) 1902 (3); v SA 1902 (1)*
Trumble, J. W. 7: v E 1884 (4); *v E 1886 (3)*
Trumper, V. T. 48: v E 1901 (5) 1903 (5) 1907 (5) 1911 (5); v SA 1910 (5); *v E 1899 (5) 1902 (5) 1905 (5) 1909 (5); v SA 1902 (3)*

Turner, A. 14: v WI 1975 (6); v P 1976 (3); *v E 1975 (3); v NZ 1976 (2)*
Turner, C. T. B. 17: v E 1886 (2) 1887 (1) 1891 (3) 1894 (3); *v E 1888 (3) 1890 (2) 1893 (3)*

Veivers, T. R. 21: v E 1965 (4); v SA 1963 (3); v P 1964 (1); *v E 1964 (5); v SA 1966 (4); v In 1964 (3); v P 1964 (1)*
Veletta, M. R. J. 8: v E 1987 (1); v WI 1988 (2); v NZ 1987 (3); v P 1989 (1); v SL 1987 (1)

Waite, M. G. 2: *v E 1938 (2)*
Walker, M. H. N. 34: v E 1974 (6) 1976 (1); v WI 1975 (3); v NZ 1973 (1); v P 1972 (2) 1976 (2); *v E 1975 (4) 1977 (5); v WI 1972 (5); v NZ 1973 (3) 1976 (2)*
Wall, T. W. 18: v E 1928 (1) 1932 (4); v SA 1931 (3); v WI 1930 (1); *v E 1930 (5) 1934 (4)*
Walters, F. H. 1: ▼ E 1884
Walters, K. D. 74: v E 1965 (5) 1970 (6) 1974 (6) 1976 (1); v WI 1968 (4); v NZ 1973 (3) 1980 (3); v In 1967 (2) 1980 (3); v P 1972 (1) 1976 (3); *v E 1968 (5) 1972 (4) 1975 (4) 1977 (5); v SA 1969 (4); v WI 1972 (5); v NZ 1973 (3) 1976 (2); v In 1969 (5)*
Ward, F. A. 4: v E 1936 (3); *v E 1938 (1)*
Warne, S. K. 71: v E 1994 (5) 1998 (1); v SA 1993 (3) 1997 (3); v WI 1992 (4) 1996 (5); v NZ 1993 (3) 1997 (3); v In 1991 (2); v P 1995 (3); v SL 1995 (3); *v E 1993 (6) 1997 (6); v SA 1993 (3) 1996 (3); v WI 1994 (4) 1998 (3); v NZ 1992 (3); v In 1997 (3); v P 1994 (3); v SL 1992 (2)*
Watkins, J. R. 1: v P 1972
Watson, G. D. 5: *v E 1972 (2); v SA 1966 (3)*
Watson, W. J. 4: v E 1954 (1); *v WI 1954 (3)*
Waugh, M. E. 90: v E 1990 (2) 1994 (5) 1998 (5); v SA 1993 (3) 1997 (3); v WI 1992 (5) 1996 (5); v NZ 1993 (3) 1997 (3); v In 1991 (4); v P 1995 (3); v SL 1995 (3); *v E 1993 (6) 1997 (6); v SA 1993 (3) 1996 (3); v WI 1990 (5) 1994 (4) 1998 (4); v NZ 1992 (2); v In 1996 (1) 1997 (3); v P 1994 (3) 1998 (3); v SL 1992 (3)*
Waugh, S. R. 115: v E 1986 (5) 1987 (1) 1990 (3) 1994 (5) 1998 (5); v SA 1993 (1) 1997 (3); v WI 1988 (5) 1992 (5) 1996 (4); v NZ 1987 (3) 1989 (1) 1993 (3) 1997 (3); v In 1985 (2); v P 1989 (3) 1995 (3); v SL 1987 (1) 1989 (2) 1995 (2); *v E 1989 (6) 1993 (6) 1997 (6); v SA 1993 (3) 1996 (3); v WI 1990 (5) 1994 (4) 1998 (4); v NZ 1985 (3) 1989 (1) 1992 (3); v In 1986 (3) 1996 (1) 1997 (2); v P 1988 (3) 1994 (2) 1998 (3)*
Wellham, D. M. 6: v E 1986 (1); v WI 1981 (1); v P 1981 (2); *v E 1981 (1) 1985 (1)*
Wessels, K. C. 24: v E 1982 (4); v WI 1984 (5); v NZ 1985 (1); v P 1983 (5); *v E 1985 (6); v WI 1983 (2); v SL 1982 (1)*
Whatmore, D. F. 7: v P 1978 (2); *v In 1979 (5)*
Whitney, M. R. 12: v WI 1988 (1) 1992 (1); v NZ 1987 (1); v In 1991 (3); *v E 1981 (2); v WI 1990 (2); v SL 1992 (2)*
Whitty, W. J. 14: v E 1911 (2); v SA 1910 (5); *v E 1909 (1) 1912 (3); v SA 1912 (3)*
Wiener, J. M. 6: v E 1979 (2); v WI 1979 (2); *v P 1979 (2)*
Wilson, J. W. 1: *v In 1956*
Wilson, P. 1: *v In 1997*
Wood, G. M. 59: v E 1978 (6) 1982 (1); v WI 1981 (3) 1984 (5) 1988 (3); v NZ 1980 (3); v In 1977 (1) 1980 (3); v P 1978 (1) 1981 (3); *v E 1980 (1) 1981 (6) 1985 (5); v WI 1977 (5) 1983 (1); v NZ 1981 (3); v In 1979 (2); v P 1982 (3) 1988 (3); v SL 1982 (1)*
Woodcock, A. J. 1: v NZ 1973
Woodfull, W. M. 35: v E 1928 (5) 1932 (5); v SA 1931 (3); v WI 1930 (5); *v E 1926 (5) 1930 (5) 1934 (5)*
Woods, S. M. J. 3: *v E 1888 (3)*
Woolley, R. D. 2: *v WI 1983 (1); v SL 1982 (1)*
Worrall, J. 11: v E 1884 (1) 1887 (1) 1894 (1) 1897 (1); *v E 1888 (3) 1899 (4)*
Wright, K. J. 10: v E 1978 (2); v P 1978 (2); *v In 1979 (6)*

Yallop, G. N. 39: v E 1978 (6); v WI 1975 (3) 1984 (1); v In 1977 (1); v P 1978 (1) 1981 (1) 1983 (5); *v E 1980 (1) 1981 (6); v WI 1977 (4); v In 1979 (6); v P 1979 (3); v SL 1982 (1)*
Yardley, B. 33: v E 1978 (4) 1982 (5); v WI 1981 (3); v In 1977 (1) 1980 (2); v P 1978 (1) 1981 (3); *v WI 1977 (5); v NZ 1981 (3); v In 1979 (3); v P 1982 (2); v SL 1982 (1)*
Young, S. 1: *v E 1997*

Zoehrer, T. J. 10: v E 1986 (4); *v NZ 1985 (3); v In 1986 (3)*

SOUTH AFRICA

Number of Test cricketers: 272

Ackerman, H. D. 4: v P 1997 (2); v SL 1997 (2)
Adams, P. R. 24: v E 1995 (2); v A 1996 (2); v WI 1998 (2); v In 1996 (2); v P 1997 (1); v SL 1997 (2); *v E 1998 (4); v A 1997 (1); v NZ 1998 (3); v In 1996 (3); v P 1997 (2)*
Adcock, N. A. T. 26: v E 1956 (5); v A 1957 (5); v NZ 1953 (5) 1961 (2); *v E 1955 (4) 1960 (5)*
Anderson, J. H. 1: v A 1902
Ashley, W. H. 1: v E 1888

Bacher, A. 12: v A 1966 (5) 1969 (4); *v E 1965 (3)*
Bacher, A. M. 17: v A 1996 (2); v WI 1998 (1); v In 1996 (3); v P 1997 (3); v SL 1997 (3); *v E 1998 (1); v A 1997 (3); v P 1997 (3)*
Balaskas, X. C. 9: v E 1930 (2) 1938 (1); v A 1935 (3); *v E 1935 (1); v NZ 1931 (2)*
Barlow, E. J. 30: v E 1964 (5); v A 1966 (5) 1969 (4); v NZ 1961 (5); *v E 1965 (3); v A 1963 (5); v NZ 1963 (3)*
Baumgartner, H. V. 1: v E 1913
Beaumont, R. 5: v E 1913 (2); *v E 1912 (1); v A 1912 (2)*
Begbie, D. W. 5: v E 1948 (3); v A 1949 (2)
Bell, A. J. 16: v E 1930 (3); *v E 1929 (3) 1935 (3); v A 1931 (5); v NZ 1931 (2)*
Bisset, M. 3: v E 1898 (2) 1909 (1)
Bissett, G. F. 4: v E 1927 (4)
Blanckenberg, J. M. 18: v E 1913 (5) 1922 (5); v A 1921 (3); *v E 1924 (5)*
Bland, K. C. 21: v E 1964 (5); v A 1966 (1); v NZ 1961 (5); *v E 1965 (3); v A 1963 (4); v NZ 1963 (3)*
Bock, E. G. 1: v A 1935
Bond, G. E. 1: v E 1938
Bosch, T. 1: *v WI 1991*
Botten, J. T. 3: *v E 1965 (3)*
Boucher, M. V. 19: v WI 1998 (5); v P 1997 (3); v SL 1997 (2); *v E 1998 (5); v NZ 1998 (3); v P 1997 (1)*
Brann, W. H. 3: v E 1922 (3)
Briscoe, A. W. 2: v E 1938 (1); v A 1935 (1)
Bromfield, H. D. 9: v E 1964 (3); v NZ 1961 (5); *v E 1965 (1)*
Brown, L. S. 2: *v A 1931 (1); v NZ 1931 (1)*
Burger, C. G. de V. 2: v A 1957 (2)
Burke, S. F. 2: v E 1964 (1); v NZ 1961 (1)
Buys, I. D. 1: v E 1922

Cameron, H. B. 26: v E 1927 (5) 1930 (5); *v E 1929 (4) 1935 (5); v A 1931 (5); v NZ 1931 (2)*
Campbell, T. 5: v E 1909 (4); *v E 1912 (1)*
Carlstein, P. R. 8: v A 1957 (1); *v E 1960 (5); v A 1963 (2)*
Carter, C. P. 10: v E 1913 (2); v A 1921 (3); *v E 1912 (1) 1924 (3)*
Catterall, R. H. 24: v E 1922 (5) 1927 (5) 1930 (4); *v E 1924 (5) 1929 (5)*
Chapman, H. W. 2: v E 1913 (1); v A 1921 (1)
Cheetham, J. E. 24: v E 1948 (1); v A 1949 (3); v NZ 1953 (5); *v E 1951 (5) 1955 (3); v A 1952 (5); v NZ 1952 (2)*
Chevalier, G. A. 1: v A 1969
Christy, J. A. J. 10: v E 1930 (1); *v E 1929 (2); v A 1931 (5); v NZ 1931 (2)*
Chubb, G. W. A. 5: *v E 1951 (5)*
Cochran, J. A. K. 1: v E 1930
Coen, S. K. 2: v E 1927 (2)
Commaille, J. M. M. 12: v E 1909 (5) 1927 (2); *v E 1924 (5)*
Commins, J. B. 3: v NZ 1994 (2); v P 1994 (1)
Conyngham, D. P. 1: v E 1922
Cook, F. J. 1: v E 1895
Cook, S. J. 3: v In 1992 (2); *v SL 1993 (1)*
Cooper, A. H. C. 1: v E 1913

Cox, J. L. 3: v E 1913 (3)

Cripps, G. 1: v E 1891

Crisp, R. J. 9: v A 1935 (4); *v E 1935 (5)*

Cronje, W. J. 59: v E 1995 (5); v A 1993 (3) 1996 (3); v WI 1998 (5); v NZ 1994 (3); v In 1992 (3) 1996 (3); v P 1994 (1) 1997 (2); v SL 1997 (2); *v E 1994 (3) 1998 (5); v A 1993 (3) 1997 (3); v WI 1991 (1); v NZ 1994 (1) 1998 (3); v In 1996 (3); v P 1997 (3); v SL 1993 (3); v Z 1995 (1)*

Cullinan, D. J. 48: v E 1995 (5); v A 1996 (3); v WI 1998 (5); v NZ 1994 (3); v In 1992 (1) 1996 (3); v P 1994 (1) 1997 (1); v SL 1997 (2); *v E 1994 (1) 1998 (5); v A 1993 (3) 1997 (1); v NZ 1994 (1) 1998 (3); v In 1996 (3); v P 1997 (3); v SL 1993 (3); v Z 1995 (1)*

Curnow, S. H. 7: v E 1930 (3); *v A 1931 (4)*

Dalton, E. L. 15: v E 1930 (1) 1938 (4); v A 1935 (1); *v E 1929 (1) 1935 (4); v A 1931 (2); v NZ 1931 (2)*

Davies, E. Q. 5: v E 1938 (3); v A 1935 (2)

Dawson, O. C. 9: v E 1948 (4); *v E 1947 (5)*

Deane, H. G. 17: v E 1927 (5) 1930 (2); *v E 1924 (5) 1929 (5)*

de Villiers, P. S. 18: v A 1993 (3); v NZ 1994 (3); v P 1994 (1) 1997 (2); *v E 1994 (3); v A 1993 (3); v NZ 1994 (1); v In 1996 (2)*

Dixon, C. D. 1: v E 1913

Donald, A. A. 54: v E 1995 (5); v A 1993 (3) 1996 (3); v WI 1998 (5); v In 1992 (4) 1996 (3); v P 1994 (1) 1997 (3); v SL 1997 (2); *v E 1994 (3) 1998 (5); v A 1993 (3) 1997 (2); v WI 1991 (1); v NZ 1994 (1) 1998 (2); v In 1996 (2); v P 1997 (2); v SL 1993 (3); v Z 1995 (1)*

Dower, R. R. 1: v E 1898

Draper, R. G. 2: v A 1949 (2)

Duckworth, C. A. R. 2: v E 1956 (2)

Dumbrill, R. 5: v A 1966 (2); *v E 1965 (3)*

Duminy, J. P. 3: v E 1927 (2); *v E 1929 (1)*

Dunell, O. R. 2: v E 1888 (2)

Du Preez, J. H. 2: v A 1966 (2)

Du Toit, J. F. 1: v E 1891

Dyer, D. V. 3: *v E 1947 (3)*

Eksteen, C. E. 6: v E 1995 (1); v NZ 1994 (2); v P 1994 (1); *v NZ 1994 (1); v SL 1993 (1)*

Elgie, M. K. 3: v NZ 1961 (3)

Elworthy, S. 2: *v E 1998 (1); v NZ 1998 (1)*

Endean, W. R. 28: v E 1956 (5); v A 1957 (5); v NZ 1953 (5); *v E 1951 (1) 1955 (5); v A 1952 (5); v NZ 1952 (2)*

Farrer, W. S. 6: v NZ 1961 (3); *v NZ 1963 (3)*

Faulkner, G. A. 25: v E 1905 (5) 1909 (5); *v E 1907 (3) 1912 (3) 1924 (1); v A 1910 (5) 1912 (3)*

Fellows-Smith, J. P. 4: *v E 1960 (4)*

Fichardt, C. G. 2: v E 1891 (1) 1895 (1)

Finlason, C. E. 1: v E 1888

Floquet, C. E. 1: v E 1909

Francis, H. H. 2: v E 1898 (2)

Francois, C. M. 5: v E 1922 (5)

Frank, C. N. 3: v A 1921 (3)

Frank, W. H. B. 1: v E 1895

Fuller, E. R. H. 7: v A 1957 (1); *v E 1955 (2); v A 1952 (2); v NZ 1952 (2)*

Fullerton, G. M. 7: v A 1949 (2); *v E 1947 (2) 1951 (3)*

Funston, K. J. 18: v E 1956 (3); v A 1957 (5); v NZ 1953 (5); *v A 1952 (5); v NZ 1952 (2)*

Gamsy, D. 2: v A 1969 (2)

Gibbs, H. H. 14: v A 1996 (1); v WI 1998 (4); v In 1996 (1); v P 1997 (1); *v A 1997 (2); v NZ 1998 (3); v In 1996 (2)*

Gleeson, R. A. 1: v E 1895

Glover, G. K. 1: v E 1895

Goddard, T. L. 41: v E 1956 (5) 1964 (5); v A 1957 (5) 1966 (5) 1969 (3); *v E 1955 (5) 1960 (5); v A 1963 (5); v NZ 1963 (3)*

Gordon, N. 5: v E 1938 (5)

Graham, R. 2: v E 1898 (2)
Grieveson, R. E. 2: v E 1938 (2)
Griffin, G. M. 2: *v E 1960 (2)*

Hall, A. E. 7: v E 1922 (4) 1927 (2) 1930 (1)
Hall, G. G. 1: v E 1964
Halliwell, E. A. 8: v E 1891 (1) 1895 (3) 1898 (1); v A 1902 (3)
Halse, C. G. 3: *v A 1963 (3)*
Hands, P. A. M. 7: v E 1913 (5); v A 1921 (1); *v E 1924 (1)*
Hands, R. H. M. 1: v E 1913
Hanley, M. A. 1: v E 1948
Harris, T. A. 3: v E 1948 (1); *v E 1947 (2)*
Hartigan, G. P. D. 5: v E 1913 (3); *v E 1912 (1); v A 1912 (1)*
Harvey, R. L. 2: v A 1935 (2)
Hathorn, C. M. H. 12: v E 1905 (5); v A 1902 (3); *v E 1907 (3); v A 1910 (1)*
Hearne, F. 4: v E 1891 (1) 1895 (3)
Hearne, G. A. L. 3: v E 1922 (2); *v E 1924 (1)*
Heine, P. S. 14: v E 1956 (5); v A 1957 (4); v NZ 1961 (1); *v E 1955 (4)*
Henry, O. 3: v In 1992 (3)
Hime, C. F. W. 1: v E 1895
Hudson, A. C. 35: v E 1995 (5); v A 1993 (3) 1996 (1); v NZ 1994 (2); v In 1992 (4) 1996 (3); v P 1997 (3); *v E 1994 (2); v A 1993 (3); v WI 1991 (1); v NZ 1994 (1); v In 1996 (3); v SL 1993 (3); v Z 1995 (1)*
Hutchinson, P. 2: v E 1888 (2)

Ironside, D. E. J. 3: v NZ 1953 (3)
Irvine, B. L. 4: v A 1969 (4)

Jack, S. D. 2: v NZ 1994 (2)
Johnson, C. L. 1: v E 1895

Kallis, J. H. 27: v E 1995 (2); v A 1996 (3); v WI 1998 (5); v P 1997 (3); v SL 1997 (2); *v E 1998 (5); v A 1997 (3); v NZ 1998 (3); v P 1997 (1)*
Keith, H. J. 8: v E 1956 (3); *v E 1955 (4); v A 1952 (1)*
Kempis, G. A. 1: v E 1888
Kirsten, G. 53: v E 1995 (5); v A 1993 (3) 1996 (3); v WI 1998 (5); v NZ 1994 (3); v In 1996 (3); v P 1994 (1) 1997 (3); v SL 1997 (2); *v E 1994 (3) 1998 (5); v A 1993 (3) 1997 (3); v NZ 1994 (1) 1998 (3); v In 1996 (3); v P 1997 (3); v Z 1995 (1)*
Kirsten, P. N. 12: v A 1993 (3); v In 1992 (4); *v E 1994 (3); v A 1993 (1); v WI 1991 (1)*
Klusener, L. 20: v E 1996 (2); v WI 1998 (1); v In 1996 (3); v P 1997 (2); *v E 1998 (3); v A 1997 (2); v NZ 1998 (3); v In 1996 (2); v P 1997 (2)*
Kotze, J. J. 3: v A 1902 (2); *v E 1907 (1)*
Kuiper, A. P. 1: *v WI 1991*
Kuys, F. 1: v E 1898

Lance, H. R. 13: v A 1966 (5) 1969 (3); v NZ 1961 (2); *v E 1965 (3)*
Langton, A. B. C. 15: v E 1938 (5); v A 1935 (5); *v E 1935 (5)*
Lawrence, G. B. 5: v NZ 1961 (5)
le Roux, F. L. 1: v E 1913
Lewis, P. T. 1: v E 1913
Liebenberg, G. F. J. 5: v SL 1997 (1); *v E 1998 (4)*
Lindsay, D. T. 19: v E 1964 (3); v A 1966 (5) 1969 (2); *v E 1965 (3); v A 1963 (3); v NZ 1963 (3)*
Lindsay, J. D. 3: *v E 1947 (3)*
Lindsay, N. V. 1: v A 1921
Ling, W. V. S. 6: v E 1922 (3); v A 1921 (3)
Llewellyn, C. B. 15: v E 1895 (1) 1898 (1); v A 1902 (3); *v E 1912 (3); v A 1910 (5) 1912 (2)*
Lundie, E. B. 1: v E 1913

Macaulay, M. J. 1: v E 1964
McCarthy, C. N. 15: v E 1948 (5); v A 1949 (5); *v E 1951 (5)*
McGlew, D. J. 34: v E 1956 (1); v A 1957 (5); v NZ 1953 (5) 1961 (5); *v E 1951 (2) 1955 (5) 1960 (5); v A 1952 (4); v NZ 1952 (2)*

McKinnon, A. H. 8: v E 1964 (2); v A 1966 (2); v NZ 1961 (1); *v E 1960 (1) 1965 (2)*
McLean, R. A. 40: v E 1956 (5) 1964 (2); v A 1957 (4); v NZ 1953 (4) 1961 (5); *v E 1951 (3) 1955 (5) 1960 (5); v A 1952 (5); v NZ 1952 (2)*
McMillan, B. M. 38: v E 1995 (5); v A 1993 (3) 1996 (2); v NZ 1994 (3); v In 1992 (4) 1996 (3); v P 1994 (1); *v E 1994 (3) 1998 (1); v A 1993 (1) 1997 (3); v In 1996 (3); v P 1997 (3); v SL 1993 (2); v Z 1995 (1)*
McMillan, Q. 13: v E 1930 (5); *v E 1929 (2); v A 1931 (4); v NZ 1931 (2)*
Mann, N. B. F. 19: v E 1948 (5); v A 1949 (5); *v E 1947 (5) 1951 (4)*
Mansell, P. N. F. 13: *v E 1951 (2) 1955 (4); v A 1952 (5); v NZ 1952 (2)*
Markham, L. A. 1: v E 1948
Marx, W. F. E. 3: v A 1921 (3)
Matthews, C. R. 18: v E 1995 (3); v A 1993 (3); v NZ 1994 (2); v In 1992 (3); *v E 1994 (3); v A 1993 (2); v NZ 1994 (1); v Z 1995 (1)*
Meintjes, D. J. 2: v E 1922 (2)
Melle, M. G. 7: v A 1949 (2); *v E 1951 (1); v A 1952 (4)*
Melville, A. 11: v E 1938 (5) 1948 (1); *v E 1947 (5)*
Middleton, J. 6: v E 1895 (2) 1898 (2); v A 1902 (2)
Mills, C. 1: v E 1891
Milton, W. H. 3: v E 1888 (2) 1891 (1)
Mitchell, B. 42: v E 1930 (5) 1938 (5) 1948 (5); v A 1935 (5); *v E 1929 (5) 1935 (5) 1947 (5); v A 1931 (5); v NZ 1931 (2)*
Mitchell, F. 3: *v E 1912 (1); v A 1912 (2)*
Morkel, D. P. B. 16: v E 1927 (5); *v E 1929 (5); v A 1931 (5); v NZ 1931 (1)*
Murray, A. R. A. 10: v NZ 1953 (4); *v A 1952 (4); v NZ 1952 (2)*

Nel, J. D. 6: v A 1949 (5) 1957 (1)
Newberry, C. 4: v E 1913 (4)
Newson, E. S. 3: v E 1930 (1) 1938 (2)
Nicholson, F. 4: v A 1935 (4)
Nicolson, J. F. W. 3: v E 1927 (3)
Norton, N. O. 1: v E 1909
Nourse, A. D. 34: v E 1938 (5) 1948 (5); v A 1935 (5) 1949 (5); *v E 1935 (4) 1947 (5) 1951 (5)*
Nourse, A. W. 45: v E 1905 (5) 1909 (5) 1913 (5) 1922 (5); v A 1902 (3) 1921 (3); *v E 1907 (3) 1912 (3) 1924 (5); v A 1910 (5) 1912 (3)*
Ntini, M. 4: v SL 1997 (2); *v E 1998 (2)*
Nupen, E. P. 17: v E 1922 (4) 1927 (5) 1930 (3); v A 1921 (2) 1935 (1); *v E 1924 (2)*

Ochse, A. E. 2: v E 1888 (2)
Ochse, A. L. 3: v E 1927 (1); *v E 1929 (2)*
O'Linn, S. 7: v NZ 1961 (2); *v E 1960 (5)*
Owen-Smith, H. G. 5: *v E 1929 (5)*

Palm, A. W. 1: v E 1927
Parker, G. M. 2: *v E 1924 (2)*
Parkin, D. C. 1: v E 1891
Partridge, J. T. 11: v E 1964 (3); *v A 1963 (5); v NZ 1963 (3)*
Pearse, O. C. 3: *v A 1910 (3)*
Pegler, S. J. 16: v E 1909 (1); *v E 1912 (3) 1924 (5); v A 1910 (4) 1912 (3)*
Pithey, A. J. 17: v E 1956 (3) 1964 (5); *v E 1960 (2); v A 1963 (4); v NZ 1963 (3)*
Pithey, D. B. 8: v A 1966 (2); *v A 1963 (3); v NZ 1963 (3)*
Plimsoll, J. B. 1: *v E 1947*
Pollock, P. M. 28: v E 1964 (5); v A 1966 (5) 1969 (4); v NZ 1961 (3); *v E 1965 (3); v A 1963 (5); v NZ 1963 (3)*
Pollock, R. G. 23: v E 1964 (5); v A 1966 (5) 1969 (4); *v E 1965 (3); v A 1963 (5); v NZ 1963 (1)*
Pollock, S. M. 33: v E 1995 (5); v A 1996 (2); v WI 1998 (5); v In 1996 (3); v P 1997 (3); v SL 1997 (2); *v E 1998 (4); v A 1997 (3); v NZ 1998 (3); v P 1997 (3)*
Poore, R. M. 3: v E 1895 (3)
Pothecary, J. E. 3: *v E 1960 (3)*
Powell, A. W. 1: v E 1898
Prince, C. F. H. 1: v E 1898
Pringle, M. W. 4: v E 1995 (1); v In 1992 (2); *v WI 1991 (1)*
Procter, M. J. 7: v A 1966 (3) 1969 (4)

Promnitz, H. L. E. 2: v E 1927 (2)

Quinn, N. A. 12: v E 1930 (1); *v E 1929 (4); v A 1931 (5); v NZ 1931 (2)*

Reid, N. 1: v A 1921
Rhodes, J. N. 44: v E 1995 (5); v A 1993 (3) 1996 (1); v WI 1998 (5); v NZ 1994 (3); v In 1992 (4); v P 1994 (1); *v E 1994 (3) 1998 (5); v A 1993 (3) 1997 (1); v NZ 1994 (1) 1998 (3); v In 1996 (1); v P 1997 (1); v SL 1993 (3); v Z 1995 (1)*
Richards, A. R. 1: v E 1895
Richards, B. A. 4: v A 1969 (4)
Richards, W. H. 1: v E 1888
Richardson, D. J. 42: v E 1995 (5); v A 1993 (3) 1996 (3); v NZ 1994 (3); v In 1992 (4) 1996 (3); v P 1994 (1); *v E 1994 (3) 1997 (3); v WI 1991 (1); v NZ 1994 (1); v In 1996 (3); v P 1997 (2); v SL 1993 (3); v Z 1995 (1)*
Robertson, J. B. 3: v A 1935 (3)
Rose-Innes, A. 2: v E 1888 (2)
Routledge, T. W. 4: v E 1891 (1) 1895 (3)
Rowan, A. M. B. 15: v E 1948 (5); *v E 1947 (5) 1951 (5)*
Rowan, E. A. B. 26: v E 1938 (4) 1948 (4); v A 1935 (3) 1949 (5); *v E 1935 (5) 1951 (5)*
Rowe, G. A. 5: v E 1895 (2) 1898 (2); v A 1902 (1)
Rushmere, M. W. 1: *v WI 1991*

Samuelson, S. V. 1: v E 1909
Schultz, B. N. 9: v E 1995 (1); v A 1996 (1); v In 1992 (2); *v P 1997 (1); v SL 1993 (3); v Z 1995 (1)*
Schwarz, R. O. 20: v E 1905 (5) 1909 (4); *v E 1907 (3) 1912 (1); v A 1910 (5) 1912 (2)*
Seccull, A. W. 1: v E 1895
Seymour, M. A. 7: v E 1964 (2); v A 1969 (1); *v A 1963 (4)*
Shalders, W. A. 12: v E 1898 (1) 1905 (5); v A 1902 (3); *v E 1907 (3)*
Shepstone, G. H. 2: v E 1895 (1) 1898 (1)
Sherwell, P. W. 13: v E 1905 (5); *v E 1907 (3); v A 1910 (5)*
Siedle, I. J. 18: v E 1927 (1) 1930 (5); v A 1935 (5); *v E 1929 (3) 1935 (4)*
Sinclair, J. H. 25: v E 1895 (3) 1898 (2) 1905 (5) 1909 (4); v A 1902 (3); *v E 1907 (3); v A 1910 (5)*
Smith, C. J. E. 3: v A 1902 (3)
Smith, F. W. 3: v E 1888 (2) 1895 (1)
Smith, V. I. 9: v A 1949 (3) 1957 (1); *v E 1947 (4) 1955 (1)*
Snell, R. P. 5: v NZ 1994 (1); *v A 1993 (1); v WI 1991 (1); v SL 1993 (2)*
Snooke, S. D. 1: *v E 1907*
Snooke, S. J. 26: v E 1905 (5) 1909 (5) 1922 (3); *v E 1907 (3) 1912 (3); v A 1910 (5) 1912 (2)*
Solomon, W. R. 1: v E 1898
Stewart, R. B. 1: v E 1888
Steyn, P. J. R. 3: v NZ 1994 (1); v P 1994 (1); *v NZ 1994 (1)*
Stricker, L. A. 13: v E 1909 (4); *v E 1912 (2); v A 1910 (5) 1912 (2)*
Susskind, M. J. 5: *v E 1924 (5)*
Symcox, P. L. 20: v A 1996 (1); v WI 1998 (3); v P 1997 (1); *v A 1993 (2) 1997 (3); v In 1996 (3); v P 1997 (3); v SL 1993 (3); v Z 1995 (1)*

Taberer, H. M. 1: v A 1902
Tancred, A. B. 2: v E 1888 (2)
Tancred, L. J. 14: v E 1905 (5) 1913 (1); v A 1902 (3); *v E 1907 (1) 1912 (2); v A 1912 (2)*
Tancred, V. M. 1: v E 1898
Tapscott, G. L. 1: v E 1913
Tapscott, L. E. 2: v E 1922 (2)
Tayfield, H. J. 37: v E 1956 (5); v A 1949 (5) 1957 (5); v NZ 1953 (5); *v E 1955 (5) 1960 (5); v A 1952 (5); v NZ 1952 (2)*
Taylor, A. I. 1: v E 1956
Taylor, D. 2: v E 1913 (2)
Taylor, H. W. 42: v E 1913 (5) 1922 (5) 1927 (5) 1930 (4); v A 1921 (3); *v E 1912 (3) 1924 (5) 1929 (3); v A 1912 (3) 1931 (5); v NZ 1931 (1)*
Terbrugge, D. J. 4: v WI 1998 (4)
Theunissen, N. H. 1: v E 1888
Thornton, P. G. 1: v A 1902

Tomlinson, D. S. 1: *v E 1935*
Traicos, A. J. 3: v A 1969 (3)
Trimborn, P. H. J. 4: v A 1966 (3) 1969 (1)
Tuckett, L. 9: v E 1948 (4); *v E 1947 (5)*
Tuckett, L. R. 1: v E 1913
Twentyman-Jones, P. S. 1: v A 1902

van der Bijl, P. G. V. 5: v E 1938 (5)
Van der Merwe, E. A. 2: v A 1935 (1); *v E 1929 (1)*
Van der Merwe, P. L. 15: v E 1964 (2); v A 1966 (3); *v E 1965 (3); v A 1963 (3); v NZ 1963 (2)*
Van Ryneveld, C. B. 19: v E 1956 (5); v A 1957 (4); v NZ 1953 (5); *v E 1951 (5)*
Varnals, G. D. 3: v E 1964 (3)
Viljoen, K. G. 27: v E 1930 (3) 1938 (4) 1948 (2); v A 1935 (4); *v E 1935 (4) 1947 (5); v A 1931 (4); v NZ 1931 (1)*
Vincent, C. L. 25: v E 1927 (5) 1930 (5); *v E 1929 (4) 1935 (4); v A 1931 (5); v NZ 1931 (2)*
Vintcent, C. H. 3: v E 1888 (2) 1891 (1)
Vogler, A. E. E. 15: v E 1905 (5) 1909 (5); *v E 1907 (3); v A 1910 (2)*

Wade, H. F. 10: v A 1935 (5); *v E 1935 (5)*
Wade, W. W. 11: v E 1938 (3) 1948 (5); v A 1949 (3)
Waite, J. H. B. 50: v E 1956 (5) 1964 (2); v A 1957 (5); v NZ 1953 (5) 1961 (5); *v E 1951 (4) 1955 (5) 1960 (5); v A 1952 (5) 1963 (4); v NZ 1952 (2) 1963 (3)*
Walter, K. A. 2: v NZ 1961 (2)
Ward, T. A. 23: v E 1913 (5) 1922 (5); v A 1921 (3); *v E 1912 (2) 1924 (5); v A 1912 (3)*
Watkins, J. C. 15: v E 1956 (2); v A 1949 (3); v NZ 1953 (3); *v A 1952 (5); v NZ 1952 (2)*
Wesley, C. 3: *v E 1960 (3)*
Wessels, K. C. 16: v A 1993 (3); v In 1992 (4); *v E 1994 (3); v A 1993 (2); v WI 1991 (1); SL 1993 (3)*
Westcott, R. J. 5: v A 1957 (2); v NZ 1953 (3)
White, G. C. 17: v E 1905 (5) 1909 (4); *v E 1907 (3) 1912 (2); v A 1912 (3)*
Willoughby, J. T. 2: v E 1895 (2)
Wimble, C. S. 1: v E 1891
Winslow, P. L. 5: v A 1949 (2); *v E 1955 (3)*
Wynne, O. E. 6: v E 1948 (3); v A 1949 (3)

Zulch, J. W. 16: v E 1909 (5) 1913 (3); v A 1921 (3); *v A 1910 (5)*

WEST INDIES

Number of Test cricketers: 230

Achong, E. 6: v E 1929 (1) 1934 (2); *v E 1933 (3)*
Adams, J. C. 37: v E 1993 (5) 1997 (4); v A 1994 (4) 1998 (4); v SA 1991 (1); v NZ 1995 (2); *v E 1995 (4); v A 1992 (3) 1996 (5); v NZ 1994 (2); v In 1994 (3)*
Alexander, F. C. M. 25: v E 1959 (5); v P 1957 (5); *v E 1957 (2); v A 1960 (5); v In 1958 (5); v P 1958 (3)*
Ali, Imtiaz 1: v In 1975
Ali, Inshan 12: v E 1973 (2); v A 1972 (3); v In 1970 (1); v P 1976 (1); v NZ 1971 (3); *v E 1973 (1); v A 1975 (1)*
Allan, D. W. 5: v A 1964 (1); v In 1961 (2); *v E 1966 (2)*
Allen, I. B. A. 2: *v E 1991 (2)*
Ambrose, C. E. L. 88: v E 1989 (3) 1993 (5) 1997 (6); v A 1990 (5) 1994 (4) 1998 (4); v SA 1991 (1); v NZ 1995 (2); v In 1988 (4) 1996 (5); v P 1987 (3) 1992 (3); v SL 1996 (2); *v E 1988 (5) 1991 (5) 1995 (5); v A 1988 (5) 1992 (5) 1996 (4); v SA 1998 (4); v NZ 1994 (2); v P 1990 (3) 1997 (2); v SL 1993 (1)*
Arthurton, K. L. T. 33: v E 1993 (5); v A 1994 (3); v SA 1991 (1); v In 1988 (4); v P 1992 (3); *v E 1988 (1) 1995 (5); v A 1992 (5); v NZ 1994 (2); v In 1994 (3); v SL 1993 (1)*
Asgarali, N. 2: *v E 1957 (2)*

Atkinson, D. St E. 22: v E 1953 (4); v A 1954 (4); v P 1957 (1); *v E 1957 (2); v A 1951 (2); v NZ 1951 (1) 1955 (4); v In 1948 (4)*

Atkinson, E. St E. 8: v P 1957 (3); *v In 1958 (3); v P 1958 (2)*

Austin, R. A. 2: v A 1977 (2)

Bacchus, S. F. A. F. 19: v A 1977 (2); *v E 1980 (5); v A 1981 (2); v In 1978 (6); v P 1980 (4)*

Baichan, L. 3: *v A 1975 (1); v P 1974 (2)*

Baptiste, E. A. E. 10: v E 1989 (1); v A 1983 (3); *v E 1984 (5); v In 1983 (1)*

Barrett, A. G. 6: v E 1973 (2); v In 1970 (2); *v In 1974 (2)*

Barrow, I. 11: v E 1929 (1) 1934 (1); *v E 1933 (3) 1939 (1); v A 1930 (5)*

Bartlett, E. L. 5: *v E 1928 (1); v A 1930 (4)*

Benjamin, K. C. G. 26: v E 1993 (5) 1997 (2); v A 1994 (4); v SA 1991 (1); *v E 1995 (5); v A 1992 (1) 1996 (3); v NZ 1994 (2); v In 1994 (3)*

Benjamin, W. K. M. 21: v E 1993 (5); v A 1994 (4); v In 1988 (1); v P 1987 (3) 1992 (2); *v E 1988 (3); v NZ 1994 (1); v In 1987 (1); v SL 1993 (1)*

Best, C. A. 8: v E 1985 (3) 1989 (3); *v P 1990 (2)*

Betancourt, N. 1: v E 1929

Binns, A. P. 5: v A 1954 (1); v In 1952 (1); *v NZ 1955 (3)*

Birkett, L. S. 4: *v A 1930 (4)*

Bishop, I. R. 43: v E 1989 (4) 1997 (3); v NZ 1995 (2); v In 1988 (4) 1996 (4); v P 1992 (2); v SL 1996 (2); *v E 1995 (6); v A 1992 (5) 1996 (5); v P 1990 (3) 1997 (3)*

Boyce, K. D. 21: v E 1973 (4); v A 1972 (4); v In 1970 (1); *v E 1973 (3); v A 1975 (4); v In 1974 (3); v P 1974 (2)*

Browne, C. O. 13: v A 1994 (1); v NZ 1995 (2); v In 1996 (3); v SL 1996 (2); *v E 1995 (2); v A 1996 (3)*

Browne, C. R. 4: v E 1929 (2); *v E 1928 (2)*

Butcher, B. F. 44: v E 1959 (2) 1967 (5); v A 1964 (5); *v E 1963 (5) 1966 (5) 1969 (3); v A 1968 (5); v NZ 1968 (3); v In 1958 (5) 1966 (3); v P 1958 (3)*

Butler, L. 1: v A 1954

Butts, C. G. 7: v NZ 1984 (1); *v NZ 1986 (1); v In 1987 (3); v P 1986 (2)*

Bynoe, M. R. 4: *v In 1966 (3); v P 1958 (1)*

Camacho, G. S. 11: v E 1967 (5); v In 1970 (2); *v E 1969 (2); v A 1968 (2)*

Cameron, F. J. 5: *v In 1948 (5)*

Cameron, J. H. 2: *v E 1939 (2)*

Campbell, S. L. 34: v E 1997 (4); v A 1994 (1) 1998 (4); v NZ 1995 (2); v In 1996 (5); v SL 1996 (2); *v E 1995 (6); v A 1996 (5); v NZ 1994 (2); v P 1997 (3)*

Carew, G. M. 4: v E 1934 (1) 1947 (2); *v In 1948 (1)*

Carew, M. C. 19: v E 1967 (1); v NZ 1971 (3); v In 1970 (3); *v E 1963 (2) 1966 (1) 1969 (1); v A 1968 (5); v NZ 1968 (3)*

Challenor, G. 3: *v E 1928 (3)*

Chanderpaul, S. 35: v E 1993 (4) 1997 (6); v NZ 1995 (2); v In 1996 (5); *v E 1995 (2); v A 1996 (5); v SA 1998 (5); v NZ 1994 (2); v In 1994 (1); v P 1997 (3)*

Chang, H. S. 1: *v In 1978*

Christiani, C. M. 4: v E 1934 (4)

Christiani, R. J. 22: v E 1947 (4) 1953 (1); v In 1952 (1); *v E 1950 (4); v A 1951 (5); v NZ 1951 (1); v In 1948 (5)*

Clarke, C. B. 3: *v E 1939 (3)*

Clarke, S. T. 11: v A 1977 (1); *v A 1981 (1); v In 1978 (5); v P 1980 (4)*

Collins, P. T. 3: v A 1998 (3)

Collymore, C. D. 1: v A 1998

Constantine, L. N. 18: v E 1929 (3) 1934 (3); *v E 1928 (3) 1933 (1) 1939 (3); v A 1930 (5)*

Croft, C. E. H. 27: v E 1980 (4); v A 1977 (2); v P 1976 (5); *v E 1980 (3); v A 1979 (3) 1981 (3); v NZ 1979 (3); v P 1980 (4)*

Cuffy, C. E. 3: *v A 1996 (1); v In 1994 (2)*

Cummins, A. C. 5: v P 1992 (2); *v A 1992 (1); v In 1994 (2)*

Da Costa, O. C. 5: v E 1929 (1) 1934 (1); *v E 1933 (3)*

Daniel, W. W. 10: v A 1983 (2); v In 1975 (1); *v E 1976 (4); v In 1983 (3)*

Davis, B. A. 4: v A 1964 (4)

Davis, C. A. 15: v A 1972 (2); v NZ 1971 (5); v In 1970 (4); *v E 1969 (3); v A 1968 (1)*

Davis, W. W. 15: v A 1983 (1); v NZ 1984 (2); v In 1982 (1); *v E 1984 (1); v In 1983 (6) 1987 (4)*

De Caires, F. I. 3: v E 1929 (3)

Depeiza, C. C. 5: v A 1954 (3); *v NZ 1955 (2)*

Dewdney, T. 9: v A 1954 (2); v P 1957 (3); *v E 1957 (1); v NZ 1955 (3)*

Dhanraj, R. 4: v NZ 1995 (1); *v E 1995 (1); v NZ 1994 (1); v In 1994 (1)*

Dillon, M. 7: v A 1998 (1); v In 1996 (2); *v SA 1998 (3); v P 1997 (1)*

Dowe, U. G. 4: v A 1972 (1); v NZ 1971 (1); v In 1970 (2)

Dujon, P. J. L. 81: v E 1985 (4) 1989 (4); v A 1983 (5) 1990 (5); v NZ 1984 (4); v In 1982 (5) 1988 (4); v P 1987 (3); *v E 1984 (5) 1988 (5) 1991 (5); v A 1981 (3) 1984 (5) 1988 (5); v NZ 1986 (3); v In 1983 (6) 1987 (4); v P 1986 (3) 1990 (3)*

Edwards, R. M. 5: *v A 1968 (2); v NZ 1968 (3)*

Ferguson, W. 8: v E 1947 (4) 1953 (1); *v In 1948 (3)*

Fernandes, M. P. 2: v E 1929 (1); *v E 1928 (1)*

Findlay, T. M. 10: v A 1972 (1); v NZ 1971 (5); v In 1970 (2); *v E 1969 (2)*

Foster, M. L. C. 14: v E 1973 (1); v A 1972 (4) 1977 (1); v NZ 1971 (3); v In 1970 (2); v P 1976 (1); *v E 1969 (1) 1973 (1)*

Francis, G. N. 10: v E 1929 (1); *v E 1928 (3) 1933 (1); v A 1930 (5)*

Frederick, M. 1: v E 1953

Fredericks, R. C. 59: v E 1973 (5); v A 1972 (5); v NZ 1971 (5); v In 1970 (4) 1975 (4); v P 1976 (5); *v E 1969 (3) 1973 (3) 1976 (5); v A 1968 (4) 1975 (6); v NZ 1968 (3); v In 1974 (5); v P 1974 (2)*

Fuller, R. L. 1: v E 1934

Furlonge, H. A. 3: v A 1954 (1); *v NZ 1955 (2)*

Ganga, D. 3: *v SA 1998 (3)*

Ganteaume, A. G. 1: v E 1947

Garner, J. 58: v E 1980 (4) 1985 (5); v A 1977 (2) 1983 (5); v NZ 1984 (4); v In 1982 (4); v P 1976 (5); *v E 1980 (5) 1984 (5); v A 1979 (3) 1981 (3) 1984 (5); v NZ 1979 (3) 1986 (2); v P 1980 (3)*

Gaskin, B. B. M. 2: v E 1947 (2)

Gibbs, G. L. 1: v A 1954

Gibbs, L. R. 79: v E 1967 (5) 1973 (5); v A 1964 (5) 1972 (5); v NZ 1971 (2); v In 1961 (5) 1970 (5); v P 1957 (4); *v E 1963 (5) 1966 (5) 1969 (3) 1973 (3); v A 1960 (3) 1968 (5) 1975 (6); v NZ 1968 (3); v In 1958 (1) 1966 (3) 1974 (5); v P 1958 (3) 1974 (2)*

Gibson, O. D. 2: *v E 1995 (1); v SA 1998 (1)*

Gilchrist, R. 13: v P 1957 (5); *v E 1957 (4); v In 1958 (4)*

Gladstone, G. 1: v E 1929

Goddard, J. D. C. 27: v E 1947 (4); *v E 1950 (4) 1957 (5); v A 1951 (4); v NZ 1951 (2) 1955 (3); v In 1948 (5)*

Gomes, H. A. 60: v E 1980 (4) 1985 (5); v A 1977 (2) 1983 (2); v NZ 1984 (4); v In 1982 (5); *v E 1976 (2) 1984 (5); v A 1981 (3) 1984 (5); v NZ 1986 (3); v In 1978 (6) 1983 (6); v P 1980 (4) 1986 (3)*

Gomez, G. E. 29: v E 1947 (4) 1953 (4); v In 1952 (4); *v E 1939 (2) 1950 (4); v A 1951 (5); v NZ 1951 (1); v In 1948 (5)*

Grant, G. C. 12: v E 1934 (4); *v E 1933 (3); v A 1930 (5)*

Grant, R. S. 7: v E 1934 (4); *v E 1939 (3)*

Gray, A. H. 5: *v NZ 1986 (2); v P 1986 (3)*

Greenidge, A. E. 6: v A 1977 (2); *v In 1978 (4)*

Greenidge, C. G. 108: v E 1980 (4) 1985 (5) 1989 (4); v A 1977 (2) 1983 (5) 1990 (5); v NZ 1984 (4); v In 1982 (5) 1988 (4); v P 1976 (5) 1987 (3); *v E 1976 (5) 1980 (5) 1984 (5) 1988 (4); v A 1975 (2) 1979 (3) 1981 (2) 1984 (5) 1988 (5); v NZ 1979 (3) 1986 (3); v In 1974 (5) 1983 (6) 1987 (3); v P 1986 (3) 1990 (3)*

Greenidge, G. A. 5: v A 1972 (3); v NZ 1971 (2)

Grell, M. G. 1: v E 1929

Griffith, A. F. G. 3: v A 1998 (2); *v A 1996 (1)*

Griffith, C. C. 28: v E 1959 (1) 1967 (4); v A 1964 (5); *v E 1963 (5) 1966 (5); v A 1968 (3); v NZ 1968 (2); v In 1966 (3)*

Griffith, H. C. 13: v E 1929 (3); *v E 1928 (3) 1933 (2); v A 1930 (5)*

Guillen, S. C. 5: *v A 1951 (3); v NZ 1951 (2)*

Hall, W. W. 48: v E 1959 (5) 1967 (4); v A 1964 (5); v In 1961 (5); *v E 1963 (5) 1966 (5); v A 1960 (5) 1968 (2); v NZ 1968 (1); v In 1958 (5) 1966 (3); v P 1958 (3)*

Harper, R. A. 25: v E 1985 (2); v A 1983 (4); v NZ 1984 (1); *v E 1984 (5) 1988 (3); v A 1984 (2) 1988 (1); v In 1983 (2) 1987 (1); v P 1986 (3); v SL 1993 (1)*

Haynes, D. L. 116: v E 1980 (4) 1985 (5) 1989 (4) 1993 (4); v A 1977 (2) 1983 (5) 1990 (5); v SA 1991 (1); v NZ 1984 (4); v In 1982 (5) 1988 (4); v P 1987 (3) 1992 (3); *v E 1980 (5) 1984 (5) 1988 (4) 1991 (5); v A 1979 (3) 1981 (3) 1984 (5) 1988 (5) 1992 (5); v NZ 1979 (3) 1986 (3); v In 1983 (6) 1987 (4); v P 1980 (4) 1986 (3) 1990 (3); v SL 1993 (1)*

Headley, G. A. 22: v E 1929 (4) 1934 (4) 1947 (1) 1953 (1); *v E 1933 (3) 1939 (3); v A 1930 (5); v In 1948 (1)*

Headley, R. G. A. 2: *v E 1973 (2)*

Hendriks, J. L. 20: v A 1964 (4); v In 1961 (1); *v E 1966 (3) 1969 (1); v A 1968 (5); v NZ 1968 (3); v In 1966 (3)*

Hoad, E. L. G. 4: v E 1929 (1); *v E 1928 (1) 1933 (2)*

Holder, R. I. C. 11: v E 1997 (2); v A 1998 (1); v In 1996 (5); v SL 1996 (2); *v P 1997 (1)*

Holder, V. A. 40: v E 1973 (1); v A 1972 (3) 1977 (3); v NZ 1971 (4); v In 1970 (3) 1975 (1); v P 1976 (1); *v E 1969 (3) 1973 (2) 1976 (4); v A 1975 (3); v In 1974 (4) 1978 (6); v P 1974 (2)*

Holding, M. A. 60: v E 1980 (4) 1985 (4); v A 1983 (3); v NZ 1984 (3); v In 1975 (4) 1982 (5); *v E 1976 (4) 1980 (5) 1984 (4); v A 1975 (5) 1979 (3) 1981 (3) 1984 (3); v NZ 1979 (3) 1986 (1); v In 1983 (6)*

Holford, D. A. J. 24: v E 1967 (4); v NZ 1971 (5); v In 1970 (1) 1975 (2); v P 1976 (1); *v E 1966 (5); v A 1968 (2); v NZ 1968 (3); v In 1966 (1)*

Holt, J. K. 17: v E 1953 (5); v A 1954 (5); *v In 1958 (5); v P 1958 (2)*

Hooper, C. L. 80: v E 1989 (3) 1997 (6); v A 1990 (5) 1994 (4) 1998 (2); v In 1996 (5); v P 1987 (3) 1992 (3); v SL 1996 (2); *v E 1988 (5) 1991 (5) 1995 (5); v A 1988 (5) 1992 (4) 1996 (5); v SA 1998 (5); v In 1987 (3) 1994 (3); v P 1990 (3) 1997 (3); v SL 1993 (1)*

Howard, A. B. 1: v NZ 1971

Hunte, C. C. 44: v E 1959 (5); v A 1964 (5); v In 1961 (5); v P 1957 (5); *v E 1963 (5) 1966 (5); v A 1960 (5); v In 1958 (5) 1966 (3); v P 1958 (1)*

Hunte, E. A. C. 3: v E 1929 (3)

Hylton, L. G. 6: v E 1934 (4); *v E 1939 (2)*

Jacobs, R. D. 9: v A 1998 (4); *v SA 1998 (5)*

Johnson, H. H. H. 3: v E 1947 (1); *v E 1950 (2)*

Johnson, T. F. 1: *v E 1939*

Jones, C. M. 4: v E 1929 (1) 1934 (3)

Jones, P. E. 9: v E 1947 (1); *v E 1950 (2); v A 1951 (1); v In 1948 (5)*

Joseph, D. R. E. 4: v A 1998 (4)

Julien, B. D. 24: v E 1973 (5); v In 1975 (4); v P 1976 (1); *v E 1973 (3) 1976 (2); v A 1975 (3); v In 1974 (4); v P 1974 (2)*

Jumadeen, R. R. 12: v A 1972 (1) 1977 (2); v NZ 1971 (1); v In 1975 (4); v P 1976 (1); *v E 1976 (1); v In 1978 (2)*

Kallicharran, A. I. 66: v E 1973 (5); v A 1972 (5) 1977 (5); v NZ 1971 (2); v In 1975 (4); v P 1976 (5); *v E 1973 (3) 1976 (3) 1980 (5); v A 1975 (6) 1979 (3); v NZ 1979 (3); v In 1974 (5) 1978 (6); v P 1974 (2) 1980 (4)*

Kanhai, R. B. 79: v E 1959 (5) 1967 (5) 1973 (5); v A 1964 (5) 1972 (5); v In 1961 (5) 1970 (5); v P 1957 (5); *v E 1957 (5) 1963 (5) 1966 (5) 1973 (3); v A 1960 (5) 1968 (5); v In 1958 (5) 1966 (3); v P 1958 (3)*

Kentish, E. S. M. 2: v E 1947 (1) 1953 (1)

King, C. L. 9: v P 1976 (1); *v E 1976 (3) 1980 (1); v A 1979 (1); v NZ 1979 (3)*

King, F. M. 14: v E 1953 (3); v A 1954 (4); v In 1952 (5); *v NZ 1955 (2)*

King, L. A. 2: v E 1967 (1); v In 1961 (1)

King, R. D. 1: *v SA 1998*

Lambert, C. B. 5: v E 1997 (2); *v E 1991 (1); v SA 1998 (2)*

Lara, B. C. 63: v E 1993 (5) 1997 (6); v A 1994 (4) 1998 (4); v SA 1991 (1); v NZ 1995 (2); v In 1996 (5); v P 1992 (3); v SL 1996 (2); *v E 1995 (6); v A 1992 (5) 1996 (5); v SA 1998 (5); v NZ 1994 (2); v In 1994 (3); v P 1990 (1) 1997 (3); v SL 1993 (1)*

Lashley, P. D. 4: *v E 1966 (2); v A 1960 (2)*

Legall, R. 4: v In 1952 (4)

Lewis, D. M. 3: v In 1970 (3)

Lewis, R. N. 3: *v SA 1998 (2); v P 1997 (1)*

Lloyd, C. H. 110: v E 1967 (5) 1973 (5) 1980 (4); v A 1972 (3) 1977 (2) 1983 (4); v NZ 1971 (2); v In 1970 (5) 1975 (4) 1982 (5); v P 1976 (5); *v E 1969 (3) 1973 (3) 1976 (5) 1980 (4) 1984 (5); v A 1968 (4) 1975 (6) 1979 (2) 1981 (3) 1984 (5); v NZ 1968 (3) 1979 (3); v In 1966 (3) 1974 (5) 1983 (6); v P 1974 (2) 1980 (4)*

Logie, A. L. 52: v E 1989 (3); v A 1983 (1) 1990 (5); v NZ 1984 (4); v In 1982 (5) 1988 (4); v P 1987 (3); *v E 1988 (5) 1991 (4); v A 1988 (5); v NZ 1986 (3); v In 1983 (3) 1987 (4); v P 1990 (3)*

McLean, N. A. M. 8: v E 1997 (4); *v SA 1998 (4)*

McMorris, E. D. A. St J. 13: v E 1959 (4); v In 1961 (4); v P 1957 (1); *v E 1963 (2) 1966 (2)*

McWatt, C. A. 6: v E 1953 (5); v A 1954 (1)

Madray, I. S. 2: *v P 1957 (2)*

Marshall, M. D. 81: v E 1980 (1) 1985 (5) 1989 (2); v A 1983 (4) 1990 (5); v NZ 1984 (4); v In 1982 (5) 1988 (3); v P 1987 (2); *v E 1980 (4) 1984 (4) 1988 (5) 1991 (5); v A 1984 (5) 1988 (5); v NZ 1986 (3); v In 1978 (3) 1983 (6); v P 1980 (4) 1986 (3) 1990 (3)*

Marshall, N. E. 1: v A 1954

Marshall, R. E. 4: *v A 1951 (2); v NZ 1951 (2)*

Martin, F. R. 9: v E 1929 (1); *v E 1928 (3); v A 1930 (5)*

Martindale, E. A. 10: v E 1934 (4); *v E 1933 (3) 1939 (3)*

Mattis, E. H. 4: v E 1980 (4)

Mendonca, I. L. 2: v In 1961 (2)

Merry, C. A. 2: *v E 1933 (2)*

Miller, R. 1: v In 1952

Moodie, G. H. 1: v E 1934

Moseley, E. A. 2: v E 1989 (2)

Murray, D. A. 19: v E 1980 (4); v A 1977 (3); *v A 1981 (2); v In 1978 (6); v P 1980 (4)*

Murray, D. L. 62: v E 1967 (5) 1973 (5); v A 1972 (4) 1977 (2); v In 1975 (4); v P 1976 (5); *v E 1963 (5) 1973 (3) 1976 (5) 1980 (5); v A 1975 (6) 1979 (3); v NZ 1979 (3); v In 1974 (5); v P 1974 (2)*

Murray, J. R. 31: v E 1993 (5) 1997 (1); v A 1994 (3); v In 1996 (2); v P 1992 (3); *v E 1995 (4); v A 1992 (3) 1996 (2); v SA 1998 (2); v NZ 1994 (2); v In 1994 (3); v SL 1993 (1)*

Nanan, R. 1: *v P 1980*

Neblett, J. M. 1: v E 1934

Noreiga, J. M. 4: v In 1970 (4)

Nunes, R. K. 4: v E 1929 (1); *v E 1928 (3)*

Nurse, S. M. 29: v E 1959 (1) 1967 (5); v A 1964 (4); v In 1961 (1); *v E 1966 (5); v A 1960 (3) 1968 (5); v NZ 1968 (3); v In 1966 (2)*

Padmore, A. L. 2: v In 1975 (1); *v E 1976 (1)*

Pairaudeau, B. H. 13: v E 1953 (2); v In 1952 (5): *v E 1957 (2); v NZ 1955 (4)*

Parry, D. R. 12: v A 1977 (5); *v NZ 1979 (1); v In 1978 (6)*

Passailaigue, C. C. 1: v E 1929

Patterson, B. P. 28: v E 1985 (5) 1989 (1); v A 1990 (5); v SA 1991 (1); v P 1987 (1); *v E 1988 (2) 1991 (3); v A 1988 (4) 1992 (1); v In 1987 (4); v P 1986 (1)*

Payne, T. R. O. 1: v E 1985

Perry, N. O. 3: v A 1998 (3)

Phillip, N. 9: v A 1977 (3); *v In 1978 (6)*

Pierre, L. R. 1: v E 1947

Rae, A. F. 15: v In 1952 (2); *v E 1950 (4); v A 1951 (3); v NZ 1951 (1); v In 1948 (5)*

Ragoonath, S. 2: v A 1998 (2)

Ramadhin, S. 43: v E 1953 (5) 1959 (4); v A 1954 (4); v In 1952 (4); *v E 1950 (4) 1957 (5); v A 1951 (5) 1960 (2); v NZ 1951 (2) 1955 (4); v In 1958 (2); v P 1958 (2)*

Ramnarine, D. 2: v E 1997 (2)

Reifer, F. L. 4: v SL 1996 (2); *v SA 1998 (2)*

Richards, I. V. A. 121: v E 1980 (4) 1985 (5) 1989 (3); v A 1977 (2) 1983 (5) 1990 (5); v NZ 1984 (4); v In 1975 (4) 1982 (5) 1988 (4); v P 1976 (5) 1987 (2); *v E 1976 (4) 1980 (5) 1984 (5) 1988 (5) 1991 (5); v A 1975 (4) 1979 (3) 1981 (3) 1984 (5) 1988 (5); v NZ 1986 (3); v In 1974 (5) 1983 (6) 1987 (4); v P 1974 (2) 1980 (4) 1986 (3)*

Richardson, R. B. 86: v E 1985 (5) 1989 (4) 1993 (4); v A 1983 (5) 1990 (5) 1994 (4); v SA 1991 (1); v NZ 1984 (4); v In 1988 (4); v P 1987 (3) 1992 (5); *v E 1988 (3) 1991 (5) 1995 (6); v A 1984 (5) 1988 (5) 1992 (5); v NZ 1986 (3); v In 1983 (1) 1987 (4); v P 1986 (3) 1990 (3); v SL 1993 (1)*

Rickards, K. R. 2: v E 1947 (1); *v A 1951 (1)*

Roach, C. A. 16: v E 1929 (4) 1934 (1); *v E 1928 (3) 1933 (3); v A 1930 (5)*

Roberts, A. M. E. 47: v E 1973 (1) 1980 (3); v A 1977 (2); v In 1975 (2) 1982 (5); v P 1976 (5); *v E 1976 (5) 1980 (3); v A 1975 (5) 1979 (3) 1981 (3); v NZ 1979 (2); v In 1974 (5) 1983 (2); v P 1974 (2)*

Roberts, A. T. 1: *v NZ 1955*

Roberts, L. A. 1: v A 1998

Rodriguez, W. V. 5: v E 1967 (1); v A 1964 (1); v In 1961 (2); *v E 1963 (1)*

Rose, F. A. 11: v E 1997 (1); v In 1996 (5); v SL 1996 (2); *v SA 1998 (1); v P 1997 (2)*

Rowe, L. G. 30: v E 1973 (5); v A 1972 (3); v NZ 1971 (3); v In 1975 (4); *v E 1976 (2); v A 1975 (6) 1979 (3); v NZ 1979 (3)*

St Hill, E. L. 2: v E 1929 (2)

St Hill, W. H. 3: v E 1929 (1); *v E 1928 (2)*

Samuels, R. G. 6: v NZ 1995 (2); *v A 1996 (4)*

Scarlett, R. O. 3: v E 1959 (3)

Scott, A. P. H. 1: v In 1952

Scott, O. C. 8: v E 1929 (1); *v E 1928 (2); v A 1930 (5)*

Sealey, B. J. 1: *v E 1933*

Sealy, J. E. D. 11: v E 1929 (2) 1934 (4); *v E 1939 (3); v A 1930 (2)*

Shepherd, J. N. 5: v In 1970 (2); *v E 1969 (3)*

Shillingford, G. C. 7: v NZ 1971 (3); v In 1970 (3); *v E 1969 (2)*

Shillingford, I. T. 4: v A 1977 (1); v P 1976 (3)

Shivnarine, S. 8: v A 1977 (3); *v In 1978 (5)*

Simmons, P. V. 26: v E 1993 (2); v SA 1991 (1); v NZ 1995 (2); v P 1987 (1) 1992 (3); *v E 1991 (5); v A 1992 (5) 1996 (1); v In 1987 (1) 1994 (3); v P 1997 (1); v SL 1993 (1)*

Singh, C. K. 2: v E 1959 (2)

Small, J. A. 3: v E 1929 (1); *v E 1928 (2)*

Small, M. A. 2: v A 1983 (1); *v E 1984 (1)*

Smith, C. W. 5: v In 1961 (1); *v A 1960 (4)*

Smith, O. G. 26: v A 1954 (4); v P 1957 (5); *v E 1957 (5); v NZ 1955 (4); v In 1958 (5); v P 1958 (3)*

Sobers, G. S. 93: v E 1953 (1) 1959 (5) 1967 (5) 1973 (4); v A 1954 (4) 1964 (5); v NZ 1971 (5); v In 1961 (5) 1970 (5); v P 1957 (5); *v E 1957 (5) 1963 (5) 1966 (5) 1969 (3) 1973 (3); v A 1960 (5) 1968 (5); v NZ 1955 (4) 1968 (3); v In 1958 (5) 1966 (3); v P 1958 (3)*

Solomon, J. S. 27: v E 1959 (4); v A 1964 (4); v In 1961 (4); *v E 1963 (5); v A 1960 (5); v In 1958 (4); v P 1958 (3)*

Stayers, S. C. 4: v In 1961 (4)

Stollmeyer, J. B. 32: v E 1947 (2) 1953 (5); v A 1954 (2); v In 1952 (5); *v E 1939 (3) 1950 (4); v A 1951 (5); v NZ 1951 (2); v In 1948 (4)*

Stollmeyer, V. H. 1: *v E 1939*

Taylor, J. 3: v P 1957 (1); *v In 1958 (1); v P 1958 (1)*

Thompson, P. I. C. 2: v NZ 1995 (1); *v A 1996 (1)*

Trim, J. 4: v E 1947 (1); *v A 1951 (1); v In 1948 (2)*

Valentine, A. L. 36: v E 1953 (3); v A 1954 (3); v In 1952 (5) 1961 (2); v P 1957 (1); *v E 1950 (4) 1957 (2); v A 1951 (5) 1960 (2); v NZ 1951 (2) 1955 (4)*

Valentine, V. A. 2: *v E 1933 (2)*

Walcott, C. L. 44: v E 1947 (4) 1953 (5) 1959 (2); v A 1954 (5); v In 1952 (5); v P 1957 (4); *v E 1950 (4) 1957 (5); v A 1951 (3); v NZ 1951 (2); v In 1948 (5)*
Walcott, L. A. 1: v E 1929
Wallace, P. A. 7: v E 1997 (2); *v SA 1998 (4); v P 1997 (1)*
Walsh, C. A. 110: v E 1985 (1) 1989 (3) 1993 (5) 1997 (6); v A 1990 (5) 1994 (4) 1998 (4); v SA 1991 (1); v NZ 1984 (1) 1995 (2); v In 1988 (4) 1996 (4); v P 1987 (3) 1992 (3); v SL 1996 (2); *v E 1988 (5) 1991 (5) 1995 (6); v A 1988 (5) 1992 (5) 1996 (5); v SA 1998 (4); v NZ 1986 (3) 1994 (2); v In 1987 (4) 1994 (3); v P 1986 (3) 1990 (3) 1997 (3); v SL 1993 (1)*
Watson, C. 7: v E 1959 (5); v In 1961 (1); *v A 1960 (1)*
Weekes, E. D. 48: v E 1947 (4) 1953 (4); v A 1954 (5); v In 1952 (5); v P 1957 (5); *v E 1950 (4) 1957 (5); v A 1951 (5); v NZ 1951 (2) 1955 (4); v In 1948 (5)*
Weekes, K. H. 2: *v E 1939 (2)*
White, W. A. 2: v A 1964 (2)
Wight, C. V. 2: v E 1929 (1); *v E 1928 (1)*
Wight, G. L. 1: v In 1952
Wiles, C. A. 1: *v E 1933*
Willett, E. T. 5: v A 1972 (3); *v In 1974 (2)*
Williams, A. B. 7: v A 1977 (3); *v In 1978 (4)*
Williams, D. 11: v E 1997 (5); v SA 1991 (1); *v A 1992 (2); v P 1997 (3)*
Williams, E. A. V. 4: v E 1947 (3); *v E 1939 (1)*
Williams, S. C. 28: v E 1993 (1) 1997 (4); v A 1994 (4); v In 1996 (5); v SL 1996 (2); *v E 1995 (2); v SA 1998 (2); v NZ 1994 (2); v In 1994 (3); v P 1997 (3)*
Wishart, K. L. 1: v E 1934
Worrell, F. M. M. 51: v E 1947 (3) 1953 (4) 1959 (4); v A 1954 (5); v In 1952 (5) 1961 (5); *v E 1950 (4) 1957 (5) 1963 (5); v A 1951 (5) 1960 (5); v NZ 1951 (2)*

NEW ZEALAND

Number of Test cricketers: 207

Alabaster, J. C. 21: v E 1962 (2); v WI 1955 (1); v In 1967 (4); *v E 1958 (2); v SA 1961 (5); v WI 1971 (2); v In 1955 (4); v P 1955 (1)*
Allcott, C. F. W. 6: v E 1929 (2); v SA 1931 (1); *v E 1931 (3)*
Allott, G. I. 10: v E 1996 (2); v SA 1998 (2); v Z 1995 (2); *v E 1999 (2); v A 1997 (2)*
Anderson, R. W. 9: v E 1977 (3); *v E 1978 (3); v P 1976 (3)*
Anderson, W. M. 1: v A 1945
Andrews, B. 2: *v A 1973 (2)*
Astle, N. J. 29: v E 1996 (3); v SA 1998 (3); v In 1998 (1); v SL 1996 (2); v Z 1995 (2) 1997 (2); *v E 1999 (4); v A 1997 (3); v WI 1995 (2); v P 1996 (2); v SL 1997 (3); v Z 1997 (2)*

Badcock, F. T. 7: v E 1929 (3) 1932 (2); v SA 1931 (2)
Barber, R. T. 1: v WI 1955
Bartlett, G. A. 10: v E 1965 (2); v In 1967 (2); v P 1964 (1); *v SA 1961 (5)*
Barton, P. T. 7: v E 1962 (3); *v SA 1961 (4)*
Beard, D. D. 4: v WI 1951 (2) 1955 (2)
Beck, J. E. F. 8: v WI 1955 (4); *v SA 1953 (4)*
Bell, M. D. 6: v SA 1998 (1); v In 1998 (2); *v E 1999 (3)*
Bell, W. 2: *v SA 1953 (2)*
Bilby, G. P. 2: v E 1965 (2)
Blain, T. E. 11: v A 1992 (2); v P 1993 (3); *v E 1986 (1); v A 1993 (3); v In 1988 (2)*
Blair, R. W. 19: v E 1954 (1) 1958 (2) 1962 (2); v SA 1952 (2) 1963 (3); v WI 1955 (2); *v E 1958 (3); v SA 1953 (4)*
Blunt, R. C. 9: v E 1929 (4); v SA 1931 (2); *v E 1931 (3)*
Bolton, B. A. 2: v E 1958 (2)
Boock, S. L. 30: v E 1977 (3) 1983 (2) 1987 (1); v WI 1979 (3) 1986 (2); v P 1978 (3) 1984 (2) 1988 (1); *v E 1978 (3); v A 1985 (1); v WI 1984 (3); v P 1984 (3); v SL 1983 (3)*
Bracewell, B. P. 6: v P 1978 (1) 1984 (1); *v E 1978 (3); v A 1980 (1)*

Bracewell, J. G. 41: v E 1987 (3); v A 1985 (2) 1989 (1); v WI 1986 (3); v In 1980 (1) 1989 (2); v P 1988 (2); *v E 1983 (4) 1986 (3) 1990 (3); v A 1980 (3) 1985 (2) 1987 (3); v WI 1984 (1); v In 1988 (3); v P 1984 (2); v SL 1983 (2) 1986 (1)*

Bradburn, G. E. 5: v SL 1990 (1); *v P 1990 (3); v SL 1992 (1)*

Bradburn, W. P. 2: v SA 1963 (2)

Brown, V. R. 2: *v A 1985 (2)*

Burgess, M. G. 50: v E 1970 (1) 1977 (3); v A 1973 (1) 1976 (2); v WI 1968 (2); v In 1967 (4) 1975 (3); v P 1972 (3) 1978 (3); *v E 1969 (2) 1973 (3) 1978 (3); v A 1980 (3); v WI 1971 (5); v In 1969 (3) 1976 (3); v P 1969 (3) 1976 (3)*

Burke, C. 1: v A 1945

Burtt, T. B. 10: v E 1946 (1) 1950 (2); v SA 1952 (1); v WI 1951 (2); *v E 1949 (4)*

Butterfield, L. A. 1: v A 1945

Cairns, B. L. 43: v E 1974 (1) 1977 (1) 1983 (3); v A 1976 (1) 1981 (3); v WI 1979 (3); v In 1975 (1) 1980 (3); v P 1978 (3) 1984 (3); v SL 1982 (2); *v E 1978 (2) 1983 (4); v A 1973 (1) 1980 (3) 1985 (1); v WI 1984 (2); v In 1976 (2); v P 1976 (2); v SL 1983 (2)*

Cairns, C. L. 39: v E 1991 (3) 1996 (3); v A 1992 (2); v In 1998 (2); v P 1993 (1) 1995 (1); v SL 1990 (1) 1996 (2); v Z 1995 (2) 1997 (2); *v E 1999 (4); v A 1989 (1) 1993 (2) 1997 (3); v In 1995 (3); v P 1996 (2); v SL 1997 (3); v Z 1997 (2)*

Cameron, F. J. 19: v E 1962 (3); v SA 1963 (3); v P 1964 (3); *v E 1965 (2); v SA 1961 (5); v In 1964 (1); v P 1964 (2)*

Cave, H. B. 19: v E 1954 (2); v WI 1955 (3); *v E 1949 (4) 1958 (2); v In 1955 (5); v P 1955 (3)*

Chapple, M. E. 14: v E 1954 (1) 1965 (1); v SA 1952 (1) 1963 (3); v WI 1955 (1); *v SA 1953 (5) 1961 (2)*

Chatfield, E. J. 43: v E 1974 (1) 1977 (1) 1983 (3) 1987 (3); v A 1976 (2) 1981 (1) 1985 (3); v WI 1986 (3); v P 1984 (3) 1988 (2); v SL 1982 (2); *v E 1983 (3) 1986 (1); v A 1985 (2) 1987 (2); v WI 1984 (4); v In 1988 (3); v P 1984 (1); v SL 1983 (2) 1986 (1)*

Cleverley, D. C. 2: v SA 1931 (1); v A 1945 (1)

Collinge, R. O. 35: v E 1970 (2) 1974 (2) 1977 (3); v A 1973 (3) 1976 (2); v P 1964 (3) 1972 (2); *v E 1965 (3) 1969 (1) 1973 (3) 1978 (3); v In 1964 (2) 1976 (1); v P 1964 (2) 1976 (2)*

Colquhoun, I. A. 2: v E 1954 (2)

Coney, J. V. 52: v E 1983 (3); v A 1973 (2) 1981 (3) 1985 (3); v WI 1979 (3) 1986 (3); v In 1980 (3); v P 1978 (3) 1984 (3); v SL 1982 (2); *v E 1983 (4) 1986 (3); v A 1973 (2) 1980 (2) 1985 (3); v WI 1984 (4); v P 1984 (3); v SL 1983 (3)*

Congdon, B. E. 61: v E 1965 (3) 1970 (2) 1974 (2) 1977 (3); v A 1973 (3) 1976 (2); v WI 1968 (3); v In 1967 (4) 1975 (3); v P 1964 (3) 1972 (3); *v E 1965 (3) 1969 (1) 1973 (3) 1978 (3); v A 1973 (3); v WI 1971 (5); v In 1964 (3) 1969 (3); v P 1964 (1) 1969 (3)*

Cowie, J. 9: v E 1946 (1); v A 1945 (1); *v E 1937 (3) 1949 (4)*

Cresswell G. F. 3: v E 1950 (2); *v E 1949 (1)*

Cromb, I. B. 5: v SA 1931 (2); *v E 1931 (3)*

Crowe, J. J. 39: v E 1983 (3) 1987 (2); v A 1989 (1); v WI 1986 (3); v P 1984 (3) 1988 (2); v SL 1982 (2); *v E 1983 (3) 1986 (3); v A 1985 (3) 1987 (3) 1989 (1); v WI 1984 (4); v P 1984 (3); v SL 1983 (3) 1986 (1)*

Crowe, M. D. 77: v E 1983 (3) 1987 (3) 1991 (3); v A 1981 (3) 1985 (3) 1992 (3); v SA 1994 (1); v WI 1986 (3); v In 1989 (3); v P 1984 (3) 1988 (2); v SL 1990 (2); *v E 1983 (4) 1986 (3) 1990 (3) 1994 (3); v A 1985 (3) 1987 (3) 1989 (1) 1993 (1); v SA 1994 (3); v WI 1984 (4); v In 1995 (3); v P 1984 (3) 1990 (3); v SL 1983 (3) 1986 (1) 1992 (2); v Z 1992 (2)*

Cunis, R. S. 20: v E 1965 (3) 1970 (2); v SA 1963 (1); v WI 1968 (3); *v E 1969 (1); v WI 1971 (5); v In 1969 (3); v P 1969 (2)*

D'Arcy, J. W. 5: *v E 1958 (5)*

Davis, H. T. 5: v E 1996 (1); v SL 1996 (2); *v E 1994 (1); v Z 1997 (1)*

de Groen, R. P. 5: v P 1993 (2); *v A 1993 (2); v SA 1994 (1)*

Dempster, C. S. 10: v E 1929 (4) 1932 (2); v SA 1931 (2); *v E 1931 (2)*

Dempster, E. W. 5: v SA 1952 (1); *v SA 1953 (4)*

Dick, A. E. 17: v E 1962 (3); v SA 1963 (2); v P 1964 (2); *v E 1965 (2); v SA 1961 (5); v P 1964 (3)*

Dickinson, G. R. 3: v E 1929 (2); v SA 1931 (1)

Donnelly, M. P. 7: *v E 1937 (3) 1949 (4)*

Doull, S. B. 30: v E 1996 (3); v SA 1998 (3); v WI 1994 (2); v In 1998 (2); v P 1993 (3); v SL 1996 (2); v Z 1997 (2); *v E 1999 (1); v A 1993 (2) 1997 (3); v SA 1994 (3); v P 1996 (2); v SL 1997 (1); v Z 1992 (1)*

Dowling, G. T. 39: v E 1962 (3) 1970 (2); v SA 1963 (1); v WI 1968 (3); v In 1967 (4); v P 1964 (2); *v E 1965 (3) 1969 (3); v SA 1961 (4); v WI 1971 (2); v In 1964 (4) 1969 (3); v P 1964 (2) 1969 (3)*

Dunning, J. A. 4: v E 1932 (1); *v E 1937 (3)*

Edgar, B. A. 39: v E 1983 (3); v A 1981 (3) 1985 (3); v WI 1979 (3); v In 1980 (3); v P 1978 (3); v SL 1982 (2); *v E 1978 (3) 1983 (4) 1986 (3); v A 1980 (3) 1985 (3); v P 1984 (3)*

Edwards, G. N. 8: v E 1977 (1); v A 1976 (2); v In 1980 (3); *v E 1978 (2)*

Emery, R. W. G. 2: v WI 1951 (2)

Fisher, F. E. 1: v SA 1952

Fleming, S. P. 43: v E 1996 (3); v SA 1994 (1); v WI 1994 (2); v In 1993 (1) 1998 (2); v P 1995 (1); v SL 1994 (2) 1996 (2); v Z 1995 (2) 1997 (2); *v E 1994 (3) 1999 (4); v A 1997 (3); SA 1994 (3); v WI 1995 (2); v In 1995 (3); v P 1996 (2); v SL 1997 (3); v Z 1997 (2)*

Foley, H. 1: v E 1929

Franklin, T. J. 21: v E 1987 (3) 1989 (1) 1989 (1); v In 1989 (3); v SL 1990 (3); *v E 1983 (1) 1990 (3); v In 1988 (3); v P 1990 (3)*

Freeman, D. L. 2: v E 1932 (2)

Gallichan, N. 1: *v E 1937*

Gedye, S. G. 4: v SA 1963 (3); v P 1964 (1)

Germon, L. K. 12: v E 1996 (2); v P 1995 (2); v Z 1995 (2); *v WI 1995 (3); v In 1995 (3); v P 1996 (2)*

Gillespie, S. R. 1: v A 1985

Gray, E. J. 10: *v E 1983 (2) 1986 (3); v A 1987 (1); v In 1988 (1); v P 1984 (2); v SL 1986 (1)*

Greatbatch, M. J. 41: v E 1987 (2) 1991 (1); v A 1989 (1) 1992 (3); v In 1989 (3) 1993 (1); v P 1988 (1) 1992 (1) 1993 (3); v SL 1990 (2) 1994 (2); *v E 1990 (3) 1994 (1); v A 1989 (1) 1993 (3); v In 1988 (3) 1995 (3); v P 1990 (3) 1996 (2); v Z 1992 (2)*

Guillen, S. C. 3: v WI 1955 (3)

Guy, J. W. 12: v E 1958 (2); v WI 1955 (2); *v SA 1961 (2); v In 1955 (5); v P 1955 (1)*

Hadlee, D. R. 26: v E 1974 (2) 1977 (1); v A 1973 (3) 1976 (1); v In 1975 (3); v P 1972 (2); *v E 1969 (2) 1973 (3); v A 1973 (3); v In 1969 (3); v P 1969 (3)*

Hadlee, R. J. 86: v E 1977 (3) 1983 (3) 1987 (1); v A 1973 (3) 1976 (2) 1981 (3) 1985 (3) 1989 (1); v WI 1979 (3) 1986 (3); v In 1975 (2) 1980 (3) 1989 (3); v P 1972 (1) 1978 (3) 1984 (3) 1988 (2); v SL 1982 (2); *v E 1973 (1) 1978 (3) 1983 (4) 1986 (3) 1990 (3); v A 1973 (3) 1980 (3) 1985 (3) 1987 (3); v WI 1984 (4); v In 1976 (3) 1988 (3); v P 1976 (3); v SL 1983 (3) 1986 (1)*

Hadlee, W. A. 11: v E 1946 (1) 1950 (2); v A 1945 (1); *v E 1937 (3) 1949 (4)*

Harford, N. S. 8: *v E 1958 (4); v In 1955 (2); v P 1955 (2)*

Harford, R. I. 3: v In 1967 (3)

Harris, C. Z. 18: v A 1992 (1); v SA 1998 (3); v P 1992 (1); *v E 1999 (1); v A 1993 (1) 1997 (1); v WI 1995 (2); v P 1996 (2); v SL 1992 (2) 1997 (2); v Z 1997 (2)*

Harris, P. G. Z. 9: v P 1964 (1); *v SA 1961 (5); v In 1955 (1); v P 1955 (2)*

Harris, R. M. 2: v E 1958 (2)

Hart, M. N. 14: v SA 1994 (1); v WI 1994 (2); v In 1993 (1); v P 1993 (2); *v E 1994 (3); v SA 1994 (3); v In 1995 (2)*

Hartland, B. R. 9: v E 1991 (3); v In 1993 (1); v P 1992 (1) 1993 (1); *v E 1994 (1); v SL 1992 (2)*

Haslam, M. J. 4: *v In 1995 (2); v Z 1992 (2)*

Hastings, B. F. 31: v E 1974 (2); v A 1973 (3); v WI 1968 (3); v In 1975 (1); v P 1972 (3); *v E 1969 (3) 1973 (3); v A 1973 (3); v WI 1971 (5); v In 1969 (2); v P 1969 (3)*

Hayes, J. A. 15: v E 1950 (2) 1954 (1); v WI 1951 (2); *v E 1958 (4); v In 1955 (5); v P 1955 (1)*

Henderson, M. 1: v E 1929

Horne, M. J. 20: v E 1996 (1); v SA 1998 (3); v In 1998 (2); v SL 1996 (2); v Z 1997 (2); *v E 1999 (4); v A 1997 (1); v SL 1997 (3); v Z 1997 (2)*

Horne, P. A. 4: v WI 1986 (1); *v A 1987 (1); v P 1990 (1); v SL 1986 (1)*

Hough, K. W. 2: v E 1958 (2)

Howarth, G. P. 47: v E 1974 (2) 1977 (3) 1983 (3); v A 1976 (2) 1981 (3); v WI 1979 (3); v In 1980 (3); v P 1978 (3) 1984 (3); v SL 1982 (2); *v E 1978 (3) 1983 (4); v A 1980 (2); v WI 1984 (4); v In 1976 (2); v P 1976 (2); v SL 1983 (3)*

Howarth, H. J. 30: v E 1970 (2) 1974 (2); v A 1973 (3) 1976 (2); v In 1975 (2); v P 1972 (3); *v E 1969 (3) 1973 (2); v WI 1971 (5); v In 1969 (3); v P 1969 (3)*

James, K. C. 11: v E 1929 (4) 1932 (2); v SA 1931 (2); *v E 1931 (3)*

Jarvis, T. W. 13: v E 1965 (1); v P 1972 (3); *v WI 1971 (4); v In 1964 (2); v P 1964 (3)*

Jones, A. H. 39: v E 1987 (1) 1991 (3); v A 1989 (1) 1992 (3); v WI 1994 (2); v In 1989 (3); v P 1988 (2) 1992 (1) 1993 (3); v SL 1990 (3); *v E 1990 (3); v A 1987 (3) 1993 (3); v In 1988 (3); v SL 1986 (1) 1992 (2); v Z 1992 (2)*

Kennedy, R. J. 4: v Z 1995 (2); *v WI 1995 (2)*

Kerr, J. L. 7: v E 1932 (2); v SA 1931 (1); *v E 1931 (2) 1937 (2)*

Kuggeleijn, C. M. 2: *v In 1988 (2)*

Larsen, G. R. 8: v SA 1994 (1); v P 1995 (1); v SL 1994 (2); v Z 1995 (1); *v E 1994 (1); v WI 1995 (2)*

Latham, R. T. 4: v E 1991 (1); v P 1992 (1); *v Z 1992 (2)*

Lees, W. K. 21: v E 1977 (2); v A 1976 (1); v WI 1979 (3); v P 1978 (3); v SL 1982 (2); *v E 1983 (2); v A 1980 (2); v In 1976 (3); v P 1976 (3)*

Leggat, I. B. 1: *v SA 1953*

Leggat, J. G. 9: v E 1954 (1); v SA 1952 (1); v WI 1951 (1) 1955 (1); *v In 1955 (3); v P 1955 (2)*

Lissette, A. F. 2: v WI 1955 (2)

Loveridge, G. R. 1: v Z 1995

Lowry, T. C. 7: v E 1929 (4); *v E 1931 (3)*

McEwan, P. E. 4: v WI 1979 (1); *v A 1980 (2); v P 1984 (1)*

MacGibbon, A. R. 26: v E 1950 (2) 1954 (2); v SA 1952 (1); v WI 1955 (3); *v E 1958 (5); v SA 1953 (5); v In 1955 (5); v P 1955 (3)*

McGirr, H. M. 2: v E 1929 (2)

McGregor, S. N. 25: v E 1954 (2) 1958 (2); v SA 1963 (3); v WI 1955 (4); v P 1964 (2); *v SA 1961 (3); v In 1955 (4); v P 1955 (3)*

McLeod E. G. 1: v E 1929

McMahon T. G. 5: v WI 1955 (1); *v In 1955 (3); v P 1955 (1)*

McMillan, C. D. 15: v SA 1998 (1); v In 1998 (2); v Z 1997 (2); *v E 1999 (4); v A 1997 (3); v SL 1997 (3)*

McRae, D. A. N. 1: v A 1945

Matheson, A. M. 2: v E 1929 (1); *v E 1931 (1)*

Meale, T. 2: *v E 1958 (2)*

Merritt, W. E. 6: v E 1929 (4); *v E 1931 (2)*

Meuli, E. M. 1: v SA 1952

Milburn, B. D. 3: v WI 1968 (3)

Miller, L. S. M. 13: v SA 1952 (2); v WI 1955 (3); *v E 1958 (4); v SA 1953 (4)*

Mills, J. E. 7: v E 1929 (3) 1932 (1); *v E 1931 (3)*

Moir, A. M. 17: v E 1950 (2) 1954 (2) 1958 (2); v SA 1952 (1); v WI 1951 (1) 1955 (1); *v E 1958 (2); v In 1955 (2); v P 1955 (3)*

Moloney D. A. R. 3: *v E 1937 (3)*

Mooney, F. L. H. 14: v E 1950 (2); v SA 1952 (2); v WI 1951 (2); *v E 1949 (3); v SA 1953 (5)*

Morgan, R. W. 20: v E 1965 (2) 1970 (2); v WI 1968 (1); v P 1964 (2); *v E 1965 (3); v WI 1971 (3); v In 1964 (4); v P 1964 (3)*

Morrison, B. D. 1: v E 1962

Morrison, D. K. 48: v E 1987 (3) 1991 (3) 1996 (1); v A 1989 (1) 1992 (3); v SA 1994 (1); v WI 1994 (2); v In 1989 (3) 1993 (1); v P 1988 (1) 1992 (1) 1993 (2) 1995 (1); v SL 1990 (3) 1994 (1); *v E 1990 (3); v A 1987 (3) 1989 (1) 1993 (3); v SA 1994 (2); v WI 1995 (2); v In 1988 (1) 1995 (3); v P 1990 (3)*

Morrison, J. F. M. 17: v E 1974 (2); v A 1973 (3) 1981 (3); v In 1975 (3); *v A 1973 (3); v In 1976 (1); v P 1976 (2)*

Motz, R. C. 32: v E 1962 (2) 1965 (3); v SA 1963 (2); v WI 1968 (3); v In 1967 (4); v P 1964 (3); *v E 1965 (3) 1969 (3); v SA 1961 (5); v In 1964 (3); v P 1964 (1)*

Murray, B. A. G. 13: v E 1970 (1); v In 1967 (4); *v E 1969 (2); v In 1969 (3); v P 1969 (3)*
Murray, D. J. 8: v SA 1994 (1); v WI 1994 (2); v SL 1994 (2); *v SA 1994 (3)*

Nash, D. J. 25: v SA 1994 (1) 1998 (3); v WI 1994 (1); v In 1993 (1) 1998 (2); v P 1995 (1); v SL 1994 (1); v Z 1997 (2); *v E 1994 (3) 1999 (4); v SA 1994 (1); v In 1995 (3); v SL 1992 (1); v Z 1992 (1)*
Newman J. 3: v E 1932 (2); v SA 1931 (1)

O'Connor, S. B. 8: v SA 1998 (1); v Z 1997 (1); *v E 1999 (1); v A 1997 (2); v SL 1997 (1); v Z 1997 (2)*
O'Sullivan, D. R. 11: v In 1975 (1); v P 1972 (1); *v A 1973 (3); v In 1976 (3); v P 1976 (3)*
Overton, G. W. F. 3: *v SA 1953 (3)*
Owens, M. B. 8: v A 1992 (2); v P 1992 (1) 1993 (1); *v E 1994 (2); v SL 1992 (2)*

Page, M. L. 14: v E 1929 (4) 1932 (2); v SA 1931 (2); *v E 1931 (3) 1937 (3)*
Parker, J. M. 36: v E 1974 (2) 1977 (3); v A 1973 (3) 1976 (2); v WI 1979 (3); v In 1975 (3); v P 1972 (1) 1978 (2); *v E 1973 (3) 1978 (2); v A 1973 (3) 1980 (3); v In 1976 (3); v P 1976 (3)*
Parker, N. M. 3: *v In 1976 (2); v P 1976 (1)*
Parore, A. C. 53: v E 1991 (1) 1996 (3); v A 1992 (1); v SA 1994 (1) 1998 (3); v WI 1994 (2); v In 1993 (1) 1998 (2); v P 1992 (1) 1995 (1); v SL 1994 (2) 1996 (2); v Z 1995 (2) 1997 (2); *v E 1990 (1) 1994 (3) 1999 (4); v A 1997 (3); v SA 1994 (3); v WI 1995 (1); v In 1995 (3); v P 1996 (2); v SL 1992 (2) 1997 (3); v Z 1992 (2) 1997 (2)*
Patel, D. N. 37: v E 1991 (3) 1996 (2); v A 1992 (3); v SA 1994 (1); v WI 1986 (3); v P 1988 (1) 1992 (1) 1995 (1); v SL 1990 (2) 1994 (1) 1996 (2); v Z 1995 (2); *v A 1987 (3) 1989 (1) 1993 (3); v WI 1995 (1); v P 1990 (3) 1996 (2); v Z 1992 (2)*
Petherick, P. J. 6: v A 1976 (1); *v In 1976 (3); v P 1976 (2)*
Petrie, E. C. 14: v E 1958 (2) 1965 (3); *v E 1958 (5); v In 1955 (2); v P 1955 (2)*
Playle, W. R. 8: v E 1962 (3); *v E 1958 (5)*
Pocock, B. A. 15: v E 1996 (3); v P 1993 (3); v SL 1996 (2); *v E 1994 (1); v A 1993 (3) 1997 (2); v Z 1997 (2)*
Pollard, V. 32: v E 1965 (3) 1970 (1); v WI 1968 (3); v In 1967 (4); v P 1972 (1); *v E 1965 (3) 1969 (3) 1973 (3); v In 1964 (4) 1969 (1); v P 1964 (3) 1969 (3)*
Poore, M. B. 14: v E 1954 (1); v SA 1952 (1); *v SA 1953 (5); v In 1955 (4); v P 1955 (2)*
Priest, M. W. 3: v Z 1997 (1); *v E 1990 (1); v SL 1997 (1)*
Pringle, C. 14: v E 1991 (1); v In 1993 (1); v P 1993 (1); v SL 1990 (2) 1994 (1); *v E 1994 (2); v SA 1994 (2); v P 1990 (3); v SL 1992 (1)*
Puna, N. 3: v E 1965 (3)

Rabone, G. O. 12: v E 1954 (2); v SA 1952 (1); v WI 1951 (2); *v E 1949 (4); v SA 1953 (3)*
Redmond, R. E. 1: v P 1972
Reid, J. F. 19: v A 1985 (3); v In 1980 (3); v P 1978 (1) 1984 (3); *v A 1985 (3); v P 1984 (3); v SL 1983 (3)*
Reid, J. R. 58: v E 1950 (2) 1954 (2) 1958 (2) 1962 (3); v SA 1952 (2) 1963 (3); v WI 1951 (2) 1955 (4); v P 1964 (3); *v E 1949 (2) 1958 (5) 1965 (3); v SA 1953 (5) 1961 (5); v In 1955 (5) 1964 (4); v P 1955 (3) 1964 (3)*
Roberts, A. D. G. 7: v In 1975 (2); *v In 1976 (3); v P 1976 (2)*
Roberts, A. W. 5: v E 1929 (1); v SA 1931 (2); *v E 1937 (3)*
Robertson, G. K. 1: v A 1985
Rowe, C. G. 1: v A 1945
Rutherford, K. R. 56: v E 1987 (2) 1991 (2); v A 1985 (3) 1989 (1) 1992 (3); v SA 1994 (1); v WI 1986 (2) 1994 (2); v In 1989 (3) 1993 (1); v P 1992 (1) 1993 (3); v SL 1990 (3) 1994 (2); *v E 1986 (1) 1990 (2) 1994 (3); v A 1987 (1) 1993 (3); v SA 1994 (3); v WI 1984 (4); v In 1988 (2); v P 1990 (3); v SL 1986 (1) 1994 (3); v Z 1992 (2)*

Scott, R. H. 1: v E 1946
Scott, V. J. 10: v E 1946 (1) 1950 (2); v A 1945 (3); v WI 1951 (2); *v E 1949 (4)*
Sewell, D. G. 1: *v Z 1997*
Shrimpton, M. J. F. 10: v E 1962 (2) 1965 (3) 1970 (2); v SA 1963 (1); *v A 1973 (2)*
Sinclair, B. W. 21: v E 1962 (3) 1965 (3); v SA 1963 (3); v In 1967 (2); v P 1964 (2); *v E 1965 (3); v In 1964 (2); v P 1964 (3)*
Sinclair, I. M. 2: v WI 1955 (2)

Smith, F. B. 4: v E 1946 (1); v WI 1951 (1); *v E 1949 (2)*

Smith, H. D. 1: v E 1932

Smith, I. D. S. 63: v E 1983 (3) 1987 (3) 1991 (2); v A 1981 (3) 1985 (3) 1989 (1); v WI 1986 (3); v In 1980 (3) 1989 (3); v P 1984 (3) 1988 (2); v SL 1990 (3); *v E 1983 (2) 1986 (2) 1990 (2); v A 1980 (1) 1985 (3) 1987 (3) 1989 (1); v WI 1984 (4); v In 1988 (3); v P 1984 (3) 1990 (3); v SL 1983 (3) 1986 (1)*

Snedden, C. A. 1: v E 1946

Snedden, M. C. 25: v E 1983 (1) 1987 (2); v A 1981 (3) 1989 (1); v WI 1986 (1); v In 1980 (3) 1989 (3); v SL 1982 (2); *v E 1983 (1) 1990 (3); v A 1985 (1) 1987 (1) 1989 (1); v In 1988 (1); v SL 1986 (1)*

Sparling, J. T. 11: v E 1958 (2) 1962 (1); v SA 1963 (2); *v E 1958 (3); v SA 1961 (3)*

Spearman, C. M. 8: v P 1995 (1); v Z 1995 (2); *v WI 1995 (2); v SL 1997 (1); v Z 1997 (2)*

Stead, G. R. 2: v SA 1998 (2)

Stirling, D. A. 6: *v E 1986 (2); v WI 1984 (1); v P 1984 (3)*

Su'a, M. L. 13: v E 1991 (2); v A 1992 (2); v WI 1994 (1); v P 1992 (1); v SL 1994 (1); *v A 1993 (2); v SL 1992 (2); v Z 1992 (2)*

Sutcliffe, B. 42: v E 1946 (1) 1950 (2) 1954 (2) 1958 (2); v SA 1952 (2); v WI 1951 (2) 1955 (2); *v E 1949 (4) 1958 (4) 1965 (1); v SA 1953 (5); v In 1955 (5) 1964 (4); v P 1955 (3) 1964 (3)*

Taylor, B. R. 30: v E 1965 (1); v WI 1968 (3); v In 1967 (3); v P 1972 (3); *v E 1965 (2) 1969 (2) 1973 (3); v WI 1971 (4); v In 1964 (3) 1969 (2); v P 1964 (3) 1969 (1)*

Taylor, D. D. 3: v E 1946 (1); v WI 1955 (2)

Thomson, K. 2: v In 1967 (2)

Thomson, S. A. 19: v E 1991 (1); v WI 1994 (2); v In 1989 (1) 1993 (1); v P 1993 (3); v SL 1990 (2) 1994 (1); *v E 1994 (3); v SA 1994 (3); v In 1995 (2)*

Tindill, E. W. T. 5: v E 1946 (1); v A 1945 (1); *v E 1937 (3)*

Troup, G. B. 15: v A 1981 (2) 1985 (2); v WI 1979 (3); v In 1980 (3); v P 1978 (2); *v A 1980 (2); v WI 1984 (1); v In 1976 (1)*

Truscott, P. B. 1: v P 1964

Turner, G. M. 41: v E 1970 (2) 1974 (2); v A 1973 (3) 1976 (2); v WI 1968 (3); v In 1975 (3); v P 1972 (3); v SL 1982 (2); *v E 1969 (2) 1973 (3); v A 1973 (2); v WI 1971 (5); v In 1969 (3) 1976 (3); v P 1969 (1) 1976 (2)*

Twose, R. G. 16: v SA 1998 (3); v In 1998 (1); v P 1995 (1); v Z 1995 (2); *v E 1999 (4); v A 1997 (1); v WI 1995 (2); v In 1995 (2)*

Vance, R. H. 4: v E 1987 (1); v P 1988 (2); *v A 1989 (1)*

Vaughan, J. T. C. 6: v E 1996 (1); *v WI 1995 (2); v P 1996 (2); v SL 1992 (1)*

Vettori, D. L. 23: v E 1996 (2); v SA 1998 (3); v In 1998 (2); v SL 1996 (2); v Z 1997 (2); *v E 1999 (4); v A 1997 (3); v SL 1997 (3); v Z 1997 (2)*

Vivian, G. E. 5: *v WI 1971 (4); v In 1964 (1)*

Vivian, H. G. 7: v E 1932 (1); v SA 1931 (1); *v E 1931 (2) 1937 (3)*

Wadsworth, K. J. 33: v E 1970 (2) 1974 (2); v A 1973 (3); v In 1975 (3); v P 1972 (3); *v E 1969 (3) 1973 (3); v A 1973 (3); v WI 1971 (5); v In 1969 (3); v P 1969 (3)*

Wallace, W. M. 13: v E 1946 (1) 1950 (2); v A 1945 (1); v SA 1952 (2); *v E 1937 (3) 1949 (4)*

Walmsley, K. P. 2: v SL 1994 (2)

Ward, J. T. 8: v SA 1963 (1); v In 1967 (1); v P 1964 (1); *v E 1965 (1); v In 1964 (4)*

Watson, W. 15: v E 1991 (1); v A 1992 (2); v SL 1990 (3); *v E 1986 (2); v A 1989 (1) 1993 (1); v P 1990 (3); v Z 1992 (2)*

Watt, L. 1: v E 1954

Webb, M. G. 3: v E 1970 (1); v A 1973 (1); *v WI 1971 (1)*

Webb, P. N. 2: v WI 1979 (2)

Weir, G. L. 11: v E 1929 (3) 1932 (2); v SA 1931 (2); *v E 1931 (3) 1937 (1)*

White, D. J. 2: *v P 1990 (2)*

Whitelaw, P. E. 2: v E 1932 (2)

Wiseman, P. J. 5: v In 1998 (2); *v SL 1997 (3)*

Wright, J. G. 82: v E 1977 (3) 1983 (3) 1987 (3) 1991 (3); v A 1981 (3) 1985 (2) 1989 (1) 1992 (3); v WI 1979 (3) 1986 (3); v In 1980 (3) 1989 (3); v P 1978 (3) 1984 (3)1988 (2); v SL 1982 (2) 1990 (3); *v E 1978 (2) 1983 (3) 1986 (3) 1990 (3); v A 1980 (3) 1985 (3) 1987 (3) 1989 (1); v WI 1984 (4); v In 1988 (3); v P 1984 (3); v SL 1983 (3) 1992 (2)*

Young, B. A. 35: v E 1996 (3); v SA 1994 (1) 1998 (2); v WI 1994 (2); v In 1993 (1); v P 1993 (3)
    1995 (1); v SL 1994 (2) 1996 (2); v Z 1997 (2); *v E 1994 (3); v A 1993 (1) 1997 (3); v SA*
    1994 (3); v In 1995 (1); v P 1996 (2); v SL 1997 (3)
Yuile, B. W. 17: v E 1962 (2); v WI 1968 (3); v In 1967 (1); v P 1964 (3); *v E 1965 (1);*
    v In 1964 (3) 1969 (1); v P 1964 (1) 1969 (2)

INDIA

Number of Test cricketers: 220

Abid Ali, S. 29: v E 1972 (4); v A 1969 (1); v WI 1974 (2); v NZ 1969 (3); *v E 1971 (3) 1974 (3);*
    v A 1967 (4); v WI 1970 (5); v NZ 1967 (4)
Adhikari, H. R. 21: v E 1951 (3); v A 1956 (2); v WI 1948 (5) 1958 (1); v P 1952 (2); *v E 1952 (3);*
    v A 1947 (5)
Agarkar, A. B. 1: *v Z 1998*
Amarnath, L. 24: v E 1933 (3) 1951 (3); v WI 1948 (5); v P 1952 (5); *v E 1946 (3); v A 1947 (5)*
Amarnath, M. 69: v E 1976 (2) 1984 (5); v A 1969 (1) 1979 (1) 1986 (3); v WI 1978 (2) 1983 (3)
    1987 (3); v NZ 1976 (3); v P 1983 (2) 1986 (5); v SL 1986 (2); *v E 1979 (2) 1986 (2); v A*
    1977 (5) 1985 (3); v WI 1975 (4) 1982 (5); v NZ 1975 (3); v P 1978 (3) 1982 (6) 1984 (2); v SL
    1985 (2)
Amarnath, S. 10: v E 1976 (2); *v WI 1975 (2); v NZ 1975 (3); v P 1978 (3)*
Amar Singh 7: v E 1933 (3); *v E 1932 (1) 1936 (3)*
Amir Elahi 1: *v A 1947*
Amre, P. K. 11: v E 1992 (3); v Z 1992 (1); *v SA 1992 (4); v SL 1993 (3)*
Ankola, S. A. 1: *v P 1989*
Apte, A. L. 1: *v E 1959*
Apte, M. L. 7: v P 1952 (2); *v WI 1952 (5)*
Arshad Ayub 13: v WI 1987 (4); v NZ 1988 (3); *v WI 1988 (4); v P 1989 (2)*
Arun, B. 2: v SL 1986 (2)
Arun Lal 16: v WI 1987 (4); v NZ 1988 (3); v P 1986 (1); v SL 1982 (1); *v WI 1988 (4); v P*
    1982 (3)
Azad, K. 7: v E 1981 (3); v WI 1983 (2); v P 1983 (1); *v NZ 1980 (1)*
Azharuddin, M. 98: v E 1984 (3) 1992 (3); v A 1986 (3) 1996 (1) 1997 (3); v SA 1996 (3); v WI
    1987 (3) 1994 (3); v NZ 1988 (3) 1995 (3); v P 1986 (5) 1998 (3); v SL 1986 (1) 1990 (1)
    1993 (3) 1997 (3); v Z 1992 (1); *v E 1986 (3) 1990 (3) 1996 (3); v A 1985 (3) 1991 (5); v SA*
    1992 (4) 1996 (3); v WI 1988 (3) 1996 (5); v NZ 1989 (3) 1993 (1) 1998 (2); v P 1989 (4); v SL
    1985 (3) 1993 (3) 1997 (2) 1998 (1); v Z 1992 (1) 1998 (1)

Baig, A. A. 10: v A 1959 (3); v WI 1966 (2); v P 1960 (3); *v E 1959 (2)*
Banerjee, S. A. 1: v WI 1948
Banerjee, S. N. 1: v WI 1948
Banerjee, S. T. 1: *v A 1991*
Baqa Jilani, M. 1: *v E 1936*
Bedi, B. S. 67: v E 1972 (5) 1976 (5); v A 1969 (5); v WI 1966 (2) 1974 (4) 1978 (3); v NZ
    1969 (3) 1976 (3); *v E 1967 (3) 1971 (3) 1974 (3) 1979 (3); v A 1967 (2) 1977 (5); v WI 1970 (5)*
    1975 (4); v NZ 1967 (4) 1975 (2); v P 1978 (3)
Bhandari, P. 3: v A 1956 (1); v NZ 1955 (1); *v P 1954 (1)*
Bhat, A. R. 2: v WI 1983 (1); v P 1983 (1)
Binny, R. M. H. 27: v E 1979 (1); v WI 1983 (6); v P 1979 (6) 1983 (2) 1986 (3); *v E 1986 (3); v A*
    1980 (1) 1985 (2); v NZ 1980 (1); v P 1984 (1); v SL 1985 (1)
Borde, C. G. 55: v E 1961 (5) 1963 (5); v A 1959 (5) 1964 (3) 1969 (1); v WI 1958 (4) 1966 (3);
    v NZ 1964 (4); v P 1960 (5); *v E 1959 (4) 1967 (3); v A 1967 (4); v WI 1961 (5); v NZ 1967 (4)*

Chandrasekhar, B. S. 58: v E 1963 (4) 1972 (5) 1976 (5); v A 1964 (2); v WI 1966 (3) 1974 (4)
    1978 (4); v NZ 1964 (2) 1976 (3); *v E 1967 (3) 1971 (3) 1974 (2) 1979 (1); v A 1967 (2) 1977(5);*
    v WI 1975 (4); v NZ 1975 (3); v P 1978 (3)
Chauhan, C. P. S. 40: v E 1972 (2); v A 1969 (1) 1979 (6); v WI 1978 (6); v NZ 1969 (2); v P
    1979 (6); *v E 1979 (4); v A 1977 (4) 1980 (3); v NZ 1980 (3); v P 1978 (3)*

Chauhan, R. K. 21: v E 1992 (3); v A 1997 (2); v WI 1994 (2); v NZ 1995 (2); v SL 1993 (3) 1997 (3); v Z 1992 (1); *v NZ 1993 (1); v SL 1993 (3) 1997 (1)*

Chowdhury, N. R. 2: v E 1951 (1); v WI 1948 (1)

Colah, S. H. M. 2: v E 1933 (1); *v E 1932 (1)*

Contractor, N. J. 31: v E 1961 (5); v A 1956 (1) 1959 (5); v WI 1958 (5); v NZ 1955 (4); v P 1960 (5); *v E 1959 (4); v WI 1961 (2)*

Dani, H. T. 1: v P 1952

Desai, R. B. 28: v E 1961 (4) 1963 (2); v A 1959 (3); v WI 1958 (5); v NZ 1964 (3); v P 1960 (5); *v E 1959 (5); v A 1967 (1); v WI 1961 (3); v NZ 1967 (1)*

Dilawar Hussain 3: v E 1933 (2); *v E 1936 (1)*

Divecha, R. V. 5: v E 1951 (2); v P 1952 (1); *v E 1952 (2)*

Doshi, D. R. 33: v E 1979 (1) 1981 (6); v A 1979 (6); v P 1979 (6) 1983 (1); v SL 1982 (1); *v E 1982 (3); v A 1980 (3); v NZ 1980 (2); v P 1982 (4)*

Dravid, R. 29: v A 1996 (1) 1997 (3); v SA 1996 (3); v P 1998 (3); v SL 1997 (3); *v E 1996 (2); v SA 1996 (3); v WI 1996 (5); v NZ 1998 (2); v SL 1997 (2) 1998 (1); v Z 1998 (1)*

Durani, S. A. 29: v E 1961 (5) 1963 (5) 1972 (3); v A 1959 (1) 1964 (3); v WI 1966 (1); v NZ 1964 (3); *v WI 1961 (5) 1970 (3)*

Engineer, F. M. 46: v E 1961 (4) 1972 (5); v A 1969 (5); v WI 1966 (1) 1974 (5); v NZ 1964 (4) 1969 (2); *v E 1967 (3) 1971 (3) 1974 (3); v A 1967 (4); v WI 1961 (3); v NZ 1967 (4)*

Gadkari, C. V. 6: *v WI 1952 (3); v P 1954 (3)*

Gaekwad, A. D. 40: v E 1976 (4) 1984 (5); v WI 1974 (3) 1978 (5) 1983 (6); v NZ 1976 (3); v P 1983 (3); *v E 1979 (2); v A 1977 (1); v WI 1975 (3) 1982 (5); v P 1984 (2)*

Gaekwad, D. K. 11: v WI 1958 (1); v P 1952 (2) 1960 (1); *v E 1952 (1) 1959 (4); v WI 1952 (2)*

Gaekwad, H. G. 1: v P 1952

Gandotra, A. 2: v A 1969 (1); v NZ 1969 (1)

Ganesh, D. 4: *v SA 1996 (2); v WI 1996 (2)*

Ganguly, S. C. 27: v A 1996 (1) 1997 (3); v SA 1996 (2); v P 1998 (3); v SL 1997 (3); *v E 1996 (2); v SA 1996 (3); v WI 1996 (4); v NZ 1998 (2); v SL 1997 (2) 1998 (1); v Z 1998 (1)*

Gavaskar, S. M. 125: v E 1972 (5) 1976 (5) 1979 (1) 1981 (6) 1984 (5); v A 1979 (6) 1986 (3); v WI 1974 (2) 1978 (6) 1983 (6); v NZ 1976 (3); v P 1979 (6) 1983 (3) 1986 (4); v SL 1982 (1) 1986 (3); *v E 1971 (3) 1974 (3) 1979 (4) 1982 (3) 1986 (3); v A 1977 (5) 1980 (3) 1985 (3); v WI 1970 (4) 1975 (4) 1982 (5); v NZ 1975 (3) 1980 (3); v P 1978 (3) 1982 (6) 1984 (2); v SL 1985 (3)*

Ghavri, K. D. 39: v E 1976 (3) 1979 (1); v A 1979 (6); v WI 1974 (3) 1978 (6); v NZ 1976 (2); v P 1979 (6); *v E 1979 (4); v A 1977 (3) 1980 (3); v NZ 1980 (1); v P 1978 (1)*

Ghorpade, J. M. 8: v A 1956 (1); v WI 1958 (1); v NZ 1955 (1); *v E 1959 (3); v WI 1952 (2)*

Ghulam Ahmed 22: v E 1951 (2); v A 1956 (2); v WI 1948 (3) 1958 (2); v NZ 1955 (1); v P 1952 (4); *v E 1952 (4); v P 1954 (4)*

Gopalan, M. J. 1: v E 1933

Gopinath, C. D. 8: v E 1951 (3); v A 1959 (1); v P 1952 (1); *v E 1952 (1); v P 1954 (2)*

Guard, G. M. 2: v A 1959 (1); v WI 1958 (1)

Guha, S. 4: v A 1969 (3); *v E 1967 (1)*

Gul Mahomed 8: v P 1952 (2); *v E 1946 (1); v A 1947 (5)*

Gupte, B. P. 3: v E 1963 (1); v NZ 1964 (1); v P 1960 (1)

Gupte, S. P. 36: v E 1951 (1) 1961 (2); v A 1956 (3); v WI 1958 (5); v NZ 1955 (5); v P 1952 (2) 1960 (1); *v E 1959 (5); v WI 1952 (5); v P 1954 (5)*

Gursharan Singh 1: *v NZ 1989*

Hafeez, A. 3: *v E 1946 (3)*

Hanumant Singh 14: v E 1963 (2); v A 1964 (3); v WI 1966 (2); v NZ 1964 (4) 1969 (1); *v E 1967 (2)*

Harbhajan Singh 6: v A 1997 (1); v P 1998 (2); *v NZ 1998 (1); v SL 1998 (1); v Z 1998 (1)*

Hardikar, M. S. 2: v WI 1958 (2)

Harvinder Singh 2: v A 1997 (2)

Hazare, V. S. 30: v E 1951 (5); v WI 1948 (5); v P 1952 (3); *v E 1946 (3) 1952 (4); v A 1947 (5); v WI 1952 (5)*

Hindlekar, D. D. 4: *v E 1936 (1) 1946 (3)*

Hirwani, N. D. 17: v SA 1996 (2); v WI 1987 (1); v NZ 1988 (3) 1995 (1); v SL 1990 (1); *v E 1990 (3); v WI 1988 (3); v NZ 1989 (3)*

Ibrahim, K. C. 4: v WI 1948 (4)
Indrajitsinhji, K. S. 4: v A 1964 (3); v NZ 1969 (1)
Irani, J. K. 2: *v A 1947 (2)*

Jadeja, A. 13: v NZ 1995 (3); *v E 1996 (2); v SA 1992 (3); v WI 1996 (2); v NZ 1998 (2); v SL 1997 (1)*
Jahangir Khan, M. 4: *v E 1932 (1) 1936 (3)*
Jai, L. P. 1: v E 1933
Jaisimha, M. L. 39: v E 1961 (5) 1963 (5); v A 1959 (1) 1964 (3); v WI 1966 (2); v NZ 1964 (3) 1969 (1); v P 1960 (4); *v E 1959 (1); v A 1967 (2); v WI 1961 (4) 1970 (3); v NZ 1967 (4)*
Jamshedji, R. J. 1: v E 1933
Jayantilal, K. 1: *v WI 1970*
Johnson, D. J. 2: v A 1996 (1); *v SA 1996 (1)*
Joshi, P. G. 12: v E 1951 (2); v A 1959 (1); v WI 1958 (1); v P 1952 (1) 1960 (1); *v E 1959 (3); v WI 1952 (3)*
Joshi, S. B. 10: v A 1996 (1); v SA 1996 (3); v P 1998 (1); *v E 1996 (1); v WI 1996 (4)*

Kambli, V. G. 17: v E 1992 (3); v WI 1994 (3); v NZ 1995 (3); v SL 1993 (3); v Z 1992 (1); *v NZ 1993 (1); v SL 1993 (3)*
Kanitkar, H. S. 2: v WI 1974 (2)
Kapil Dev 131: v E 1979 (1) 1981 (6) 1984 (4) 1992 (3); v A 1979 (6) 1986 (3); v WI 1978 (6) 1983 (6) 1987 (4); v NZ 1988 (3); v P 1979 (6) 1983 (3) 1986 (5); v SL 1982 (1) 1986 (3) 1990 (1) 1993 (3); v Z 1992 (1); *v E 1979 (4) 1982 (3) 1986 (3) 1990 (3); v A 1980 (3) 1985 (3) 1991 (5); v SA 1992 (4); v WI 1982 (5) 1988 (4); v NZ 1980 (3) 1989 (3) 1993 (1); v P 1978 (3) 1982 (6) 1984 (2) 1989 (4); v SL 1985 (3) 1993 (3); v Z 1992 (1)*
Kapoor, A. R. 4: v A 1996 (1); v SA 1996 (1); v WI 1994 (1); v NZ 1995 (1)
Kardar, A. H. (*see* Hafeez)
Kenny, R. B. 5: v A 1959 (4); v WI 1958 (1)
Kirmani, S. M. H. 88: v E 1976 (5) 1979 (1) 1981 (6) 1984 (5); v A 1979 (6); v WI 1978 (6) 1983 (6); v NZ 1976 (3); v P 1979 (6) 1983 (3); v SL 1982 (1); *v E 1982 (3); v A 1977 (5) 1980 (3) 1985 (3); v WI 1975 (4) 1982 (5); v NZ 1975 (3) 1980 (3); v P 1978 (3) 1982 (6) 1984 (2)*
Kischenchand, G. 5: v P 1952 (1); *v A 1947 (4)*
Kripal Singh, A. G. 14: v E 1961 (3) 1963 (2); v A 1956 (2) 1964 (1); v WI 1958 (1); v NZ 1955 (4); *v E 1959 (1)*
Krishnamurthy, P. 5: *v WI 1970 (5)*
Kulkarni, N. M. 2: v SL 1997 (1); *v SL 1997 (1)*
Kulkarni, R. R. 3: v A 1986 (1); v P 1986 (2)
Kulkarni, U. N. 4: *v A 1967 (3); v NZ 1967 (1)*
Kumar, V. V. 2: v E 1961 (1); v P 1960 (1)
Kumble, A. 53: v E 1992 (3); v A 1996 (1) 1997 (3); v SA 1996 (3); v WI 1994 (3); v NZ 1995 (3); v P 1998 (3); v SL 1993 (3) 1997 (3); v Z 1992 (1); *v E 1990 (1) 1996 (3); v SA 1992 (4) 1996 (3); v WI 1996 (5); v NZ 1993 (1) 1998 (2); v SL 1993 (3) 1997 (2) 1998 (1); v Z 1992 (1) 1998 (1)*
Kunderan, B. K. 18: v E 1961 (1) 1963 (5); v A 1959 (3); v WI 1966 (2); v NZ 1964 (1); v P 1960 (2); *v E 1967 (2); v WI 1961 (2)*
Kuruvilla, A. 10: v SL 1997 (3); *v WI 1996 (5); v SL 1997 (2)*

Lall Singh 1: *v E 1932*
Lamba, R. 4: v WI 1987 (1); v SL 1986 (3)
Laxman, V. V. S. 14: v A 1997 (2); v SA 1996 (2); v P 1998 (3); *v SA 1996 (2); v WI 1996 (4); v SL 1998 (1)*

Madan Lal 39: v E 1976 (2) 1981 (6); v WI 1974 (2) 1983 (3); v NZ 1976 (1); v P 1983 (3); v SL 1982 (1); *v E 1974 (2) 1982 (3) 1986 (1); v A 1977 (2); v WI 1975 (4) 1982 (2); v NZ 1975 (3); v P 1982 (3) 1984 (1)*
Maka, E. S. 2: v P 1952 (1); *v WI 1952 (1)*
Malhotra, A. 7: v E 1981 (2) 1984 (1); v WI 1983 (3); *v E 1982 (1)*
Maninder Singh 35: v A 1986 (3); v WI 1983 (4) 1987 (3); v P 1986 (4); v SL 1986 (3); v Z 1992 (1); *v E 1986 (3); v WI 1982 (3); v P 1982 (5) 1984 (1) 1989 (3); v SL 1985 (2)*
Manjrekar, S. V. 37: v SA 1996 (1); v WI 1987 (1) 1994 (3); v NZ 1995 (1); v SL 1990 (1) 1993 (3); *v E 1990 (3) 1996 (2); v A 1991 (5); v SA 1992 (4); v WI 1988 (4); v NZ 1989 (3) 1993 (1); v P 1989 (4); v Z 1992 (1)*

Manjrekar, V. L. 55: v E 1951 (2) 1961 (5) 1963 (4); v A 1956 (3) 1964 (3); v WI 1958 (4); v NZ 1955 (5) 1964 (1); v P 1952 (3) 1960 (5); *v E 1952 (4) 1959 (2); v WI 1952 (4) 1961 (5); v P 1954 (5)*

Mankad, A. V. 22: v E 1976 (1); v A 1969 (5); v WI 1974 (1); v NZ 1969 (2) 1976 (3); *v E 1971 (3) 1974 (1); v A 1977 (3); v WI 1970 (3)*

Mankad, V. 44: v E 1951 (5); v A 1956 (3); v WI 1948 (5) 1958 (2); v NZ 1955 (4); v P 1952 (4); *v E 1946 (3) 1952 (3); v A 1947 (5); v WI 1952 (5); v P 1954 (5)*

Mansur Ali Khan (*see* Pataudi)

Mantri, M. K. 4: v E 1951 (1); *v E 1952 (2); v P 1954 (1)*

Meherhomji, K. R. 1: *v E 1936*

Mehra, V. L. 8: v E 1961 (1) 1963 (2); v NZ 1955 (2); *v WI 1961 (3)*

Merchant, V. M. 10: v E 1933 (3) 1951 (1); *v E 1936 (3) 1946 (3)*

Mhambrey, P. L. 2: *v E 1996 (2)*

Milkha Singh, A. G. 4: v E 1961 (1); v A 1959 (1); v P 1960 (2)

Modi, R. S. 10: v E 1951 (1); v WI 1948 (5); v P 1952 (1); *v E 1946 (3)*

Mohanty, D. S. 2: v SL 1997 (1); *v SL 1997 (1)*

Mongia, N. R. 40: v A 1996 (1) 1997 (3); v SA 1996 (3); v WI 1994 (3); v NZ 1995 (3); v P 1998 (3); v SL 1993 (3) 1997 (3); *v E 1996 (3); v SA 1996 (3); v WI 1996 (5); v NZ 1993 (1) 1998 (2); v SL 1997 (2) 1998 (1); v Z 1998 (1)*

More, K. S. 49: v E 1992 (3); v A 1986 (2); v WI 1987 (4); v NZ 1988 (3); v P 1986 (5); v SL 1986 (3) 1990 (1); *v E 1986 (3) 1990 (3); v A 1991 (3); v SA 1992 (4); v WI 1988 (4); v NZ 1989 (3); v P 1989 (4); v SL 1993 (3); v Z 1992 (1)*

Muddiah, V. M. 2: v A 1959 (1); v P 1960 (1)

Mushtaq Ali, S. 11: v E 1933 (2) 1951 (1); v WI 1948 (3); *v E 1936 (3) 1946 (2)*

Nadkarni, R. G. 41: v E 1961 (1) 1963 (5); v A 1959 (5) 1964 (3); v WI 1958 (1) 1966 (1); v NZ 1955 (1) 1964 (4); v P 1960 (4); *v E 1959 (4); v A 1967 (3); v WI 1961 (5); v NZ 1967 (4)*

Naik, S. S. 3: v WI 1974 (2); *v E 1974 (1)*

Naoomal Jeoomal 3: v E 1933 (2); *v E 1932 (1)*

Narasimha Rao, M. V. 4: v A 1979 (2); v WI 1978 (2)

Navle, J. G. 2: v E 1933 (1); *v E 1932 (1)*

Nayak, S. V. 2: *v E 1982 (2)*

Nayudu, C. K. 7: v E 1933 (3); *v E 1932 (1) 1936 (3)*

Nayudu, C. S. 11: v E 1933 (2) 1951 (1); *v E 1936 (2) 1946 (2); v A 1947 (4)*

Nazir Ali, S. 2: v E 1933 (1); *v E 1932 (1)*

Nehra, A. 1: *v SL 1998*

Nissar, Mahomed 6: v E 1933 (2); *v E 1932 (1) 1936 (3)*

Nyalchand, S. 1: v P 1952

Pai, A. M. 1: v NZ 1969

Palia, P. E. 2: *v E 1932 (1) 1936 (1)*

Pandit, C. S. 5: v A 1986 (2); *v E 1986 (1); v A 1991 (2)*

Parkar, G. A. 1: *v E 1982*

Parkar, R. D. 2: v E 1972 (2)

Parsana, D. D. 2: v WI 1978 (2)

Patankar, C. T. 1: v NZ 1955

Pataudi sen., Nawab of, 3: *v E 1946 (3)*

Pataudi jun., Nawab of (now Mansur Ali Khan) 46: v E 1961 (3) 1963 (5) 1972 (3); v A 1964 (3) 1969 (5); v WI 1966 (3) 1974 (4); v NZ 1964 (4) 1969 (3); *v E 1967 (3); v A 1967 (3); v WI 1961 (3); v NZ 1967 (4)*

Patel, B. P. 21: v E 1976 (5); v WI 1974 (3); v NZ 1976 (3); *v E 1974 (2); v A 1977 (2); v WI 1975 (3); v NZ 1975 (3)*

Patel, J. M. 7: v A 1956 (2) 1959 (3); v NZ 1955 (1); *v P 1954 (1)*

Patel, R. 1: v NZ 1988

Patiala, Yuvraj of, 1: v E 1933

Patil, S. M. 29: v E 1979 (1) 1981 (4) 1984 (2); v WI 1983 (2); v P 1979 (2) 1983 (3); v SL 1982 (1); *v E 1982 (2); v A 1980 (3); v NZ 1980 (3); v P 1982 (4) 1984 (2)*

Patil, S. R. 1: v NZ 1955

Phadkar, D. G. 31: v E 1951 (4); v A 1956 (1); v WI 1948 (4) 1958 (1); v NZ 1955 (4); v P 1952 (2); *v E 1952 (4); v A 1947 (4); v WI 1952 (4); v P 1954 (3)*

Prabhakar, M. 39: v E 1984 (2) 1992 (3); v WI 1994 (3); v NZ 1995 (3); v SL 1990 (1) 1993 (3); v Z 1992 (1); *v E 1990 (3); v A 1991 (5); v SA 1992 (4); v NZ 1989 (3); v P 1989 (4); v SL 1993 (3); v Z 1992 (1)*

Prasad, B. K. V. 24: v A 1996 (1); v SA 1996 (3); v P 1998 (3); v SL 1997 (1); *v E 1996 (3); v SA 1996 (3); v WI 1996 (5); v NZ 1998 (2); v SL 1997 (2) 1998 (1)*

Prasanna, E. A. S. 49: v E 1961 (1) 1972 (3) 1976 (4); v A 1969 (5); v WI 1966 (1) 1974 (5); v NZ 1969 (3); *v E 1967 (3) 1974 (2); v A 1967 (4) 1977 (4); v WI 1961 (1) 1970 (3) 1975 (1); v NZ 1967 (4) 1975 (3); v P 1978 (2)*

Punjabi, P. H. 5: *v P 1954 (5)*

Rai Singh, K. 1: *v A 1947*

Rajinder Pal 1: v E 1963

Rajindernath, V. 1: v P 1952

Rajput, L. S. 2: *v SL 1985 (2)*

Raju, S. L. V. 27: v E 1992 (3); v A 1997 (3); v WI 1994 (3); v NZ 1995 (2); v SL 1990 (1) 1993 (3); *v E 1996 (1); v A 1991 (4); v SA 1992 (2); v NZ 1989 (2) 1993 (1); v SL 1993 (1); v Z 1992 (1)*

Raman, W. V. 11: v SA 1996 (1); v WI 1987 (1); v NZ 1988 (1); *v SA 1992 (1) 1996 (2); v WI 1988 (1); v NZ 1989 (3); v Z 1992 (1)*

Ramaswami, C. 2: *v E 1936 (2)*

Ramchand, G. S. 33: v A 1956 (3) 1959 (5); v WI 1958 (3); v NZ 1955 (5); v P 1952 (3); *v E 1952 (4); v WI 1952 (5); v P 1954 (5)*

Ramesh, S. 4: v P 1998 (3); *v SL 1998 (1)*

Ramji, L. 1: v E 1933

Rangachari, C. R. 4: v WI 1948 (2); *v A 1947 (2)*

Rangnekar, K. M. 3: *v A 1947 (3)*

Ranjane, V. B. 7: v E 1961 (3) 1963 (1); v A 1964 (1); v WI 1958 (1); *v WI 1961 (1)*

Rathore, V. 6: v A 1996 (1); *v E 1996 (3); v SA 1996 (2)*

Razdan, V. 2: *v P 1989 (2)*

Reddy, B. 4: *v E 1979 (4)*

Rege, M. R. 1: v WI 1948

Roy, A. 4: v A 1969 (2); v NZ 1969 (2)

Roy, Pankaj 43: v E 1951 (5); v A 1956 (3) 1959 (5); v WI 1958 (5); v NZ 1955 (3); v P 1952 (3) 1960 (1); *v E 1952 (4) 1959 (5); v WI 1952 (4); v P 1954 (5)*

Roy, Pranab 2: v E 1981 (2)

Sandhu, B. S. 8: v WI 1983 (1); *v WI 1982 (4); v P 1982 (3)*

Sardesai, D. N. 30: v E 1961 (1) 1963 (5) 1972 (1); v A 1964 (3) 1969 (1); v WI 1966 (2); v NZ 1964 (3); *v E 1967 (1) 1971 (3); v A 1967 (2); v WI 1961 (3) 1970 (5)*

Sarwate, C. T. 9: v E 1951 (1); v WI 1948 (2); *v E 1946 (1); v A 1947 (5)*

Saxena, R. C. 1: *v E 1967*

Sekar, T. A. P. 2: *v P 1982 (2)*

Sen, P. 14: v E 1951 (2); v WI 1948 (5); v P 1952 (2); *v E 1952 (2); v A 1947 (3)*

Sen Gupta, A. K. 1: v WI 1958

Sharma, Ajay 1: v WI 1987

Sharma, Chetan 23: v E 1984 (3); v A 1986 (2); v WI 1987 (3); v SL 1986 (2); *v E 1986 (2); v A 1985 (2); v WI 1988 (4); v P 1984 (2); v SL 1985 (3)*

Sharma, Gopal 5: v E 1984 (1); v P 1986 (2); v SL 1990 (1); *v SL 1985 (1)*

Sharma, P. 5: v E 1976 (2); v WI 1974 (2); *v WI 1975 (1)*

Sharma, Sanjeev 2: v NZ 1988 (1); *v E 1990 (1)*

Shastri, R. J. 80: v E 1981 (6) 1984 (5); v A 1986 (3); v WI 1983 (6) 1987 (4); v NZ 1988 (3); v P 1983 (2) 1986 (5); v SL 1986 (3) 1990 (1); *v E 1982 (3) 1986 (3) 1990 (3); v A 1985 (3) 1991 (3); v SA 1992 (3); v WI 1982 (5) 1988 (4); v NZ 1980 (3); v P 1982 (2) 1984 (2) 1989 (4); v SL 1985 (3); v Z 1992 (1)*

Shinde, S. G. 7: v E 1951 (3); v WI 1948 (1); *v E 1946 (1) 1952 (2)*

Shodhan, R. H. 3: v P 1952 (1); *v WI 1952 (2)*

Shukla, R. C. 1: v SL 1982

Sidhu, N. S. 51: v E 1992 (3); v A 1997 (3); v WI 1983 (2) 1994 (3); v NZ 1988 (3) 1995 (2); v SL 1993 (3) 1997 (3); v Z 1992 (1); *v E 1990 (3); v A 1991 (3); v WI 1988 (4) 1996 (4); v NZ 1989 (1) 1993 (1) 1998 (2); v P 1989 (4); v SL 1993 (3) 1997 (2); v Z 1998 (1)*

Singh, R. 1: *v NZ 1998*

Singh, R. R. 1: *v Z 1998*

Sivaramakrishnan, L. 9: v E 1984 (5); *v A 1985 (2); v WI 1982 (1); v SL 1985 (1)*

Sohoni, S. W. 4: v E 1951 (1); *v E 1946 (2); v A 1947 (1)*

Solkar, E. D. 27: v E 1972 (5) 1976 (1); v A 1969 (4); v WI 1974 (4); v NZ 1969 (1); *v E 1971 (3) 1974 (3); v WI 1970 (5) 1975 (1)*

Sood, M. M. 1: v A 1959

Srikkanth, K. 43: v E 1981 (4) 1984 (2); v A 1986 (3); v WI 1987 (4); v NZ 1988 (3); v P 1986 (5); v SL 1986 (3); *v E 1986 (3); v A 1985 (3) 1991 (4); v P 1982 (2) 1989 (4); v SL 1985 (3)*

Srinath, J. 38: v A 1997 (2); v SA 1996 (3); v WI 1994 (3); v NZ 1995 (3); v P 1998 (3); v SL 1997 (3); *v E 1996 (3); v A 1991 (5); v SA 1992 (3) 1996 (3); v NZ 1993 (1) 1998 (2); v SL 1993 (2); v Z 1992 (1) 1998 (1)*

Srinivasan, T. E. 1: *v NZ 1980*

Subramanya, V. 9: v WI 1966 (2); v NZ 1964 (1); *v E 1967 (2); v A 1967 (2); v NZ 1967 (2)*

Sunderram, G. 2: v NZ 1955 (2)

Surendranath, R. 11: v A 1959 (2); v WI 1958 (2); v P 1960 (2); *v E 1959 (5)*

Surti, R. F. 26: v E 1963 (1); v A 1964 (2) 1969 (1); v WI 1966 (2); v NZ 1964 (1) 1969 (2); v P 1960 (2); *v E 1967 (2); v A 1967 (4); v WI 1961 (5); v NZ 1967 (4)*

Swamy, V. N. 1: v NZ 1955

Tamhane, N. S. 21: v A 1956 (3) 1959 (1); v WI 1958 (4); v NZ 1955 (4); v P 1960 (2); *v E 1959 (2); v P 1954 (5)*

Tarapore, K. K. 1: v WI 1948

Tendulkar, S. R. 68: v E 1992 (3); v A 1996 (1) 1997 (3); v SA 1996 (3); v WI 1994 (3); v NZ 1995 (3); v P 1998 (3); v SL 1990 (1) 1993 (3) 1997 (3); *v E 1990 (3) 1996 (3); v A 1991 (5); v SA 1992 (4) 1996 (3); v WI 1996 (5); v NZ 1989 (3) 1993 (1) 1998 (2); v P 1989 (4); v SL 1993 (3) 1997 (2) 1998 (1); v Z 1992 (1) 1998 (1)*

Umrigar, P. R. 59: v E 1951 (5) 1961 (4); v A 1956 (3) 1959 (3); v WI 1948 (1) 1958 (5); v NZ 1955 (5); v P 1952 (5) 1960 (5); *v E 1952 (4) 1959 (4); v WI 1952 (5) 1961 (5); v P 1954 (5)*

Vengsarkar, D. B. 116: v E 1976 (1) 1979 (1) 1981 (6) 1984 (5); v A 1979 (6) 1986 (2); v WI 1978 (6) 1983 (5) 1987 (3); v NZ 1988 (3); v P 1979 (5) 1983 (1) 1986 (5); v SL 1982 (1) 1986 (3) 1990 (1); *v E 1979 (4) 1982 (3) 1986 (3) 1990 (3); v A 1977 (5) 1980 (3) 1985 (3) 1991 (5); v WI 1975 (2) 1982 (5) 1988 (4); v NZ 1975 (3) 1980 (3) 1989 (2); v P 1978 (3) 1982 (6) 1984 (2); v SL 1985 (3)*

Venkataraghavan, S. 57: v E 1972 (2) 1976 (1); v A 1969 (5) 1979 (3); v WI 1966 (2) 1974 (2) 1978 (6); v NZ 1964 (4) 1969 (2) 1976 (3); v P 1983 (2); *v E 1967 (1) 1971 (3) 1974 (2) 1979 (4); v A 1977 (1); v WI 1970 (5) 1975 (3) 1982 (5); v NZ 1975 (1)*

Venkataramana, M. 1: *v WI 1988*

Viswanath, G. R. 91: v E 1972 (5) 1976 (5) 1979 (1) 1981 (6); v A 1969 (4) 1979 (6); v WI 1974 (5) 1978 (6); v NZ 1976 (3); v P 1979 (6); v SL 1982 (1); *v E 1971 (3) 1974 (3) 1979 (4) 1982 (3); v A 1977 (5) 1980 (3); v WI 1970 (3) 1975 (4); v NZ 1975 (3) 1980 (3); v P 1978 (3) 1982 (6)*

Viswanath, S. 3: *v SL 1985 (3)*

Vizianagram, Maharaj Kumar of, Sir Vijay A. 3: *v E 1936 (3)*

Wadekar, A. L. 37: v E 1972 (5); v A 1969 (5); v WI 1966 (2); v NZ 1969 (3); *v E 1967 (3) 1971 (3) 1974 (3); v A 1967 (4); v WI 1970 (5); v NZ 1967 (4)*

Wassan, A. S. 4: *v E 1990 (1); v NZ 1989 (3)*

Wazir Ali, S. 7: v E 1933 (3); *v E 1932 (1) 1936 (3)*

Yadav, N. S. 35: v E 1979 (1) 1981 (1) 1984 (4); v A 1979 (5) 1986 (3); v WI 1983 (3); v P 1979 (5) 1986 (4); v SL 1986 (2); *v A 1980 (2) 1985 (3); v NZ 1980 (1); v P 1984 (1)*

Yadav, V. S. 1: v Z 1992

Yajurvindra Singh 4: v E 1976 (2); v A 1979 (1); *v E 1979 (1)*

Yashpal Sharma 37: v E 1979 (1) 1981 (2); v A 1979 (6); v WI 1983 (1); v P 1979 (6) 1983 (3); v SL 1982 (1); *v E 1979 (3) 1982 (3); v A 1980 (3); v WI 1982 (5); v NZ 1980 (1); v P 1982 (2)*

Yograj Singh 1: *v NZ 1980*

Note: Hafeez, on going later to Oxford University, took his correct name, Kardar.

PAKISTAN

Number of Test cricketers: 156

Aamer Malik 14: v E 1987 (2); v A 1988 (1) 1994 (1); v WI 1990 (1); v In 1989 (4); *v A 1989 (2); v WI 1987 (1); v NZ 1988 (2)*

Aamir Nazir 6: v SL 1995 (1); *v SA 1994 (1); v WI 1992 (1); v NZ 1993 (1); v Z 1994 (2)*

Aamir Sohail 45: v A 1994 (3) 1998 (3); v SA 1997 (1); v WI 1997 (3); v SL 1995 (3); v Z 1993 (3) 1996 (2) 1998 (1); *v E 1992 (5) 1996 (2); v A 1995 (3); v SA 1994 (1) 1997 (3); v WI 1992 (2); v NZ 1992 (1) 1993 (3) 1995 (1); v SL 1994 (2); v Z 1994 (3)*

Abdul Kadir 4: v A 1964 (1); *v A 1964 (1); v NZ 1964 (2)*

Abdul Qadir 67: v E 1977 (3) 1983 (3) 1987 (3); v A 1982 (3) 1988 (3); v WI 1980 (2) 1986 (3) 1990 (2); v NZ 1984 (3) 1990 (2); v In 1982 (5) 1984 (1) 1989 (4); v SL 1985 (3); *v E 1982 (3) 1987 (4); v A 1983 (5); v WI 1987 (3); v NZ 1984 (2) 1988 (2); v In 1979 (3) 1986 (3); v SL 1985 (2)*

Afaq Hussain 2: v E 1961 (1); *v A 1964 (1)*

Aftab Baloch 2: v WI 1974 (1); v NZ 1969 (1)

Aftab Gul 6: v E 1968 (2); v NZ 1969 (1); *v E 1971 (3)*

Agha Saadat Ali 1: v NZ 1955

Agha Zahid 1: v WI 1974

Akram Raza 9: v A 1994 (2); v WI 1990 (1); v In 1989 (1); v SL 1991 (1); *v NZ 1993 (2); v SL 1994 (1); v Z 1994 (1)*

Ali Hussain Rizvi 1: v SA 1997

Alim-ud-Din 25: v A 1956 (1) 1959 (1); v WI 1958 (1); v NZ 1955 (3); v In 1954 (5); *v E 1954 (3) 1962 (3); v WI 1957 (5); v In 1960 (1)*

Ali Naqvi 5: v SA 1997 (3); *v Z 1997 (2)*

Amir Elahi 5: *v In 1952 (5)*

Anil Dalpat 9: v E 1983 (3); v NZ 1984 (3); *v NZ 1984 (3)*

Anwar Hussain 4: *v In 1952 (4)*

Anwar Khan 1: *v NZ 1978*

Aqib Javed 22: v A 1994 (1); v NZ 1990 (3); v SL 1991 (3) 1995 (3); v Z 1998 (1); *v E 1992 (5); v A 1989 (1); v SA 1994 (1); v NZ 1988 (1) 1992 (1); v Z 1994 (2)*

Arif Butt 3: *v A 1964 (1); v NZ 1964 (2)*

Arshad Khan 3: v A 1998 (1); v WI 1997 (1); *v SL 1998 (1)*

Ashfaq Ahmed 1: v Z 1993

Ashraf Ali 8: v E 1987 (3); v In 1984 (2); v SL 1981 (2) 1985 (1)

Asif Iqbal 58: v E 1968 (3) 1972 (3); v A 1964 (1); v WI 1974 (2); v NZ 1964 (3) 1969 (3) 1976 (3); v In 1978 (3); *v E 1967 (3) 1971 (3) 1974 (3); v A 1964 (1) 1972 (3) 1976 (3) 1978 (2); v WI 1976 (5); v NZ 1964 (3) 1972 (3) 1978 (2); v In 1979 (6)*

Asif Masood 16: v E 1968 (2) 1972 (1); v WI 1974 (2); v NZ 1969 (1); *v E 1971 (3) 1974 (3); v A 1972 (3) 1976 (1)*

Asif Mujtaba 25: v E 1987 (1); v WI 1986 (2); v Z 1993 (3); *v E 1992 (5) 1996 (2); v SA 1994 (1); v WI 1992 (2); v NZ 1992 (1) 1993 (2); v SL 1994 (2) 1996 (2); v Z 1994 (1)*

Ata-ur-Rehman 13: v SL 1995 (1); v Z 1993 (3); *v E 1992 (1) 1996 (2); v WI 1992 (3); v NZ 1993 (2) 1995 (1)*

Atif Rauf 1: *v NZ 1993*

Azam Khan 1: v Z 1996

Azeem Hafeez 18: v E 1983 (2); v NZ 1984 (3); v In 1984 (2); *v A 1983 (5); v NZ 1984 (3); v In 1983 (3)*

Azhar Khan 1: v A 1979

Azhar Mahmood 15: v A 1998 (2); v SA 1997 (3); v WI 1997 (3); v Z 1998 (1); *v SA 1997 (3); v In 1998 (1); v Z 1997 (2)*

Azmat Rana 1: v A 1979

Basit Ali 19: v A 1994 (2); v SL 1995 (1); v Z 1993 (3); *v A 1995 (3); v WI 1992 (3); v NZ 1993 (3) 1995 (1); v SL 1994 (2); v Z 1994 (1)*

Burki, J. 25: v E 1961 (3); v A 1964 (1); v NZ 1964 (1); *v E 1962 (5) 1967 (3); v A 1964 (1); v NZ 1964 (3); v In 1960 (5)*

D'Souza, A. 6: v E 1961 (2); v WI 1958 (1); *v E 1962 (3)*

Ehtesham-ud-Din 5: v A 1979 (1); *v E 1982 (1); v In 1979 (3)*

Farooq Hamid 1: *v A 1964*
Farrukh Zaman 1: v NZ 1976
Fazal Mahmood 34: v E 1961 (1); v A 1956 (1) 1959 (2); v WI 1958 (3); v NZ 1955 (2); v In 1954 (4); *v E 1954 (4) 1962 (2); v WI 1957 (5); v In 1952 (5) 1960 (5)*
Fazl-e-Akbar 2: v SL 1998 (1); *v SA 1997 (1)*

Ghazali, M. E. Z. 2: *v E 1954 (2)*
Ghulam Abbas 1: *v E 1967*
Gul Mahomed 1: v A 1956

Hanif Mohammad 55: v E 1961 (3) 1968 (3); v A 1956 (1) 1959 (3) 1964 (1); v WI 1958 (1); v NZ 1955 (3) 1964 (3) 1969 (1); v In 1954 (5); *v E 1954 (4) 1962 (5) 1967 (3); v A 1964 (1); v WI 1957 (5); v NZ 1964 (3); v In 1952 (5) 1960 (5)*
Haroon Rashid 23: v E 1977 (3); v A 1979 (2) 1982 (3); v In 1982 (1); v SL 1981 (2); *v E 1978 (3) 1982 (1); v A 1976 (1) 1978 (1); v WI 1976 (5); v NZ 1978 (1)*
Hasan Raza 2: v Z 1996 (1) 1998 (1)
Haseeb Ahsan 12: v E 1961 (2); v A 1959 (1); v WI 1958 (1); *v WI 1957 (3); v In 1960 (5)*

Ibadulla, K. 4: v A 1964 (1); *v E 1967 (2); v NZ 1964 (1)*
Ijaz Ahmed, sen. 54: v E 1987 (3); v A 1988 (3) 1994 (1) 1998 (2); v SA 1997 (3); v WI 1990 (3) 1997 (3); v NZ 1996 (2); v Z 1996 (2) 1998 (2); *v E 1987 (4) 1996 (3); v A 1989 (3) 1995 (2); v SA 1994 (1) 1997 (3); v WI 1987 (2); v NZ 1995 (1); v In 1986 (1) 1998 (3); v SL 1996 (2) 1998 (1); v Z 1994 (3) 1997 (1)*
Ijaz Ahmed, jun. 2: v SL 1995 (2)
Ijaz Butt 8: v A 1959 (2); v WI 1958 (3); *v E 1962 (3)*
Ijaz Faqih 5: v WI 1980 (1); *v A 1981 (1); v WI 1987 (2); v In 1986 (1)*
Imran Khan 88: v E 1979 (2) 1982 (3); v WI 1980 (4) 1986 (3) 1990 (3); v NZ 1976 (3); v In 1978 (3) 1982 (6) 1989 (4); v SL 1981 (1) 1985 (3) 1991 (3); *v E 1971 (1) 1974 (3) 1982 (3) 1987 (5); v A 1976 (3) 1978 (2) 1981 (3) 1983 (2) 1989 (3); v WI 1976 (5) 1987 (3); v NZ 1978 (2) 1988 (2); v In 1979 (5) 1986 (5); v SL 1985 (3)*
Imran Nazir 1: v SL 1998
Imtiaz Ahmed 41: v E 1961 (3); v A 1956 (1) 1959 (3); v WI 1958 (3); v NZ 1955 (3); v In 1954 (3); *v E 1954 (4) 1962 (4); v WI 1957 (5); v In 1952 (5) 1960 (5)*
Intikhab Alam 47: v E 1961 (2) 1968 (3) 1972 (3); v A 1959 (1) 1964 (1); v WI 1974 (2); v NZ 1964 (3) 1969 (3) 1976 (3); *v E 1962 (3) 1967 (3) 1971 (3) 1974 (3); v A 1964 (1) 1972 (3); v WI 1976 (1); v NZ 1964 (3) 1972 (3); v In 1960 (3)*
Inzamam-ul-Haq 55: v A 1994 (3) 1998 (3); v SA 1997 (3); v WI 1997 (3); v NZ 1996 (2); v SL 1995 (3) 1998 (1); v Z 1993 (3) 1998 (1); *v E 1992 (4) 1996 (3); v A 1995 (3); v SA 1994 (1) 1997 (2); v WI 1992 (3); v NZ 1992 (1) 1993 (3) 1995 (1); v In 1998 (2); v SL 1994 (2) 1996 (2) 1998 (1); v Z 1994 (3) 1997 (2)*
Iqbal Qasim 50: v E 1977 (3) 1987 (3); v A 1979 (3) 1982 (2) 1988 (3); v WI 1980 (4); v NZ 1984 (3); v In 1978 (3) 1982 (2); v SL 1981 (3); *v E 1978 (3); v A 1976 (3) 1981 (2); v WI 1976 (2); v NZ 1984 (1); v In 1979 (6) 1983 (1) 1986 (3)*
Israr Ali 4: v A 1959 (2); *v In 1952 (2)*

Jalal-ud-Din 6: v A 1982 (1); v In 1982 (2) 1984 (2); v SL 1985 (1)
Javed Akhtar 1: *v E 1962*
Javed Miandad 124: v E 1977 (3) 1987 (3); v A 1979 (3) 1982 (3) 1988 (3); v WI 1980 (4) 1986 (3) 1990 (3); v NZ 1976 (3) 1984 (3) 1990 (3); v In 1978 (3) 1982 (6) 1984 (2) 1989 (4); v SL 1981 (3) 1985 (3) 1991 (3); v Z 1993 (3); *v E 1978 (3) 1982 (3) 1987 (5) 1992 (5); v A 1976 (3) 1978 (2) 1981 (3) 1983 (5) 1989 (3); v WI 1976 (1) 1987 (3) 1992 (3); v NZ 1978 (3) 1984 (3) 1988 (2) 1992 (1); v In 1979 (6) 1983 (3) 1986 (4); v SL 1985 (3)*

Kabir Khan 4: *v SA 1994 (1); v SL 1994 (1); v Z 1994 (2)*
Kardar, A. H. 23: v A 1956 (1); v NZ 1955 (3); v In 1954 (5); *v E 1954 (4); v WI 1957 (5); v In 1952 (5)*
Khalid Hassan 1: *v E 1954*

Khalid Wazir 2: v *E 1954 (2)*

Khan Mohammad 13: v A 1956 (1); v NZ 1955 (3); v In 1954 (4); *v E 1954 (2); v WI 1957 (2); v In 1952 (1)*

Liaqat Ali 5: v E 1977 (2); v WI 1974 (1); *v E 1978 (2)*

Mahmood Hussain 27: v E 1961 (1); v WI 1958 (3); v NZ 1955 (1); v In 1954 (5); *v E 1954 (2) 1962 (3); v WI 1957 (3); v In 1952 (4) 1960 (5)*

Majid Khan 63: v E 1968 (3) 1972 (3); v A 1964 (1) 1979 (3); v WI 1974 (2) 1980 (4); v NZ 1964 (3) 1976 (3); v In 1978 (3) 1982 (1); v SL 1981 (1); *v E 1967 (3) 1971 (2) 1974 (3) 1982 (1); v A 1972 (3) 1976 (3) 1978 (2) 1981 (3); v WI 1976 (5); v NZ 1972 (3) 1978 (2); v In 1979 (6)*

Mansoor Akhtar 19: v A 1982 (3); v WI 1980 (2); v In 1982 (3); v SL 1981 (1); *v E 1982 (3) 1987 (5); v A 1981 (1) 1989 (1)*

Manzoor Elahi 6: v NZ 1984 (1); v In 1984 (1); *v In 1986 (2); v Z 1994 (2)*

Maqsood Ahmed 16: v NZ 1955 (2); v In 1954 (5); *v E 1954 (4); v In 1952 (5)*

Masood Anwar 1: v WI 1990

Mathias, Wallis 21: v E 1961 (1); v A 1956 (1) 1959 (2); v WI 1958 (3); v NZ 1955 (1); *v E 1962 (3); v WI 1957 (5); v In 1960 (5)*

Miran Bux 2: v In 1954 (2)

Mohammad Akram 6: v NZ 1996 (1); v SL 1995 (2); *v E 1996 (1); v A 1995 (2)*

Mohammad Aslam 1: *v E 1954*

Mohammad Farooq 7: v NZ 1964 (3); *v E 1962 (2); v In 1960 (2)*

Mohammad Hussain 2: v A 1998 (1); v Z 1996 (1)

Mohammad Ilyas 10: v E 1968 (2); v NZ 1964 (3); *v E 1967 (1); v A 1964 (1); v NZ 1964 (3)*

Mohammad Munaf 4: v E 1961 (2); v A 1959 (2)

Mohammad Nazir 14: v E 1972 (1); v WI 1980 (4); v NZ 1969 (3); *v A 1983 (3); v In 1983 (3)*

Mohammad Ramzan 1: v SA 1997

Mohammad Wasim 11: v A 1998 (1); v NZ 1996 (1); *v SL 1996 (2)*

Mohammad Zahid 4: v A 1998 (1); v NZ 1996 (1); v SL 1997 (3); v WI 1997 (3); v NZ 1996 (2); *v SA 1997 (2); v Z 1997 (1)*

Mohsin Kamal 9: v E 1983 (1); v A 1994 (2); v SL 1985 (1); *v E 1987 (4); v SL 1985 (1)*

Mohsin Khan 48: v E 1977 (1) 1983 (3); v A 1982 (3); v WI 1986 (3); v NZ 1984 (2); v In 1982 (6) 1984 (2); v SL 1981 (2) 1985 (2); *v E 1978 (3) 1982 (3); v A 1978 (1) 1981 (2) 1983 (5); v NZ 1978 (1) 1984 (3); v In 1983 (3); v SL 1985 (3)*

Moin Khan 47: v A 1994 (1) 1998 (3); v SA 1997 (3); v WI 1990 (2) 1997 (3); v NZ 1996 (2); v SL 1991 (3) 1995 (3) 1998 (1); v Z 1996 (2) 1998 (2); *v E 1992 (4) 1996 (2); v A 1995 (2); v SA 1994 (1) 1997 (3); v WI 1992 (2); v In 1998 (3); v SL 1996 (2) 1998 (1); v Z 1997 (2)*

Mudassar Nazar 76: v E 1977 (3) 1983 (1) 1987 (3); v A 1979 (3) 1982 (3) 1988 (3); v WI 1986 (2); v NZ 1984 (3); v In 1978 (2) 1982 (6) 1984 (2); v SL 1981 (1) 1985 (3) ; *v E 1978 (3) 1982 (3) 1987 (5); v A 1976 (1) 1978 (1) 1981 (3) 1983 (5); v WI 1987 (5); v NZ 1978 (1) 1984 (3) 1988 (2); v In 1979 (5) 1983 (3); v SL 1985 (3)*

Mufasir-ul-Haq 1: *v NZ 1964*

Munir Malik 3: v A 1959 (1); *v E 1962 (2)*

Mushtaq Ahmed 42: v A 1994 (3) 1998 (2); v SA 1997 (3); v WI 1990 (2) 1997 (3); v NZ 1996 (2); v Z 1993 (2) 1998 (1); *v E 1992 (5) 1996 (3); v A 1989 (1) 1995 (2); v SA 1997 (3); v WI 1992 (1); v NZ 1992 (1) 1993 (1) 1995 (1); v In 1998 (1); v SL 1994 (2) 1996 (2); v Z 1997 (1)*

Mushtaq Mohammad 57: v E 1961 (3) 1968 (3) 1972 (3); v WI 1958 (1) 1974 (2); v NZ 1969 (2) 1976 (3); v In 1978 (3); *v E 1962 (3) 1967 (3) 1971 (3) 1974 (3); v A 1967 (3) 1976 (3) 1978 (2); v WI 1976 (5); v NZ 1972 (2) 1978 (3); v In 1960 (5)*

Nadeem Abbasi 3: v In 1989 (3)

Nadeem Ghauri 1: *v A 1989*

Nadeem Khan 2: *v WI 1992 (1); v In 1998 (1)*

Nasim-ul-Ghani 29: v E 1961 (2); v A 1959 (2) 1964 (1); v WI 1958 (3); *v E 1962 (5) 1967 (2); v A 1964 (1) 1972 (1); v WI 1957 (5); v NZ 1964 (3); v In 1960 (4)*

Naushad Ali 6: v NZ 1964 (3); *v NZ 1964 (3)*

Naved Anjum 2: v NZ 1990 (1); v In 1989 (1)

Naved Ashraf 1: v Z 1998

Nazar Mohammad 5: *v In 1952 (5)*

Nazir Junior (*see* Mohammad Nazir)
Niaz Ahmed 2: v E 1968 (1); *v E 1967 (1)*

Pervez Sajjad 19: v E 1968 (1) 1972 (2); v A 1964 (1); v NZ 1964 (3) 1969 (3); *v E 1971 (3); v NZ 1964 (3) 1972 (3)*

Qasim Omar 26: v E 1983 (3); v WI 1986 (3); v NZ 1984 (3); v In 1984 (2); v SL 1985 (3); *v A 1983 (5); v NZ 1984 (3); v In 1983 (1); v SL 1985 (3)*

Ramiz Raja 57: v E 1983 (2) 1987 (3); v A 1988 (3); v WI 1986 (3) 1990 (2); v NZ 1990 (3); v In 1989 (4); v SL 1985 (1) 1991 (3) 1995 (3); *v E 1987 (2) 1992 (5); v A 1989 (2) 1995 (3); v WI 1987 (3) 1992 (3); v NZ 1992 (1) 1995 (1); v In 1986 (5); v SL 1985 (3) 1996 (2)*

Rashid Khan 4: v SL 1981 (2); *v A 1983 (1); v NZ 1984 (1)*
Rashid Latif 22: v A 1994 (2); v Z 1993 (3); *v E 1992 (1) 1996 (1); v A 1995 (1); v SA 1997 (1); v WI 1992 (1); v NZ 1992 (1) 1993 (3) 1995 (1); v SL 1994 (2); v Z 1994 (3) 1997 (2)*
Rehman, S. F. 1: *v WI 1957*
Rizwan-uz-Zaman 11: v WI 1986 (1); v SL 1981 (2); *v A 1981 (1); v NZ 1988 (2); v In 1986 (5)*

Sadiq Mohammad 41: v E 1972 (3) 1977 (2); v WI 1974 (1) 1980 (3); v NZ 1969 (3) 1976 (3); v In 1978 (1); *v E 1971 (3) 1974 (3) 1978 (3); v A 1972 (3) 1976 (2); v WI 1976 (5); v NZ 1972 (3); v In 1979 (3)*
Saeed Ahmed 41: v E 1961 (3) 1968 (3); v A 1959 (3) 1964 (1); v WI 1958 (3); v NZ 1964 (3); *v E 1962 (5) 1967 (3) 1971 (1); v A 1964 (1) 1972 (2); v WI 1957 (5); v NZ 1964 (3); v In 1960 (5)*
Saeed Anwar 41: v A 1994 (3) 1998 (2); v SA 1997 (3); v WI 1990 (1) 1997 (3); v NZ 1996 (2); v SL 1995 (2) 1998 (1); v Z 1996 (2) 1998 (1); *v E 1992 (5); v A 1994 (1) 1997 (3); v NZ 1993 (3); v In 1998 (3); v SL 1994 (2) 1998 (1); v Z 1994 (2) 1997 (2)*
Salah-ud-Din 5: v E 1968 (1); v NZ 1964 (3) 1969 (1)
Saleem Jaffer 14: v E 1987 (1); v A 1988 (2); v WI 1986 (1); v NZ 1990 (1); v In 1989 (1); v SL 1991 (2); *v WI 1987 (1); v NZ 1988 (2); v In 1986 (2)*
Salim Altaf 21: v E 1972 (3); v NZ 1969 (2); v In 1978 (1); *v E 1967 (2) 1971 (2); v A 1972 (3) 1976 (2); v WI 1976 (3); v NZ 1972 (3)*
Salim Elahi 4: *v A 1995 (2); v SL 1996 (2)*
Salim Malik 103: v E 1983 (3) 1987 (3); v A 1988 (3) 1994 (3) 1998 (3); v WI 1986 (1) 1990 (3); v NZ 1984 (3) 1990 (3) 1996 (2); v In 1982 (6) 1984 (2) 1989 (4); v SL 1981 (2) 1985 (3) 1991 (3); v Z 1996 (2) 1998 (1); *v E 1987 (5) 1992 (5) 1996 (3); v A 1983 (3) 1989 (1) 1995 (2); v SA 1994 (1); v WI 1987 (3); v NZ 1984 (3) 1988 (2) 1992 (1) 1993 (3) 1995 (1); v In 1983 (2) 1986 (5) 1998 (3); v SL 1985 (3) 1994 (2) 1996 (2); v Z 1994 (3)*
Salim Yousuf 32: v A 1988 (3); v WI 1986 (3) 1990 (1); v NZ 1990 (3); v In 1989 (1); v SL 1981 (1) 1985 (2); *v E 1987 (5); v A 1989 (3); v WI 1987 (3); v NZ 1988 (2); v In 1986 (5)*
Saqlain Mushtaq 22: v A 1998 (1); v SA 1997 (3); v WI 1997 (1); v NZ 1996 (1); v SL 1995 (2) 1998 (1); v Z 1996 (2) 1998 (1); *v A 1995 (2); v SA 1997 (1); v In 1998 (3); v SL 1996 (2) 1998 (1); v Z 1997 (1)*
Sarfraz Nawaz 55: v E 1968 (1) 1972 (2) 1977 (2) 1983 (3); v A 1979 (3); v WI 1974 (2) 1980 (2); v NZ 1976 (3); v In 1978 (3) 1982 (6); *v E 1974 (3) 1978 (2) 1982 (1); v A 1972 (2) 1976 (2) 1978 (2) 1981 (3) 1983 (3); v WI 1976 (4); v NZ 1972 (3) 1978 (3)*
Shadab Kabir 3: v Z 1996 (1); *v E 1996 (2)*
Shafiq Ahmed 6: v E 1977 (3); v WI 1980 (2); *v E 1974 (1)*
Shafqat Rana 5: v E 1968 (2); v A 1964 (1); v NZ 1969 (2)
Shahid Afridi 6: v A 1998 (1); v SL 1998 (1); *v In 1998 (3); v SL 1998 (1)*
Shahid Israr 1: v NZ 1976
Shahid Mahboob 1: v In 1989
Shahid Mahmood 1: *v E 1962*
Shahid Nazir 8: v WI 1997 (1); v NZ 1996 (2); v SL 1998 (1); v Z 1996 (2); *v SL 1996 (2)*
Shahid Saeed 1: v In 1989
Shakeel Ahmed, sen. 1: v A 1998
Shakeel Ahmed, jun. 3: *v WI 1992 (1); v Z 1994 (2)*
Sharpe, D. 3: v A 1959 (3)
Shoaib Akhtar 10: v A 1998 (2); v WI 1997 (1); v Z 1998 (1); *v SA 1997 (3); v In 1998 (1); v SL 1998 (1); v Z 1997 (1)*
Shoaib Mohammad 45: v E 1983 (1) 1987 (1); v A 1988 (3); v WI 1990 (3); v NZ 1984 (1) 1990 (3); v In 1989 (4); v SL 1985 (1) 1991 (3) 1995 (3); v Z 1993 (3); *v E 1987 (4) 1992 (1); v A 1989 (3); v WI 1987 (3); v NZ 1984 (1) 1988 (2); v In 1983 (2) 1986 (3)*

Shuja-ud-Din 19: v E 1961 (2); v A 1959 (3); v WI 1958 (3); v NZ 1955 (3); v In 1954 (5); *v E 1954 (3)*

Sikander Bakht 26: v E 1977 (2); v WI 1980 (1); v NZ 1976 (1); v In 1978 (2) 1982 (1); *v E 1978 (3) 1982 (2); v A 1978 (2) 1981 (3); v WI 1976 (1); v NZ 1978 (3); v In 1979 (5)*

Tahir Naqqash 15: v A 1982 (3); v In 1982 (2); v SL 1981 (3); *v E 1982 (2); v A 1983 (1); v NZ 1984 (1); v In 1983 (3)*

Talat Ali 10: v E 1972 (3); *v E 1978 (2); v A 1972 (1); v NZ 1972 (1) 1978 (3)*

Taslim Arif 6: v A 1979 (3); v WI 1980 (2); *v In 1979 (1)*

Tauseef Ahmed 34: v E 1983 (2) 1987 (2); v A 1979 (3) 1988 (3); v WI 1986 (3); v NZ 1984 (1) 1990 (2); v In 1984 (1); v SL 1981 (3) 1985 (1); v Z 1993 (1); *v E 1987 (2); v A 1989 (3); v NZ 1988 (1); v In 1986 (4); v SL 1985 (2)*

Wajahatullah Wasti 3: v SL 1998 (1); *v In 1998 (1); v SL 1998 (1)*

Waqar Hassan 21: v A 1956 (1) 1959 (1); v WI 1958 (1); v NZ 1955 (3); v In 1954 (5); *v E 1954 (4); v WI 1957 (1); v In 1952 (5)*

Waqar Younis 57: v E 1994 (2); v SA 1997 (2); v WI 1990 (3) 1997 (2); v NZ 1990 (3) 1996 (1); v In 1989 (2); v SL 1991 (3) 1995 (1); v Z 1993 (3) 1996 (2) 1998 (2); *v E 1992 (5) 1996 (3); v A 1989 (3) 1995 (3); v SA 1997 (3); v WI 1992 (3); v NZ 1992 (1) 1993 (3) 1995 (1); v In 1998 (2); v SL 1994 (2); v Z 1997 (2)*

Wasim Akram 88: v E 1987 (2); v A 1994 (2) 1998 (2); v SA 1997 (2); v WI 1986 (2) 1990 (3) 1997 (3); v NZ 1990 (2); v In 1989 (4); v SL 1985 (3) 1991 (3) 1995 (2) 1998 (1); v Z 1993 (2) 1996 (2) 1998 (2); *v E 1987 (5) 1992 (4) 1996 (3); v A 1989 (3) 1995 (3) 1999 (1) 1997 (1); v WI 1987 (3) 1992 (3); v NZ 1984 (2) 1992 (1) 1993 (3) 1995 (1); v In 1986 (5) 1998 (3); v SL 1985 (3) 1994 (2) 1998 (1); v Z 1994 (3) 1997 (1)*

Wasim Bari 81: v E 1968 (3) 1972 (3) 1977 (3); v A 1982 (3); v WI 1974 (2) 1980 (2); v NZ 1969 (3) 1976 (2); v In 1978 (3) 1982 (6); *v E 1967 (3) 1971 (3) 1974 (3) 1978 (3) 1982 (3); v A 1972 (3) 1976 (3) 1978 (2) 1981 (3) 1983 (5); v WI 1976 (5); v NZ 1972 (3) 1978 (3); v In 1979 (6) 1983 (3)*

Wasim Raja 57: v E 1972 (1) 1977 (3) 1983 (3); v A 1979 (3); v WI 1974 (2) 1980 (4); v NZ 1976 (1) 1984 (1); v In 1982 (1) 1984 (1); v SL 1981 (3); *v E 1974 (2) 1978 (3) 1982 (1); v A 1978 (1) 1981 (3) 1983 (2); v WI 1976 (5); v NZ 1972 (3) 1978 (3) 1984 (2); v In 1979 (6) 1983 (3)*

Wazir Mohammad 20: v A 1956 (1) 1959 (1); v WI 1958 (3); v NZ 1955 (3); v In 1954 (5); *v E 1954 (2); v WI 1957 (5); v In 1952 (1)*

Younis Ahmed 4: v NZ 1969 (2); *v In 1986 (2)*

Yousuf Youhana 12: v A 1998 (2); v SL 1998 (1); v Z 1998 (2); *v SA 1997 (1); v In 1998 (3); v SL 1998 (1); v Z 1997 (2)*

Zaheer Abbas 78: v E 1972 (2) 1983 (3); v A 1979 (2) 1982 (3); v WI 1974 (2) 1980 (3); v NZ 1969 (1) 1976 (3) 1984 (3); v In 1978 (3) 1982 (6) 1984 (2); v SL 1981 (1) 1985 (2); *v E 1971 (3) 1974 (3) 1982 (3); v A 1972 (3) 1976 (3) 1978 (2) 1981 (2) 1983 (5); v WI 1976 (3); v NZ 1972 (3) 1978 (2) 1984 (2); v In 1979 (5) 1983 (3)*

Zahid Fazal 9: v A 1994 (2); v WI 1990 (2); v SL 1991 (3) 1995 (1)

Zahoor Elahi 2: v NZ 1996 (2)

Zakir Khan 2: v In 1989 (1); *v SL 1985 (1)*

Zulfiqar Ahmed 9: v A 1956 (1); v NZ 1955 (3); *v E 1954 (2); v In 1952 (3)*

Zulqarnain 3: *v SL 1985 (3)*

SRI LANKA

Number of Test cricketers: 77

Ahangama, F. S. 3: v In 1985 (3)

Amalean, K. N. 2: v P 1985 (1); *v A 1987 (1)*

Amerasinghe, A. M. J. G. 2: v NZ 1983 (2)

Anurasiri, S. D. 18: v A 1992 (3); v WI 1993 (1); v NZ 1986 (1) 1992 (2); v P 1985 (2); v Z 1997 (1); *v E 1991 (1); v In 1986 (1) 1993 (3); v P 1991 (3)*

Arnold, R. P. 6: v In 1998 (1); v P 1996 (2); *v WI 1996 (1); v P 1998 (2)*

Atapattu, M. S. 23: v A 1992 (1); v NZ 1997 (3); v In 1997 (2) 1998 (1); v P 1996 (2); v Z 1997 (2); *v E 1998 (1); v SA 1997 (2); v WI 1996 (1); v NZ 1996 (1); v In 1990 (1) 1993 (1) 1997 (3); v P 1998 (2)*

Bandara, C. M. 1: v NZ 1997
Bandaratilleke, M. R. C. N. 4: v NZ 1997 (3); *v P 1998 (1)*

Chandana, U. D. U. 1: *v P 1998*

Dassanayake, P. B. 11: v SA 1993 (3); v WI 1993 (1); v P 1994 (2); *v In 1993 (3); v Z 1994 (2)*
de Alwis, R. G. 11: v A 1982 (1); v NZ 1983 (3); v P 1985 (2); *v A 1987 (1); v NZ 1982 (1); v In 1986 (3)*
de Mel, A. L. F. 17: v E 1981 (1); v A 1982 (1); v In 1985 (3); v P 1985 (3); *v E 1984 (1); v In 1982 (1) 1986 (1); v P 1981 (3) 1985 (3)*
de Silva, A. M. 3: v E 1992 (1); v In 1993 (2)
de Silva, D. S. 12: v E 1981 (1); v A 1982 (1); v NZ 1983 (3); *v E 1984 (1); v NZ 1982 (2); v In 1982 (1); v P 1981 (3)*
de Silva, E. A. R. 10: v In 1985 (1); v P 1985 (1); *v A 1989 (2); v NZ 1990 (3); v In 1986 (3)*
de Silva, G. R. A. 4: v E 1981 (1); *v In 1982 (1); v P 1981 (2)*
de Silva, K. S. C. 8: v In 1997 (1); v P 1996 (1); *v WI 1996 (2); v NZ 1996 (1); v In 1997 (1); v P 1998 (2)*
de Silva, P. A. 76: v E 1992 (1); v A 1992 (3); v SA 1993 (3); v WI 1993 (1); v NZ 1992 (2) 1997 (3); v In 1985 (3) 1993 (3) 1997 (2) 1998 (1); v P 1985 (3) 1994 (2) 1996 (2); v Z 1996 (2) 1997 (2); *v E 1984 (1) 1988 (1) 1991 (1) 1998 (1); v A 1987 (1) 1989 (2) 1995 (3); v NZ 1990 (3) 1994 (2); v WI 1996 (2); v NZ 1990 (3) 1994 (2) 1996 (2); v In 1986 (3) 1990 (1) 1993 (3) 1997 (3); v P 1985 (3) 1991 (3) 1995 (2) 1998 (1); v Z 1994 (3)*
de Silva, S. K. L. 3: *v In 1997 (3)*
Dharmasena, H. D. P. K. 20: v SA 1993 (2); v NZ 1997 (2); v P 1994 (2) 1996 (1); v Z 1996 (1); *v E 1998 (1); v A 1995 (2); v WI 1996 (2); v NZ 1996 (1); v In 1997 (2); v P 1995 (2); v Z 1994 (2)*
Dias, R. L. 20: v E 1981 (1); v A 1982 (1); v NZ 1983 (2) 1986 (1); v In 1985 (3); v P 1985 (1); *v E 1984 (1); v In 1982 (1) 1986 (3); v P 1981 (3) 1985 (3)*
Dunusinghe, C. I. 5: *v NZ 1994 (2); v P 1995 (3)*

Fernando, E. R. N. S. 5: v A 1982 (1); v NZ 1983 (2); *v NZ 1982 (2)*

Goonatillake, H. M. 5: v E 1981 (1); *v In 1982 (1); v P 1981 (3)*
Gunasekera, Y. 2: *v NZ 1982 (2)*
Gunawardene, D. A. 2: *v P 1998 (2)*
Guneratne, R. P. W. 1: v A 1982
Gurusinha, A. P. 41: v E 1992 (1); v A 1992 (3); v SA 1993 (1); v NZ 1986 (1) 1992 (2); v In 1993 (3); v P 1985 (2) 1994 (1); v Z 1996 (2); *v E 1991 (1); v A 1989 (2) 1995 (3); v NZ 1990 (3) 1994 (2); v In 1986 (3) 1990 (1); v P 1985 (1) 1991 (3) 1995 (3); v Z 1994 (3)*

Hathurusinghe, U. C. 26: v E 1992 (1); v A 1992 (3); v SA 1993 (3); v NZ 1992 (2); v In 1993 (3) 1998 (1); *v E 1991 (1); v A 1995 (3); v NZ 1990 (2); v P 1991 (3) 1995 (3) 1998 (1)*

Jayasekera, R. S. A. 1: *v P 1981*
Jayasuriya, S. T. 38: v E 1992 (1); v A 1992 (2); v SA 1993 (2); v WI 1993 (1); v NZ 1997 (3); v In 1993 (1) 1997 (2); v P 1994 (1) 1996 (2); v Z 1996 (2) 1997 (2); *v E 1991 (1) 1998 (1); v A 1995 (1); v SA 1997 (2); v WI 1996 (1); v NZ 1990 (2) 1996 (2); v In 1993 (1) 1997 (3); v P 1991 (3); v Z 1994 (1)*
Jayawardene, D. P. M. D. 9: v NZ 1997 (3); v In 1997 (2) 1998 (1); *v E 1998 (1); v P 1998 (2)*
Jeganathan, S. 2: *v NZ 1982 (2)*
John, V. B. 6: v NZ 1983 (3); *v E 1984 (1); v NZ 1982 (2)*
Jurangpathy, B. R. 2: v In 1985 (1); *v In 1986 (1)*

Kalpage, R. S. 11: v SA 1993 (1); v WI 1993 (1); v NZ 1997 (1); v In 1993 (1); v P 1994 (1) 1996 (1); *v In 1993 (3); v P 1998 (1); v Z 1994 (1)*

Kaluperuma, L. W. 2: v E 1981 (1); *v P 1981 (1)*

Kaluperuma, S. M. S. 4: v NZ 1983 (3); *v A 1987 (1)*

Kaluwitharana, R. S. 27: v A 1992 (2); v NZ 1997 (3); v In 1993 (1) 1997 (2) 1998 (1); v P 1996 (2); v Z 1996 (2) 1997 (2); *v E 1998 (1); A 1995 (3); v SA 1997 (2); v WI 1996 (2); v NZ 1996 (2); v P 1998 (2)*

Kuruppu, D. S. B. P. 4: v NZ 1986 (1); *v E 1988 (1) 1991 (1); v A 1987 (1)*

Kuruppuarachchi, A. K. 2: v NZ 1986 (1); v P 1985 (1)

Labrooy, G. F. 9: *v E 1988 (1); v A 1987 (1) 1989 (2); v NZ 1990 (3); v In 1986 (1) 1990 (1)*

Liyanage, D. K. 8: v A 1992 (2); v SA 1993 (1); v NZ 1992 (2); v In 1993 (2); *v In 1993 (1)*

Madugalle, R. S. 21: v E 1981 (1); v A 1982 (1); v NZ 1983 (3) 1986 (1); v In 1985 (3); *v E 1984 (1) 1988 (1); v A 1987 (1); v NZ 1982 (2); v In 1982 (1); v P 1981 (3) 1985 (3)*

Madurasinghe, A. W. R. 3: v A 1992 (1); *v E 1988 (1); v In 1990 (1)*

Mahanama, R. S. 52: v E 1992 (1); v A 1992 (3); v SA 1993 (1); v WI 1993 (1); v NZ 1986 (1) 1992 (2); v In 1993 (3) 1997 (2); v P 1985 (2) 1994 (2); v Z 1996 (2) 1997 (2); *v E 1991 (1); v A 1987 (1) 1989 (2) 1995 (2); v SA 1997 (2); v WI 1996 (2); v NZ 1990 (1) 1996 (2); v In 1990 (1) 1993 (3) 1997 (3); v P 1991 (2) 1995 (3); v Z 1994 (3)*

Mendis, L. R. D. 24: v E 1981 (1); v A 1982 (1); v NZ 1983 (3) 1986 (1); v In 1985 (3); v P 1985 (3); *v E 1984 (1) 1988 (1); v In 1982 (1) 1986 (3); v P 1981 (3) 1985 (3)*

Muralitharan, M. 42: v E 1992 (1); v A 1992 (2); v SA 1993 (3); v WI 1993 (1); v NZ 1992 (1) 1997 (3); v In 1993 (2) 1997 (2); v P 1994 (1) 1996 (1); v Z 1996 (2) 1997 (2); *v E 1998 (1); v A 1995 (2); v SA 1997 (2); v WI 1996 (2); v NZ 1994 (2) 1996 (2); v In 1993 (3) 1997 (2); v P 1995 (3); v Z 1994 (2)*

Perera, A. S. A. 1: *v E 1998*

Perera, P. D. R. L. 1: v In 1998

Pushpakumara, K. R. 18: v In 1997 (2); v P 1994 (1); v Z 1996 (1) 1997 (2); *v A 1995 (1); v SA 1997 (2); v WI 1996 (2); v NZ 1994 (2); v In 1997 (2); v P 1995 (1); v Z 1994 (2)*

Ramanayake, C. P. H. 18: v E 1992 (1); v A 1992 (3); v SA 1993 (2); v NZ 1992 (1); v In 1993 (1); *v E 1988 (1) 1991 (1); v A 1987 (1) 1989 (2); v NZ 1990 (3); v P 1991 (2)*

Ranasinghe, A. N. 2: *v In 1982 (1); v P 1981 (1)*

Ranatunga, A. 83: v E 1981 (1) 1992 (1); v A 1982 (1) 1992 (3); v SA 1993 (3); v WI 1993 (1); v NZ 1983 (3) 1986 (1) 1992 (2) 1997 (3); v In 1985 (3) 1993 (3) 1997 (2) 1998 (1); v P 1985 (3) 1994 (2) 1996 (2); v Z 1996 (2) 1997 (2); *v E 1984 (1) 1988 (1) 1998 (1); v A 1987 (1) 1989 (2) 1995 (2); v SA 1997 (2); v WI 1996 (2); v NZ 1990 (3) 1994 (2) 1996 (2); v In 1982 (1) 1986 (3) 1990 (1) 1993 (3) 1997 (3); v P 1981 (2) 1985 (3) 1991 (3) 1995 (3); v Z 1994 (3)*

Ranatunga, D. 2: *v A 1989 (2)*

Ranatunga, S. 9: v P 1994 (1); *v A 1995 (1); v WI 1996 (1); v NZ 1994 (2); v P 1995 (1); 1994 (3)*

Ratnayake, R. J. 23: v A 1982 (1); v NZ 1983 (1) 1986 (1); v In 1985 (3); v P 1985 (1); *v E 1991 (1); v A 1989 (1); v NZ 1982 (2) 1990 (3); v In 1986 (2) 1990 (1); v P 1985 (3) 1991 (3)*

Ratnayeke, J. R. 22: v NZ 1983 (2) 1986 (1); v P 1985 (3); *v E 1984 (1) 1988 (1); v A 1987 (1) 1989 (2); v NZ 1982 (2); v In 1982 (1) 1986 (3); v P 1981 (2) 1985 (3)*

Samarasekera, M. A. R. 4: *v E 1988 (1); v A 1989 (1); v In 1990 (1); v P 1991 (1)*

Samaraweera, D. P. 7: v WI 1993 (1); v P 1994 (1); *v NZ 1994 (2); v In 1993 (3)*

Senanayake, C. P. 3: *v NZ 1990 (3)*

Silva, K. J. 7: v In 1997 (1); v P 1996 (1); v Z 1996 (2) 1997 (1); *v A 1995 (1); v In 1997 (1)*

Silva, S. A. R. 9: v In 1985 (3); v P 1985 (1); *v E 1984 (1) 1988 (1); v NZ 1982 (1); v P 1985 (2)*

Tillekeratne, H. P. 56: v E 1992 (1); v A 1992 (1); v SA 1993 (3); v WI 1993 (1); v NZ 1992 (2) 1997 (2); v In 1993 (3) 1998 (1); v P 1994 (2) 1996 (2); v Z 1996 (2) 1997 (2); *v E 1991 (1) 1998 (1); v A 1989 (1) 1995 (3); v SA 1997 (2); v WI 1996 (1); v NZ 1990 (3) 1994 (2) 1996 (2); v In 1990 (1) 1993 (3) 1997 (3); v P 1991 (3) 1995 (3) 1998 (2); v Z 1994 (3)*

Upashantha, K. E. A. 1: v In 1998

Vaas, W. P. U. J. C. 28: v In 1997 (2) 1998 (1); v P 1994 (1) 1996 (2); v Z 1996 (2) 1997 (2); *v A 1995 (3); v SA 1997 (1); v NZ 1994 (2) 1996 (2); v In 1997 (3); v P 1995 (3) 1998 (1); v Z 1994 (3)*

Warnapura, B. 4: v E 1981 (1); *v In 1982 (1); v P 1981 (2)*
Warnaweera, K. P. J. 10: v E 1992 (1); v NZ 1992 (2); v In 1993 (3); v P 1985 (1) 1994 (1); *v NZ 1990 (1); v In 1990 (1)*
Weerasinghe, C. D. U. S. 1: v In 1985
Wettimuny, M. D. 2: *v NZ 1982 (2)*
Wettimuny, S. 23: v E 1981 (1); v A 1982 (1); v NZ 1983 (3); v In 1985 (3); v P 1985 (3); *v E 1984 (1); v NZ 1982 (2); v In 1986 (3); v P 1981 (3) 1985 (3)*
Wickremasinghe, A. G. D. 3: v NZ 1992 (2); *v A 1989 (1)*
Wickremasinghe, G. P. 33: v A 1992 (1); v SA 1993 (1); v WI 1993 (1); v NZ 1997 (3); v In 1993 (2); v P 1994 (1); *v E 1998 (1); v A 1995 (3); v SA 1997 (2); v NZ 1994 (2) 1996 (1); v In 1993 (3) 1997 (1); v P 1991 (3) 1995 (3) 1998 (2); v Z 1994 (2)*
Wijegunawardene, K. I. W. 2: *v E 1991 (1); v P 1991 (1)*
Wijesuriya, R. G. C. E. 4: *v P 1981 (1) 1985 (3)*
Wijetunge, P. K. 1: v SA 1993

Zoysa, D. N. T. 4: v P 1996 (1); *v SA 1997 (1); v NZ 1996 (2)*

ZIMBABWE

Number of Test cricketers: 40

Arnott, K. J. 4: v NZ 1992 (2); v In 1992 (1); *v In 1992 (1)*

Brain, D. H. 9: v NZ 1992 (1); v P 1994 (3); v SL 1994 (2); *v In 1992 (1); v P 1993 (2)*
Brandes, E. A. 9: v E 1996 (1); v NZ 1992 (1); v In 1992 (1); *v P 1995 (2); v In 1992 (1); v P 1993 (3)*
Briant, G. A. 1: *v In 1992*
Bruk-Jackson, G. K. 2: *v P 1993 (2)*
Burmester, M. G. 3: v NZ 1992 (2); v In 1992 (1)
Butchart, I. P. 1: v P 1994

Campbell, A. D. R. 33: v E 1996 (2); v SA 1995 (1); v NZ 1992 (2) 1997 (2); v In 1992 (1) 1998 (1); v P 1994 (3) 1997 (2); v SL 1994 (3); *v NZ 1995 (2) 1997 (2); v In 1992 (1); v P 1993 (3) 1996 (2) 1998 (2); v SL 1996 (2) 1997 (2)*
Carlisle, S. V. 6: v E 1996 (1); v P 1994 (3); *v NZ 1995 (2)*
Crocker, G. J. 3: v NZ 1992 (2); v In 1992 (1)

Dekker, M. H. 14: v E 1996 (1); v SA 1995 (1); v P 1994 (2); v SL 1994 (3); *v P 1993 (3) 1996 (2); v SL 1996 (2)*

Evans, C. N. 2: v In 1998 (1); *v SL 1996 (1)*

Flower, A. 33: v E 1996 (2); v SA 1995 (1); v NZ 1992 (2) 1997 (2); v In 1992 (1) 1998 (1); v P 1994 (3) 1997 (2); v SL 1994 (3); *v NZ 1995 (2) 1997 (2); v In 1992 (1); v P 1993 (3) 1996 (2) 1998 (2); v SL 1996 (2) 1997 (2)*
Flower, G. W. 32: v E 1996 (2); v SA 1995 (1); v NZ 1992 (2) 1997 (2); v In 1992 (1); v P 1994 (3) 1997 (2); v SL 1994 (3); *v NZ 1995 (2) 1997 (2); v In 1992 (1); v P 1993 (3) 1996 (2) 1998 (2); v SL 1996 (2) 1997 (2)*

Goodwin, M. W. 9: v In 1998 (1); v P 1997 (2); *v NZ 1997 (2); v P 1998 (2); v SL 1997 (2)*

Houghton, D. L. 22: v E 1996 (2); v SA 1995 (1); v NZ 1992 (2) 1997 (2); v In 1992 (1); v P 1994 (3); v SL 1994 (3); *v NZ 1995 (2); v In 1992 (1); v P 1993 (3) 1996 (2)*
Huckle, A. G. 8: v NZ 1997 (2); v In 1998 (1); v P 1997 (1); *v NZ 1997 (2); v P 1998 (1); v SL 1997 (1)*

James, W. R. 4: v SL 1994 (3); *v P 1993 (1)*
Jarvis, M. P. 5: v NZ 1992 (1); v SL 1994 (3)
Johnson, N. C. 3: v In 1998 (1); *v P 1998 (2)*

Lock, A. C. I. 1: v SA 1995

Madondo, T. N. 2: v P 1997 (2)
Matambanadzo, E. 2: v NZ 1997 (1); *v P 1996 (1)*
Mbangwa, M. 9: v In 1998 (1); v P 1997 (2); *v NZ 1997 (2); v P 1996 (1) 1998 (2); v SL 1997 (1)*

Olonga, H. K. 10: v E 1996 (2); v In 1998 (1); v P 1994 (1); *v NZ 1995 (1); v P 1996 (1) 1998 (2); v SL 1996 (2)*

Peall, S. G. 4: v SL 1994 (2); *v P 1993 (2)*
Pycroft, A. J. 3: v NZ 1992 (1); v In 1992 (1)

Ranchod, U. 1: *v In 1992*
Rennie, G. J. 10: v NZ 1997 (2); v In 1998 (1); v P 1997 (1); *v NZ 1997 (2); v P 1998 (2); v SL 1997 (1)*
Rennie, J. A. 4: v NZ 1997 (1); v SL 1994 (1); *v P 1993 (2)*

Shah, A. H. 3: v NZ 1992 (1); *v In 1992 (1); v SL 1996 (1)*
Strang, B. C. 13: v E 1996 (1); v SA 1995 (1); v NZ 1997 (2); v P 1994 (2) 1997 (1); *v NZ 1995 (2); v P 1996 (2); v SL 1996 (1) 1997 (1)*
Strang, P. A. 20: v E 1996 (2); v SA 1995 (1); v NZ 1997 (2); v P 1994 (3) 1997 (1); v SL 1994 (1); *v NZ 1995 (2) 1997 (2); v P 1996 (2); v SL 1996 (2) 1997 (2)*
Streak, H. H. 26: v E 1996 (2); v SA 1995 (1); v NZ 1997 (2); v In 1998 (1); v P 1994 (3) 1997 (2); v SL 1994 (3); *v NZ 1995 (2) 1997 (2); v P 1993 (3) 1998 (2); v SL 1996 (1) 1997 (2)*

Traicos, A. J. 4: v NZ 1992 (2); v In 1992 (1); *v In 1992 (1)*

Viljoen, D. P. 1: v P 1997

Waller, A. C. 2: v E 1996 (2)
Whittall, A. R. 9: v P 1997 (1); *v NZ 1997 (2); v P 1996 (1) 1998 (1); v SL 1996 (2) 1997 (2)*
Whittall, G. J. 25: v E 1996 (2); v SA 1995 (1); v NZ 1997 (2); v P 1994 (3) 1997 (2); v SL 1994 (3); *v NZ 1995 (2) 1997 (2); v P 1993 (3) 1996 (2); v SL 1996 (1) 1997 (1)*
Wishart, C. B. 11: v SA 1995 (1); v In 1998 (1); *v NZ 1995 (2); v P 1996 (2) 1998 (2); v SL 1996 (2) 1997 (2)*

TWO COUNTRIES

Fourteen cricketers have appeared for two countries in Test matches, namely:

Amir Elahi, *India and Pakistan.*
J. J. Ferris, *Australia and England.*
S. C. Guillen, *West Indies and NZ.*
Gul Mahomed, *India and Pakistan.*
F. Hearne, *England and South Africa.*
A. H. Kardar, *India and Pakistan.*
W. E. Midwinter, *England and Australia.*

F. Mitchell, *England and South Africa.*
W. L. Murdoch, *Australia and England.*
Nawab of Pataudi, sen., *England and India.*
A. J. Traicos, *South Africa and Zimbabwe.*
A. E. Trott, *Australia and England.*
K. C. Wessels, *Australia and South Africa.*
S. M. J. Woods, *Australia and England*

ENGLAND v REST OF THE WORLD

In 1970, owing to the cancellation of the South African tour to England, a series of matches was arranged, with the trappings of a full Test series, between England and the Rest of the World. It was played for the Guinness Trophy.

The following were awarded England caps for playing against the Rest of the World in that series, although the five matches played are now generally considered not to have rated as full Tests: D. L. Amiss (1), G. Boycott (2), D. J. Brown (2), M. C. Cowdrey (4), M. H. Denness (1), B. L. D'Oliveira (4), J. H. Edrich (2), K. W. R. Fletcher (4), A. W. Greig (3), R. Illingworth (5), A. Jones (1), A. P. E. Knott (5), P. Lever (1), B. W. Luckhurst (5), C. M. Old (2), P. J. Sharpe (1), K. Shuttleworth (1), J. A. Snow (3), D. L. Underwood (3), A. Ward (1), D. Wilson (2).

The following players represented the Rest of the World: E. J. Barlow (5), F. M. Engineer (2), L. R. Gibbs (4), Intikhab Alam (5), R. B. Kanhai (5), C. H. Lloyd (5), G. D. McKenzie (3), D. L. Murray (3), Mushtaq Mohammad (2), P. M. Pollock (1), R. G. Pollock (5), M. J. Procter (5), B. A. Richards (5), G. S. Sobers (5).

LIMITED-OVERS INTERNATIONAL CRICKETERS

The following players have appeared for Test-playing countries in limited-overs internationals but had not represented their countries in Test matches by August 21, 1999:

England C. J. Adams, M. W. Alleyne, I. D. Austin, A. D. Brown, D. R. Brown, M. V. Fleming, I. J. Gould, G. W. Humpage, T. E. Jesty, G. D. Lloyd, J. D. Love, M. A. Lynch, M. J. Smith, N. M. K. Smith, S. D. Udal, C. M. Wells, V. J. Wells.

Australia G. A. Bishop, M. J. Di Venuto, A. C. Gilchrist, S. F. Graf, I. J. Harvey, S. Lee, R. J. McCurdy, K. H. MacLeay, J. P. Maher, G. D. Porter, J. D. Siddons, A. M. Stuart, A. Symonds, G. S. Trimble, B. E. Young, A. K. Zesers.

South Africa D. M. Benkenstein, N. Boje, R. E. Bryson, D. J. Callaghan, D. N. Crookes, A. C. Dawson, A. J. Hall, L. J. Koen, P. V. Mpitsang, S. J. Palframan, C. E. B. Rice, M. J. R. Rindel, D. B. Rundle, T. G. Shaw, E. O. Simons, E. L. R. Stewart, R. Telemachus, C. J. P. G. van Zyl, H. S. Williams, M. Yachad.

West Indies H. A. G. Anthony, B. St A. Browne, H. R. Bryan, V. C. Drakes, R. S. Gabriel, R. C. Haynes, N. C. McGarrell, R. L. Powell, M. R. Pydanna, K. F. Semple, C. M. Tuckett, L. R. Williams.

New Zealand M. D. Bailey, B. R. Blair, C. E. Bulfin, P. G. Coman, M. W. Douglas, C. J. Drum, B. G. Hadlee, R. T. Hart, R. L. Hayes, L. G. Howell, B. J. McKechnie, E. B. McSweeney, J. P. Millmow, A. J. Penn, R. G. Petrie, R. B. Reid, S. J. Roberts, L. W. Stott, A. R. Tait, R. J. Webb, J. W. Wilson.

India S. V. Bahutule, A. C. Bedade, Bhupinder Singh, sen., G. Bose, V. B. Chandrasekhar, U. Chatterjee, N. Chopra, N. A. David, P. Dharmani, R. S. Ghai, H. H. Kanitkar, S. S. Karim, S. C. Khanna, G. K. Khoda, A. R. Khurasiya, S. P. Mukherjee, G. K. Pandey, J. V. Paranjpe, A. K. Patel, M. S. K. Prasad, Randhir Singh, S. S. Raul, R. Sanghvi, V. Shewag, L. R. Shukla, R. P. Singh, S. Somasunder, Sudhakar Rao, P. S. Vaidya.

Pakistan Aamer Hameed, Aamer Hanif, Abdur Razzaq, Akhtar Sarfraz, Arshad Pervez, Asif Mahmood, Ghulam Ali, Haafiz Shahid, Hasan Jamil, Iqbal Sikandar, Irfan Bhatti, Javed Qadir, Mahmood Hamid, Mansoor Rana, Manzoor Akhtar, Maqsood Rana, Masood Iqbal, Moin-ul-Atiq, Mujahid Jamshed, Naeem Ahmed, Naeem Ashraf, Naseer Malik, Parvez Mir, Saadat Ali, Saeed Azad, Sajid Ali, Sajjad Akbar, Salim Pervez, Shahid Anwar, Shakil Khan, Sohail Fazal, Tanvir Mehdi, Wasim Haider, Zafar Iqbal, Zahid Ahmed.

Sri Lanka H. Boteju, D. L. S. de Silva, G. N. de Silva, E. R. Fernando, T. L. Fernando, U. N. K. Fernando, J. C. Gamage, F. R. M. Goonatillake, A. A. W. Gunawardene, P. D. Heyn, S. A. Jayasinghe, S. H. U. Karnain, C. Mendis, A. M. N. Munasinghe, M. N. Nawaz, A. R. M. Opatha, S. P. Pasqual, K. G. Perera, H. S. M. Pieris, S. K. Ranasinghe, N. Ranatunga, N. L. K. Ratnayake, T. T. Samaraweera, A. P. B. Tennekoon, M. H. Tissera, D. M. Vonhagt, A. P. Weerakkody, S. R. de S. Wettimuny, R. P. A. H. Wickremaratne.

Zimbabwe G. B. Brent, R. D. Brown, K. M. Curran, S. G. Davies, K. G. Duers, E. A. Essop-Adam, D. A. G. Fletcher, J. G. Heron, V. R. Hogg, T. N. Madondo, G. C. Martin, M. A. Meman, M. L. Nkala, G. A. Paterson, G. E. Peckover, P. W. E. Rawson.

Shahid Afridi appeared for Pakistan in 66 limited-overs internationals before making his Test debut.

PRESIDENTS OF MCC SINCE 1946

1946	General Sir Ronald Adam, Bart	1970-71	Sir Cyril Hawker
1947	Captain Lord Cornwallis	1971-72	F. R. Brown
1948	Brig.-Gen. The Earl of Gowrie	1972-73	A. M. Crawley
1949	HRH The Duke of Edinburgh	1973-74	Lord Caccia
1950	Sir Pelham Warner	1974-75	HRH The Duke of Edinburgh
1951-52	W. Findlay	1975-76	C. G. A. Paris
1952-53	The Duke of Beaufort	1976-77	W. H. Webster
1953-54	The Earl of Rosebery	1977-78	D. G. Clark
1954-55	Viscount Cobham	1978-79	C. H. Palmer
1955-56	Field Marshal Earl Alexander of Tunis	1979-80	S. C. Griffith
		1980-81	P. B. H. May
1956-57	Viscount Monckton of Brenchley	1981-82	G. H. G. Doggart
1957-58	The Duke of Norfolk	1982-83	Sir Anthony Tuke
1958-59	Marshal of the RAF Viscount Portal of Hungerford	1983-84	A. H. A. Dibbs
		1984-85	F. G. Mann
1959-60	H. S. Altham	1985-86	J. G. W. Davies
1960-61	Sir Hubert Ashton	1986-87	M. C. Cowdrey
1961-62	Col. Sir William Worsley, Bart	1987-88	J. J. Warr
1962-63	Lt.-Col. Lord Nugent	1988-89	Field Marshal The Lord Bramall
1963-64	G. O. B. Allen	1989-90	The Hon. Sir Denys Roberts
1964-65	R. H. Twining	1990-91	The Rt Hon. The Lord Griffiths
1965-66	Lt-Gen. Sir Oliver Leese, Bart	1991-92	M. E. L. Melluish
1966-67	Sir Alec Douglas-Home	1992-94	D. R. W. Silk
1967-68	A. E. R. Gilligan	1994-96	The Hon. Sir Oliver Popplewell
1968-69	R. Aird	1996-98	A. C. D. Ingleby-Mackenzie
1969-70	M. J. C. Allom	1998-	A. R. Lewis

Since 1951, Presidents of MCC have taken office on October 1. Previously they took office immediately after the annual general meeting at the start of the season. Since 1992, Presidents have been eligible for two consecutive years of office.

BIRTHS AND DEATHS OF PAST CRICKETERS

Details of current first-class players are no longer listed in this section but may be found in the Register of Players on pages 201–219.

The qualifications for inclusion are as follows:

1. All players who have appeared in a Test match and are no longer playing first-class cricket.

2. All players who have appeared in a one-day international for a Test-match playing country and are no longer playing first-class cricket.

3. County players who appeared in 200 or more first-class matches during their careers, or 100 after the Second World War, and are no longer playing first-class cricket.

4. English county captains who captained their county in three seasons or more since 1890 and are no longer playing first-class cricket.

5. All *Wisden* Cricketers of the Year who are no longer playing first-class cricket, including the Public Schoolboys chosen for the 1918 and 1919 Almanacks. Cricketers of the Year are identified by the italic notation *CY* and year of appearance. A list of the Cricketers of the Year from 1889 to 2000 appears on pages 220–222.

6. Players or personalities not otherwise qualified who are thought to be of sufficient interest to merit inclusion.

Key to abbreviations and symbols

CU – Cambridge University, OU – Oxford University.

Australian states: NSW – New South Wales, Qld – Queensland, S. Aust. – South Australia, Tas. – Tasmania, Vic. – Victoria, W. Aust. – Western Australia.

Indian teams: Eur. – Europeans, Guj. – Gujarat, H'bad – Hyderabad, H. Pradesh – Himachal Pradesh, Ind. Rlwys – Indian Railways, Ind. Serv. – Indian Services, J/K – Jammu and Kashmir, Karn. – Karnataka (Mysore to 1972-73), M. Pradesh – Madhya Pradesh (Central India [C. Ind.] to 1939-40, Holkar to 1954-55, Madhya Bharat to 1956-57), M'tra – Maharashtra, Naw. – Nawanagar, Raja. – Rajasthan, S'tra – Saurashtra (West India [W. Ind.] to 1945-46, Kathiawar to 1949-50), S. Punjab – Southern Punjab (Patiala to 1958-59, Punjab since 1968-69), TC – Travancore-Cochin (Kerala since 1956-57), TN – Tamil Nadu (Madras to 1959-60), U. Pradesh – Uttar Pradesh (United Provinces [U. Prov.] to 1948-49), Vidarbha (CP & Berar to 1949-50, Madhya Pradesh to 1956-57).

New Zealand provinces: Auck. – Auckland, Cant. – Canterbury, C. Dist. – Central Districts, N. Dist. – Northern Districts, Wgtn – Wellington.

Pakistani teams: ADBP – Agricultural Development Bank of Pakistan, B'pur – Bahawalpur, Customs – Pakistan Customs, F'bad – Faisalabad, HBFC – House Building Finance Corporation, HBL – Habib Bank Ltd, I'bad – Islamabad, IDBP – Industrial Development Bank of Pakistan, Kar. – Karachi, KRL – Khan Research Laboratories, MCB – Muslim Commercial Bank, NBP – National Bank of Pakistan, NWFP – North-West Frontier Province, PACO – Pakistan Automobile Corporation, Pak. Rlwys – Pakistan Railways, Pak. Us – Pakistan Universities, PIA – Pakistan International Airlines, PNSC – Pakistan National Shipping Corporation, PWD – Public Works Department, R'pindi – Rawalpindi, UBL – United Bank Ltd, WAPDA – Water and Power Development Authority.

South African provinces: E. Prov. – Eastern Province, E. Tvl – Eastern Transvaal (Easterns since 1995-96), Griq. W. – Griqualand West, N. Tvl – Northern Transvaal, NE Tvl – North-Eastern Transvaal, OFS – Orange Free State (Free State [FS] since 1995-96), Rhod. – Rhodesia, Tvl – Transvaal (Gauteng since 1997-98), W. Prov. – Western Province, W. Tvl – Western Transvaal (North West since 1995-96).

Sri Lankan teams: Ant. – Antonians, Bloom. – Bloomfield Cricket and Athletic Club, BRC – Burgher Recreation Club, CCC – Colombo Cricket Club, Mor. – Moratuwa Sports Club, NCC – Nondescripts Cricket Club, Pan. – Panadura Sports Club, Seb. – Sebastianites, SLAF – Air Force, SSC – Sinhalese Sports Club, TU – Tamil Union Cricket and Athletic Club, Under-23 – Board Under-23 XI, WPC – Western Province (City), WPN – Western Province (North), WPS – Western Province (South).

West Indies islands: B'dos – Barbados, BG – British Guiana (Guyana since 1966), Comb. Is. – Combined Islands, Jam. – Jamaica, T/T – Trinidad & Tobago.

Zimbabwean teams: Mash. – Mashonaland, Mat. – Matabeleland, MCD – Mashonaland Country Districts, Under-24 – Mashonaland Under-24, Zimb. – Zimbabwe.

* *Denotes Test player.* ** *Denotes appeared for two countries. There is a list of Test players country by country from page 99.*
† *Denotes also played for team under its previous name.*

Aamer Hameed (Pak. Us, Lahore, Punjab & OU) b Oct. 18, 1954

Abberley, R. N. (Warwicks) b April 22, 1944

*a'Beckett, E. L. (Vic.) b Aug. 11, 1907, d June 2, 1989

*Abdul Kadir (Kar. & NBP) b May 10, 1944

*Abdul Qadir (HBL, Lahore & Punjab) b Sept. 15, 1955

*Abel, R. (Surrey; *CY 1890*) b Nov. 30, 1857, d Dec. 10, 1936

*Abid Ali, S. (H'bad) b Sept. 9, 1941

Abrahams, J. (Lancs) b July 21, 1952

*Absolom, C. A. (CU & Kent) b June 7, 1846, d July 30, 1889

Acfield, D. L. (CU & Essex) b July 24, 1947

*Achong, E. (T/T) b Feb. 16, 1904, d Aug. 29, 1986

Ackerman, H. M. (Border, NE Tvl, Northants, Natal & W. Prov.) b April 28, 1947

Adams, P. W. (Cheltenham & Sussex; *CY 1919*) b Sept. 5, 1900, d Sept. 28, 1962

*Adcock, N. A. T. (Tvl & Natal; *CY 1961*) b March 8, 1931

*Adhikari, H. R. (Guj., Baroda & Ind. Serv.) b July 31, 1919

*Afaq Hussain (Kar., Pak Us, PIA & PWD) b Dec. 31, 1939

Afford, J. A. (Notts) b May 12, 1964

*Aftab Baloch (PWD, Kar., Sind, NBP & PIA) b April 1, 1953

*Aftab Gul (Punjab U., Pak. Us & Lahore) b March 31, 1946

*Agha Saadat Ali (Pak. Us, Punjab, B'pur & Lahore) b June 21, 1929, d Oct. 26, 1995

*Agha Zahid (Pak Us, Punjab & HBL) b Jan. 7, 1953

*Agnew, J. P. (Leics; *CY 1988;* broadcaster) b April 4, 1960

*Ahangama, F. S. (SSC) b Sept. 14, 1959

Aird, R. (CU & Hants; Sec. MCC 1953-62, Pres. MCC 1968-69) b May 4, 1902, d Aug. 16, 1986

Aislabie, B. (Surrey, Hants, Kent & Sussex; Sec. MCC 1822-42) b Jan. 14, 1774, d June 2, 1842

Aitchison, Rev. J. K. (Scotland) b May 26, 1920, d Feb. 13, 1994

*Alabaster, J. C. (Otago) b July 11, 1930

Alcock, C. W. (Sec. Surrey CCC 1872-1907; Editor *Cricket* 1882-1907) b Dec. 2, 1842, d Feb. 26, 1907

Alderman, A. E. (Derbys) b Oct. 30, 1907, d June 4, 1990

*Alderman, T. M. (W. Aust., Kent & Glos; *CY 1982*) b June 12, 1956

*Alexander, F. C. M. (CU & Jam.) b Nov. 2, 1928

*Alexander, G. (Vic.) b April 22, 1851, d Nov. 6, 1930

*Alexander, H. H. (Vic.) b June 9, 1905, d April 15, 1993

Alikhan, R. I. (Sussex, PIA, Surrey & PNSC) b Dec. 28, 1962

*Alim-ud-Din (Rajputana, Guj., Sind, B'pur, Kar. & PWD) b Dec. 15, 1930

*Allan, D. W. (B'dos) b Nov. 5, 1937

*Allan, F. E. (Vic.) b Dec. 2, 1849, d Feb. 9, 1917

Allan, J. M. (OU, Kent, Warwicks & Scotland) b April 2, 1932

*Allan, P. J. (Qld) b Dec. 31, 1935

*Allcott, C. F. W. (Auck.) b Oct. 7, 1896, d Nov. 19, 1973

Allen, B. O. (CU & Glos) b Oct. 13, 1911, d May 1, 1981

*Allen, D. A. (Glos) b Oct. 29, 1935

*Allen, Sir George O. B. (CU & Middx; Pres. MCC 1963-64) b July 31, 1902, d Nov. 29, 1989

*Allen, I. B. A. (Windwards) b Oct. 6, 1965

Allen, M. H. J. (Northants & Derbys) b Jan. 7, 1933, d Oct. 6, 1995

*Allen, R. C. (NSW) b July 2, 1858, d May 2, 1952

Alletson, E. B. (Notts) b March 6, 1884, d July 5, 1963

Alley, W. E. (NSW & Som; Test umpire; *CY 1962*) b Feb. 3, 1919

*Allom, M. J. C. (CU & Surrey; Pres. MCC 1969-70) b March 23, 1906, d April 8, 1995

*Allott, P. J. W. (Lancs & Wgtn) b Sept. 14, 1956

Altham, H. S. CBE (OU, Surrey & Hants; historian; Pres. MCC 1959-60) b Nov. 30, 1888, d March 11, 1965

*Amalean, K. N. (SL) b April 7, 1965

*Amarnath, Lala (N. B.) (N. Ind., S. Punjab, Guj., Patiala, U. Pradesh & Ind. Rlwys) b Sept. 11, 1911

*Amarnath, M. (Punjab & Delhi; *CY 1984*) b Sept. 24, 1950

*Amarnath, S. (Punjab & Delhi) b Dec. 30, 1948

*Amar Singh, L. (Patiala, W. Ind. & Naw.) b Dec. 4, 1910, d May 20, 1940

*Amerasinghe, A. M. J. G. (Nomads & Ant.) b Feb. 2, 1954

*Ames, L. E. G. CBE (Kent; *CY 1929*) b Dec. 3, 1905, d Feb. 26, 1990

**Amir Elahi (Baroda, N. Ind., S. Punjab & B'pur) b Sept. 1, 1908, d Dec. 28, 1980

*Amiss, D. L. MBE (Warwicks; *CY 1975*) b April 7, 1943

Anderson, I. S. (Derbys & Boland) b April 24, 1960

*Anderson, J. H. (W. Prov.) b April 26, 1874, d March 11, 1926

*Anderson, R. W. (Cant., N. Dist., Otago & C. Dist.) b Oct. 2, 1948

*Anderson, W. M. (Cant.) b Oct. 8, 1919, d Dec. 21, 1979

*Andrew, K. V. (Northants) b Dec. 15, 1929

Andrew, S. J. W. (Hants & Essex) b Jan. 27, 1966

*Andrews, B. (Cant., C. Dist. & Otago) b April 4, 1945

*Andrews, T. J. E. (NSW) b Aug. 26, 1890, d Jan. 28, 1970

Andrews, W. H. R. (Som) b April 14, 1908, d Jan. 9, 1989

Angell, F. L. (Som) b June 29, 1922

*Anil Dalpat (Kar. & PIA) b Sept. 20, 1963

Anisur Rehman (Bangladesh) b March 1, 1971

*Ankola, S. A. (M'tra & †Mumbai) b March 1, 1968

Anthony, H. A. G. (Leewards & Glam) b Jan 16, 1971

*Anurasiri, S. D. (Pan. & WPS) b Feb. 25, 1966

*Anwar Hussain (N. Ind., Bombay, Sind & Kar.) b July 16, 1920

*Anwar Khan (Kar., Sind & NBP) b Dec. 24, 1955

*Appleyard, R. (Yorks; *CY 1952*) b June 27, 1924

*Apte, A. L. (Ind. Us, Bombay & Raja.) b Oct. 24, 1934

*Apte, M. L. (Bombay & Bengal) b Oct. 5, 1932

*Archer, A. G. (Worcs) b Dec. 6, 1871, d July 15, 1935

*Archer, K. A. (Qld) b Jan. 17, 1928

*Archer, R. G. (Qld) b Oct. 25, 1933

*Arif Butt (Lahore & Pak. Rlwys) b May 17, 1944

Arlott, John OBE (Writer & broadcaster) b Feb. 25, 1914, d Dec. 14, 1991

*Armitage, T. (Yorks) b April 25, 1848, d Sept. 21, 1922

Armstrong, N. F. (Leics) b Dec. 22, 1892, d Jan. 19, 1990

*Armstrong, W. W. (Vic.; *CY 1903*) b May 22, 1879, d July 13, 1947

Arnold, A. P. (Cant. & Northants) b Oct. 16, 1926

*Arnold, E. G. (Worcs) b Nov. 7, 1876, d Oct. 25, 1942

*Arnold, G. G. (Surrey & Sussex; *CY 1972*) b Sept. 3, 1944

*Arnold, J. (Hants) b Nov. 30, 1907, d April 4, 1984

*Arnott, K. J. (MCD) b March 8, 1961

Arnott, T. (Glam) b Feb. 16, 1902, d Feb. 2, 1975

*Arshad Ayub (H'bad) b Aug. 2, 1958

Arshad Pervez (Sargodha, Lahore, Pak. Us, Servis Ind., HBL & Punjab) b Oct. 1, 1952

*Arun, B. (TN) b Dec. 14, 1962

*Arun Lal (Delhi & Bengal) b Aug. 1 1955

*Asgarali, N. (T/T) b Dec. 28, 1920

Ashdown, W. H. (Kent) b Dec. 27, 1898, d Sept. 15, 1979

*Ashley, W. H. (W. Prov.) b Feb. 10, 1862, d July 14, 1930

*Ashraf Ali (Lahore, Income Tax, Pak. Us, Pak. Rlwys & UBL) b April 22, 1958

Ashton, C. T. (CU & Essex) b Feb. 19, 1901, d Oct. 31, 1942

Ashton, G. (CU & Worcs) b Sept. 27, 1896, d Feb. 6, 1981

Ashton, Sir Hubert (CU & Essex; *CY 1922*; Pres. MCC 1960-61) b Feb. 13, 1898, d June 17, 1979

Asif Din, M. (Warwicks) b Sept. 21, 1960

*Asif Iqbal (H'bad, Kar., Kent, PIA & NBP; *CY 1968*) b June 6, 1943

*Asif Masood (Lahore, Punjab U. & PIA) b Jan. 23, 1946

Aslett, D. G. (Kent) b Feb. 12, 1958

*Astill, W. E. (Leics; *CY 1933*) b March 1, 1888, d Feb. 10, 1948

Athar Zaidi (Test umpire) b Nov. 12, 1946

Ather Ali Khan (Bangladesh) b Feb. 10, 1962

*Athey, C. W. J. (Yorks, Glos & Sussex) b Sept. 27, 1957

Atkinson, C. R. M. CBE (Som) b July 23, 1931, d June 25, 1991

*Atkinson, D. St E. (B'dos & T/T) b Aug. 9, 1926

*Atkinson, E. St E. (B'dos) b Nov. 6, 1927, d May 29, 1998

Atkinson, G. (Som & Lancs) b March 29, 1938

*Attewell, W. (Notts; *CY 1892*) b June 12, 1861, d June 11, 1927

Austin, Sir Harold B. G. (B'dos) b July 15, 1877, d July 27, 1943

*Austin, R. A. (Jam.) b Sept. 5, 1954

Avery, A. V. (Essex) b Dec. 19, 1914, d May 10, 1997

Aylward, James (Hants & All-England) b 1741, *buried* Dec. 27, 1827

*Azad, K. (Delhi) b Jan. 2, 1959

*Azeem Hafeez (Kar., Allied Bank & PIA) b July 29, 1963

*Azhar Khan (Lahore, Punjab, Pak. Us, PIA & HBL) b Sept. 7, 1955

*Azmat Rana (B'pur, PIA, Punjab, Lahore & MCB) b Nov. 3, 1951

*Bacchus, S. F. A. F. (Guyana, W. Prov. & Border) b Jan. 31, 1954

*Bacher, Dr A. (Tvl; Managing Director UCBSA) b May 24, 1942

*Badcock, C. L. (Tas. & S. Aust.) b April 10, 1914, d Dec. 13, 1982

*Badcock, F. T. (Wgtn & Otago) b Aug. 9, 1897, d Sept. 19, 1982

Baggallay, R. R. C. (Derbys) b May 4, 1884, d Dec. 12, 1975

*Baichan, L. (Guyana) b May 12, 1946

*Baig, A. A. (H'bad, OU & Som) b March 19, 1939

Bailey, J. (Hants) b April 6, 1908, d Feb. 9, 1988

Bailey, J. A. (Essex & OU; Sec. MCC 1974-87) b June 22, 1930

*Bailey, T. E. CBE (Essex & CU; *CY 1950*) b Dec. 3, 1923

Baillie, A. W. (Sec. MCC 1858-63) b June 22, 1830, d May 10, 1867

Bainbridge, H. W. (Surrey, CU & Warwicks) b Oct. 29, 1862, d March 3, 1940

Bainbridge, P. (Glos & Durham; *CY 1986*) b April 16, 1958

*Bairstow, D. L. (Yorks & Griq. W.) b Sept. 1, 1951, d Jan. 5, 1998

Baker, C. S. (Warwicks) b Jan. 5, 1883, d Dec. 16, 1976

Baker, G. R. (Yorks & Lancs) b April 18, 1862, d Dec. 6, 1938

*Bakewell, A. H. (Northants; *CY 1934*) b Nov. 2, 1908, d Jan. 23, 1983

*Balaskas, X. C. (Griq. W., Border, W. Prov., Tvl & NE Tvl) b Oct. 15, 1910, d May 12, 1994

*Balderstone, J. C. (Yorks & Leics) b Nov. 16, 1940

Baldry, D. O. (Middx & Hants) b Dec. 26, 1931

*Banerjee, S. A. (Bengal & Bihar) b Nov. 1, 1919, d Sept. 14, 1992

*Banerjee, S. N. (Bengal, Naw., Bihar & M. Pradesh) b Oct. 3, 1911, d Oct. 14, 1980

*Bannerman, A. C. (NSW) b March 22, 1854, d Sept. 19, 1924

*Bannerman, Charles (NSW) b July 23, 1851, d Aug. 20, 1930

Bannister, J. D. (Warwicks) b Aug. 23, 1930

*Baqa Jilani, M. (N. Ind.) b July 20, 1911, d July 2, 1941

*Barber, R. T. (Wgton & C. Dist.) b June 3, 1925

*Barber, R. W. (Lancs, CU & Warwicks; *CY 1967*) b Sept. 26, 1935

*Barber, W. (Yorks) b April 18, 1901, d Sept. 10, 1968

Barclay, J. R. T. (Sussex & OFS) b Jan. 22, 1954

*Bardsley, W. (NSW; *CY 1910*) b Dec. 6, 1882, d Jan. 20, 1954

Barker, G. (Essex) b July 6, 1931

Barling, T. H. (Surrey) b Sept. 1, 1906, d Jan. 2, 1993

*Barlow, E. J. (Tvl, E. Prov., W. Prov., Derbys & Boland) b Aug. 12, 1940

Barlow, G. D. (Middx) b March 26, 1950

*Barlow, R. G. (Lancs) b May 28, 1851, d July 31, 1919

Barnard, H. M. (Hants) b July 18, 1933

*Barnes, S. F. (Warwicks & Lancs; *CY 1910*) b April 19, 1873, d Dec. 26, 1967

*Barnes, S. G. (NSW) b June 5, 1916, d Dec. 16, 1973

*Barnes, W. (Notts; *CY 1890*) b May 27, 1852, d March 24, 1899

*Barnett, B. A. (Vic.) b March 23, 1908, d June 29, 1979

*Barnett, C. J. (Glos; *CY 1937*) b July 3, 1910, d May 28, 1993

Baroda, Maharaja of (Manager, Ind. in Eng. 1959) b April 2, 1930, d Sept. 1, 1988

*Barratt, F. (Notts) b April 12, 1894, d Jan. 29, 1947

*Barrett, A. G. (Jam.) b April 5, 1942

*Barrett, Dr J. E. (Vic.) b Oct. 15, 1866, d Feb. 6, 1916

Barrick, D. W. (Northants) b April 28, 1926

*Barrington, K. F. (Surrey; *CY 1960*) b Nov. 24, 1930, d March 14, 1981

Barron, W. (Lancs & Northants) b Oct. 26, 1917

*Barrow, I. (Jam.) b Jan. 6, 1911, d April 2, 1979

*Bartlett, E. L. (B'dos) b March 10, 1906, d Dec. 21, 1976

*Bartlett, G. A. (C. Dist. & Cant.) b Feb. 3, 1941

Bartlett, H. T. (CU, Surrey & Sussex; *CY 1939*) b Oct. 7, 1914, d June 26, 1968

Bartley, T. J. (Test umpire) b March 19, 1908, d April 2, 1964

Barton, M. R. (OU & Surrey) b Oct. 14, 1914

*Barton, P. T. (Wgtn) b Oct. 9, 1935

*Barton, V. A. (Kent & Hants) b Oct. 6, 1867, d March 23, 1906

Barwick, S. R. (Glam) b Sept. 6, 1960

Base, S. J. (W. Prov., Glam, Derbys, Boland & Border) b Jan. 2, 1960

*Basit Ali (Kar. & UBL) b Dec. 13, 1970

Bates, D. L. (Sussex) b May 10, 1933

Bates, L. A. (Warwicks) b March 20, 1895, d March 11, 1971

*Bates, W. (Yorks) b Nov. 19, 1855, d Jan. 8, 1900

Bates, W. E. (Yorks & Glam) b March 5, 1884, d Jan. 17, 1957

*Baumgartner, H. V. (OFS & Tvl) b Nov. 17, 1883, d April 8, 1938

*Bean, G. (Notts & Sussex) b March 7, 1864, d March 16, 1923

Bear, M. J. (Essex & Cant.) b Feb. 23, 1934

*Beard, D. D. (C. Dist. & N. Dist.) b Jan. 14, 1920, d July 15, 1982

*Beard, G. R. (NSW) b Aug. 19, 1950

Beauclerk, Lord Frederick (Middx, Surrey & MCC) b May 8, 1773, d April 22, 1850

*Beaumont, R. (Tvl) b Feb. 4, 1884, d May 25, 1958

Beck, J. E. F. (Wgtn) b Aug. 1, 1934

*Bedi, B. S. (N. Punjab, Delhi & Northants) b Sept. 25, 1946

*Bedser, Sir Alec V. (Surrey; *CY 1947*) b July 4, 1918

Bedser, E. A. (Surrey) b July 4, 1918

Beet, G. (Derbys; Test umpire) b April 24, 1886, d Dec. 13, 1946

*Begbie, D. W. (Tvl) b Dec. 12, 1914

Beldham, W. (Hambledon & Surrey) b Feb. 5, 1766, d Feb. 20, 1862

*Bell, A. J. (W. Prov. & Rhod.) b April 15, 1906, d Aug. 1, 1985

Bell, R. V. (Middx & Sussex) b Jan. 7, 1931, d Oct. 26, 1989

*Bell, W. (Cant.) b Sept. 5, 1931

Bellamy, B. W. (Northants) b April 22, 1891, d Dec. 22, 1985

*Benaud, J. (NSW) b May 11, 1944

*Benaud, R. OBE (NSW; *CY 1962;* broadcaster) b Oct. 6, 1930

*Benjamin, W. K. M. (Leewards, Leics & Hants) b Dec. 31, 1964

Bencraft, Sir H. W. Russell (Hants) b March 4, 1858, d Dec. 25, 1943

Bennett, D. (Middx) b Dec. 18, 1933

*Bennett, M. J. (NSW) b Oct. 6, 1956

*Benson, M. R. (Kent) b July 6, 1958

Berry, L. G. (Leics) b April 28, 1906, d Feb. 5, 1985

*Berry, R. (Lancs, Worcs & Derbys) b Jan. 29, 1926

Berry, Scyld (Writer) b April 28, 1954

*Best, C. A. (B'dos & W. Prov.) b May 14, 1959

Bestwick, W. (Derbys) b Feb. 24, 1875, d May 2, 1938

*Betancourt, N. (T/T) b June 4, 1887, d Oct. 12, 1947

Bhalekar, R. B. (M'tra) b Feb. 17, 1952

*Bhandari, P. (Delhi & Bengal) b Nov. 27, 1935

*Bhat, A. R. (Karn.) b April 16, 1958

Bhupinder Singh (Punjab) b April 1, 1965

Bick, D. A. (Middx) b Feb. 22, 1936, d Jan. 13, 1992

Bicknell, D. J. (Surrey) b June 24, 1967

*Bilby, G. P. (Wgtn) b May 7, 1941

*Binks, J. G. (Yorks; *CY 1969*) b Oct. 5, 1935

*Binns, A. P. (Jam.) b July 24, 1929

*Binny, R. M. H. (Karn.) b July 19, 1955

Birch, J. D. (Notts) b June 18, 1955

Bird, H. D. MBE (Yorks & Leics; Test umpire) b April 19, 1933

*Bird, M. C. (Lancs & Surrey) b March 25, 1888, d Dec. 9, 1933

Bird, R. E. (Worcs) b April 4, 1915, d Feb. 20, 1985

*Birkenshaw, J. (Yorks, Leics & Worcs) b Nov. 13, 1940

*Birkett, L. S. (B'dos, BG & T/T) b April 14, 1904, d Jan. 16, 1998

Bishop, G. A. (S. Aust.) b Feb. 25, 1960

*Bisset, Sir Murray (M.) (W. Prov.) b April 14, 1876, d Oct. 24, 1931

*Bissett, G. F. (Griq. W., W. Prov. & Tvl) b Nov. 5, 1905, d Nov. 14, 1965

Bissex, M. (Glos) b Sept. 28, 1944

*Blackham, J. McC. (Vic; *CY 1891*) b May 11, 1854, d Dec. 28, 1932

*Blackie, D. D. (Vic.) b April 5, 1882, d April 18, 1955

*Blain, T. E. (C. Dist.) b Feb. 17, 1962

Blair, B. R. (Otago) b Dec. 27, 1957

*Blair, R. W. (Wgtn & C. Dist.) b June 23, 1932

*Blanckenberg, J. M. (W. Prov. & Natal) b Dec. 31, 1892, dead

*Bland, K. C. (Rhod., E. Prov. & OFS; *CY 1966*) b April 5, 1938

Blenkiron, W. (Warwicks) b July 21, 1942

*Bligh, Hon. Ivo (I. F. W.) (8th Earl of Darnley) (CU & Kent; Pres. MCC 1900) b March 13, 1859, d April 10, 1927

Blofeld, H. C. (CU; writer & broadcaster) b Sept. 23, 1939

*Blunt, R. C. MBE (Cant. & Otago; *CY 1928*) b Nov. 3, 1900, d June 22, 1966

*Blythe, C. (Kent; *CY 1904*) b May 30, 1879, d Nov. 8, 1917

*Board, J. H. (Glos) b Feb. 23, 1867, d April 15, 1924

*Bock, E. G. (Griq. W., Tvl & W. Prov.) b Sept. 17, 1908, d Sept. 5, 1961

*Bolton, B. A. (Cant. & Wgtn) b May 31, 1935

*Bolus, J. B. (Yorks, Notts & Derbys) b Jan. 31, 1934

*Bond, G. E. (W. Prov.) b April 5, 1909, d Aug. 27, 1965

Bond, J. D. (Lancs & Notts; *CY 1971*) b May 6, 1932

*Bonnor, G. J. (Vic. & NSW) b Feb. 25, 1855, d June 27, 1912

*Boock, S. L. (Otago & Cant.) b Sept. 20, 1951

Boon, T. J. (Leics) b Nov. 1, 1961

*Booth, B. C. MBE (NSW) b Oct. 19, 1933

Booth, B. J. (Lancs & Leics) b Dec. 3, 1935

Booth, C. (CU & Hants) b May 11, 1842, d July 14, 1926

*Booth, M. W. (Yorks; *CY 1914*) b Dec. 10, 1886, d July 1, 1916

Booth, R. (Yorks & Worcs) b Oct. 1, 1926

*Borde, C. G. (Baroda & M'tra) b July 21, 1933

*Border, A. R. (NSW, Glos, Qld & Essex; *CY 1982*) b July 27, 1955

Bore, M. K. (Yorks & Notts) b June 2, 1947

Borrington, A. J. (Derbys) b Dec. 8, 1948

*Bosanquet, B. J. T. (OU & Middx; *CY 1905*) b Oct. 13, 1877, d Oct. 12, 1936

*Bosch, T. (N. Tvl & Natal) b March 14, 1966

Bose, G. (Bengal) b May 20, 1947

Boshier, B. S. (Leics) b March 6, 1932

*Botham, I. T. OBE (Som, Worcs, Durham & Qld; *CY 1978*) b Nov. 24, 1955

*Botten, J. T. (NE Tvl & N. Tvl) b June 21, 1938

Boucher, J. C. (Ireland) b Dec. 22, 1910, d Dec. 25, 1995

Bowden, J. (Derbys) b Oct. 8, 1884, d March 1, 1958

*Bowden, M. P. (Surrey & Tvl) b Nov. 1, 1865, d Feb. 19, 1892

Bowell, A. (Hants) b April 27, 1880, d Aug. 28, 1957

*Bowes, W. E. (Yorks; *CY 1932*) b July 25, 1908, d Sept. 5, 1987

*Bowley, E. H. (Sussex & Auck.; *CY 1930*) b June 6, 1890, d July 9, 1974

Bowley, F. L. (Worcs) b Nov. 9 1873, d May 31, 1943

Box, T. (Sussex) b Feb. 7, 1808, d July 12, 1876

*Boyce, K. D. (B'dos & Essex; *CY 1974*) b Oct. 11, 1943, d Oct. 11, 1996

*Boycott, G. OBE (Yorks & N. Tvl; *CY 1965*) b Oct. 21, 1940

Boyd-Moss, R. J. (CU & Northants) b Dec. 16, 1959

Boyes, G. S. (Hants) b March 31, 1899, d Feb. 11, 1973

*Boyle, H. F. (Vic.) b Dec. 10, 1847, d Nov. 21, 1907

*Bracewell, B. P. (C. Dist., Otago & N. Dist.) b Sept. 14, 1959

*Bracewell, J. G. (Otago & Auck.) b April 15, 1958

*Bradburn, W. P. (N. Dist.) b Nov. 24, 1938

*Bradley, W. M. (Kent) b Jan. 2, 1875, d June 19, 1944

*Bradman, Sir Donald G. (NSW & S. Aust.; *CY 1931*) b Aug. 27, 1908

Brain, B. M. (Worcs & Glos) b Sept. 13, 1940

*Brain, D. H. (Mash.) b Oct. 4, 1964

Brann, G. (Sussex) b April 23, 1865, d June 14, 1954

*Brann, W. H. (E. Prov.) b April 4, 1899, d Sept. 2, 1953

Brassington, A. J. (Glos) b Aug. 9, 1954

*Braund, L. C. (Surrey & Som; *CY 1902*) b Oct. 18, 1875, d Dec. 23, 1955

Bray, C. (Essex) b April 6, 1898, d Sept. 12, 1993

Brayshaw, I. J. (W. Aust.) b Jan. 14, 1942

Breakwell, D. (Northants & Som) b July 2, 1948

*Brearley, J. M. OBE (CU & Middx; *CY 1977*) b April 28, 1942

*Brearley, W. (Lancs; *CY 1909*) b March 11, 1876, d Jan. 13, 1937

*Brennan, D. V. (Yorks) b Feb. 10, 1920, d Jan. 9, 1985

*Briant, G. A. (Mash.) b April 11, 1969

Bridges, J. J. (Som) b June 28, 1887, d Sept. 26, 1966

Brierley, T. L. (Glam, Lancs & Canada) b June 15, 1910, d Jan. 7, 1989

Briers, N. E. (Leics; *CY 1993*) b Jan. 15, 1955

*Briggs, John (Lancs; *CY 1889*) b Oct. 3, 1862, d Jan. 11, 1902

*Bright, R. J. (Vic.) b July 13, 1954

*Briscoe, A. W. (Tvl) b Feb. 6, 1911, d April 22, 1941

*Broad, B. C. (Glos & Notts) b Sept. 29, 1957

Broadbent, R. G. (Worcs) b June 21, 1924, d April 26, 1993

*Brockwell, W. (Surrey & Kimberley; *CY 1895*) b Jan. 21, 1865, d June 30, 1935

Broderick, V. (Northants) b Aug. 17, 1920

*Bromfield, H. D. (W. Prov.) b June 26, 1932

*Bromley, E. H. (W. Aust. & Vic.) b Sept. 2, 1912, d Feb. 1, 1967

*Bromley-Davenport, H. R. (CU, Eur., & Middx) b Aug. 18, 1870, d May 23, 1954

*Brookes, D. (Northants; *CY 1957*) b Oct. 29, 1915

Brookes, Wilfrid H. (Editor of *Wisden* 1936-39) b Dec. 5, 1894, d May 28, 1955

Brown, A. (Kent) b Oct. 17, 1935

Brown, A. D. (Surrey) b Feb. 11, 1970

Brown, A. S. (Glos) b June 24, 1936

*Brown, D. J. (Warwicks) b Jan. 30, 1942

*Brown, F. R. MBE (CU, Surrey & Northants; *CY 1933; Pres. MCC 1971-72*) b Dec. 16, 1910, d July 24, 1991

*Brown, G. (Hants) b Oct. 6, 1887, d Dec. 3, 1964

Brown, J. MBE (Scotland) b Sept. 24, 1931

*Brown, J. T. (Yorks; *CY 1895*) b Aug. 20, 1869, d Nov. 4, 1904

Brown, K. R. (Middx) b March 18, 1963

*Brown, L. S. (Tvl, NE Tvl & Rhod.) b Nov. 24, 1910, d Sept. 1, 1983

Brown, R. D. (Mash.) b March 11, 1951

Brown, S. M. (Middx) b Dec. 8, 1917, d Dec. 28, 1987

*Brown, V. R. (Cant. & Auck.) b Nov. 3, 1959

*Brown, W. A. (NSW & Qld; *CY 1939*) b July 31, 1912

Brown, W. C. (Northants) b Nov. 13, 1900, d Jan. 20, 1986

Browne, B. St A. (Guyana) b Sept. 16, 1967

*Browne, C. R. (B'dos & BG) b Oct. 8, 1890, d Jan. 12, 1964

*Bruce, W. (Vic.) b May 22, 1864, d Aug. 3, 1925

*Bruk-Jackson, G. K. (MCD & Mash.) b April 25, 1969

Bryan, G. J. CBE (Kent) b Dec. 29, 1902, d April 4, 1991

Bryan, J. L. (CU & Kent; *CY 1922*) b May 26, 1896, d April 23, 1985

Bryan, R. T. (Kent) b July 30, 1898, d July 27, 1970

*Buckenham, C. P. (Essex) b Jan. 16, 1876, d Feb. 23, 1937

Bucknor, S. A. (Test umpire) b May 31, 1946

Buckston, R. H. R. (Derbys) b Oct. 10, 1908, d May 16, 1967

Budd, E. H. (Middx & All-England) b Feb. 23, 1785, d March 29, 1875

Budd, W. L. (Hants; Test umpire) b Oct. 25, 1913, d Aug. 23, 1986

Bull, F. G. (Essex; *CY 1898*) b April 2, 1875, d Sept. 16, 1910

Buller, J. S. MBE (Yorks & Worcs; Test umpire) b Aug. 23, 1909, d Aug. 7, 1970

Burden, M. D. (Hants) b Oct. 4, 1930, d Nov. 9, 1987

*Burge, P. J. (Qld; *CY 1965;* ICC referee) b May 17, 1932

*Burger, C. G. de V. (Natal) b July 12, 1935

Burgess, G. I. (Som) b May 5, 1943

Burgess, M. G. (Auck.) b July 12, 1944

*Burke, C. (Auck.) b March 22, 1914, d Aug. 4, 1997

*Burke, J. W. (NSW; *CY 1957*) b June 12, 1930, d Feb. 2, 1979

*Burke, S. F. (NE Tvl & OFS) b March 11, 1934

*Burki, Javed (Pak. Us, OU, Punjab, Lahore, Kar., R'pindi & NWFP; ICC referee) b May 8, 1938

*Burmester, M. G. (Mash.) b Jan. 24, 1968

*Burn, K. E. (Tas.) b Sept. 17, 1862, d July 20, 1956

Burns, N. D. (Essex, W. Prov., Som) b Sept. 19, 1965

Burns, W. B. (Worcs) b Aug. 29, 1883, d July 7, 1916

Burnup, C. J. (CU & Kent; *CY 1903*) b Nov. 21, 1875, d April 5, 1960

Burrough, H. D. (Som) b Feb. 6, 1909, d April 9, 1994

Burrows, R. D. (Worcs) b June 6, 1871, d Feb. 12, 1943

Burton, D. C. F. (Yorks) b Sept. 13, 1887, d Sept. 24, 1971

*Burton, F. J. (Vic. & NSW) b Nov. 2, 1865, d Aug. 25, 1929

*Burtt, T. B. (Cant.) b Jan. 22, 1915, d May 24, 1988

Buse, H. T. F. (Som) b Aug. 5, 1910, d Feb. 23, 1992

Buss, A. (Sussex) b Sept. 1, 1939

Buss, M. A. (Sussex & OFS) b Jan. 24, 1944

*Butchart, I. P. (MCD) b May 9, 1960

*Butcher, A. R. (Surrey & Glam; *CY 1991*) b Jan. 7, 1954

*Butcher, B. F. (Guyana; *CY 1970*) b Sept. 3, 1933

Butcher, I. P. (Leics & Glos) b July 1, 1962

*Butcher, R. O. (Middx, B'dos & Tas.) b Oct. 14, 1953

*Butler, H. J. (Notts) b March 12, 1913, d July 17, 1991

*Butler, L. (T/T) b Feb. 9, 1929

*Butt, H. R. (Sussex) b Dec. 27, 1865, d Dec. 21, 1928

*Butterfield, L. A. (Cant.) b Aug. 29, 1913, d July 7, 1999

*Butts, C. G. (Guyana) b July 8, 1957

Buxton, I. R. (Derbys) b April 17, 1938

*Buys, I. D. (W. Prov.) b Feb. 3, 1895, dead

*Bynoe, M. R. (B'dos) b Feb. 23, 1941

Byrne, J. F. (Warwicks) b June 19, 1871, d May 10, 1954

Cadman, S. (Derbys) b Jan. 29, 1877, d May 6, 1952

Caesar, Julius (Surrey & All-England) b March 25, 1830, d March 6, 1878

Caffyn, W. (Surrey & NSW) b Feb. 2, 1828, d Aug. 28, 1919

Caine, C. Stewart (Editor of *Wisden* 1926-33) b Oct. 28, 1861, d April 15, 1933

*Cairns, B. L. (C. Dist., Otago & N. Dist.) b Oct. 10, 1949

Calder, H. L. (Cranleigh; *CY 1918*) b Jan. 24, 1901, d Sept. 15, 1995

*Callaway, S. T. (NSW & Cant.) b Feb. 6, 1868, d Nov. 25, 1923

*Callen, I. W. (Vic. & Boland) b May 2, 1955

*Calthorpe, Hon. F. S. Gough- (CU, Sussex & Warwicks) b May 27, 1892, d Nov. 19, 1935

*Camacho, G. S. (Guyana; Chief Exec. WICB) b Oct. 15, 1945

*Cameron, F. J. (Jam.) b June 22, 1923, d Feb. 1995

*Cameron, F. J. MBE (Otago) b June 1, 1932

*Cameron, H. B. (Tvl, E. Prov. & W. Prov.; *CY 1936*) b July 5, 1905, d Nov. 2, 1935

*Cameron, J. H. (CU, Jam. & Som) b April 8, 1914

*Campbell, G. D. (Tas.) b March 10, 1964

*Campbell, T. (Tvl) b Feb. 9, 1882, d Oct. 5, 1924

Cannings, V. H. D. (Warwicks & Hants) b April 3, 1919

*Capel, D. J. (Northants & E. Prov.) b Feb. 6, 1963

Cardus, Sir Neville (Writer) b April 3, 1888, d Feb. 27, 1975

*Carew, G. M. (B'dos) b June 4, 1910, d Dec. 9, 1974

*Carew, M. C. (T/T) b Sept. 15, 1937

*Carkeek, W. (Vic.) b Oct. 17, 1878, d Feb. 20, 1937

*Carlisle, S. V. (Zimb. U-24) b May 10, 1972

*Carlson, P. H. (Qld) b Aug. 8, 1951

*Carlstein, P. R. (OFS, Tvl, Natal & Rhod.) b Oct. 28, 1938

*Carpenter, D. (Glos) b Sept. 12, 1935

Carpenter, H. A. (Essex) b July 12, 1869, d Dec. 12, 1933

Carpenter, R. (Cambs & Utd England XI) b Nov. 18, 1830, d July 13, 1901

*Carr, A. W. (Notts; *CY 1923*) b May 21, 1893, d Feb. 7, 1963

*Carr, D. B. OBE (OU & Derbys; *CY 1960*; Sec. TCCB 1974-86) b Dec. 28, 1926

*Carr, D. W. (Kent; *CY 1910*) b March 17, 1872, d March 23, 1950

Carr, J. D. (OU & Middx) b June 15, 1963

Carrick, P. (Yorks & E. Prov.) b July 16, 1952, d Jan. 11, 2000

*Carter, C. P. (Natal & Tvl) b April 23, 1881, d Nov. 8, 1952

*Carter, H. (NSW) b March 15, 1878, d June 8, 1948

Carter, R. G. M. (Worcs) b July 11, 1937

*Cartwright, T. W. (Warwicks, Som & Glam) b July 22, 1935

Case, C. C. C. (Som) b Sept. 7, 1895, d Nov. 11, 1969

Cass, G. R. (Essex, Worcs & Tas.) b April 23, 1940

Catt, A. W. (Kent & W. Prov.) b Oct. 2, 1933

*Catterall, R. H. (Tvl, Rhod., Natal & OFS; *CY 1925*) b July 10, 1900, d Jan. 3, 1961

*Cave, H. B. (Wgtn & C. Dist.) b Oct. 10, 1922, d Sept. 15, 1989

*Chalk, F. G. H. (OU & Kent) b Sept. 7, 1910, d Feb. 17, 1943

*Challenor, G. (B'dos) b June 28, 1888, d July 30, 1947

Chamberlain, W. R. F. (Northants; Chairman TCCB 1990-94) b April 13, 1925

*Chandrasekhar, B. S. (†Karn.; *CY 1972*) b May 17, 1945

Chandrasekhar, V. B. (Goa) b Aug. 21, 1961

*Chang, H. S. (Jam.) b July 22, 1952

Chaplin, H. P. (Sussex & Eur.) b March 1, 1883, d March 6, 1970

*Chapman, A. P. F. (Uppingham, OU & Kent; *CY 1919*) b Sept. 3, 1900, d Sept. 16, 1961

*Chapman, H. W. (Natal) b June 30, 1890, d Dec. 1, 1941

Chapman, J. (Derbys) b March 11, 1877, d Aug. 12, 1956

*Chappell, G. S. MBE (S. Aust., Som & Qld; *CY 1973*) b Aug. 7, 1948

*Chappell, I. M. (S. Aust. & Lancs; *CY 1976*; broadcaster) b Sept. 26, 1943

*Chappell, T. M. (S. Aust., W. Aust. & NSW) b Oct. 21, 1952

*Chapple, M. E. (Cant. & C. Dist.) b July 25, 1930, d July 31, 1985

Charlesworth, C. (Warwicks) b Feb. 12, 1875, d June 15, 1953

*Charlton, P. C. (NSW) b April 9, 1867, d Sept. 30, 1954

*Charlwood, H. R. J. (Sussex) b Dec. 19, 1846, d June 6, 1888

*Chatfield, E. J. MBE (Wgtn) b July 3, 1950

*Chatterton, W. (Derbys) b Dec. 27, 1861, d March 19, 1913

*Chauhan, C. P. S. (M'tra & Delhi) b July 21, 1947

*Cheetham, J. E. (W. Prov.) b May 26, 1920, d Aug. 21, 1980

Chester, F. (Worcs; Test umpire) b Jan. 20, 1895, d April 8, 1957

*Chevalier, G. A. (W. Prov.) b March 9, 1937

*Childs, J. H. (Glos & Essex; *CY 1987*) b Aug. 15, 1951

*Chipperfield, A. G. (NSW) b Nov. 17, 1905, d July 29, 1987

Chisholm, R. H. E. (Scotland) b May 22, 1927

*Chowdhury, N. R. (Bihar & Bengal) b May 23, 1923, d Dec. 14, 1979

*Christiani, C. M. (BG) b Oct. 28, 1913, d April 4, 1938

*Christiani, R. J. (BG) b July 19, 1920

*Christopherson, S. (Kent; Pres. MCC 1939-45) b Nov. 11, 1861, d April 6, 1949

*Christy, J. A. J. (Tvl & Qld) b Dec. 12, 1904, d Feb. 1, 1971

*Chubb, G. W. A. (Border & Tvl) b April 12, 1911, d Aug. 28, 1982

Clark, D. G. (Kent; Pres. MCC 1977-78) b Jan. 27, 1919

Clark, E. A. (Middx) b April 15, 1937

*Clark, E. W. (Northants) b Aug. 9, 1902, d April 28, 1982

Clark, T. H. (Surrey) b Oct. 5, 1924, d June 14, 1981

*Clark, W. M. (W. Aust.) b Sept. 19, 1953
*Clarke, Dr C. B. OBE (B'dos, Northants & Essex) b April 7, 1918, d Oct. 14, 1993
Clarke, R. W. (Northants) b April 22, 1924, d Aug. 3, 1981
*Clarke, S. T. (B'dos, Surrey, Tvl, OFS & N. Tvl) b Dec. 11, 1954, d Dec. 4, 1999
Clarke, William (Notts; founded All-England XI & Trent Bridge ground) b Dec. 24, 1798, d Aug. 25, 1856
Clarkson, A. (Yorks & Som) b Sept. 5, 1939
*Clay, J. C. (Glam) b March 18, 1898, d Aug. 12, 1973
Clay, J. D. (Notts) b Oct. 15, 1924
Clayton, G. (Lancs & Som) b Feb. 3, 1938
*Cleverley, D. C. (Auck.) b Dec. 23, 1909
Clift, Patrick B. (Rhod., Leics & Natal) b July 14, 1953, d Sept. 2, 1996
Clift, Phil B. (Glam) b Sept. 3, 1918
Clinton, G. S. (Kent, Surrey & Zimb.-Rhod.) b May 5, 1953
*Close, D. B. CBE (Yorks & Som; *CY 1964*) b Feb. 24, 1931
Cobb, R. A. (Leics & N. Tvl) b May 18, 1961
Cobham, 10th Visct (Hon. C. J. Lyttelton) (Worcs; Pres. MCC 1954) b Aug. 8, 1909, d March 20, 1977
*Cochrane, J. A. K. (Tvl & Griq. W.) b July 15, 1909, d June 15, 1987
Coe, S. (Leics) b June 3, 1873, d Nov. 4, 1955
*Coen, S. K. (OFS, W. Prov., Tvl & Border) b Oct. 14, 1902, d Jan. 28, 1967
*Colah, S. M. H. (Bombay, W. Ind. & Naw.) b Sept. 22, 1902, d Sept. 11, 1950
Colchin, Robert ("Long Robin") (Kent & All-England) b Nov. 1713, d April 1750
*Coldwell, L. J. (Worcs) b Jan. 10, 1933, d Aug. 6, 1996
*Colley, D. J. (NSW) b March 15, 1947
*Collinge, R. O. (C. Dist., Wgtn & N. Dist.) b April 2, 1946
Collins, A. E. J. (Clifton Coll. & Royal Engineers) b Aug. 18, 1885, d Nov. 11, 1914
Collins, G. C. (Kent) b Sept. 21, 1889, d Jan. 23, 1949
*Collins, H. L. (NSW) b Jan. 21, 1888, d May 28, 1959
Collins, R. (Lancs) b March 10, 1934
*Colquhoun, I. A. (C. Dist.) b June 8, 1924
Coman, P. G. (Cant.) b April 13, 1943
*Commaille, J. M. M. (W. Prov., Natal, OFS & Griq. W.) b Feb. 21, 1883, d July 28, 1956
*Compton, D. C. S. CBE (Middx & Holkar; *CY 1939*) b May 23, 1918, d April 23, 1997
Compton, L. H. (Middx) b Sept. 12, 1912, d Dec. 27, 1984
*Coney, J. V. MBE (Wgtn; *CY 1984*) b June 21, 1952

*Congdon, B. E. OBE (C. Dist., Wgtn, Otago & Cant.; *CY 1974*) b Feb. 11, 1938
*Coningham, A. (NSW & Qld) b July 14, 1863, d June 13, 1939
*Connolly, A. N. (Vic. & Middx) b June 29, 1939
Connor, C. A. (Hants) b March 24, 1961
Constable, B. (Surrey) b Feb. 19, 1921, d May 15, 1997
Constant, D. J. (Kent & Leics; Test umpire) b Nov. 9, 1941
*Constantine, L. N. (later Baron Constantine of Maraval and Nelson) (T/T & B'dos; *CY 1940*) b Sept. 21, 1902, d July 1, 1971
Constantine, L. S. (T/T) b May 25, 1874, d Jan. 5, 1942
*Contractor, N. J. (Guj. & Ind. Rlwys) b March 7, 1934
*Conyngham, D. P. (Natal, Tvl & W. Prov.) b May 10, 1897, d July 7, 1979
*Cook, C. (Glos) b Aug. 23, 1921, d Sept. 4, 1996
*Cook, F. J. (E. Prov.) b 1870, d Nov. 30, 1914
*Cook, G. (Northants & E. Prov.) b Oct. 9, 1951
Cook, L. W. (Lancs) b March 28, 1885, d Dec. 2, 1933
*Cook, N. G. B. (Leics & Northants) b June 17, 1956
*Cook, S. J. (Tvl & Som; *CY 1990*) b July 31, 1953
Cook, T. E. R. (Sussex) b Jan. 5, 1901, d Jan. 15, 1950
*Cooper, A. H. C. (Tvl) b Sept. 2, 1893, d July 18, 1963
*Cooper, B. B. (Middx, Kent & Vic.) b March 15, 1844, d Aug. 7, 1914
Cooper, E. (Worcs) b Nov. 30, 1915, d Oct. 29, 1968
Cooper, F. S. Ashley- (Historian) b March 22, 1877, d Jan. 31, 1932
Cooper, G. C. (Sussex) b Sept. 2, 1936
Cooper, K. E. (Notts & Glos) b Dec. 27, 1957
*Cooper, W. H. (Vic.) b Sept. 11, 1849, d April 5, 1939
Cooray, B. C. (Test umpire) b May 15, 1941
*Cope, G. A. (Yorks) b Feb. 23, 1947
*Copson, W. H. (Derbys; *CY 1937*) b April 27, 1908, d Sept. 14, 1971
Cordle, A. E. (Glam) b Sept. 21, 1940
*Corling, G. E. (NSW) b July 13, 1941
Cornford, J. H. (Sussex) b Dec. 9, 1911, d June 17, 1985
*Cornford, W. L. (Sussex) b Dec. 25, 1900, d Feb. 6, 1964
Cornwallis, W. S. (later 2nd Baron) (Kent) b March 14, 1892, d Jan. 4, 1982
Corrall, P. (Leics) b July 16, 1906, d Feb. 1994
Corran, A. J. (OU & Notts) b Nov. 25, 1936

*Cosier, G. J. (Vic., S. Aust. & Qld) b April 25, 1953

*Cottam, J. T. (NSW) b Sept. 5, 1867, d Jan. 30, 1897

*Cottam, R. M. H. (Hants & Northants) b Oct. 16, 1944

*Cotter, A. (NSW) b Dec. 3, 1884, d Oct. 31, 1917

Cotton, J. (Notts & Leics) b Nov. 7, 1940

*Coulthard, G. (Vic.; Test umpire) b Aug. 1, 1856, d Oct. 22, 1883

*Coventry, Hon. C. J. (Worcs) b Feb. 26, 1867, d June 2, 1929

*Cowans, N. G. (Middx & Hants) b April 17, 1961

*Cowdrey, C. S. (Kent & Glam) b Oct. 20, 1957

Cowdrey, G. R. (Kent) b June 27, 1964

*Cowdrey, M. C. (later Baron Cowdrey of Tonbridge) (OU & Kent; *CY 1956;* Pres. MCC 1986-87) b Dec. 24, 1932

Cowie, D. B. (Test umpire) b Dec. 2, 1946

*Cowie, J. OBE (Auck.) b March 30, 1912, d June 3, 1994

Cowley, N. G. (Hants & Glam) b March 1, 1953

*Cowper, R. M. (Vic. & W. Aust.) b Oct. 5, 1940

Cox, A. L. (Northants) b July 22, 1907, d Nov. 13, 1986

Cox, G., jun. (Sussex) b Aug. 23, 1911, d March 30, 1985

Cox, G., sen. (Sussex) b Nov. 29, 1873, d March 24, 1949

*Cox, J. L. (Natal) b June 28, 1886, d July 4, 1971

*Coxon, A. (Yorks) b Jan. 18, 1916

Cozier, Tony (Writer & broadcaster) b July 10, 1940

*Craig, I. D. (NSW) b June 12, 1935

Cranfield, L. M. (Glos) b Aug. 29, 1909, d Nov. 18, 1993

Cranmer, P. (Warwicks & Eur.) b Sept. 10, 1914, d May 29, 1994

*Cranston, J. (Glos) b Jan. 9, 1859, d Dec. 10, 1904

*Cranston, K. (Lancs) b Oct. 20, 1917

*Crapp, J. F. (Glos; Test umpire) b Oct. 14, 1912, d Feb. 15, 1981

*Crawford, J. N. (Surrey, S. Aust., Wgtn & Otago; *CY 1907*) b Dec. 1, 1886, d May 2, 1963

*Crawford, P. (NSW) b Aug. 3, 1933

Crawford, V. F. S. (Surrey & Leics) b April 11, 1879, d Aug. 21, 1922

Crawley, A. M. MBE (OU & Kent; Pres. MCC 1972-73) b April 10, 1908, d Nov. 3, 1993

Cray, S. J. (Essex) b May 29, 1921

Creese, W. L. (Hants) b Dec. 27, 1907, d March 9, 1974

*Cresswell, G. F. (Wgtn & C. Dist.) b March 22, 1915, d Jan. 10, 1966

*Cripps, G. (W. Prov.) b Oct. 19, 1865, d July 27, 1943

*Crisp, R. J. (Rhod., W. Prov. & Worcs) b May 28, 1911, d March 3, 1994

*Crocker, G. J. (MCD) b May 16, 1962

*Croft, C. E. H. (Guyana & Lancs) b March 15, 1953

*Cromb, I. B. (Cant.) b June 25, 1905, d March 6, 1984

Croom, A. J. (Warwicks) b May 23, 1896, d Aug. 16, 1947

*Crowe, J. J. (S. Aust. & Auck.) b Sept. 14, 1958

*Crowe, M. D. MBE (Auck., C. Dist., Som & Wgtn; *CY 1985*) b Sept. 22, 1962

Crump, B. S. (Northants) b April 25, 1938

Cuffe, J. A. (NSW & Worcs) b June 26, 1880, d May 16, 1931

Cumbes, J. (Lancs, Surrey, Worcs & Warwicks) b May 4, 1944

*Cummins, A. C. (B'dos & Durham) b May 7, 1966

*Cunis, R. S. (Auck. & N. Dist.) b Jan. 5, 1941

*Curnow, S. H. (Tvl) b Dec. 16, 1907, d July 28, 1986

*Curtis, T. S. (Worcs & CU) b Jan. 15, 1960

Cutmore, J. A. (Essex) b Dec. 28, 1898, d Nov. 30, 1985

*Cuttell, W. R. (Lancs; *CY 1898*) b Sept. 13, 1864, d Dec. 9, 1929

*Da Costa, O. C. (Jam.) b Sept. 11, 1907, d Oct. 1, 1936

Dacre, C. C. (Auck. & Glos) b May 15, 1899, d Nov. 2, 1975

Daft, H. B. (Notts) b April 5, 1866, d Jan. 12, 1945

Daft, Richard (Notts & All-England) b Nov. 2, 1835, d July 18, 1900

Dalmeny, Lord (later 6th Earl of Rosebery) (Middx, Surrey & Scotland) b Jan. 8, 1882, d May 30, 1974

Dalmiya, J. (President ICC 1997-) b May 30, 1940

*Dalton, E. L. (Natal) b Dec. 2, 1906, d June 3, 1981

*Dani, H. T. (M'tra & Ind. Serv.) b May 24, 1933, d Dec. 19, 1999

*Daniel, W. W. (B'dos, Middx & W. Aust.) b Jan. 16, 1956

*D'Arcy, J. W. (Cant., Wgtn & Otago) b April 23, 1936

Dare, R. (Hants) b Nov. 26, 1921

*Darling, J. (S. Aust.; *CY 1900*) b Nov. 21, 1870, d Jan. 2, 1946

*Darling, L. S. (Vic.) b Aug. 14, 1909, d June 24, 1992

*Darling, W. M. (S. Aust.) b May 1, 1957

Davey, J. (Glos) b Sept. 4, 1944

*Davidson, A. K. OBE (NSW; *CY 1962*) b June 14, 1929

Davidson, G. (Derbys) b June 29, 1866, d Feb. 8, 1899

Davies, Dai (Glam; Test umpire) b Aug. 26, 1896, d July 16, 1976

Davies, Emrys (Glam; Test umpire) b June 27, 1904, d Nov. 10, 1975

*Davies, E. Q. (E. Prov., Tvl & NE Tvl) b Aug. 26, 1909, d Nov. 11, 1976

Davies, H. G. (Glam) b April 23, 1912, d Sept. 4, 1993

Davies, J. G. W. OBE (CU & Kent; Pres. MCC 1985-86) b Sept. 10, 1911, d Nov. 5, 1992

Davies, S. G. (Mat.) b May 12, 1977

Davies, T. (Glam) b Oct. 25, 1960

*Davis, B. A. (T/T & Glam) b May 2, 1940

*Davis, C. A. (T/T) b Jan. 1, 1944

Davis, E. (Northants) b March 8, 1922

*Davis, I. C. (NSW & Qld) b June 25, 1953

Davis, P. (Northants) b May 24, 1915

Davis, R. C. (Glam) b Jan. 1, 1946

Davis, R. P. (Kent, Warwicks & Glos) b March 18, 1966

*Davis, S. P. (Vic.) b Nov. 8, 1959

*Davis, W. W. (Windwards, Glam, Tas., Northants & Wgtn) b Sept. 18, 1958

Davison, B. F. (Rhod., Leics, Tas. & Glos) b Dec. 21, 1946

Davison, I. J. (Notts) b Oct. 4, 1937

Dawkes, G. O. (Leics & Derbys) b July 19, 1920

*Dawson, E. W. (CU & Leics) b Feb. 13, 1904, d June 4, 1979

*Dawson, O. C. (Natal & Border) b Sept. 1, 1919

Day, A. P. (Kent; *CY 1910*) b April 10, 1885, d Jan. 22, 1969

*de Alwis, R. G. (SSC) b Feb. 15, 1959

*Dean, H. (Lancs) b Aug. 13, 1884, d March 12, 1957

Dean, J., sen. (Sussex) b Jan. 4, 1816, d Dec. 25, 1881

*Deane, H. G. (Natal & Tvl) b July 21, 1895, d Oct. 21, 1939

*De Caires, F. I. (BG) b May 12, 1909, d Feb. 2, 1959

*De Courcy, J. H. (NSW) b April 18, 1927

*de Groen, R. P. (Auck. & N. Dist.) b Aug. 5, 1962

*Dekker, M. H. (Mat.) b Dec. 5, 1969

*Dell, A. R. (Qld) b Aug. 6, 1947

*de Mel, A. L. F. (SL) b May 9, 1959

*Dempster, C. S. (Wgtn, Leics, Scotland & Warwicks; *CY 1932*) b Nov. 15, 1903, d Feb. 14, 1974

*Dempster, E. W. (Wgtn) b Jan. 25, 1925

*Denness, M. H. (Scotland, Kent & Essex; *CY 1975*; ICC referee) b Dec. 1, 1940

Dennett, G. (Glos) b April 27, 1880, d Sept. 14, 1937

Denning, P. W. (Som) b Dec. 16, 1949

Dennis, F. (Yorks) b June 11, 1907

Dennis, S. J. (Yorks, OFS & Glam) b Oct. 18, 1960

*Denton, D. (Yorks; *CY 1906*) b July 4, 1874, d Feb. 16, 1950

Deodhar, D. B. (M'tra) b Jan. 14, 1892, d Aug. 24, 1993

*Depeiza, C. C. (B'dos) b Oct. 10, 1928, d Nov. 10, 1995

*Desai, R. B. (Bombay) b June 20, 1939, d April 27, 1998

*de Silva, A. M. (CCC) b Dec. 3, 1963

de Silva, D. L. S. (SL) b Nov. 17, 1956, d April 12, 1980

*de Silva, D. S. (Bloom.) b June 11, 1942

*de Silva, E. A. R. (NCC & Galle) b March 28, 1956

de Silva, G. N. (SL) b March 12, 1955

*de Silva, G. R. A. (SL) b Dec. 12, 1952

de Smidt, R. W. (W. Prov.) b Nov. 24, 1883, d Aug. 3, 1986

De Trafford, C. E. (Lancs & Leics) b May 21, 1864, d Nov. 11, 1951

Devereux, L. N. (Middx, Worcs & Glam) b Oct. 20, 1931

*de Villiers, P. S. (Northerns, N. Tvl & Kent) b Oct. 13, 1964

*Dewdney, C. T. (Jam.) b Oct. 23, 1933

*Dewes, J. G. (CU & Middx) b Oct. 11, 1926

Dews, G. (Worcs) b June 5, 1921

*Dexter, E. R. (CU & Sussex; *CY 1961*) b May 15, 1935

*Dhanraj, R. (T/T) b Feb. 6, 1969

*Dias, R. L. (CCC) b Oct. 18, 1952

*Dick, A. E. (Otago & Wgtn) b Oct. 10, 1936

*Dickinson, G. R. (Otago) b March 11, 1903, d March 17, 1978

*Dilawar Hussain (C. Ind. and U. Prov.) b March 19, 1907, d Aug. 26, 1967

*Dilley, G. R. (Kent, Natal & Worcs) b May 18, 1959

Dillon, E. W. (Kent & OU) b Feb. 15, 1881, d April 20, 1941

*Dipper, A. E. (Glos) b Nov. 9, 1885, d Nov. 7, 1945

*Divecha, R. V. (Bombay, OU, Northants, Vidarbha & S'tra) b Oct. 18, 1927

Diver, A. J. D. (Cambs., Middx, Notts & All-England) b June 6, 1824, d March 25, 1876

Diver, E. J. (Surrey & Warwicks) b March 20, 1861, d Dec. 27, 1924

Dixon, A. L. (Kent) b Nov. 27, 1933

*Dixon, C. D. (Tvl) b Feb. 12, 1891, d Sept. 9, 1969

Dixon, J. A. (Notts) b May 27, 1861, d June 8, 1931

Dodds, T. C. (Essex) b May 29, 1919

*Dodemaide, A. I. C. (Vic. & Sussex) b Oct. 5, 1963

*Doggart, G. H. G. OBE (CU & Sussex; Pres. MCC 1981-82) b July 18, 1925

*D'Oliveira, B. L. OBE (Worcs; *CY 1967*) b Oct. 4, 1931

D'Oliveira, D. B. (Worcs) b Oct. 19, 1960

*Dollery, H. E. (Warwicks & Wgtn; *CY 1952*) b Oct. 14, 1914, d Jan. 20, 1987

*Dolphin, A. (Yorks) b Dec. 24, 1885, d Oct. 23, 1942

*Donnan, H. (NSW) b Nov. 12, 1864, d Aug. 13, 1956

*Donnelly, M. P. (Wgtn, Cant., OU, Middx & Warwicks; *CY 1948*) b Oct. 17, 1917, d Oct. 22, 1999

*Dooland, B. (S. Aust. & Notts; *CY 1955*) b Nov. 1, 1923, d Sept. 8, 1980

Dorrinton, W. (Kent & All-England) b April 29, 1809, d Nov. 8, 1848

Dorset, 3rd Duke of (Kent) b March 24, 1745, d July 19, 1799

*Doshi, D. R. (Bengal, Notts, Warwicks & S'tra) b Dec. 22, 1947

*Douglas, J. W. H. T. (Essex; *CY 1915*) b Sept. 3, 1882, d Dec. 19, 1930

Dovey, R. R. (Kent) b July 18, 1920, d Dec. 27, 1974

*Dowe, U. G. (Jam.) b March 29, 1949

*Dower, R. R. (E. Prov.) b June 4, 1876, d Sept. 15, 1964

*Dowling, G. T. OBE (Cant.; ICC referee) b March 4, 1937

*Downton, P. R. (Kent & Middx) b April 4, 1957

*Draper, R. G. (E. Prov. & Griq. W.) b Dec. 24, 1926

Dredge, C. H. (Som) b Aug. 4, 1954

*Druce, N. F. (CU & Surrey; *CY 1898*) b Jan. 1, 1875, d Oct. 27, 1954

Drybrough, C. D. (OU & Middx) b Aug. 31, 1938

*D'Souza, A. (Kar., Peshawar & PIA) b Jan. 17, 1939

*Ducat, A. (Surrey; *CY 1920*) b Feb. 16, 1886, d July 23, 1942

*Duckworth, C. A. R. (Natal & Rhod.) b March 22, 1933

*Duckworth, G. (Lancs; *CY 1929*) b May 9, 1901, d Jan. 5, 1966

Dudleston, B. (Leics, Glos & Rhod.; Test umpire) b July 16, 1945

Duers, K. G. (Mash.) b June 30, 1960

*Duff, R. A. (NSW) b Aug. 17, 1878, d Dec. 13, 1911

*Dujon, P. J. L. (Jam.; *CY 1989*) b May 28, 1956

*Duleepsinhji, K. S. (CU & Sussex; *CY 1930*) b June 13, 1905, d Dec. 5, 1959

*Dumbrill, R. (Natal & Tvl) b Nov. 19, 1938

*Duminy, J. P. (OU, W. Prov. & Tvl) b Dec. 16, 1897, d Jan. 31, 1980

*Duncan, J. R. F. (Qld & Vic.) b March 25, 1944

*Dunell, O. R. (E. Prov.) b July 15, 1856, d Oct. 21, 1929

Dunne, R. S. (Otago; Test umpire) b April 22, 1943

*Dunning, J. A. (Otago & OU) b Feb. 6, 1903, d June 24, 1971

*Dunusinghe, C. I. (Ant. & NCC) b Oct. 19, 1970

*Du Preez, J. H. (Rhod. & Zimb.) b Nov. 14, 1942

*Durani, S. A. (S'tra, Guj. & Raja.) b Dec. 11, 1934

*Durston, F. J. (Middx) b July 11, 1893, d April 8, 1965

*Du Toit, J. F. (SA) b April 5, 1868, d July 10, 1909

Dye, J. C. J. (Kent, Northants & E. Prov.) b July 24, 1942

*Dyer, D. V. (Natal) b May 2, 1914, d June 18, 1990

*Dyer, G. C. (NSW) b March 16, 1959

*Dymock, G. (Qld) b July 21, 1945

Dyson, A. H. (Glam) b July 10, 1905, d June 7, 1978

Dyson, Jack (Lancs) b July 8, 1934

*Dyson, John (NSW) b June 11, 1954

*Eady, C. J. (Tas.) b Oct. 29, 1870, d Dec. 20, 1945

Eagar, E. D. R. (OU, Glos & Hants) b Dec. 8, 1917, d Sept. 13, 1977

Ealham, A. G. E. (Kent) b Aug. 30, 1944

East, D. E. (Essex) b July 27, 1959

East, R. E. (Essex) b June 20, 1947

Eastman, L. C. (Essex & Otago) b June 3, 1897, d April 17, 1941

*Eastwood, K. H. (Vic.) b Nov. 23, 1935

*Ebeling, H. I. MBE (Vic.) b Jan. 1, 1905, d Jan. 12, 1980

Ebrahim, Ahmed (ICC referee) b Dec. 2, 1937

Eckersley, P. T. (Lancs) b July 2, 1904, d Aug. 13, 1940

*Edgar, B. A. (Wgtn) b Nov. 23, 1956

Edinburgh, HRH Duke of (Pres. MCC 1948-49, 1974-75) b June 10, 1921

Edmeades, B. E. A. (Essex) b Sept. 17, 1941

*Edmonds, P. H. (CU, Middx & E. Prov.) b March 8, 1951

Edrich, B. R. (Kent & Glam) b Aug. 18, 1922

Edrich, E. H. (Lancs) b March 27, 1914, d July 9, 1993

Edrich, G. A. (Lancs) b July 13, 1918

*Edrich, J. H. MBE (Surrey; *CY 1966*) b June 21, 1937

*Edrich, W. J. (Middx; *CY 1940*) b March 26, 1916, d April 24, 1986

*Edwards, G. N. (C. Dist.) b May 27, 1955

*Edwards, J. D. (Vic.) b June 12, 1862, d July 31, 1911

Edwards, M. J. (CU & Surrey) b March 1, 1940

*Edwards, R. (W. Aust. & NSW) b Dec. 1, 1942

*Edwards, R. M. (B'dos) b June 3, 1940

*Edwards, W. J. (W. Aust.) b Dec. 23, 1949

*Ehtesham-ud-Din (Lahore, Punjab, PIA, NBP & UBL) b Sept. 4, 1950

*Elgie, M. K. (Natal) b March 6, 1933

Elliott, C. S. MBE (Derbys; Test umpire) b April 24, 1912

*Elliott, Harold (Lancs; Test umpire) b June 15, 1904, d April 15, 1969

Elliott, Harry (Derbys) b Nov. 2, 1891, d Feb. 2, 1976

*Ellison, R. M. (Kent & Tas.; *CY 1986*) b Sept. 21, 1959

*Emburey, J. E. (Middx, W. Prov. & Northants; *CY 1984*) b Aug. 20, 1952

*Emery, R. W. G. (Auck. & Cant.) b March 28, 1915, d Dec. 18, 1982

*Emery, S. H. (NSW) b Oct. 16, 1885, d Jan. 7, 1967

*Emmett, G. M. (Glos) b Dec. 2, 1912, d Dec. 18, 1976

*Emmett, T. (Yorks) b Sept. 3, 1841, d June 30, 1904

*Endean, W. R. (Tvl) b May 31, 1924

*Engineer, F. M. (Bombay & Lancs) b Feb. 25, 1938

Enthoven, H. J. (CU & Middx) b June 4, 1903, d June 29, 1975

Essop-Adam, E. A. (Mash.) b Nov. 16, 1968

*Evans, A. J. (OU, Hants & Kent) b May 1, 1889, d Sept. 18, 1960

Evans, D. G. L. (Glam; Test umpire) b July 27, 1933, d March 25, 1990

*Evans, E. (NSW) b March 26, 1849, d July 2, 1921

Evans, K. P. (Notts) b Sept. 10, 1963

*Evans, T. G. CBE (Kent; *CY 1951*) b Aug. 18, 1920, d May 3, 1999

Evershed, Sir Sydney H. (Derbys) b Jan. 13, 1861, d March 7, 1937

Every, T. (Glam) b Dec. 19, 1909, d Jan. 20, 1990

Eyre, T. J. P. (Derbys) b Oct. 17, 1939

*Fagg, A. E. (Kent; Test umpire) b June 18, 1915, d Sept. 13, 1977

*Fairfax, A. G. (NSW) b June 16, 1906, d May 17, 1955

Fairservice, W. J. (Kent) b May 16, 1881, d June 26, 1971

*Fane, F. L. (OU & Essex) b April 27, 1875, d Nov. 27, 1960

*Farnes, K. (CU & Essex; *CY 1939*) b July 8, 1911, d Oct. 20, 1941

*Farooq Hamid (Lahore & PIA) b March 3, 1945

*Farrer, W. S. (Border) b Dec. 8, 1936

*Farrimond, W. (Lancs) b May 23, 1903, d Nov. 14, 1979

*Farrukh Zaman (Peshawar, NWFP, Punjab & MCB) b April 2, 1956

*Faulkner, G. A. (Tvl) b Dec. 17, 1881, d Sept. 10, 1930

*Favell, L. E. MBE (S. Aust.) b Oct. 4, 1929, d June 14, 1987

*Fazal Mahmood (N. Ind., Punjab & Lahore; *CY 1955*) b Feb. 18, 1927

Fearnley, C. D. (Worcs; bat-maker) b April 12, 1940

Featherstone, N. G. (Tvl, N. Tvl, Middx & Glam) b Aug. 20, 1949

'Felix', N. (Wanostrocht) (Kent, Surrey & All-England) b Oct. 4, 1804, d Sept. 3, 1876

*Fellows-Smith, J. P. (OU, Tvl & Northants) b Feb. 3, 1932

Feltham, M. A. (Surrey & Middx) b June 26, 1963

Felton, N. A. (Som & Northants) b Oct. 24, 1960

*Fender, P. G. H. (Sussex & Surrey; *CY 1915*) b Aug. 22, 1892, d June 15, 1985

*Ferguson, W. (T/T) b Dec. 14, 1917, d Feb. 23, 1961

Ferguson, W. H. BEM (Scorer) b June 6, 1880, d Sept. 22, 1957

*Fernandes, M. P. (BG) b Aug. 12, 1897, d May 8, 1981

Fernando, E. R. (SL) b Feb. 22, 1944

*Fernando, E. R. N. S. (SLAF) b Dec. 19, 1955

Fernando, T. L. (Colts & BRC) b Dec. 27, 1962

Ferreira, A. M. (N. Tvl & Warwicks) b April 13, 1955

**Ferris, J. J. (NSW, Glos & S. Aust.; *CY 1889*) b May 21, 1867, d Nov. 21, 1900

*Fichardt, C. G. (OFS) b March 20, 1870, d May 30, 1923

Fiddling, K. (Yorks & Northants) b Oct. 13, 1917, d June 19, 1992

*Field, F. E. (Warwicks) b Sept. 23, 1874, d Aug. 25, 1934

*Fielder, A. (Kent; *CY 1907*) b July 19, 1877, d Aug. 30, 1949

*Findlay, T. M. MBE (Comb. Is. & Windwards) b Oct. 19, 1943

Findlay, W. (OU & Lancs; Sec. Surrey CCC 1907-19; Sec. MCC 1926-36) b June 22, 1880, d June 19, 1953

*Fingleton, J. H. OBE (NSW; writer) b April 28, 1908, d Nov. 22, 1981

*Finlason, C. E. (Tvl & Griq. W.) b Feb. 19, 1860, d July 31, 1917

Finney, R. J. (Derbys) b Aug. 2, 1960

Firth, Canon J. D'E. E. (Winchester, OU & Notts; *CY 1918*) b Jan. 21, 1900, d Sept. 21, 1957

Firth, J. (Yorks & Leics) b June 27, 1917, d Sept. 7, 1981

*Fisher, F. E. (Wgtn & C. Dist.) b July 28, 1924, d June 19, 1996

*Fishlock, L. B. (Surrey; *CY 1947*) b Jan. 2, 1907, d June 26, 1986

Fishwick, T. S. (Warwicks) b July 24, 1876, d Feb. 21, 1950

Fitzgerald, R. A. (CU & Middx; Sec. MCC 1863-76) b Oct. 1, 1834, d Oct. 28, 1881

Fitzroy-Newdegate, Hon. J. M. (Northants) b March 20, 1897, d May 7, 1976

*Flavell, J. A. (Worcs; *CY 1965*) b May 15, 1929

Fleetwood-Smith, L. O'B. (Vic.) b March 30, 1908, d March 16, 1971

Fletcher, D. A. G. (Rhod. & Zimb.) b Sept. 27, 1948

Fletcher, D. G. W. (Surrey) b July 6, 1924

*Fletcher, K. W. R. OBE (Essex; *CY 1974*) b May 20, 1944

Fletcher, S. D. (Yorks & Lancs) b June 8, 1964

*Floquet, C. E. (Tvl) b Nov. 3, 1884, d Nov. 22, 1963

*Flowers, W. (Notts) b Dec. 7, 1856, d Nov. 1, 1926

*Foley, H. (Wgtn) b Jan. 28, 1906, d Oct. 16, 1948

Folley, I. (Lancs & Derbys) b Jan. 9, 1963, d Aug. 30, 1993

Forbes, C. (Notts) b Aug. 9, 1936

*Ford, F. G. J. (CU & Middx) b Dec. 14, 1866, d Feb. 7, 1940

Fordham, A. (Northants) b Nov. 9, 1964

Foreman, D. J. (W. Prov. & Sussex) b Feb. 1, 1933

*Foster, F. R. (Warwicks; *CY 1912*) b Jan. 31, 1889, d May 3, 1958

Foster, G. N. (OU, Worcs & Kent) b Oct. 16, 1884, d Aug. 11, 1971

Foster, H. K. (OU & Worcs; *CY 1911*) b Oct. 30, 1873, d June 23, 1950

Foster, M. K. (Worcs) b Jan. 1, 1889, d Dec. 3, 1940

*Foster, M. L. C. (Jam.) b May 9, 1943

*Foster, N. A. (Essex & Tvl; *CY 1988*) b May 6, 1962

*Foster, R. E. (OU & Worcs; *CY 1901*) b April 16, 1878, d May 13, 1914

*Fothergill, A. J. (Som) b Aug. 26, 1854, d Aug. 1, 1932

Fowke, G. H. S. (Leics) b Oct. 14, 1880, d June 24, 1946

*Fowler, G. (Lancs & Durham) b April 20, 1957

*Francis, B. C. (NSW & Essex) b Feb. 18, 1948

Francis, D. A. (Glam) b Nov. 29, 1953

*Francis, G. N. (B'dos) b Dec. 11, 1897, d Jan. 7, 1942

*Francis, H. H. (Glos & W. Prov.) b May 26, 1868, d Jan. 7, 1936

Francis, K. T. (Test umpire) b Oct. 15, 1949

Francke, F. M. (SL & Qld) b March 29, 1941

*Francois, C. M. (Griq. W.) b June 20, 1897, d May 26, 1944

*Frank, C. N. (Tvl) b Jan. 27, 1891, d Dec. 25, 1961

*Frank, W. H. B. (SA) b Nov. 23, 1872, d Feb. 16, 1945

*Franklin, T. J. (Auck.) b March 18, 1962

*Frederick, M. (B'dos, Derbys & Jam.) b May 6, 1927

*Fredericks, R. C. (†Guyana & Glam; *CY 1974*) b Nov. 11, 1942

*Freeman, A. P. (Kent; *CY 1923*) b May 17, 1888, d Jan. 28, 1965

*Freeman, D. L. (Wgtn) b Sept. 8, 1914, d May 31, 1994

*Freeman, E. W. (S. Aust.) b July 13, 1944

Freeman, J. R. (Essex) b Sept. 3, 1883, d Aug. 8, 1958

*Freer, F. W. (Vic.) b Dec. 4, 1915, d Nov. 2 1998

*French, B. N. (Notts) b Aug. 13, 1959

Frost, G. (Notts) b Jan. 15, 1947

*Fry, C. B. (OU, Sussex & Hants; *CY 1895*) b April 25, 1872, d Sept. 7, 1956

*Fuller, E. R. H. (W. Prov.) b Aug. 2, 1931

*Fuller, R. L. (Jam.) b Jan. 30, 1913, d May 3, 1987

*Fullerton, G. M. (Tvl) b Dec. 8, 1922

*Funston, K. J. (NE Tvl, OFS & Tvl) b Dec. 3, 1925

*Furlonge, H. A. (T/T) b June 19, 1934

Gabriel, R. S. (T/T) b June 5, 1952

*Gadkari, C. V. (M'tra & Ind. Serv.) b Feb. 3, 1928, d Jan. 11, 1998

*Gaekwad, A. D. (Baroda) b Sept. 23, 1952

*Gaekwad, D. K. (Baroda) b Oct. 27, 1928

*Gaekwad, H. G. (†M. Pradesh) b Aug. 29, 1923

Gale, R. A. (Middx) b Dec. 10, 1933

*Gallichan, N. (Wgtn) b June 3, 1906, d March 25, 1969

*Gamsy, D. (Natal) b Feb. 17, 1940

*Gandotra, A. (Delhi & Bengal) b Nov. 24, 1948

*Gannon, J. B. (W. Aust.) b Feb. 8, 1947

*Ganteaume, A. G. (T/T) b Jan. 22, 1921

Gard, T. (Som) b June 2, 1957

Gardiner, Howard (ICC referee) b Jan. 1, 1944

Gardner, F. C. (Warwicks) b June 4, 1922, d Jan. 12, 1979

Gardner, L. R. (Leics) b Feb. 23, 1934

Garland-Wells, H. M. (OU & Surrey) b Nov. 14, 1907, d May 28, 1993

Garlick, R. G. (Lancs & Northants) b April 11, 1917, d May 16, 1988

*Garner, J. MBE (B'dos, Som & S. Aust.; *CY 1980*) b Dec. 16, 1952

Garnham, M. A. (Glos, Leics & Essex) b Aug. 20, 1960

*Garrett, T. W. (NSW) b July 26, 1858, d Aug. 6, 1943

*Gaskin, B. B. M. (BG) b March 21, 1908, d May 1, 1979

*Gatting, M. W. OBE (Middx; *CY 1984*) b June 6, 1957

*Gaunt, R. A. (W. Aust. & Vic.) b Feb. 26, 1934

*Gavaskar, S. M. (Bombay & Som; *CY 1980*) b July 10, 1949

*Gay, L. H. (CU, Hants & Som) b March 24, 1871, d Nov. 1, 1949

*Geary, G. (Leics; *CY 1927*) b July 9, 1893, d March 6, 1981

*Gedye, S. G. (Auck.) b May 2, 1929

*Gehrs, D. R. A. (S. Aust.) b Nov. 29, 1880, d June 25, 1953

*Germon, L. K. (Cant.) b Nov. 4, 1968

Ghai, R. S. (Punjab) b June 12, 1960

*Ghavri, K. D. (S'tra & Bombay) b Feb. 28, 1951

*Ghazali, M. E. Z. (M'tra & Pak. Serv.) b June 15, 1924

*Ghorpade, J. M. (Baroda) b Oct. 2, 1930, d March 29, 1978

*Ghulam Abbas (Kar., NBP & PIA) b May 1, 1947

*Ghulam Ahmed (H'bad) b July 4, 1922, d Oct. 28, 1998

*Gibb, P. A. (CU, Scotland, Yorks & Essex) b July 11, 1913, d Dec. 7, 1977

Gibbons, H. H. (Worcs) b Oct. 10, 1904, d Feb. 16, 1973

*Gibbs, G. L. (BG) b Dec. 27, 1925, d Feb. 21, 1979

*Gibbs, L. R. (†Guyana, S. Aust. & Warwicks; *CY 1972*) b Sept. 29, 1934

Gibbs, P. J. K. (OU & Derbys) b Aug. 17, 1944

Gibson, C. H. (Eton, CU & Sussex; *CY 1918*) b Aug. 23, 1900, d Dec. 31, 1976

Gibson, D. (Surrey) b May 1, 1936

*Giffen, G. (S. Aust.; *CY 1894*) b March 27, 1859, d Nov. 29, 1927

*Giffen, W. F. (S. Aust.) b Sept. 20, 1861, d June 29, 1949

*Gifford, N. MBE (Worcs & Warwicks; *CY 1975*) b March 30, 1940

*Gilbert, D. R. (NSW, Tas. & Glos) b Dec. 29, 1960

*Gilchrist, R. (Jam. & H'bad) b June 28, 1934

Giles, R. J. (Notts) b Oct. 17, 1919

Gilhouley, K. (Yorks & Notts) b Aug. 8, 1934

*Gillespie, S. R. (Auck.) b March 2, 1957

Gilliat, R. M. C. (OU & Hants) b May 20, 1944

*Gilligan, A. E. R. (CU, Surrey & Sussex; *CY 1924;* Pres. MCC 1967-68) b Dec. 23, 1894, d Sept. 5, 1976

*Gilligan, A. H. H. (Sussex) b June 29, 1896, d May 5, 1978

Gilligan, F. W. (OU & Essex) b Sept. 20, 1893, d May 4, 1960

Gillingham, Canon F. H. (Essex) b Sept. 6, 1875, d April 1, 1953

*Gilmour, G. J. (NSW) b June 26, 1951

*Gimblett, H. (Som; *CY 1953*) b Oct. 19, 1914, d March 30, 1978

Gladstone, G. (*see* Marais, G. G.)

*Gladwin, Cliff (Derbys) b April 3, 1916, d April 10, 1988

*Gleeson, J. W. (NSW & E. Prov.) b March 14, 1938

*Gleeson, R. A. (E. Prov.) b Dec. 6, 1873, d Sept. 27, 1919

Glover, A. C. S. (Warwicks) b April 19, 1872, d May 22, 1904

*Glover, G. K. (Kimberley & Griq. W.) b May 13, 1870, d Nov. 15, 1938

*Goddard, J. D. C. OBE (B'dos) b April 21, 1919, d Aug. 26, 1987

*Goddard, T. L. (Natal & NE Tvl) b Aug. 1, 1931

*Goddard, T. W. (Glos; *CY 1938*) b Oct. 1, 1900, d May 22, 1966

Goel, R. (Patiala & Haryana) b Sept. 29, 1942

*Gomes, H. A. (T/T & Middx; *CY 1985*) b July 13, 1953

*Gomez, G. E. (T/T) b Oct. 10, 1919, d Aug. 6, 1996

*Gooch, G. A. OBE (Essex & W. Prov.; *CY 1980*) b July 23, 1953

Goodwin, K. (Lancs) b June 25, 1938

Goodwin, T. J. (Leics) b Jan. 22, 1929

*Goonatillake, F. R. M. de S. (SL) b Aug. 15, 1951

*Goonatillake, H. M. (SL) b Aug. 16, 1952

Goonesena, G. (Ceylon, Notts, CU & NSW) b Feb. 16, 1931

Gopalan, M. J. (Madras) b June 6, 1909

*Gopinath, C. D. (Madras) b March 1, 1930

Gordon, N. (Tvl) b Aug. 6, 1911

Gore, A. C. (Eton & Army; *CY 1919*) b May 14, 1900, d June 7, 1990

Gould, I. J. (Middx, Auck. & Sussex) b Aug. 19, 1957

*Gover, A. R. MBE (Surrey; *CY 1937;* oldest surviving CY and oldest living Test cricketer at end of 1999) b Feb. 29, 1908

*Gower, D. I. OBE (Leics & Hants; *CY 1979*) b April 1, 1957

Grace, C. B. (London County; son of W. G.) b March 1882, d June 6, 1938

*Grace, Dr E. M. (Glos; brother of W. G.) b Nov. 28, 1841, d May 20, 1911

*Grace, G. F. (Glos; brother of W. G.) b Dec. 13, 1850, d Sept. 22, 1880

Grace, Dr Henry (Glos; brother of W. G.) b Jan. 31, 1833, d Nov. 15, 1895

Grace, Dr H. M. (father of W. G.) b Feb. 21, 1808, d Dec. 23, 1871

Grace, Mrs H. M. (mother of W. G.) b July 18, 1812, d July 25, 1884

*Grace, Dr W. G. (Glos; CY 1896) b July 18, 1848, d Oct. 23, 1915

Grace, W. G., jun. (CU & Glos; son of W. G.) b July 6, 1874, d March 2, 1905

Graf, S. F. (Vic., W. Aust. & Hants) b May 19, 1957

*Graham, H. (Vic. & Otago) b Nov. 22, 1870, d Feb. 7, 1911

Graham, J. N. (Kent) b May 8, 1943

*Graham, R. (W. Prov.) b Sept. 16, 1877, d April 21, 1946

*Grant, G. C. (CU, T/T & Rhod.) b May 9, 1907, d Oct. 26, 1978

*Grant, R. S. (CU & T/T) b Dec. 15, 1909, d Oct. 18, 1977

Graveney, D. A. (Glos, Som & Durham) b Jan. 2, 1953

Graveney, J. K. (Glos) b Dec. 16, 1924

*Graveney, T. W. OBE (Glos, Worcs & Qld; CY 1953) b June 16, 1927

Graves, P. J. (Sussex & OFS) b May 19, 1946

*Gray, A. H. (T/T, Surrey & W. Tvl) b May 23, 1963

*Gray, E. J. (Wgtn) b Nov. 18, 1954

*Gray, J. R. (Hants) b May 19, 1926

Gray, L. H. (Middx) b Dec. 15, 1915, d Jan. 3, 1983

*Greatbatch, M. J. (C. Dist.) b Dec. 11, 1963

Green, A. M. (Sussex & OFS) b May 28, 1960

Green, D. M. (OU, Lancs & Glos; CY 1969) b Nov. 10, 1939

Green, Major A. (Lancs) b Feb. 1, 1890, d March 2, 1963

*Greenhough, T. (Lancs) b Nov. 9, 1931

*Greenidge, A. E. (B'dos) b Aug. 20, 1956

*Greenidge, C. G. MBE (Hants & B'dos; CY 1977) b May 1, 1951

*Greenidge, G. A. (B'dos & Sussex) b May 26, 1948

Greensmith, W. T. (Essex) b Aug. 16, 1930

*Greenwood, A. (Yorks) b Aug. 20, 1847, d Feb. 12, 1889

Greetham, C. (Som) b Aug. 28, 1936

*Gregory, D. W. (NSW; first Australian captain) b April 15, 1845, d Aug. 4, 1919

*Gregory, E. J. (NSW) b May 29, 1839, d April 22, 1899

*Gregory, J. M. (NSW; CY 1922) b Aug. 14, 1895, d Aug. 7, 1973

*Gregory, R. G. (Vic.) b Feb. 28, 1916, d June 10, 1942

Gregory, R. J. (Surrey) b Aug. 26, 1902, d Oct. 6, 1973

*Gregory, S. E. (NSW; CY 1897) b April 14, 1870, d Aug. 1, 1929

*Greig, A. W. (Border, E. Prov. & Sussex; CY 1975) b Oct. 6, 1946

*Greig, I. A. (CU, Border, Sussex & Surrey) b Dec. 8, 1955

*Grell, M. G. (T/T) b Dec. 18, 1899, d Jan. 11, 1976

*Grieve, B. A. F. (Eng.) b May 28, 1864, d Nov. 19, 1917

Grieves, K. J. (NSW & Lancs) b Aug. 27, 1925, d Jan. 3, 1992

*Grieveson, R. E. OBE (Tvl) b Aug. 24, 1909, d July 24, 1998

*Griffin, G. M. (Natal & Rhod.) b June 12, 1939

*Griffith, C. C. (B'dos; CY 1964) b Dec. 14, 1938

Griffith, G. ("Ben") (Surrey & Utd England XI) b Dec. 20, 1833, d May 3, 1879

*Griffith, H. C. (B'dos) b Dec. 1, 1893, d March 18, 1980

Griffith, M. G. (CU & Sussex) b Nov. 25, 1943

*Griffith, S. C. CBE (CU, Surrey & Sussex; Sec. MCC 1962-74; Pres. MCC 1979-80) b June 16, 1914, d April 7, 1993

Griffiths, B. J. (Northants) b June 13, 1949

*Grimmett, C. V. (Wgtn, Vic., & S. Aust.; CY 1931) b Dec. 25, 1891, d May 2, 1980

*Groube, T. U. (Vic.) b Sept. 2, 1857, d Aug. 5, 1927

*Grout, A. T. W. (Qld) b March 30, 1927, d Nov. 9, 1968

Grove, C. W. (Warwicks & Worcs) b Dec. 16, 1912, d Feb. 15, 1982

Grundy, James (Notts & Utd England XI) b March 5, 1824, d Nov. 24, 1873

*Guard, G. M. (Bombay & Guj.) b Dec. 12, 1925, d March 13, 1978

*Guest, C. E. J. (Vic. & W. Aust.) b Oct. 7, 1937

*Guha, S. (Bengal) b Jan. 31, 1946

**Guillen, S. C. (T/T & Cant.) b Sept. 24, 1924

**Gul Mahomed (N. Ind., Baroda, H'bad, Punjab & Lahore) b Oct. 15, 1921, d May 8, 1992

*Gunasekera, Y. (SL) b Nov. 8, 1957

*Guneratne, R. P. W. (Nomads) b Jan. 26, 1962

*Gunn, G. (Notts; CY 1914) b June 13, 1879, d June 29, 1958

Gunn, G. V. (Notts) b June 21, 1905, d Oct. 14, 1957

*Gunn, J. (Notts; CY 1904) b July 19, 1876, d Aug. 21, 1963

*Gunn, W. (Notts; CY 1890) b Dec. 4, 1858, d Jan. 29, 1921

*Gupte, B. P. (Bombay, Bengal & Ind. Rlwys) b Aug. 30, 1934

*Gupte, S. P. (Bombay, Bengal, Raja. & T/T) b Dec. 11, 1929

*Gursharan Singh (Punjab) b March 8, 1963

*Gurusinha, A. P. (SSC & NCC) b Sept. 16, 1966

*Guy, J. W. (C. Dist., Wgtn, Northants, Cant., Otago & N. Dist.) b Aug. 29, 1934

Haafiz Shahid (WAPDA) b May 10, 1963

Habibul Bashar (Bangladesh) b Aug. 17, 1972

Hadlee, B. G. (Cant.) b Dec. 14, 1941

*Hadlee, D. R. (Cant.) b Jan. 6, 1948

*Hadlee, Sir Richard J. (Cant., Notts & Tas.; *CY 1982*) b July 3, 1951

*Hadlee, W. A. CBE (Cant. & Otago) b June 4, 1915

*Hafeez, A. (*see* Kardar)

*Haig, N. E. (Middx) b Dec. 12, 1887, d Oct. 27, 1966

*Haigh, S. (Yorks; *CY 1901*) b March 19, 1871, d Feb. 27, 1921

Hair, D. B. (Test umpire) b Sept. 30, 1952

Halfyard, D. J. (Kent & Notts) b April 3, 1931, d Aug. 23, 1996

*Hall, A. E. (Tvl & Lancs) b Jan. 23, 1896, d Jan. 1, 1964

*Hall, G. G. (NE Tvl & E. Prov.) b May 24, 1938, d June 26, 1987

Hall, I. W. (Derbys) b Dec. 27, 1939

Hall, L. (Yorks; *CY 1890*) b Nov. 1, 1852, d Nov. 19, 1915

*Hall, W. W. (B'dos, T/T & Qld) b Sept. 12, 1937

Hallam, A. W. (Lancs & Notts; *CY 1908*) b Nov. 12, 1869, d July 24, 1940

Hallam, M. R. (Leics) b Sept. 10, 1931, d Jan. 1, 2000

Halliday, H. (Yorks) b Feb. 9, 1920, d Aug. 27, 1967

*Halliwell, E. A. (Tvl & Middx; *CY 1905*) b Sept. 7, 1864, d Oct. 2, 1919

*Hallows, C. (Lancs; *CY 1928*) b April 4, 1895, d Nov. 10, 1972

Hallows, J. (Lancs; *CY 1905*) b Nov. 14, 1873, d May 20, 1910

*Halse, C. G. (Natal) b Feb. 28, 1935

*Hamence, R. A. (S. Aust.) b Nov. 25, 1915

Hamer, A. (Yorks & Derbys) b Dec. 8, 1916, d Nov. 3, 1993

Hammond, H. E. (Sussex) b Nov. 7, 1907, d June 16, 1985

*Hammond, J. R. (S. Aust.) b April 19, 1950

*Hammond, W. R. (Glos; *CY 1928*) b June 19, 1903, d July 1, 1965

*Hampshire, J. H. (Yorks, Derbys & Tas.; Test umpire) b Feb. 10, 1941

*Hands, P. A. M. (W. Prov.) b March 18, 1890, d April 27, 1951

*Hands, R. H. M. (W. Prov.) b July 26, 1888, d April 20, 1918

*Hanif Mohammad (B'pur, Kar. & PIA; *CY 1968*) b Dec. 21, 1934

*Hanley, M. A. (Border & W. Prov.) b Nov. 10, 1918

*Hanumant Singh (M. Pradesh & Raja.; ICC referee) b March 29, 1939

Hardie, B. R. (Scotland & Essex) b Jan. 14, 1950

*Hardikar, M. S. (Bombay) b Feb. 8, 1936, d Feb. 4, 1995

*Hardinge, H. T. W. (Kent; *CY 1915*) b Feb. 25, 1886, d May 8, 1965

*Hardstaff, J. (Notts; Test umpire) b Nov. 9, 1882, d April 2, 1947

*Hardstaff, J., jun. (Notts & Auck.; *CY 1938*) b July 3, 1911, d Jan. 1, 1990

Hardy, J. J. E. (Hants, Som, W. Prov. & Glos) b Oct. 2, 1960

*Harford, N. S. (C. Dist. & Auck.) b Aug. 30, 1930, d March 30, 1981

*Harford, R. I. (Auck.) b May 30, 1936

Hargreave, S. (Warwicks) b Sept. 22, 1875, d Jan. 1, 1929

Harman, R. (Surrey) b Dec. 28, 1941

*Haroon Rashid (Kar., Sind, NBP, PIA & UBL) b March 25, 1953

*Harper, D. J. (Test umpire) b Oct. 23, 1951

*Harper, R. A. (Guyana & Northants) b March 17, 1963

*Harris, 4th Lord (OU & Kent; Pres. MCC 1895) b Feb. 3, 1851, d March 24, 1932

Harris, C. B. (Notts) b Dec. 6, 1907, d Aug. 8, 1954

Harris, David (Hants & All-England) b 1755, d May 19, 1803

Harris, J. H. (Som; umpire) b Feb. 13, 1936

Harris, M. J. (Middx, Notts, E. Prov. & Wgtn) b May 25, 1944

*Harris, P. G. Z. (Cant.) b July 18, 1927, d Dec. 1, 1991

*Harris, R. M. (Auck.) b July 27, 1933

*Harris, T. A. (Griq. W. & Tvl) b Aug. 27, 1916, d March 7, 1993

Harrison, L. (Hants) b June 8, 1922

*Harry, J. (Vic.) b Aug. 1, 1857, d Oct. 27, 1919

Hart, R. T. (C. Dist. & Wgtn) b Nov. 7, 1961

*Hartigan, G. P. D. (Border) b Dec. 30, 1884, d Jan. 7, 1955

*Hartigan, R. J. (NSW & Qld) b Dec. 12, 1879, d June 7, 1958

*Hartkopf, A. E. V. (Vic.) b Dec. 28, 1889, d May 20, 1968

*Hartland, B. R. (Cant.) b Oct. 22, 1966

Hartley, A. (Lancs; *CY 1911*) b April 11, 1879, d Oct. 9, 1918

*Hartley, J. C. (OU & Sussex) b Nov. 15, 1874, d March 8, 1963

Hartley, S. N. (Yorks & OFS) b March 18, 1956

Harvey, J. F. (Derbys) b Sept. 27, 1939

*Harvey, M. R. (Vic.) b April 29, 1918, d March 20, 1995

Harvey, P. F. (Notts) b Jan. 15, 1923

*Harvey, R. L. (Natal) b Sept. 14, 1911

*Harvey, R. N. MBE (Vic. & NSW; *CY 1954*) b Oct. 8, 1928

Hasan Jamil (Kalat, Kar., Pak. Us & PIA) b July 25, 1952

*Haseeb Ahsan (Peshawar, Pak. Us, Kar. & PIA) b July 15, 1939

Hassan, B. (Notts) b March 24, 1944

*Hassett, A. L. MBE (Vic.; *CY 1949*) b Aug. 28, 1913, d June 16, 1993

*Hastings, B. F. (Wgtn, C. Dist. & Cant.; ICC referee) b March 23, 1940

*Hathorn, C. M. H. (Tvl) b April 7, 1878, d May 17, 1920

*Hawke, 7th Lord (CU & Yorks; *CY 1909*; Pres. MCC 1914-18) b Aug. 16, 1860, d Oct. 10, 1938

*Hawke, N. J. N. (W. Aust., S. Aust. & Tas.) b June 27, 1939

Hawkins, D. G. (Glos) b May 18, 1935

*Hayes, E. G. (Surrey & Leics; *CY 1907*) b Nov. 6, 1876, d Dec. 2, 1953

*Hayes, F. C. (Lancs) b Dec. 6, 1946

Hayes, J. A. (Auck. & Cant.) b Jan. 11, 1927

Hayes, R. L. (N. Dist.) b May 9, 1971

Haygarth, A. (Sussex; Historian) b Aug. 4, 1825, d May 1, 1903

Hayhurst, A. N. (Lancs, Som & Derbys) b Nov. 23, 1962

*Haynes, D. L. (B'dos, Middx & W. Prov.; *CY 1991*) b Feb. 15, 1956

Haynes, R. C. (Jam.) b Nov. 11, 1964

Hayward, T. (Cambs. & All-England) b March 21, 1835, d July 21, 1876

*Hayward, T. W. (Surrey; *CY 1895*) b March 29, 1871, d July 19, 1939

*Hazare, V. S. (M'tra, C. Ind. & Baroda) b March 11, 1915

Hazell, H. L. (Som) b Sept. 30, 1909, d March 31, 1990

Hazlerigg, Sir A. G. Bt (later 1st Lord) (Leics) b Nov. 17, 1878, d May 25, 1949

Hazlitt, G. R. (Vic. & NSW) b Sept. 4, 1888, d Oct. 30, 1915

*Headley, G. A. MBE (Jam.; *CY 1934*) b May 30, 1909, d Nov. 30, 1983

*Headley, R. G. A. (Worcs & Jam.) b June 29, 1939

Heane, G. F. H. (Notts) b Jan. 2, 1904, d Oct. 24, 1969

Heap, J. S. (Lancs) b Aug. 12, 1882, d Jan. 30, 1951

Hearn, P. (Kent) b Nov. 18, 1925

*Hearne, A. (Kent; *CY 1894*) b July 22, 1863, d May 16, 1952

**Hearne, F. (Kent & W. Prov.) b Nov. 23, 1858, d July 14, 1949

*Hearne, G. A. L. (W. Prov.) b March 27, 1888, d Nov. 13, 1978

*Hearne, G. G. (Kent) b July 7, 1856, d Feb. 13, 1932

*Hearne, J. T. (Middx; *CY 1892*) b May 3, 1867, d April 17, 1944

*Hearne, J. W. (Middx; *CY 1912*) b Feb. 11, 1891, d Sept. 14, 1965

Hearne, T. (Middx) b Sept. 4, 1826, d May 13, 1900

Heath, G. E. M. (Hants) b Feb. 20, 1913

Heath, M. (Hants) b March 9, 1934

Hedges, B. (Glam) b Nov. 10, 1927

Hedges, L. P. (Tonbridge, OU, Kent & Glos; *CY 1919*) b July 13, 1900, d Jan. 12, 1933

Heine, P. S. (NE Tvl, OFS & Tvl) b June 28, 1928

*Hemmings, E. E. (Warwicks, Notts & Sussex) b Feb. 20, 1949

Hemsley, E. J. O. (Worcs) b Sept. 1, 1943

Henderson, M. (Wgtn) b Aug. 2, 1895, d June 17, 1970

Henderson, R. (Surrey; *CY 1890*) b March 30, 1865, d Jan. 29, 1931

*Hendren, E. H. (Middx; *CY 1920*) b Feb. 5, 1889, d Oct. 4, 1962

*Hendrick, M. (Derbys & Notts; *CY 1978*) b Oct. 22, 1948

Hendriks, J. L. (Jam.; ICC referee) b Dec. 21, 1933

*Hendry, H. L. (NSW & Vic.) b May 24, 1895, d Dec. 16, 1988

*Henry, O. (W. Prov., Boland, OFS & Scotland) b Jan. 23, 1952

Herman, O. W. (Hants) b Sept. 18, 1907, d June 24, 1987

Herman, R. S. (Middx, Border, Griq. W. & Hants) b Nov. 30, 1946

Heron, J. G. (Zimb.) b Nov. 8, 1948

*Heseltine, C. (Hants) b Nov. 26, 1869, d June 13, 1944

Hever, N. G. (Middx & Glam) b Dec. 17, 1924, d Sept. 11, 1987

Hewett, H. T. (OU & Som; *CY 1893*) b May 25, 1864, d March 4, 1921.

Heyhoe-Flint, Rachael (England Women) b June 11, 1939

Heyn, P. D. (SL) b June 26, 1945

*Hibbert, P. A. (Vic.) b July 23, 1952

Hide, M. E. (Molly) (England Women) b Oct 24, 1913, d Sept. 10, 1995

*Higgs, J. D. (Vic.) b July 11, 1950

*Higgs, K. (Lancs & Leics; *CY 1968*) b Jan. 14, 1937

Hignell, A. J. (CU & Glos) b Sept. 4, 1955

*Hilditch, A. M. J. (NSW & S. Aust.) b May 20, 1956

Hill, Alan (Derbys & OFS) b June 29, 1950

*Hill, Allen (Yorks) b Nov. 14, 1843, d Aug. 29, 1910

*Hill, A. J. L. (CU & Hants) b July 26, 1871, d Sept. 6, 1950

*Hill, C. (S. Aust.; *CY 1900*) b March 18, 1877, d Sept. 5, 1945

Hill, E. (Som) b July 9, 1923

Hill, G. (Hants) b April 15, 1913

*Hill, J. C. (Vic.) b June 25, 1923, d Aug. 11, 1974

Hill, M. (Notts, Derbys & Som) b Sept. 14, 1935

Hill, N. W. (Notts) b Aug. 22, 1935

Hill, W. A. (Warwicks) b April 27, 1910, d Aug. 11, 1995

Hill-Wood, Sir Samuel H. (Derbys) b March 21, 1872, d Jan. 4, 1949

Hillyer, W. R. (Kent & Surrey) b March 5, 1813, d Jan. 8, 1861

Hilton, C. (Lancs & Essex) b Sept. 26, 1937

*Hilton, M. J. (Lancs; *CY 1957*) b Aug. 2, 1928, d July 8, 1990

*Hime, C. F. W. (Natal) b Oct. 24, 1869, d Dec. 6, 1940

*Hindlekar, D. D. (Bombay) b Jan. 1, 1909, d March 30, 1949

Hinks, S. G. (Kent & Glos) b Oct. 12, 1960

Hipkin, A. B. (Essex) b Aug. 8, 1900, d Feb. 11, 1957

*Hirst, G. H. (Yorks; *CY 1901*) b Sept. 7, 1871, d May 10, 1954

*Hitch, J. W. (Surrey; *CY 1914*) b May 7, 1886, d July 7, 1965

Hitchcock, R. E. (Cant. & Warwicks) b Nov. 28, 1929

*Hoad, E. L. G. (B'dos) b Jan. 29, 1896, d March 5, 1986

*Hoare, D. E. (W. Aust.) b Oct. 19, 1934

*Hobbs, Sir John B. "Jack" (Surrey; *CY 1909, special portrait 1926*) b Dec. 16, 1882, d Dec. 21, 1963

*Hobbs, R. N. S. (Essex & Glam) b May 8, 1942

*Hodges, J. (Vic.) b Aug. 11, 1855, death unknown

Hodgson, A. (Northants) b Oct. 27, 1951

Hodgson, G. D. (Glos) b Oct. 22, 1966

*Hogan, T. G. (W. Aust.) b Sept. 23, 1956

*Hogg, R. M. (S. Aust.) b March 5, 1951

Hogg, V. R. (Zimb.) b July 3, 1952

*Hohns, T. V. (Qld) b Jan. 23, 1954

Holder, J. W. (Hants; Test umpire) b March 19, 1945

*Holder, V. A. (B'dos, Worcs & OFS) b Oct. 8, 1945

*Holding, M. A. (Jam., Lancs, Derbys, Tas. & Cant.; *CY 1977*) b Feb. 16, 1954

*Hole, G. B. (NSW & S. Aust.) b Jan. 6, 1931, d Feb. 14, 1990

*Holford, D. A. J. (B'dos & T/T) b April 16, 1940

Holland, F. C. (Surrey) b Feb. 10, 1876, d Feb. 5, 1957

*Holland, R. G. (NSW & Wgtn) b Oct. 19, 1946

*Hollies, W. E. (Warwicks; *CY 1955*) b June 5, 1912, d April 16, 1981

Holmes, Gp Capt. A. J. (Sussex) b June 30, 1899, d May 21, 1950

*Holmes, E. R. T. (OU & Surrey; *CY 1936*) b Aug. 21, 1905, d Aug. 16, 1960

Holmes, G. C. (Glam) b Sept. 16, 1958

*Holmes, P. (Yorks; *CY 1920*) b Nov. 25, 1886, d Sept. 3, 1971

Holt, A. G. (Hants) b April 8, 1911, d July 28, 1994

*Holt, J. K., jun. (Jam.) b Aug. 12, 1923, d July 2, 1997

Home of the Hirsel, Lord (Middx; Pres. MCC 1966-67) b July 2, 1903, d Oct. 9, 1995

*Hone, L. (MCC) b Jan. 30, 1853, d Dec. 31, 1896

Hooker, R. W. (Middx) b Feb. 22, 1935

*Hookes, D. W. (S. Aust.) b May 3, 1955

*Hopkins, A. J. (NSW) b May 3, 1874, d April 25, 1931

Hopkins, J. A. (Glam & E. Prov.) b June 16, 1953

Hopkins, V. (Glos) b Jan. 21, 1911, d Aug. 6, 1984

*Hopwood, J. L. (Lancs) b Oct. 30, 1903, d June 15, 1985

*Horan, T. P. (Vic.) b March 8, 1854, d April 16, 1916

*Hordern, Dr H. V. (NSW & Philadelphia) b Feb. 10, 1884, d June 17, 1938

Hornby, A. H. (CU & Lancs) b July 29, 1877, d Sept. 6, 1952

*Hornby, A. N. (Lancs) b Feb. 10, 1847, d Dec. 17, 1925

*Horne, P. A. (Auck.) b Jan. 21, 1960

Horner, N. F. (Yorks & Warwicks) b May 10, 1926

*Hornibrook, P. M. (Qld) b July 27, 1899, d Aug. 25, 1976

Horsfall, R. (Essex & Glam) b June 26, 1920, d Aug. 25, 1981

Horton, H. (Worcs & Hants) b April 18, 1923, d Nov. 2, 1998

*Horton, M. J. (Worcs & N. Dist.) b April 21, 1934

*Hough, K. W. (Auck.) b Oct. 24, 1928

*Houghton, D. L. (Mash.) b June 23, 1957

*Howard, A. B. (B'dos) b Aug. 27, 1946

*Howard, N. D. (Lancs) b May 18, 1925, d May 31, 1979

Howard, Major R. (Lancs; MCC Team Manager) b April 17, 1890, d Sept. 10, 1967

*Howarth, G. P. OBE (Auck., Surrey & N. Dist.) b March 29, 1951

*Howarth, H. J. (Auck.) b Dec. 25, 1943

*Howell, H. (Warwicks) b Nov. 29, 1890, d July 9, 1932

*Howell, W. P. (NSW) b Dec. 29, 1869, d July 14, 1940

*Howorth, R. (Worcs) b April 26, 1909, d April 2, 1980

Hubble, J. C. (Kent) b Feb. 10, 1881, d Feb. 26, 1965

Huggins, H. J. (Glos) b March 15, 1877, d Nov. 20, 1942

Hughes, D. P. (Lancs & Tas.; *CY 1988*) b May 13, 1947

*Hughes, K. J. (W. Aust. & Natal; *CY 1981*) b Jan. 26, 1954

*Hunter, J. (Yorks) b Aug. 3, 1855, d Jan. 4, 1891

*Hurst, A. G. (Vic.) b July 15, 1950

Hurst, R. J. (Middx) b Dec. 29, 1933, d Feb. 10, 1996

*Hurwood, A. (Qld) b June 17, 1902, d Sept. 26, 1982

*Hutchings, K. L. (Kent; *CY 1907*) b Dec. 7, 1882, d Sept. 3, 1916

Hutchinson, J. M. (Derbys; *believed to be oldest living first-class cricketer at end 1999*) b Nov. 29, 1896

FIRST-CLASS CRICKETERS WHO HAVE LIVED TO 100

Hutchinson, J. M. (Derbys)	**b Nov. 29, 1896**	*First cricketer to attain 103 years*
de Smidt, R. W. (W. Prov.)	b Nov. 24, 1883, d Aug. 3, 1986	102 years 252 days
English, E. A. (Hants)	b Jan. 1, 1864, d Sept. 5, 1966	102 years 247 days
Wheatley, J. (Cant.)	b Jan. 8, 1860, d April 20, 1962	102 years 102 days
Deodhar, D. B. (M'tra)	b Jan. 14, 1892, d Aug. 24, 1993	101 years 222 days
Harman, G. R. U. (Dublin U.)	b June 6, 1874, d Dec. 14, 1975	101 years 191 days
Braithwaite, C. H.		
(English Residents – USA)	b Sept 10, 1845, d April 15, 1946	100 years 217 days
Deane, G. O. (Hants)	b Dec. 11, 1828, d Feb. 26, 1929	100 years 77 days

Research: Robert Brooke

---

*Hughes, M. G. (Vic. & Essex; *CY 1994*) b Nov. 23, 1961

Hughes, S. P. (Middx, N. Tvl & Durham) b Dec. 20, 1959

Huish, F. H. (Kent) b Nov. 15, 1869, d March 16, 1957

Hulme, J. H. A. (Middx) b Aug. 26, 1904, d Sept. 26, 1991

Humpage, G. W. (Warwicks & OFS; *CY 1985*) b April 24, 1954

Humphrey, T. (Surrey) b Jan. 16, 1839, d Sept. 3, 1878

Humphreys, E. (Kent & Cant.) b Aug. 24, 1881, d Nov. 6, 1949

Humphreys, W. A. (Sussex & Hants) b Oct. 28, 1849, d March 23, 1924

Humphries, D. J. (Leics & Worcs) b Aug. 6, 1953

*Humphries, J. (Derbys) b May 19, 1876, d May 7, 1946

Hunt, A. V. (Scotland & Bermuda) b Oct. 1, 1910, d March 3, 1999

Hunt, G. E. (Som) b Sept. 30, 1896, d Jan. 22, 1959

*Hunt, W. A. (NSW) b Aug. 26, 1908, d Dec. 30, 1983

*Hunte, Sir Conrad C. (B'dos; *CY 1964*) b May 9, 1932, d Dec. 3, 1999

*Hunte, E. A. C. (T/T) b Oct. 3, 1905, d June 26, 1967

Hunter, D. (Yorks) b Feb. 23, 1860, d Jan. 11, 1927

*Hutchinson, P. (SA) b Jan. 26, 1862, d Sept. 30, 1925

*Hutton, Sir Leonard (Yorks; *CY 1938*) b June 23, 1916, d Sept. 6, 1990

*Hutton, R. A. (CU, Yorks & Tvl) b Sept. 6, 1942

*Hylton, L. G. (Jam.) b March 29, 1905, d May 17, 1955

*Ibadulla, K. (Punjab, Warwicks, Tas. & Otago) b Dec. 20, 1935

*Ibrahim, K. C. (Bombay) b Jan. 26, 1919

Iddison, R. (Yorks & Lancs) b Sept. 15, 1834, d March 19, 1890

*Iddon, J. (Lancs) b Jan. 8, 1902, d April 17, 1946

*Igglesden, A. P. (Kent & W. Prov.) b Oct. 8, 1964

Ijaz Butt (Pak. Us, Punjab, Lahore, R'pindi & Multan) b March 10, 1938

*Ijaz Faqih (Kar., Sind, PWD & MCB) b March 24, 1956

*Ikin, J. T. (Lancs) b March 7, 1918, d Sept. 15, 1984

*Illingworth, R. CBE (Yorks & Leics; *CY 1960*) b June 8, 1932

*Imran Khan (Lahore, Dawood, Worcs, OU, PIA, Sussex & NSW; *CY 1983*) b Nov. 25, 1952

*Imtiaz Ahmed (N. Ind., Comb. Us, NWFP, Pak. Servs, Peshawar & PAF) b Jan. 5, 1928

*Imtiaz Ali (T/T) b July 28, 1954

Inchmore, J. D. (Worcs & N. Tvl) b Feb. 22, 1949

*Indrajitsinhji, K. S. (S'tra & Delhi) b June 15, 1937

Ingle, R. A. (Som) b Nov. 5, 1903, d Dec. 19, 1992

Ingleby-Mackenzie, A. C. D. (Hants; Pres. MCC 1996-98) b Sept. 15, 1933

Inman, C. C. (Ceylon & Leics) b Jan. 29, 1936

*Inshan Ali (T/T) b Sept. 25, 1949, d June 24, 1995

*Insole, D. J. CBE (CU & Essex; *CY 1956*; Chairman TCCB 1975-78) b April 18, 1926

*Intikhab Alam (Kar., PIA, Surrey, PWD, Sind, Punjab; ICC referee) b Dec. 28, 1941

*Inverarity, R. J. (W. Aust. & S. Aust.) b Jan. 31, 1944

*Iqbal Qasim (Kar., Sind & NBP) b Aug. 6, 1953

*Irani, J. K. (Sind) b Aug. 18, 1923, d Feb. 25, 1982

*Iredale, F. A. (NSW) b June 19, 1867, d April 15, 1926

Iremonger, J. (Notts; *CY 1903*) b March 5, 1876, d March 25, 1956

*Ironmonger, H. (Qld & Vic.) b April 7, 1882, d June 1, 1971

*Ironside, D. E. J. (Tvl) b May 2, 1925

*Irvine, B. L. (W. Prov., Natal, Essex & Tvl) b March 9, 1944

Isaacs, E. (ICC referee) b Jan. 26, 1945

*Israr Ali (S. Punjab, B'pur & Multan) b May 1, 1927

*Iverson, J. B. (Vic.) b July 27, 1915, d Oct. 24, 1973

*Jack, S. D. (Tvl) b Aug. 4, 1970

*Jackman, R. D. (Surrey, W. Prov. & Rhod.; *CY 1981*) b Aug. 13, 1945

*Jackson, A. A. (NSW) b Sept. 5, 1909, d Feb. 16, 1933

Jackson, A. B. (Derbys) b Aug. 21, 1933

*Jackson, Rt Hon. Sir F. Stanley (CU & Yorks; *CY 1894*; Pres. MCC 1921) b Nov. 21, 1870, d March 9, 1947

Jackson, G. R. (Derbys) b June 23, 1896, d Feb. 21, 1966

*Jackson, H. L. (Derbys; *CY 1959*) b April 5, 1921

Jackson, J. (Notts & All-England) b May 21, 1833, d Nov. 4, 1901

Jackson, P. F. (Worcs) b May 11, 1911, d April 27, 1999

Jackson, V. E. (NSW & Leics) b Oct. 25, 1916, d Jan. 30, 1965

*Jahangir Khan (N. Ind. & CU) b Feb. 1, 1910, d July 23, 1988

*Jai, L. P. (Bombay) b April 1, 1902, d Jan. 29, 1968

*Jaisimha, M. L. (H'bad) b March 3, 1939, d July 6, 1999

Jakeman, F. (Yorks & Northants) b Jan. 10, 1920, d May 18, 1986

*Jalal-ud-Din (PWD, Kar., IDBP & Allied Bank) b June 12, 1959

James, A. E. (Sussex) b Aug. 7, 1924

James, C. L. R. (Writer) b Jan. 4, 1901, d May 31, 1989

*James, K. C. (Wgtn & Northants) b March 12, 1904, d Aug. 21, 1976

*James, W. R. (Mat.) b Aug. 27, 1965

*Jameson, J. A. (Warwicks) b June 30, 1941

*Jamshedji, R. J. (Bombay) b Nov. 18, 1892, d April 5, 1976

*Jardine, D. R. (OU & Surrey; *CY 1928*) b Oct. 23, 1900, d June 18, 1958

*Jarman, B. N. (S. Aust.; ICC referee) b Feb. 17, 1936

*Jarvis, A. H. (S. Aust.) b Oct. 19, 1860, d Nov. 15, 1933

Jarvis, K. B. S. (Kent & Glos) b April 23, 1953

Jarvis, M. P. (Mash.) b Dec. 6, 1955

*Jarvis, T. W. (Auck. & Cant.) b July 29, 1944

*Javed Akhtar (R'pindi & Pak. Serv.; Test umpire) b Nov. 21, 1940

*Javed Miandad (Kar., Sind, Sussex, HBL & Glam; *CY 1982*) b June 12, 1957

*Jayantilal, K. (H'bad) b Jan. 13, 1948

Jayaprakash, A. V. (Test umpire) b March 14, 1950

*Jayasekera, R. S. A. (SL) b Dec. 7, 1957

Jayasinghe, S. (Ceylon & Leics) b Jan. 19, 1931

Jayasinghe, S. A. (SL) b July 15, 1955, d April 20, 1995

Jeeves, P. (Warwicks) b March 5, 1888, d July 22, 1916

Jefferies, S. T. (W. Prov., Derbys, Lancs, Hants & Boland) b Dec. 8, 1959

*Jeganathan, S. (SL) b July 11, 1951, d May 14, 1996

*Jenkins, R. O. (Worcs; *CY 1950*) b Nov. 24, 1918, d July 21, 1995

*Jenner, T. J. (W. Aust. & S. Aust.) b Sept. 8, 1944

*Jennings, C. B. (S. Aust. & Qld) b June 5, 1884, d June 20, 1950

Jennings, R. V. (Tvl & N. Tvl) b Aug. 9, 1954

Jephson, D. L. A. (CU & Surrey) b Feb. 23, 1871, d Jan. 19, 1926

Jepson, A. (Notts; Test umpire) b July 12, 1915, d July 17, 1997

*Jessop, G. L. (CU & Glos; *CY 1898*) b May 19, 1874, d May 11, 1955

Jesty, T. E. (Hants, Border, Griq. W., Cant., Surrey & Lancs; *CY 1983*) b June 2, 1948

Jewell, Major M. F. S. (Worcs & Sussex) b Sept. 15, 1885, d May 28, 1978

*John, V. B. (SL) b May 27, 1960

*Johnson, C. L. (Tvl) b 1871, d May 31, 1908

*Johnson, D. J. (Karn.) b Oct. 16, 1971

Johnson, G. W. (Kent & Tvl) b Nov. 8, 1946

*Johnson, H. H. H. (Jam.) b July 17, 1910, d June 24, 1987

Johnson, H. L. (Derbys) b Nov. 8, 1927

*Johnson, I. W. OBE (Vic.) b Dec. 8, 1917, d Oct. 9, 1998

Johnson, L. A. (Northants) b Aug. 12, 1936

*Johnson, L. J. (Qld) b March 18, 1919, d April 20, 1977

Johnson, P. R. (CU & Som) b Aug. 5, 1880, d July 1, 1936

*Johnson, T. F. (T/T) b Jan. 10, 1917, d April 5, 1985

Johnston, Brian A. CBE (Broadcaster) b June 24, 1912, d Jan. 5, 1994

*Johnston, W. A. (Vic.; *CY 1949*) b Feb. 26, 1922

Jones, A. MBE (Glam, W. Aust., N. Tvl & Natal; *CY 1978*) b Nov. 4, 1938

Jones, A. A. (Sussex, Som, Middx, Glam, N. Tvl & OFS) b Dec. 9, 1947

*Jones, A. H. (Wgtn & C. Dist.) b May 9, 1959

Jones, A. L. (Glam) b June 1, 1957

Jones, A. N. (Sussex, Border & Som) b July 22, 1961

*Jones, A. O. (Notts & CU; *CY 1900*) b Aug. 16, 1872, d Dec. 21, 1914

*Jones, C. M. (BG) b Nov. 3, 1902, d Dec. 10, 1959

*Jones, D. M. (Vic., Durham & Derbys) b March 24, 1961

*Jones, Ernest (S. Aust. & W. Aust.) b Sept. 30, 1869, d Nov. 23, 1943

Jones, E. C. (Glam) b Dec. 14, 1911, d April 14, 1989

Jones, E. W. (Glam) b June 25, 1942

*Jones, I. J. (Glam) b Dec. 10, 1941

Jones, K. V. (Middx) b March 28, 1942

*Jones, P. E. (T/T) b June 6, 1917, d Nov. 21, 1991

Jones, P. H. (Kent) b June 19, 1935

*Jones, S. P. (NSW, Qld & Auck.) b Aug. 1, 1861, d July 14, 1951

Jones, W. E. (Glam) b Oct. 31, 1916, d July 25, 1996

Jordon, R. C. (Vic.) b Feb. 17, 1937

*Joshi, P. G. (M'tra) b Oct. 27, 1926, d Jan. 8, 1987

Joshi, U. C. (S'tra, Ind. Rlwys, Guj. & Sussex) b Dec. 23, 1944

*Joslin, L. R. (Vic.) b Dec. 13, 1947

Julian, A. (Leics) b Aug. 23, 1936

*Julien, B. D. (T/T & Kent) b March 13, 1950

*Jumadeen, R. R. (T/T) b April 12, 1948

*Jupp, H. (Surrey) b Nov. 19, 1841, d April 8, 1889

*Jupp, V. W. C. (Sussex & Northants; *CY 1928*) b March 27, 1891, d July 9, 1960

*Jurangpathy, B. R. (CCC) b June 25, 1967

*Kallicharran, A. I. (Guyana, Warwicks, Qld, Tvl & OFS; *CY 1983*) b March 21, 1949

*Kaluperuma, L. W. (SL) b May 25, 1949

*Kaluperuma, S. M. S. (SL) b Oct. 22, 1961

*Kanhai, R. B. (†Guyana, T/T, W. Aust., Warwicks & Tas.; *CY 1964*) b Dec. 26, 1935

*Kanitkar, H. S. (M'tra) b Dec. 8, 1942

*Kapil Dev (Haryana, Northants & Worcs; *CY 1983*) b Jan. 6, 1959

**Kardar, A. H. (formerly Abdul Hafeez) (N. Ind., OU, Warwicks & Pak. Serv.) b Jan. 17, 1925, d April 21, 1996

*Keeton, W. W. (Notts; *CY 1940*) b April 30, 1905, d Oct. 10, 1980

*Keith, H. J. (Natal) b Oct. 25, 1927, d Nov. 17, 1997

*Kelleway, C. (NSW) b April 25, 1886, d Nov. 16, 1944

*Kelly, J. J. (NSW; *CY 1903*) b May 10, 1867, d Aug. 14, 1938

Kelly, J. M. (Lancs & Derbys) b March 19, 1922, d Nov. 13, 1979

*Kelly, T. J. D. (Vic.) b May 3, 1844, d July 20, 1893

*Kempis, G. A. (Natal) b Aug. 4, 1865, d May 19, 1890

*Kendall, T. (Vic. & Tas.) b Aug. 24, 1851, d Aug. 17, 1924

Kennedy, A. (Lancs) b Nov. 4, 1949

*Kennedy, A. S. (Hants; *CY 1933*) b Jan. 24, 1891, d Nov. 15, 1959

*Kenny, R. B. (Bombay & Bengal) b Sept. 29, 1930, d Nov. 21, 1985

*Kent, M. F. (Qld) b Nov. 23, 1953

*Kentish, E. S. M. (Jam. & OU) b Nov. 21, 1916

*Kenyon, D. (Worcs; *CY 1963*) b May 15, 1924, d Nov. 12, 1996

Kenyon, M. N. (Lancs) b Dec. 25, 1886, d Nov. 21, 1960

*Kerr, J. L. (Cant.) b Dec. 28, 1910

*Kerr, R. B. (Qld) b June 16, 1961

Key, Sir Kingsmill J. (Surrey & OU) b Oct. 11, 1864, d Aug. 9, 1932

*Khalid Hassan (Punjab & Lahore) b July 14, 1937

*Khalid Wazir (Pak.) b April 27, 1936

*Khan Mohammad (N. Ind., Pak. Us, Som, B'pur, Sind, Kar. & Lahore) b Jan. 1, 1928

Khanna, S. C. (Delhi) b June 3, 1956

Killick, E. H. (Sussex) b Jan. 17, 1875, d Sept. 29, 1948

*Killick, Rev. E. T. (CU & Middx) b May 9, 1907, d May 18, 1953

Kilner, N. (Yorks & Warwicks) b July 21, 1895, d April 28, 1979

*Kilner, R. (Yorks; *CY 1924*) b Oct. 17, 1890, d April 5, 1928

King, B. P. (Worcs & Lancs) b April 22, 1915, d March 31, 1970

*King, C. L. (B'dos, Glam, Worcs & Natal) b June 11, 1951

*King, F. M. (B'dos) b Dec. 14, 1926, d Dec. 23, 1990

King, J. B. (Philadelphia) b Oct. 19, 1873, d Oct. 17, 1965

*King, J. H. (Leics) b April 16, 1871, d Nov. 18, 1946

*King, L. A. (Jam. & Bengal) b Feb. 27, 1939, d July 9, 1998

*Kinneir, S. P. (Warwicks; *CY 1912*) b May 13, 1871, d Oct. 16, 1928

*Kippax, A. F. (NSW) b May 25, 1897, d Sept. 4, 1972

Kirby, D. (CU & Leics) b Jan. 18, 1939

*Kirmani, S. M. H. (†Karn.) b Dec. 29, 1949

*Kirsten, P. N. (W. Prov., Sussex, Derbys & Border) b May 14, 1955

*Kischenchand, G. (W. Ind., Guj. & Baroda) b April 14, 1925, d April 16, 1997

Kitchen, M. J. (Som; Test umpire) b Aug. 1, 1940

*Kline, L. F. (Vic.) b Sept. 29, 1934

*Knight, A. E. (Leics; *CY 1904*) b Oct. 8, 1872, d April 25, 1946

*Knight, B. R. (Essex & Leics) b Feb. 18, 1938

*Knight, D. J. (OU & Surrey; *CY 1915*) b May 12, 1894, d Jan. 5, 1960

Knight, R. D. V. (CU, Surrey, Glos & Sussex; Sec. MCC 1994–   ) b Sept. 6, 1946

Knight, W. H. (Editor of *Wisden* 1870-79) b Nov. 29, 1812, d Aug. 16, 1879

*Knott, A. P. E. (Kent & Tas.; *CY 1970*) b April 9, 1946

Knott, C. J. (Hants) b Nov. 26, 1914

Knowles, J. (Notts) b March 25, 1910

*Knox, N. A. (Surrey; *CY 1907*) b Oct. 10, 1884, d March 3, 1935

Koertzen, R. E. (Test umpire) b March 26, 1949

Kortright, C. J. (Essex) b Jan. 9, 1871, d Dec. 12, 1952

*Kotze, J. J. (Tvl & W. Prov.) b Aug. 7, 1879, d July 7, 1931

*Kripal Singh, A. G. (Madras & H'bad) b Aug. 6, 1933, d July 23, 1987

*Krishnamurthy, P. (H'bad) b July 12, 1947, d Jan. 28, 1999

*Kuggeleijn, C. M. (N. Dist.) b May 10, 1956

*Kuiper, A. P. (W. Prov., Derbys & Boland) b Aug. 24, 1959

*Kulkarni, R. R. (Bombay) b Sept. 25, 1962

*Kulkarni, U. N. (Bombay) b March 7, 1942

*Kumar, V. V. (†TN) b June 22, 1935

*Kunderan, B. K. (Ind. Rlwys & Mysore) b Oct. 2, 1939

*Kuruppu, D. S. B. P. (BRC) b Jan. 5, 1962

*Kuruppuarachchi, A. K. (NCC) b Nov. 1, 1964

*Kuys, F. (W. Prov.) b March 21, 1870, d Sept. 12, 1953

Kynaston, R. (Middx; Sec. MCC 1846-58) b Nov. 5, 1805, d June 21, 1874

*Labrooy, G. F. (CCC) b June 7, 1964

Lacey, Sir Francis E. (CU & Hants; Sec. MCC 1898-1926) b Oct. 19, 1859, d May 26, 1946

*Laird, B. M. (W. Aust.) b Nov. 21, 1950

*Laker, J. C. (Surrey, Auck. & Essex; *CY 1952*) b Feb. 9, 1922, d April 23, 1986

*Lall Singh (S. Punjab) b Dec. 16, 1909, d Nov. 19, 1985

*Lamb, A. J. (W. Prov., Northants & OFS; *CY 1981*) b June 20, 1954

Lamb, Hon. T. M. (OU, Middx & Northants; Chief Exec. ECB, 1997–   ) b March 24, 1953

*Lamba, R. (Delhi) b Jan. 2, 1960, d Feb. 23, 1998

Lambert, G. E. (Glos & Som) b May 11, 1918, d Oct. 31, 1991

Lambert, R. H. (Ireland) b July 18, 1874, d March 24, 1956

Lambert, Wm (Surrey) b 1779, d April 19, 1851

*Lance, H. R. (NE Tvl & Tvl) b June 6, 1940

Langdon, T. (Glos) b Jan. 8, 1879, d Nov. 30, 1944

Langford, B. A. (Som) b Dec. 17, 1935

*Langley, G. R. A. (S. Aust.; *CY 1957*) b Sept. 14, 1919

*Langridge, James (Sussex; *CY 1932*) b July 10, 1906, d Sept. 10, 1966

Langridge, John G. MBE (Sussex; Test umpire; *CY 1950*) b Feb. 10, 1910, d June 27, 1999

Langridge, R. J. (Sussex) b April 13, 1939

*Langton, A. B. C. (Tvl) b March 2, 1912, d Nov. 27, 1942

*Larkins, W. (Northants, E. Prov. & Durham) b Nov. 22, 1953

*Larter, J. D. F. (Northants) b April 24, 1940

*Larwood, H. MBE (Notts; *CY 1927*) b Nov. 14, 1904, d July 22, 1995

*Lashley, P. D. (B'dos) b Feb. 11, 1937

Latchman, H. C. (Middx & Notts) b July 26, 1943

*Latham, R. T. (Cant.) b June 12, 1961

*Laughlin, T. J. (Vic.) b Jan. 30, 1951

*Laver, F. (Vic.) b Dec. 7, 1869, d Sept. 24, 1919

Lavis, G. (Glam) b Aug. 17, 1908, d July 29, 1956

*Lawrence, D. V. (Glos) b Jan. 28, 1964

*Lawrence, G. B. (Rhod. & Natal) b March 31, 1932

Lawrence, J. (Som) b March 29, 1914, d Dec. 10, 1988

*Lawry, W. M. (Vic.; *CY 1962*) b Feb. 11, 1937

*Lawson, G. F. (NSW & Lancs) b Dec. 7, 1957

Lawton, A. E. (Derbys & Lancs) b March 31, 1879, d Dec. 25, 1955

Leach, G. (Sussex) b July 18, 1881, d Jan. 10, 1945

Leadbeater, B. (Yorks) b Aug. 14, 1943

*Leadbeater, E. (Yorks & Warwicks) b Aug. 15, 1927

Leary, S. E. (Kent) b April 30, 1933, d Aug. 21, 1988

Lee, C. (Yorks & Derbys) b March 17, 1924, d Sept. 3, 1999

Lee, F. S. (Middx & Som; Test umpire) b July 24, 1905, d March 30, 1982

Lee, G. M. (Notts & Derbys) b June 7, 1887, d Feb. 29, 1976

*Lee, H. W. (Middx) b Oct. 26, 1890, d April 21, 1981

Lee, J. W. (Middx & Som) b Feb. 1, 1904, d June 20, 1944

Lee, P. G. (Northants & Lancs; *CY 1976*) b Aug. 27, 1945

*Lee, P. K. (S. Aust.) b Sept. 15, 1904, d Aug. 9, 1980

*Lees, W. K. MBE (Otago) b March 19, 1952

*Lees, W. S. (Surrey; *CY 1906*) b Dec. 25, 1875, d Sept. 10, 1924

Lefebvre, R. P. (Holland, Som, Cant. & Glam) b Feb. 7, 1963

*Legall, R. (B'dos & T/T) b Dec. 1, 1925

*Leggat, I. B. (C. Dist.) b June 7, 1930

*Leggat, J. G. (Cant.) b May 27, 1926, d March 9, 1973

*Legge, G. B. (OU & Kent) b Jan. 26, 1903, d Nov. 21, 1940

Lenham, L. J. (Sussex) b May 24, 1936

Lenham, N. J. (Sussex) b Dec. 17, 1965

*le Roux, F. L. (Tvl & E. Prov.) b Feb. 5, 1882, d Sept. 22, 1963

le Roux, G. S. (W. Prov. & Sussex) b Sept. 4, 1955

*Leslie, C. F. H. (OU & Middx) b Dec. 8, 1861, d Feb. 12, 1921

Lester, E. (Yorks) b Feb. 18, 1923

Lester, G. (Leics) b Dec. 27, 1915, d Jan. 26, 1998

Lester, Dr J. A. (Philadelphia) b Aug. 1, 1871, d Sept. 3, 1969

*Lever, J. K. MBE (Essex & Natal; *CY 1979*) b Feb. 24, 1949

*Lever, P. (Lancs & Tas.) b Sept. 17, 1940

*Leveson Gower, Sir H. D. G. (OU & Surrey) b May 8, 1873, d Feb. 1, 1954

*Levett, W. H. V. (Kent) b Jan. 25, 1908, d Nov. 30, 1995

*Lewis, A. R. (Glam & CU; Pres. MCC 1998- ; writer & broadcaster) b July 6, 1938

Lewis, A. E. (Som) b Jan. 20, 1877, d Feb. 22, 1956

Lewis, C. BEM (Kent) b July 27, 1908, d April 26, 1993

*Lewis, D. M. (Jam.) b Feb. 21, 1946

Lewis, E. J. (Glam & Sussex) b Jan. 31, 1942

*Lewis, P. T. (W. Prov.) b Oct. 2, 1884, d Jan. 30, 1976

*Leyland, M. (Yorks; *CY 1929*) b July 20, 1900, d Jan. 1, 1967

*Liaqat Ali (Kar., Sind, HBL & PIA) b May 21, 1955

Lightfoot, A. (Northants) b Jan. 8, 1936

*Lillee, D. K. MBE (W. Aust., Tas. & Northants; *CY 1973*) b July 18, 1949

*Lilley, A. A. (Warwicks; *CY 1897*) b Nov. 28, 1866, d Nov. 17, 1929

Lilley, A. W. (Essex) b May 8, 1959

Lilley, B. (Notts) b Feb. 11, 1895, d Aug. 4, 1950

Lillywhite, Fred (Sussex; Editor of *Lillywhite's Guide to Cricketers*) b July 23, 1829, d Sept. 15, 1866

Lillywhite, F. W. ("William") (Sussex) b June 13, 1792, d Aug. 21, 1854

*Lillywhite, James, jun. (Sussex) b Feb. 23, 1842, d Oct. 25, 1929

*Lindsay, D. T. (NE Tvl, N. Tvl & Tvl) b Sept. 4, 1939

*Lindsay, J. D. (Tvl & NE Tvl) b Sept. 8, 1909, d Aug. 31, 1990

*Lindsay, N. V. (Tvl & OFS) b July 30, 1886, d Feb. 2, 1976

*Lindwall, R. R. MBE (NSW & Qld; *CY 1949*) b Oct. 3, 1921, d June 22, 1996

*Ling, W. V. S. (Griq. W. & E. Prov.) b Oct. 3, 1891, d Sept. 26, 1960

*Lissette, A. F. (Auck. & N. Dist.) b Nov. 6, 1919, d Jan. 24, 1973

Lister, W. H. L. (CU & Lancs) b Oct. 7, 1911, d July 29, 1998

Livingston, L. (NSW & Northants) b May 3, 1920, d Jan. 16, 1998

Livingstone, D. A. (Hants) b Sept. 21, 1933, d Sept. 8, 1988

Livsey, W. H. (Hants) b Sept. 23, 1893, d Sept. 12, 1978

*Llewellyn, C. B. (Natal & Hants; *CY 1911*) b Sept. 26, 1876, d June 7, 1964

Llewellyn, M. J. (Glam) b Nov. 27, 1953

Lloyd, B. J. (Glam) b Sept. 6, 1953

*Lloyd, C. H. OBE (†Guyana & Lancs; *CY 1971*) b Aug. 31, 1944

*Lloyd, D. (Lancs) b March 18, 1947

*Lloyd, T. A. (Warwicks & OFS) b Nov. 5, 1956

Lloyds, J. W. (Som, OFS & Glos) b Nov. 17, 1954

*Loader, P. J. (Surrey & W. Aust.; *CY 1958*) b Oct. 25, 1929

Lobb, B. (Warwicks & Som) b Jan. 11, 1931

*Lock, A. C. I. (Mash.) b Sept. 10, 1962

*Lock, G. A. R. (Surrey, W. Aust. & Leics; *CY 1954*) b July 5, 1929, d March 29, 1995

Lock, H. C. (Surrey; first TCCB pitch inspector) b May 8, 1903, d May 19, 1978

Lockwood, Ephraim (Yorks) b April 4, 1845, d Dec. 19, 1921

*Lockwood, W. H. (Notts & Surrey; *CY 1899*) b March 25, 1868, d April 26, 1932

Lockyer, T. (Surrey & All-England) b Nov. 1, 1826, d Dec. 22, 1869

Logan, J. D., jun. (SA) b June 24, 1880, d Jan. 3, 1960

*Logie, A. L. (T/T) b Sept. 28, 1960

*Lohmann, G. A. (Surrey, W. Prov. & Tvl; *CY 1889*) b June 2, 1865, d Dec. 1, 1901

Lomax, J. G. (Lancs & Som) b May 5, 1925, d May 21, 1992

Long, A. (Surrey & Sussex) b Dec. 18, 1940

Longrigg, E. F. (Som & CU) b April 16, 1906, d July 23, 1974

Lord, Thomas (Middx; founder of Lord's) b Nov. 23, 1755, d Jan. 13, 1832

*Love, H. S. B. (NSW & Vic.) b Aug. 10, 1895, d July 22, 1969

Love, J. D. (Yorks) b April 22, 1955

*Lowry, T. C. (Wgtn, CU & Som) b Feb. 17, 1898, d July 20, 1976

*Lowson, F. A. (Yorks) b July 1, 1925, d Sept. 8, 1984

*Loxton, S. J. E. (Vic.) b March 29, 1921

*Lucas, A. P. (CU, Surrey, Middx & Essex) b Feb. 20, 1857, d Oct. 12, 1923

Luckes, W. T. (Som) b Jan. 1, 1901, d Oct. 27, 1982

*Luckhurst, B. W. (Kent; *CY 1971*) b Feb. 5, 1939

Lumb, R. G. (Yorks) b Feb. 27, 1950

*Lundie, E. B. (E. Prov., W. Prov. & Tvl) b March 15, 1888, d Sept. 12, 1917

Lupton, A. W. (Yorks) b Feb. 23, 1879, d April 14, 1944

Lynch, M. A. (Surrey, Glos & Guyana) b May 21, 1958

Lyon, B. H. (OU & Glos; *CY 1931*) b Jan. 19, 1902, d June 22, 1970

Lyon, M. D. (CU & Som) b April 22, 1898, d Feb. 17, 1964

*Lyons, J. J. (S. Aust.) b May 21, 1863, d July 21, 1927

*Lyttelton, Hon. Alfred (CU & Middx; Pres. MCC 1898) b Feb. 7, 1857, d July 5, 1913

Lyttelton, Rev. Hon. C. F. (CU & Worcs) b Jan. 25, 1887, d Oct. 3, 1931

Lyttelton, Hon. C. G. (CU) b Oct. 27, 1842, d June 9, 1922

Lyttelton, Hon. C. J. (*see* 10th Visct Cobham)

*McAlister, P. A. (Vic.) b July 11, 1869, d May 10, 1938

*Macartney, C. G. (NSW & Otago; *CY 1922*) b June 27, 1886, d Sept. 9, 1958

*Macaulay, G. G. (Yorks; *CY 1924*) b Dec. 7, 1897, d Dec. 13, 1940

*Macaulay, M. J. (Tvl, W. Prov., OFS, NE Tvl & E. Prov.) b April 1939

*MacBryan, J. C. W. (CU & Som; *CY 1925*) b July 22, 1892, d July 14, 1983

*McCabe, S. J. (NSW; *CY 1935*) b July 16, 1910, d Aug. 25, 1968

*McCarthy, C. N. (Natal & CU) b March 24, 1929

*McConnon, J. E. (Glam) b June 21, 1922

*McCool, C. L. (NSW, Qld & Som) b Dec. 9, 1916, d April 5, 1986

McCorkell, N. (Hants) b March 23, 1912

*McCormick, E. L. (Vic.) b May 16, 1906, d June 28, 1991

*McCosker, R. B. (NSW; *CY 1976*) b Dec. 11, 1946

McCurdy, R. J. (Vic., Derbys, S. Aust., E. Prov. & Natal) b Dec. 30, 1959

*McDermott, C. J. (Qld; *CY 1986*) b April 14, 1965

*McDonald, C. C. (Vic.) b Nov. 17, 1928

*McDonald, E. A. (Tas., Vic. & Lancs; *CY 1922*) b Jan. 6, 1891, d July 22, 1937

*McDonnell, P. S. (Vic., NSW & Qld) b Nov. 13, 1858, d Sept. 24, 1896

McEwan, K. S. (E. Prov., W. Prov., Essex & W. Aust.; *CY 1978*) b July 16, 1952

*McEwan, P. E. (Cant.) b Dec. 19, 1953

*McGahey, C. P. (Essex; *CY 1902*) b Feb. 12, 1871, d Jan. 10, 1935

*MacGibbon, A. R. (Cant.) b Aug. 28, 1924

McGilvray, A. D. (NSW; broadcaster) b Dec. 6, 1909, d July 16, 1996

*McGirr, H. M. (Wgtn) b Nov. 5, 1891, d April 14, 1964

*McGlew, D. J. (Natal; *CY 1956*) b March 11, 1929, d June 9, 1998

*MacGregor, G. (CU & Middx; *CY 1891*) b Aug. 31, 1869, d Aug. 20, 1919

*McGregor, S. N. (Otago) b Dec. 18, 1931

*McIlwraith, J. (Vic.) b Sept. 7, 1857, d July 5, 1938

*McIntyre, A. J. (Surrey; *CY 1958*) b May 14, 1918

*Mackay, K. D. MBE (Qld) b Oct. 24, 1925, d June 13, 1982

McKechnie, B. J. (Otago) b Nov. 6, 1953

*McKenzie, G. D. (W. Aust. & Leics; *CY 1965*) b June 24, 1941

*McKibbin, T. R. (NSW) b Dec. 10, 1870, d Dec. 15, 1939

*McKinnon, A. H. (E. Prov. & Tvl) b Aug. 20, 1932, d Dec. 1, 1983

*MacKinnon, F. A. (CU & Kent; *believed to be longest-lived Test cricketer*) b April 9, 1848, d Feb. 27, 1947

*MacLaren, A. C. (Lancs; *CY 1895*) b Dec. 1, 1871, d Nov. 17, 1944

*McLaren, J. W. (Qld) b Dec. 24, 1887, d Nov. 17, 1921

MacLaurin of Knebworth, Lord (Chairman ECB 1997-   ) b March 30, 1937

*Maclean, J. A. (Qld) b April 27, 1946

*McLean, R. A. (Natal; *CY 1961*) b July 9, 1930

MacLeay, K. H. (W. Aust. & Som) b April 2, 1959

*McLeod, C. E. (Vic.) b Oct. 24, 1869, d Nov. 26, 1918

*McLeod, E. G. (Auck. & Wgtn) b Oct. 14, 1900, d Sept. 14, 1989

*McLeod, R. W. (Vic.) b Jan. 19, 1868, d June 14, 1907

McMahon, J. W. (Surrey & Som) b Dec. 28, 1919

*McMahon, T. G. (Wgtn) b Nov. 8, 1929

*McMaster, J. E. P. (Eng.) b March 16, 1861, d June 7, 1929

*McMillan, Q. (Tvl) b June 23, 1904, d July 3, 1948

McMorris, E. D. A. (Jam.) b April 4, 1935

*McRae, D. A. N. (Cant.) b Dec. 25, 1912, d Aug. 10, 1986

*McShane, P. G. (Vic.) b 1857, d Dec. 11, 1903

McSweeney, E. B. (C. Dist. & Wgtn) b March 8, 1957

McVicker, N. M. (Warwicks & Leics) b Nov. 4, 1940

*McWatt, C. A. (BG) b Feb. 1, 1922, d July 12, 1997

*Madan Lal (Punjab & Delhi) b March 20, 1951

*Maddocks, L. V. (Vic. & Tas.) b May 24, 1926

*Madray, I. S. (BG) b July 2, 1934

*Madugalle, B. S. (NCC; ICC referee) b April 22, 1959

Mafizur Rehman (Bangladesh) b Nov. 10, 1978

*Maguire, J. N. (Qld, E. Prov. & Leics) b Sept. 15, 1956

Maher, B. J. M. (Derbys) b Feb. 11, 1958

*Mahmood Hussain (Pak. Us, Punjab, Kar., E. Pak. & NTB) b April 2, 1932, d Dec. 25, 1991

*Mailey, A. A. (NSW; writer) b Jan. 3, 1886, d Dec. 31, 1967

*Majid Khan (Lahore, Pak. Us, CU, Glam, PIA, Qld, Punjab; *CY 1970*) b Sept. 28, 1946

*Maka, E. S. (Bombay) b March 5, 1922, dead

*Makepeace, H. (Lancs) b Aug. 22, 1881, d Dec. 19, 1952

*Malhotra, A. (Haryana, Bengal & Delhi) b Jan. 26, 1957

*Mallender, N. A. (Northants, Otago & Som) b Aug. 13, 1961

*Mallett, A. A. (S. Aust.) b July 13, 1945

*Malone, M. F. (W. Aust. & Lancs) b Oct. 9, 1950

*Maninder Singh (Delhi) b June 13, 1965

*Manjrekar, V. L. (Bombay, Bengal, Andhra, U. Pradesh, Raja. & M'tra) b Sept. 26, 1931, d Oct. 18, 1983

*Manjrekar, S. V. (†Mumbai) b July 12, 1965

*Mankad, A. V. (Bombay) b Oct. 12, 1946

*Mankad, V. (M. H.) (W. Ind., Naw., M'tra, Guj., Bengal, Bombay & Raja.; *CY 1947*) b April 12, 1917, d Aug. 21, 1978

*Mann, A. L. (W. Aust.) b Nov. 8, 1945

*Mann, F. G. CBE (CU & Middx; Chairman TCCB 1978-83; Pres. MCC 1984-85) b Sept. 6, 1917

*Mann, F. T. (CU & Middx) b March 3, 1888, d Oct. 6, 1964

*Mann, N. B. F. (Natal & E. Prov.) b Dec. 28, 1920, d July 31, 1952

Manning, J. S. (S. Aust. & Northants) b June 11, 1924 d May 5, 1988

Manning, T. E. (Northants) b Sept. 2, 1884, d Nov. 22, 1975

*Mansell, P. N. F. MBE (Rhod.) b March 16, 1920, d May 9, 1995

*Mansoor Akhtar (Kar., UBL & Sind) b Dec. 25, 1957

Mansur Ali Khan (*see* Pataudi, Mansur Ali, Nawab of)

*Mantri, M. K. (Bombay & M'tra) b Sept. 1, 1921

Manuel, P. (Test umpire) b Nov. 18, 1950

*Maqsood Ahmed (S. Punjab, R'pindi, B'pur & Kar.) b March 26, 1925, d Jan. 4, 1999

*Marais, G. G. ("G. Gladstone") (Jam.) b Jan. 14, 1901, d May 19, 1978

Marchant, F. (Kent & CU) b May 22, 1864, d April 13, 1946

*Markham, L. A. (Natal) b Sept. 12, 1924

*Marks, V. J. (OU, Som & W. Aust.; writer) b June 25, 1955

Marlar, R. G. (CU & Sussex; writer) b Jan. 2, 1931

Marlow, F. W. (Sussex) b Oct. 8, 1867, d Aug. 7, 1952

Marner, P. T. (Lancs & Leics) b March 31, 1936

*Marr, A. P. (NSW) b March 28, 1862, d March 15, 1940

*Marriott, C. S. (CU, Lancs & Kent) b Sept. 14, 1895, d Oct. 13, 1966

Marsden, Tom (Eng.) b 1805, d Feb. 27, 1843

*Marsh, G. R. (W. Aust.) b Dec. 31, 1958

*Marsh, R. W. MBE (W. Aust.; *CY 1982*) b Nov. 4, 1947

Marshal, Alan (Qld & Surrey; *CY 1909*) b June 12, 1883, d July 23, 1915

*Marshall, M. D. (B'dos, Hants & Natal; *CY 1983*) b April 18, 1958, d Nov. 4, 1999

*Marshall, N. E. (B'dos & T/T) b Feb. 27, 1924

*Marshall, R. E. (B'dos & Hants; *CY 1959*) b April 25, 1930, d Oct. 27, 1992

Marsham, C. H. B. (OU & Kent) b Feb. 10, 1879, d July 19, 1928

Martin, E. J. (Notts) b Aug. 17, 1925

*Martin, F. (Kent; *CY 1892*) b Oct. 12, 1861, d Dec. 13, 1921

*Martin, F. R. (Jam.) b Oct. 12, 1893, d Nov. 23, 1967

Martin, G. C. (Mash.) b May 30, 1966

*Martin, J. W. (NSW & S. Aust.) b July 28, 1931, d July 16, 1992

*Martin, J. W. (Kent) b Feb. 16, 1917, d Jan. 4, 1987

Martin, S. H. (Worcs, Natal & Rhod.) b Jan. 11, 1909, d Feb. 17, 1988

*Martindale, E. A. (B'dos) b Nov. 25, 1909, d March 17, 1972

Martin-Jenkins, Christopher (Writer & broadcaster) b Jan. 20, 1945

Maru, R. J. (Middx & Hants) b Oct. 28, 1962

*Marx, W. F. E. (Tvl) b July 4, 1895, d June 2, 1974

*Mason, J. R. (Kent; *CY 1898*) b March 26, 1874, d Oct. 15, 1958

*Masood Anwar (UBL, Multan & F'bad) b Dec. 12, 1967

Masood Iqbal (Lahore, Punjab U., Pak. Us & HBL) b April 17, 1952

*Massie, H. H. (NSW) b April 11, 1854, d Oct. 12, 1938

*Massie, R. A. L. (W. Aust.; *CY 1973*) b April 14, 1947

*Matheson, A. M. (Auck.) b Feb. 27, 1906, d Dec. 31, 1985

*Mathias, Wallis (Sind, Kar. & NBP) b Feb. 4, 1935, d Sept. 1, 1994

*Matthews, A. D. G. (Northants & Glam) b May 3, 1904, d July 29, 1977

*Matthews, C. D. (W. Aust. & Lancs) b Sept. 22, 1962

*Matthews, G. R. J. (NSW) b Dec. 15, 1959

*Matthews, T. J. (Vic.) b April 3, 1884, d Oct. 14, 1943

*Mattis, E. H. (Jam.) b April 11, 1957

*May, P. B. H. CBE (CU & Surrey; *CY 1952;* Pres. MCC 1980-81) b Dec. 31, 1929, d Dec. 27, 1994

*May, T. B. A. (S. Aust.) b Jan. 26, 1962

Mayer, J. H. (Warwicks) b March 2, 1902, d Sept. 6, 1981

Maynard, C. (Warwicks & Lancs) b April 8, 1958

*Mayne, E. R. (S. Aust. & Vict.) b July 2, 1882, d Oct. 26, 1961

*Mayne, L. C. (W. Aust.) b Jan. 23, 1942

*Mead, C. P. (Hants; *CY 1912*) b March 9, 1887, d March 26, 1958

*Mead, W. (Essex; *CY 1904*) b March 25, 1868, d March 18, 1954

Meads, E. A. (Notts) b Aug. 17, 1916

*Meale, T. (Wgtn) b Nov. 11, 1928

*Meckiff, I. (Vic.) b Jan. 6, 1935

Medlycott, K. T. (Surrey & N. Tvl) b May 12, 1965

*Meherhomji, K. R. (W. Ind. & Bombay) b Aug. 9, 1911, d Feb. 10, 1982

*Mehra, V. L. (E. Punjab, Ind. Rlwys & Delhi) b March 12, 1938

*Meintjes, D. J. (Tvl) b June 9, 1890, d July 17, 1979

*Melle, M. G. (Tvl & W. Prov.) b June 3, 1930

Melville, A. (OU, Sussex, Natal & Tvl; *CY 1948*) b May 19, 1910, d April 18, 1983

Meman, M. A. (Zimb.) b June 26, 1952

Mendis, G. D. (Sussex & Lancs) b April 20, 1955

*Mendis, L. R. D. (SSC) b Aug. 25, 1952

Mendis, M. C. (Colts) b Dec. 28, 1968

Mendonca, I. L. (BG) b July 13, 1934

*Mercer, J. (Sussex, Glam & Northants; *CY 1927*) b April 22, 1895, d Aug. 31, 1987

*Merchant, V. M. (Bombay; *CY 1937*) b Oct. 12, 1911, d Oct. 27, 1987

*Merritt, W. E. (Cant. & Northants) b Aug. 18, 1908, d June 9, 1977

*Merry, C. A. (T/T) b Jan. 20, 1911, d April 19, 1964

Metcalfe, A. A. (Yorks & Notts) b Dec. 25, 1963

Metson, C. P. (Middx & Glam) b July 2, 1963

*Meuleman, K. D. (Vic. & W. Aust.) b Sept. 5, 1923

Meuli, E. M. (C. Dist.) b Feb. 20, 1926

Meyer, B. J. (Glos; Test umpire) b Aug. 21, 1932

Meyer, R. J. O. OBE (CU, Som & W. Ind.) b March 15, 1905, d March 9, 1991

Mian Mohammed Saeed (N. India, Patiala & S. Punjab) b Aug. 31, 1910, d Aug. 23, 1979

*Middleton, J. (W. Prov.) b Sept. 30, 1865, d Dec. 23, 1913

Middleton, T. C. (Hants) b Feb. 1, 1964

**Midwinter, W. E. (Vic. & Glos) b June 19, 1851, d Dec. 3, 1890

*Milburn, B. D. (Otago) b Nov. 24, 1943

*Milburn, C. (Northants & W. Aust.; *CY 1967*) b Oct. 23, 1941, d Feb. 28, 1990

Milkha Singh, A. G. (Madras) b Dec. 31, 1941

*Miller, A. M. (Eng.) b Oct. 19, 1869, d June 26, 1959

Miller, F. P. (Surrey) b July 29, 1828, d Nov. 22, 1875

*Miller, G. (Derbys, Natal & Essex) b Sept. 8, 1952

*Miller, K. R. MBE (Vic., NSW & Notts; *CY 1954*) b Nov. 28, 1919

*Miller, L. S. M. (C. Dist. & Wgtn) b March 31, 1923, d Dec. 17, 1996

Miller, R. (Warwicks) b Jan. 6, 1941, d May 7, 1996

*Miller, R. C. (Jam.) b Dec. 24, 1924

*Milligan, F. W. (Yorks) b March 19, 1870, d March 31, 1900

*Millman, G. (Notts) b Oct. 2, 1934

Millmow, J. P. (Wgtn) b Sept. 22, 1967

*Mills, C. H. (Surrey, Kimberley & W. Prov.) b Nov. 26, 1867, d July 26, 1948

*Mills, J. E. (Auck.) b Sept. 3, 1905, d Dec. 11, 1972

Mills, P. T. (Glos) b May 7, 1879, d Dec. 8, 1950

*Milton, C. A. (Glos; *CY 1959*) b March 10, 1928

*Milton, Sir William H. (W. Prov.) b Dec. 3, 1854, d March 6, 1930

*Minnett, R. B. (NSW) b June 13, 1888, d Oct. 21, 1955

Minshull, John (scorer of first recorded century) b *circa* 1741, d Oct. 1793

*Miran Bux (Pak. Serv., Punjab & R'pindi) b April 20, 1907, d Feb. 8, 1991

*Misson, F. M. (NSW) b Nov. 19, 1938

*Mitchell, A. (Yorks) b Sept. 13, 1902, d Dec. 25, 1976

*Mitchell, B. (Tvl; *CY 1936*) b Jan. 8, 1909, d July 2, 1995

**Mitchell, F. (CU, Yorks & Tvl; *CY 1902*) b Aug. 13, 1872, d Oct. 11, 1935

*Mitchell, T. B. (Derbys) b Sept. 4, 1902, d Jan. 27, 1996

*Mitchell-Innes, N. S. (OU & Som) b Sept. 7, 1914

Mitchley, C. J. (Tvl; Test umpire) b July 4, 1938

*Modi, R. S. (Bombay) b Nov. 11, 1924, d May 17, 1996

*Mohammad Aslam (N. Ind. & Pak. Rlwys) b Jan. 5, 1920

*Mohammad Farooq (Kar.) b April 8, 1938

*Mohammad Ilyas (Lahore & PIA) b March 19, 1946

*Mohammad Munaf (Sind, E. Pak., Kar. & PIA) b Nov. 2, 1935

*Mohammad Nazir (Pak. Rlwys) b March 8, 1946

*Mohammad Zahid (PIA) b Aug. 2, 1976

*Mohsin Kamal (Lahore, Allied Bank & PNSC) b June 16, 1963

*Mohsin Khan (Pak. Rlwys, Kar., Sind, Pak. Us & HBL) b March 15, 1955

*Moir, A. M. (Otago) b July 17, 1919

*Mold, A. (Lancs; *CY 1892*) b May 27, 1863, d April 29, 1921

Moles, A. J. (Warwicks & Griq. W.) b Feb. 12, 1961

*Moloney, D. A. R. (Wgtn, Otago & Cant.) b Aug. 11, 1910, d July 15, 1942

*Moodie, G. H. (Jam.) b Nov. 25, 1915

*Moon, L. J. (CU & Middx) b Feb. 9, 1878, d Nov. 23, 1916

*Mooney, F. L. H. (Wgtn) b May 26, 1921

Moore, H. I. (Notts) b Feb. 28, 1941

Moore, R. H. (Hants) b Nov. 14, 1913

Moores, P. (Worcs & Sussex) b Dec. 18, 1962

Moorhouse, R. (Yorks) b Sept. 7, 1866, d Jan. 7, 1921

*More, K. S. (Baroda) b Sept. 4, 1962

Morgan, D. C. (Derbys) b Feb. 26, 1929

Morgan, R. W. (Auck.) b Feb. 12, 1941

*Morkel, D. P. B. (W. Prov.) b Jan. 25, 1906, d Oct. 6, 1980

*Morley, F. (Notts) b Dec. 16, 1850, d Sept. 28, 1884

*Moroney, J. (NSW) b July 24, 1917, d July 1, 1999

*Morris, A. R. MBE (NSW; *CY 1949*) b Jan. 19, 1922

*Morris, H. (Glam) b Oct. 5, 1963

Morris, H. M. (Essex & CU) b April 16, 1898, d Nov. 18, 1984

*Morris, S. (Vic.) b June 22, 1855, d Sept. 20, 1931

*Morrison, B. D. (Wgtn) b Dec. 17, 1933

*Morrison, D. K. (Auck. & Lancs) b Feb. 3, 1966

*Morrison, J. F. M. (C. Dist. & Wgtn) b Aug. 27, 1947

Morshed Ali Khan (Bangladesh) b May 14, 1972

Mortensen, O. H. (Denmark & Derbys) b Jan. 29, 1958

*Mortimore, J. B. (Glos) b May 14, 1933

Mortlock, W. (Surrey & Utd Eng. XI) b July 18, 1832, d Jan. 23, 1884

Morton, A., jun. (Derbys) b May 7, 1883, d Dec. 19, 1935

*Moseley, E. A. (B'dos, Glam, E. Prov. & N. Tvl) b Jan. 5, 1958

Moseley, H. R. (B'dos & Som) b May 28, 1948

*Moses, H. (NSW) b Feb. 13, 1858, d Dec. 7, 1938

*Moss, A. E. (Middx) b Nov. 14, 1930

*Moss, J. K. (Vic.) b June 29, 1947

*Motz, R. C. (Cant.; *CY 1966*) b Jan. 12, 1940

*Moule, W. H. (Vic.) b Jan. 31, 1858, d Aug. 24, 1939

*Moxon, M. D. (Yorks and Griq. W.; *CY 1993*) b May 4, 1960

*Mudassar Nazar (Lahore, Punjab, Pak. Us, HBL, PIA & UBL) b April 6, 1956

*Muddiah, V. M. (Mysore & Ind. Servs) b June 8, 1929

*Mufasir-ul-Haq (Kar., Dacca, PWD, E. Pak. & NBP) b Aug. 16, 1944, d July 27, 1983

Mukherjee, S. P. (Bengal) b Oct. 5, 1964

Munasinghe, A. M. N. (SSC) b Dec. 10, 1971

Muncer, B. L. (Glam & Middx) b Oct. 23, 1913, d Jan. 18, 1982

*Munden, V. S. (Leics) b Jan. 2, 1928

*Munir Malik (Punjab, R'pindi, Pak. Serv. & Kar.) b July 10, 1934

**Murdoch, W. L. (NSW & Sussex) b Oct. 18, 1854, d Feb. 18, 1911

*Murray, A. R. A. (E. Prov.) b April 30, 1922, d April 17, 1995

*Murray, B. A. G. (Wgtn) b Sept. 18, 1940

*Murray, D. A. (B'dos) b Sept. 29, 1950

*Murray, D. J. (Cant.) b Sept. 4, 1967

*Murray, D. L. (T/T, CU, Notts & Warwicks) b May 20, 1943

*Murray, J. T. MBE (Middx; *CY 1967*) b April 1, 1935

Murray-Wood, W. (OU & Kent) b June 30, 1917, d Dec. 21, 1968

Murrell, H. R. (Kent & Middx) b Nov. 19, 1879, d Aug. 15, 1952

*Musgrove, H. (Vic.) b Nov. 27, 1860, d Nov. 2, 1931

*Mushtaq Ali, S. (C. Ind., Guj., †M. Pradesh & U. Pradesh) b Dec. 17, 1914

*Mushtaq Mohammad (Kar., Northants & PIA; *CY 1963*) b Nov. 22, 1943

Mynn, Alfred (Kent & All-Eng.) b Jan. 19, 1807, d Nov. 1, 1861

*Nadkarni, R. G. (M'tra & Bombay) b April 4, 1932

Naeem Ahmed (Kar., Pak Us, NBP, UBL & PIA) b Sept. 20, 1952

*Nagel, L. E. (Vic.) b March 6, 1905, d Nov. 23, 1971

*Naik, S. S. (Bombay) b Feb. 21, 1945

*Nanan, R. (T/T) b May 29, 1953

*Naoomal Jeoomal, M. (N. Ind. & Sind) b April 17, 1904, d July 18, 1980

*Narasimha Rao, M. V. (H'bad) b Aug. 11, 1954

Naseer Malik (Khairpair & NBP) b Feb. 1, 1950, d Aug. 1, 1999

*Nash, L. J. (Tas. & Vic.) b May 2, 1910, d July 24, 1986

Nash, M. A. (Glam) b May 9, 1945

*Nasim-ul-Ghani (Kar., Pak. Us, Dacca, E. Pak., PWD & NBP) b May 14, 1941

*Naushad Ali (Kar., E. Pak., R'pindi, Peshawar, NWFP, Punjab & Pak. Serv.; ICC referee) b Oct. 1, 1943

*Navle, J. G. (Rajputna, C. Ind., Holkar & Gwalior) b Dec. 7, 1902, d Sept. 7, 1979

*Nayak, S. V. (Bombay) b Oct. 20, 1954

*Nayudu, Col. C. K. (C. Ind., Andhra, U. Pradesh & Holkar; *CY 1933*) b Oct. 31, 1895, d Nov. 14, 1967

*Nayudu, C. S. (C. Ind., Holkar, Baroda, Bengal, Andhra & U. Pradesh) b April 18, 1914

*Nazar Mohammad (N. Ind. & Punjab) b March 5, 1921, d July 12, 1996

*Nazir Ali, S. (S. Punjab & Sussex) b June 8, 1906, d Feb. 18, 1975

Neale, P. A. (Worcs; *CY 1989*) b June 5, 1954

Neale, W. L. (Glos) b March 3, 1904, d Oct. 26, 1955

*Neblett, J. M. (B'dos & BG) b Nov. 13, 1901, d March 28, 1959

Needham, A. (Surrey & Middx) b March 23, 1957

*Nel, J. D. (W. Prov.) b July 10, 1928

Nelson, R. P. (Middx, CU & Northants) b Aug. 7, 1912, d Oct. 29, 1940

*Newberry, C. (Tvl) b 1889, d Aug. 1, 1916

Newell, M. (Notts) b Feb. 25, 1965

*Newham, W. (Sussex) b Dec. 12, 1860, d June 26, 1944

Newland, Richard (Sussex) b circa 1718, d May 29, 1791

*Newman, Sir Jack (Wgtn & Cant.) b July 3, 1902, d Sept. 23, 1996

Newman, J. A. (Hants & Cant.) b Nov. 12, 1884, d Dec. 21, 1973

Newman, P. G. (Derbys) b Jan. 10, 1959

*Newson, E. S. OBE (Tvl & Rhod.) b Dec. 2, 1910, d April 24, 1988

Newstead, J. T. (Yorks; *CY 1909*) b Sept. 8, 1877, d March 25, 1952

Newton, A. E. (OU & Som) b Sept. 12, 1862, d Sept. 15, 1952

Niaz Ahmed (Dacca, E. Pak., PWD & Pak. Rlwys) b Nov. 11, 1945

Nicholas, M. C. J. (Hants) b Sept. 29, 1957

Nicholls, D. (Kent) b Dec. 8, 1943

Nicholls, E. A. (Test umpire) b Dec. 10, 1947

Nicholls, R. B. (Glos) b Dec. 4, 1933, d July 21, 1994

*Nichols, M. S. (Essex; *CY 1934*) b Oct. 6, 1900, d Jan. 26, 1961

Nicholson, A. G. (Yorks) b June 25, 1938, d Nov. 4, 1985

*Nicholson, F. (Griq. W.) b Sept. 17, 1909, d July 30, 1982

*Nicolson, J. F. W. (Natal & OU) b July 19, 1899, d Dec. 13, 1935

*Nissar, Mahomed (Patiala, S. Punjab & U. Pradesh) b Aug. 1, 1910, d March 11, 1963

*Nitschke, H. C. (S. Aust.) b April 14, 1905, d Sept. 29, 1982

*Noble, M. A. (NSW; *CY 1900*) b Jan. 28, 1873, d June 22, 1940

*Noblet, G. (S. Aust.) b Sept. 14, 1916

*Noreiga, J. M. (T/T) b April 15, 1936

Norman, M. E. J. C. (Northants & Leics) b Jan. 19, 1933

*Norton, N. O. (W. Prov. & Border) b May 11, 1881, d June 27, 1968

*Nothling, O. E. (NSW & Qld) b Aug. 1, 1900, d Sept. 26, 1965

*Nourse, A. D. ("Dudley") (Natal; *CY 1948*) b Nov. 12, 1910, d Aug. 14, 1981

*Nourse, A. W. ("Dave") (Natal, Tvl & W. Prov.) b Jan. 26, 1878, d July 8, 1948

*Nunes, R. K. (Jam.) b June 7, 1894, d July 22, 1958

*Nupen, E. P. (Tvl) b Jan. 1, 1902, d Jan. 29, 1977

Parish, R. J. (Aust. Administrator) b May 7, 1916

*Park, Dr R. L. (Vic.) b July 30, 1892, d Jan. 23, 1947

*Parkar, G. A. (Bombay) b Oct. 24, 1955

*Parkar, R. D. (Bombay) b Oct. 31, 1946, d Aug. 11, 1999

Parkar, Z. (Bombay) b Nov. 22, 1957

*Parker, C. W. L. (Glos; *CY 1923*) b Oct. 14, 1882, d July 11, 1959

*Parker, G. M. (SA) b May 27, 1899, d May 1, 1969

Parker, J. F. (Surrey) b April 23, 1913, d Jan. 27, 1983

*Parker, J. M. (N. Dist. & Worcs) b Feb. 21, 1951

*Parker, N. M. (Otago & Cant.) b Aug. 28, 1948

*Parker, P. W. G. (CU, Sussex, Natal & Durham) b Jan. 15, 1956

*Parkhouse, W. G. A. (Glam) b Oct. 12, 1925

*Parkin, C. H. (Yorks & Lancs; *CY 1924*) b Feb. 18, 1886, d June 15, 1943

*Parkin, D. C. (E. Prov., Tvl & Griq. W.) b Feb. 20, 1873, d March 20, 1936

Parks, H. W. (Sussex) b July 18, 1906, d May 7, 1984

*Parks, J. H. (Sussex & Cant.; *CY 1938*) b May 12, 1903, d Nov. 21, 1980

*Parks, J. M. (Sussex & Som; *CY 1968*) b Oct. 21, 1931

Parks, R. J. (Hants & Kent) b June 15, 1959

Parr, George (Notts & All-England) b May 22, 1826, d June 23, 1891

*Parry, D. R. (Comb. Is. & Leewards) b Dec. 22, 1954

*Parsana, D. D. (S'tra, Ind. Rlwys & Guj.) b Dec. 2, 1947

Parsons, A. B. D. (CU & Surrey) b Sept. 20, 1933, d Feb. 11, 1999

Parsons, G. J. (Leics, Warwicks, Boland, Griq. W. & OFS) b Oct. 17, 1959

Parsons, Canon J. H. (Warwicks) b May 30, 1890, d Feb. 2, 1981

*Partridge, J. T. (Rhod.) b Dec. 9, 1932, d June 7, 1988

Partridge, N. E. (Malvern, CU & Warwicks; *CY 1919*) b Aug. 10, 1900, d March 10, 1982

Partridge, R. J. (Northants) b Feb. 11, 1912, d Feb. 1, 1997

Parvez Mir (R'pindi, Lahore, Punjab, Pak. Us, Derbys, HBL & Glam) b Sept. 24, 1953

*Pascoe, L. S. (NSW) b Feb. 13, 1950

Pasqual, S. P. (SL) b Oct. 15, 1961

*Passailaigue, C. C. (Jam.) b Aug. 1902, d Jan. 7, 1972

*Patankar, C. T. (Bombay) b Nov. 24, 1930

**Pataudi, Iftiqar Ali, Nawab of (OU, Worcs, Patiala, N. Ind. & S. Punjab; *CY 1932*) b March 16, 1910, d Jan. 5, 1952

*Pataudi, Mansur Ali, Nawab of (Sussex, OU, Delhi & H'bad; *CY 1968*) b Jan. 5, 1941

Patel, A. K. (S'tra) b March 6, 1957

*Patel, B. P. (Karn.) b Nov. 24, 1952

*Patel, D. N. (Worcs & Auck.) b Oct. 25, 1958

*Patel, J. M. (Guj.) b Nov. 26, 1924, d Dec. 12, 1992

*Patel, R. G. M. (Baroda) b June 1, 1964

Paterson, G. A. (Zimb.) b June 9, 1960

*Patiala, Maharaja of (N. Ind., Patiala & S. Punjab) b Jan. 17, 1913, d June 17, 1974

*Patil, S. M. (Bombay & M. Pradesh) b Aug. 18, 1956

*Patil, S. R. (M'tra) b Oct. 10, 1933

*Patterson, B. P. (Jam., Tas. & Lancs) b Sept. 15, 1961

Patterson, W. H. (OU & Kent) b March 11, 1859, d May 3, 1946

*Payne, T. R. O. (B'dos) b Feb. 13, 1957

*Paynter, E. (Lancs; *CY 1938*) b Nov. 5, 1901, d Feb. 5, 1979

Payton, W. R. D. (Notts) b Feb. 13, 1882, d May 2, 1943

Peach, H. A. (Surrey) b Oct. 6, 1890, d Oct. 8, 1961

*Peall, S. G. (MCD) b Sept. 2, 1969

Pearce, T. N. (Essex) b Nov. 3, 1905, d April 10, 1994

*Pearse, O. C. (Natal) b Oct. 10, 1884, d May 7, 1953

Pearson, F. (Worcs & Auck.) b Sept. 23, 1880, d Nov. 10, 1963

*Peate, E. (Yorks) b March 2, 1855, d March 11, 1900

Peckover, G. E. (Zimb.) b June 2, 1955

*Peebles, I. A. R. (OU, Middx & Scotland; writer; *CY 1931*) b Jan. 20, 1908, d Feb. 28, 1980

*Peel, R. (Yorks; *CY 1889*) b Feb. 12, 1857, d Aug. 12, 1941

*Pegler, S. J. (Tvl) b July 28, 1888, d Sept. 10, 1972

*Pellew, C. E. (S. Aust.) b Sept. 21, 1893, d May 9, 1981

Penn, C. (Kent) b June 19, 1963

*Penn, F. (Kent) b March 7, 1851, d Dec. 26, 1916

Pepper, C. G. (NSW & Aust. Serv.; umpire) b Sept. 15, 1916, d March 24, 1993

Perkins, H. (CU & Cambs; Sec. MCC 1876-97) b Dec. 10, 1832, d May 6, 1916

*Perks, R. T. D. (Worcs) b Oct. 4, 1911, d Nov. 22, 1977

Perrin, P. A. (Essex; *CY 1905*) b May 26, 1876, d Nov. 20, 1945

Perryman, S. P. (Warwicks & Worcs) b Oct. 22, 1955

*Pervez Sajjad (Lahore, PIA & Kar.) b Aug. 30, 1942

*Petherick, P. J. (Otago & Wgtn) b Sept. 25, 1942

*Petrie, E. C. (Auck. & N. Dist.) b May 22, 1927

Pettiford, J. (NSW & Kent) b Nov. 29, 1919, d Oct. 11, 1964

*Phadkar, D. G. (M'tra, Bombay, Bengal & Ind. Rlwys) b Dec. 10, 1925, d March 17, 1985

Phebey, A. H. (Kent) b Oct. 1, 1924, d June 28, 1998

Phelan, P. J. (Essex) b Feb. 9, 1938

*Philipson, H. (OU & Middx) b June 8, 1866, d Dec. 4, 1935

*Phillip, N. (Comb. Is., Windwards & Essex) b June 12, 1948

Phillips, H. (Sussex) b Oct. 14, 1844, d July 3, 1919

Phillips, R. B. (NSW & Qld) b May 23, 1954

*Phillips, W. B. (S. Aust.) b March 1, 1958

*Phillips, W. N. (Vic.) b Nov. 7, 1962

Phillipson, C. P. (Sussex) b Feb. 10, 1952

Phillipson, W. E. (Lancs; Test umpire) b Dec. 3, 1910, d Aug. 24, 1991

*Philpott, P. I. (NSW) b Nov. 21, 1934

Pick, R. A. (Notts & Wgtn) b Nov. 19, 1963

Pieris, H. S. M. (SL) b Feb. 16, 1946

*Pierre, L. R. (T/T) b June 5, 1921, d April 14, 1989

*Pigott, A. C. S. (Sussex, Wgtn & Surrey) b June 4, 1958

Pilch, Fuller (Norfolk & Kent) b March 17, 1804, d May 1, 1870

Pilling, H. (Lancs) b Feb. 23, 1943

*Pilling, R. (Lancs; *CY 1891*) b July 5, 1855, d March 28, 1891

*Pithey, A. J. (Rhod. & W. Prov.) b July 17, 1933

*Pithey, D. B. (Rhod., OU, Northants, W. Prov., Natal & Tvl) b Oct. 4, 1936

*Place, W. (Lancs) b Dec. 7, 1914

Platt, R. K. (Yorks & Northants) b Dec. 21, 1932

*Playle, W. R. (Auck. & W. Aust.) b Dec. 1, 1938

Pleass, J. E. (Glam) b May 21, 1923

Plews, N. T. (Test umpire) b Sept. 5, 1934

*Plimsoll, J. B. (W. Prov. & Natal) b Oct. 27, 1917, d Nov. 11, 1999

Pocock, N. E. J. (Hants) b Dec. 15, 1951

*Pocock, P. I. (Surrey & N. Tvl) b Sept. 24, 1946

*Pollard, R. (Lancs) b June 19, 1912, d Dec. 16, 1985

*Pollard, V. (C. Dist. & Cant.) b Sept. 7, 1945

*Pollock, P. M. (E. Prov.; *CY 1966*) b June 30, 1941

*Pollock, R. G. (E. Prov. & Tvl; *CY 1966*) b Feb. 27, 1944

*Ponsford, W. H. MBE (Vic.; *CY 1935*) b Oct. 19, 1900, d April 6, 1991

Pont, K. R. (Essex) b Jan. 16, 1953

*Poole, C. J. (Notts) b March 13, 1921, d Feb. 11, 1996

Pooley, E. (Surrey & first England tour) b Feb. 13, 1838, d July 18, 1907

*Poore, M. B. (Cant.) b June 1, 1930

*Poore, Brig.-Gen. R. M. (Hants & SA; *CY 1900*) b March 20, 1866, d July 14, 1938

Pope, A. V. (Derbys) b Aug. 15, 1909, d May 11, 1996

*Pope, G. H. (Derbys) b Jan. 27, 1911, d Oct. 29, 1993

*Pope, Dr R. J. (NSW) b Feb. 18, 1864, d July 27, 1952

Popplewell, N. F. M. (CU & Som) b Aug. 8, 1957

Popplewell, Hon. Sir Oliver B. (CU; Pres. MCC 1994-96) b Aug. 15, 1927

Porter, G. D. (W. Aust.) b March 18, 1955

Pothecary, A. E. (Hants) b March 1, 1906, d May 21, 1991

*Pothecary, J. E. (W. Prov.) b Dec. 6, 1933

Potter, L. (Kent, Griq. W., Leics & OFS) b Nov. 7, 1962

*Pougher, A. D. (Leics) b April 19, 1865, d May 20, 1926

*Powell, A. W. (Griq. W.) b July 18, 1873, d Sept. 11, 1948

*Prabhakar, M. (Delhi & Durham) b April 15, 1963

*Prasanna, E. A. S. (†Karn.) b May 22, 1940

Prentice, F. T. (Leics) b April 22, 1912, d July 10, 1978

Pressdee, J. S. (Glam & NE Tvl) b June 19, 1933

Preston, Hubert (Editor of *Wisden* 1944-51) b Dec. 16, 1868, d Aug. 6, 1960

Preston, K. C. (Essex) b Aug. 22, 1925

Preston, Norman MBE (Editor of *Wisden* 1952-80) b March 18, 1903, d March 6, 1980

Pretlove, J. F. (CU & Kent) b Nov. 23, 1932

*Price, J. S. E. (Middx) b July 22, 1937

*Price, W. F. (Middx; Test umpire) b April 25, 1902, d Jan. 13, 1969

*Prideaux, R. M. (CU, Kent, Northants, Sussex & OFS) b July 31, 1939

Pridgeon, A. P. (Worcs) b Feb. 22, 1954

*Prince, C. F. H. (W. Prov., Border & E. Prov.) b Sept. 11, 1874, d Feb. 2, 1949

*Pringle, C. (Auck.) b Jan. 26, 1968

*Pringle, D. R. (CU & Essex) b Sept. 18, 1958

Pritchard, T. L. (Wgtn, Warwicks & Kent) b March 10, 1917

*Procter, M. J. (Glos, Natal, W. Prov., Rhod. & OFS; *CY 1970*) b Sept. 15, 1946

Prodger, J. M. (Kent) b Sept. 1, 1935

*Promnitz, H. L. E. (Border, Griq. W. & OFS) b Feb. 23, 1904, d Sept. 7, 1983

*Pullar, G. (Lancs & Glos; *CY 1960*) b Aug. 1, 1935

*Puna, N. (N. Dist.) b Oct. 28, 1929, d June 7, 1996

*Punjabi, P. H. (Sind & Guj.) b Sept. 20, 1921

*Pycroft, A. J. (Zimb.) b June 6, 1956

Pydanna, M. R. (Guyana) b Jan. 27, 1950

*Qasim Omar (Kar. & MCB) b Feb. 9, 1957

Quaife, B. W. (Warwicks & Worcs) b Nov. 24, 1899, d Nov. 28, 1984

Quaife, Walter (Sussex & Warwicks) b April 1, 1864, d Jan. 18, 1943

*Quaife, William (W. G.) (Warwicks & Griq. W.; *CY 1902*) b March 17, 1872, d Oct. 13, 1951

*Quinn, N. A. (Griq. W. & Tvl) b Feb. 21, 1908, d Aug. 5, 1934

*Rabone, G. O. (Wgtn & Auck.) b Nov. 6, 1921

*Rackemann, C. G. (Qld & Surrey) b June 3, 1960

Radcliffe, Sir Everard J. Bt (Yorks) b Jan. 27, 1884, d Nov. 23, .1969

*Radford, N. V. (Lancs, Tvl & Worcs; *CY 1986*) b June 7, 1957

*Radley, C. T. (Middx; *CY 1979*) b May 13, 1944

*Rae, A. F. (Jam.) b Sept. 30, 1922

Raees Mohammad (Kar.) b Dec. 24, 1932

*Rai Singh, K. (S. Punjab & Ind. Serv.) b Feb. 24, 1922

Rait Kerr, Col. R. S. (Eur.; Sec. MCC 1936-52) b April 13, 1891, d April 2, 1961

Rajab Ali (Kenya) b Nov. 19, 1965

Rajadurai, B. E. A. (SSC) b Aug. 24, 1965

*Rajindernath, V. (N. Ind., U. Prov., S. Punjab, Bihar & E. Punjab) b Jan. 7, 1928, d Nov. 22, 1989

*Rajinder Pal (Delhi, S. Punjab & Punjab) b Nov. 18, 1937

Ralph, L. H. R. (Essex) b May 22, 1920

*Ramadhin, S. (T/T & Lancs; *CY 1951*) b May 1, 1929

*Ramaswami, C. (Madras) b June 18, 1896, presumed dead.

Ramaswamy, V. K. (Test umpire) b April 26, 1946

*Ramchand, G. S. (Sind, Bombay & Raja.) b July 26, 1927

*Ramiz Raja (Lahore, Allied Bank, PNSC & I'bad) b Aug. 14, 1962

*Ramji, L. (W. Ind.) b Oct. 2, 1902, d Dec. 20, 1948

*Ranasinghe, A. N. (BRC) b Oct. 13, 1956, d Nov. 9, 1998

Ranasinghe, S. K. (SL) b July 4, 1962

*Ranatunga, D. (SSC) b Oct. 12, 1962

Ranatunga, N. (Colts & WPN) b Jan. 22, 1966

*Ranchod, U. (Mash.) b May 17, 1969

*Randall, D. W. (Notts; *CY 1980*) b Feb. 24, 1951

Randhir Singh (Orissa & Bihar) b Aug. 16, 1957

*Rangachari, C. R. (Madras) b April 14, 1916, d Oct. 9, 1993

*Rangnekar, K. M. (M'tra, Bombay & †M. Pradesh) b June 27, 1917, d Oct. 11, 1984

*Ranjane, V. B. (M'tra & Ind. Rlwys) b July 22, 1937

*Ranjitsinhji, K. S., (later H. H. the Jam Sahib of Nawanagar) (CU & Sussex; *CY 1897*) b Sept. 10, 1872, d April 2, 1933

*Ransford, V. S. (Vic.; *CY 1910*) b March 20, 1885, d March 19, 1958

*Rashid Khan (PWD, Kar. & PIA) b Dec. 15, 1959

Ratnayake, N. L. K. (SSC) b Nov. 22, 1968

*Ratnayeke, J. R. (NCC) b May 2, 1960

Rawlin, J. T. (Yorks & Middx) b Nov. 10, 1856, d Jan. 19, 1924

Rawson, P. W. E. (Zimb. & Natal) b May 25, 1957

Rayment, A. W. H. (Hants) b May 29, 1928

*Razdan, V. (Delhi) b Aug. 25, 1969

*Read, H. D. (Surrey & Essex) b Jan. 28, 1910, d Jan. 5, 2000

*Read, J. M. (Surrey; *CY 1890*) b Feb. 9, 1859, d Feb. 17, 1929

*Read, W. W. (Surrey; *CY 1893*) b Nov. 23, 1855, d Jan. 6, 1907

*Reddy, B. (TN) b Nov. 12, 1954

*Redmond, R. E. (Wgtn & Auck.) b Dec. 29, 1944

*Redpath, I. R. MBE (Vic.) b May 11, 1941

Reed, B. L. (Hants) b Sept. 17, 1937

*Reedman, J. C. (S. Aust.) b Oct. 9, 1865, d March 25, 1924

Rees, A. (Glam) b Feb. 17, 1938

*Reeve, D. A. OBE (Sussex & Warwicks; *CY 1996*) b April 2, 1963

Reeves, W. (Essex; Test umpire) b Jan. 22, 1875, d March 22, 1944

*Rege, M. R. (M'tra) b March 18, 1924

*Rehman, S. F. (Punjab, Pak. Us & Lahore) b June 11, 1935

*Reid, B. A. (W. Aust.) b March 14, 1963

*Reid, J. F. (Auck.) b March 3, 1956

*Reid, J. R. OBE (Wgtn & Otago; *CY 1959*; ICC referee) b June 3, 1928

*Reid, N. (W. Prov.) b Dec. 26, 1890, d June 6, 1947

Reid, R. B. (Wgtn & Auck.) b Dec. 3, 1958

Reidy, B. W. (Lancs) b Sept. 18, 1953

*Relf, A. E. (Sussex & Auck.; *CY 1914*) b June 26, 1874, d March 26, 1937

Relf, R. R. (Sussex) b Sept. 1, 1883, d April 28, 1965

*Renneburg, D. A. (NSW) b Sept. 23, 1942

Revill, A. C. (Derbys & Leics) b March 27, 1923, d July 6, 1998

Reynolds, B. L. (Northants) b June 10, 1932

Rhodes, A. E. G. (Derbys; Test umpire) b Oct. 10, 1916, d Oct. 18, 1983

*Rhodes, H. J. (Derbys) b July 22, 1936

*Rhodes, W. (Yorks; *CY 1899*) b Oct. 29, 1877, d July 8, 1973

Riazuddin (Test umpire) b Dec. 15, 1958

Rice, C. E. B. (Tvl & Notts; *CY 1981*) b July 23, 1949

Rice, J. M. (Hants) b Oct. 23, 1949

*Richards, A. R. (W. Prov.) b Dec. 14, 1867, d Jan. 9, 1904

*Richards, B. A. (Natal, Glos, Hants & S. Aust.; *CY 1969*) b July 21, 1945

*Richards, C. J. (Surrey & OFS) b Aug. 10, 1958

Richards, D. L. (Chief Exec. ICC 1993-) b July 28, 1946

Richards, G. (Glam) b Nov. 29, 1951

*Richards, Sir Vivian (I. V. A.) OBE (Comb. Is., Leewards, Som, Qld & Glam; *CY 1977*) b March 7, 1952

*Richards, W. H. (SA) b March 26, 1862, d Jan. 4, 1903

*Richardson, A. J. (S. Aust.) b July 24, 1888, d Dec. 23, 1973

Richardson, A. W. (Derbys) b March 4, 1907, d July 29, 1983

*Richardson, D. J. (E. Prov & N. Tvl) b Sept. 16, 1959

*Richardson, D. W. (Worcs) b Nov. 3, 1934

*Richardson, P. E. (Worcs & Kent; *CY 1957*) b July 4, 1931

*Richardson, R. B. (Leewards, Yorks, N. Tvl & Windwards; *CY 1992*) b Jan. 12, 1962

*Richardson, T. (Surrey & Som; *CY 1897*) b Aug. 11, 1870, d July 2, 1912

*Richardson, V. Y. (S. Aust.) b Sept. 7, 1894, d Oct. 29, 1969

Riches, N. V. H. (Glam) b June 9, 1883, d Nov. 6, 1975

*Richmond, T. L. (Notts) b June 23, 1890, d Dec. 29, 1957

*Rickards, K. R. (Jam. & Essex) b Aug. 23, 1923, d Aug. 21, 1995

Riddington, A. (Leics) b Dec. 22, 1911, d Feb. 25, 1998

*Ridgway, F. (Kent) b Aug. 10, 1923

*Rigg, K. E. (Vic.) b May 21, 1906, d Feb. 28, 1995

*Ring, D. T. (Vic.) b Oct. 14, 1918

*Ritchie, G. M. (Qld) b Jan. 23, 1960

*Rixon, S. J. (NSW) b Feb. 25, 1954

*Roach, C. A. (T/T) b March 13, 1904, d April 16, 1988

*Roberts, A. D. G. (N. Dist.) b May 6, 1947, d Oct. 26, 1989

*Roberts, A. M. E. CBE (Comb. Is., Leewards, Hants, NSW & Leics; *CY 1975*) b Jan. 29, 1951

*Roberts, A. T. (Windwards & T/T) b Sept. 18, 1937, d July 24, 1996

*Roberts, A. W. (Cant. & Otago) b Aug. 20, 1909, d May 13, 1978

Roberts, B. (Tvl & Derbys) b May 30, 1962

Roberts, F. G. (Glos) b April 1, 1862, d April 7, 1936

Roberts, S. J. (Lancs) b March 22, 1965

Roberts, W. B. (Lancs & Victory Tests) b Sept. 27, 1914, d Aug. 24, 1951

*Robertson, G. K. (C. Dist.) b July 15, 1960

*Robertson, J. B. (W. Prov.) b June 5, 1906, d July 5, 1985

*Robertson, J. D. (Middx; *CY 1948*) b Feb. 22, 1917, d Oct. 12, 1996

*Robertson, W. R. (Vic.) b Oct. 6, 1861, d June 24, 1938

Robertson-Glasgow, R. C. (OU & Som; writer) b July 15, 1901, d March 4, 1965

Robins, D. H. (Warwicks) b June 26, 1914

*Robins, R. W. V. (CU & Middx; *CY 1930*) b June 3, 1906, d Dec. 12, 1968

Robinson, D. C. (Glos & Essex) b April 20, 1884, d July 29, 1963

Robinson, E. (Yorks) b Nov. 16, 1883, d Nov. 17, 1969

Robinson, E. P. (Yorks & Som) b Aug. 10, 1911, d Nov. 10, 1998

Robinson, Sir Foster G. (Glos) b Sept. 19, 1880, d Oct. 31, 1967

Robinson, I. D. (Test umpire) b March 11, 1947

Robinson, P. E. (Yorks & Leics) b Aug. 3, 1963

Robinson, P. J. (Worcs & Som) b Feb. 9, 1943

*Robinson, R. D. (Vic.) b June 8, 1946

*Robinson, R. H. (NSW, S. Aust. & Otago) b March 26, 1914, d Aug. 10, 1965

Robson, C. (Hants) b June 20, 1859, d Sept. 27, 1943

Robson, E. (Som) b May 1, 1870, d May 23, 1924

*Rodriguez, W. V. (T/T) b June 25, 1934

Roe, B. (Som) b Jan. 27, 1939

Roebuck, P. M. (CU & Som; *CY 1988*) b March 6, 1956

Rogers, N. H. (Hants) b March 9, 1918

Rogers, S. S. (Eur. & Som) b March 18, 1923, d Nov. 6, 1969

Romaines, P. W. (Northants, Glos & Griq. W.) b Dec. 25, 1955

*Roope, G. R. J. (Surrey & Griq. W.) b July 12, 1946

*Root, C. F. (Derbys & Worcs) b April 16, 1890, d Jan. 20, 1954

*Rorke, G. F. (NSW) b June 27, 1938

*Rose, B. C. (Som; *CY 1980*) b June 4, 1950

*Rose-Innes, A. (Kimberley & Tvl) b Feb. 16, 1868, d Nov. 22, 1946

Rotherham, G. A. (Rugby, CU, Warwicks & Wgtn.; *CY 1918*) b May 28, 1899, d Jan. 31, 1985

Rouse, S. J. (Warwicks) b Jan. 20, 1949

*Routledge, T. W. (W. Prov. & Tvl) April 18, 1867, d May 9, 1927

*Rowan, A. M. B. (Tvl) b Feb. 7, 1921, d Feb. 21, 1998

*Rowan, E. A. B. (Tvl; *CY 1952*) b July 20, 1909, d April 30, 1993

Rowbotham, J. (Yorks; Test umpire) b July 8, 1831, d Dec. 22, 1899

*Rowe, C. G. (Wgtn & C. Dist.) b June 30, 1915, d June 9, 1995

Rowe, C. J. C. (Kent & Glam) b Nov. 11, 1951

Rowe, E. J. (Notts) b July 21, 1920, d Dec. 17, 1989

*Rowe, G. A. (W. Prov.) b June 15, 1874, d Jan. 8, 1950

*Rowe, L. G. (Jam. & Derbys) b Jan. 8, 1949

*Roy, A. (Bengal) b June 5, 1945, d Sept. 19, 1997

*Roy, Pankaj (Bengal) b May 31, 1928

*Roy, Pranab (Bengal) b Feb. 10, 1957

*Royle, Rev. V. P. F. A. (OU & Lancs) b Jan. 29, 1854, d May 21, 1929

*Rumsey, F. E. (Worcs, Som & Derbys) b Dec. 4, 1935

Rundle, D. B. (W. Prov.) b Sept. 25, 1965

Rushby, T. (Surrey) b Sept. 6, 1880, d July 13, 1962

*Russell, A. C. (Essex; *CY 1923*) b Oct. 7, 1887, d March 23, 1961

Russell, P. E. (Derbys) b May 9, 1944

Russell, S. E. J. (Middx & Glos) b Oct. 4, 1937, d June 18, 1994

*Russell, W. E. (Middx) b July 3, 1936

*Rutherford, J. W. (W. Aust.) b Sept. 25, 1929

Ryan, F. (Hants & Glam) b Nov. 14, 1888, d Jan. 5, 1954

Ryan, M. (Yorks) b June 23, 1933

*Ryder, J. (Vic.) b Aug. 8, 1889, d April 3, 1977

Saadat Ali (Lahore, UBL & HBFC) b Feb. 6, 1955

*Sadiq Mohammad (Kar., PIA, Tas., Essex, Glos & UBL) b May 3, 1945

*Saeed Ahmed (Punjab, Pak. Us, Lahore, PIA, Kar., PWD & Sind) b Oct. 1, 1937

*Saggers, R. A. (NSW) b May 15, 1917, d March 17, 1987

Saiful Islam (Bangladesh) b April 14, 1969

Sainsbury, P. J. (Hants; *CY 1974*) b June 13, 1934

*St Hill, E. L. (T/T) b March 9, 1904, d May 21, 1957

*St Hill, W. H. (T/T) b July 6, 1893, d *circa* 1957

*Salah-ud-Din (Kar., PIA & Pak. Us) b Feb. 14, 1947

*Saleem Altaf (Lahore & PIA) b April 19, 1944

*Saleem Jaffer (Kar. & UBL) b Nov. 19, 1962

Salim Badar (Test umpire) b May 16, 1953

Salim Pervez (NBP) b Sept. 9, 1947

*Salim Yousuf (Sind, Kar., IDBP, Allied Bank & Customs) b Dec. 7, 1959

Samaranayake, A. D. A. (SL) b Feb. 25, 1962

*Samarasekera, M. A. R. (CCC) b Aug. 5, 1961

Sampson, H. (Yorks & All-England) b March 13, 1813, d March 29, 1885

*Samuelson, S. V. (Natal) b Nov. 21, 1883, d Nov. 18, 1958

*Sandham, A. (Surrey; *CY 1923*) b July 6, 1890, d April 20, 1982

*Sandhu, B. S. (Bombay) b Aug. 3, 1956

Santall, F. R. (Warwicks) b July 12, 1903, d Nov. 3, 1950

Santall, S. (Warwicks) b June 10, 1873, d March 19, 1957

Sanuar Hossain (Bangladesh) b Aug. 5, 1973

*Sardesai, D. N. (Bombay) b Aug. 8, 1940

*Sarfraz Nawaz (Lahore, Punjab, Northants, Pak. Rlwys & UBL) b Dec. 1, 1948

*Sarwate, C. T. (CP & B, M'tra, Bombay & †M. Pradesh) b June 22, 1920

*Saunders, J. V. (Vic. & Wgtn) b March 21, 1876, d Dec. 21, 1927

Savage, J. S. (Leics & Lancs) b March 3, 1929

Savill, L. A. (Essex) b June 30, 1935

Saville, G. J. (Essex) b Feb. 5, 1944

Saxelby, K. (Notts) b Feb. 23, 1959

*Saxena, R. C. (Delhi & Bihar) b Sept. 20, 1944

Sayer, D. M. (OU & Kent) b Sept. 19, 1936

*Scarlett, R. O. (Jam.) b Aug. 15, 1934

*Schultz, B. N. (E. Prov. & W. Prov) b Aug. 26, 1970

*Schultz, S. S. (CU & Lancs) b Aug. 29, 1857, d Dec. 18, 1937

*Schwarz, R. O. (Middx & Natal; *CY 1908*) b May 4, 1875, d Nov. 18, 1918

*Scott, A. P. H. (Jam.) b July 29, 1934

Scott, C. J. (Glos) b May 1, 1919, d Nov. 22, 1992

Scott, C. W. (Notts & Durham) b Jan. 23, 1964

*Scott, H. J. H. (Vic.) b Dec. 26, 1858, d Sept. 23, 1910

Scott, M. E. (Northants) b May 8, 1936

*Scott, O. C. (Jam.) b Aug. 14, 1893, d June 15, 1961

*Scott, R. H. (Cant.) b March 6, 1917

*Scott, S. W. (Middx; *CY 1893*) b March 24, 1854, d Dec. 8, 1933

*Scott, V. J. (Auck.) b July 31, 1916, d Aug. 2, 1980

*Scotton, W. H. (Notts) b Jan. 15, 1856, d July 9, 1893

*Sealey, B. J. (T/T) b Aug. 12, 1899, d Sept. 12, 1963

*Sealy, J. E. D. (B'dos & T/T) b Sept. 11, 1912, d Jan. 3, 1982

*Seccull, A. W. (Kimberley, W. Prov. & Tvl) b Sept. 14, 1868, d July 20, 1945

*Sekar, T. A. P. (TN) b March 28, 1955

*Selby, J. (Notts) b July 1, 1849, d March 11, 1894

Sellers, A. B. MBE (Yorks; *CY 1940*) b March 5, 1907, d Feb. 20, 1981

*Sellers, R. H. D. (S. Aust.) b Aug. 20, 1940

*Selvey, M. W. W. (CU, Surrey, Middx, Glam & OFS; writer) b April 25, 1948

*Sen, P. (Bengal) b May 31, 1926, d Jan. 27, 1970

*Sen Gupta, A. K. (Ind. Serv.) b Aug. 3, 1939

*Senanayake, C. P. (CCC) b Dec. 19, 1962

*Serjeant, C. S. (W. Aust.) b Nov. 1, 1951

Seymour, James (Kent) b Oct. 25, 1879, d Sept. 30, 1930

*Seymour, M. A. (W. Prov.) b June 5, 1936

*Shackleton, D. (Hants; *CY 1959*) b Aug. 12, 1924

*Shafiq Ahmed (Lahore, Punjab, NBP & UBL) b March 28, 1949

*Shafqat Rana (Lahore & PIA) b Aug. 10, 1943

*Shah, A. H. (Mash.) b Aug. 7, 1959

*Shahid Israr (Kar. & Sind) b March 1, 1950

*Shahid Mahmood (Kar., Pak. Us & PWD) b March 17, 1939

*Shahid Saeed (HBFC, Lahore & PACO) b Jan. 6, 1966

*Shalders, W. A. (Griq. W. & Tvl) b Feb. 12, 1880, d March 18, 1917

Shariful Haq (Bangladesh) b Jan. 15, 1976

*Sharma, Chetan (Haryana & Bengal) b Jan. 3, 1966

*Sharma, Gopal (U. Pradesh) b Aug. 3, 1960

*Sharma, P. (Raja.) b Jan. 5, 1948

Sharma, Sanjeev (Delhi & H. Pradesh) b Aug. 25, 1965

Sharp, G. (Northants; Test umpire) b March 12, 1950

Sharp, H. P. (Middx) b Oct. 6, 1917, d Jan. 15, 1995

*Sharp, J. (Lancs) b Feb. 15, 1878, d Jan. 28, 1938

Sharp, K. (Yorks & Griq. W.) b April 6, 1959

*Sharpe, D. (Punjab, Pak. Rlwys, Lahore & S. Aust.) b Aug. 3, 1937

*Sharpe, J. W. (Surrey & Notts; *CY 1892*) b Dec. 9, 1866, d June 19, 1936

*Sharpe, P. J. (Yorks & Derbys; *CY 1963*) b Dec. 27, 1936

*Shastri, R. J. (Bombay & Glam) b May 27, 1962

*Shaw, Alfred (Notts & Sussex) b Aug. 29, 1842, d Jan. 16, 1907

Shaw, T. G. (E. Prov.) b July 5, 1959

*Sheahan, A. P. (Vic.) b Sept. 30, 1946

Sheffield, J. R. (Essex & Wgtn) b Nov. 19, 1906, d Nov. 16, 1997

Sheikh Salahuddin (Bangladesh) b Feb. 10, 1969

*Shepherd, B. K. (W. Aust.) b April 23, 1937

Shepherd, D. J. (Glam; *CY 1970*) b Aug. 12, 1927

Shepherd, D. R. MBE (Glos; Test umpire) b Dec. 27, 1940

*Shepherd, J. N. (B'dos, Kent, Rhod. & Glos; *CY 1979*) b Nov. 9, 1943

Shepherd, T. F. (Surrey) b Dec. 5, 1889, d Feb. 13, 1957

*Sheppard, Rt Rev. D. S. (Bishop of Liverpool; later Baron Sheppard) (CU & Sussex; *CY 1953*) b March 6, 1929

*Shepstone, G. H. (Tvl) b April 9, 1876, d July 3, 1940

*Sherwell, P. W. (Tvl) b Aug. 17, 1880, d April 17, 1948

*Sherwin, M. (Notts; *CY 1891*) b Feb. 26, 1851, d July 3, 1910

Shields, J. (Leics) b Feb. 1, 1882, d May 11, 1960

*Shillingford, G. C. (Comb. Is. & Windwards) b Sept. 25, 1944

*Shillingford, I. T. (Comb. Is. & Windwards) b April 18, 1944

*Shinde, S. G. (Baroda, M'tra & Bombay) b Aug. 18, 1923, d June 22, 1955

Shine, K. J. (Hants, Middx & Somerset) b Feb. 22, 1969

Shipman, A. W. (Leics) b March 7, 1901, d Dec. 12, 1979

Shirreff, A. C. (CU, Hants, Kent & Som) b Feb. 12, 1919

*Shivnarine, S. (Guyana) b May 13, 1952

*Shodhan, R. H. (Guj. & Baroda) b Oct. 18, 1928

*Shrewsbury, A. (Notts; *CY 1890*) b April 11, 1856, d May 19, 1903

*Shrimpton, M. J. F. (C. Dist. & N. Dist.) b June 23, 1940

*Shuja-ud-Din, Col. (N. Ind., Pak. Us, Pak. Serv., B'pur & R'pindi) b April 10, 1930

*Shukla, R. C. (Bihar & Delhi) b Feb. 4, 1948

*Shuter, J. (Kent & Surrey) b Feb. 9, 1855, d July 5, 1920

*Shuttleworth, K. (Lancs & Leics) b Nov. 13, 1944

Sibbles, F. M. (Lancs) b March 15, 1904, d July 20, 1973

*Sidebottom, A. (Yorks & OFS) b April 1, 1954

Sidwell, T. E. (Leics) b Jan. 30, 1888, d Dec. 8, 1958

*Siedle, I. J. (Natal) b Jan. 11, 1903, d Aug. 24, 1982

*Sievers, M. W. (Vic.) b April 13, 1912, d May 10, 1968

*Sikander Bakht (PWD, PIA, Sind, Kar. & UBL) b Aug. 25, 1957

Silk, D. R. W. CBE (CU & Som; Pres. MCC 1992-94; Chairman TCCB 1994-96) b Oct. 8, 1931

*Silva, S. A. R. (NCC) b Dec. 12, 1960

Sime, W. A. MBE (OU & Notts) b Feb. 8, 1909, d May 5, 1983

Simmons, J. MBE (Lancs & Tas.; *CY 1985*) b March 28, 1941

*Simpson, R. B. (NSW & W. Aust.; *CY 1965*) b Feb. 3, 1936

*Simpson, R. T. (Sind & Notts; *CY 1950*) b Feb. 27, 1920

*Simpson-Hayward, G. H. (Worcs) b June 7, 1875, d Oct. 2, 1936

Sims, Sir Arthur (Cant.) b July 22, 1877, d April 27, 1969

*Sims, J. M. (Middx) b May 13, 1903, d April 27, 1973

*Sinclair, B. W. (Wgtn) b Oct. 23, 1936

*Sinclair, I. M. (Cant.) b June 1, 1933

*Sinclair, J. H. (Tvl) b Oct. 16, 1876, d Feb. 23, 1913

*Sincock, D. J. (S. Aust.) b Feb. 1, 1942

*Sinfield, R. A. (Glos) b Dec. 24, 1900, d March 17, 1988

*Singh, Charan K. (T/T) b Nov. 27, 1935

Singh, R. P. (U. Pradesh) b Jan. 6, 1963

Singleton, A. P. (OU, Worcs & Rhod.) b Aug. 5, 1914, d March 22, 1999

Skelding, A. (Leics; umpire) b Sept. 5, 1886, d April 17, 1960

*Slack, W. N. (Middx & Windwards) b Dec. 12, 1954, d Jan. 15, 1989

Slade, D. N. F. (Worcs) b Aug. 24, 1940

Slater, A. G. (Derbys) b Nov. 22, 1890, d July 22, 1949

*Slater, K. N. (W. Aust.) b March 12, 1935

*Sleep, P. R. (S. Aust.) b May 4, 1957

*Slight, J. (Vic.) b Oct. 20, 1855, d Dec. 9, 1930

Slocombe, P. A. (Som) b Sept. 6, 1954

*Smailes, T. F. (Yorks) b March 27, 1910, d Dec. 1, 1970

Smales, K. (Yorks & Notts) b Sept. 15, 1927

*Small, G. C. (Warwicks & S. Aust.) b Oct. 18, 1961

Small, John, sen. (Hants & All-England) b April 19, 1737, d Dec. 31, 1826

*Small, J. A. (T/T) b Nov. 3, 1892, d April 26, 1958

*Small, M. A. (B'dos) b Feb. 12, 1964

Smart, C. C. (Warwicks & Glam) b July 23, 1898, d May 21, 1975

Smart, J. A. (Warwicks) b April 12, 1891, d Oct. 3, 1979

Smedley, M. J. (Notts) b Oct. 28, 1941

*Smith, A. C. CBE (OU & Warwicks; Chief Exec. TCCB 1987-96; ICC referee) b Oct. 25, 1936

*Smith, Sir C. Aubrey (CU, Sussex & Tvl) b July 21, 1863, d Dec. 20, 1948

*Smith, C. I. J. (Middx; *CY 1935*) b Aug. 25, 1906, d Feb. 9, 1979

*Smith, C. J. E. (Tvl) b Dec. 25, 1872, d March 27, 1947

*Smith, C. L. (Natal, Glam & Hants; *CY 1984*) b Oct. 15, 1958

Smith, C. L. A. (Sussex) b Jan. 1, 1879, d Nov. 22, 1949

Smith, C. S. (later Sir Colin Stansfield-) (CU & Lancs) b Oct. 1, 1932

*Smith, C. W. (B'dos; ICC referee) b July 29, 1933

*Smith, Denis (Derbys; *CY 1936*) b Jan. 24, 1907, d Sept. 12, 1979

*Smith, D. B. M. (Vic.) b Sept. 14, 1884, d July 29, 1963

Smith, D. H. K. (Derbys & OFS) b June 29, 1940

*Smith, D. M. (Surrey, Worcs & Sussex) b Jan. 9, 1956

*Smith, D. R. (Glos) b Oct. 5, 1934

*Smith, D. V. (Sussex) b June 14, 1923

Smith, Edwin (Derbys) b Jan. 2, 1934

Smith, Ernest (OU & Yorks) b Oct. 19, 1869, d April 9, 1945

*Smith, E. J. (Warwicks) b Feb. 6, 1886, d Aug. 31, 1979

*Smith, F. B. (Cant.) b March 13, 1922, d July 6, 1997

*Smith, F. W. (Tvl) b unknown, d April 17, 1914, aged 53

Smith, G. J. (Essex) b April 2, 1935

*Smith, Harry (Glos) b May 21, 1890, d Nov. 12, 1937

Smith, H. A. (Leics) b March 29, 1901, d Aug. 7, 1948

*Smith, H. D. (Otago & Cant.) b Jan. 8, 1913, d Jan. 25, 1986

*Smith, I. D. S. MBE (C. Dist. & Auck.) b Feb. 28, 1957

Smith, K. D. (Warwicks) b July 9, 1956

Smith, M. J. (Middx) b Jan. 4, 1942

*Smith, M. J. K. OBE (Leics, OU & Warwicks; *CY 1960*) b June 30, 1933

Smith, N. (Yorks & Essex) b April 1, 1949

*Smith, O. G. ("Collie") (Jam.; *CY 1958*) b May 5, 1933, d Sept. 9, 1959

Smith, P. A. (Warwicks) b April 5, 1964

Smith, Ray (Essex) b Aug. 10, 1914, d Feb. 21, 1996

Smith, Roy (Som) b April 14, 1930

Smith, R. C. (Leics) b Aug. 3, 1935

*Smith, S. B. (NSW & Tvl) b Oct. 18, 1961

Smith, S. G. (T/T, Northants & Auck.; *CY 1915*) b Jan. 15, 1881, d Oct. 25, 1963

*Smith, T. P. B. (Essex; *CY 1947*) b Oct. 30, 1908, d Aug. 4, 1967

*Smith, V. I. (Natal) b Feb. 23, 1925

Smith, W. A. (Surrey) b Sept. 15, 1937

Smith, W. C. (Surrey; *CY 1911*) b Oct. 4, 1877, d July 16, 1946

*Smithson, G. A. (Yorks & Leics) b Nov. 1, 1926, d Sept. 6, 1970

*Snedden, C. A. (Auck.) b Jan. 7, 1918

*Snedden, M. C. (Auck.) b Nov. 23, 1958

*Snell, R. P. (Natal, Tvl, Somerset & Gauteng) b Sept. 12, 1968

Snellgrove, K. L. (Lancs) b Nov. 12, 1941

*Snooke, S. D. (W. Prov. & Tvl) b Nov. 11, 1878, d April 6, 1959

*Snooke, S. J. (Border, W. Prov. & Tvl) b Feb. 1, 1881, d Aug. 14, 1966

*Snow, J. A. (Sussex; *CY 1973*) b Oct. 13, 1941

*Sobers, Sir Garfield S. (B'dos, S. Aust. & Notts; *CY 1964*) b July 28, 1936

Sohail Fazal (HBL) b Nov. 11, 1967

*Sohoni, S. W. (M'tra, Baroda & Bombay) b March 5, 1918, d May 19, 1993

*Solkar, E. D. (Bombay & Sussex) b March 18, 1948

*Solomon, J. S. (BG) b Aug. 26, 1930

*Solomon, W. R. (Tvl & E. Prov.) b April 23, 1872, d July 12, 1964

*Sood, M. M. (Delhi) b July 6, 1939

Southern, J. W. (Hants) b Sept. 2, 1952

*Southerton, James (Surrey, Hants & Sussex) b Nov. 16, 1827, d June 16, 1880

Southerton, S. J. (Editor of *Wisden* 1934-35) b July 7, 1874, d March 12, 1935

*Sparling, J. T. (Auck.) b July 24, 1938

Spencer, C. T. (Leics) b Aug. 18, 1931

Spencer, J. (CU & Sussex) b Oct. 6, 1949

Spencer, T. W. OBE (Kent; Test umpire) b March 22, 1914

Sperry, J. (Leics) b March 19, 1910, d April 21, 1997

*Spofforth, F. R. (NSW & Vic.) b Sept. 9, 1853, d June 4, 1926

*Spooner, R. H. (Lancs; *CY 1905*) b Oct. 21, 1880, d Oct. 2, 1961

*Spooner, R. T. (Warwicks) b Dec. 30, 1919, d Dec. 20, 1997

Springall, J. D. (Notts) b Sept. 19, 1932

Sprot, E. M. (Hants) b Feb. 4, 1872, d Oct. 8, 1945

Squires, H. S. (Surrey) b Feb. 22, 1909, d Jan. 24, 1950

*Srikkanth, K. (TN) b Dec. 21, 1959

*Srinivasan, T. E. (TN) b Oct. 26, 1950

*Stackpole, K. R. MBE (Vic.; *CY 1973*) b July 10, 1940

Standen, J. A. (Worcs) b May 30, 1935

*Stanyforth, Lt.-Col. R. T. (Yorks) b May 30, 1892, d Feb. 20, 1964

Staples, A. (Notts) b Feb. 4, 1899, d Sept. 9, 1965

*Staples, S. J. (Notts; *CY 1929*) b Sept. 18, 1892, d June 4, 1950

*Statham, J. B. CBE (Lancs; *CY 1955*) b June 17, 1930

*Stayers, S. C. (†Guyana & Bombay) b June 9, 1937

Stead, B. (Yorks, Essex, Notts & N. Tvl) b June 21, 1939, d April 15, 1980

*Steel, A. G. (CU & Lancs; Pres. MCC 1902) b Sept. 24, 1858, d June 15, 1914

*Steele, D. S. OBE (Northants & Derbys; *CY 1976*) b Sept. 29, 1941

Steele, J. F. (Leics, Natal & Glam) b July 23, 1946

Stephens, E. J. (Glos) b March 23, 1909, d April 3, 1983

Stephenson, F. D. (B'dos, Glos, Tas., Notts, Sussex & †FS; *CY 1989*) b April 8, 1959

Stephenson, G. R. (Derbys & Hants) b Nov. 19, 1942

Stephenson, H. H. (Surrey & All-England) b May 3, 1832, d Dec. 17, 1896

Stephenson, H. W. (Som) b July 18, 1920

Stephenson, Lt.-Col. J. R. CBE (Sec. MCC 1987-93) b Feb. 25, 1931

Stephenson, Lt.-Col. J. W. A. (Essex, Worcs, Army, Europeans & Victory Tests) b Aug. 1, 1907, d May 20, 1982

Stevens, Edward ("Lumpy") (Hants) b *circa* 1735, d Sept. 7, 1819

*Stevens, G. B. (S. Aust.) b Feb. 29, 1932

*Stevens, G. T. S. (UCS, OU & Middx; *CY 1918*) b Jan. 7, 1901, d Sept. 19, 1970

*Stevenson, G. B. (Yorks & Northants) b Dec. 16, 1955

Stevenson, K. (Derbys & Hants) b Oct. 6, 1950

*Stewart, M. J. OBE (Surrey; *CY 1958*) b Sept. 16, 1932

*Stewart, R. B. (SA) b Sept. 3, 1856, d Sept. 12, 1913

Stewart, W. J. (Warwicks & Northants) b Oct. 31, 1934

*Stirling, D. A. (C. Dist.) b Oct. 5, 1961

Stocks, F. W. (Notts) b Nov. 6, 1918, d Feb. 23, 1996

*Stoddart, A. E. (Middx; *CY 1893*) b March 11, 1863, d April 3, 1915

*Stollmeyer, J. B. (T/T) b April 11, 1921, d Sept. 10, 1989

*Stollmeyer, V. H. (T/T) b Jan. 24, 1916, d Sept. 21, 1999

Stone, J. (Hants & Glam) b Nov. 29, 1876, d Nov. 15, 1942

Storer, H. jun. (Derbys) b Feb. 2, 1898, d Sept. 1, 1967

*Storer, W. (Derbys; *CY 1899*) b Jan. 25, 1867, d Feb. 28, 1912

Storey, S. J. (Surrey & Sussex) b Jan. 6, 1941

Stott, L. W. (Auck.) b Dec. 8, 1946

Stott, W. B. (Yorks) b July 18, 1934

Stovold, A. W. (Glos & OFS) b March 19, 1953

Street, G. B. (Sussex) b Dec. 6, 1889, d April 24, 1924

*Stricker, L. A. (Tvl) b May 26, 1884, d Feb. 5, 1960

*Strudwick, H. (Surrey; *CY 1912*) b Jan. 28, 1880, d Feb. 14, 1970

*Studd, C. T. (CU & Middx) b Dec. 2, 1860, d July 16, 1931

*Studd, G. B. (CU & Middx) b Oct. 20, 1859, d Feb. 13, 1945

Studd, Sir J. E. Kynaston (Middx & CU; Pres. MCC 1930) b July 26, 1858, d Jan. 14, 1944

*Su'a, M. L. (N. Dist. & Auck.) b Nov. 7, 1966

*Subba Row, R. CBE (CU, Surrey & Northants; *CY 1961*; Chairman TCCB 1985-90; ICC referee) b Jan. 29, 1932

*Subramanya, V. (Mysore) b July 16, 1936

Sudhakar Rao, R. (Karn.) b Aug. 8, 1952

Sueter, T. (Hants & Surrey) b *circa* 1749, d Feb. 17, 1827

*Sugg, F. H. (Yorks, Derbys & Lancs; *CY 1890*) b Jan. 11, 1862, d May 29, 1933

Sullivan, J. (Lancs) b Feb. 5, 1945

Sully, H. (Som & Northants) b Nov. 1, 1939

*Sunderram, G. (Bombay & Raja.) b March 29, 1930

*Surendranath, R. (Ind. Serv.) b Jan. 4, 1937

Surridge, W. S. (Surrey; *CY 1953*) b Sept. 3, 1917, d April 13, 1992

*Surti, R. F. (Guj., Raja., & Qld) b May 25, 1936

*Susskind, M. J. (CU, Middx & Tvl) b June 8, 1891, d July 9, 1957

*Sutcliffe, B. MBE (Auck., Otago & N. Dist.; *CY 1950*) b Nov. 17, 1923

*Sutcliffe, H. (Yorks; *CY 1920*) b Nov. 24, 1894, d Jan. 22, 1978

Sutcliffe, W. H. H. (Yorks) b Oct. 10, 1926, d Sept. 16, 1998

Suttle, K. G. (Sussex) b Aug. 25, 1928

*Swamy, V. N. (Ind. Serv.) b May 23, 1924, d May 1, 1983

Swanton, E. W. CBE (Middx; writer & broadcaster) b Feb. 11, 1907, d Jan. 22, 2000

Swarbrook, F. W. (Derbys, Griq. W. & OFS) b Dec. 17, 1950

Swart, P. D. (Rhod., W. Prov., Glam & Boland) b April 27, 1946

*Swetman, R. (Surrey, Notts & Glos) b Oct. 25, 1933

Sydenham, D. A. D. (Surrey) b April 6, 1934

*Taber, H. B. (NSW) b April 29, 1940

*Taberer, H. M. (OU & Natal) b Oct. 7, 1870, d June 5, 1932

*Tahir Naqqash (Servls Ind., MCB, Punjab & Lahore) b July 6, 1959

*Talat Ali (Lahore, PIA & UBL; ICC referee) b May 29, 1950

*Tallon, D. (Qld; *CY 1949*) b Feb. 17, 1916, d Sept. 7, 1984

*Tamhane, N. S. (Bombay) b Aug. 4, 1931

*Tancred, A. B. (Kimberley, Griq. W. & Tvl) b Aug. 20, 1865, d Nov. 23, 1911

*Tancred, L. J. (Tvl) b Oct. 7, 1876, d July 28, 1934

*Tancred, V. M. (Tvl) b July 7, 1875, d June 3, 1904

Tanvir Mehdi (Lahore & UBL) b Nov. 7, 1972

*Tapscott, G. L. (Griq. W.) b Nov. 7, 1889, d Dec. 13, 1940

*Tapscott, L. E. (Griq. W.) b March 18, 1894, d July 7, 1934

*Tarapore, K. K. (Bombay) b Dec. 17, 1910, d June 15, 1986

Tarbox, C. V. (Worcs) b July 2, 1891, d June 15, 1978

*Tarrant, F. A. (Vic., Middx & Patiala; *CY 1908*) b Dec. 11, 1880, d Jan. 29, 1951

Tarrant, G. F. (Cambs. & All-England) b Dec. 7, 1838, d July 2, 1870

*Taslim Arif (Kar., Sind & NBP) b May 1, 1954

*Tate, F. W. (Sussex) b July 24, 1867, d Feb. 24, 1943

*Tate, M. W. (Sussex; *CY 1924*) b May 30, 1895, d May 18, 1956

*Tattersall, R. (Lancs) b Aug. 17, 1922

*Tauseef Ahmed (PWD, UBL, Kar. & Customs) b May 10, 1958

*Tavaré, C. J. (OU, Kent & Som) b Oct. 27, 1954

Tayfield, H. J. (Natal, Rhod. & Tvl; *CY 1956*) b Jan. 30, 1929, d Feb. 25, 1994

*Taylor, A. I. (Tvl) b July 25, 1925

Taylor, B. (Essex; *CY 1972*) b June 19, 1932

Taylor, B. R. (Cant. & Wgtn) b July 12, 1943

Taylor, C. G. (CU & Sussex) b Nov. 21, 1816, d Sept. 10, 1869

*Taylor, Daniel (Natal) b Jan. 9, 1887, d Jan. 24, 1957

*Taylor, D. D. (Auck. & Warwicks) b March 2, 1923, d Dec. 5, 1980

Taylor, D. J. S. (Surrey, Som & Griq. W.) b Nov. 12, 1942

*Taylor, H. W. (Natal, Tvl & W. Prov.; *CY 1925*) b May 5, 1889, d Feb. 8, 1973

*Taylor, J. (T/T) b Jan. 3, 1932, d Nov. 13, 1999

*Taylor, J. M. (NSW) b Oct. 10, 1895, d May 12, 1971

*Taylor, K. (Yorks & Auck.) b Aug. 21, 1935

*Taylor, L. B. (Leics & Natal) b Oct. 25, 1953

Taylor, M. N. S. (Notts & Hants) b Nov. 12, 1942

Taylor, N. R. (Kent & Sussex) b July 21, 1959

*Taylor, P. L. (NSW & Qld) b Aug. 22, 1956

Taylor, R. M. (Essex) b Nov. 30, 1909, d Jan. 7, 1984

*Taylor, R. W. MBE (Derbys; *CY 1977*) b July 17, 1941

Taylor, T. L. (CU & Yorks; *CY 1901*) b May 25, 1878, d March 16, 1960

Telemachus, R. (Boland) b March 27, 1973

Tennekoon, A. P. B. (SL) b Oct. 29, 1946

*Tennyson, 3rd Lord (Hon. L. H.) (Hants; *CY 1914*) b Nov. 7, 1889, d June 6, 1951

*Terry, V. P. (Hants) b Jan. 14, 1959

*Theunissen, N. H. (W. Prov.) b May 4, 1867, d Nov. 9, 1929

Thomas, A. E. (Northants) b June 7, 1893, d March 21, 1965

Thomas, D. J. (Surrey, N. Tvl, Natal & Glos) b June 30, 1959

*Thomas, G. (NSW) b March 21, 1938

*Thomas, J. G. (Glam, Border, E. Prov. & Northants) b Aug. 12, 1960

Thompson, A. (Middx) b April 17, 1916

*Thompson, G. J. (Northants; Test umpire; *CY 1906*) b Oct. 27, 1877, d March 3, 1943

Thompson, R. G. (Warwicks) b Sept. 26, 1932

*Thoms, G. R. (Vic.) b March 22, 1927

*Thomson, A. L. (Vic.) b Dec. 2, 1945

*Thomson, J. R. (NSW, Qld & Middx) b Aug. 16, 1950

*Thomson, K. (Cant.) b Feb. 26, 1941

*Thomson, N. F. D. (NSW) b May 29, 1839, d Sept. 2, 1896

*Thomson, N. I. (Sussex) b Jan. 23, 1929

*Thomson, S. A. (N. Dist.) b Jan. 27, 1969

Thornton, C. I. (CU, Kent & Middx) b March 20, 1850, d Dec. 10, 1929

*Thornton, Dr P. G. (Yorks, Middx & SA) b Dec. 24, 1867, d Jan. 31, 1939

*Thurlow, H. M. (Qld) b Jan. 10, 1903, d Dec. 3, 1975

Tiffin, R. B. (Test umpire) b June 4, 1959

Timms, B. S. V. (Hants & Warwicks) b Dec. 17, 1940

Timms, J. E. (Northants) b Nov. 3, 1906, d May 18, 1980

Tindall, R. A. E. (Surrey) b Sept. 23, 1935

*Tindill, E. W. T. (Wgtn) b Dec. 18, 1910

Tissera, M. H. (SL) b March 23, 1939

*Titmus, F. J. MBE (Middx, Surrey & OFS; *CY 1963*) b Nov. 24, 1932

Todd, L. J. (Kent) b June 19, 1907, d Aug. 20, 1967

Todd, P. A. (Notts & Glam) b March 12, 1953

*Tolchard, R. W. (Leics) b June 15, 1946

Tomlins, K. P. (Middx & Glos) b Oct. 23, 1957

*Tomlinson, D. S. (Rhod. & Border) b Sept. 4, 1910, d July 11, 1993

Tompkin, M. (Leics) b Feb. 17, 1919, d Sept. 27, 1956

*Toohey, P. M. (NSW) b April 20, 1954

Topley, T. D. (Surrey, Essex & Griq. W.) b Feb. 25, 1964

*Toshack, E. R. H. (NSW) b Dec. 15, 1914

Townsend, A. (Warwicks) b Aug. 26, 1921

Townsend, A. F. (Derbys) b March 29, 1912, d Feb. 25, 1994

*Townsend, C. L. (Glos; *CY 1899*) b Nov. 7, 1876, d Oct. 17, 1958

*Townsend, D. C. H. (OU) b April 20, 1912, d Jan. 27, 1997

*Townsend, L. F. (Derbys & Auck.; *CY 1934*) b June 8, 1903, d Feb. 17, 1993

**Traicos, A. J. (Rhod. & Mash.) b May 17, 1947

*Travers, J. P. F. (S. Aust.) b Jan. 10, 1871, d Sept. 15, 1942

*Tremlett, M. F. (Som & C. Dist.) b July 5, 1923, d July 30, 1984

Tremlett, T. M. (Hants) b July 26, 1956

*Tribe, G. E. (Vic. & Northants; *CY 1955*) b Oct. 4, 1920

*Trim, J. (BG) b Jan. 25, 1915, d Nov. 12, 1960

Trimble, G. S. (Qld) b Jan. 1, 1963

*Trimborn, P. H. J. (Natal) b May 18, 1940

**Trott, A. E. (Vic., Middx & Hawkes Bay; *CY 1899*) b Feb. 6, 1873, d July 30, 1914

*Trott, G. H. S. (Vic.; *CY 1894*) b Aug. 5, 1866, d Nov. 10, 1917

Troughton, L. H. W. (Kent) b May 17, 1879, d Aug. 31, 1933

*Troup, G. B. (Auck.) b Oct. 3, 1952

*Trueman, F. S. OBE (Yorks; *CY 1953*) b Feb. 6, 1931

*Trumble, H. (Vic.; *CY 1897*) b May 12, 1867, d Aug. 14, 1938

*Trumble, J. W. (Vic.) b Sept. 16, 1863, d Aug. 17, 1944

*Trumper, V. T. (NSW; *CY 1903*) b Nov. 2, 1877, d June 28, 1915

Truscott, P. B. (Wgtn) b Aug. 14, 1941

*Tuckett, L. (OFS) b Feb. 6, 1919

*Tuckett, L. R. (Natal & OFS) b April 19, 1885, d April 8, 1963

*Tufnell, N. C. (CU & Surrey) b June 13, 1887, d Aug. 3, 1951

Tunnicliffe, C. J. (Derbys) b Aug. 11, 1951

Tunnicliffe, J. (Yorks; *CY 1901*) b Aug. 26, 1866. d July 11, 1948

*Turnbull, M. J. (CU & Glam; *CY 1931*) b March 16, 1906, d Aug. 5, 1944

*Turner, A. (NSW) b July 23, 1950

Turner, C. (Yorks) b Jan. 11, 1902, d Nov. 19, 1968

*Turner, C. T. B. (NSW; *CY 1889*) b Nov. 16, 1862, d Jan. 1, 1944

Turner, D. R. (Hants & W. Prov.) b Feb. 5, 1949

Turner, F. M. MBE (Leics) b Aug. 8, 1934

*Turner, G. M. (Otago, N. Dist. & Worcs; *CY 1971*) b May 26, 1947

Turner, S. (Essex & Natal) b July 18, 1943

*Twentyman-Jones, Sir Percy S. (W. Prov.) b Sept. 13, 1876, d March 8, 1954

*Tyldesley, E. (Lancs; *CY 1920*) b Feb. 5, 1889, d May 5, 1962

*Tyldesley, J. T. (Lancs; *CY 1902*) b Nov. 22, 1873, d Nov. 27, 1930

*Tyldesley, R. K. (Lancs; *CY 1925*) b March 11, 1897, d Sept. 17, 1943

*Tylecote, E. F. S. (OU & Kent) b June 23, 1849, d March 15, 1938

*Tyler, E. J. (Som) b Oct. 13, 1864, d Jan. 25, 1917

*Tyson, F. H. (Northants; *CY 1956*) b June 6, 1930

Ufton, D. G. (Kent) b May 31, 1928

*Ulyett, G. (Yorks) b Oct. 21, 1851, d June 18, 1898

*Umrigar, P. R. (Bombay & Guj.) b March 28, 1926

*Underwood, D. L. MBE (Kent; *CY 1969*) b June 8, 1945

Vaidya, P. S. (Bengal) b Sept. 23, 1967

*Valentine, A. L. (Jam.; *CY 1951*) b April 29, 1930

*Valentine, B. H. (CU & Kent) b Jan. 17, 1908, d Feb. 2, 1983

*Valentine, V. A. (Jam.) b April 4, 1908, d July 6, 1972

*Vance, R. H. (Wgtn) b March 31, 1955

*van der Bijl, P. G. (W. Prov. & OU) b Oct. 21, 1907, d Feb. 16, 1973

van der Bijl, V. A. P. (Natal, Middx & Tvl; *CY 1981*) b March 19, 1948

*Van der Merwe, E. A. (Tvl) b Nov. 9, 1904, d Feb. 26, 1971

*Van der Merwe, P. L. (W. Prov. & E. Prov.; ICC referee) b March 14, 1937

van Geloven, J. (Yorks & Leics) b Jan. 4, 1934

*Van Ryneveld, C. B. (W. Prov. & OU) b March 19, 1928

van Zyl, C. J. P. G. (OFS & Glam) b Oct. 1, 1961

*Varnals, G. D. (E. Prov., Tvl & Natal) b July 24, 1935

*Vaughan, J. T. C. (Auck.) b Aug. 30, 1967

*Veivers, T. R. (Qld) b April 6, 1937

*Veletta, M. R. J. (W. Aust.) b Oct. 30, 1963

*Vengsarkar, D. B. (Bombay; *CY 1987*) b April 6, 1956

*Venkataraghavan, S. (†TN & Derbys; Test umpire) b April 21, 1946

*Verity, H. (Yorks; *CY 1932*) b May 18, 1905, d July 31, 1943

*Vernon, G. F. (Middx) b June 20, 1856, d Aug. 10, 1902

Vials, G. A. T. (Northants) b March 18, 1887, d April 26, 1974

Vigar, F. H. (Essex) b July 7, 1917

*Viljoen, K. G. (Griq. W., OFS & Tvl) b May 14, 1910, d Jan. 21, 1974

*Vincent, C. L. (Tvl) b Feb. 16, 1902, d Aug. 24, 1968

*Vine, J. (Sussex; *CY 1906*) b May 15, 1875, d April 25, 1946

*Vintcent, C. H. (Tvl & Griq. W.) b Sept. 2, 1866, d Sept. 28, 1943

Virgin, R. T. (Som, Northants & W. Prov.; *CY 1971*) b Aug. 26, 1939

*Viswanath, G. R. (†Karn.; ICC referee) b Feb. 12, 1949

*Viswanath, S. (Karn.) b Nov. 29, 1962

*Vivian, G. E. (Auck.) b Feb. 28, 1946

*Vivian, H. G. (Auck.) b Nov. 4, 1912, d Aug. 12, 1983

*Vizianagram, Maharaj Kumar of, Sir Vijay A., (U. Prov.) b Dec. 28, 1905, d Dec. 2, 1965

*Voce, W. (Notts; *CY 1933*) b Aug. 8, 1909, d June 6, 1984

*Vogler, A. E. E. (Middx, Natal, Tvl & E. Prov.; *CY 1908*) b Nov. 28, 1876, d Aug. 9, 1946

Vonhagt, D. M. (Moors) b March 31, 1965

*Waddington, A. (Yorks) b Feb. 4, 1893, d Oct. 28, 1959

*Wade, H. F. (Natal) b Sept. 14, 1905, d Nov. 23, 1980

Wade, T. H. (Essex) b Nov. 24, 1910, d July 25, 1987

*Wade, W. W. (Natal) b June 18, 1914

*Wadekar, A. L. (Bombay) b April 1, 1941

*Wadsworth, K. J. (C. Dist. & Cant.) b Nov. 30, 1946, d Aug. 19, 1976

*Wainwright, E. (Yorks; *CY 1894*) b April 8, 1865, d Oct. 28, 1919

*Waite, J. H. B. (E. Prov. & Tvl) b Jan. 19, 1930

*Waite, M. G. (S. Aust.) b Jan. 7, 1911, d Dec. 16, 1985

*Walcott, Sir Clyde L. (B'dos & BG; *CY 1958*) b Jan. 17, 1926

*Walcott, L. A. (B'dos) b Jan. 18, 1894, d Feb. 27, 1984

Walden, F. (Northants; Test umpire) b March 1, 1888, d May 3, 1949

Walker, A. (Northants & Durham) b July 7, 1962

Walker, C. (Yorks & Hants) b June 27, 1919, d Dec. 3, 1992

Walker, I. D. (Middx) b Jan. 8, 1844, d July 6, 1898

*Walker, M. H. N. (Vic.) b Sept. 12, 1948

*Walker, P. M. (Glam, Tvl & W. Prov.) b Feb. 17, 1936

Walker, V. E. (Middx) b April 20, 1837, d Jan. 3, 1906

Walker, W. (Notts) b Nov. 24, 1892, d Dec. 3, 1991

*Wall, T. W. (S. Aust.) b May 13, 1904, d March 25, 1981

*Wallace, W. M. (Auck.) b Dec. 19, 1916

*Waller, A. C. (Mash.) b Sept. 25, 1959

Waller, C. E. (Surrey & Sussex) b Oct. 3, 1948

Walsh, J. E. (NSW & Leics) b Dec. 4, 1912, d May 20, 1980

*Walter, K. A. (Tvl) b Nov. 5, 1939

*Walters, C. F. (Glam & Worcs; *CY 1934*) b Aug. 28, 1905, d Dec. 23, 1992

*Walters, F. H. (Vic. & NSW) b Feb. 9, 1860, d June 1, 1922

*Walters, K. D. MBE (NSW) b Dec. 21, 1945

*Waqar Hassan (Pak. Us, Punjab, Pak. Serv. & Kar.) b Sept. 12, 1932

*Ward, Alan (Derbys, Leics & Border) b Aug. 10, 1947

*Ward, Albert (Yorks & Lancs; *CY 1890*) b Nov. 21, 1865, d Jan. 6, 1939

Ward, B. (Essex) b Feb. 28, 1944

Ward, D. (Glam) b Aug. 30, 1934

Ward, D. M. (Surrey) b Feb. 10, 1961

*Ward, F. A. (S. Aust.) b Feb. 23, 1906, d March 25, 1974

*Ward, J. T. (Cant.) b March 11, 1937

*Ward, T. A. (Tvl) b Aug. 2, 1887, d Feb. 16, 1936

Ward, William (MCC & Hants) b July 24, 1787, d June 30, 1849

*Wardle, J. H. (Yorks; *CY 1954*) b Jan. 8, 1923, d July 23, 1985

*Warnapura, B. (SL) b March 1, 1953

*Warnaweera, K. P. J. (Galle & Singha) b Nov. 23, 1960

Warner, A. E. (Worcs & Derbys) b May 12, 1959

*Warner, Sir Pelham F. (OU & Middx; *CY 1904, special portrait 1921*; Pres. MCC 1950-51) b Oct. 2, 1873, d Jan. 30, 1963

*Warr, J. J. (CU & Middx; Pres. MCC 1987-88) b July 16, 1927

*Warren, A. R. (Derbys) b April 2, 1875, d Sept. 3, 1951

*Washbrook, C. CBE (Lancs; *CY 1947*) b Dec. 6, 1914, d April 27, 1999

*Wasim Bari (Kar., PIA & Sind) b March 23, 1948

Wasim Haider (PIA & F'bad) b June 6, 1967

*Wasim Raja (Lahore, Sargodha, Pak. Us, PIA, Punjab & NBP) b July 3, 1952

Wass, T. G. (Notts; *CY 1908*) b Dec. 26, 1873, d Oct. 27, 1953

*Wassan, A. S. (Delhi) b March 23, 1968

Wassell, A. (Hants) b April 15, 1940

*Watkins, A. J. (Glam) b April 21, 1922

*Watkins, J. C. (Natal) b April 10, 1923

*Watkins, J. R. (NSW) b April 16, 1943

Watson, A. (Lancs) b Nov. 4, 1844, d Oct. 26, 1920

*Watson, C. (Jam. & Delhi) b July 1, 1938

Watson, F. (Lancs) b Sept. 17, 1898, d Feb. 1, 1976

*Watson, G. D. (Vic., W. Aust. & NSW) b March 8, 1945

Watson, G. S. (Kent & Leics) b April 10, 1907, d April 1, 1974

*Watson, W. (Yorks & Leics; *CY 1954*) b March 7, 1920

*Watson, W. (Auck.) b Aug. 31, 1965

*Watson, W. J. (NSW) b Jan. 31, 1931

Watt, A. E. (Kent) b June 19, 1907, d Feb. 3, 1974

*Watt, L. (Otago) b Sept. 17, 1924, d Nov. 15, 1996

Watts, E. A. (Surrey) b Aug. 1, 1911, d May 2, 1982

Watts, P. D. (Northants & Notts) b March 31, 1938

Watts, P. J. (Northants) b June 16, 1940

*Wazir, Ali, S. (C. Ind., S. Punjab & Patiala) b Sept. 15, 1903, d June 17, 1950

*Wazir Mohammad (B'pur & Kar.) b Dec. 22, 1929

*Webb, M. G. (Otago & Cant.) b June 22, 1947

*Webb, P. N. (Auck.) b July 14, 1957

Webb, R. J. (Otago) b Sept. 15, 1952

Webb, R. T. (Sussex) b July 11, 1922

*Webbe, A. J. (OU & Middx) b Jan. 16, 1855, d Feb. 19, 1941

Webber, Roy (Statistician) b July 23, 1914, d Nov. 14, 1962

*Weekes, Sir Everton D. (B'dos; *CY 1951*) b Feb. 26, 1925

*Weekes, K. H. (Jam.) b Jan. 24, 1912, d Feb. 9, 1998

Weekes, R. T. (Warwicks) b April 30, 1930

Weerakkody, A. P. (NCC) b Oct. 1, 1970

*Weerasinghe, C. D. U. S. (TU & NCC) b March 1, 1968

Weigall, G. J. V. (CU & Kent) b Oct. 19, 1870, d May 17, 1944

*Weir, G. L. (Auck.) b June 2, 1908

*Wellard, A. W. (Som; *CY 1936*) b April 8, 1902, d Dec. 31, 1980

*Wellham, D. M. (NSW, Tas. & Qld) b March 13, 1959

Wells, B. D. (Glos & Notts) b July 27, 1930

Wells, C. M. (Sussex, Border, W. Prov. & Derbys) b March 3, 1960

Wells, W. (Northants) b March 14, 1881, d March 18, 1939

Wenman, E. G. (Kent & England) b Aug. 18, 1803, d Dec. 31, 1879

Wensley, A. F. (Sussex, Auck., Naw. & Eur.) b May 23, 1898, d June 17, 1970

*Wesley, C. (Natal) b Sept. 5, 1937

West, G. H. (Editor of *Wisden* 1880-86) b 1851, d Oct. 6, 1896

*Westcott, R. J. (W. Prov.) b Sept. 19, 1927

Weston, M. J. (Worcs) b April 8, 1959

*Wettimuny, M. D. (SL) b June 11, 1951

*Wettimuny, S. (SL; *CY 1985*; ICC referee) b Aug. 12, 1956

Wettimuny, S. R. de S. (SL) b Feb. 7, 1949

*Wharton, A. (Lancs & Leics) b April 30, 1923, d Aug. 26, 1993

*Whatmore, D. F. (Vic.) b March 16, 1954

Wheatley, O. S. CBE (CU, Warwicks & Glam; *CY 1969*) b May 28, 1935

Whitaker, Haddon OBE (Editor of *Wisden* 1940-43) b Aug. 30, 1908, d Jan. 5, 1982

White, A. F. T. (CU, Warwicks & Worcs) b Sept. 5, 1915, d March 16, 1993

White, Sir Archibald W. 4th Bt (Yorks) b Oct. 14, 1877, d Dec. 16, 1945

*White, D. J. (N. Dist.) b June 26, 1961

*White, D. W. (Hants & Glam) b Dec. 14, 1935

*White, G. C. (Tvl) b Feb. 5, 1882, d Oct. 17, 1918

*White, J. C. (Som; *CY 1929*) b Feb. 19, 1891, d May 2, 1961

White, Hon. L. R. (5th Lord Annaly) (Middx & Victory Test) b March 15, 1927, d Sept. 30, 1990

White, R. A. (Middx & Notts) b Oct. 6, 1936

White, R. C. (CU, Glos & Tvl) b Jan. 29, 1941

*White, W. A. (B'dos) b Nov. 20, 1938

Whitehead, A. G. T. (Som; Test umpire) b Oct. 28, 1940

Whitehead, H. (Leics) b Sept. 19, 1874, d Sept. 14, 1944

Whitehouse, J. (Warwicks) b April 8, 1949

*Whitelaw, P. E. (Auck.) b Feb. 10, 1910, d Aug. 28, 1988

Whiteside, J. P. (Lancs & Leics) b June 11, 1861, d March 8, 1946

Whitfield, E. W. (Surrey & Northants) b May 31, 1911, d Aug. 10, 1996

Whitington, R. S. (S. Aust. & Victory Tests; writer) b June 30, 1912, d March 13, 1984

*Whitney, M. R. (NSW & Glos) b Feb. 24, 1959

Whittaker, G. J. (Surrey) b May 29, 1916, d April 20, 1997

Whitticase, P. (Leics) b March 15, 1965

Whittingham, N. B. (Notts) b Oct. 22, 1940

*Whitty, W. J. (S. Aust.) b Aug. 15, 1886, d Jan. 30, 1974

*Whysall, W. W. (Notts; *CY 1925*) b Oct. 31, 1887, d Nov. 11, 1930

*Wickremasinghe, A. G. D. (NCC) b Dec. 27, 1965

Wiener, J. M. (Vic.) b May 1, 1955

*Wight, C. V. (BG) b July 28, 1902, d Oct. 4, 1969

*Wight, G. L. (BG) b May 28, 1929

Wight, P. B. (BG, Som & Cant.) b June 25, 1930

*Wijegunawardene, K. I. W. (CCC) b Nov. 23, 1964

*Wijesuriya, R. G. C. E. (Mor. & Colts) b Feb. 18, 1960

*Wijetunge, P. K. (SSC & Moors) b Aug. 6, 1971

Wilcox, D. R. (Essex & CU) b June 4, 1910, d Feb. 6, 1953

Wild, D. J. (Northants) b Nov. 28, 1962

*Wiles, C. A. (B'dos & T/T) b Aug. 11, 1892, d Nov. 4, 1957

Wilkins, C. P. (Derbys, Border, E. Prov. & Natal) b July 31, 1944

*Wilkinson, C. T. A. (Surrey) b Oct. 4, 1884, d Dec. 16, 1970

*Wilkinson, L. L. (Lancs) b Nov. 5, 1916

Willatt, G. L. (CU, Notts & Derbys) b May 7, 1918

*Willett, E. T. (Comb. Is. & Leewards) b May 1, 1953

Willett, M. D. (Surrey) b April 21, 1933

*Willey, P. (Northants, E. Prov. & Leics; Test umpire) b Dec. 6, 1949

*Williams, A. B. (Jam.) b Nov. 21, 1949

Williams, D. L. (Glam) b Nov. 20, 1946

*Williams, E. A. V. (B'dos) b April 10, 1914, d April 13, 1997

*Williams, N. F. (Middx, Essex, Windwards & Tas.) b July 2, 1962

Williams, R. G. (Northants) b Aug. 10, 1957

*Willis, R. G. D. MBE (Surrey, Warwicks & N. Tvl; *CY 1978*) b May 30, 1949

*Willoughby, J. T. (SA) b Nov. 7, 1874, d March 11, 1952

Willsher, E. (Kent & All-England) b Nov. 22, 1828, d Oct. 7, 1885

Wilson, A. (Lancs) b April 24, 1921

Wilson, A. E. (Middx & Glos) b May 18, 1910

*Wilson, Rev. C. E. M. (CU & Yorks) b May 15, 1875, d Feb. 8, 1944

*Wilson, D. (Yorks) b Aug. 7, 1937

Wilson, E. R. (Betty) (Australia Women) b Nov. 21, 1921

*Wilson, E. R. (CU & Yorks) b March 25, 1879, d July 21, 1957

Wilson, G. (CU & Yorks) b Aug. 21, 1895, d Nov. 29, 1960

Wilson, H. L. (Sussex) b June 27, 1881, d March 15, 1937

Wilson, J. V. (Yorks; *CY 1961*) b Jan. 17, 1921

Wilson, J. W. (Otago) b Oct. 24, 1973

*Wilson, J. W. (Vic. & S. Aust.) b Aug. 20, 1921, d Oct. 13, 1985

Wilson, R. C. (Kent) b Feb. 18, 1928

*Wimble, C. S. (Tvl) b April 22, 1861, d Jan. 28, 1930

Windows, A. R. (Glos & CU) b Sept. 25, 1942

Winfield, H. M. (Notts) b June 13, 1933

Winrow, H. F. (Notts) b Jan. 17, 1916, d Aug. 19, 1973

*Winslow, P. L. (Sussex, Tvl & Rhod.) b May 21, 1929

Wisden, John (Sussex; founder John Wisden & Co and *Wisden's Cricketers' Almanack; special portrait 1913*) b Sept. 5, 1826, d April 5, 1884

*Wishart, K. L. (BG) b Nov. 28, 1908, d Oct. 18, 1972

Wolton, A. V. (Warwicks) b June 12, 1919, d Sept. 9, 1990

*Wood, A. (Yorks; *CY 1939*) b Aug. 25, 1898, d April 1, 1973

*Wood, B. (Yorks, Lancs, Derbys & E. Prov.) b Dec. 26, 1942

Wood, C. J. B. (Leics) b Nov. 21, 1875, d June 5, 1960

Wood, D. J. (Sussex) b May 19, 1914, d March 12, 1989

*Wood, G. E. C. (CU & Kent) b Aug. 22, 1893, d March 18, 1971

*Wood, G. M. (W. Aust.) b Nov. 6, 1956

*Wood, H. (Kent & Surrey; *CY 1891*) b Dec. 14, 1854, d April 30, 1919

*Wood, R. (Lancs & Vic.) b March 7, 1860, d Jan. 6, 1915

*Woodcock, A. J. (S. Aust.) b Feb. 27, 1948

Woodcock, John C. OBE (Writer; Editor of *Wisden* 1981-86) b Aug. 7, 1926

*Woodfull, W. M. OBE (Vic.; *CY 1927*) b Aug. 22, 1897, d Aug. 11, 1965

Woodhead, F. G. (Notts) b Oct. 30, 1912, d May 24, 1991

**Woods, S. M. J. (CU & Som; *CY 1889*) b April 13, 1867, d April 30, 1931

Wooller, W. (CU & Glam) b Nov. 20, 1912, d March 10, 1997

*Woolley, C. N. (Glos & Northants) b May 5, 1886, d Nov. 3, 1962

*Woolley, F. E. (Kent; *CY 1911*) b May 27, 1887, d Oct. 18, 1978

*Woolley, R. D. (Tas.) b Sept. 16, 1954

*Woolmer, R. A. (Kent, Natal & W. Prov.; *CY 1976*) b May 14, 1948

*Worrall, J. (Vic.) b June 21, 1861, d Nov. 17, 1937

*Worrell, Sir Frank M. M. (B'dos & Jam.; *CY 1951*) b Aug. 1, 1924, d March 13, 1967

Worsley, D. R. (OU & Lancs) b July 18, 1941

*Worthington, T. S. (Derbys; *CY 1937*) b Aug. 21, 1905, d Aug. 31, 1973

Wrathall, H. (Glos) b Feb. 1, 1869, d June 1, 1944

Wright, A. C. (Kent) b April 4, 1895, d May 26, 1959

Wright, A. J. (Glos) b June 27, 1962

*Wright, C. W. (CU & Notts) b May 27, 1863, d Jan. 10, 1936

*Wright, D. V. P. (Kent; *CY 1940*) b Aug. 21, 1914, d Nov. 13, 1998

Wright, Graeme A. (Editor of *Wisden* 1987-92) b April 23, 1943

*Wright, J. G. MBE (N. Dist., Derbys, Cant. & Auck.) b July 5, 1954

*Wright, K. J. (W. Aust. & S. Aust.) b Dec. 27, 1953

Wright, L. G. (Derbys; *CY 1906*) b June 15, 1862, d Jan. 11, 1953

Wright, W. (Notts & Kent) b Feb. 29, 1856, d March 22, 1940

*Wyatt, R. E. S. (Warwicks & Worcs; *CY 1930*) b May 2, 1901, d April 20, 1995

*Wynne, O. E. (Tvl & W. Prov.) b June 1, 1919, d July 13, 1975

*Wynyard, E. G. (Hants) b April 1, 1861, d Oct. 30, 1936

Yachad, M. (Tvl) b Nov. 17, 1960

*Yadav, N. S. (H'bad) b Jan. 26, 1957

*Yajurvindra Singh (M'tra & S'tra) b Aug. 1, 1952

*Yallop, G. N. (Vic.) b Oct. 7, 1952

*Yardley, B. (W. Aust.) b Sept. 5, 1947

*Yardley, N. W. D. (CU & Yorks; *CY 1948*) b March 19, 1915, d Oct. 4, 1989

Yardley, T. J. (Worcs & Northants) b Oct. 27, 1946

Yarnold, H. (Worcs) b July 6, 1917, d Aug. 13, 1974

*Yashpal Sharma (Punjab) b Aug. 11, 1954

Yawar Saeed (Som & Punjab) b Jan. 22, 1935

*Yograj Singh (Haryana & Punjab) b March 25, 1958

Young, A. (Som) b Nov. 6, 1890, d April 2, 1936

Young, D. M. (Worcs & Glos) b April 15, 1924, d June 18, 1993

Young, H. I. (Essex) b Feb. 5, 1876, d Dec. 12, 1964

*Young, J. A. (Middx) b Oct. 14, 1912, d Feb. 5, 1993

*Young, R. A. (CU & Sussex) b Sept. 16, 1885, d July 1, 1968

*Younis Ahmed (Lahore, Kar., Surrey, PIA, S. Aust., Worcs & Glam) b Oct. 20, 1947

*Yuile, B. W. (C. Dist.) b Oct. 29, 1941

*Zaheer Abbas (Kar., Glos, PWD, Dawood Ind., Sind & PIA; *CY 1972*) b July 24, 1947

Zakir Hassan (Bangladesh) b Dec. 1, 1972

*Zakir Khan (Sind, Peshawar & ADBP) b April 3, 1963

Zesers, A. K. (S. Aust.) b March 11, 1967

*Zoehrer, T. J. (W. Aust.) b Sept. 25, 1961

*Zulch, J. W. (Tvl) b Jan. 2, 1886, d May 19, 1924

*Zulfiqar Ahmed (B'pur & PIA) b Nov. 22, 1926

*Zulqarnain (Pak. Rlwys, Lahore, HBFC & PACO) b May 25, 1962

REGISTER OF CURRENT PLAYERS

The qualifications for inclusion are as follows:

1. All players who appeared in Tests or one-day internationals for a Test-playing country in 1998-99 or 1999.

2. All players who appeared in the County Championship in 1999.

3. All players who appeared in the Sheffield Shield, Supersport Series, Busta Cup, Shell Conference and Duleep Trophy in 1998-99.

4. All players who appeared in first-class domestic cricket in 1998-99, who have also played in Tests or one-day international cricket.

5. All players who appeared in one-day internationals for Bangladesh, Kenya and Scotland in 1998-99.

Notes: The forename by which the player is known is underlined if it is not his first name.

Teams are those played for in 1998-99 and/or 1999, or the last domestic team for which that player appeared.

Countries are those for which players are qualified.

The country of birth is given if it is not the one for which a player is qualified. It is also given to differentiate between nations in the Leeward and Windward Islands, and where it is essential for clarity.

    * *Denotes Test player.*

	Team	Country	Born	Birthplace
Aamer Hanif	Karachi/Allied Bank	P	4.10.71	Karachi
* **Aamer Malik**	Lahore/PIA	P	3.1.63	Mandi Bahauddin
* **Aamir Nazir**	Islamabad	P	2.1.71	Lahore
* **Aamir Sohail**	Lahore	P	14.9.66	Lahore
Abdur Razzaq	Lahore/KRL	P	2.12.79	Lahore
Abrahams Shafiek	Eastern Province	SA	4.3.68	Port Elizabeth
* **Ackerman** Hylton Deon	Western Province	SA	14.2.73	Cape Town
Adam Shaun Michael	KwaZulu-Natal	SA	13.9.79	Durban
Adams Christopher John	Sussex	E	6.5.70	Whitwell
Adams Fabian **Alex**	Leeward Islands	WI	7.1.75	The Valley, Anguilla
* **Adams** James Clive	Jamaica	WI	9.1.68	Port Maria
* **Adams** Paul Regan	Western Province	SA	20.1.77	Cape Town
Adcock Nathan Tennyson	South Australia	A	22.4.78	Adelaide
Afzaal Usman	Nottinghamshire	E	9.6.77	Rawalpindi, Pakistan
* **Agarkar** Ajit Bhalchandra	Mumbai	I	4.12.77	Bombay
Akhtar Sarfraz	Peshawar/National Bank	P	20.2.76	Peshawar
Akram Khan	Bangladesh	B	1.11.68	Chittagong
* **Akram Raza**	Sargodha/Habib Bank	P	22.11.64	Lahore
Albanie James Daniel	Boland	SA	1.5.68	Touwsrivier
Aldred Paul	Derbyshire	E	4.2.69	Chellaston
Ali Kabir	Worcestershire	E	24.11.80	Moseley
* **Ali** Hussain Rizvi	Karachi	P	6.1.74	Karachi
* **Ali** Naqvi	Karachi/PNSC	P	19.3.77	Lahore
Alleyne Mark Wayne	Gloucestershire	E	23.5.68	Tottenham
Allingham Michael James de Grey	Scotland	S	6.1.65	Inverness
* **Allott** Geoffrey Ian	Canterbury	NZ	24.12.71	Christchurch
Almeida Renato	Gauteng	SA	9.4.77	Salisbury, Rhodesia
Al-Shahriar Rokon	Bangladesh	B	23.4.78	Dhaka
* **Ambrose** Curtly Elconn Lynwall	Leeward Islands	WI	21.9.63	Swetes Village, Antigua
Amin Rupesh Mahesh	Surrey	E	20.8.77	Clapham
Aminul Islam, jun.	Bangladesh	B	1.4.75	Rajshahi
Aminul Islam, sen.	Bangladesh	B	2.2.68	Dhaka
* **Amre** Pravin Kalyan	Mumbai	I	14.8.68	Bombay
Anderson Ricaldo Sherman Glenroy	Essex	E	22.9.76	Hammersmith
Angara Joseph Oduol	Kenya	K	8.11.71	Nairobi
* **Angel** Jo	Western Australia	A	22.4.68	Mount Lawley

	Team	Country	Born	Birthplace
* **Aqib Javed**	Allied Bank	P	5.8.72	Sheikhupura
Archer Graeme Francis	Nottinghamshire	E	26.9.70	Carlisle
Arnberger Jason Lee	Victoria	A	18.11.72	Penrith
* **Arnold** Russel Premakumaran	Nondescripts	SL	25.10.73	Colombo
Arothe Tushar Bhalchandra	Baroda	I	17.9.66	Baroda
* **Arshad Khan**	Peshawar/Allied Bank	P	22.3.71	Peshawar
Arthur John Michael	Griqualand West	SA	17.5.68	Johannesburg
* **Arthurton** Keith Lloyd Thomas	Leeward Islands	WI	21.2.65	Charlestown, Nevis
Arvind Kumar Gangashetty	Hyderabad	I	4.10.73	Hyderabad
* **Ashfaq Ahmed**	PIA	P	6.6.73	Lahore
Asif Mahmood	Rawalpindi/KRL	P	18.12.75	Rawalpindi
* **Asif Mujtaba**	Karachi/PIA	P	4.11.67	Karachi
Asim Butt	Scotland	S	24.10.67	Lahore, Pakistan
* **Astle** Nathan John	Canterbury	NZ	15.9.71	Christchurch
* **Atapattu** Marvan Samson	Sinhalese	SL	22.11.70	Kalutara
* **Ata-ur-Rehman**	Allied Bank	P	28.3.75	Lahore
* **Atherton** Michael Andrew	Lancashire	E	23.3.68	Manchester
* **Atif Rauf**	ADBP	P	3.3.64	Lahore
Atkinson Mark Neville	Tasmania	A	11.2.69	Sydney
Atkinson Mark Peter	Western Australia	A	27.11.70	Bentley
Austin Ian David	Lancashire	E	30.5.66	Haslingden
Averis James Maxwell Michael	Gloucestershire	E	28.5.74	Bristol
Aymes Adrian Nigel	Hampshire	E	4.6.64	Southampton
* **Azam Khan**	Karachi/Customs	P	1.3.69	Karachi
* **Azhar Mahmood**	Rawalpindi	P	28.2.75	Rawalpindi
* **Azharuddin** Mohammad	Hyderabad	I	8.2.63	Hyderabad
* **Bacher** Adam Marc	Gauteng	SA	29.10.73	Johannesburg
Badat Mehmood	KwaZulu-Natal	SA	13.5.70	Durban
Bahutule Sairaj Vasant	Mumbai	I	6.1.73	Bombay
Bailey Mark David	Northern Districts	NZ	26.11.70	Hamilton
* **Bailey** Robert John	Northamptonshire	E	28.10.63	Biddulph
Bailey Tobin Michael Barnaby	Northamptonshire	E	28.8.76	Kettering
Baker Robert Michael	Western Australia	A	24.7.75	Osborne Park
Bakker Jason Richard	Victoria	A	12.11.67	Geelong
Bakkes Herman Charles	Free State	SA	24.12.69	Port Elizabeth
Ball Martyn Charles John	Gloucestershire	E	26.4.70	Bristol
Balliram Anil	Trinidad & Tobago	WI	27.2.74	Trinidad
* **Bandara** Charitha Malinga	Nondescripts	SL	31.12.79	Kalutara
* **Bandaratilleke** Mapa Rallage Chandima Niroshan	Tamil Union	SL	16.5.75	Colombo
* **Banerjee** Subroto Tara	Bengal	I	13.2.69	Patna
Banes Matthew John	Kent	E	10.12.79	Pembury
Bangar Sanjay Bapusaheb	Railways	I	11.10.72	Beed
* **Baptiste** Eldine Ashworth Elderfield	Eastern Province	WI	12.3.60	Liberta, Antigua
Barnard Pieter Hendrik	Griqualand West	SA	8.5.70	Nelspruit
* **Barnett** Kim John	Gloucestershire	E	17.7.60	Stoke-on-Trent
Base Simon John	Derbyshire	E	2.1.60	Maidstone
Bastow Jonathan Edward	KwaZulu-Natal	SA	12.2.74	Pietermaritzburg
Bates Justin Jonathan	Sussex	E	9.4.76	Farnborough, Hants
Bates Richard Terry	Nottinghamshire	E	17.6.72	Stamford
Batson Nathan Evan	Worcestershire	E	24.7.78	Basildon
Batty Jonathan Neil	Surrey	E	18.4.74	Chesterfield
Bedade Atul Chandrakant	Baroda	I	24.9.66	Bombay
Bell Ian Ronald	Warwickshire	E	11.4.82	Coventry
* **Bell** Matthew David	Wellington	NZ	25.2.77	Dunedin
* **Benjamin** Joseph Emmanuel	Surrey	E	2.2.61	Christ Church, St Kitts
* **Benjamin** Kenneth Charlie Griffith	Leeward Islands	WI	8.4.67	St John's, Antigua
Benkenstein Dale Martin	KwaZulu-Natal	SA	9.6.74	Salisbury, Rhodesia

	Team	Country	Born	Birthplace
Berry Darren Shane	Victoria	A	10.12.69	*Melbourne*
Betts Melvyn Morris	Durham	E	26.3.75	*Sacriston*
Beukes Jonathan Alan	Free State	SA	15.3.79	*Kimberley*
*Bevan** Michael Gwyl	New South Wales	A	8.5.70	*Belconnen*
Bhandari Amit	Delhi	I	1.10.78	*Delhi*
Bharadwaj Raghvendrarao Vijay	Karnataka	I	15.8.75	*Bangalore*
*Bichel** Andrew John	Queensland	A	27.8.70	*Laidley*
Bicknell Darren John	Surrey	E	24.6.67	*Guildford*
*Bicknell** Martin Paul	Surrey	E	14.1.69	*Guildford*
Bishop Ian Emlyn	Surrey	E	26.8.77	*Taunton*
*Bishop** Ian Raphael	Trinidad & Tobago	WI	24.10.67	*Port-of-Spain*
Black Marlon Ian	Trinidad & Tobago	WI	7.6.75	*Trinidad*
Blackwell Ian David	Derbyshire	E	10.6.78	*Chesterfield*
Blain John Angus Rae	Scotland	S	4.1.79	*Edinburgh*
*Blakey** Richard John	Yorkshire	E	15.1.67	*Huddersfield*
*Blewett** Gregory Scott	South Australia/Yorkshire	A	29.10.71	*Adelaide*
Blignaut Arnoldus Mauritius	Mashonaland	Z	1.8.78	*Salisbury*
Bloomfield Timothy Francis	Middlesex	E	31.5.73	*Ashford, Middlesex*
Bodi Ghulam Hussain	Gauteng	SA	4.1.79	*Hathuran, India*
Boje Nico	Free State	SA	20.3.73	*Bloemfontein*
*Boon** David Clarence	Tasmania/Durham	A	29.12.60	*Launceston*
Bosman Lungile Loots	Griqualand West	SA	14.4.77	*Kimberley*
Bossenger Wendell	Griqualand West	SA	23.10.76	*Cape Town*
Boswell Scott Antony John	Leicestershire	E	11.9.74	*Fulford*
Boteju Hemantha	Colombo	SL	3.11.77	*Colombo*
Botha Andre Cornelius	Griqualand West	SA	12.9.75	*Johannesburg*
Botha Anthony Greyvensteyn	KwaZulu-Natal	SA	17.11.76	*Pretoria*
Botha Peterus Johannes	Border	SA	28.9.66	*Vereeniging*
*Boucher** Mark Verdon	Border	SA	3.12.76	*East London*
Bowen Mark Nicholas	Nottinghamshire	E	6.12.67	*Redcar*
Bowler Peter Duncan	Somerset	E	30.7.63	*Plymouth*
Bracken Nathan Wade	New South Wales	A	12.9.77	*Penrith*
*Bradburn** Grant Eric	Northern Districts	NZ	26.5.66	*Hamilton*
Bradfield Carl Crispin	Eastern Province	SA	18.1.75	*Grahamstown*
Bradstreet Shawn David	New South Wales	A	28.2.72	*Wollongong*
*Brandes** Eddo Andre	Mashonaland	Z	5.3.63	*Port Shepstone, SA*
Brent Gary Bazil	Mashonaland	Z	13.1.76	*Sinoia*
Bridge Graeme David	Durham	E	4.9.80	*Sunderland*
Brimson Matthew Thomas	Leicestershire	E	1.12.70	*Plumstead*
Brinkley James Edward	Scotland	S	13.3.74	*Helensburgh*
Brooker Finley Clint	Griqualand West	SA	26.12.72	*Kimberley*
Brophy Gerard Louis	Gauteng	SA	26.11.75	*Welkom*
Brown Alistair Duncan	Surrey	E	11.2.70	*Beckenham*
Brown Douglas Robert	Warwickshire	E	29.10.69	*Stirling, Scotland*
Brown Jason Fred	Northamptonshire	E	10.10.74	*Newcastle-under-Lyme*
Brown Michael James	Middlesex	E	9.2.80	*Burnley*
*Brown** Simon John Emmerson	Durham	E	29.6.69	*Cleadon*
*Browne** Courtney Oswald	Barbados	WI	7.12.70	*Lambeth, England*
Bruyns Mark Lloyd	KwaZulu-Natal	SA	8.11.73	*Pietermaritzburg*
Bryan Henderson Ricardo	Barbados	WI	21.3.70	*Barbados*
Bryant James Douglas Campbell	Eastern Province	SA	4.2.76	*Durban*
Bryson Rudi Edwin	Northerns	SA	25.7.68	*Springs*
Bulbeck Matthew Paul Leonard	Somerset	E	8.11.79	*Taunton*
Bulfin Carl Edwin	Central Districts	NZ	19.8.73	*Blenheim*
Bundela Devendra Singh	Madhya Pradesh	I	22.2.77	*Indore*
Burns Michael	Somerset	E	2.6.69	*Barrow-in-Furness*
Butcher Gary Paul	Surrey	E	11.3.75	*Clapham*
*Butcher** Mark Alan	Surrey	E	23.8.72	*Croydon*
Byas David	Yorkshire	E	26.8.63	*Kilham*

	Team	Country	Born	Birthplace
* **Caddick** Andrew Richard	Somerset	E	21.11.68	Christchurch, NZ
* **Cairns** Christopher Lance	Canterbury	NZ	13.6.70	Picton
Callaghan David John	Eastern Province	SA	1.2.65	Queenstown
* **Campbell** Alistair Douglas Ross	Mashonaland	Z	23.9.72	Salisbury
Campbell Ryan John	Western Australia	A	7.2.72	Osborne Park
* **Campbell** Sherwin Legay	Barbados	WI	1.11.70	Bridgetown
* **Carlisle** Stuart Vance	Mashonaland A	Z	10.5.72	Salisbury
Carseldine Lee Andrew	Queensland	A	17.11.75	Nambour
Cary Sean Ross	Western Australia	A	10.3.71	Subiaco
Cassar Matthew Edward	Derbyshire	E	16.10.72	Sydney, Australia
Catterall Duncan Neil	Worcestershire	E	17.9.78	Preston
Cawdron Michael John	Gloucestershire	E	7.10.74	Luton
* **Chandana** Umagiliya Durage <u>Upul</u>	Tamil Union	SL	7.5.72	Galle
* **Chanderpaul** Shivnarine	Guyana	WI	18.8.74	Unity Village
Chapman Steven	Durham	E	2.10.71	Crook
Chapple Glen	Lancashire	E	23.1.74	Skipton
Chatterjee Utpal	Bengal	I	13.7.64	Calcutta
* **Chauhan** Rajesh Kumar	Madhya Pradesh	I	19.12.66	Ranchi
Chillingworth Garry Andrew	South Australia	A	23.1.70	Sutherland
Chilton Mark James	Lancashire	E	2.10.76	Sheffield
Chopra Nikhil	Delhi	I	26.12.73	Allahabad
Chudasama Dipak Nanalal	Kenya	K	20.5.63	Mombasa
Cilliers Sarel Arnold	Free State	SA	6.6.71	Klerksdorp
Clark Stuart Rupert	New South Wales	A	28.4.75	Carringbah
Collingwood Paul David	Durham	E	26.5.76	Shotley Bridge
* **Collins** Pedro Tyrone	Barbados	WI	12.8.76	Boscobelle
* **Collymore** Corey Dalanelo	Barbados	WI	21.12.77	Boscobelle
* **Commins** John Brian	Western Province	SA	19.2.65	East London
Cook Simon Hewitt	New South Wales	A	29.1.72	Hastings
Cook Simon James	Middlesex	E	15.1.77	Oxford
* **Cork** Dominic Gerald	Derbyshire	E	7.8.71	Newcastle-under-Lyme
Cornwall Wilden Winston	Leeward Islands	WI	29.4.73	Antigua
Cosker Dean Andrew	Glamorgan	E	7.1.78	Weymouth
Cotterell Thomas Paul	Gloucestershire	E	9.3.77	Hounslow
Cottey Phillip <u>Anthony</u>	Sussex	E	2.6.66	Swansea
Cowan Ashley Preston	Essex	E	7.5.75	Hitchin
Cox Jamie	Tasmania/Somerset	A	15.10.69	Burnie
Craig Shawn Andrew Jacob	Victoria	A	23.6.73	Carlton
* **Crawley** John Paul	Lancashire	E	21.9.71	Maldon
Creed Murray	Eastern Province	SA	5.3.79	Port Elizabeth
Creevey Brendan Neville	Queensland	A	18.2.70	Charleville
* **Croft** Robert Damien Bale	Glamorgan	E	25.5.70	Morriston
* **Cronje** Wessel <u>Johannes</u> (Hansie)	Free State	SA	25.9.69	Bloemfontein
Crookes Derek Norman	Gauteng	SA	5.3.69	Mariannhill
Crowe Carl Daniel	Leicestershire	E	25.11.75	Leicester
Croy Martyn Gilbert	Otago	NZ	23.1.74	Hamilton
* **Cuffy** Cameron Eustace	Windward Islands	WI	8.2.70	South Rivers, St Vincent
* **Cullinan** Daryll John	Gauteng	SA	4.3.67	Kimberley
Cumming Craig Derek	Canterbury	NZ	31.8.75	Timaru
Cunliffe Robert John	Gloucestershire	E	8.11.73	Oxford
Curran Kevin Malcolm	Northamptonshire	E	7.9.59	Rusape, Rhodesia
Cush Lennox Joseph	Guyana	WI	12.12.74	Guyana
Dahiya Vijay	Delhi	I	10.5.73	Delhi
Dakin Jonathan Michael	Leicestershire	E	28.2.73	Hitchin
* **Dale** Adam Craig	Queensland	A	30.12.68	Ivanhoe
Dale Adrian	Glamorgan	E	24.10.68	Germiston, South Africa
Daley James Arthur	Durham	E	24.9.73	Sunderland

	Team	Country	Born	Birthplace
Dani Ashu	Delhi	I	3.10.74	Delhi
Darlington Kevin Godfrey	Guyana	WI	26.4.72	Guyana
Das Shiv Sunder	Orissa	I	5.11.77	Bhubaneshwar
* **Dassanayake** Pubudu Bathiya	Bloomfield	SL	11.7.70	Kandy
David Noel Arthur	Hyderabad	I	26.2.71	Hyderabad
Davies Alec George	Scotland	S	18.4.62	Rawalpindi, Pakistan
Davies Christopher James	South Australia	A	15.11.78	Adelaide
Davies Michael Kenton	Northamptonshire	E	17.7.76	Ashby-de-la-Zouch
Davis Casper Andre	Windward Islands	WI	14.3.66	St Vincent
* **Davis** Heath Te-Ihi-O-Te-Rangi	Wellington	NZ	30.11.71	Lower Hutt
Davis Mark Jeffrey Gronow	Northerns	SA	10.10.71	Port Elizabeth
Davison John Michael	Victoria	A	9.5.70	Campbell River, Canada
Davison Rodney John	New South Wales	A	26.6.69	Kogarah
Dawes Joseph Henry	Queensland	A	29.8.70	Herston
Dawood Ismail	Glamorgan	E	23.7.76	Dewsbury
Dawson Alan Charles	Western Province	SA	27.11.69	Cape Town
Dawson Robert Ian	Gloucestershire	E	29.3.70	Exmouth
Dean Kevin James	Derbyshire	E	16.10.75	Derby
Deane Michael John	Derbyshire	E	9.3.77	Chesterfield
de Bruyn Pierre	Northerns	SA	31.3.77	Pretoria
de Bruyn Zander	Gauteng	SA	5.7.75	Johannesburg
* **DeFreitas** Phillip Anthony Jason	Derbyshire	E	18.2.66	Scotts Head, Dominica
De Groot Nicholas Alexander	Guyana	WI	22.10.75	Guyana
Deitz Shane Andrew	South Australia	A	4.5.75	Bankstown
de Kock Grant Andrew	Griqualand West	SA	18.11.76	Bellville
de la Pena Jason Michael	Worcestershire	E	16.9.72	Hammersmith
Denton Gerard John	Tasmania	A	7.8.75	Mount Isa
de Saram Samantha Indika	Colts	SL	2.9.73	Matara
* **de Silva** Karunakalage Sajeewa Chanaka	Nondescripts	SL	11.1.71	Kalutara
* **de Silva** Pinnaduwage Aravinda	Nondescripts	SL	17.10.65	Colombo
* **de Silva** Sanjeewa Kumara Lanka	Colombo	SL	29.7.75	Kurunegala
de Vos Dirk Johannes Jacobus	Northerns	SA	15.6.75	Pretoria
Dharmani Pankaj	Punjab	I	27.9.74	Delhi
* **Dharmasena** Handunnettige Deepthi Priyantha Kumar	Bloomfield	SL	24.4.71	Colombo
Dighe Samir Sudhakar	Mumbai	I	8.10.68	Bombay
Dighton Michael Gray	Western Australia	A	24.7.76	Toowoomba
* **Dillon** Mervyn	Trinidad & Tobago	WI	5.6.74	Toco
Dilshan Tillekeratne Mudiyansilage	Sebastianites	SL	14.10.76	Kalutara
Dippenaar Hendrik Human	Free State	SA	14.6.77	Kimberley
Di Venuto Michael James	Tasmania/Sussex	A	12.12.73	Hobart
* **Donald** Allan Anthony	Free State/Warwickshire	SA	20.10.66	Bloemfontein
Douglas Mark William	Central Districts	NZ	20.10.68	Nelson
* **Doull** Simon Blair	Northern Districts	NZ	6.8.69	Pukekohe
Dowlin Travis Montague	Guyana	WI	24.2.77	Georgetown
Dowman Mathew Peter	Nottinghamshire	E	10.5.74	Grantham
Drakes Vasbert Conniel	Barbados/Border/Notts	WI	5.8.69	St James
* **Dravid** Rahul	Karnataka	I	11.1.73	Indore
Drew Bryan John	Boland	SA	23.1.71	Durban
Dreyer Jan Nicolaas	KwaZulu-Natal	SA	9.9.76	Amanzimtoti
Driver Ryan Craig	Worcestershire	E	30.4.79	Truro
Dros Gerald	Northerns	SA	2.4.73	Pretoria
Drum Christopher James	Auckland	NZ	10.7.74	Auckland
Dry Willem Moolman	Griqualand West	SA	9.1.71	Vryburg
Dumas Vernon	Windward Islands	WI	27.5.78	Dominica
Dutch Keith Philip	Middlesex	E	21.3.73	Harrow
du Toit Willem Johannes	Boland	SA	18.3.81	Cape Town
Dyer Nicholas Rayner	Scotland	S	10.6.69	Edinburgh
Dykes James Andrew	Tasmania	A	15.11.71	Hobart

	Team	Country	Born	Birthplace
Eagleson Ryan Logan	Derbyshire	E	17.12.74	Carrickfergus, Ireland
***Ealham** Mark Alan	Kent	E	27.8.69	Willesborough
Edwards Alexander David	Sussex	E	2.8.75	Cuckfield
Eime Andrew Barry	South Australia	A	3.7.71	North Adelaide
***Eksteen** Clive Edward	Gauteng	SA	2.12.66	Johannesburg
***Elliott** Matthew Thomas Gray	Victoria	A	28.9.71	Chelsea
***Elworthy** Steven	Northerns	SA	23.2.65	Bulawayo, Rhodesia
***Emery** Philip Allen	New South Wales	A	25.6.64	St Ives
Emslie Peter Arthur Norman	Border	SA	21.10.68	Grahamstown
Enamul Haque	Bangladesh	B	27.2.67	Comilla
Engelke Justin Marc	Gauteng	SA	3.4.76	Cape Town
English Cedric Vaughan	Boland	SA	13.9.73	Kimberley
Evans Alun Wyn	Glamorgan	E	20.8.75	Glanamman
***Evans** Craig Neil	Mashonaland	Z	29.11.69	Salisbury
***Fairbrother** Neil Harvey	Lancashire	E	9.9.63	Warrington
Faruq Ahmed	Bangladesh	B	24.7.66	Dhaka
Faull Martin Peter	South Australia	A	10.5.68	Darwin
***Fazl-e-Akbar**	Peshawar/Customs	P	20.10.80	Peshawar
Fellows Gary Matthew	Yorkshire	E	30.7.78	Halifax
Fernando Ungamandalige <u>Nisal</u> Kumudusiri	Sinhalese	SL	10.3.70	Colombo
Ferreira Evert Johann	Boland	SA	29.4.76	Pretoria
Ferreira Lloyd Douglas	Western Province	SA	6.5.74	Johannesburg
Ferreira Quentin	Northerns	SA	28.12.72	East London
Fisher Ian Douglas	Yorkshire	E	31.5.76	Bradford
Fitzgerald David Andrew	South Australia	A	30.11.72	Osborne Park
Flanagan Ian Nicholas	Essex	E	5.6.80	Colchester
***Fleming** Damien William	Victoria	A	24.4.70	Bentley
Fleming Matthew Valentine	Kent	E	12.12.64	Macclesfield
***Fleming** Stephen Paul	Canterbury	NZ	1.4.73	Christchurch
***Flintoff** Andrew	Lancashire	E	6.12.77	Preston
***Flower** Andrew	Mashonaland	Z	28.4.68	Cape Town, SA
***Flower** Grant William	Mashonaland	Z	20.12.70	Salisbury
Foley Geoffrey Ian	Queensland	A	11.10.67	Jandowae
Follett David	Northamptonshire	E	14.10.68	Newcastle-under-Lyme
Ford Shane George Bancroft	Jamaica	WI	8.9.69	Kingston
Forde Keith Adrian	KwaZulu-Natal	SA	12.7.69	Pietermaritzburg
Francis Simon Richard George	Hampshire	E	15.8.78	Bromley
Franks Paul John	Nottinghamshire	E	3.2.79	Mansfield
***Fraser** Angus Robert Charles	Middlesex	E	8.8.65	Billinge
Freedman David Andrew	New South Wales	A	19.6.64	Sydney
Frost Tony	Warwickshire	E	17.11.75	Stoke-on-Trent
Fulton David Paul	Kent	E	15.11.71	Lewisham
Gain Douglas Robert	Boland	SA	29.12.76	Johannesburg
Gait Andrew Ian	Free State	SA	19.12.78	Bulawayo, Rhodesia
***Gallian** Jason Edward Riche	Nottinghamshire	E	25.6.71	Sydney, Australia
Gamage Janaka Champika	Galle	SL	17.4.64	Matara
Gandhe Pritam Vithal	Vidarbha	I	6.8.71	Nagpur
***Ganesh** Doddanarasiah	Karnataka	I	30.6.73	Bangalore
***Ganga** Daren	Trinidad & Tobago	WI	14.1.79	Barrackpore
***Ganguly** Sourav Chandidas	Bengal	I	8.7.72	Calcutta
Gannon Benjamin Ward	Gloucestershire	E	5.9.75	Oxford
Garrick Leon Vivian	Jamaica	WI	11.11.76	St Ann
Gayle Christopher Henry	Jamaica	WI	21.9.79	Kingston
George Mulligan Frank	Western Province	SA	10.9.76	Cape Town
Ghare Yogesh Trimbak	Vidarbha	I	5.7.71	Nagpur
Ghulam Ali	PIA	P	8.9.66	Karachi
***Gibbs** Herschelle Herman	Western Province	SA	23.2.74	Cape Town

	Team	Country	Born	Birthplace
* **Gibson** Ottis Delroy	Griqualand West	WI	16.3.69	Sion Hill, Barbados
* **Giddins** Edward Simon Hunter	Warwickshire	E	20.7.71	Eastbourne
Gidley Martyn Ian	Griqualand West	SA	30.9.68	Leicester, England
Gie Noel Addison	Nottinghamshire	E	12.4.77	Pretoria, South Africa
Gilbert Ashley Stephen	Victoria	A	26.11.71	Preston
Gilchrist Adam Craig	Western Australia	A	14.11.71	Bellingen
Gilder Gary Michael	KwaZulu-Natal	SA	6.7.74	Salisbury, Rhodesia
* **Giles** Ashley Fraser	Warwickshire	E	19.3.73	Chertsey
* **Gillespie** Jason Neil	South Australia	A	19.4.75	Darlinghurst
* **Goodwin** Murray William	Mashonaland	Z	11.12.72	Salisbury, Rhodesia
* **Gough** Darren	Yorkshire	E	18.9.70	Barnsley
Gough Michael Andrew	Durham	E	18.12.79	Hartlepool
Grace Graham Vernon	Eastern Province	SA	16.8.75	Salisbury
Graham Hattian Rodney O'Brien	Barbados	WI	22.6.73	Barbados
Grainger Chad	Boland	SA	23.9.72	Johannesburg
Grayson Adrian Paul	Essex	E	31.3.71	Ripon
Green Richard James	Lancashire	E	13.3.76	Warrington
Greenidge Carl Gary	Surrey	E	20.4.78	Basingstoke
* **Griffith** Adrian Frank Gordon	Barbados	WI	19.11.71	Barbados
Griffiths Steven Paul	Derbyshire	E	31.5.73	Hertford
Grove Jamie Oliver	Essex	E	3.7.79	Bury St Edmunds
Gunawardene Aruna Alwis Wijesiri	Sinhalese	SL	31.3.69	Colombo
* **Gunawardene** Dihan Avishka	Sinhalese	SL	26.5.77	Colombo
Gupta Sandeep Kumar	Kenya	K	7.4.67	Nairobi
* **Habib** Aftab	Leicestershire	E	7.2.72	Reading
Hafeez Abdul	Worcestershire	E	21.3.77	Birmingham
Haldipur Nikhil	Bengal	I	19.12.77	Calcutta
Hall Andrew James	Gauteng	SA	31.7.75	Johannesburg
Hamilton Gavin Mark	Yorkshire/Scotland	S/E	16.9.74	Broxburn
Hancock Timothy Harold Coulter	Gloucestershire	E	20.4.72	Reading
Haniff Azeemul	Guyana	WI	24.10.77	Guyana
Haniff Azib Ally	Guyana	WI		Port Mourant
Hansen Thomas Munkholt	Hampshire	E	25.3.76	Glostrup, Denmark
* **Harbhajan Singh**	Punjab	I	3.7.80	Jullundur
Harden Richard John	Yorkshire	E	16.8.65	Bridgwater
Hardinges Mark Andrew	Gloucestershire	E	5.2.78	Gloucester
Harmison Stephen James	Durham	E	23.10.78	Ashington
Harper Laurence Damien	Victoria	A	10.12.70	Deniliquin
Harris Andrew James	Derbyshire	E	26.6.73	Ashton-under-Lyne
* **Harris** Chris Zinzan	Canterbury	NZ	20.11.69	Christchurch
Harrison David Stuart	Glamorgan	E	30.7.81	Newport
Harrity Mark Andrew	South Australia	A	9.3.74	Semaphore
* **Hart** Matthew Norman	Northern Districts	NZ	16.5.72	Hamilton
Hart Robert Garry	Northern Districts	NZ	2.12.74	Hamilton
Hartley Peter John	Hampshire	E	18.4.60	Keighley
Harvey Ian Joseph	Victoria/Gloucestershire	A	10.4.72	Wonthaggi
Harvey Kade Murray	Western Australia	A	7.10.75	Subiaco
* **Harvinder Singh**	Punjab	I	23.12.77	Amritsar
* **Hasan Raza**	Karachi/Customs	P	11.3.82	Karachi
Hasibul Hussain	Bangladesh	B	3.6.77	Dhaka
* **Haslam** Mark James	Auckland	NZ	26.9.72	Bury, England
* **Hathurusinghe** Upul Chandika	Moors	SL	13.9.68	Colombo
* **Hayden** Matthew Lawrence	Queensland/Northants	A	29.10.71	Kingaroy
Haynes Gavin Richard	Worcestershire	E	29.9.69	Stourbridge
Hayward Mornantau	Eastern Province	SA	6.3.77	Uitenhage
Haywood Giles Ronald	Sussex	E	8.9.79	Chichester
* **Headley** Dean Warren	Kent	E	27.1.70	Stourbridge
* **Healy** Ian Andrew	Queensland	A	30.4.64	Spring Hill

	Team	Country	Born	Birthplace
* **Hegg** Warren Kevin	Lancashire	E	23.2.68	*Whitefield*
Hemp David Lloyd	Warwickshire	E	8.11.70	*Hamilton, Bermuda*
Henderson Claude William	Western Province	SA	14.6.72	*Worcester*
Henderson James Michael	Boland	SA	6.8.75	*Worcester*
Henderson Tyron	Border	SA	1.8.74	*Durban*
Herath Rangana	Moors	SL	19.3.78	*Kurunegala*
Hewitt James Peter	Middlesex	E	26.2.76	*Southwark*
Hewson Dominic Robert	Gloucestershire	E	3.10.74	*Cheltenham*
* **Hick** Graeme Ashley	Worcestershire	E	23.5.66	*Salisbury, Rhodesia*
Higgs Mark Anthony	New South Wales	A	30.6.76	*Queanbeyan*
Hills Dene Fleetwood	Tasmania	A	27.8.70	*Wynyard*
Hinds Ryan O'Neal	Barbados	WI	17.2.81	*Holders Hill*
Hinds Wavell Wayne	Jamaica	WI	7.9.76	*Kingston*
* **Hirwani** Narendra Deepchand	Madhya Pradesh	I	18.10.68	*Gorakhpur*
Hockley James Bernard	Kent	E	16.4.79	*Beckenham*
Hodge Bradley John	Victoria	A	29.12.74	*Sandringham*
* **Hogg** George Bradley	Western Australia	A	6.2.71	*Narrogin*
Hoggard Matthew James	Yorkshire/Free State	E	31.12.76	*Leeds*
* **Holder** Roland Irwin Christopher	Barbados	WI	22.12.67	*Port-of-Spain, Trinidad*
* **Hollioake** Adam John	Surrey	E	5.9.71	*Melbourne, Australia*
* **Hollioake** Benjamin Caine	Surrey	E	11.11.77	*Melbourne, Australia*
Holloway Piran Charles Laity	Somerset	E	1.10.70	*Helston*
* **Hooper** Carl Llewellyn	Guyana	WI	15.12.66	*Georgetown*
* **Horne** Matthew Jeffery	Otago	NZ	5.2.70	*Takapuna*
Howell Llorne Gregory	Central Districts	NZ	8.7.72	*Napier*
Hoyte Ricardo Lawrence	Barbados	WI	15.10.69	*Bridgetown*
Huckle Adam George	Matabeleland	Z	21.9.71	*Bulawayo*
Hughes Bruce Kilvy	KwaZulu-Natal	SA	19.7.76	*Port Elizabeth*
Hudson Andrew Charles	KwaZulu-Natal	SA	17.3.65	*Eshowe*
Humphries Shaun	Sussex	E	11.1.73	*Horsham*
* **Hussain** Nasser	Essex	E	28.3.68	*Madras, India*
Hussey Michael Edward	Western Australia	A	27.5.75	*Morley*
Hutchison Paul Michael	Yorkshire	E	9.6.77	*Leeds*
Hutton Benjamin Leonard	Middlesex	E	29.1.77	*Johannesburg, S. Africa*
Hyam Barry James	Essex	E	9.9.75	*Romford*
* **Ijaz Ahmed**, sen.	Habib Bank	P	20.9.68	*Sialkot*
* **Ijaz Ahmed**, jun.	Faisalabad/Allied Bank	P	2.2.69	*Lyallpur*
* **Illingworth** Richard Keith	Worcestershire	E	23.8.63	*Bradford*
* **Ilott** Mark Christopher	Essex	E	27.8.70	*Watford*
* **Imran Nazir**	WAPDA	P	16.12.81	*Gujranwala*
Innes Kevin John	Northamptonshire	E	24.9.75	*Wellingborough*
Inness Mathew William Hunter	Victoria	A	13.1.78	*East Melbourne*
* **Inzamam-ul-Haq**	Faisalabad	P	3.3.70	*Multan*
Iqbal Khan Badruddin	Assam	I	4.6.68	*Bombay*
Iqbal Sikandar	Bahawalpur	P	19.12.58	*Karachi*
* **Irani** Ronald Charles	Essex	E	26.10.71	*Leigh*
Irfan Bhatti	Rawalpindi	P	28.9.64	*Peshawar*
Jackson Kenneth Charles	Boland	SA	16.8.64	*Kitwe, Zambia*
Jackson Paul William	Queensland	A	1.11.61	*East Melbourne*
* **Jacobs** Ridley Detamore	Leeward Islands	WI	26.11.67	*Swetes Village, Antigua*
* **Jadeja** Ajaysinhji	Haryana	I	1.2.71	*Jamnagar*
Jahangir Alam	Bangladesh	B	5.3.73	*Narayangonj*
Jain Pradeep	Haryana	I	22.5.65	*Delhi*
Jain Vineet	Haryana	I	16.5.72	*Malerkotla*
James Kevan David	Hampshire	E	18.3.61	*Lambeth*
* **James** Stephen Peter	Glamorgan	E	7.9.67	*Lydney*
* **Jarvis** Paul William	Somerset	E	29.6.65	*Redcar*
Javed Omar	Bangladesh	B	25.11.76	*Dhaka*
Javed Qadir	Karachi/PIA	P	25.8.76	*Karachi*

	Team	Country	Born	Birthplace
* **Jayasuriya** Sanath Teran	Bloomfield	SL	30.6.69	Matara
* **Jayawardene** Denagamage Proboth <u>Mahela</u> De Silva	Sinhalese	SL	27.5.77	Colombo
Jefferson Mark Robin	Wellington	NZ	28.6.76	Oamaru
Jeremy Kerry Clifford Bryan	Leeward Islands	WI	6.2.80	Antigua
Jitender Singh	Haryana	I	10.1.76	Rohtak
Joffe Ryan	Western Province	SA	19.4.75	Cape Town
Johnson Benjamin Andrew	South Australia	A	1.8.73	Naracoorte
* **Johnson** Neil Clarkson	Matabeleland	Z	24.1.70	Salisbury
Johnson Paul	Nottinghamshire	E	24.4.65	Newark
Johnson Richard Leonard	Middlesex	E	29.12.74	Chertsey
Johnston David <u>Trent</u>	New South Wales	A	29.4.74	Wollongong
Jones Ian	Somerset	E	11.3.77	Edmonton
Jones Philip <u>Steffan</u>	Somerset	E	9.2.74	Llanelli
Jones Simon <u>Philip</u>	Glamorgan	E	25.12.78	Swansea
Jordaan Deon	Northerns	SA	3.12.70	Bloemfontein
* **Joseph** David Rolston Emmanuel	Leeward Islands	WI	15.11.69	Antigua
Joseph Dawnley Alister	Windward Islands	WI	20.8.66	Stubbs, St Vincent
Joseph Sylvester Cleofoster	Leeward Islands	WI	5.9.78	New Winthorpes, Antigua
* **Joshi** Sunil Bandacharya	Karnataka	I	6.6.69	Gadag
Joubert Pierre	Northerns	SA	2.5.78	Pretoria
Joyce Edmund Christopher	Middlesex	E	22.9.78	Dublin, Ireland
* **Julian** Brendon Paul	Western Australia	A	10.8.70	Hamilton, New Zealand
Jurgensen Shayne John	Western Australia	A	28.4.76	Redcliffe
* **Kabir Khan**	Peshawar/Habib Bank	P	12.4.74	Peshawar
Kale Abhijit Vasant	Maharashtra	I	3.7.73	Ahmednagar
* **Kallis** Jacques Henry	W. Province/Glamorgan	SA	16.10.75	Cape Town
* **Kalpage** Ruwan Senani	Nondescripts	SL	19.2.70	Kandy
* **Kaluwitharana** Romesh Shantha	Colts	SL	24.11.69	Colombo
Kamande James Kabatha	Kenya	K	12.12.78	Muranga
* **Kambli** Vinod Ganpat	Mumbai	I	18.1.72	Bombay
Kanitkar Hrishikesh Hemant	Maharashtra	I	14.11.74	Poona
* **Kapoor** Aashish Rakesh	Rajasthan	I	25.3.71	Madras
Karim Aasif Yusuf	Kenya	K	15.12.63	Mombasa
Karim Syed Saba	Bengal	I	14.11.67	Patna
Karnain Shaul Hameed Uvais	Moors	SL	11.8.62	Colombo
Kartik Murali	Railways	I	11.9.76	Madras
* **Kasprowicz** Michael Scott	Queensland/Leicestershire	A	10.2.72	South Brisbane
Katich Simon Mathew	Western Australia	A	21.8.75	Middle Swan
Keech Matthew	Hampshire	E	21.10.70	Hampstead
Keedy Gary	Lancashire	E	27.11.74	Wakefield
Kemp Justin Miles	Eastern Province	SA	2.10.77	Queenstown
Kendall William Salwey	Hampshire	E	18.12.73	Wimbledon
* **Kennedy** Robert John	Otago	NZ	3.6.72	Dunedin
Kennis Gregor John	Somerset	E	9.3.74	Yokohama, Japan
Kent John Carter	KwaZulu-Natal	SA	7.5.79	Cape Town
Kenway Derek Anthony	Hampshire	E	12.6.78	Fareham
Kerr Jason Ian Douglas	Somerset	E	7.4.74	Bolton
Kettleborough Richard Allan	Middlesex	E	15.3.73	Sheffield
Key Robert William Trevor	Kent	E	12.5.79	East Dulwich
Khaled Mahmud	Bangladesh	B	26.7.71	Dhaka
Khaled Masud	Bangladesh	B	8.2.76	Rajshahi
Khan Aamer Ali	Leicestershire	E	5.11.69	Lahore, Pakistan
Khan Wasim Gulzar	Sussex	E	26.2.71	Birmingham
Khoda Gagan Kishanlal	Rajasthan	I	24.10.74	Barmer
Khurasiya Amay Ramsevak	Madhya Pradesh	I	18.5.72	Jabalpur
Kidwell Errol Wayne	Gauteng	SA	6.6.75	Vereeniging
Killeen Neil	Durham	E	17.10.75	Shotley Bridge
* **King** Reon Dane	Guyana	WI	6.10.75	Berbice
* **Kirsten** Gary	Western Province	SA	23.11.67	Cape Town

	Team	Country	Born	Birthplace
Kirsten Paul	Western Province	SA	30.10.69	Cape Town
Kirtley Robert James	Sussex	E	10.1.75	Eastbourne
***Klusener** Lance	KwaZulu-Natal	SA	4.9.71	Durban
***Knight** Nicholas Verity	Warwickshire	E	28.11.69	Watford
Koch Donovan Marius	Boland	SA	11.10.76	Somerset West
Koen Louis Johannes	Eastern Province	SA	28.3.67	Paarl
Koenig Sven Gaetan	Gauteng	SA	9.12.73	Durban
Kotak Shitanshu Hargovindbhai	Saurashtra	I	19.10.72	Rajkot
Krikken Karl Matthew	Derbyshire	E	9.4.69	Bolton
Kruis Gideon Jacobus	Griqualand West	SA	9.5.74	Pretoria
***Kulkarni** Nilesh Moreshwar	Mumbai	I	3.4.73	Dombivili
***Kumble** Anil	Karnataka	I	17.10.70	Bangalore
***Kuruvilla** Abey	Mumbai	I	8.8.68	Mannar
Lacey Simon James	Derbyshire	E	9.3.75	Nottingham
Lake Anthony Jermaine Alphonso	Leeward Islands	WI	22.3.74	Antigua
***Lambert** Clayton Benjamin	Guyana	WI	10.2.62	New Amsterdam
Lampitt Stuart Richard	Worcestershire	E	29.7.66	Wolverhampton
Laney Jason Scott	Hampshire	E	27.4.73	Winchester
***Langer** Justin Lee	W. Australia/Middlesex	A	21.11.70	Perth
Langeveldt Charl Kenneth	Boland	SA	17.12.74	Stellenbosch
***Lara** Brian Charles	Trinidad & Tobago	WI	2.5.69	Santa Cruz
***Larsen** Gavin Rolf	Wellington	NZ	27.9.62	Wellington
†***Lathwell** Mark Nicholas	Somerset	E	26.12.71	Bletchley
Law Danny Richard	Essex	E	15.7.75	Lambeth
***Law** Stuart Grant	Queensland/Essex	A	18.10.68	Herston
Law Wayne Lincoln	Glamorgan	E	4.9.78	Swansea
***Laxman** Vangipurappu Venkata Sai	Hyderabad	I	1.11.74	Hyderabad
Leatherdale David Antony	Worcestershire	E	26.11.67	Bradford
Lee Brett	New South Wales	A	8.11.76	Wollongong
Lee Shane	New South Wales	A	8.8.73	Wollongong
***Lehmann** Darren Scott	South Australia	A	5.2.70	Gawler
***Lewis** Clairmonte Christopher	Leicestershire	E	14.2.68	Georgetown, Guyana
Lewis Jonathan	Gloucestershire	E	26.8.75	Aylesbury
Lewis Jonathan James Benjamin	Durham	E	21.5.70	Isleworth
***Lewis** Rawl Nicholas	Windward Islands	WI	5.9.74	Grenada
Lewry Jason David	Sussex	E	2.4.71	Worthing
Liburd Merlin Dave	Leeward Islands	WI	15.12.69	Nevis
***Liebenberg** Gerhardus Frederick Johannes	Free State	SA	7.4.72	Upington
Liptrot Christopher George	Worcestershire	E	13.2.80	Wigan
***Liyanage** Dulip Kapila	Colts	SL	6.6.72	Kalutara
Lloyd Graham David	Lancashire	E	1.7.69	Accrington
Looch Ernest Michael	Boland	SA	21.4.75	Pretoria
Love Geoff Terry	Eastern Province	SA	19.9.76	Port Elizabeth
Love Martin Lloyd	Queensland	A	30.3.74	Mundubbera
***Loveridge** Greg Riaka	Cambridge U.	NZ	15.1.75	Palmerston North
Loye Malachy Bernard	Northamptonshire	E	27.9.72	Northampton
Lucas David Scott	Nottinghamshire	E	19.8.78	Nottingham
***McCague** Martin John	Kent	E	24.5.69	Larne, N. Ireland
McGarrell Neil Christopher	Guyana	WI	12.7.72	Guyana
***MacGill** Stuart Charles Glyndwr	New South Wales	A	25.2.71	Mount Lawley
McGrath Anthony	Yorkshire	E	6.10.75	Bradford
***McGrath** Glenn Donald	New South Wales	A	9.2.70	Dubbo
***McIntyre** Peter Edward	South Australia	A	27.4.66	Gisborne
McKenzie Neil Douglas	Gauteng	SA	24.11.75	Johannesburg
McKeown Patrick Christopher	Lancashire	E	1.6.76	Liverpool
***McLean** Nixon Alexei McNamara	Windward Islands/Hants	WI	20.7.73	Stubbs, St Vincent

† *Lathwell did not play in 1999, but was expected to return in 2000.*

	Team	Country	Born	Birthplace
McLean Reynold Julius Jefferson	Windward Islands	WI	9.4.73	Stubbs, St Vincent
***McMillan** Brian Mervin	Western Province	SA	22.12.63	Welkom
***McMillan** Craig Douglas	Canterbury	NZ	13.9.76	Christchurch
McNamara Bradley Edward	New South Wales	A	30.12.65	Sydney
MacQueen Robert Bruce	KwaZulu-Natal	SA	6.9.77	Durban
Maddy Darren Lee	Leicestershire	E	23.5.74	Leicester
***Madondo** Trevor Nyasha	Mashonaland	Z	22.11.76	Mount Darwin
Madurasinghe Arachchige Wijaysiri Raniith	Kurunegala Youth	SL	30.1.61	Kurunegala
***Mahanama** Roshan Siriwardene	Bloomfield	SL	31.5.66	Colombo
Mahbubur Rahman	Bangladesh	B	1.2.69	Mymensingh
Maher James Patrick	Queensland	A	27.2.74	Innistail
Mahmood Hamid	Karachi/PIA	P	19.1.69	Karachi
Mais Dwight Hugh	Jamaica	WI	27.10.77	St Catherine
***Malcolm** Devon Eugene	Northamptonshire	E	22.2.63	Kingston, Jamaica
Mall Ashraf	KwaZulu-Natal	SA	8.10.78	Durban
Manjurul Islam	Bangladesh	B	7.11.79	Khulna
Mansoor Rana	ADBP	P	27.12.62	Lahore
Manzoor Akhtar	Islamabad/Allied Bank	P	16.4.68	Karachi
***Manzoor Elahi**	ADBP	P	15.4.63	Sahiwal
Maqsood Rana	National Bank	P	1.8.72	Lahore
Marsh Daniel James	Tasmania	A	14.6.73	Subiaco
Marsh Steven Andrew	Kent	E	27.1.61	Westminster
Marshall Dave Kerwin	Barbados	WI	24.5.72	Barbados
Marshall Roy Ashworth	Windward Islands	WI	1.4.65	St Joseph, Dominica
Martin Jacob Joseph	Baroda	I	11.5.72	Baroda
***Martin** Peter James	Lancashire	E	15.11.68	Accrington
Martin-Jenkins Robin Simon Christopher	Sussex	E	28.10.75	Guildford
***Martyn** Damien Richard	Western Australia	A	21.10.71	Darwin
***Mascarenhas** Adrian Dimitri	Hampshire	E	30.10.77	Chiswick
Masikazana Lulama	Eastern Province	SA	6.2.73	Port Elizabeth
Masimula Walter Bafana	Gauteng	SA	23.10.75	Johannesburg
Mason Scott Robert	Tasmania	A	27.7.76	Launceston
Mason Timothy James	Leicestershire	E	12.4.75	Leicester
***Masood Anwar**	Lahore	P	12.12.67	Khanewal
***Matambanadzo** Everton Zvikomborero	Mashonaland	Z	13.4.76	Salisbury
Mather Stephen Robert	Otago	NZ	13.8.73	Napier
***Matthews** Craig Russell	Western Province	SA	15.2.65	Cape Town
Maynard John Carl	Leeward Islands	WI	18.5.69	Nevis
***Maynard** Matthew Peter	Glamorgan	E	21.3.66	Oldham
***Mbangwa** Mpumelelo	Matabeleland	Z	26.6.76	Plumtree
Mehrab Hossain	Bangladesh	B	22.9.78	Dhaka
Mendis Chaminda	Colts	SL	28.12.68	Galle
***Mhambrey** Paras Laxmikant	Mumbai	I	20.6.72	Bombay
***Miller** Colin Reid	Tasmania	A	6.2.64	Footscray
Miller Michael Christian	Queensland	A	30.5.79	Toowoomba
Millns David James	Leicestershire	E	27.2.65	Clipstone
Minhas Mithun	Delhi	I	12.9.77	Jammu
Minhazul Abedin	Bangladesh	B	25.9.65	Chittagong
Mitchell Ian	Border	SA	14.12.77	Johannesburg
Modi Hitesh Subhash	Kenya	K	13.10.71	Kisumu
***Mohammad Akram**	Rawalpindi/Allied Bank	P	10.9.74	Islamabad
***Mohammad Hussain**	Lahore/National Bank	P	8.10.76	Lahore
Mohammad Kaif	Uttar Pradesh	I	1.12.80	Allahabad
Mohammad Rafiq	Bangladesh	B	15.5.70	Dhaka
***Mohammad Ramzan**	Faisalabad/PNSC	P	25.12.70	Lyallpur
Mohammad Sheikh	Kenya	K	29.8.80	Nairobi
***Mohammad Wasim**	Rawalpindi/KRL	P	8.8.77	Rawalpindi

	Team	Country	Born	Birthplace
*Mohammad Zahid	PIA	P	2.8.76	Gaggu Mandi
Mohammed Ricardo A. A.	Guyana	WI		
*Mohanty Debasis Sarbeswar	Orissa	I	20.7.76	Bhubaneshwar
Mohsin Kamal	PNSC	P	16.6.63	Lyallpur
*Moin Khan	PIA	P	23.9.71	Rawalpindi
Moin-ul-Atiq	Habib Bank	P	5.8.64	Karachi
Mongia Dinesh	Punjab	I	17.4.77	Chandigarh
*Mongia Nayan Ramlal	Baroda	I	19.12.69	Baroda
Montgomerie Richard Robert	Sussex	E	3.7.71	Rugby
*Moody Thomas Masson	W. Australia/Worcs	A	2.10.65	Adelaide
Morgan Grant	Northerns	SA	19.5.71	Port Elizabeth
Morgan McNeil Junior	Windward Islands	WI	18.10.70	St Vincent
Morris Alexander Corfield	Hampshire	E	4.10.76	Barnsley
*Morris John Edward	Durham	E	1.4.64	Crewe
Morris Robin Francis	Orissa	I	6.11.76	Bombay
Morris Zachary Clegg	Hampshire	E	4.9.78	Barnsley
Mott Matthew Peter	Victoria	A	3.10.73	Charleville
Mpitsang Phenyo Victor	Free State	SA	28.3.80	Kimberley
Mudgal Manoj Sitaram	Uttar Pradesh	I	18.10.72	Meerut
Mujahid Jamshed	Sargodha/Habib Bank	P	1.12.71	Muredke
Mulder Bret	Western Australia	A	6.2.64	Subiaco
*Mullally Alan David	Leicestershire	E	12.7.69	Southend-on-Sea
Muller Scott Andrew	Queensland	A	11.7.71	Herston
Munnik Renier	Western Province	SA	7.1.78	Cape Town
*Munton Timothy Alan	Warwickshire	E	30.7.65	Melton Mowbray
*Muralitharan Muttiah	Tamil Union/Lancashire	SL	17.4.72	Kandy
Murphy Brian Samuel	Jamaica	WI	7.4.73	Jamaica
*Murray Junior Randalph	Windward Islands	WI	20.1.68	St Georges, Grenada
*Mushtaq Ahmed	Peshawar	P	28.6.70	Sahiwal
*Nadeem Abbasi	Rawalpindi/KRL	P	15.4.64	Rawalpindi
*Nadeem Ghauri	Habib Bank	P	12.10.62	Lahore
*Nadeem Khan	Karachi/PIA	P	10.12.69	Rawalpindi
Naeem Ashraf	Lahore/National Bank	P	10.11.72	Lahore
Nagamootoo Mahendra Veeren	Guyana	WI	9.10.75	Guyana
Nagamootoo Vishal	Guyana	WI	7.1.77	Guyana
Naimur Rahman	Bangladesh	B	19.9.74	Dhaka
Nash David Charles	Middlesex	E	19.1.78	Chertsey
*Nash Dion Joseph	Auckland	NZ	20.11.71	Auckland
*Naved Anjum	Habib Bank	P	27.7.63	Lahore
*Naved Ashraf	Rawalpindi/KRL	P	4.9.74	Rawalpindi
Nawaz Mohamed Naveed	Nondescripts	SL	20.9.73	Colombo
Nayyar Rajiv	Himachal Pradesh	I	28.3.70	Delhi
Nedd Gavin Hilton	Guyana	WI	21.7.72	Guyana
Neeyamur Rashid	Bangladesh	B	1.1.75	Pabna
*Nehra Ashish	Delhi	I	29.4.79	Delhi
Nevin Christopher John	Wellington	NZ	3.8.75	Dunedin
Newell Keith	Glamorgan	E	25.3.72	Crawley
Newell Mark	Derbyshire	E	19.12.73	Crawley
*Newport Philip John	Worcestershire	E	11.10.62	High Wycombe
*Nicholson Matthew James	Western Australia	A	2.10.74	St Leonards
Nielsen Timothy John	South Australia	A	5.5.68	Forest Gate, England
Nikitaras Steven	Western Australia	A	31.8.70	Port Kembla
Nixon Paul Andrew	Leicestershire	E	21.10.70	Carlisle
Nkala Mluleki Luke	Zimbabwe	Z	1.4.81	Bulawayo
Noon Wayne Michael	Nottinghamshire	E	5.2.71	Grimsby
*Ntini Makhaya	Border	SA	6.7.77	Zwelitsha

	Team	Country	Born	Birthplace
Obaid Kamal	Uttar Pradesh	I	4.9.72	Allahabad
* **O'Connor** Shayne Barry	Otago	NZ	15.11.73	Hastings
Odoyo Thomas Migai	Kenya	K	12.5.78	Nairobi
Odumbe Maurice Omondi	Kenya	K	15.6.69	Nairobi
Oldroyd Bradley John	Western Australia	A	5.11.73	Bentley
* **Olonga** Henry Khaaba	Matabeleland	Z	3.7.76	Lusaka, Zambia
Ontong Justin Lee	Boland	SA	4.1.80	Paarl
Ormond James	Leicestershire	E	20.8.77	Walsgrave
Ostler Dominic Piers	Warwickshire	E	15.7.70	Solihull
Otieno Kennedy Obhya	Kenya	K	11.3.72	Nairobi
Padmanabhan Karumanaseri Narayanaiyer Anantha	Kerala	I	8.9.69	Trivandrum
Palframan Steven John	Boland	SA	12.5.70	East London
Pandey Gyanendrakumar Kedarnath	Uttar Pradesh	I	12.8.72	Lucknow
* **Pandit** Chandrakant Sitaram	Madhya Pradesh	I	30.9.61	Bombay
Pangarker Hassan	Western Province	SA	31.8.68	Cape Town
Paranjpe Jatin Vasudeo	Mumbai	I	17.4.72	Bombay
Parida Kulamani Shankar	Railways	I	9.3.77	Cuttack
Parillon Joseph	Windward Islands	WI	4.1.79	Dominica
Parker Geoffrey Ross	South Australia	A	31.3.68	Malvern
Parkin Owen Thomas	Glamorgan	E	24.9.72	Coventry
Parlane Michael Edward	Northern Districts	NZ	22.7.72	Pukekohe
* **Parore** Adam Craig	Auckland	NZ	23.1.71	Auckland
Parsons Keith Alan	Somerset	E	2.5.73	Taunton
Pascoe Matthew David	Queensland	A	10.1.77	Camperdown
* **Patel** Minal Mahesh	Kent	E	7.7.70	Bombay, India
Patterson Bruce Mathew Winston	Scotland	S	29.1.65	Ayr
Patterson Mark William	Surrey	E	2.2.74	Belfast, N. Ireland
Peirce Michael Toby Edward	Sussex	E	14.6.73	Maidenhead
Penberthy Anthony Leonard	Northamptonshire	E	1.9.69	Troon, Cornwall
Penn Andrew Jonathan	Central Districts	NZ	27.7.74	Wanganui
Penney Trevor Lionel	Warwicks/Mashonaland A	E	12.6.68	Salisbury, Rhodesia
Percival Andre Ricardo	Guyana	WI	5.1.75	New Amsterdam
* **Perera** Anhettige Suresh Asanka	Sinhalese	SL	16.2.78	Colombo
* **Perera** Kahawalege Gamini	Galle	SL	22.5.64	Colombo
* **Perera** Panagodage Don Ruchira Laksiri	Sinhalese	SL	27.10.76	Colombo
Perren Clinton Terrence	Queensland	A	22.2.75	Herston
* **Perry** Nehemiah Odolphus	Jamaica	WI	16.6.68	Jamaica
Persad Mukesh	Trinidad & Tobago	WI	1.5.70	Trinidad
Persad-Maharaj Vishal	Trinidad & Tobago	WI	6.8.76	Trinidad
Peters Stephen David	Essex	E	10.12.78	Harold Wood
Peterson Robin John	Eastern Province	SA	4.8.79	Port Elizabeth
Petrie Richard George	Wellington	NZ	23.8.67	Christchurch
Phelps Matthew James	New South Wales	A	1.9.72	Lismore
Philip Iain Lindsay	Scotland	S	9.6.58	Falkirk
Phillip Wayne	Windward Islands	WI	25.11.77	Dominica
Phillip Warrington Dexter	Leeward Islands	WI	23.7.68	Nevis
Phillips Nicholas Charles	Durham	E	10.5.74	Pembury
Phillips Timothy James	Essex	E	13.3.81	Cambridge
Pienaar Roy Francois	Northern Transvaal	SA	17.7.61	Johannesburg
Pierson Adrian Roger Kirshaw	Somerset	E	21.7.63	Enfield, Middlesex
Piper Keith John	Warwickshire	E	18.12.69	Leicester
Player Bradley Thomas	Western Province	SA	18.1.67	Benoni
* **Pocock** Blair Andrew	Auckland	NZ	18.6.71	Papakura
Pollard Paul Raymond	Worcestershire	E	24.9.68	Nottingham
* **Pollock** Shaun Maclean	KwaZulu-Natal	SA	16.7.73	Port Elizabeth
* **Ponting** Ricky Thomas	Tasmania	A	19.12.74	Launceston
Pooran Homchand	Guyana	WI	14.2.79	Albion

	Team	Country	Born	Birthplace
Shahriar Hossain	Bangladesh	B	1.6.76	*Narayangonj*
*** Shakeel Ahmed**, jun	Easterns	P	12.11.71	*Daska*
*** Shakeel Ahmed**, sen.	Rawalpindi/KRL	P	12.2.66	*Kuwait City, Kuwait*
Shakeel Khan	Habib Bank	P	28.5.68	*Lahore*
Sharath Sridharan	Tamil Nadu	I	31.10.72	*Madras*
*** Sharma** Ajay	Delhi	I	3.4.64	*Delhi*
Shaw Adrian David	Glamorgan	E	17.2.72	*Neath*
Sheikh Mohamed Avez	Warwickshire	E	2.7.73	*Birmingham*
Shepard David John	Victoria	A	30.12.70	*Berwick*
Sheriyar Alamgir	Worcestershire	E	15.11.73	*Birmingham*
Shewag Virender	Delhi	I	20.10.78	*Delhi*
*** Shoaib** Akhtar	Rawalpindi	P	13.8.75	*Rawalpindi*
*** Shoaib** Mohammad	Karachi/PIA	P	8.1.61	*Karachi*
Shukla Laxmi Ratan	Bengal	I	6.5.81	*Howrah*
Siddiqui Iqbal	Maharashtra	I	26.12.74	*Aurangabad*
Siddons James Darren	South Australia	A	25.4.64	*Robinvale*
Sidebottom Ryan Jay	Yorkshire	E	15.6.78	*Huddersfield*
*** Sidhu** Navjot Singh	Punjab	I	20.10.63	*Patiala*
*** Silva** Kelaniyage Jayantha	Sinhalese	SL	2.6.73	*Kalutara*
Silva Lindamlilage Prageeth Chamara	Panadura	SL	14.12.79	*Panadura*
*** Silverwood** Christopher Eric Wilfred	Yorkshire	E	5.3.75	*Pontefract*
*** Simmons** Philip Verant	Trinidad & Tobago	WI	18.4.63	*Arima*
Simons Eric Owen	Western Province	SA	9.3.62	*Cape Town*
Sinclair Matthew George	Jamaica	WI	26.1.80	*St Elizabeth*
Sinclair Mathew Stuart	Central Districts	NZ	9.11.75	*Katherine, Australia*
Singh Anurag	Warwickshire	E	9.9.75	*Kanpur, India*
Singh Narender Pal	Hyderabad	I	10.9.73	*Dehra Dun*
*** Singh** Rabindra Ramanarayan	Tamil Nadu	I	14.9.63	*Princes Town, Trinidad*
*** Singh** Robin	Delhi	I	1.1.70	*Delhi*
*** Sivaramakrishnan** Laxman	Baroda	I	31.12.65	*Madras*
*** Slater** Michael Jonathon	New South Wales/Derbys	A	21.2.70	*Wagga Wagga*
Smethurst Michael Paul	Lancashire	E	11.10.76	*Oldham*
*** Smith** Andrew Michael	Gloucestershire	E	1.10.67	*Dewsbury*
Smith Benjamin Francis	Leicestershire	E	3.4.72	*Corby*
Smith Dennis James	Northerns	SA	26.11.71	*Durban*
Smith Devon Sheldon	Windward Islands	WI	21.10.81	*Grenada*
Smith Edward Thomas	Kent	E	19.7.77	*Pembury*
Smith Gregory James	Northerns	SA	30.10.71	*Pretoria*
Smith Michael Jonathon	Scotland	S	30.3.66	*Edinburgh*
Smith Neil Michael Knight	Warwickshire	E	27.7.67	*Birmingham*
Smith Richard Andrew Mortimer	Trinidad & Tobago	WI	17.7.71	*Trinidad*
*** Smith** Robin Arnold	Hampshire	E	13.9.63	*Durban, South Africa*
Smith Trevor Mark	Derbyshire	E	18.1.77	*Derby*
Snape Jeremy Nicholas	Gloucestershire	E	27.4.73	*Stoke-on-Trent*
Solanki Vikram Singh	Worcestershire	E	1.4.76	*Udaipur, India*
Solomons Mario Theodore	Western Province	SA	24.2.71	*Kuils River*
Somasekhar Shiraguppi	Karnataka	I	14.6.74	*Dharwad*
Somasunder Sujith	Karnataka	I	2.12.72	*Bangalore*
Speak Nicholas Jason	Durham	E	21.11.66	*Manchester*
*** Spearman** Craig Murray	Central Districts	NZ	4.7.72	*Auckland*
Speight Martin Peter	Durham	E	24.10.67	*Walsall*
Spendlove Benjamin Lee	Derbyshire	E	4.11.78	*Belper*
Spiring Karl Reuben	Worcestershire	E	13.11.74	*Southport*
*** Srinath** Javagal	Karnataka	I	31.8.69	*Mysore*
Sriram Sridharan	Tamil Nadu	I	21.2.76	*Madras*
Stanger Ian Michael	Scotland	S	5.10.71	*Glasgow*
*** Stead** Gary Raymond	Canterbury	NZ	9.1.72	*Christchurch*
Stemp Richard David	Nottinghamshire	E	11.12.67	*Birmingham*

	Team	Country	Born	Birthplace
* **Stephenson** John Patrick	Hampshire	E	14.3.65	Stebbing
Stevens Darren Ian	Leicestershire	E	30.4.76	Leicester
* **Stewart** Alec James	Surrey	E	8.4.63	Merton
Stewart Errol Leslie Rae	KwaZulu-Natal	SA	30.7.69	Durban
* **Steyn** Philippus Jeremia Rudolf	Northerns	SA	30.6.67	Kimberley
Storey Keith Graham	KwaZulu-Natal	SA	25.1.69	Salisbury, Rhodesia
* **Strang** Bryan Colin	Mashonaland	Z	9.6.72	Bulawayo
* **Strang** Paul Andrew	Mashonaland	Z	28.7.70	Bulawayo
Strauss Andrew John	Middlesex	E	2.3.77	Johannesburg, SA
* **Streak** Heath Hilton	Matabeleland	Z	16.3.74	Bulawayo
Strong Michael Richard	Sussex	E	28.6.74	Cuckfield
Strydom Pieter Coenraad	Border	SA	10.6.69	Somerset East
Stuart Anthony Mark	New South Wales	A	2.1.70	Newcastle
Stuart Colin Ellsworth Laurie	Guyana	WI	28.9.73	Guyana
Stubbings Stephen David	Derbyshire	E	31.3.78	Huddersfield
* **Such** Peter Mark	Essex	E	12.6.64	Helensburgh, Scotland
Sugden Craig Brian	Border	SA	7.3.74	Durban
Suji Anthony Ondik	Kenya	K	5.2.76	Nairobi
Suji Martin Armon	Kenya	K	2.6.71	Nairobi
Sutcliffe Iain John	Leicestershire	E	20.12.74	Leeds
Swain Brett Andrew	South Australia	A	14.5.72	Stirling
Swanepoel Adriaan Johannes	Griqualand West	SA	19.3.72	Kimberley
Swann Alec James	Northamptonshire	E	26.10.76	Northampton
Swann Graeme Peter	Northamptonshire	E	24.3.79	Northampton
* **Symcox** Patrick Leonard	Griqualand West	SA	14.4.60	Kimberley
Symonds Andrew	Queensland/Kent	A	9.6.75	Birmingham, England
Tait Alex Ross	Northern Districts	NZ	13.6.72	Paparoa
Taljard Dion	Border	SA	7.1.70	East London
Targett Benjamin Stuart	Tasmania	A	27.12.72	Paddington
Tariq-ur-Rehman	Bihar	I	22.2.74	Darbanga
Tatton Craig Ross	KwaZulu-Natal	SA	29.1.75	Bulawayo
Taylor Billy Victor	Sussex	E	11.1.77	Southampton
* **Taylor** Jonathan Paul	Northamptonshire	E	8.8.64	Ashby-de-la-Zouch
* **Taylor** Mark Anthony	New South Wales	A	27.10.64	Leeton
Tendulkar Sachin Ramesh	Mumbai	I	24.4.73	Bombay
* **Terbrugge** David John	Gauteng	SA	31.1.77	Ladysmith
Thomas Dennison	Windward Islands	WI	3.3.68	Grenada
Thomas Paul Anthony	Derbyshire	E	3.6.71	Perry Barr, Birmingham
Thomas Stuart Darren	Glamorgan	E	25.1.75	Morriston
Thompson David James	Essex	E	11.3.76	Wandsworth
Thompson Julian Barton DeCourcy	Kent	E	28.10.68	Cape Town, SA
* **Thompson** Patterson Ian Chesterfield	Barbados	WI	26.9.71	Barbados
Thompson Scott Michael	New South Wales	A	4.5.72	Bankstown
* **Thorpe** Graham Paul	Surrey	E	1.8.69	Farnham
Tikolo Stephen Ogomji	Kenya	K	25.6.71	Nairobi
* **Tillekeratne** Hashan Prasantha	Nondescripts	SL	14.7.67	Colombo
Titchard Stephen Paul	Derbyshire	E	17.12.67	Warrington
Tolley Christopher Mark	Nottinghamshire	E	30.12.67	Kidderminster
Townsend David Hume	Northerns	SA	22.12.77	Port Elizabeth
Toyana Geoffrey	Gauteng	SA	27.2.74	Soweto
Trescothick Marcus Edward	Somerset	E	25.12.75	Keynsham
Tucker Rodney James	Tasmania	A	28.8.64	Auburn
Tuckett Carl McArthur	Leeward Islands	WI	18.5.70	Nevis
* **Tudor** Alex Jeremy	Surrey	E	23.10.77	Kensington
* **Tufnell** Philip Charles Roderick	Middlesex	E	29.4.66	Barnet

	Team	Country	Born	Birthplace
Turner Robert Julian	Somerset	E	25.11.67	Malvern
Tweats Timothy Andrew	Derbyshire	E	18.4.74	Stoke-on-Trent
*****Twose** Roger Graham	Wellington	NZ	17.4.68	Torquay, England
Udal Shaun David	Hampshire	E	18.3.69	Farnborough, Hants
*****Upashantha** Kalutarage <u>Eric</u> Amila	Colts	SL	10.6.72	Kurunegala
*****Vaas** Warnakulasooriya Patabendige Ushantha Joseph <u>Chaminda</u>	Colts	SL	27.1.74	Mattumagala
Vadher Alpesh Vallabhdas	Kenya	K	7.9.74	Nairobi
van der Merwe Casparus Cornelius	Border	SA	11.7.73	Johannesburg
van der Wath Johannes Jacobus	Free State	SA	10.1.78	Newcastle
van Jaarsveld Martin	Northerns	SA	18.6.74	Klerksdorp
van Wyk Jacques Merlin	Boland	SA	27.1.78	Stellenbosch
van Wyk Morne Nico	Free State	SA	20.3.79	Bloemfontein
van Zyl Daniel Jacobus	Boland	SA	8.1.71	Pretoria
Vaughan Jeffrey Mark	South Australia	A	26.3.74	Blacktown
Vaughan Michael Paul	Yorkshire	E	29.10.74	Manchester
Veenstra Ross Edward	Gauteng	SA	22.4.72	Estcourt
Venkataramana Margashayam	Tamil Nadu	I	24.4.66	Secunderabad
Venter Hermanus	Boland	SA	25.8.75	Roodepoort
Venter Jacobus Francois	Free State	SA	1.10.69	Bloemfontein
Ventura Mario Dimitri	Jamaica	WI	21.4.74	Jamaica
*****Vettori** Daniel Luca	Northern Districts	NZ	27.1.79	Auckland
*****Viljoen** Dirk Peter	Mashonaland	Z	11.3.77	Salisbury
Vimpani Graeme Ronald	Victoria	A	27.1.72	Herston
Volsteedt Andre Kenne	Free State	SA	6.5.75	Bloemfontein
Vorster Christiaan Jakobus	Free State	SA	17.8.76	Paarl
Wagh Mark Anant	Warwicks/Mashonaland A	E	20.10.76	Birmingham
*****Wajahatullah Wasti**	Peshawar/Allied Bank	P	11.11.74	Peshawar
Waldron Earl	Leeward Islands	WI	31.8.66	All Saints, Antigua
Waldron Horace Ricardo	Barbados	WI	22.9.71	Barbados
Walker Brooke Graeme Keith	Auckland	NZ	25.3.77	Auckland
Walker Matthew Jonathan	Kent	E	2.1.74	Gravesend
Wallace Mark Alexander	Glamorgan	E	19.11.81	Abergavenny
*****Wallace** Philo Alphonso	Barbados	WI	2.8.70	Haynesville
Walmsley Kerry Peter	Auckland	NZ	23.8.73	Dunedin
*****Walsh** Courtney Andrew	Jamaica	WI	30.10.62	Kingston
Walsh Mark Jason	Western Australia	A	28.4.72	Townsville
Walton Timothy Charles	Essex	E	8.11.72	Low Head
*****Waqar Younis**	Multan	P	16.11.71	Vehari
Ward Ian James	Surrey	E	30.9.72	Plymouth
Ward Trevor Robert	Kent	E	18.1.68	Farningham
*****Warne** Shane Keith	Victoria	A	13.9.69	Ferntree Gully
Warren Russell John	Northamptonshire	E	10.9.71	Northampton
*****Wasim Akram**	Lancashire	P	3.6.66	Lahore
Wasim Haider	Faisalabad/PIA	P	6.6.67	Lyallpur
Wasim Jaffer	Mumbai	I	16.2.78	Bombay
*****Watkin** Steven Llewellyn	Glamorgan	E	15.9.64	Maesteg
*****Watkinson** Michael	Lancashire	E	1.8.61	Westhoughton
Watson Douglas James	KwaZulu-Natal	SA	15.5.73	Pietermaritzburg
Watt Balthazar Michael	Windward Islands	WI	12.4.75	Dominica
*****Waugh** Mark Edward	New South Wales	A	2.6.65	Sydney
*****Waugh** Stephen Rodger	New South Wales	A	2.6.65	Sydney
Weekes Paul Nicholas	Middlesex	E	8.7.69	Hackney
Welch Graeme	Warwickshire	E	21.3.72	Durham
*****Wells** Alan Peter	Kent	E	2.10.61	Newhaven
Wells Vincent John	Leicestershire	E	6.8.65	Dartford
Welton Guy Edward	Nottinghamshire	E	4.5.78	Grimsby

	Team	Country	Born	Birthplace
* **Wessels** Kepler Christoffel	Griqualand West	SA	14.9.57	*Bloemfontein*
Weston Robin Michael Swann	Derbyshire	E	7.6.75	*Durham*
Weston William Philip Christopher	Worcestershire	E	16.6.73	*Durham*
Wharf Alexander George	Nottinghamshire	E	4.6.75	*Bradford*
* **Whitaker** John James	Leicestershire	E	5.5.62	*Skipton*
White Brad Middleton	Border	SA	15.5.70	*Johannesburg*
* **White** Craig	Yorkshire	E	16.12.69	*Morley*
White Giles William	Hampshire	E	23.3.72	*Barnstaple*
* **Whittall** Andrew Richard	Matabeleland	Z	28.3.73	*Mutare*
* **Whittall** Guy James	Matabeleland	Z	5.9.72	*Chipinga*
Wiblin Wayne	Border	SA	13.2.69	*Grahamstown*
Wickremaratne Ranasinghe Pattikirikoralalage Aruna Hemantha	Sinhalese	SL	21.2.71	*Colombo*
* **Wickremasinghe** Gallage Pramodya	Sinhalese	SL	14.8.71	*Matara*
Wigney Bradley Neil	South Australia	A	30.6.65	*Leongatha*
Wilkinson Louis Johannes	Free State	SA	19.11.66	*Vereeniging*
Williams Brad Andrew	Victoria	A	20.11.74	*Frankston*
* **Williams** David	Trinidad & Tobago	WI	4.11.63	*San Fernando*
Williams Henry Smith	Boland	SA	11.6.67	*Stellenbosch*
Williams Jason	Leeward Islands	WI		*St Kitts*
Williams Laurie Rohan	Jamaica	WI	12.12.68	*Jamaica*
* **Williams** Stuart Clayton	Leeward Islands	WI	12.8.69	*Government Road, Nevis*
Williamson Dominic	Leicestershire	E	15.11.75	*Durham*
Williamson John Greig	Scotland	S	20.12.68	*Glasgow*
Willis Simon Charles	Kent	E	19.3.74	*Greenwich*
Willoughby Charl Myles	Boland	SA	3.12.74	*Cape Town*
Wilson Elliott James	Worcestershire	E	3.11.76	*St Pancras*
* **Wilson** Paul	South Australia	A	12.1.72	*Newcastle*
Wilton Nicholas James	Sussex	E	23.9.78	*Pembury*
Windows Matthew Guy Norman	Gloucestershire	E	5.4.73	*Bristol*
Wingfield Wade Richard	KwaZulu-Natal	SA	17.12.77	*Scottburgh*
Wiseman Paul John	Otago	NZ	4.5.70	*Auckland*
* **Wishart** Craig Brian	Mashonaland	Z	9.1.74	*Salisbury*
Wood John	Durham	E	22.7.70	*Crofton*
Wood Matthew James	Yorkshire	E	6.4.77	*Huddersfield*
Wood Nathan Theodore	Lancashire	E	4.10.74	*Thornhill Edge*
Woolley Anthony Paul	Derbyshire	E	4.12.71	*Derby*
Wright Damien Geoffrey	Tasmania	A	25.7.75	*Casino*
Yadav Jai Prakash	Madhya Pradesh	I	7.8.74	*Bhopal*
Yadav Jyoti Prasad	Uttar Pradesh	I	26.9.77	*Allahabad*
* **Yadav** Vijay Singh	Haryana	I	14.3.67	*Gonda*
Yates Gary	Lancashire	E	20.9.67	*Ashton-under-Lyne*
Young Bradley Evan	South Australia	A	23.2.73	*Semaphore*
* **Young** Bryan Andrew	Auckland	NZ	3.11.64	*Whangarei*
Young Shaun	Tasmania	A	13.6.70	*Burnie*
* **Yousuf** Youhana	Lahore/WAPDA	P	27.8.74	*Lahore*
Zafar Iqbal	Karachi/Nat. Bank	P	6.3.69	*Karachi*
Zahid Ahmed	Hyderabad/PIA	P	15.11.61	*Karachi*
* **Zahid Fazal**	Gujranwala/PIA	P	10.11.73	*Sialkot*
* **Zahoor Elahi**	Lahore/ADBP	P	1.3.71	*Sahiwal*
Zaidi Ashish Winston	Uttar Pradesh	I	16.9.71	*Allahabad*
* **Zoysa** Demuni Nuwan Tharanga	Sinhalese	SL	13.5.78	*Colombo*

WISDEN'S CRICKETERS OF THE YEAR, 1889-2000

Year	
1889	*Six Great Bowlers of the Year:* J. Briggs, J. J. Ferris, G. A. Lohmann, R. Peel, C. T. B. Turner, S. M. J. Woods.
1890	*Nine Great Batsmen of the Year:* R. Abel, W. Barnes, W. Gunn, L. Hall, R. Henderson, J. M. Read, A. Shrewsbury, F. H. Sugg, A. Ward.
1891	*Five Great Wicket-Keepers:* J. McC. Blackham, G. MacGregor, R. Pilling, M. Sherwin, H. Wood.
1892	*Five Great Bowlers:* W. Attewell, J. T. Hearne, F. Martin, A. W. Mold, J. W. Sharpe.
1893	*Five Batsmen of the Year:* H. T. Hewett, L. C. H. Palairet, W. W. Read, S. W. Scott, A. E. Stoddart.
1894	*Five All-Round Cricketers:* G. Giffen, A. Hearne, F. S. Jackson, G. H. S. Trott, E. Wainwright.
1895	*Five Young Batsmen of the Season:* W. Brockwell, J. T. Brown, C. B. Fry, T. W. Hayward, A. C. MacLaren.
1896	W. G. Grace.
1897	*Five Cricketers of the Season:* S. E. Gregory, A. A. Lilley, K. S. Ranjitsinhji, T. Richardson, H. Trumble.
1898	*Five Cricketers of the Year:* F. G. Bull, W. R. Cuttell, N. F. Druce, G. L. Jessop, J. R. Mason.
1899	*Five Great Players of the Season:* W. H. Lockwood, W. Rhodes, W. Storer, C. L. Townsend, A. E. Trott.
1900	*Five Cricketers of the Season:* J. Darling, C. Hill, A. O. Jones, M. A. Noble, Major R. M. Poore.
1901	*Mr R. E. Foster and Four Yorkshiremen:* R. E. Foster, S. Haigh, G. H. Hirst, T. L. Taylor, J. Tunnicliffe.
1902	L. C. Braund, C. P. McGahey, F. Mitchell, W. G. Quaife, J. T. Tyldesley.
1903	W. W. Armstrong, C. J. Burnup, J. Iremonger, J. J. Kelly, V. T. Trumper.
1904	C. Blythe, J. Gunn, A. E. Knight, W. Mead, P. F. Warner.
1905	B. J. T. Bosanquet, E. A. Halliwell, J. Hallows, P. A. Perrin, R. H. Spooner.
1906	D. Denton, W. S. Lees, G. J. Thompson, J. Vine, L. G. Wright.
1907	J. N. Crawford, A. Fielder, E. G. Hayes, K. L. Hutchings, N. A. Knox.
1908	A. W. Hallam, R. O. Schwarz, F. A. Tarrant, A. E. E. Vogler, T. G. Wass.
1909	*Lord Hawke and Four Cricketers of the Year:* W. Brearley, Lord Hawke, J. B. Hobbs, A. Marshal, J. T. Newstead.
1910	W. Bardsley, S. F. Barnes, D. W. Carr, A. P. Day, V. S. Ransford.
1911	H. K. Foster, A. Hartley, C. B. Llewellyn, W. C. Smith, F. E. Woolley.
1912	*Five Members of the MCC's Team in Australia:* F. R. Foster, J. W. Hearne, S. P. Kinneir, C. P. Mead, H Strudwick.
1913	John Wisden: Personal Recollections.
1914	M. W. Booth, G. Gunn, J. W. Hitch, A. E. Relf, Hon. L. H. Tennyson.
1915	J. W. H. T. Douglas, P. G. H. Fender, H. T. W. Hardinge, D. J. Knight, S. G. Smith.
1916-17	No portraits appeared.
1918	*School Bowlers of the Year:* H. L. Calder, J. E. D'E. Firth, C. H. Gibson, G. A. Rotherham, G. T. S. Stevens.
1919	*Five Public School Cricketers of the Year:* P. W. Adams, A. P. F. Chapman, A. C. Gore, L. P. Hedges, N. E. Partridge.
1920	*Five Batsmen of the Year:* A. Ducat, E. H. Hendren, P. Holmes, H. Sutcliffe, E. Tyldesley.
1921	P. F. Warner.
1922	H. Ashton, J. L. Bryan, J. M. Gregory, C. G. Macartney, E. A. McDonald.
1923	A. W. Carr, A. P. Freeman, C. W. L. Parker, A. C. Russell, A. Sandham.
1924	*Five Bowlers of the Year:* A. E. R. Gilligan, R. Kilner, G. G. Macaulay, C. H. Parkin, M. W. Tate.
1925	R. H. Catterall, J. C. W. MacBryan, H. W. Taylor, R. K. Tyldesley, W. W. Whysall.
1926	J. B. Hobbs.

1927	G. Geary, H. Larwood, J. Mercer, W. A. Oldfield, W. M. Woodfull.
1928	R. C. Blunt, C. Hallows, W. R. Hammond, D. R. Jardine, V. W. C. Jupp.
1929	L. E. G. Ames, G. Duckworth, M. Leyland, S. J. Staples, J. C. White.
1930	E. H. Bowley, K. S. Duleepsinhji, H. G. Owen-Smith, R. W. V. Robins, R. E. S. Wyatt.
1931	D. G. Bradman, C. V. Grimmett, B. H. Lyon, I. A. R. Peebles, M. J. Turnbull.
1932	W. E. Bowes, C. S. Dempster, James Langridge, Nawab of Pataudi sen., H. Verity.
1933	W. E. Astill, F. R. Brown, A. S. Kennedy, C. K. Nayudu, W. Voce.
1934	A. H. Bakewell, G. A. Headley, M. S. Nichols, L. F. Townsend, C. F. Walters.
1935	S. J. McCabe, W. J. O'Reilly, G. A. E. Paine, W. H. Ponsford, C. I. J. Smith.
1936	H. B. Cameron, E. R. T. Holmes, B. Mitchell, D. Smith, A. W. Wellard.
1937	C. J. Barnett, W. H. Copson, A. R. Gover, V. M. Merchant, T. S. Worthington.
1938	T. W. J. Goddard, J. Hardstaff jun., L. Hutton, J. H. Parks, E. Paynter.
1939	H. T. Bartlett, W. A. Brown, D. C. S. Compton, K. Farnes, A. Wood.
1940	L. N. Constantine, W. J. Edrich, W. W. Keeton, A. B. Sellers, D. V. P. Wright.
1941-46	No portraits appeared.
1947	A. V. Bedser, L. B. Fishlock, V. (M. H.) Mankad, T. P. B. Smith, C. Washbrook.
1948	M. P. Donnelly, A. Melville, A. D. Nourse, J. D. Robertson, N. W. D. Yardley.
1949	A. L. Hassett, W. A. Johnston, R. R. Lindwall, A. R. Morris, D. Tallon.
1950	T. E. Bailey, R. O. Jenkins, John Langridge, R. T. Simpson, B. Sutcliffe.
1951	T. G. Evans, S. Ramadhin, A. L. Valentine, E. D. Weekes, F. M. M. Worrell.
1952	R. Appleyard, H. E. Dollery, J. C. Laker, P. B. H. May, E. A. B. Rowan.
1953	H. Gimblett, T. W. Graveney, D. S. Sheppard, W. S. Surridge, F. S. Trueman.
1954	R. N. Harvey, G. A. R. Lock, K. R. Miller, J. H. Wardle, W. Watson.
1955	B. Dooland, Fazal Mahmood, W. E. Hollies, J. B. Statham, G. E. Tribe.
1956	M. C. Cowdrey, D. J. Insole, D. J. McGlew, H. J. Tayfield, F. H. Tyson.
1957	D. Brookes, J. W. Burke, M. J. Hilton, G. R. A. Langley, P. E. Richardson.
1958	P. J. Loader, A. J. McIntyre, O. G. Smith, M. J. Stewart, C. L. Walcott.
1959	H. L. Jackson, R. E. Marshall, C. A. Milton, J. R. Reid, D. Shackleton.
1960	K. F. Barrington, D. B. Carr, R. Illingworth, G. Pullar, M. J. K. Smith.
1961	N. A. T. Adcock, E. R. Dexter, R. A. McLean, R. Subba Row, J. V. Wilson.
1962	W. E. Alley, R. Benaud, A. K. Davidson, W. M. Lawry, N. C. O'Neill.
1963	D. Kenyon, Mushtaq Mohammad, P. H. Parfitt, P. J. Sharpe, F. J. Titmus.
1964	D. B. Close, C. C. Griffith, C. C. Hunte, R. B. Kanhai, G. S. Sobers.
1965	G. Boycott, P. J. Burge, J. A. Flavell, G. D. McKenzie, R. B. Simpson.
1966	K. C. Bland, J. H. Edrich, R. C. Motz, P. M. Pollock, R. G. Pollock.
1967	R. W. Barber, B. L. D'Oliveira, C. Milburn, J. T. Murray, S. M. Nurse.
1968	Asif Iqbal, Hanif Mohammad, K. Higgs, J. M. Parks, Nawab of Pataudi jun.
1969	J. G. Binks, D. M. Green, B. A. Richards, D. L. Underwood, O. S. Wheatley.
1970	B. F. Butcher, A. P. E. Knott, Majid Khan, M. J. Procter, D. J. Shepherd.
1971	J. D. Bond, C. H. Lloyd, B. W. Luckhurst, G. M. Turner, R. T. Virgin.
1972	G. G. Arnold, B. S. Chandrasekhar, L. R. Gibbs, B. Taylor, Zaheer Abbas.
1973	G. S. Chappell, D. K. Lillee, R. A. L. Massie, J. A. Snow, K. R. Stackpole.
1974	K. D. Boyce, B. E. Congdon, K. W. R. Fletcher, R. C. Fredericks, P. J. Sainsbury.
1975	D. L. Amiss, M. H. Denness, N. Gifford, A. W. Greig, A. M. E. Roberts.
1976	I. M. Chappell, P. G. Lee, R. B. McCosker, D. S. Steele, R. A. Woolmer.
1977	J. M. Brearley, C. G. Greenidge, M. A. Holding, I. V. A. Richards, R. W. Taylor.
1978	I. T. Botham, M. Hendrick, A. Jones, K. S. McEwan, R. G. D. Willis.
1979	D. I. Gower, J. K. Lever, C. M. Old, C. T. Radley, J. N. Shepherd.
1980	J. Garner, S. M. Gavaskar, G. A. Gooch, D. W. Randall, B. C. Rose.
1981	K. J. Hughes, R. D. Jackman, A. J. Lamb, C. E. B. Rice, V. A. P. van der Bijl.
1982	T. M. Alderman, A. R. Border, R. J. Hadlee, Javed Miandad, R. W. Marsh.
1983	Imran Khan, T. E. Jesty, A. I. Kallicharran, Kapil Dev, M. D. Marshall.
1984	M. Amarnath, J. V. Coney, J. E. Emburey, M. W. Gatting, C. L. Smith.
1985	M. D. Crowe, H. A. Gomes, G. W. Humpage, J. Simmons, S. Wettimuny.
1986	P. Bainbridge, R. M. Ellison, C. J. McDermott, N. V. Radford, R. T. Robinson.
1987	J. H. Childs, G. A. Hick, D. B. Vengsarkar, C. A. Walsh, J. J. Whitaker.
1988	J. P. Agnew, N. A. Foster, D. P. Hughes, P. M. Roebuck, Salim Malik.
1989	K. J. Barnett, P. J. L. Dujon, P. A. Neale, F. D. Stephenson, S. R. Waugh.

1990	S. J. Cook, D. M. Jones, R. C. Russell, R. A. Smith, M. A. Taylor.
1991	M. A. Atherton, M. Azharuddin, A. R. Butcher, D. L. Haynes, M. E. Waugh.
1992	C. E. L. Ambrose, P. A. J. DeFreitas, A. A. Donald, R. B. Richardson, Waqar Younis.
1993	N. E. Briers, M. D. Moxon, I. D. K. Salisbury, A. J. Stewart, Wasim Akram.
1994	D. C. Boon, I. A. Healy, M. G. Hughes, S. K. Warne, S. L. Watkin.
1995	B. C. Lara, D. E. Malcolm, T. A. Munton, S. J. Rhodes, K. C. Wessels.
1996	D. G. Cork, P. A. de Silva, A. R. C. Fraser, A. Kumble, D. A. Reeve.
1997	S. T. Jayasuriya, Mushtaq Ahmed, Saeed Anwar, P. V. Simmons, S. R. Tendulkar.
1998	M. T. G. Elliott, S. G. Law, G. D. McGrath, M. P. Maynard, G. P. Thorpe.
1999	I. D. Austin, D. Gough, M. Muralitharan, A. Ranatunga, J. N. Rhodes.
2000	C. L. Cairns, R. Dravid, L. Klusener, T. M. Moody, Saqlain Mushtaq.

Cricketers of the Century D. G. Bradman, G. S. Sobers, J. B. Hobbs, S. K. Warne, I. V. A. Richards.

CRICKETERS OF THE YEAR: AN ANALYSIS

The five players selected to be Cricketers of the Year for 2000 bring the number chosen since selection began in 1889 to 507. They have been chosen from 36 different teams as follows:

Derbyshire	13	Northants	13	Cambridge Univ.	10
Essex	22	Nottinghamshire	25	Australians	63
Glamorgan	10	Somerset	16	South Africans	21
Gloucestershire	15	Surrey	46	West Indians	23
Hampshire	14	Sussex	20	New Zealanders	8
Kent	25	Warwickshire	19	Indians	12
Lancashire	31	Worcestershire	15	Pakistanis	11
Leicestershire	8	Yorkshire	39	Sri Lankans	4
Middlesex	25	Oxford Univ.	6	Staffordshire	1

Cheltenham College	1
Cranleigh School	1
Eton College	2
Malvern College	1
Rugby School	1
Tonbridge School	1
Univ. Coll. School	1
Uppingham School	1
Winchester College	1

Durham and the Zimbabweans have as yet had no team members chosen as Cricketers of the Year.

Notes: schoolboys were chosen in 1918 and 1919 when first-class cricket was suspended due to war. The total of sides comes to 525 because 18 players played regularly for two teams (England excluded) in the year for which they were chosen. John Wisden, listed as a Sussex player, retired 50 years before his posthumous selection.

Types of Players

Of the 507 Cricketers of the Year, 256 are best classified as batsmen, 145 as bowlers, 74 as all-rounders and 32 as wicket-keepers.

Nationalities

At the time they were chosen, 323 players (63.70 per cent) were qualified to play for England, 72 for Australia, 36 West Indies, 31 South Africa, 14 Pakistan, 13 India, 12 New Zealand, 5 Sri Lanka and 1 Zimbabwe.

Note: nationalities and teams are not necessarily identical.

Ages

On April 1 in the year of selection

Youngest: 17 years 67 days H. L. Calder, 1918. The youngest first-class cricketer was Mushtaq Mohammad, 19 years 130 days in 1963.

Oldest: 48 years 228 days Lord Hawke, 1909. (This excludes John Wisden, whose portrait appeared 87 years after his birth and 29 years after his death.)

An analysis of post-war Cricketers of the Year may be found in Wisden *1998, page 174.*

Research: Robert Brooke

PART FOUR: RECORDS

CRICKET RECORDS

First-class and limited-overs records by PHILIP BAILEY
Test match records by PHILIP BAILEY and GORDON VINCE

**Records in the England v South Africa section (pages 312–316) have been updated to
include the 1999-2000 series. These figures are NOT included elsewhere. The deadline
for other sections is the end of the 1999 season in England.**

Updated Test records can be found on the Wisden web site, www.wisden.com.

Unless otherwise stated, all records apply only to first-class cricket. This is considered to have
started in 1815, after the Napoleonic War.
  * Denotes not out or an unbroken partnership.
  (A), (SA), (WI), (NZ), (I), (P), (SL) or (Z) indicates either the nationality of the player, or the
country in which the record was made.

FIRST-CLASS RECORDS

BATTING RECORDS

BOWLING RECORDS

ALL-ROUND RECORDS

WICKET-KEEPING RECORDS

FIELDING RECORDS

TEAM RECORDS

TEST MATCH RECORDS

BATTING RECORDS

BOWLING RECORDS

ALL-ROUND RECORDS

WICKET-KEEPING RECORDS

FIELDING RECORDS

TEAM RECORDS

PLAYERS

CAPTAINCY

UMPIRING

TEST SERIES

LIMITED-OVERS INTERNATIONAL RECORDS

WORLD CUP RECORDS

MISCELLANEOUS

FIRST-CLASS RECORDS

BATTING RECORDS

HIGHEST INDIVIDUAL SCORES

501*	B. C. Lara	Warwickshire v Durham at Birmingham	1994
499	Hanif Mohammad	Karachi v Bahawalpur at Karachi.	1958-59
452*	D. G. Bradman	NSW v Queensland at Sydney.	1929-30
443*	B. B. Nimbalkar	Maharashtra v Kathiawar at Poona	1948-49
437	W. H. Ponsford	Victoria v Queensland at Melbourne	1927-28
429	W. H. Ponsford	Victoria v Tasmania at Melbourne	1922-23
428	Aftab Baloch	Sind v Baluchistan at Karachi	1973-74
424	A. C. MacLaren	Lancashire v Somerset at Taunton	1895
405*	G. A. Hick	Worcestershire v Somerset at Taunton	1988
385	B. Sutcliffe	Otago v Canterbury at Christchurch	1952-53
383	C. W. Gregory	NSW v Queensland at Brisbane.	1906-07
377	S. V. Manjrekar	Bombay v Hyderabad at Bombay.	1990-91
375	B. C. Lara	West Indies v England at St John's	1993-94
369	D. G. Bradman	South Australia v Tasmania at Adelaide	1935-36
366	N. H. Fairbrother	Lancashire v Surrey at The Oval	1990
366	M. V. Sridhar	Hyderabad v Andhra at Secunderabad	1993-94
365*	C. Hill	South Australia v NSW at Adelaide	1900-01
365*	G. S. Sobers	West Indies v Pakistan at Kingston	1957-58
364	L. Hutton	England v Australia at The Oval	1938
359*	V. M. Merchant	Bombay v Maharashtra at Bombay.	1943-44
359	R. B. Simpson	NSW v Queensland at Brisbane.	1963-64
357*	R. Abel	Surrey v Somerset at The Oval	1899
357	D. G. Bradman	South Australia v Victoria at Melbourne	1935-36
356	B. A. Richards	South Australia v Western Australia at Perth	1970-71
355*	G. R. Marsh	Western Australia v South Australia at Perth	1989-90
355	B. Sutcliffe	Otago v Auckland at Dunedin	1949-50
352	W. H. Ponsford	Victoria v NSW at Melbourne.	1926-27
350	Rashid Israr	Habib Bank v National Bank at Lahore	1976-77
345	C. G. Macartney	Australians v Nottinghamshire at Nottingham	1921
344*	G. A. Headley	Jamaica v Lord Tennyson's XI at Kingston	1931-32
344	W. G. Grace	MCC v Kent at Canterbury.	1876
343*	P. A. Perrin	Essex v Derbyshire at Chesterfield	1904
341	G. H. Hirst	Yorkshire v Leicestershire at Leicester	1905
340*	D. G. Bradman	NSW v Victoria at Sydney.	1928-29
340	S. M. Gavaskar	Bombay v Bengal at Bombay	1981-82
340	S. T. Jayasuriya	Sri Lanka v India at Colombo.	1997-98
338*	R. C. Blunt	Otago v Canterbury at Christchurch	1931-32
338	W. W. Read	Surrey v Oxford University at The Oval	1888
337*	Pervez Akhtar	Railways v Dera Ismail Khan at Lahore	1964-65
337*	D. J. Cullinan	Transvaal v Northern Transvaal at Johannesburg	1993-94
337	Hanif Mohammad	Pakistan v West Indies at Bridgetown	1957-58
336*	W. R. Hammond	England v New Zealand at Auckland	1932-33
336	W. H. Ponsford	Victoria v South Australia at Melbourne	1927-28
334*	M. A. Taylor	Australia v Pakistan at Peshawar	1998-99
334	D. G. Bradman	Australia v England at Leeds	1930
333	K. S. Duleepsinhji	Sussex v Northamptonshire at Hove	1930
333	G. A. Gooch	England v India at Lord's.	1990
332	W. H. Ashdown	Kent v Essex at Brentwood	1934
331*	J. D. Robertson	Middlesex v Worcestershire at Worcester	1949
325*	H. L. Hendry	Victoria v New Zealanders at Melbourne	1925-26
325	A. Sandham	England v West Indies at Kingston	1929-30
325	C. L. Badcock	South Australia v Victoria at Adelaide	1935-36
324*	D. M. Jones	Victoria v South Australia at Melbourne	1994-95

324	J. B. Stollmeyer	Trinidad v British Guiana at Port-of-Spain	1946-47
324	Waheed Mirza	Karachi Whites v Quetta at Karachi	1976-77
323	A. L. Wadekar	Bombay v Mysore at Bombay	1966-67
323	D. Gandhi	Bengal v Assam at Gauhati	1998-99
322*	M. B. Loye	Northamptonshire v Glamorgan at Northampton	1998
322	E. Paynter	Lancashire v Sussex at Hove	1937
322	I. V. A. Richards	Somerset v Warwickshire at Taunton	1985
321	W. L. Murdoch	NSW v Victoria at Sydney	1881-82
320	R. Lamba	North Zone v West Zone at Bhilai	1987-88
319	Gul Mahomed	Baroda v Holkar at Baroda	1946-47
318*	W. G. Grace	Gloucestershire v Yorkshire at Cheltenham	1876
317	W. R. Hammond	Gloucestershire v Nottinghamshire at Gloucester	1936
317	K. R. Rutherford	New Zealanders v D. B. Close's XI at Scarborough. . .	1986
316*	J. B. Hobbs	Surrey v Middlesex at Lord's	1926
316*	V. S. Hazare	Maharashtra v Baroda at Poona	1939-40
316	R. H. Moore	Hampshire v Warwickshire at Bournemouth	1937
315*	T. W. Hayward	Surrey v Lancashire at The Oval	1898
315*	P. Holmes	Yorkshire v Middlesex at Lord's	1925
315*	A. F. Kippax	NSW v Queensland at Sydney	1927-28
314*	C. L. Walcott	Barbados v Trinidad at Port-of-Spain	1945-46
314*	Wasim Jaffer	Mumbai v Saurashtra at Rajkot	1996-97
313*	S. J. Cook	Somerset v Glamorgan at Cardiff	1990
313	H. Sutcliffe	Yorkshire v Essex at Leyton	1932
313	W. V. Raman‡	Tamil Nadu v Goa at Panjim	1988-89
312*	W. W. Keeton	Nottinghamshire v Middlesex at The Oval†	1939
312*	J. M. Brearley	MCC Under-25 v North Zone at Peshawar	1966-67
312	R. Lamba	Delhi v Himachal Pradesh at Delhi	1994-95
312	J. E. R. Gallian	Lancashire v Derbyshire at Manchester	1996
311*	G. M. Turner	Worcestershire v Warwickshire at Worcester	1982
311	J. T. Brown	Yorkshire v Sussex at Sheffield	1897
311	R. B. Simpson	Australia v England at Manchester	1964
311	Javed Miandad	Karachi Whites v National Bank at Karachi	1974-75
310*	J. H. Edrich	England v New Zealand at Leeds	1965
310	H. Gimblett	Somerset v Sussex at Eastbourne	1948
309	V. S. Hazare	The Rest v Hindus at Bombay	1943-44
308*	F. M. M. Worrell	Barbados v Trinidad at Bridgetown	1943-44
307*	T. N. Lazard	Boland v W. Province at Worcester, Cape Province . . .	1993-94
307	M. C. Cowdrey	MCC v South Australia at Adelaide	1962-63
307	R. M. Cowper	Australia v England at Melbourne	1965-66
306*	A. Ducat	Surrey v Oxford University at The Oval	1919
306*	E. A. B. Rowan	Transvaal v Natal at Johannesburg	1939-40
306*	D. W. Hookes	South Australia v Tasmania at Adelaide	1986-87
305*	F. E. Woolley	MCC v Tasmania at Hobart	1911-12
305*	F. R. Foster	Warwickshire v Worcestershire at Dudley	1914
305*	W. H. Ashdown	Kent v Derbyshire at Dover	1935
304*	A. W. Nourse	Natal v Transvaal at Johannesburg	1919-20
304*	P. H. Tarilton	Barbados v Trinidad at Bridgetown	1919-20
304*	E. D. Weekes	West Indians v Cambridge University at Cambridge. . .	1950
304	R. M. Poore	Hampshire v Somerset at Taunton	1899
304	D. G. Bradman	Australia v England at Leeds	1934
303*	W. W. Armstrong	Australians v Somerset at Bath	1905
303*	Mushtaq Mohammad	Karachi Blues v Karachi University at Karachi	1967-68
303*	Abdul Azeem	Hyderabad v Tamil Nadu at Hyderabad	1986-87
303*	S. Chanderpaul	Guyana v Jamaica at Kingston	1995-96
303*	G. A. Hick	Worcestershire v Hampshire at Southampton	1997
303*	D. J. Sales	Northamptonshire v Essex at Northampton	1999
302*	P. Holmes	Yorkshire v Hampshire at Portsmouth	1920
302*	W. R. Hammond	Gloucestershire v Glamorgan at Bristol	1934
302*	Arjan Kripal Singh‡	Tamil Nadu v Goa at Panjim	1988-89
302	W. R. Hammond	Gloucestershire v Glamorgan at Newport	1939
302	L. G. Rowe	West Indies v England at Bridgetown	1973-74

J. W. Hearne 96	P. H. Parfitt 58	C. L. Smith 47
C. B. Fry 94	W. Rhodes 58	A. R. Butcher 46
M. W. Gatting 94	P. N. Kirsten 57	J. Iddon 46
C. G. Greenidge 92	L. B. Fishlock 56	A. R. Morris 46
A. J. Lamb 89	A. Jones 56	C. T. Radley 46
A. I. Kallicharran 87	C. A. Milton 56	**A. P. Wells** **46**
W. J. Edrich 86	**R. A. Smith** **56**	Younis Ahmed 46
G. S. Sobers 86	C. W. J. Athey 55	W. W. Armstrong 45
J. T. Tyldesley 86	**K. J. Barnett** **55**	Asif Iqbal 45
P. B. H. May 85	C. Hallows 55	L. G. Berry 45
R. E. S. Wyatt 85	Hanif Mohammad 55	J. M. Brearley 45
J. Hardstaff, jun 83	D. M. Jones 55	A. W. Carr 45
R. B. Kanhai 83	D. B. Vengsarkar 55	C. Hill 45
S. M. Gavaskar 81	W. Watson 55	**M. P. Maynard** **45**
Javed Miandad 80	D. J. Insole 54	M. D. Moxon 45
M. Leyland 80	W. W. Keeton 54	N. C. O'Neill 45
B. A. Richards 80	W. Bardsley 53	E. Paynter 45
C. H. Lloyd 79	B. F. Davison 53	Rev. D. S. Sheppard . . . 45
K. F. Barrington 76	A. E. Dipper 53	N. R. Taylor 45
J. G. Langridge 76	D. I. Gower 53	K. D. Walters 45
C. Washbrook 76	G. L. Jessop 53	**R. J. Bailey** **44**
H. T. W. Hardinge 75	H. Morris 53	H. H. Gibbons 44
R. Abel 74	James Seymour 53	V. M. Merchant 44
G. S. Chappell 74	Shafiq Ahmad 53	A. Mitchell 44
D. Kenyon 74	**S. R. Waugh** **53**	P. E. Richardson 44
K. S. McEwan 74	E. H. Bowley 52	**A. J. Stewart** **44**
Majid Khan 73	D. B. Close 52	B. Sutcliffe 44
Mushtaq Mohammad . . . 72	A. Ducat 52	G. R. Viswanath 44
J. O'Connor 72	D. W. Randall 52	P. Willey 44
W. G. Quaife 72	**M. Azharuddin** **51**	E. J. Barlow 43
K. S. Ranjitsinhji 72	E. R. Dexter 51	T. S. Curtis 43
D. Brookes 71	J. M. Parks 51	B. L. D'Oliveira 43
M. D. Crowe 71	W. W. Whysall 51	J. H. Hampshire 43
A. C. Russell 71	B. C. Broad 50	A. F. Kippax 43
M. E. Waugh **71**	G. Cox, jun. 50	J. W. H. Makepeace 43
A. R. Border 70	H. E. Dollery 50	**Salim Malik** **43**
D. Denton 69	K. S. Duleepsinhji 50	James Langridge 42
M. J. K. Smith 69	H. Gimblett 50	Mudassar Nazar 42
D. C. Boon **68**	W. M. Lawry 50	H. W. Parks 42
R. E. Marshall 68	Sadiq Mohammad 50	T. F. Shepherd 42
R. N. Harvey 67	F. B. Watson 50	V. T. Trumper 42
P. Holmes 67	**C. L. Hooper** **49**	M. J. Harris 41
J. D. Robertson 67	C. G. Macartney 49	**N. Hussain** **41**
P. A. Perrin 66	**J. E. Morris** **49**	**S. G. Law** **41**
K. C. Wessels **66**	M. J. Stewart 49	G. D. Mendis 41
S. J. Cook 64	K. G. Suttle 49	K. R. Miller 41
T. M. Moody **64**	P. R. Umrigar 49	A. D. Nourse 41
R. G. Pollock 64	W. M. Woodfull 49	J. H. Parks 41
R. T. Simpson 64	**M. A. Atherton** **48**	R. M. Prideaux 41
K. W. R. Fletcher 63	C. J. Barnett 48	G. Pullar 41
R. T. Robinson **63**	M. R. Benson 48	W. E. Russell 41
G. Gunn 62	W. Gunn 48	**M. A. Taylor** **41**
D. L. Haynes 61	E. G. Hayes 48	**M. G. Bevan** **40**
V. S. Hazare 60	B. W. Luckhurst 48	**N. H. Fairbrother** **40**
G. H. Hirst 60	M. J. Procter 48	R. C. Fredericks 40
R. B. Simpson 60	C. E. B. Rice 48	J. Gunn 40
P. F. Warner 60	C. J. Tavaré 48	M. J. Smith 40
I. M. Chappell 59	A. C. MacLaren 47	C. L. Walcott 40
A. L. Hassett 59	P. W. G. Parker 47	D. M. Young 40
W. Larkins 59	W. H. Ponsford 47	Arshad Pervez 39
A. Shrewsbury 59	**M. R. Ramprakash** . . . **47**	W. H. Ashdown 39
J. G. Wright 59		
A. E. Fagg 58		

Asif Mujtaba **39**	Rev. J. H. Parsons 38	Ajay Sharma **37**
J. B. Bolus 39	W. W. Read 38	H. S. Squires 37
W. A. Brown 39	**Rizwan-uz-Zaman** **38**	R. T. Virgin 37
R. J. Gregory 39	J. Sharp 38	C. J. B. Wood 37
S. P. James **39**	**S. R. Tendulkar** **38**	N. F. Armstrong 36
M. A. Lynch 39	V. P. Terry 38	G. Fowler 36
W. R. D. Payton 39	L. J. Todd 38	M. C. J. Nicholas 36
J. R. Reid 39	**J. J. Whitaker** **38**	E. Oldroyd 36
F. M. M. Worrell 39	J. Arnold 37	W. Place 36
I. T. Botham 38	G. Brown 37	A. L. Wadekar 36
F. L. Bowley 38	G. Cook 37	E. D. Weekes 36
P. J. Burge 38	**P. A. de Silva** **37**	C. S. Dempster 35
J. F. Crapp 38	G. M. Emmett 37	D. R. Jardine 35
M. L. Hayden **38**	**P. Johnson** **37**	T. E. Jesty 35
B. C. Lara **38**	H. W. Lee 37	**G. P. Thorpe** **35**
D. Lloyd 38	**D. S. Lehmann** **37**	B. H. Valentine 35
V. L. Manjrekar 38	M. A. Noble 37	G. M. Wood 35
A. W. Nourse 38	B. P. Patel 37	
N. Oldfield 38	R. B. Richardson 37	

Bold type denotes those who played in 1998-99 and 1999 seasons.

MOST RUNS IN A SEASON

	Season	I	NO	R	HS	100s	Avge
D. C. S. Compton	1947	50	8	3,816	246	18	90.85
W. J. Edrich	1947	52	8	3,539	267*	12	80.43
T. W. Hayward	1906	61	8	3,518	219	13	66.37
L. Hutton	1949	56	6	3,429	269*	12	68.58
F. E. Woolley	1928	59	4	3,352	198	12	60.94
H. Sutcliffe	1932	52	7	3,336	313	14	74.13
W. R. Hammond	1933	54	5	3,323	264	13	67.81
E. H. Hendren	1928	54	7	3,311	209*	13	70.44
R. Abel	1901	68	8	3,309	247	7	55.15

Notes: 3,000 in a season has been surpassed on 19 other occasions (a full list can be found in *Wisden* 1999 and earlier editions). W. R. Hammond, E. H. Hendren and H. Sutcliffe are the only players to achieve the feat three times. M. J. K. Smith (3,245 in 1959) and W. E. Alley (3,019 in 1961) are the only players except those listed above to have reached 3,000 since World War II.

2,000 RUNS IN A SEASON

Since Reduction of Championship Matches in 1969

Five times: G. A. Gooch 2,746 (1990), 2,559 (1984), 2,324 (1988), 2,208 (1985), 2,023 (1993).

Three times: D. L. Amiss 2,239 (1984), 2,110 (1976), 2,030 (1978); S. J. Cook 2,755† (1991), 2,608 (1990), 2,241 (1989); M. W. Gatting 2,257 (1984), 2,057 (1991), 2,000 (1992); G. A. Hick 2,713 (1988), 2,347 (1990), 2,004 (1986); G. M. Turner 2,416 (1973), 2,379 (1970), 2,101 (1981).

Twice: G. Boycott 2,503 (1971), 2,051 (1970); J. H. Edrich 2,238 (1969), 2,031 (1971); A. I. Kallicharran 2,301 (1984), 2,120 (1982); Zaheer Abbas 2,554 (1976), 2,306 (1981).

Once: M. Azharuddin 2,016 (1991); J. B. Bolus 2,143 (1970); P. D. Bowler 2,044 (1992); B. C. Broad 2,226 (1990); A. R. Butcher 2,116 (1990); C. G. Greenidge 2,035 (1986); M. J. Harris 2,238 (1971); D. L. Haynes 2,346 (1990); Javed Miandad 2,083 (1981); A. J. Lamb 2,049 (1981); B. C. Lara 2,066 (1994); K. S. McEwan 2,176 (1983); Majid Khan 2,074 (1972); A. A. Metcalfe 2,047 (1990); H. Morris 2,276 (1990); M. R. Ramprakash 2,258 (1995); D. W. Randall 2,151 (1985); I. V. A. Richards 2,161 (1977); R. T. Robinson 2,032 (1984); M. A. Roseberry 2,044 (1992); C. L. Smith 2,000 (1985); R. T. Virgin 2,223 (1970); D. M. Ward 2,072 (1990); M. E. Waugh 2,072 (1990).

Notes: W. G. Grace scored 2,739 runs in 1871 – the first batsman to reach 2,000 runs in a season. He made ten hundreds and twice exceeded 200, with an average of 78.25 in all first-class matches.

† *Highest since the reduction of Championship matches in 1969.*

1,000 RUNS IN A SEASON MOST TIMES

(Includes Overseas Tours and Seasons)

28 times: W. G. Grace 2,000 (6); F. E. Woolley 3,000 (1), 2,000 (12).

27 times: M. C. Cowdrey 2,000 (2); C. P. Mead 3,000 (2), 2,000 (9).

26 times: G. Boycott 2,000 (3); J. B. Hobbs 3,000 (1), 2,000 (16).

25 times: E. H. Hendren 3,000 (3), 2,000 (12).

24 times: D. L. Amiss 2,000 (3); W. G. Quaife 2,000 (1); H. Sutcliffe 3,000 (3), 2,000 (12).

23 times: A. Jones.

22 times: T. W. Graveney 2,000 (7); W. R. Hammond 3,000 (3), 2,000 (9).

21 times: D. Denton 2,000 (5); J. H. Edrich 2,000 (6); G. A. Gooch 2,000 (5); W. Rhodes 2,000 (3).

20 times: D. B. Close; K. W. R. Fletcher; M. W. Gatting 2,000 (3); G. Gunn; T. W. Hayward 3,000 (2), 2,000 (8); James Langridge 2,000 (1); J. M. Parks 2,000 (3); A. Sandham 2,000 (8); M. J. K. Smith 3,000 (1), 2,000 (5); C. Washbrook 2,000 (2).

19 times: J. W. Hearne 2,000 (4); G. H. Hirst 2,000 (3); D. Kenyon 2,000 (7); E. Tyldesley 3,000 (1), 2,000 (5); J. T. Tyldesley 3,000 (1), 2,000 (4).

18 times: L. G. Berry 2,000 (1); H. T. W. Hardinge 2,000 (5); R. E. Marshall 2,000 (6); P. A. Perrin; G. M. Turner 2,000 (3); R. E. S. Wyatt 2,000 (5).

17 times: L. E. G. Ames 3,000 (1), 2,000 (5); T. E. Bailey 2,000 (1); D. Brookes 2,000 (6); D. C. S. Compton 3,000 (1), 2,000 (5); C. G. Greenidge 2,000 (1); L. Hutton 3,000 (1), 2,000 (8); J. G. Langridge 2,000 (11); M. Leyland 2,000 (3); I. V. A. Richards 2,000 (1); K. G. Suttle 2,000 (1); Zaheer Abbas 2,000 (2).

16 times: D. G. Bradman 2,000 (4); D. E. Davies 2,000 (1); E. G. Hayes 2,000 (2); G. A. Hick 2,000 (3); C. A. Milton 2,000 (1); J. O'Connor 2,000 (4); C. T. Radley; James Seymour 2,000 (1); C. J. Tavaré.

15 times: G. Barker; K. J. Barnett; K. F. Barrington 2,000 (3); E. H. Bowley 2,000 (4); M. H. Denness; A. E. Dipper 2,000 (5); H. E. Dollery 2,000 (2); W. J. Edrich 3,000 (1), 2,000 (8); J. H. Hampshire; P. Holmes 2,000 (7); Mushtaq Mohammad; R. B. Nicholls 2,000 (1); P. H. Parfitt 2,000 (3); W. G. A. Parkhouse 2,000 (1); B. A. Richards 2,000 (1); J. D. Robertson 2,000 (9); G. S. Sobers; M. J. Stewart 2,000 (1).

Notes: F. E. Woolley reached 1,000 runs in 28 consecutive seasons (1907-1938), C. P. Mead in 27 (1906-1936).

Outside England, 1,000 runs in a season has been reached most times by D. G. Bradman (in 12 seasons in Australia).

Three batsmen have scored 1,000 runs in a season in each of four different countries: G. S. Sobers in West Indies, England, India and Australia; M. C. Cowdrey and G. Boycott in England, South Africa, West Indies and Australia.

HIGHEST AGGREGATES OUTSIDE ENGLAND

	Season	I	NO	R	HS	100s	Avge
In Australia D. G. Bradman	1928-29	24	6	1,690	340*	7	93.88
In South Africa J. R. Reid	1961-62	30	2	1,915	203	7	68.39
In West Indies E. H. Hendren	1929-30	18	5	1,765	254*	6	135.76
In New Zealand M. D. Crowe	1986-87	21	3	1,676	175*	8	93.11
In India C. G. Borde	1964-65	28	3	1,604	168	6	64.16
In Pakistan Saadat Ali	1983-84	27	1	1,649	208	4	63.42

In Sri Lanka	*Season*	*I*	*NO*	*R*	*HS*	*100s*	*Avge*
R. P. Arnold	1995-96	24	3	1,475	217*	5	70.23

In Zimbabwe	*Season*	*I*	*NO*	*R*	*HS*	*100s*	*Avge*
G. W. Flower	1994-95	20	3	983	201*	4	57.82

Note: in more than one country, the following aggregates of over 2,000 runs have been recorded:

M. Amarnath (P/I/WI)	1982-83	34	6	2,234	207	9	79.78
J. R. Reid (SA/A/NZ)	1961-62	40	2	2,188	203	7	57.57
S. M. Gavaskar (I/P)	1978-79	30	6	2,121	205	10	88.37
R. B. Simpson (I/P/A/WI).	1964-65	34	4	2,063	201	8	68.76

LEADING BATSMEN IN AN ENGLISH SEASON

(Qualification: 8 completed innings)

Season	*Leading scorer*	*Runs*	*Avge*	*Top of averages*	*Runs*	*Avge*
1946	D. C. S. Compton . . .	2,403	61.61	W. R. Hammond	1,783	84.90
1947	D. C. S. Compton . . .	3,816	90.85	D. C. S. Compton . . .	3,816	90.85
1948	L. Hutton	2,654	64.73	D. G. Bradman	2,428	89.92
1949	L. Hutton	3,429	68.58	J. Hardstaff	2,251	72.61
1950	R. T. Simpson	2,576	62.82	E. Weekes	2,310	79.65
1951	J. D. Robertson	2,917	56.09	P. B. H. May	2,339	68.79
1952	L. Hutton	2,567	61.11	D. S. Sheppard	2,262	64.62
1953	W. J. Edrich	2,557	47.35	R. N. Harvey	2,040	65.80
1954	D. Kenyon	2,636	51.68	D. C. S. Compton . . .	1,524	58.61
1955	D. J. Insole	2,427	42.57	D. J. McGlew	1,871	58.46
1956	T. W. Graveney	2,397	49.93	K. Mackay	1,103	52.52
1957	T. W. Graveney	2,361	49.18	P. B. H. May	2,347	61.76
1958	P. B. H. May	2,231	63.74	P. B. H. May	2,231	63.74
1959	M. J. K. Smith	3,245	57.94	V. L. Manjrekar	755	68.63
1960	M. J. K. Smith	2,551	45.55	R. Subba Row	1,503	55.66
1961	W. E. Alley	3,019	56.96	W. M. Lawry	2,019	61.18
1962	J. H. Edrich	2,482	51.70	R. T. Simpson	867	54.18
1963	J. B. Bolus	2,190	41.32	G. S. Sobers	1,333	47.60
1964	T. W. Graveney	2,385	54.20	K. F. Barrington	1,872	62.40
1965	J. H. Edrich	2,319	62.67	M. C. Cowdrey	2,093	63.42
1966	A. R. Lewis	2,198	41.47	G. S. Sobers	1,349	61.31
1967	C. A. Milton	2,089	46.42	K. F. Barrington	2,059	68.63
1968	B. A. Richards	2,395	47.90	G. Boycott	1,487	64.65
1969	J. H. Edrich	2,238	69.93	J. H. Edrich	2,238	69.93
1970	G. M. Turner	2,379	61.00	G. S. Sobers	1,742	75.73
1971	G. Boycott	2,503	100.12	G. Boycott	2,503	100.12
1972	Majid Khan	2,074	61.00	G. Boycott	1,230	72.35
1973	G. M. Turner	2,416	67.11	G. M. Turner	2,416	67.11
1974	R. T. Virgin	1,936	56.94	C. H. Lloyd	1,458	63.39
1975	G. Boycott	1,915	73.65	R. B. Kanhai	1,073	82.53
1976	Zaheer Abbas	2,554	75.11	Zaheer Abbas	2,554	75.11
1977	I. V. A. Richards . . .	2,161	65.48	G. Boycott	1,701	68.04
1978	D. L. Amiss	2,030	53.42	C. E. B. Rice	1,871	66.82
1979	K. C. Wessels.	1,800	52.94	G. Boycott	1,538	102.53
1980	P. N. Kirsten	1,895	63.16	A. J. Lamb	1,797	66.55
1981	Zaheer Abbas	2,306	88.69	Zaheer Abbas	2,306	88.69
1982	A. I. Kallicharran . . .	2,120	66.25	G. M. Turner	1,171	90.07
1983	K. S. McEwan	2,176	64.00	I. V. A. Richards . . .	1,204	75.25
1984	G. A. Gooch	2,559	67.34	C. G. Greenidge	1,069	82.23
1985	G. A. Gooch	2,208	71.22	I. V. A. Richards . . .	1,836	76.50
1986	C. G. Greenidge	2,035	67.83	C. G. Greenidge	2,035	67.83

		Career	R	I	NO	HS	100s	Avge
98	M. H. Denness	1959-80	25,886	838	65	195	33	33.48
99	S. M. Gavaskar	1966-87	25,834	563	61	340	81	51.46
100	J. W. H. Makepeace . .	1906-30	25,799	778	66	203	43	36.23
101	W. Gunn	1880-1904	25,691	850	72	273	48	33.02
102	W. Watson	1939-64	25,670	753	109	257	55	39.86
103	G. Brown	1908-33	25,649	1,012	52	232*	37	26.71
104	G. M. Emmett	1936-59	25,602	865	50	188	37	31.41
105	J. B. Bolus	1956-75	25,598	833	81	202*	39	34.03
106	W. E. Russell	1956-72	25,525	796	64	193	41	34.87
107	C. W. J. Athey	1976-97	25,453	784	71	184	55	35.69
108	C. J. Barnett	1927-53	25,389	821	45	259	48	32.71
109	L. B. Fishlock	1931-52	25,376	699	54	253	56	39.34
110	D. J. Insole	1947-63	25,241	743	72	219*	54	37.61
111	J. M. Brearley	1961-83	25,185	768	102	312*	45	37.81
112	J. Vine	1896-1922	25,171	920	79	202	34	29.92
113	R. M. Prideaux	1958-74	25,136	808	75	202*	41	34.29
114	J. H. King	1895-1925	25,122	988	69	227*	34	27.33
115	J. G. Wright	1975-92	25,073	636	44	192	59	42.35

Bold type denotes those who played in 1998-99 and 1999 seasons.

Note: some works of reference provide career figures which differ from those in this list, owing to the exclusion or inclusion of matches recognised or not recognised as first-class by *Wisden*.

Current Players with 20,000 Runs

	Career	R	I	NO	HS	100s	Avge
K. C. Wessels	1973-98	24,703	537	50	254	66	50.72
R. A. Smith	1980-99	23,608	622	83	209*	56	43.79
D. C. Boon	1978-99	23,413	585	53	227	68	44.00
A. J. Stewart	1981-99	22,507	626	68	271*	44	40.33
M. E. Waugh	1985-98	22,131	472	59	229*	71	53.58
A. P. Wells	1981-99	20,802	609	79	253*	46	39.24
T. M. Moody	1985-99	20,677	487	46	272	64	46.88
R. J. Bailey	1982-99	20,601	584	84	224*	44	41.20
J. E. Morris	1982-99	20,298	576	33	229	49	37.38
M. P. Maynard	1985-99	20,181	527	55	243	45	42.75

CAREER AVERAGE OVER 50

(Qualification: 10,000 runs)

Avge		Career	I	NO	R	HS	100s
95.14	D. G. Bradman	1927-48	338	43	28,067	452*	117
71.22	V. M. Merchant	1929-51	229	43	13,248	359*	44
65.18	W. H. Ponsford	1920-34	235	23	13,819	437	47
64.99	W. M. Woodfull	1921-34	245	39	13,388	284	49
59.75	**S. R. Tendulkar**	**1988-98**	**224**	**22**	**12,070**	**204***	**38**
58.24	A. L. Hassett	1932-53	322	32	16,890	232	59
58.19	V. S. Hazare	1934-66	365	45	18,621	316*	60
57.22	A. F. Kippax	1918-35	256	33	12,762	315*	43
56.83	G. Boycott	1962-86	1,014	162	48,426	261*	151
56.55	C. L. Walcott	1941-63	238	29	11,820	314*	40
56.37	K. S. Ranjitsinhji . . .	1893-1920	500	62	24,692	285*	72
56.22	R. B. Simpson	1952-77	436	62	21,029	359	60
56.10	W. R. Hammond	1920-51	1,005	104	50,551	336*	167
56.02	M. D. Crowe	1979-95	412	62	19,608	299	71
55.51	L. Hutton	1934-60	814	91	40,140	364	129
55.34	E. D. Weekes	1944-64	241	24	12,010	304*	36

Avge		Career	I	NO	R	HS	100s
55.11	S. V. Manjrekar	*1984-97*	217	31	10,252	377	31
55.02	**G. A. Hick**	***1983-99***	**628**	**60**	**31,252**	**405***	**108**
54.87	G. S. Sobers	*1952-74*	609	93	28,315	365*	86
54.74	B. A. Richards	*1964-82*	576	58	28,358	356	80
54.67	R. G. Pollock	*1960-86*	437	54	20,940	274	64
54.56	**M. G. Bevan**	***1989-98***	**269**	**48**	**12,059**	**203***	**40**
54.24	F. M. M. Worrell	*1941-64*	326	49	15,025	308*	39
53.78	R. M. Cowper	*1959-69*	228	31	10,595	307	26
53.67	A. R. Morris	*1940-63*	250	15	12,614	290	46
53.58	**M. E. Waugh**	***1985-98***	**472**	**59**	**22,131**	**229***	**71**
53.44	Javed Miandad	*1973-93*	631	95	28,647	311	80
53.30	**M. L. Hayden**	***1991-99***	**249**	**26**	**11,886**	**235***	**38**
53.08	**D. S. Lehmann**	***1987-98***	**245**	**15**	**12,210**	**255**	**37**
52.86	D. B. Vengsarkar	*1975-91*	390	52	17,868	284	55
52.62	**S. R. Waugh**	***1984-98***	**414**	**71**	**18,052**	**216***	**53**
52.32	Hanif Mohammad	*1951-76*	371	45	17,059	499	55
52.27	P. R. Umrigar	*1944-67*	350	41	16,154	252*	49
52.20	G. S. Chappell	*1966-83*	542	72	24,535	247*	74
51.95	H. Sutcliffe	*1919-45*	1,088	123	50,138	313	149
51.85	D. M. Jones	*1981-97*	415	45	19,188	324*	55
51.85	D. C. S. Compton	*1936-64*	839	88	38,942	300	123
51.54	Zaheer Abbas	*1965-86*	768	92	34,843	274	108
51.53	A. D. Nourse	*1931-52*	269	27	12,472	260*	41
51.53	**J. L. Langer**	***1991-99***	**248**	**31**	**11,183**	**274***	**33**
51.46	S. M. Gavaskar	*1966-87*	563	61	25,834	340	81
51.44	W. A. Brown	*1932-49*	284	15	13,838	265*	39
51.38	A. R. Border	*1976-95*	625	97	27,131	205	70
51.00	P. B. H. May	1948-63	618	77	27,592	285*	85
50.95	N. C. O'Neill	*1955-67*	306	34	13,859	284	45
50.93	R. N. Harvey	*1946-62*	461	35	21,699	231*	67
50.92	**M. Azharuddin**	***1981-98***	**328**	**35**	**14,920**	**226**	**51**
50.90	W. M. Lawry	*1955-71*	417	49	18,734	266	50
50.90	A. V. Mankad	*1963-82*	326	71	12,980	265	31
50.87	**B. C. Lara**	***1987-98***	**278**	**8**	**13,737**	**501***	**38**
50.80	E. H. Hendren	1907-38	1,300	166	57,611	301*	170
50.72	**K. C. Wessels**	***1973-98***	**537**	**50**	**24,703**	**254**	**66**
50.65	J. B. Hobbs	1905-34	1,315	106	61,237	316*	197
50.58	S. J. Cook	*1972-94*	475	57	21,143	313*	64
50.27	**Asif Mujtaba**	***1984-98***	**353**	**70**	**14,229**	**208**	**39**
50.22	C. B. Fry	*1892-1921*	658	43	30,886	258*	94
50.01	Shafiq Ahmad	*1967-90*	449	58	19,555	217*	53

Note: G. A. Headley (*1927-1954*) scored 9,921 runs, average 69.86.

Bold type denotes those who played in 1998-99 and 1999 seasons.

FASTEST FIFTIES

Minutes			
11	C. I. J. Smith (66)	Middlesex v Gloucestershire at Bristol	1938
14	S. J. Pegler (50)	South Africans v Tasmania at Launceston	1910-11
14	F. T. Mann (53)	Middlesex v Nottinghamshire at Lord's	1921
14	H. B. Cameron (56)	Transvaal v Orange Free State at Johannesburg . . .	1934-35
14	C. I. J. Smith (52)	Middlesex v Kent at Maidstone	1935

Note: the following fast fifties were scored in contrived circumstances when runs were given from full tosses and long hops to expedite a declaration: C. C. Inman (8 minutes), Leicestershire v Nottinghamshire at Nottingham, 1965; G. Chapple (10 minutes), Lancashire v Glamorgan at Manchester, 1993; T. M. Moody (11 minutes), Warwickshire v Glamorgan at Swansea, 1990; A. J. Stewart (14 minutes), Surrey v Kent at Dartford, 1986; M. P. Maynard (14 minutes), Glamorgan v Yorkshire at Cardiff, 1987.

FASTEST HUNDREDS

Minutes

35	P. G. H. Fender (113*)	Surrey v Northamptonshire at Northampton	1920
40	G. L. Jessop (101)	Gloucestershire v Yorkshire at Harrogate	1897
40	Ahsan-ul-Haq (100*)	Muslims v Sikhs at Lahore	1923-24
42	G. L. Jessop (191)	Gentlemen of South v Players of South at Hastings	1907
43	A. H. Hornby (106)	Lancashire v Somerset at Manchester	1905
43	D. W. Hookes (107)	South Australia v Victoria at Adelaide	1982-83
44	R. N. S. Hobbs (100)	Essex v Australians at Chelmsford	1975

Notes: the fastest recorded authentic hundred in terms of balls received was scored off 34 balls by D. W. Hookes (above).

Research of the scorebook has shown that P. G. H. Fender scored his hundred from between 40 and 46 balls. He contributed 113 to an unfinished sixth-wicket partnership of 171 in 42 minutes with H. A. Peach.

E. B. Alletson (Nottinghamshire) scored 189 out of 227 runs in 90 minutes against Sussex at Hove in 1911. It has been estimated that his last 139 runs took 37 minutes.

The following fast hundreds were scored in contrived circumstances when runs were given from full tosses and long hops to expedite a declaration: G. Chapple (21 minutes), Lancashire v Glamorgan at Manchester, 1993; T. M. Moody (26 minutes), Warwickshire v Glamorgan at Swansea, 1990; S. J. O'Shaughnessy (35 minutes), Lancashire v Leicestershire at Manchester, 1983; C. M. Old (37 minutes), Yorkshire v Warwickshire at Birmingham, 1977; N. F. M. Popplewell (41 minutes), Somerset v Gloucestershire at Bath, 1983.

FASTEST DOUBLE-HUNDREDS

Minutes

113	R. J. Shastri (200*)	Bombay v Baroda at Bombay	1984-85
120	G. L. Jessop (286)	Gloucestershire v Sussex at Hove	1903
120	C. H. Lloyd (201*)	West Indians v Glamorgan at Swansea	1976
130	G. L. Jessop (234)	Gloucestershire v Somerset at Bristol	1905
131	V. T. Trumper (293)	Australians v Canterbury at Christchurch	1913-14

FASTEST TRIPLE-HUNDREDS

Minutes

181	D. C. S. Compton (300)	MCC v N. E. Transvaal at Benoni	1948-49
205	F. E. Woolley (305*)	MCC v Tasmania at Hobart	1911-12
205	C. G. Macartney (345)	Australians v Nottinghamshire at Nottingham	1921
213	D. G. Bradman (369)	South Australia v Tasmania at Adelaide	1935-36

300 RUNS IN ONE DAY

390*	B. C. Lara	Warwickshire v Durham at Birmingham	1994
345	C. G. Macartney	Australians v Nottinghamshire at Nottingham	1921
334	W. H. Ponsford	Victoria v New South Wales at Melbourne	1926-27
333	K. S. Duleepsinhji	Sussex v Northamptonshire at Hove	1930
331*	J. D. Robertson	Middlesex v Worcestershire at Worcester	1949
325*	B. A. Richards	S. Australia v W. Australia at Perth	1970-71
322†	E. Paynter	Lancashire v Sussex at Hove	1937
322	I. V. A. Richards	Somerset v Warwickshire at Taunton	1985
318	C. W. Gregory	New South Wales v Queensland at Brisbane	1906-07
317	K. R. Rutherford	New Zealanders v D. B. Close's XI at Scarborough	1986

316†	R. H. Moore	Hampshire v Warwickshire at Bournemouth......	1937
315*	R. C. Blunt	Otago v Canterbury at Christchurch	1931-32
312*	J. M. Brearley	MCC Under-25 v North Zone at Peshawar	1966-67
311*	G. M. Turner	Worcestershire v Warwickshire at Worcester.....	1982
311*	N. H. Fairbrother	Lancashire v Surrey at The Oval	1990
309*	D. G. Bradman	Australia v England at Leeds	1930
307*	W. H. Ashdown	Kent v Essex at Brentwood	1934
306*	A. Ducat	Surrey v Oxford University at The Oval	1919
305*	F. R. Foster	Warwickshire v Worcestershire at Dudley	1914

† *E. Paynter's 322 and R. H. Moore's 316 were scored on the same day: July 28, 1937.*

These scores do not necessarily represent the complete innings. See pages 228–230.

LONGEST INNINGS

In India on November 3, 1999, after the deadline for this section, Rajiv Nayyar of Himachal Pradesh became the first player to bat longer than 1,000 minutes in one first-class innings. Against Jammu and Kashmir at Chamba, he batted 16 hours 55 minutes (1,015 minutes), scoring 271. The innings lasted almost three full playing days. Unconfirmed reports say he faced 728 balls and hit 26 fours and a six. Prior to this, the three longest innings were all in Test matches:

Mins			
970	Hanif Mohammad (337)	Pakistan v West Indies at Bridgetown......	1957-58
	Hanif believes he batted 999 minutes.		
799	S. T. Jayasuriya (340)	Sri Lanka v India at Colombo...........	1997-98
797	L. Hutton (364)	England v Australia at The Oval	1938

1,000 RUNS IN MAY

	Runs	*Avge*
W. G. Grace, May 9 to May 30, 1895 (22 days):		
13, 103, 18, 25, 288, 52, 257, 73*, 18, 169	1,016	112.88
Grace was within two months of completing his 47th year.		
W. R. Hammond, May 7 to May 31, 1927 (25 days):		
27, 135, 108, 128, 17, 11, 99, 187, 4, 30, 83, 7, 192, 14	1,042	74.42
Hammond scored his 1,000th run on May 28, thus equalling		
Grace's record of 22 days.		
C. Hallows, May 5 to May 31, 1928 (27 days):		
100, 101, 51*, 123, 101*, 22, 74, 104, 58, 34*, 232	1,000	125.00

1,000 RUNS IN APRIL AND MAY

	Runs	*Avge*
T. W. Hayward, April 16 to May 31, 1900:		
120*, 55, 108, 131*, 55, 193, 120, 5, 6, 3, 40, 146, 92	1,074	97.63
D. G. Bradman, April 30 to May 31, 1930:		
236, 185*, 78, 9, 48*, 66, 4, 44, 252*, 32, 47*	1,001	143.00
On April 30 Bradman was 75 not out.		
D. G. Bradman, April 30 to May 31, 1938:		
258, 58, 137, 278, 2, 143, 145*, 5, 30*	1,056	150.85
Bradman scored 258 on April 30, and his 1,000th run on May 27.		
W. J. Edrich, April 30 to May 31, 1938:		
104, 37, 115, 63, 20*, 182, 71, 31, 53*, 45, 15, 245, 0, 9, 20*	1,010	84.16
Edrich was 21 not out on April 30. All his runs were scored at Lord's.		
G. M. Turner, April 24 to May 31, 1973:		
41, 151*, 143, 85, 7, 8, 17*, 81, 13, 53, 44, 153*, 3, 2, 66*, 30, 10*, 111	1,018	78.30
G. A. Hick, April 17 to May 29, 1988:		
61, 37, 212, 86, 14, 405*, 8, 11, 6, 7, 172	1,019	101.90
Hick scored a record 410 runs in April, and his 1,000th run on May 28.		

1,000 RUNS IN TWO SEPARATE MONTHS

Only four batsmen, C. B. Fry, K. S. Ranjitsinhji, H. Sutcliffe and L. Hutton, have scored over 1,000 runs in each of two months in the same season. L. Hutton, by scoring 1,294 in June 1949, made more runs in a single month than anyone else. He also made 1,050 in August 1949.

MOST RUNS SCORED OFF ONE OVER

(All instances refer to six-ball overs)

36	G. S. Sobers	off M. A. Nash, Nottinghamshire v Glamorgan at Swansea (six sixes)	1968
36	R. J. Shastri	off Tilak Raj, Bombay v Baroda at Bombay (six sixes)	1984-85
34	E. B. Alletson	off E. H. Killick, Nottinghamshire v Sussex at Hove (46604446; including two no-balls)	1911
34	F. C. Hayes	off M. A. Nash, Lancashire v Glamorgan at Swansea (646666)	1977
34†	A. Flintoff	off A. J. Tudor, Lancashire v Surrey at Manchester (64444660; including two no-balls)	1998
32	I. T. Botham	off I. R. Snook, England XI v Central Districts at Palmerston North (466466)	1983-84
32	P. W. G. Parker	off A. I. Kallicharran, Sussex v Warwickshire at Birmingham (466664)	1982
32	I. R. Redpath	off N. Rosendorff, Australians v Orange Free State at Bloemfontein (666644)	1969-70
32	C. C. Smart	off G. Hill, Glamorgan v Hampshire at Cardiff (664664)	1935

† *Altogether 38 runs were scored off this over, the two no-balls counting for two extra runs each under ECB regulations.*

Notes: the following instances have been excluded from the above table because of the bowlers' compliance: 34 – M. P. Maynard off S. A. Marsh, Glamorgan v Kent at Swansea, 1992; 34 – G. Chapple off P. A. Cottey, Lancashire v Glamorgan at Manchester, 1993; 34 – F. B. Touzel off F. J. J. Viljoen, Western Province B v Griqualand West at Kimberley, 1993-94; 32 – C. C. Inman off N. W. Hill, Leicestershire v Nottinghamshire at Nottingham, 1965; 32 – T. E. Jesty off R. J. Boyd-Moss, Hampshire v Northamptonshire at Southampton, 1984; 32 – M. A. Ealham off G. D. Hodgson, Kent v Gloucestershire at Bristol, 1992; 32 – G. Chapple off P. A. Cottey, Lancashire v Glamorgan at Manchester, 1993. Chapple's 34 and 32 came off successive overs from Cottey.

There were 35 runs off an over received by A. T. Reinholds off H. T. Davis, Auckland v Wellington at Auckland 1995-96, but this included six no-balls (counting as two runs each), four byes and only 19 off the bat.

The greatest number of runs scored off an eight-ball over is 34 (40446664) by R. M. Edwards off M. C. Carew, Governor-General's XI v West Indians at Auckland, 1968-69.

In a Shell Trophy match against Canterbury at Christchurch in 1989-90, R. H. Vance (Wellington), acting on the instructions of his captain, deliberately conceded 77 runs in an over of full tosses which contained 17 no-balls and, owing to the umpire's understandable miscalculation, only five legitimate deliveries.

MOST SIXES IN AN INNINGS

16	A. Symonds (254*)	Gloucestershire v Glamorgan at Abergavenny	1995
15	J. R. Reid (296)	Wellington v Northern Districts at Wellington	1962-63
14	Shakti Singh (128)	Himachal Pradesh v Haryana at Dharmsala	1990-91
13	Majid Khan (147*)	Pakistanis v Glamorgan at Swansea	1967
13	C. G. Greenidge (273*)	D. H. Robins' XI v Pakistanis at Eastbourne	1974
13	C. G. Greenidge (259)	Hampshire v Sussex at Southampton	1975
13	G. W. Humpage (254)	Warwickshire v Lancashire at Southport	1982
13	R. J. Shastri (200*)	Bombay v Baroda at Bombay	1984-85
12	Gulfraz Khan (207)	Railways v Universities at Lahore	1976-77
12	I. T. Botham (138*)	Somerset v Warwickshire at Birmingham	1985

12	R. A. Harper (234)	Northamptonshire v Gloucestershire at Northampton .	1986
12	D. M. Jones (248)	Australians v Warwickshire at Birmingham	1989
12	U. N. K. Fernando (160)	Sinhalese SC v Sebastianites C and AC at Colombo. .	1990-91
12	D. N. Patel (204)	Auckland v Northern Districts at Auckland.	1991-92
12	W. V. Raman (206)	Tamil Nadu v Kerala at Madras	1991-92
12	G. D. Lloyd (241)	Lancashire v Essex at Chelmsford	1996
12	Wasim Akram (257*)	Pakistan v Zimbabwe at Sheikhupura.	1996-97
11	C. K. Nayudu (153)	Hindus v MCC at Bombay	1926-27
11	C. J. Barnett (194)	Gloucestershire v Somerset at Bath	1934
11	R. Benaud (135)	Australians v T. N. Pearce's XI at Scarborough	1953
11	R. Bora (126)	Assam v Tripura at Gauhati.	1987-88
11	G. A. Hick (405*)	Worcestershire v Somerset at Taunton	1988
11	A. S. Jayasinghe (183)	Tamil Union v Burgher RC at Colombo	1996-97

Note: F. B. Touzel (128*) hit 13 sixes for Western Province B v Griqualand West in contrived circumstances at Kimberley in 1993-94.

MOST SIXES IN A MATCH

| 20 | A. Symonds (254*, 76) | Gloucestershire v Glamorgan at Abergavenny . . . . . . | 1995 |
| 17 | W. J. Stewart (155, 125) | Warwickshire v Lancashire at Blackpool . . . . | 1959 |

MOST SIXES IN A SEASON

80	I. T. Botham	1985		49	I. V. A. Richards	1985
66	A. W. Wellard	1935		48	A. W. Carr	1925
57	A. W. Wellard	1936		48	J. H. Edrich	1965
57	A. W. Wellard	1938		48	A. Symonds	1995
51	A. W. Wellard	1933				

MOST BOUNDARIES IN AN INNINGS

	4s/6s			
72	62/10	B. C. Lara (501*)	Warwickshire v Durham at Birmingham .	1994
68	68/–	P. A. Perrin (343*)	Essex v Derbyshire at Chesterfield	1904
65	64/1	A. C. MacLaren (424)	Lancashire v Somerset at Taunton.	1895
64	64/–	Hanif Mohammad (499)	Karachi v Bahawalpur at Karachi	1958-59
57	52/5	J. H. Edrich (310*)	England v New Zealand at Leeds	1965
55	55/–	C. W. Gregory (383)	NSW v Queensland at Brisbane	1906-07
55	51/3†	S. V. Manjrekar (377)	Bombay v Hyderabad at Bombay	1990-91
55	53/2	G. R. Marsh (355*)	W. Australia v S. Australia at Perth. . . .	1989-90
54	53/1	G. H. Hirst (341)	Yorkshire v Leicestershire at Leicester . .	1905
53	53/–	A. W. Nourse (304*)	Natal v Transvaal at Johannesburg	1919-20
53	45/8	K. R. Rutherford (317)	New Zealanders v D. B. Close's XI at Scarborough	1986
52	47/5	N. H. Fairbrother (366)	Lancashire v Surrey at The Oval	1990
51	51/–	W. G. Grace (344)	MCC v Kent at Canterbury	1876
51	47/4	C. G. Macartney (345)	Australians v Notts at Nottingham	1921
51	50/1	B. B. Nimbalkar (443*)	Maharashtra v Kathiawar at Poona	1948-49
50	46/4	D. G. Bradman (369)	S. Australia v Tasmania at Adelaide	1935-36
50	47/–‡	A. Ducat (306*)	Surrey v Oxford U. at The Oval.	1919
50	35/15	J. R. Reid (296)	Wellington v N. Districts at Wellington .	1962-63
50	42/8	I. V. A. Richards (322)	Somerset v Warwickshire at Taunton . . .	1985

† *Plus one five.*
‡ *Plus three fives.*

PARTNERSHIPS OVER 500

577	V. S. Hazare (288) and Gul Mahomed (319), fourth wicket, Baroda v Holkar at Baroda	1946-47
576	S. T. Jayasuriya (340) and R. S. Mahanama (225), second wicket, Sri Lanka v India at Colombo	1997-98
574*	F. M. M. Worrell (255*) and C. L. Walcott (314*), fourth wicket, Barbados v Trinidad at Port-of-Spain	1945-46
561	Waheed Mirza (324) and Mansoor Akhtar (224*), first wicket, Karachi Whites v Quetta at Karachi	1976-77
555	P. Holmes (224*) and H. Sutcliffe (313), first wicket, Yorkshire v Essex at Leyton	1932
554	J. T. Brown (300) and J. Tunnicliffe (243), first wicket, Yorkshire v Derbyshire at Chesterfield	1898
502*	F. M. M. Worrell (308*) and J. D. C. Goddard (218*), fourth wicket, Barbados v Trinidad at Bridgetown	1943-44

HIGHEST PARTNERSHIPS FOR EACH WICKET

The following lists include all stands above 400; otherwise the top ten for each wicket.

First Wicket

561	Waheed Mirza and Mansoor Akhtar, Karachi Whites v Quetta at Karachi	1976-77
555	P. Holmes and H. Sutcliffe, Yorkshire v Essex at Leyton	1932
554	J. T. Brown and J. Tunnicliffe, Yorkshire v Derbyshire at Chesterfield	1898
490	E. H. Bowley and J. G. Langridge, Sussex v Middlesex at Hove	1933
464	R. Sehgal and R. Lamba, Delhi v Himachal Pradesh at Delhi	1994-95
459	Wasim Jaffer and S. K. Kulkarni, Mumbai v Saurashtra at Rajkot	1996-97
456	E. R. Mayne and W. H. Ponsford, Victoria v Queensland at Melbourne.	1923-24
451*	S. Desai and R. M. H. Binny, Karnataka v Kerala at Chikmagalur.	1977-78
431	M. R. J. Veletta and G. R. Marsh, Western Australia v South Australia at Perth.	1989-90
428	J. B. Hobbs and A. Sandham, Surrey v Oxford University at The Oval	1926
424	I. J. Siedle and J. F. W. Nicolson, Natal v Orange Free State at Bloemfontein	1926-27
421	S. M. Gavaskar and G. A. Parkar, Bombay v Bengal at Bombay	1981-82
418	Kamal Najamuddin and Khalid Alvi, Karachi v Railways at Karachi	1980-81
413	V. Mankad and Pankaj Roy, India v New Zealand at Madras	1955-56
405	C. P. S. Chauhan and M. S. Gupte, Maharashtra v Vidarbha at Poona.	1972-73

Second Wicket

576	S. T. Jayasuriya and R. S. Mahanama, Sri Lanka v India at Colombo.	1997-98
475	Zahir Alam and L. S. Rajput, Assam v Tripura at Gauhati	1991-92
465*	J. A. Jameson and R. B. Kanhai, Warwicks v Gloucestershire at Birmingham	1974
455	K. V. Bhandarkar and B. B. Nimbalkar, Maharashtra v Kathiawar at Poona	1948-49
451	W. H. Ponsford and D. G. Bradman, Australia v England at The Oval	1934
446	C. C. Hunte and G. S. Sobers, West Indies v Pakistan at Kingston	1957-58
429*	J. G. Dewes and G. H. G. Doggart, Cambridge U. v Essex at Cambridge	1949
426	Arshad Pervez and Mohsin Khan, Habib Bank v Income Tax at Lahore	1977-78
417†	K. J. Barnett and T. A. Tweats, Derbyshire v Yorkshire at Derby	1997
415	A. Jadeja and S. V. Manjrekar, Indians v Bowl XI at Springs	1992-93
403	G. A. Gooch and P. J. Prichard, Essex v Leicestershire at Chelmsford	1990

Third Wicket

467	A. H. Jones and M. D. Crowe, New Zealand v Sri Lanka at Wellington	1990-91
456	Khalid Irtiza and Aslam Ali, United Bank v Multan at Karachi	1975-76
451	Mudassar Nazar and Javed Miandad, Pakistan v India at Hyderabad	1982-83
445	P. E. Whitelaw and W. N. Carson, Auckland v Otago at Dunedin	1936-37
438*†	G. A. Hick and T. M. Moody, Worcestershire v Hampshire at Southampton . . .	1997
434	J. B. Stollmeyer and G. E. Gomez, Trinidad v British Guiana at Port-of-Spain .	1946-47
424*	W. J. Edrich and D. C. S. Compton, Middlesex v Somerset at Lord's.	1948
413	D. J. Bicknell and D. M. Ward, Surrey v Kent at Canterbury	1990
410*	R. S. Modi and L. Amarnath, India in England v The Rest at Calcutta.	1946-47
405	A. Jadeja and A. S. Kaypee, Haryana v Services at Faridabad.	1991-92

Fourth Wicket

577	V. S. Hazare and Gul Mahomed, Baroda v Holkar at Baroda	1946-47
574*	C. L. Walcott and F. M. M. Worrell, Barbados v Trinidad at Port-of-Spain . . .	1945-46
502*	F. M. M. Worrell and J. D. C. Goddard, Barbados v Trinidad at Bridgetown . .	1943-44
470	A. I. Kallicharran and G. W. Humpage, Warwicks v Lancs at Southport	1982
462*	D. W. Hookes and W. B. Phillips, South Australia v Tasmania at Adelaide	1986-87
448	R. Abel and T. W. Hayward, Surrey v Yorkshire at The Oval	1899
436	S. Abbas Ali and P. K. Dwevedi, Madhya Pradesh v Railways at Indore	1997-98
425*†	A. Dale and I. V. A. Richards, Glamorgan v Middlesex at Cardiff	1993
424	I. S. Lee and S. O. Quin, Victoria v Tasmania at Melbourne	1933-34
411	P. B. H. May and M. C. Cowdrey, England v West Indies at Birmingham. . . .	1957
410	G. Abraham and P. Balan Pandit, Kerala v Andhra at Palghat	1959-60
402	W. Watson and T. W. Graveney, MCC v British Guiana at Georgetown.	1953-54
402	R. B. Kanhai and K. Ibadulla, Warwicks v Notts at Nottingham	1968

Fifth Wicket

464*†	M. E. Waugh and S. R. Waugh, New South Wales v Western Australia at Perth	1990-91
405	S. G. Barnes and D. G. Bradman, Australia v England at Sydney	1946-47
401†	M. B. Loye and D. Ripley, Northamptonshire v Glamorgan at Northampton . .	1998
397	W. Bardsley and C. Kelleway, New South Wales v South Australia at Sydney . .	1920-21
393	E. G. Arnold and W. B. Burns, Worcestershire v Warwickshire at Birmingham.	1909
391	A. Malhotra and S. Dogra, Delhi v Services at Delhi	1995-96
385	S. R. Waugh and G. S. Blewett, Australia v South Africa at Johannesburg	1996-97
377*	G. P. Thorpe and M. R. Ramprakash, England XI v South Australia at Adelaide	1998-99
360	U. M. Merchant and M. N. Raiji, Bombay v Hyderabad at Bombay.	1947-48
355	Altaf Shah and Tariq Bashir, HBFC v Multan at Multan	1976-77
355	A. J. Lamb and J. J. Strydom, OFS v Eastern Province at Bloemfontein	1987-88

Sixth Wicket

487*	G. A. Headley and C. C. Passailaigue, Jamaica v Lord Tennyson's XI at Kingston	1931-32
428	W. W. Armstrong and M. A. Noble, Australians v Sussex at Hove	1902
411	R. M. Poore and E. G. Wynyard, Hampshire v Somerset at Taunton	1899
376	R. Subba Row and A. Lightfoot, Northamptonshire v Surrey at The Oval	1958
371	V. M. Merchant and R. S. Modi, Bombay v Maharashtra at Bombay	1943-44
356	W. V. Raman and A. Kripal Singh, Tamil Nadu v Goa at Panjim	1988-89
353	Salah-ud-Din and Zaheer Abbas, Karachi v East Pakistan at Karachi	1968-69
346	J. H. W. Fingleton and D. G. Bradman, Australia v England at Melbourne . . .	1936-37
337†	R. R. Montgomerie and D. J. Capel, Northamptonshire v Kent at Canterbury. .	1995
332	N. G. Marks and G. Thomas, New South Wales v South Australia at Sydney. . .	1958-59

Seventh Wicket

460	Bhupinder Singh, jun. and P. Dharmani, Punjab v Delhi at Delhi	1994-95
347	D. St E. Atkinson and C. C. Depeiza, West Indies v Australia at Bridgetown . . .	1954-55
344	K. S. Ranjitsinhji and W. Newham, Sussex v Essex at Leyton	1902
340	K. J. Key and H. Philipson, Oxford University v Middlesex at Chiswick Park .	1887
336	F. C. W. Newman and C. R. N. Maxwell, Sir J. Cahn's XI v Leicestershire at Nottingham	1935
335	C. W. Andrews and E. C. Bensted, Queensland v New South Wales at Sydney .	1934-35
325	G. Brown and C. H. Abercrombie, Hampshire v Essex at Leyton	1913
323	E. H. Hendren and L. F. Townsend, MCC v Barbados at Bridgetown	1929-30
308	Waqar Hassan and Imtiaz Ahmed, Pakistan v New Zealand at Lahore	1955-56
301	C. C. Lewis and B. N. French, Nottinghamshire v Durham at Chester-le-Street	1993

Eighth Wicket

433	V. T. Trumper and A. Sims, A. Sims' Aust. XI v Canterbury at Christchurch .	1913-14
313	Wasim Akram and Saqlain Mushtaq, Pakistan v Zimbabwe at Sheikhupura . . .	1996-97
292	R. Peel and Lord Hawke, Yorkshire v Warwickshire at Birmingham	1896
270	V. T. Trumper and E. P. Barbour, New South Wales v Victoria at Sydney	1912-13
263	Dr R. Wilcox and R. M. Taylor, Essex v Warwickshire at Southend	1946
255	E. A. V. Williams and E. A. Martindale, Barbados v Trinidad at Bridgetown . .	1935-36
249*	Shaukat Mirza and Akram Raza, Habib Bank v PNSC at Lahore	1993-94
246	L. E. G. Ames and G. O. B. Allen, England v New Zealand at Lord's	1931
243	R. J. Hartigan and C. Hill, Australia v England at Adelaide	1907-08
242*	T. J. Zoehrer and K. H. MacLeay, W. Australia v New South Wales at Perth . .	1990-91

Ninth Wicket

283	J. Chapman and A. Warren, Derbyshire v Warwickshire at Blackwell	1910
268	J. B. Commins and N. Boje, South Africa A v Mashonaland at Harare	1994-95
251	J. W. H. T. Douglas and S. N. Hare, Essex v Derbyshire at Leyton	1921
245	V. S. Hazare and N. D. Nagarwalla, Maharashtra v Baroda at Poona	1939-40
244*	Arshad Ayub and M. V. Ramanamurthy, Hyderabad v Bihar at Hyderabad	1986-87
239	H. B. Cave and I. B. Leggat, Central Districts v Otago at Dunedin	1952-53
232	C. Hill and E. Walkley, South Australia v New South Wales at Adelaide	1900-01
231	P. Sen and J. Mitter, Bengal v Bihar at Jamshedpur	1950-51
230	D. A. Livingstone and A. T. Castell, Hampshire v Surrey at Southampton	1962
226	C. Kelleway and W. A. Oldfield, New South Wales v Victoria at Melbourne . .	1925-26

Tenth Wicket

307	A. F. Kippax and J. E. H. Hooker, New South Wales v Victoria at Melbourne .	1928-29
249	C. T. Sarwate and S. N. Banerjee, Indians v Surrey at The Oval	1946
235	F. E. Woolley and A. Fielder, Kent v Worcestershire at Stourbridge	1909
233	Ajay Sharma and Maninder Singh, Delhi v Bombay at Bombay	1991-92
230	R. W. Nicholls and W. Roche, Middlesex v Kent at Lord's	1899
228	R. Illingworth and K. Higgs, Leicestershire v Northamptonshire at Leicester . .	1977
218	F. H. Vigar and T. P. B. Smith, Essex v Derbyshire at Chesterfield	1947
211	M. Ellis and T. J. Hastings, Victoria v South Australia at Melbourne	1902-03
196*	Nadim Yousuf and Maqsood Kundi, MCB v National Bank at Lahore	1981-82
192	H. A. W. Bowell and W. H. Livsey, Hampshire v Worcs at Bournemouth	1921

† *Partnerships affected by ECB or ACB regulations governing no-balls and wides.*

UNUSUAL DISMISSALS

Handled the Ball

J. Grundy	MCC v Kent at Lord's	1857
G. Bennett	Kent v Sussex at Hove	1872
W. H. Scotton	Smokers v Non-Smokers at East Melbourne.	1886-87
C. W. Wright	Nottinghamshire v Gloucestershire at Bristol	1893
E. Jones	South Australia v Victoria at Melbourne	1894-95
A. W. Nourse	South Africans v Sussex at Hove	1907
E. T. Benson	MCC v Auckland at Auckland	1929-30
A. W. Gilbertson	Otago v Auckland at Auckland	1952-53
W. R. Endean	South Africa v England at Cape Town	1956-57
P. J. Burge	Queensland v New South Wales at Sydney	1958-59
Dildar Awan	Services v Lahore at Lahore	1959-60
M. Mehra	Railways v Delhi at Delhi	1959-60
Mahmood-ul-Hasan	Karachi University v Railways-Quetta at Karachi . .	1960-61
Ali Raza	Karachi Greens v Hyderabad at Karachi	1961-62
Mohammad Yusuf	Rawalpindi v Peshawar at Peshawar	1962-63
A. Rees	Glamorgan v Middlesex at Lord's	1965
Pervez Akhtar	Multan v Karachi Greens at Sahiwal	1971-72
Javed Mirza	Railways v Punjab at Lahore	1972-73
R. G. Pollock	Eastern Province v Western Province at Cape Town	1973-74
C. I. Dey	Northern Transvaal v Orange Free State at Bloemfontein	1973-74
Nasir Valika	Karachi Whites v National Bank at Karachi	1974-75
Haji Yousuf	National Bank v Railways at Lahore	1974-75
Masood-ul-Hasan	PIA v National Bank B at Lyallpur	1975-76
Hanif Solangi	Hyderabad v Karachi B at Hyderabad	1977-78
D. K. Pearse	Natal v Western Province at Cape Town	1978-79
A. M. J. Hilditch	Australia v Pakistan at Perth	1978-79
Musleh-ud-Din	Railways v Lahore at Lahore	1979-80
Jalal-ud-Din	IDBP v Habib Bank at Bahawalpur	1981-82
Mohsin Khan	Pakistan v Australia at Karachi	1982-83
D. L. Haynes	West Indies v India at Bombay	1983-84
K. Azad	Delhi v Punjab at Amritsar	1983-84
Athar A. Khan	Allied Bank v HBFC at Sialkot	1983-84
A. N. Pandya	Saurashtra v Baroda at Baroda	1984-85
G. L. Linton	Barbados v Windward Islands at Bridgetown	1985-86
R. B. Gartrell	Tasmania v Victoria at Melbourne	1986-87
R. Nayyar	Himachal Pradesh v Punjab at Una	1988-89
R. Weerawardene	Moratuwa v Nomads SC at Colombo	1988-89
A. M. Kane	Vidarbha v Railways at Nagpur	1989-90
P. Bali	Jammu and Kashmir v Services at Delhi	1991-92
M. J. G. Davis	Northern Transvaal B v OFS B at Bloemfontein . .	1991-92
J. T. C. Vaughan	Emerging Players v England XI at Hamilton	1991-92
G. A. Gooch	England v Australia at Manchester	1993
A. C. Waller	Mashonaland CD v Mashonaland Under-24 at Harare	1994-95
K. M. Krikken	Derbyshire v Indians at Derby	1996
A. Badenhorst	Eastern Province B v North West at Fochville	1998-99

Obstructing the Field

C. A. Absolom	Cambridge University v Surrey at The Oval.	1868
T. Straw	Worcestershire v Warwickshire at Worcester	1899
T. Straw	Worcestershire v Warwickshire at Birmingham	1901
J. P. Whiteside	Leicestershire v Lancashire at Leicester	1901
L. Hutton	England v South Africa at The Oval	1951
J. A. Hayes	Canterbury v Central Districts at Christchurch	1954-55
D. D. Deshpande	Madhya Pradesh v Uttar Pradesh at Benares	1956-57
K. Ibadulla	Warwickshire v Hampshire at Coventry	1963
Qaiser Khan	Dera Ismail Khan v Railways at Lahore	1964-65

Note: the following instances were achieved in 12-a-side matches:

	O	M	R		
E. M. Grace (MCC)............	32.2	7	69	v Gents of Kent at Canterbury..	1862
W. G. Grace (MCC)............	46.1	15	92	v Kent at Canterbury........	1873
†D. C. S. Hinds (A. B. St Hill's XII)	19.1	6	36	v Trinidad at Port-of-Spain	1900-01

* J. Wisden and W. E. Hollies achieved the feat without the direct assistance of a fielder. Wisden's ten were all bowled; Hollies bowled seven and had three lbw.

† On debut in first-class cricket.   ‡ Pennsylvania.   § Mitchells & Butlers Ground.

OUTSTANDING ANALYSES

	O	M	R	W		
H. Verity (Yorkshire)	19.4	16	10	10	v Nottinghamshire at Leeds ..	1932
G. Elliott (Victoria)	19	17	2	9	v Tasmania at Launceston ..	1857-58
Ahad Khan (Railways)	6.3	4	7	9	v Dera Ismail Khan at Lahore	1964-65
J. C. Laker (England)	14	12	2	8	v The Rest at Bradford	1950
D. Shackleton (Hampshire) ...	11.1	7	4	8	v Somerset at Weston-s-Mare .	1955
E. Peate (Yorkshire)	16	11	5	8	v Surrey at Holbeck	1883
F. R. Spofforth (Australians) ..	8.3	6	3	7	v England XI at Birmingham .	1884
W. A. Henderson (North-Eastern Transvaal)	9.3	7	4	7	v Orange Free State at Bloemfontein	1937-38
Rajinder Goel (Haryana)	7	4	4	7	v Jammu and Kashmir at Chandigarh	1977-78
V. I. Smith (South Africans)..	4.5	3	1	6	v Derbyshire at Derby......	1947
S. Coststick (Victoria)	21.1	20	1	6	v Tasmania at Melbourne....	1868-69
Israr Ali (Bahawalpur)	11	10	1	6	v Dacca U. at Bahawalpur ...	1957-58
A. D. Pougher (MCC)	3	3	0	5	v Australians at Lord's	1896
G. R. Cox (Sussex)	6	6	0	5	v Somerset at Weston-s-Mare .	1921
R. K. Tyldesley (Lancashire) ..	5	5	0	5	v Leicestershire at Manchester	1924
P. T. Mills (Gloucestershire)...	6.4	6	0	5	v Somerset at Bristol	1928

MOST WICKETS IN A MATCH

19-90	J. C. Laker	England v Australia at Manchester	1956
17-48†	C. Blythe	Kent v Northamptonshire at Northampton.......	1907
17-50	C. T. B. Turner	Australians v England XI at Hastings	1888
17-54	W. P. Howell	Australians v Western Province at Cape Town	1902-03
17-56	C. W. L. Parker	Gloucestershire v Essex at Gloucester	1925
17-67	A. P. Freeman	Kent v Sussex at Hove	1922
17-89	W. G. Grace	Gloucestershire v Nottinghamshire at Cheltenham ..	1877
17-89	F. C. L. Matthews	Nottinghamshire v Northants at Nottingham	1923
17-91	H. Dean	Lancashire v Yorkshire at Liverpool	1913
17-91†	H. Verity	Yorkshire v Essex at Leyton	1933
17-92	A. P. Freeman	Kent v Warwickshire at Folkestone	1932
17-103	W. Mycroft	Derbyshire v Hampshire at Southampton	1876
17-106	G. R. Cox	Sussex v Warwickshire at Horsham	1926
17-106†	T. W. J. Goddard	Gloucestershire v Kent at Bristol	1939
17-119	W. Mead	Essex v Hampshire at Southampton	1895
17-137	W. Brearley	Lancashire v Somerset at Manchester	1905
17-159	S. F. Barnes	England v South Africa at Johannesburg........	1913-14
17-201	G. Giffen	South Australia v Victoria at Adelaide	1885-86
17-212	J. C. Clay	Glamorgan v Worcestershire at Swansea	1937

† Achieved in a single day.

FOUR WICKETS WITH CONSECUTIVE BALLS

J. Wells	Kent v Sussex at Brighton	1862
G. Ulyett	Lord Harris's XI v New South Wales at Sydney	1878-79
G. Nash	Lancashire v Somerset at Manchester	1882
J. B. Hide	Sussex v MCC and Ground at Lord's	1890
F. J. Shacklock	Nottinghamshire v Somerset at Nottingham	1893
A. D. Downes	Otago v Auckland at Dunedin	1893-94
F. Martin	MCC and Ground v Derbyshire at Lord's	1895
A. W. Mold	Lancashire v Nottinghamshire at Nottingham	1895
W. Brearley†	Lancashire v Somerset at Manchester	1905
S. Haigh	MCC v Army XI at Pretoria	1905-06
A. E. Trott‡	Middlesex v Somerset at Lord's	1907
F. A. Tarrant	Middlesex v Gloucestershire at Bristol.	1907
A. Drake	Yorkshire v Derbyshire at Chesterfield.	1914
S. G. Smith	Northamptonshire v Warwickshire at Birmingham	1914
H. A. Peach	Surrey v Sussex at The Oval	1924
A. F. Borland	Natal v Griqualand West at Kimberley.	1926-27
J. E. H. Hooker†	New South Wales v Victoria at Sydney	1928-29
R. K. Tyldesley†	Lancashire v Derbyshire at Derby	1929
R. J. Crisp	Western Province v Griqualand West at Johannesburg.	1931-32
R. J. Crisp	Western Province v Natal at Durban	1933-34
A. R. Gover	Surrey v Worcestershire at Worcester.	1935
W. H. Copson	Derbyshire v Warwickshire at Derby	1937
W. A. Henderson	N.E. Transvaal v Orange Free State at Bloemfontein	1937-38
F. Ridgway	Kent v Derbyshire at Folkestone	1951
A. K. Walker§	Nottinghamshire v Leicestershire at Leicester	1956
S. N. Mohol	President's XI v Combined XI at Poona	1965-66
P. I. Pocock	Surrey v Sussex at Eastbourne	1972
S. S. Saini†	Delhi v Himachal Pradesh at Delhi.	1988-89
D. Dias	W. Province (Suburbs) v Central Province at Colombo	1990-91
Ali Gauhar	Karachi Blues v United Bank at Peshawar	1994-95
K. D. James**	Hampshire v Indians at Southampton	1996

† *Not all in the same innings.*

‡ *Trott achieved another hat-trick in the same innings of this, his benefit match.*

§ *Having bowled Firth with the last ball of the first innings, Walker achieved a unique feat by dismissing Lester, Tompkin and Smithson with the first three balls of the second.*

** *James also scored a century, a unique double.*

Notes: in their match with England at The Oval in 1863, Surrey lost four wickets in the course of a four-ball over from G. Bennett.

Sussex lost five wickets in the course of the final (six-ball) over of their match with Surrey at Eastbourne in 1972. P. I. Pocock, who had taken three wickets in his previous over, captured four more, taking in all seven wickets with 11 balls, a feat unique in first-class matches. (The eighth wicket fell to a run-out.)

HAT-TRICKS

Double Hat-Trick

Besides Trott's performance, which is given in the preceding section, the following instances are recorded of players having performed the hat-trick twice in the same match, Rao doing so in the same innings.

A. Shaw	Nottinghamshire v Gloucestershire at Nottingham	1884
T. J. Matthews	Australia v South Africa at Manchester	1912
C. W. L. Parker	Gloucestershire v Middlesex at Bristol.	1924
R. O. Jenkins	Worcestershire v Surrey at Worcester.	1949
J. S. Rao	Services v Northern Punjab at Amritsar	1963-64
Amin Lakhani	Combined XI v Indians at Multan	1978-79

Five Wickets in Six Balls

W. H. Copson	Derbyshire v Warwickshire at Derby	1937
W. A. Henderson	N.E. Transvaal v Orange Free State at Bloemfontein	1937-38
P. I. Pocock	Surrey v Sussex at Eastbourne	1972

Most Hat-Tricks

Seven times: D. V. P. Wright.

Six times: T. W. J. Goddard, C. W. L. Parker.

Five times: S. Haigh, V. W. C. Jupp, A. E. G. Rhodes, F. A. Tarrant.

Four times: R. G. Barlow, A. P. Freeman, J. T. Hearne, J. C. Laker, G. A. R. Lock, G. G. Macaulay, T. J. Matthews, M. J. Procter, T. Richardson, F. R. Spofforth, F. S. Trueman.

Three times: W. M. Bradley, H. J. Butler, S. T. Clarke, W. H. Copson, R. J. Crisp, J. W. H. T. Douglas, J. A. Flavell, G. Giffen, D. W. Headley, K. Higgs, A. Hill, W. A. Humphreys, R. D. Jackman, R. O. Jenkins, A. S. Kennedy, W. H. Lockwood, E. A. McDonald, T. L. Pritchard, J. S. Rao, A. Shaw, J. B. Statham, M. W. Tate, H. Trumble, Wasim Akram, D. Wilson, G. A. Wilson.

Twice (current players only): D. G. Cork, D. Gough, A. Kumble, A. Sheriyar.

Hat-Trick on Debut

H. Hay	South Australia v Lord Hawke's XI at Unley, Adelaide	1902-03
H. A. Sedgwick	Yorkshire v Worcestershire at Hull	1906
R. Wooster	Northamptonshire v Dublin University at Northampton	1925
J. C. Treanor	New South Wales v Queensland at Brisbane	1954-55
V. B. Ranjane	Maharashtra v Saurashtra at Poona	1956-57
N. Frederick	Ceylon v Madras at Colombo	1963-64
J. S. Rao	Services v Jammu and Kashmir at Delhi	1963-64
Mehboodullah	Uttar Pradesh v Madhya Pradesh at Lucknow	1971-72
R. O. Estwick	Barbados v Guyana at Bridgetown	1982-83
S. A. Ankola	Maharashtra v Gujarat at Poona	1988-89
J. Srinath	Karnataka v Hyderabad at Secunderabad	1989-90
S. P. Mukherjee	Bengal v Hyderabad at Secunderabad	1989-90

Notes: R. R. Phillips (Border) took a hat-trick in his first over in first-class cricket (v Eastern Province at Port Elizabeth, 1939-40) having previously played in four matches without bowling.

J. S. Rao took two more hat-tricks in his next match.

250 WICKETS IN A SEASON

	Season	O	M	R	W	Avge
A. P. Freeman	1928	1,976.1	423	5,489	304	18.05
A. P. Freeman	1933‡	2,039	651	4,549	298	15.26
T. Richardson	1895‡	1,690.1	463	4,170	290	14.37
C. T. B. Turner	1888†	2,427.2	1,127	3,307	283	11.68
A. P. Freeman	1931	1,618	360	4,307	276	15.60
A. P. Freeman	1930	1,914.3	472	4,632	275	16.84
T. Richardson	1897‡	1,603.4	495	3,945	273	14.45
A. P. Freeman	1929	1,670.5	381	4,879	267	18.27
W. Rhodes	1900	1,553	455	3,606	261	13.81
J. T. Hearne	1896	2,003.1	818	3,670	257	14.28
A. P. Freeman	1932	1,565.5	404	4,149	253	16.39
W. Rhodes	1901	1,565	505	3,797	251	15.12

† Indicates 4-ball overs; ‡ 5-ball overs.

Notes: in four consecutive seasons (1928-31), A. P. Freeman took 1,122 wickets, and in eight consecutive seasons (1928-35), 2,090 wickets. In each of these eight seasons he took over 200 wickets.

T. Richardson took 1,005 wickets in four consecutive seasons (1894-97).

In 1896, J. T. Hearne took his 100th wicket as early as June 12. In 1931, C. W. L. Parker did the same and A. P. Freeman obtained his 100th wicket a day later.

LEADING BOWLERS IN AN ENGLISH SEASON

(Qualification: 10 wickets in 10 innings)

Season	Leading wicket-taker	Wkts	Avge	Top of averages	Wkts	Avge
1946	W. E. Hollies	184	15.60	A. Booth	111	11.61
1947	T. W. J. Goddard	238	17.30	J. C. Clay	65	16.44
1948	J. E. Walsh	174	19.56	J. C. Clay	41	14.17
1949	R. O. Jenkins	183	21.19	T. W. J. Goddard	160	19.18
1950	R. Tattersall	193	13.59	R. Tattersall	193	13.59
1951	R. Appleyard	200	14.14	R. Appleyard	200	14.14
1952	J. H. Wardle	177	19.54	F. S. Trueman	61	13.78
1953	B. Dooland	172	16.58	C. J. Knott	38	13.71
1954	B. Dooland	196	15.48	J. B. Statham	92	14.13
1955	G. A. R. Lock	216	14.49	R. Appleyard	85	13.01
1956	D. J. Shepherd	177	15.36	G. A. R. Lock	155	12.46
1957	G. A. R. Lock	212	12.02	G. A. R. Lock	212	12.02
1958	G. A. R. Lock	170	12.08	H. L. Jackson	143	10.99
1959	D. Shackleton	148	21.55	J. B. Statham	139	15.01
1960	F. S. Trueman	175	13.98	J. B. Statham	135	12.31
1961	J. A. Flavell	171	17.79	J. A. Flavell	171	17.79
1962	D. Shackleton	172	20.15	C. Cook	58	17.13
1963	D. Shackleton	146	16.75	C. C. Griffith	119	12.83
1964	D. Shackleton	142	20.40	J. A. Standen	64	13.00
1965	D. Shackleton	144	16.08	H. J. Rhodes	119	11.04
1966	D. L. Underwood	157	13.80	D. L. Underwood	157	13.80
1967	T. W. Cartwright	147	15.52	D. L. Underwood	136	12.39
1968	R. Illingworth	131	14.36	O. S. Wheatley	82	12.95
1969	R. M. H. Cottam	109	21.04	A. Ward	69	14.82
1970	D. J. Shepherd	106	19.16	Majid Khan	11	18.81
1971	L. R. Gibbs	131	18.89	G. G. Arnold	83	17.12
1972	{ T. W. Cartwright	98	18.64	I. M. Chappell	10	10.60
	{ B. Stead	98	20.38			
1973	B. S. Bedi	105	17.94	T. W. Cartwright	89	15.84
1974	A. M. E. Roberts	119	13.62	A. M. E. Roberts	119	13.62
1975	P. G. Lee	112	18.45	A. M. E. Roberts	57	15.80
1976	G. A. Cope	93	24.13	M. A. Holding	55	14.38
1977	M. J. Procter	109	18.04	R. A. Woolmer	19	15.21
1978	D. L. Underwood	110	14.49	D. L. Underwood	110	14.49
1979	{ D. L. Underwood	106	14.85	J. Garner	55	13.83
	{ J. K. Lever	106	17.30			
1980	R. D. Jackman	121	15.40	J. Garner	49	13.93
1981	R. J. Hadlee	105	14.89	R. J. Hadlee	105	14.89
1982	M. D. Marshall	134	15.73	R. J. Hadlee	61	14.57
1983	{ J. K. Lever	106	16.28	Imran Khan	12	7.16
	{ D. L. Underwood	106	19.28			
1984	R. J. Hadlee	117	14.05	R. J. Hadlee	117	14.05
1985	N. V. Radford	101	24.68	R. M. Ellison	65	17.20
1986	C. A. Walsh	118	18.17	M. D. Marshall	100	15.08
1987	N. V. Radford	109	20.81	R. J. Hadlee	97	12.64
1988	T. D. Stephenson	125	18.31	M. D. Marshall	42	13.16
1989	{ D. R. Pringle	94	18.64	T. M. Alderman	70	15.64
	{ S. L. Watkin	94	25.09			
1990	N. A. Foster	94	26.61	I. R. Bishop	59	19.05
1991	Waqar Younis	113	14.65	Waqar Younis	113	14.65
1992	C. A. Walsh	92	15.96	C. A. Walsh	92	15.96
1993	S. L. Watkin	92	22.80	Wasim Akram	59	19.27
1994	M. M. Patel	90	22.86	C. E. L. Ambrose	77	14.45
1995	A. Kumble	105	20.40	A. A. Donald	89	16.07

Season	Leading wicket-taker	Wkts	Avge	Top of averages	Wkts	Avge
1996	C. A. Walsh	85	16.84	C. E. L. Ambrose	43	16.67
1997	A. M. Smith	83	17.63	A. A. Donald	60	15.63
1998	C. A. Walsh.	106	17.31	V. J. Wells.	36	14.27
1999	A. Sheriyar	· 92	24.70	Saqlain Mushtaq	58	11.37

100 WICKETS IN A SEASON

Since Reduction of Championship Matches in 1969

Five times: D. L. Underwood 110 (1978), 106 (1979), 106 (1983), 102 (1971), 101 (1969).

Four times: J. K. Lever 116 (1984), 106 (1978), 106 (1979), 106 (1983).

Twice: B. S. Bedi 112 (1974), 105 (1973); T. W. Cartwright 108 (1969), 104 (1971); N. A. Foster 105 (1986), 102 (1991); N. Gifford 105 (1970), 104 (1983); R. J. Hadlee 117 (1984), 105 (1981); P. G. Lee 112 (1975), 101 (1973); M. D. Marshall 134 (1982), 100 (1986); M. J. Procter 109 (1977), 108 (1969); N. V. Radford 109 (1987), 101 (1985); F. J. Titmus 105 (1970), 104 (1971); C. A. Walsh 118 (1986), 106 (1998).

Once: J. P. Agnew 101 (1987); I. T. Botham 100 (1978); A. R. Caddick 105 (1998); K. E. Cooper 101 (1988); R. M. H. Cottam 109 (1969); D. R. Doshi 101 (1980); J. E. Emburey 103 (1983); L. R. Gibbs 131 (1971); R. N. S. Hobbs 102 (1970); Intikhab Alam 104 (1971); R. D. Jackman 121 (1980); A. Kumble 105 (1995); A. M. E. Roberts 119 (1974); P. J. Sainsbury 107 (1971); Sarfraz Nawaz 101 (1975); M. W. W. Selvey 101 (1978); D. J. Shepherd 106 (1970); F. D. Stephenson 125 (1988); Waqar Younis 113 (1991); D. Wilson 102 (1969).

100 WICKETS IN A SEASON MOST TIMES

(Includes Overseas Tours and Seasons)

23 times: W. Rhodes 200 wkts (3).

20 times: D. Shackleton (In successive seasons – 1949 to 1968 inclusive).

17 times: A. P. Freeman 300 wkts (1), 200 wkts (7).

16 times: T. W. J. Goddard 200 wkts (4), C. W. L. Parker 200 wkts (5), R. T. D. Perks, F. J. Titmus.

15 times: J. T. Hearne 200 wkts (3), G. H. Hirst 200 wkts (1), A. S. Kennedy 200 wkts (1).

14 times: C. Blythe 200 wkts (1), W. E. Hollies, G. A. R. Lock 200 wkts (2), M. W. Tate 200 wkts (3), J. C. White.

13 times: J. B. Statham.

12 times: J. Briggs, E. G. Dennett 200 wkts (1), C. Gladwin, D. J. Shepherd, N. I. Thomson, F. S. Trueman.

11 times: A. V. Bedser, G. Geary, S. Haigh, J. C. Laker, M. S. Nichols, A. E. Relf.

10 times: W. Attewell, W. G. Grace, R. Illingworth, H. L. Jackson, V. W. C. Jupp, G. G. Macaulay 200 wkts (1), W. Mead, T. B. Mitchell, T. Richardson 200 wkts (1), J. Southerton 200 wkts (1), R. K. Tyldesley, D. L. Underwood, J. H. Wardle, T. G. Wass, D. V. P. Wright.

100 WICKETS IN A SEASON OUTSIDE ENGLAND

W		Season	Country	R	Avge
116	M. W. Tate.	1926-27	India/Ceylon	1,599	13.78
113	Kabir Khan	1998-99	Pakistan	1,706	15.09
107	Ijaz Faqih	1985-86	Pakistan	1,719	16.06
106	C. T. B. Turner.	1887-88	Australia	1,441	13.59
106	R. Benaud	1957-58	South Africa	2,056	19.39
105	Murtaza Hussain	1995-96	Pakistan	1,882	17.92
104	S. F. Barnes	1913-14	South Africa	1,117	10.74
104	Sajjad Akbar.	1989-90	Pakistan	2,328	22.38
103	Abdul Qadir	1982-83	Pakistan	2,367	22.98

1,500 WICKETS IN A CAREER

Dates in italics denote the first half of an overseas season; i.e. *1970* denotes the 1970-71 season.

		Career	*W*	*R*	*Avge*
1	W. Rhodes	1898-1930	4,187	69,993	16.71
2	A. P. Freeman	1914-36	3,776	69,577	18.42
3	C. W. L. Parker	1903-35	3,278	63,817	19.46
4	J. T. Hearne	1888-1923	3,061	54,352	17.75
5	T. W. J. Goddard	1922-52	2,979	59,116	19.84
6	W. G. Grace	1865-1908	2,876	51,545	17.92
7	A. S. Kennedy	1907-36	2,874	61,034	21.23
8	D. Shackleton	1948-69	2,857	53,303	18.65
9	G. A. R. Lock	1946-*70*	2,844	54,709	19.23
10	F. J. Titmus	1949-82	2,830	63,313	22.37
11	M. W. Tate	1912-37	2,784	50,571	18.16
12	G. H. Hirst	1891-1929	2,739	51,282	18.72
13	C. Blythe	1899-1914	2,506	42,136	16.81
14	D. L. Underwood	1963-87	2,465	49,993	20.28
15	W. E. Astill	1906-39	2,431	57,783	23.76
16	J. C. White	1909-37	2,356	43,759	18.57
17	W. E. Hollies	1932-57	2,323	48,656	20.94
18	F. S. Trueman	1949-69	2,304	42,154	18.29
19	J. B. Statham	1950-68	2,260	36,999	16.37
20	R. T. D. Perks	1930-55	2,233	53,770	24.07
21	J. Briggs	1879-1900	2,221	35,431	15.95
22	D. J. Shepherd	1950-72	2,218	47,302	21.32
23	E. G. Dennett	1903-26	2,147	42,571	19.82
24	T. Richardson	1892-1905	2,104	38,794	18.43
25	T. E. Bailey	1945-67	2,082	48,170	23.13
26	R. Illingworth	1951-83	2,072	42,023	20.28
27	{ N. Gifford	1960-88	2,068	48,731	23.56
	{ F. E. Woolley	1906-38	2,068	41,066	19.85
29	G. Geary	1912-38	2,063	41,339	20.03
30	D. V. P. Wright	1932-57	2,056	49,307	23.98
31	J. A. Newman	1906-30	2,032	51,111	25.15
32	†A. Shaw	1864-97	2,027	24,580	12.12
33	S. Haigh	1895-1913	2,012	32,091	15.94
34	H. Verity	1930-39	1,956	29,146	14.90
35	W. Attewell	1881-1900	1,951	29,896	15.32
36	J. C. Laker	1946-*64*	1,944	35,791	18.41
37	A. V. Bedser	1939-60	1,924	39,279	20.41
38	W. Mead	1892-1913	1,916	36,388	18.99
39	A. E. Relf	1900-21	1,897	39,724	20.94
40	P. G. H. Fender	1910-36	1,894	47,458	25.05
41	J. W. H. T. Douglas	1901-30	1,893	44,159	23.32
42	J. H. Wardle	1946-*67*	1,846	35,027	18.97
43	G. R. Cox	1895-1928	1,843	42,136	22.86
44	G. A. Lohmann	1884-97	1,841	25,295	13.73
45	J. W. Hearne	1909-36	1,839	44,926	24.42
46	G. G. Macaulay	1920-35	1,837	32,440	17.65
47	M. S. Nichols	1924-39	1,833	39,666	21.63
48	J. B. Mortimore	1950-75	1,807	41,904	23.18
49	C. Cook	1946-64	1,782	36,578	20.52
50	R. Peel	1882-99	1,752	28,442	16.23
51	H. L. Jackson	1947-63	1,733	30,101	17.36
52	J. K. Lever	1967-89	1,722	41,772	24.25
53	T. P. B. Smith	1929-52	1,697	45,059	26.55
54	J. Southerton	1854-79	1,681	24,290	14.44
55	A. E. Trott	*1892*-1911	1,674	35,317	21.09
56	A. W. Mold	1889-1901	1,673	26,010	15.54

		Career	W	R	Avge
57	C. A. Walsh	*1981-98*	**1,670**	**36,565**	21.89
58	T. G. Wass	1896-1920	1,666	34,092	20.46
59	V. W. C. Jupp	1909-38	1,658	38,166	23.01
60	C. Gladwin	1939-58	1,653	30,265	18.30
61	M. D. Marshall	*1977-95*	1,651	31,548	19.10
62	W. E. Bowes	1928-47	1,639	27,470	16.76
63	A. W. Wellard	1927-50	1,614	39,302	24.35
64	J. E. Emburey	1973-97	1,608	41,958	26.09
65	P. I. Pocock	1964-86	1,607	42,648	26.53
66	N. I. Thomson	1952-72	1,597	32,867	20.58
67	J. Mercer	1919-47	1,591	37,210	23.38
	G. J. Thompson	1897-1922	1,591	30,058	18.89
69	J. M. Sims	1929-53	1,581	39,401	24.92
70	T. Emmett	1866-88	1,571	21,314	13.56
	Intikhab Alam	*1957-82*	1,571	43,474	27.67
72	B. S. Bedi	*1961-81*	1,560	33,843	21.69
73	W. Voce	1927-52	1,558	35,961	23.08
74	A. R. Gover	1928-48	1,555	36,753	23.63
75	T. W. Cartwright	1952-77	1,536	29,357	19.11
	K. Higgs	1958-86	1,536	36,267	23.61
77	James Langridge	1924-53	1,530	34,524	22.56
78	J. A. Flavell	1949-67	1,529	32,847	21.48
79	E. E. Hemmings	1966-95	1,515	44,403	29.30
80	C. F. Root	1910-33	1,512	31,933	21.11
	F. A. Tarrant	*1898-1936*	1,512	26,450	17.49
82	R. K. Tyldesley	1919-35	1,509	25,980	17.21

Bold type denotes those who played in 1998-99 and 1999 seasons.

† *The figures for A. Shaw exclude one wicket for which no analysis is available.*

Note: some works of reference provide career figures which differ from those in this list, owing to the exclusion or inclusion of matches recognised or not recognised as first-class by *Wisden*.

Current Players with 1,000 Wickets

	Career	W	R	Avge
A. A. Donald	*1985-99*	1,073	23,970	22.33
P. A. J. DeFreitas	1985-99	1,027	28,263	27.51

ALL-ROUND RECORDS

HUNDRED RUNS AND TEN WICKETS IN AN INNINGS

V. E. Walker, England v Surrey at The Oval; 20*, 108, ten for 74, and four for 17 . .   1859
W. G. Grace, MCC v Oxford University at Oxford; 104, two for 60, and ten for 49 . .   1886

Note: E. M. Grace, for MCC v Gentlemen of Kent in a 12-a-side match at Canterbury in 1862, scored 192* and took five for 77 and ten for 69.

TWO HUNDRED RUNS AND SIXTEEN WICKETS

G. Giffen, South Australia v Victoria at Adelaide; 271, nine for 96, and seven for 70 . . 1891-92

HUNDRED IN EACH INNINGS AND FIVE WICKETS TWICE

G. H. Hirst, Yorkshire v Somerset at Bath; 111, 117*, six for 70, and five for 45 . . .   1906

HUNDRED IN EACH INNINGS AND TEN WICKETS

B. J. T. Bosanquet, Middlesex v Sussex at Lord's; 103, 100*, three for 75, and eight for 53. 1905

F. D. Stephenson, Nottinghamshire v Yorkshire at Nottingham; 111, 117, four for 105, and seven for 117 1988

HUNDRED AND FOUR WICKETS WITH CONSECUTIVE BALLS

K. D. James, Hampshire v Indians at Southampton; 103 and five for 74 including four wickets with consecutive balls. 1996

HUNDRED AND HAT-TRICK

G. Giffen, Australians v Lancashire at Manchester 1884
W. E. Roller, Surrey v Sussex at The Oval. *Unique instance of 200 and hat-trick* . . 1885
W. B. Burns, Worcestershire v Gloucestershire at Worcester 1913
V. W. C. Jupp, Sussex v Essex at Colchester 1921
R. E. S. Wyatt, MCC v Ceylon at Colombo 1926-27
L. N. Constantine, West Indians v Northamptonshire at Northampton. 1928
D. E. Davies, Glamorgan v Leicestershire at Leicester 1937
V. M. Merchant, Dr C. R. Pereira's XI v Sir Homi Mehta's XI at Bombay 1946-47
M. J. Procter, Gloucestershire v Essex at Westcliff-on-Sea 1972
M. J. Procter, Gloucestershire v Leicestershire at Bristol 1979

SEASON DOUBLES

2,000 Runs and 200 Wickets

1906   G. H. Hirst   2,385 runs and 208 wickets

3,000 Runs and 100 Wickets

1937   J. H. Parks   3,003 runs and 101 wickets

2,000 Runs and 100 Wickets

	Season	R	W		Season	R	W
W. G. Grace	1873	2,139	106	F. E. Woolley	1914	2,272	125
W. G. Grace	1876	2,622	130	J. W. Hearne	1920	2,148	142
C. L. Townsend	1899	2,440	101	V. W. C. Jupp	1921	2,169	121
G. L. Jessop	1900	2,210	104	F. E. Woolley	1921	2,101	167
G. H. Hirst	1904	2,501	132	F. E. Woolley	1922	2,022	163
G. H. Hirst	1905	2,266	110	F. E. Woolley	1923	2,091	101
W. Rhodes	1909	2,094	141	L. F. Townsend	1933	2,268	100
W. Rhodes	1911	2,261	117	D. E. Davies	1937	2,012	103
F. A. Tarrant	1911	2,030	111	James Langridge	1937	2,082	101
J. W. Hearne	1913	2,036	124	T. E. Bailey.	1959	2,011	100
J. W. Hearne	1914	2,116	123				

1,000 Runs and 200 Wickets

	Season	R	W		Season	R	W
A. E. Trott	1899	1,175	239	M. W. Tate	1923	1,168	219
A. E. Trott	1900	1,337	211	M. W. Tate	1924	1,419	205
A. S. Kennedy	1922	1,129	205	M. W. Tate	1925	1,290	228

1,000 Runs and 100 Wickets

Sixteen times: W. Rhodes.
Fourteen times: G. H. Hirst.
Ten times: V. W. C. Jupp.
Nine times: W. E. Astill.
Eight times: T. E. Bailey, W. G. Grace, M. S. Nichols, A. E. Relf, F. A. Tarrant, M. W. Tate†, F. J. Titmus, F. E. Woolley.
Seven times: G. E. Tribe.

† *M. W. Tate also scored 1,193 runs and took 116 wickets for MCC in first-class matches on the 1926-27 MCC tour of India and Ceylon.*

Note: R. J. Hadlee (1984) and F. D. Stephenson (1988) are the only players to perform the feat since the reduction of County Championship matches. A complete list of those performing the feat before then will be found on page 202 of the 1982 *Wisden*.

Wicket-Keeper's Double

	Season	R	D
L. E. G. Ames	1928	1,919	122
L. E. G. Ames	1929	1,795	128
L. E. G. Ames	1932	2,482	104
J. T. Murray	1957	1,025	104

20,000 RUNS AND 2,000 WICKETS IN A CAREER

	Career	R	Avge	W	Avge	Doubles
W. E. Astill	1906-39	22,731	22.55	2,431	23.76	9
T. E. Bailey	1945-67	28,641	33.42	2,082	23.13	8
W. G. Grace	1865-1908	54,896	39.55	2,876	17.92	8
G. H. Hirst	1891-1929	36,323	34.13	2,739	18.72	14
R. Illingworth	1951-83	24,134	28.06	2,072	20.28	6
W. Rhodes	1898-1930	39,802	30.83	4,187	16.71	16
M. W. Tate	1912-37	21,717	25.01	2,784	18.16	8†
F. J. Titmus	1949-82	21,588	23.11	2,830	22.37	8
F. E. Woolley	1906-38	58,969	40.75	2,068	19.85	8

† *Plus one double overseas (see above).*

WICKET-KEEPING RECORDS

MOST DISMISSALS IN AN INNINGS

9 (8ct, 1st)	Tahir Rashid	Habib Bank v PACO at Gujranwala	1992-93
9 (7ct, 2st)	W. R. James*	Matabeleland v Mashonaland CD at Bulawayo	1995-96
8 (all ct)	A. T. W. Grout	Queensland v Western Australia at Brisbane	1959-60

8 (all ct)†	D. E. East	Essex v Somerset at Taunton	1985
8 (all ct)	S. A. Marsh‡	Kent v Middlesex at Lord's	1991
8 (6ct, 2st)	T. J. Zoehrer	Australians v Surrey at The Oval	1993
8 (7ct, 1st)	D. S. Berry	Victoria v South Australia at Melbourne	1996-97
7 (4ct, 3st)	E. J. Smith	Warwickshire v Derbyshire at Birmingham	1926
7 (6ct, 1st)	W. Farrimond	Lancashire v Kent at Manchester	1930
7 (all ct)	W. F. F. Price	Middlesex v Yorkshire at Lord's	1937
7 (3ct, 4st)	D. Tallon	Queensland v Victoria at Brisbane	1938-39
7 (all ct)	R. A. Saggers	New South Wales v Combined XI at Brisbane	1940-41
7 (1ct, 6st)	H. Yarnold	Worcestershire v Scotland at Dundee	1951
7 (4ct, 3st)	J. Brown	Scotland v Ireland at Dublin	1957
7 (6ct, 1st)	N. Kirsten	Border v Rhodesia at East London	1959-60
7 (all ct)	M. S. Smith	Natal v Border at East London	1959-60
7 (all ct)	K. V. Andrew	Northamptonshire v Lancashire at Manchester	1962
7 (all ct)	A. Long	Surrey v Sussex at Hove	1964
7 (all ct)	R. M. Schofield	Central Districts v Wellington at Wellington	1964-65
7 (all ct)	R. W. Taylor	Derbyshire v Glamorgan at Derby	1966
7 (6ct, 1st)	H. B. Taber	New South Wales v South Australia at Adelaide . . .	1968-69
7 (6ct, 1st)	E. W. Jones	Glamorgan v Cambridge University at Cambridge . . .	1970
7 (6ct, 1st)	S. Benjamin	Central Zone v North Zone at Bombay	1973-74
7 (all ct)	R. W. Taylor	Derbyshire v Yorkshire at Chesterfield	1975
7 (6ct, 1st)	Shahid Israr	Karachi Whites v Quetta at Karachi	1976-77
7 (4ct, 3st)	Wasim Bari	PIA v Sind at Lahore	1977-78
7 (all ct)	J. A. Maclean	Queensland v Victoria at Melbourne	1977-78
7 (5ct, 2st)	Taslim Arif	National Bank v Punjab at Lahore	1978-79
7 (all ct)	Wasim Bari	Pakistan v New Zealand at Auckland	1978-79
7 (all ct)	R. W. Taylor	England v India at Bombay	1979-80
7 (all ct)	D. L. Bairstow	Yorkshire v Derbyshire at Scarborough	1982
7 (6ct, 1st)	R. B. Phillips	Queensland v New Zealanders at Bundaberg	1982-83
7 (3ct, 4st)	Masood Iqbal	Habib Bank v Lahore at Lahore	1982-83
7 (3ct, 4st)	Arif-ud-Din	United Bank v PACO at Sahiwal	1983-84
7 (6ct, 1st)	R. J. East	OFS v Western Province B at Cape Town	1984-85
7 (all ct)	B. A. Young	Northern Districts v Canterbury at Christchurch	1986-87
7 (all ct)	D. J. Richardson	Eastern Province v OFS at Bloemfontein	1988-89
7 (6ct, 1st)	Dildar Malik	Multan v Faisalabad at Sahiwal	1988-89
7 (all ct)	W. K. Hegg	Lancashire v Derbyshire at Chesterfield	1989
7 (all ct)	Imran Zia	Bahawalpur v Faisalabad at Faisalabad	1989-90
7 (all ct)	I. D. S. Smith	New Zealand v Sri Lanka at Hamilton	1990-91
7 (all ct)	J. F. Holyman	Tasmania v Western Australia at Hobart	1990-91
7 (all ct)	P. J. L. Radley	OFS v Western Province at Cape Town	1990-91
7 (all ct)	C. P. Metson	Glamorgan v Derbyshire at Chesterfield	1991
7 (all ct)	H. M. de Vos	W. Transvaal v E. Transvaal at Potchefstroom	1993-94
7 (all ct)	P. Kirsten	Griqualand West v W. Transvaal at Potchefstroom . .	1993-94
7 (6ct, 1st)	S. A. Marsh	Kent v Durham at Canterbury	1994
7 (all ct)	K. J. Piper	Warwickshire v Essex at Birmingham	1994
7 (6ct, 1st)	K. J. Piper	Warwickshire v Derbyshire at Chesterfield	1994
7 (all ct)	H. H. Devapriya	Colts CC v Sinhalese SC at Colombo	1995-96
7 (all ct)	D. J. R. Campbell	Mashonaland CD v Matabeleland at Bulawayo	1995-96
7 (all ct)	A. C. Gilchrist	Western Australia v South Australia at Perth	1995-96
7 (all ct)	C. W. Scott	Durham v Yorkshire at Chester-le-Street	1996
7 (all ct)	Zahid Umar	WAPDA v Habib Bank at Sheikhupura	1997-98
7 (all ct)	K. S. M. Iyer	Vidarbha v Uttar Pradesh at Allahabad	1997-98
7 (all ct)	W. M. Noon	Nottinghamshire v Kent at Nottingham	1999

* W. R. James also scored 99 and 99 not out.
† The first eight wickets to fall.
‡ S. A. Marsh also scored 108 not out.

WICKET-KEEPERS' HAT-TRICKS

W. H. Brain, Gloucestershire v Somerset at Cheltenham, 1893 – three stumpings off successive balls from C. L. Townsend.

G. O. Dawkes, Derbyshire v Worcestershire at Kidderminster, 1958 – three catches off successive balls from H. L. Jackson.

R. C. Russell, Gloucestershire v Surrey at The Oval, 1986 – three catches off successive balls from C. A. Walsh and D. V. Lawrence (2).

MOST DISMISSALS IN A MATCH

13 (11ct, 2st)	W. R. James*	Matabeleland v Mashonaland CD at Bulawayo. . .	1995-96
12 (8ct, 4st)	E. Pooley	Surrey v Sussex at The Oval	1868
12 (9ct, 3st)	D. Tallon	Queensland v New South Wales at Sydney	1938-39
12 (9ct, 3st)	H. B. Taber	New South Wales v South Australia at Adelaide. .	1968-69
11 (all ct)	A. Long	Surrey v Sussex at Hove	1964
11 (all ct)	R. W. Marsh	Western Australia v Victoria at Perth	1975-76
11 (all ct)	D. L. Bairstow	Yorkshire v Derbyshire at Scarborough.	1982
11 (all ct)	W. K. Hegg	Lancashire v Derbyshire at Chesterfield	1989
11 (all ct)	A. J. Stewart	Surrey v Leicestershire at Leicester	1989
11 (all ct)	T. J. Nielsen	South Australia v Western Australia at Perth	1990-91
11 (10ct, 1st)	I. A. Healy	Australians v N. Transvaal at Verwoerdburg	1993-94
11 (10ct, 1st)	K. J. Piper	Warwickshire v Derbyshire at Chesterfield	1994
11 (all ct)	D. S. Berry	Victoria v Pakistanis at Melbourne	1995-96
11 (10ct, 1st)	W. A. Seccombe	Queensland v Western Australia at Brisbane	1995-96
11 (all ct)	R. C. Russell	England v South Africa (Second Test) at Johannesburg	1995-96
11 (10ct, 1st)	D. S. Berry	Victoria v South Australia at Melbourne	1996-97
11 (all ct)	Wasim Yousufi	Peshawar v Bahawalpur at Peshawar	1997-98

* W. R. James also scored 99 and 99 not out.

MOST DISMISSALS IN A SEASON

128 (79ct, 49st)	L. E. G. Ames	1929	104 (82ct, 22st)	J. T. Murray	1957
122 (70ct, 52st)	L. E. G. Ames	1928	102 (69ct, 33st)	F. H. Huish	1913
110 (63ct, 47st)	H. Yarnold	1949	102 (95ct, 7st)	J. T. Murray	1960
107 (77ct, 30st)	G. Duckworth	1928	101 (62ct, 39st)	F. H. Huish	1911
107 (96ct, 11st)	J. G. Binks	1960	101 (85ct, 16st)	R. Booth	1960
104 (40ct, 64st)	L. E. G. Ames	1932	100 (91ct, 9st)	R. Booth	1964

MOST DISMISSALS IN A CAREER

Dates in italics denote the first half of an overseas season; i.e. *1914* denotes the 1914-15 season.

		Career	*M*	*Ct*	*St*	*Total*
1	R. W. Taylor	1960-88	639	1,473	176	1,649
2	J. T. Murray	1952-75	635	1,270	257	1,527
3	H. Strudwick	1902-27	675	1,242	255	1,497
4	A. P. E. Knott	1964-85	511	1,211	133	1,344
5	F. H. Huish	1895-*1914*.	497	933	377	1,310
6	B. Taylor	1949-73	572	1,083	211	1,294
7	D. Hunter	1889-*1909*.	548	906	347	1,253
8	H. R. Butt	1890-1912	550	953	275	1,228

		Career	M	Ct	St	Total
9	J. H. Board.	1891-*1914*	525	852	355	1,207
10	H. Elliott	1920-47	532	904	302	1,206
11	J. M. Parks	1949-76	739	1,088	93	1,181
12	**R. C. Russell . . . .**	**1981-99**	**409**	**1,027**	**116**	**1,143**
13	R. Booth	1951-70	468	948	178	1,126
14	L. E. G. Ames	1926-51	593	703	418†	1,121
15	D. L. Bairstow	1970-90	459	961	138	1,099
16	G. Duckworth	1923-47	504	753	343	1,096
17	H. W. Stephenson	1948-64	462	748	334	1,082
18	J. G. Binks	1955-75	502	895	176	1,071
19	T. G. Evans	1939-69	465	816	250	1,066
20	A. Long	1960-80	452	922	124	1,046
21	G. O. Dawkes	1937-61	482	895	148	1,043
22	R. W. Tolchard	1965-83	483	912	125	1,037
23	**S. J. Rhodes . . . . . .**	**1981-99**	**364**	**915**	**112**	**1,027**
24	W. L. Cornford	1921-47	496	675	342	1,017

Bold type denotes those who played in 1998-99 and 1999 seasons.

　† *Record.*

Current Players with 500 Dismissals

	Career	M	Ct	St	Total
S. A. Marsh	1982-99	291	688	61	749
I. A. Healy.	*1986-98*	224	678	67	745
W. K. Hegg	1986-99	258	624	70	694
R. J. Blakey	1985-99	292	627	48	675
D. Ripley.	1984-99	279	595	78	673
Tahir Rashid.	*1979-99*	165	450	60	510
P. A. Nixon	1989-99	181	469	40	509

Note: in 376 matches since 1981, A. J. Stewart has achieved 536 catches and 19 stumpings, but 213 of his catches were taken as a fielder.

FIELDING RECORDS

(Excluding wicket-keepers)

MOST CATCHES IN AN INNINGS

7	M. J. Stewart	Surrey v Northamptonshire at Northampton.	1957
7	A. S. Brown	Gloucestershire v Nottinghamshire at Nottingham. . .	1966

MOST CATCHES IN A MATCH

10	W. R. Hammond†	Gloucestershire v Surrey at Cheltenham	1928
8	W. B. Burns	Worcestershire v Yorkshire at Bradford.	1907
8	F. G. Travers	Europeans v Parsees at Bombay	1923-24
8	A. H. Bakewell	Northamptonshire v Essex at Leyton	1928
8	W. R. Hammond	Gloucestershire v Worcestershire at Cheltenham	1932
8	K. J. Grieves	Lancashire v Sussex at Manchester	1951
8	C. A. Milton	Gloucestershire v Sussex at Hove	1952
8	G. A. R. Lock	Surrey v Warwickshire at The Oval	1957
8	J. M. Prodger	Kent v Gloucestershire at Cheltenham	1961
8	P. M. Walker	Glamorgan v Derbyshire at Swansea	1970
8	Masood Anwar	Rawalpindi v Lahore Division at Rawalpindi.	1983-84
8	M. C. J. Ball	Gloucestershire v Yorkshire at Cheltenham	1994
8	J. D. Carr	Middlesex v Warwickshire at Birmingham	1995

　† *Hammond also scored a hundred in each innings.*

MOST CATCHES IN A SEASON

78	W. R. Hammond	1928	69	P. M. Walker	1960
77	M. J. Stewart	1957	66	J. Tunnicliffe	1895
73	P. M. Walker	1961	65	W. R. Hammond	1925
71	P. J. Sharpe	1962	65	P. M. Walker	1959
70	J. Tunnicliffe	1901	65	D. W. Richardson	1961
69	J. G. Langridge	1955			

Note: the most catches by a fielder since the reduction of County Championship matches in 1969 is 49 by C. J. Tavaré in 1978.

MOST CATCHES IN A CAREER

Dates in italics denote the first half of an overseas season; i.e. *1970* denotes the 1970-71 season.

1,018	F. E. Woolley (1906-38)	784	J. G. Langridge (1928-55)
887	W. G. Grace (1865-1908)	764	W. Rhodes (1898-1930)
830	G. A. R. Lock (1946-*70*)	758	C. A. Milton (1948-74)
819	W. R. Hammond (1920-51)	754	E. H. Hendren (1907-38)
813	D. B. Close (1949-86)		

Most Catches by Current Player

474   G. A. Hick (*1983*-99)

TEAM RECORDS

HIGHEST INNINGS TOTALS

1,107	Victoria v New South Wales at Melbourne	1926-27
1,059	Victoria v Tasmania at Melbourne	1922-23
952-6 dec.	Sri Lanka v India at Colombo	1997-98
951-7 dec.	Sind v Baluchistan at Karachi	1973-74
944-6 dec.	Hyderabad v Andhra at Secunderabad	1993-94
918	New South Wales v South Australia at Sydney	1900-01
912-8 dec.	Holkar v Mysore at Indore	1945-46
912-6 dec.†	Tamil Nadu v Goa at Panjim	1988-89
910-6 dec.	Railways v Dera Ismail Khan at Lahore	1964-65
903-7 dec.	England v Australia at The Oval	1938
887	Yorkshire v Warwickshire at Birmingham	1896
868†	North Zone v West Zone at Bhilai	1987-88
863	Lancashire v Surrey at The Oval	1990
855-6 dec.†	Bombay v Hyderabad at Bombay	1990-91
849	England v West Indies at Kingston	1929-30
843	Australians v Oxford & Cambridge U P & P at Portsmouth	1893
839	New South Wales v Tasmania at Sydney	1898-99
826-4	Maharashtra v Kathiawar at Poona	1948-49
824	Lahore Greens v Bahawalpur at Lahore	1965-66

821-7 dec.	South Australia v Queensland at Adelaide	1939-40
815	New South Wales v Victoria at Sydney.	1908-09
811	Surrey v Somerset at The Oval	1899
810-4 dec.	Warwickshire v Durham at Birmingham	1994
807	New South Wales v South Australia at Adelaide	1899-1900
805	New South Wales v Victoria at Melbourne.	1905-06
803-4 dec.	Kent v Essex at Brentwood.	1934
803	Non-Smokers v Smokers at East Melbourne	1886-87
802-8 dec.	Karachi Blues v Lahore City at Peshawar	1994-95
802	New South Wales v South Australia at Sydney.	1920-21
801	Lancashire v Somerset at Taunton	1895
798	Maharashtra v Northern India at Poona	1940-41
793	Victoria v Queensland at Melbourne.	1927-28
791-6 dec.	Karnataka v Bengal at Calcutta	1990-91
790-3 dec.	West Indies v Pakistan at Kingston	1957-58
786	New South Wales v South Australia at Adelaide	1922-23
784	Baroda v Holkar at Baroda.	1946-47
783-8 dec.	Hyderabad v Bihar at Secunderabad	1986-87
781-7 dec.	Northamptonshire v Nottinghamshire at Northampton	1995
780-8	Punjab v Delhi at Delhi.	1994-95
777	Canterbury v Otago at Christchurch	1996-97
775	New South Wales v Victoria at Sydney.	1881-82

† *Tamil Nadu's total of 912-6 dec. included 52 penalty runs from their opponents' failure to meet the required bowling rate. North Zone's total of 868 included 68, and Bombay's total of 855-6 dec. included 48.*

HIGHEST FOURTH-INNINGS TOTALS

(Unless otherwise stated, the side making the runs won the match.)

654-5	England v South Africa at Durban	1938-39
	After being set 696 to win. The match was left drawn on the tenth day.	
604	Maharashtra (*set 959 to win*) v Bombay at Poona	1948-49
576-8	Trinidad (*set 672 to win*) v Barbados at Port-of-Spain	1945-46
572	New South Wales (*set 593 to win*) v South Australia at Sydney	1907-08
529-9	Combined XI (*set 579 to win*) v South Africans at Perth.	1963-64
518	Victoria (*set 753 to win*) v Queensland at Brisbane	1926-27
507-7	Cambridge University v MCC and Ground at Lord's	1896
506-6	South Australia v Queensland at Adelaide	1991-92
502-6	Middlesex v Nottinghamshire at Nottingham.	1925
502-8	Players v Gentlemen at Lord's	1900
500-7	South African Universities v Western Province at Stellenbosch	1978-79

HIGHEST MATCH AGGREGATES

Runs	*Wkts*		
2,376	37	Maharashtra v Bombay at Poona	1948-49
2,078	40	Bombay v Holkar at Bombay	1944-45
1,981	35	England v South Africa at Durban	1938-39
1,945	18	Canterbury v Wellington at Christchurch	1994-95
1,929	39	New South Wales v South Australia at Sydney.	1925-26
1,911	34	New South Wales v Victoria at Sydney.	1908-09
1,905	40	Otago v Wellington at Dunedin	1923-24

In Britain

Runs	*Wkts*		
1,808	20	Sussex v Essex at Hove....................	1993
1,723	31	England v Australia at Leeds	1948
1,706	23	Hampshire v Warwickshire at Southampton	1997
1,650	19	Surrey v Lancashire at The Oval	1990
1,642	29	Nottinghamshire v Kent at Nottingham.............	1995
1,641	16	Glamorgan v Worcestershire at Abergavenny	1990
1,614	30	England v India at Manchester	1990
1,606	34	Somerset v Derbyshire at Taunton	1996
1,603	28	England v India at Lord's	1990
1,601	29	England v Australia at Lord's	1930
1,601	35	Kent v Surrey at Canterbury.................	1995

LOWEST INNINGS TOTALS

12	Oxford University v MCC and Ground at Oxford	†1877
12	Northamptonshire v Gloucestershire at Gloucester.................	1907
13	Auckland v Canterbury at Auckland	1877-78
13	Nottinghamshire v Yorkshire at Nottingham	1901
14	Surrey v Essex at Chelmsford	1983
15	MCC v Surrey at Lord's	1839
15	Victoria v MCC at Melbourne	†1903-04
15	Northamptonshire v Yorkshire at Northampton	†1908
15	Hampshire v Warwickshire at Birmingham	1922

Following on, Hampshire scored 521 and won by 155 runs.

16	MCC and Ground v Surrey at Lord's	1872
16	Derbyshire v Nottinghamshire at Nottingham	1879
16	Surrey v Nottinghamshire at The Oval	1880
16	Warwickshire v Kent at Tonbridge	1913
16	Trinidad v Barbados at Bridgetown.	1942-43
16	Border v Natal at East London (first innings).	1959-60
17	Gentlemen of Kent v Gentlemen of England at Lord's	1850
17	Gloucestershire v Australians at Cheltenham	1896
18	The Bs v England at Lord's	1831
18	Kent v Sussex at Gravesend	†1867
18	Tasmania v Victoria at Melbourne	1868-69
18	Australians v MCC and Ground at Lord's	†1896
18	Border v Natal at East London (second innings).	1959-60
18	Sussex v Surrey at Godalming	1830
19	Sussex v Nottinghamshire at Hove	†1873
19	MCC and Ground v Australians at Lord's	1878
19	Wellington v Nelson at Nelson	1885-86

† *Signifies that one man was absent.*

Note: at Lord's in 1810, The Bs, with one man absent, were dismissed by England for 6.

LOWEST TOTAL IN A MATCH

34	(16 and 18) Border v Natal at East London	1959-60
42	(27 and 15) Northamptonshire v Yorkshire at Northampton	1908

Note: Northamptonshire batted one man short in each innings.

LOWEST AGGREGATE IN A COMPLETED MATCH

Runs	*Wkts*		
105	31	MCC v Australians at Lord's	1878

Note: the lowest aggregate since 1900 is 157 for 22 wickets, Surrey v Worcestershire at The Oval, 1954.

LARGEST VICTORIES

Largest Innings Victories

Inns and 851 runs:	Railways (910-6 dec.) v Dera Ismail Khan at Lahore	1964-65
Inns and 666 runs:	Victoria (1,059) v Tasmania at Melbourne	1922-23
Inns and 656 runs:	Victoria (1,107) v New South Wales at Melbourne	1926-27
Inns and 605 runs:	New South Wales (918) v South Australia at Sydney	1900-01
Inns and 579 runs:	England (903-7 dec.) v Australia at The Oval	1938
Inns and 575 runs:	Sind (951-7 dec.) v Baluchistan at Karachi	1973-74
Inns and 527 runs:	New South Wales (713) v South Australia at Adelaide	1908-09
Inns and 517 runs:	Australians (675) v Nottinghamshire at Nottingham	1921

Largest Victories by Runs Margin

685 runs:	New South Wales (235 and 761-8 dec.) v Queensland at Sydney	1929-30
675 runs:	England (521 and 342-8 dec.) v Australia at Brisbane	1928-29
638 runs:	New South Wales (304 and 770) v South Australia at Adelaide	1920-21
609 runs:	Muslim Commercial Bank (575 and 282-0 dec.) v WAPDA at Lahore. . .	1977-78
585 runs:	Sargodha (336 and 416) v Lahore Municipal Corporation at Faisalabad . .	1978-79
573 runs:	Sinhalese SC (395-7 dec. and 350-2 dec.) v Sebastianites C and AC at Colombo	1990-91
571 runs:	Victoria (304 and 649) v South Australia at Adelaide	1926-27
562 runs:	Australia (701 and 327) v England at The Oval	1934
556 runs:	Nondescripts (397-8 dec. and 313-6 dec.) v Matara at Colombo.	1998-99

Victory Without Losing a Wicket

Lancashire (166-0 dec. and 66-0) beat Leicestershire by ten wickets at Manchester . .	1956
Karachi A (277-0 dec.) beat Sind A by an innings and 77 runs at Karachi.	1957-58
Railways (236-0 dec. and 16-0) beat Jammu and Kashmir by ten wickets at Srinagar.	1960-61
Karnataka (451-0 dec.) beat Kerala by an innings and 186 runs at Chikmagalur	1977-78

TIED MATCHES

Since 1948 a tie has been recognised only when the scores are level with all the wickets down in the fourth innings.

The following are the instances since then:

Hampshire v Kent at Southampton	1950
Sussex v Warwickshire at Hove	1952
Essex v Lancashire at Brentwood	1952
Northamptonshire v Middlesex at Peterborough.	1953
Yorkshire v Leicestershire at Huddersfield	1954
Sussex v Hampshire at Eastbourne	1955
Victoria v New South Wales at Melbourne	1956-57
T. N. Pearce's XI v New Zealanders at Scarborough	1958
Essex v Gloucestershire at Leyton	1959
Australia v West Indies (First Test) at Brisbane.	1960-61
Bahawalpur v Lahore B at Bahawalpur	1961-62
Hampshire v Middlesex at Portsmouth	1967
England XI v England Under-25 XI at Scarborough	1968
Yorkshire v Middlesex at Bradford	1973
Sussex v Essex at Hove	1974
South Australia v Queensland at Adelaide	1976-77
Central Districts v England XI at New Plymouth	1977-78
Victoria v New Zealanders at Melbourne	1982-83

Muslim Commercial Bank v Railways at Sialkot	1983-84
Sussex v Kent at Hastings	1984
Northamptonshire v Kent at Northampton	1984
Eastern Province B v Boland at Albany SC, Grahamstown	1985-86
Natal B v Eastern Province B at Pietermaritzburg	1985-86
India v Australia (First Test) at Madras	1986-87
Gloucestershire v Derbyshire at Bristol	1987
Bahawalpur v Peshawar at Bahawalpur	1988-89
Wellington v Canterbury at Wellington	1988-89
Sussex v Kent at Hove	†1991
Nottinghamshire v Worcestershire at Nottingham	1993

† *Sussex (436) scored the highest total to tie a first-class match.*

MATCHES BEGUN AND FINISHED ON FIRST DAY

Since World War II.

Derbyshire v Somerset at Chesterfield, June 11	1947
Lancashire v Sussex at Manchester, July 12	1950
Surrey v Warwickshire at The Oval, May 16	1953
Somerset v Lancashire at Bath, June 6 (H. F. T. Buse's benefit)	1953
Kent v Worcestershire at Tunbridge Wells, June 15	1960

PWC TEST RATINGS

Introduced in 1987, the PricewaterhouseCoopers (PwC) Ratings – originally the Deloitte Ratings, and later the Coopers & Lybrand Ratings – rank Test cricketers on a scale up to 1,000 according to their performances in Test matches. The ratings take into account playing conditions, the quality of the opposition and the result of the matches. In August 1998, a similar set of ratings for one-day internationals was added (see page 1294).

The leading 20 batsmen and bowlers in the Test ratings after the 1999 Test series between England and New Zealand which ended on August 22 were:

	Batsmen	Rating		Bowlers	Rating
1.	B. C. Lara (*WI*)	917	1.	A. A. Donald (*SA*)	886
2.	S. R. Waugh (*Aus.*)	884	2.	G. D. McGrath (*Aus.*)	871
3.	S. R. Tendulkar (*Ind.*)	811	3.	S. M. Pollock (*SA*)	865
4.	R. Dravid (*Ind.*)	796	4.	C. E. L. Ambrose (*WI*)	832
5.	Saeed Anwar (*Pak.*)	793	5. {	M. Muralitharan (*SL*)	764
6.	D. J. Cullinan (*SA*)	730		Wasim Akram (*Pak.*)	764
7.	M. E. Waugh (*Aus.*)	722	7.	A. Kumble (*Ind.*)	761
8.	P. A. de Silva (*SL*)	712	8.	C. A. Walsh (*WI*)	748
9.	A. J. Stewart (*Eng.*)	706	9. {	Saqlain Mushtaq (*Pak.*)	696
10.	N. Hussain (*Eng.*)	704		J. Srinath (*Ind.*)	696
11.	W. J. Cronje (*SA*)	691	11.	A. R. C. Fraser (*Eng.*)	692
12.	M. W. Goodwin (*Zimb.*)	684	12.	S. C. G. MacGill (*Aus.*)	686
13.	M. J. Slater (*Aus.*)	679	13.	S. B. Doull (*NZ*)	681
14.	S. C. Ganguly (*Ind.*)	676	14. {	H. H. Streak (*Zimb.*)	671
15.	G. Kirsten (*SA*)	663		Waqar Younis (*Pak.*)	671
16.	J. H. Kallis (*SA*)	661	16.	J. N. Gillespie (*Aus.*)	644
17.	A. Flower (*Zimb.*)	650	17.	Mushtaq Ahmed (*Pak.*)	627
18.	S. Chanderpaul (*WI*)	648	18.	D. Gough (*Eng.*)	616
19.	Ijaz Ahmed, sen. (*Pak.*)	647	19.	D. J. Nash (*NZ*)	614
20.	Inzamam-ul-Haq (*Pak.*)	644	20.	A. R. Caddick (*Eng.*)	605

TEST MATCH RECORDS

Note: This section covers all Tests up to September 8, 1999.

BATTING RECORDS

HIGHEST INDIVIDUAL INNINGS

375	B. C. Lara	West Indies v England at St John's	1993-94
365*	G. S. Sobers	West Indies v Pakistan at Kingston	1957-58
364	L. Hutton	England v Australia at The Oval	1938
340	S. T. Jayasuriya	Sri Lanka v India at Colombo (RPS)	1997-98
337	Hanif Mohammad	Pakistan v West Indies at Bridgetown	1957-58
336*	W. R. Hammond	England v New Zealand at Auckland	1932-33
334*	M. A. Taylor	Australia v Pakistan at Peshawar	1998-99
334	D. G. Bradman	Australia v England at Leeds	1930
333	G. A. Gooch	England v India at Lord's	1990
325	A. Sandham	England v West Indies at Kingston	1929-30
311	R. B. Simpson	Australia v England at Manchester	1964
310*	J. H. Edrich	England v New Zealand at Leeds	1965
307	R. M. Cowper	Australia v England at Melbourne	1965-66
304	D. G. Bradman	Australia v England at Leeds	1934
302	L. G. Rowe	West Indies v England at Bridgetown	1973-74
299*	D. G. Bradman	Australia v South Africa at Adelaide	1931-32
299	M. D. Crowe	New Zealand v Sri Lanka at Wellington	1990-91
291	I. V. A. Richards	West Indies v England at The Oval	1976
287	R. E. Foster	England v Australia at Sydney	1903-04
285*	P. B. H. May	England v West Indies at Birmingham	1957
280*	Javed Miandad	Pakistan v India at Hyderabad	1982-83
278	D. C. S. Compton	England v Pakistan at Nottingham	1954
277	B. C. Lara	West Indies v Australia at Sydney	1992-93
275*	D. J. Cullinan	South Africa v New Zealand at Auckland	1998-99
274	R. G. Pollock	South Africa v Australia at Durban	1969-70
274	Zaheer Abbas	Pakistan v England at Birmingham	1971
271	Javed Miandad	Pakistan v New Zealand at Auckland	1988-89
270*	G. A. Headley	West Indies v England at Kingston	1934-35
270	D. G. Bradman	Australia v England at Melbourne	1936-37
268	G. N. Yallop	Australia v Pakistan at Melbourne	1983-84
267*	B. A. Young	New Zealand v Sri Lanka at Dunedin	1996-97
267	P. A. de Silva	Sri Lanka v New Zealand at Wellington	1990-91
266	W. H. Ponsford	Australia v England at The Oval	1934
266	D. L. Houghton	Zimbabwe v Sri Lanka at Bulawayo	1994-95
262*	D. L. Amiss	England v West Indies at Kingston	1973-74
261	F. M. M. Worrell	West Indies v England at Nottingham	1950
260	C. C. Hunte	West Indies v Pakistan at Kingston	1957-58
260	Javed Miandad	Pakistan v England at The Oval	1987
259	G. M. Turner	New Zealand v West Indies at Georgetown	1971-72
258	T. W. Graveney	England v West Indies at Nottingham	1957
258	S. M. Nurse	West Indies v New Zealand at Christchurch	1968-69
257*	Wasim Akram	Pakistan v Zimbabwe at Sheikhupura	1996-97
256	R. B. Kanhai	West Indies v India at Calcutta	1958-59
256	K. F. Barrington	England v Australia at Manchester	1964
255*	D. J. McGlew	South Africa v New Zealand at Wellington	1952-53
254	D. G. Bradman	Australia v England at Lord's	1930
251	W. R. Hammond	England v Australia at Sydney	1928-29
250	K. D. Walters	Australia v New Zealand at Christchurch	1976-77
250	S. F. A. F. Bacchus	West Indies v India at Kanpur	1978-79

The highest individual innings for India is:

236*	S. M. Gavaskar	India v West Indies at Madras	1983-84

HUNDRED ON TEST DEBUT

C. Bannerman (165*)	Australia v England at Melbourne	1876-77
W. G. Grace (152)	England v Australia at The Oval	1880
H. Graham (107)	Australia v England at Lord's	1893
† K. S. Ranjitsinhji (154*) . . .	England v Australia at Manchester	1896
† P. F. Warner (132*)	England v South Africa at Johannesburg	1898-99
† R. A. Duff (104)	Australia v England at Melbourne	1901-02
R. E. Foster (287)	England v Australia at Sydney	1903-04
G. Gunn (119)	England v Australia at Sydney	1907-08
† R. J. Hartigan (116)	Australia v England at Adelaide	1907-08
† H. L. Collins (104)	Australia v England at Sydney	1920-21
W. H. Ponsford (110)	Australia v England at Sydney	1924-25
A. A. Jackson (164)	Australia v England at Adelaide	1928-29
† G. A. Headley (176)	West Indies v England at Bridgetown	1929-30
J. E. Mills (117)	New Zealand v England at Wellington	1929-30
Nawab of Pataudi sen. (102) .	England v Australia at Sydney	1932-33
B. H. Valentine (136)	England v India at Bombay	1933-34
† L. Amarnath (118)	India v England at Bombay . . . . : . . .	1933-34
† P. A. Gibb (106)	England v South Africa at Johannesburg	1938-39
S. C. Griffith (140)	England v West Indies at Port-of-Spain	1947-48
A. G. Ganteaume (112)	West Indies v England at Port-of-Spain	1947-48
† J. W. Burke (101*)	Australia v England at Adelaide	1950-51
P. B. H. May (138)	England v South Africa at Leeds	1951
R. H. Shodhan (110)	India v Pakistan at Calcutta	1952-53
B. H. Pairaudeau (115)	West Indies v India at Port-of-Spain	1952-53
† O. G. Smith (104)	West Indies v Australia at Kingston	1954-55
A. G. Kripal Singh (100*) . .	India v New Zealand at Hyderabad	1955-56
C. C. Hunte (142)	West Indies v Pakistan at Bridgetown	1957-58
C. A. Milton (104*)	England v New Zealand at Leeds	1958
† A. A. Baig (112)	India v England at Manchester	1959
Hanumant Singh (105)	India v England at Delhi	1963-64
Khalid Ibadulla (166)	Pakistan v Australia at Karachi	1964-65
B. R. Taylor (105)	New Zealand v India at Calcutta	1964-65
K. D. Walters (155)	Australia v England at Brisbane	1965-66
J. H. Hampshire (107)	England v West Indies at Lord's	1969
† G. R. Viswanath (137)	India v Australia at Kanpur	1969-70
G. S. Chappell (108)	Australia v England at Perth	1970-71
‡ L. G. Rowe (214, 100*) . . .	West Indies v New Zealand at Kingston	1971-72
A. I. Kallicharran (100*) . . .	West Indies v New Zealand at Georgetown . . .	1971-72
R. E. Redmond (107)	New Zealand v Pakistan at Auckland	1972-73
† F. C. Hayes (106*)	England v West Indies at The Oval	1973
† C. G. Greenidge (107)	West Indies v India at Bangalore	1974-75
† L. Baichan (105*)	West Indies v Pakistan at Lahore	1974-75
G. J. Cosier (109)	Australia v West Indies at Melbourne	1975-76
S. Amarnath (124)	India v New Zealand at Auckland	1975-76
Javed Miandad (163)	Pakistan v New Zealand at Lahore	1976-77
† A. B. Williams (100)	West Indies v Australia at Georgetown	1977-78
† D. M. Wellham (103)	Australia v England at The Oval	1981
† Salim Malik (100*)	Pakistan v Sri Lanka at Karachi	1981-82
K. C. Wessels (162)	Australia v England at Brisbane	1982-83
W. B. Phillips (159)	Australia v Pakistan at Perth	1983-84
§ M. Azharuddin (110)	India v England at Calcutta	1984-85
D. S. B. P. Kuruppu (201*) . .	Sri Lanka v New Zealand at Colombo (CCC) . .	1986-87
† M. J. Greatbatch (107*)	New Zealand v England at Auckland	1987-88
M. E. Waugh (138)	Australia v England at Adelaide	1990-91
A. C. Hudson (163)	South Africa v West Indies at Bridgetown	1991-92
R. S. Kaluwitharana (132*) . .	Sri Lanka v Australia at Colombo (SSC)	1992-93
D. L. Houghton (121)	Zimbabwe v India at Harare	1992-93
P. K. Amre (103)	India v South Africa at Durban	1992-93

†G. P. Thorpe (114*)	England v Australia at Nottingham	1993
G. S. Blewett (102*)	Australia v England at Adelaide	1994-95
S. C. Ganguly (131)	India v England at Lord's	1996
†Mohammad Wasim (109*) . .	Pakistan v New Zealand at Lahore	1996-97
Ali Naqvi (115)	Pakistan v South Africa at Rawalpindi	1997-98
Azhar Mahmood (128*)	Pakistan v South Africa at Rawalpindi	1997-98

† *In his second innings of the match.*

‡ *L. G. Rowe is the only batsman to score a hundred in each innings on debut.*

§ *M. Azharuddin is the only batsman to score hundreds in each of his first three Tests.*

Notes: L. Amarnath and S. Amarnath were father and son.

Ali Naqvi and Azhar Mahmood achieved the feat in the same innings.

M. S. Sinclair scored 214 for New Zealand v West Indies at Wellington in 1999-2000, after the deadline for this section. He was the fourth player to reach 200 on Test debut.

300 RUNS IN FIRST TEST

| 314 | L. G. Rowe (214, 100*) | West Indies v New Zealand at Kingston . . . . . . | 1971-72 |
| 306 | R. E. Foster (287, 19) | England v Australia at Sydney . . . . | 1903-04 |

TWO SEPARATE HUNDREDS IN A TEST

Three times: S. M. Gavaskar.

Twice in one series: C. L. Walcott v Australia (1954-55).

Twice: †A. R. Border; G. S. Chappell; ‡P. A. de Silva; G. A. Headley; H. Sutcliffe.

Once: W. Bardsley; D. G. Bradman; I. M. Chappell; D. C. S. Compton; R. Dravid; G. W. Flower; G. A. Gooch; C. G. Greenidge; A. P. Gurusinha; W. R. Hammond; Hanif Mohammad; V. S. Hazare; G. P. Howarth; Javed Miandad; A. H. Jones; D. M. Jones; R. B. Kanhai; G. Kirsten; A. Melville; L. R. D. Mendis; B. Mitchell; J. Moroney; A. R. Morris; E. Paynter; §L. G. Rowe; A. C. Russell; R. B. Simpson; G. S. Sobers; A. J. Stewart; G. M. Turner; Wajahatullah Wasti; K. D. Walters; S. R. Waugh; E. D. Weekes.

† *A. R. Border scored 150* and 153 against Pakistan in 1979-80 to become the first to score 150 in each innings of a Test match.*

‡ *P. A. de Silva scored 138* and 103* against Pakistan in 1996-97 to become the first to score two not out hundreds in a Test match.*

§ *L. G. Rowe's two hundreds were on his Test debut.*

TRIPLE-HUNDRED AND HUNDRED IN SAME TEST

| G. A. Gooch (England) | 333 and 123 v India at Lord's . . . . | 1990 |

The only instance in first-class cricket. M. A. Taylor (Australia) scored 334 and 92 v Pakistan at Peshawar in 1998-99.*

DOUBLE-HUNDRED AND HUNDRED IN SAME TEST

K. D. Walters (Australia)	242 and 103 v West Indies at Sydney	1968-69
S. M. Gavaskar (India)	124 and 220 v West Indies at Port-of-Spain	1970-71
†L. G. Rowe (West Indies)	214 and 100* v New Zealand at Kingston	1971-72
G. S. Chappell (Australia)	247* and 133 v New Zealand at Wellington	1973-74

† *On Test debut.*

HIGHEST CAREER AVERAGES

(Qualification: 20 innings)

Avge		*T*	*I*	*NO*	*R*	*HS*	*100s*
99.94	D. G. Bradman (A).	52	80	10	6,996	334	29
60.97	R. G. Pollock (SA).	23	41	4	2,256	274	7
60.83	G. A. Headley (WI)	22	40	4	2,190	270*	10
60.73	H. Sutcliffe (E)	54	84	9	4,555	194	16
59.23	E. Paynter (E)	20	31	5	1,540	243	4
58.67	K. F. Barrington (E)	82	131	15	6,806	256	20
58.61	E. D. Weekes (WI)	48	81	5	4,455	207	15
58.45	W. R. Hammond (E).	85	140	16	7,249	336*	22
57.78	G. S. Sobers (WI)	93	160	21	8,032	365*	26
56.94	J. B. Hobbs (E)	61	102	7	5,410	211	15
56.68	C. L. Walcott (WI)	44	74	7	3,798	220	15
56.67	L. Hutton (E)	79	138	15	6,971	364	19
55.00	E. Tyldesley (E).	14	20	2	990	122	3
54.49	**S. R. Tendulkar (I)**	**68**	**105**	**10**	**5,177**	**179**	**19**
54.43	**R. Dravid (I)**	**29**	**48**	**4**	**2,395**	**190**	**5**
54.20	C. A. Davis (WI)	15	29	5	1,301	183	4
54.20	V. G. Kambli (I)	17	21	1	1,084	227	4
53.86	G. S. Chappell (A)	87	151	19	7,110	247*	24
53.81	A. D. Nourse (SA)	34	62	7	2,960	231	9
52.57	Javed Miandad (P)	124	189	21	8,832	280*	23
51.98	**B. C. Lara (WI)**	**63**	**108**	**4**	**5,406**	**375**	**13**
51.62	J. Ryder (A)	20	32	5	1,394	201*	3
51.12	S. M. Gavaskar (I)	125	214	16	10,122	236*	34
50.81	**S. R. Waugh (A)**	**115**	**185**	**35**	**7,622**	**200**	**19**
50.56	A. R. Border (A)	156	265	44	11,174	205	27
50.23	I. V. A. Richards (WI).	121	182	12	8,540	291	24
50.06	D. C. S. Compton (E)	78	131	15	5,807	278	17

Bold type denotes those who played Test cricket in 1998-99 and 1999 seasons.

MOST HUNDREDS

							Opponents					
	Total	*200+*	*Inns*	*E*	*A*	*SA*	*WI*	*NZ*	*I*	*P*	*SL*	*Z*
S. M. Gavaskar (I) . .	34	4	214	4	8	–	13	2	–	5	2	–
D. G. Bradman (A). .	29	12	80	19	–	4	2	–	4	–	–	–
A. R. Border (A) . . .	27	2	265	8	–	0	3	5	4	6	1	–
G. S. Sobers (WI). . .	26	2	160	10	4	–	–	1	8	3	–	–
G. S. Chappell (A) . .	24	4	151	9	–	–	5	3	1	6	0	–
I. V. A. Richards (WI	24	3	182	8	5	–	–	1	8	2	–	–
Javed Miandad (P) . .	23	6	189	2	6	–	2	7	5	–	1	–
G. Boycott (E).	22	1	193	–	7	1	5	2	4	3	–	–
M. C. Cowdrey (E). .	22	0	188	–	5	3	6	2	3	3	–	–
W. R. Hammond (E). .	22	7	140	–	9	6	1	4	2	–	–	–
M. Azharuddin (I). .	**21**	**0**	**145**	**6**	**2**	**3**	**0**	**2**	**–**	**3**	**5**	**0**
D. C. Boon (A) . . .	21	1	190	7	–	–	3	3	6	1	1	–
R. N. Harvey (A) . . .	21	2	137	6	–	8	3	–	4	0	–	–
K. F. Barrington (E) .	20	1	131	–	5	2	3	3	3	4	–	–
G. A. Gooch (E). . . .	20	2	215	–	4	–	5	4	5	1	1	–

Notes: the most hundreds for New Zealand is 17 by M. D. Crowe in 131 innings, for Sri Lanka 17 by **P. A. de Silva** in 131 innings, for South Africa 9 by A. D. Nourse in 62 innings and by **G. Kirsten** in 95 innings, and for Zimbabwe 5 by **A. Flower** and **G. W. Flower,** both in 58 innings.

The most double-hundreds by batsmen not qualifying for the above list is four by C. G. Greenidge (West Indies), L. Hutton (England) and Zaheer Abbas (Pakistan).

Bold type denotes those who played Test cricket in 1998-99 and 1999 seasons. Dashes indicate that a player did not play against the country concerned.

CARRYING BAT THROUGH TEST INNINGS

(Figures in brackets show side's total)

A. B. Tancred	26* (47)	South Africa v England at Cape Town	1888-89
J. E. Barrett	67* (176)	Australia v England at Lord's	1890
R. Abel	132* (307)	England v Australia at Sydney	1891-92
P. F. Warner	132* (237)	England v South Africa at Johannesburg	1898-99
W. W. Armstrong . .	159* (309)	Australia v South Africa at Johannesburg . . .	1902-03
J. W. Zulch	43* (103)	South Africa v England at Cape Town	1909-10
W. Bardsley.	193* (383)	Australia v England at Lord's	1926
W. M. Woodfull . . .	30* (66)‡	Australia v England at Brisbane	1928-29
W. M. Woodfull . . .	73* (193)†	Australia v England at Adelaide	1932-33
W. A. Brown	206* (422)	Australia v England at Lord's	1938
L. Hutton	202* (344)	England v West Indies at The Oval	1950
L. Hutton	156* (272)	England v Australia at Adelaide	1950-51
Nazar Mohammad§.	124* (331)	Pakistan v India at Lucknow	1952-53
F. M. M. Worrell . .	191* (372)	West Indies v England at Nottingham.	1957
T. L. Goddard	56* (99)	South Africa v Australia at Cape Town	1957-58
D. J. McGlew	127* (292)	South Africa v New Zealand at Durban	1961-62
C. C. Hunte	60* (131)	West Indies v Australia at Port-of-Spain	1964-65
G. M. Turner	43* (131)	New Zealand v England at Lord's	1969
W. M. Lawry.	49* (107)	Australia v India at Delhi	1969-70
W. M. Lawry.	60* (116)†	Australia v England at Sydney	1970-71
G. M. Turner	223* (386)	New Zealand v West Indies at Kingston	1971-72
I. R. Redpath.	159* (346)	Australia v New Zealand at Auckland	1973-74
G. Boycott	99* (215)	England v Australia at Perth	1979-80
S. M. Gavaskar . . .	127* (286)	India v Pakistan at Faisalabad	1982-83
Mudassar Nazar§ . .	152* (323)	Pakistan v India at Lahore	1982-83
S. Wettimuny.	63* (144)	Sri Lanka v New Zealand at Christchurch . . .	1982-83
D. C. Boon	58* (103)	Australia v New Zealand at Auckland	1985-86
D. L. Haynes	88* (211)	West Indies v Pakistan at Karachi	1986-87
G. A. Gooch	154* (252)	England v West Indies at Leeds.	1991
D. L. Haynes	75* (176)	West Indies v England at The Oval	1991
A. J. Stewart	69* (175)	England v Pakistan at Lord's	1992
D. L. Haynes	143* (382)	West Indies v Pakistan at Port-of-Spain. . . .	1992-93
M. H. Dekker	68* (187)	Zimbabwe v Pakistan at Rawalpindi	1993-94
M. A. Atherton . . .	94* (228)	England v New Zealand at Christchurch	1996-97
G. Kirsten.	100* (239)	South Africa v Pakistan at Faisalabad	1997-98
M. A. Taylor	169* (350)	Australia v South Africa at Adelaide	1997-98
G. W. Flower.	156* (321)	Zimbabwe v Pakistan at Bulawayo.	1997-98
Saeed Anwar	188* (316)	Pakistan v India at Calcutta	1998-99

† *One man absent.* ‡ *Two men absent.* § *Father and son.*

Notes: G. M. Turner (223*) holds the record for the highest score by a player carrying his bat through a Test innings. He is also the youngest player to do so, being 22 years 63 days old when he first achieved the feat (1969).

D. L. Haynes, who is alone in achieving this feat on three occasions, also opened the batting and was last man out in each innings for West Indies v New Zealand at Dunedin, 1979-80.

OUTSTANDING ANALYSES

	O	M	R	W		
J. C. Laker (E)	51.2	23	53	10	v Australia at Manchester	1956
A. Kumble (I)	26.3	9	74	10	v Pakistan at Delhi	1998-99
G. A. Lohmann (E)	14.2	6	28	9	v South Africa at Johannesburg	1895-96
J. C. Laker (E)	16.4	4	37	9	v Australia at Manchester.	1956
G. A. Lohmann (E)	9.4	5	7	8	v South Africa at Port Elizabeth	1895-96
J. Briggs (E)	14.2	5	11	8	v South Africa at Cape Town	1888-89
J. Briggs (E)	19.1	11	17	7	v South Africa at Cape Town	1888-89
M. A. Noble (A)	7.4	2	17	7	v England at Melbourne	1901-02
W. Rhodes (E)	11	3	17	7	v Australia at Birmingham	1902
A. E. R. Gilligan (E)	6.3	4	7	6	v South Africa at Birmingham	1924
S. Haigh (E)	11.4	6	11	6	v South Africa at Cape Town	1898-99
D. L. Underwood (E)	11.6	7	12	6	v New Zealand at Christchurch	1970-71
S. L. V. Raju (I)	17.5	13	12	6	v Sri Lanka at Chandigarh	1990-91
H. J. Tayfield (SA)	14	7	13	6	v New Zealand at Johannesburg	1953-54
C. T. B. Turner (A)	18	11	15	6	v England at Sydney.	1886-87
M. H. N. Walker (A)	16	8	15	6	v Pakistan at Sydney	1972-73
E. R. H. Toshack (A)	2.3	1	2	5	v India at Brisbane	1947-48
H. Ironmonger (A)	7.2	5	6	5	v South Africa at Melbourne	1931-32
T. B. A. May (A)	6.5	3	9	5	v West Indies at Adelaide	1992-93
Pervez Sajjad (P)	12	8	5	4	v New Zealand at Rawalpindi	1964-65
K. Higgs (E)	9	7	5	4	v New Zealand at Christchurch	1965-66
P. H. Edmonds (E)	8	6	6	4	v Pakistan at Lord's	1978
J. C. White (E)	6.3	2	7	4	v Australia at Brisbane	1928-29
J. H. Wardle (E)	5	2	7	4	v Australia at Manchester	1953
R. Appleyard (E)	6	3	7	4	v New Zealand at Auckland	1954-55
R. Benaud (A)	3.4	3	0	3	v India at Delhi	1959-60

MOST WICKETS IN A MATCH

19-90	J. C. Laker	England v Australia at Manchester	1956
17-159	S. F. Barnes	England v South Africa at Johannesburg	1913-14
16-136†	N. D. Hirwani	India v West Indies at Madras	1987-88
16-137†	R. A. L. Massie . . .	Australia v England at Lord's	1972
16-220	M. Muralitharan . . .	Sri Lanka v England at The Oval	1998
15-28	J. Briggs	England v South Africa at Cape Town	1888-89
15-45	G. A. Lohmann . . .	England v South Africa at Port Elizabeth	1895-96
15-99	C. Blythe	England v South Africa at Leeds	1907
15-104	H. Verity	England v Australia at Lord's	1934
15-123	R. J. Hadlee	New Zealand v Australia at Brisbane	1985-86
15-124	W. Rhodes	England v Australia at Melbourne	1903-04
14-90	F. R. Spofforth	Australia v England at The Oval	1882
14-99	A. V. Bedser	England v Australia at Nottingham	1953
14-102	W. Bates	England v Australia at Melbourne	1882-83
14-116	Imran Khan	Pakistan v Sri Lanka at Lahore	1981-82
14-124	J. M. Patel	India v Australia at Kanpur	1959-60
14-144	S. F. Barnes	England v South Africa at Durban	1913-14
14-149	M. A. Holding	West Indies v England at The Oval	1976
14-149	A. Kumble	India v Pakistan at Delhi.	1998-99
14-199	C. V. Grimmett	Australia v South Africa at Adelaide	1931-32

† *On Test debut.*

Note: the best for South Africa is 13-165 by H. J. Tayfield against Australia at Melbourne, 1952-53, and for Zimbabwe 11-255 by A. G. Huckle v New Zealand at Bulawayo, 1997-98.

MOST WICKETS IN A SERIES

	T	R	W	Avge		
S. F. Barnes	4	536	49	10.93	England v South Africa . . .	1913-14
J. C. Laker	5	442	46	9.60	England v Australia	1956
C. V. Grimmett	5	642	44	14.59	Australia v South Africa . .	1935-36
T. M. Alderman	6	893	42	21.26	Australia v England	1981
R. M. Hogg	6	527	41	12.85	Australia v England	1978-79
T. M. Alderman	6	712	41	17.36	Australia v England	1989
Imran Khan.	6	558	40	13.95	Pakistan v India	1982-83
A. V. Bedser	5	682	39	17.48	England v Australia	1953
D. K. Lillee	6	870	39	22.30	Australia v England	1981
M. W. Tate	5	881	38	23.18	England v Australia	1924-25
W. J. Whitty	5	632	37	17.08	Australia v South Africa . .	1910-11
H. J. Tayfield	5	636	37	17.18	South Africa v England . . .	1956-57
A. E. E. Vogler	5	783	36	21.75	South Africa v England . . .	1909-10
A. A. Mailey	5	946	36	26.27	Australia v England	1920-21
G. D. McGrath	6	701	36	19.47	Australia v England	1997
G. A. Lohmann	3	203	35	5.80	England v South Africa . . .	1895-96
B. S. Chandrasekhar	5	662	35	18.91	India v England	1972-73
M. D. Marshall	5	443	35	12.65	West Indies v England . . .	1988

Notes: the most for New Zealand is 33 by R. J. Hadlee against Australia in 1985-86, for Sri Lanka 20 by R. J. Ratnayake against India in 1985-86, and for Zimbabwe 22 by H. H. Streak against Pakistan in 1994-95.

MOST WICKETS IN A CALENDAR YEAR

	T	R	W	Avge	5W/i	10W/m	Year
D. K. Lillee (A).	13	1,781	85	20.95	5	2	1981
A. A. Donald (SA).	14	1,571	80	19.63	7	–	1998
J. Garner (WI).	15	1,604	77	20.83	4	–	1984
Kapil Dev (I)	18	1,739	75	23.18	5	1	1983
Kapil Dev (I)	18	1,720	74	23.24	5	–	1979
M. D. Marshall (WI) . . .	13	1,471	73	20.15	9	1	1984
S. K. Warne (A)	16	1,697	72	23.56	2	–	1993
G. D. McKenzie (A). . . .	14	1,737	71	24.46	4	1	1964
S. K. Warne (A)	10	1,274	70	18.20	6	2	1994

MOST WICKETS IN A CAREER

(Qualification: 100 wickets)

ENGLAND

		T	Balls	R	W	Avge	5W/i	10W/m
1	I. T. Botham	102	21,815	10,878	383	28.40	27	4
2	R. G. D. Willis	90	17,357	8,190	325	25.20	16	—
3	F. S. Trueman	67	15,178	6,625	307	21.57	17	3
4	D. L. Underwood . . .	86	21,862	7,674	297	25.83	17	6
5	J. B. Statham	70	16,056	6,261	252	24.84	9	1
6	A. V. Bedser	51	15,918	5,876	236	24.89	15	5
7	J. A. Snow	49	12,021	5,387	202	26.66	8	1
8	J. C. Laker	46	12,027	4,101	193	21.24	9	3
9	S. F. Barnes	27	7,873	3,106	189	16.43	24	7
10	**A. R. C. Fraser . . . .**	**46**	**10,876**	**4,836**	**177**	**27.32**	**13**	**2**
11	G. A. R. Lock	49	13,147	4,451	174	25.58	9	3

PAKISTAN

		T	Balls	R	W	Avge	5W/i	10W/m
1	**Wasim Akram**	**88**	**19,796**	**8,574**	**378**	**22.68**	**22**	**4**
2	Imran Khan	88	19,458	8,258	362	22.81	23	6
3	**Waqar Younis**	**57**	**11,389**	**6,084**	**277**	**21.96**	**21**	**5**
4	Abdul Qadir	67	17,126	7,742	236	32.80	15	5
5	Sarfraz Nawaz	55	13,927	5,798	177	32.75	4	1
6	Iqbal Qasim	50	13,019	4,807	171	28.11	8	2
7	**Mushtaq Ahmed** . . .	**42**	**10,552**	**4,938**	**169**	**29.21**	**10**	**3**
8	Fazal Mahmood	34	9,834	3,434	139	24.70	13	4
9	Intikhab Alam	47	10,474	4,494	125	35.95	5	2

SRI LANKA

		T	Balls	R	W	Avge	5W/i	10W/m
1	M. Muralitharan	42	13,041	5,464	203	26.91	16	2

ZIMBABWE

		T	Balls	R	W	Avge	5W/i	10W/m
1	**H. H. Streak**	**26**	**5,961**	**2,633**	**106**	**24.83**	**3**	**—**

Bold type denotes those who played Test cricket in 1998-99 and 1999 seasons.

WICKET WITH FIRST BALL IN TEST CRICKET

	Batsman dismissed				
A. Coningham	A. C. MacLaren	A v E	Melbourne	1894-95
W. M. Bradley	F. Laver	E v A	Manchester	1899
E. G. Arnold	V. T. Trumper	E v A	Sydney	1903-04
G. G. Macaulay	G. A. L. Hearne	E v SA	Cape Town	1922-23
M. W. Tate	M. J. Susskind	E v SA	Birmingham	1924
M. Henderson	E. W. Dawson	NZ v E	Christchurch . . .	1929-30
H. D. Smith	E. Paynter	NZ v E	Christchurch . . .	1932-33
T. F. Johnson	W. W. Keeton	WI v E	The Oval	1939
R. Howorth	D. V. Dyer	E v SA	The Oval	1947
Intikhab Alam	C. C. McDonald	P v A	Karachi	1959-60
R. K. Illingworth	P. V. Simmons	E v WI	Nottingham	1991
N. M. Kulkarni	M. S. Atapattu	I v SL	Colombo (RPS) . . .	1997-98

HAT-TRICKS

F. R. Spofforth	Australia v England at Melbourne	1878-79
W. Bates	England v Australia at Melbourne	1882-83
J. Briggs	England v Australia at Sydney	1891-92
G. A. Lohmann	England v South Africa at Port Elizabeth	1895-96
J. T. Hearne	England v Australia at Leeds	1899
H. Trumble	Australia v England at Melbourne	1901-02
H. Trumble	Australia v England at Melbourne	1903-04
T. J. Matthews† . . . . }	Australia v South Africa at Manchester	1912
T. J. Matthews		
M. J. C. Allom‡	England v New Zealand at Christchurch	1929-30
T. W. J. Goddard	England v South Africa at Johannesburg	1938-39
P. J. Loader	England v West Indies at Leeds	1957
L. F. Kline	Australia v South Africa at Cape Town	1957-58

W. W. Hall	West Indies v Pakistan at Lahore	1958-59
G. M. Griffin	South Africa v England at Lord's	1960
L. R. Gibbs	West Indies v Australia at Adelaide	1960-61
P. J. Petherick‡	New Zealand v Pakistan at Lahore	1976-77
C. A. Walsh§	West Indies v Australia at Brisbane	1988-89
M. G. Hughes§	Australia v West Indies at Perth	1988-89
D. W. Fleming‡	Australia v Pakistan at Rawalpindi	1994-95
S. K. Warne	Australia v England at Melbourne	1994-95
D. G. Cork	England v West Indies at Manchester	1995
D. Gough	England v Australia at Sydney	1998-99
Wasim Akram**	Pakistan v Sri Lanka at Lahore	1998-99
Wasim Akram**	Pakistan v Sri Lanka at Dhaka	1998-99

† *T. J. Matthews did the hat-trick in each innings of the same match.*
‡ *On Test debut.*
§ *Not all in the same innings.*
** *Wasim Akram did the hat-trick in successive matches.*

Note: Nuwan Zoysa took a hat-trick with the first three balls of the second over for Sri Lanka v Zimbabwe at Harare in 1999-2000, after the deadline for this section.

FOUR WICKETS IN FIVE BALLS

M. J. C. Allom	England v New Zealand at Christchurch	1929-30
	On debut, in his eighth over: W-WWW	
C. M. Old	England v Pakistan at Birmingham	1978
	Sequence interrupted by a no-ball: WW-WW	
Wasim Akram	Pakistan v West Indies at Lahore (*WW-WW*)	1990-91

MOST BALLS BOWLED IN A TEST

S. Ramadhin (West Indies) sent down 774 balls in 129 overs against England at Birmingham, 1957. It was the most delivered by any bowler in a Test, beating H. Verity's 766 for England against South Africa at Durban, 1938-39. In this match Ramadhin also bowled the most balls (588) in any single first-class innings, including Tests.

ALL-ROUND RECORDS
100 RUNS AND FIVE WICKETS IN AN INNINGS

England

A. W. Greig	148	6-164	v West Indies	Bridgetown	1973-74
I. T. Botham	103	5-73	v New Zealand	Christchurch	1977-78
I. T. Botham	108	8-34	v Pakistan	Lord's	1978
I. T. Botham	114	6-58 } 7-48 }	v India	Bombay	1979-80
I. T. Botham	149*	6-95	v Australia	Leeds	1981
I. T. Botham	138	5-59	v New Zealand	Wellington	1983-84

Australia

C. Kelleway	114	5-33	v South Africa	Manchester	1912
J. M. Gregory	100	7-69	v England	Melbourne	1920-21
K. R. Miller	109	6-107	v West Indies	Kingston	1954-55
R. Benaud	100	5-84	v South Africa	Johannesburg	1957-58

South Africa

J. H. Sinclair	106	6-26	v England	Cape Town	1898-99
G. A. Faulkner	123	5-120	v England	Johannesburg	1909-10
J. H. Kallis	110	5-90	v West Indies	Cape Town	1998-99

West Indies

D. St E. Atkinson	219	5-56	v Australia	Bridgetown	1954-55
O. G. Smith	100	5-90	v India	Delhi	1958-59
G. S. Sobers	104	5-63	v India	Kingston	1961-62
G. S. Sobers	174	5-41	v England	Leeds	1966

New Zealand

B. R. Taylor†	105	5-86	v India	Calcutta	1964-65

India

V. Mankad	184	5-196	v England	Lord's	1952
P. R. Umrigar	172*	5-107	v West Indies	Port-of-Spain	1961-62

Pakistan

Mushtaq Mohammad	201	5-49	v New Zealand	Dunedin	1972-73
Mushtaq Mohammad	121	5-28	v West Indies	Port-of-Spain	1976-77
Imran Khan	117	6-98 } 5-82 }	v India	Faisalabad	1982-83
Wasim Akram	123	5-100	v Australia	Adelaide	1989-90

Zimbabwe

P. A. Strang	106*	5-212	v Pakistan	Sheikhupura	1996-97

† *On debut.*

100 RUNS AND FIVE DISMISSALS IN AN INNINGS

D. T. Lindsay	182	6ct	SA v A.	Johannesburg	1966-67
I. D. S. Smith	113*	4ct, 1st	NZ v E.	Auckland.	1983-84
S. A. R. Silva	111	5ct	SL v I	Colombo (PSS).	1985-86

100 RUNS AND TEN WICKETS IN A TEST

A. K. Davidson	44 80	5-135 } 6-87 }	A v WI.	Brisbane	1960-61
I. T. Botham	114	6-58 } 7-48 }	E v I	Bombay	1979-80
Imran Khan	117	6-98 } 5-82 }	P v I	Faisalabad	1982-83

1,000 RUNS AND 100 WICKETS IN A CAREER

	Tests	Runs	Wkts	Tests for Double
England				
T. E. Bailey.	61	2,290	132	47
†I. T. Botham	102	5,200	383	21
J. E. Emburey	64	1,713	147	46
A. W. Greig	58	3,599	141	37
R. Illingworth	61	1,836	122	47
W. Rhodes	58	2,325	127	44
M. W. Tate	39	1,198	155	33
F. J. Titmus	53	1,449	153	40

	Tests	Runs	Wkts	Tests for Double
Australia				
R. Benaud	63	2,201	248	32
A. K. Davidson	44	1,328	186	34
G. Giffen	31	1,238	103	30
M. G. Hughes	53	1,032	212	52
I. W. Johnson.	45	1,000	109	45
R. R. Lindwall.	61	1,502	228	38
K. R. Miller	55	2,958	170	33
M. A. Noble	42	1,997	121	27
S. K. Warne	**71**	**1,378**	**317**	**58**
South Africa				
T. L. Goddard	41	2,516	123	36
S. M. Pollock	**33**	**1,255**	**133**	**26**
West Indies				
C. E. L. Ambrose	**88**	**1,297**	**369**	**69**
M. D. Marshall	81	1,810	376	49
†G. S. Sobers	93	8,032	235	48
New Zealand				
J. G. Bracewell	41	1,001	102	41
C. L. Cairns	**39**	**1,818**	**128**	**33**
R. J. Hadlee	86	3,124	431	28
India				
Kapil Dev	131	5,248	434	25
V. Mankad	44	2,109	162	23
R. J. Shastri	80	3,830	151	44
Pakistan				
Abdul Qadir	67	1,029	236	62
Imran Khan.	88	3,807	362	30
Intikhab Alam	47	1,493	125	41
Sarfraz Nawaz	55	1,045	177	55
Wasim Akram	**88**	**2,270**	**378**	**45**

Bold type denotes those who played Test cricket in 1998-99 and 1999 seasons.

† I. T. Botham (120 catches) and G. S. Sobers (109) are the only players to have achieved the treble of 1,000 runs, 100 wickets and 100 catches.

WICKET-KEEPING RECORDS

MOST DISMISSALS IN AN INNINGS

7 (all ct)	Wasim Bari	Pakistan v New Zealand at Auckland	1978-79
7 (all ct)	R. W. Taylor	England v India at Bombay.	1979-80
7 (all ct)	I. D. S. Smith	New Zealand v Sri Lanka at Hamilton	1990-91
6 (all ct)	A. T. W. Grout	Australia v South Africa at Johannesburg . . .	1957-58
6 (all ct)	D. T. Lindsay.	South Africa v Australia at Johannesburg . . .	1966-67
6 (all ct)	J. T. Murray	England v India at Lord's	1967
6 (5ct, 1st)	S. M. H. Kirmani . . .	India v New Zealand at Christchurch	1975-76
6 (all ct)	R. W. Marsh	Australia v England at Brisbane	1982-83
6 (all ct)	S. A. R. Silva	Sri Lanka v India at Colombo (SSC).	1985-86
6 (all ct)	R. C. Russell	England v Australia at Melbourne.	1990-91
6 (all ct)	R. C. Russell	England v South Africa at Johannesburg . . .	1995-96
6 (all ct)	I. A. Healy	Australia v England at Birmingham	1997
6 (all ct)	A. J. Stewart	England v Australia at Manchester	1997

MOST CATCHES IN A SERIES

15	J. M. Gregory	Australia v England	1920-21
14	G. S. Chappell	Australia v England (6 Tests)	1974-75
13	R. B. Simpson	Australia v South Africa	1957-58
13	R. B. Simpson	Australia v West Indies	1960-61
13	B. C. Lara	West Indies v England (6 Tests)	1997-98

MOST CATCHES IN A CAREER

M. A. Taylor (Australia)	**157**	R. B. Simpson (Australia)	110
A. R. Border (Australia)	156	G. S. Sobers (West Indies)	109
G. S. Chappell (Australia)	122	S. M. Gavaskar (India)	108
I. V. A. Richards (West Indies)	122	**M. E. Waugh (Australia)**	**107**
I. T. Botham (England)	120	**M. Azharuddin (India)**	**105**
M. C. Cowdrey (England)	120	I. M. Chappell (Australia)	105
W. R. Hammond (England)	110	G. A. Gooch (England)	103

The most catches in the field for other countries are South Africa 56 (B. Mitchell); New Zealand **75 (S. P. Fleming)**; Pakistan 93 (Javed Miandad); Sri Lanka 56 (R. S. Mahanama); Zimbabwe **33 (A. D. R. Campbell)**.

Bold type denotes those who played Test cricket in 1998-99 and 1999 seasons.

TEAM RECORDS

HIGHEST INNINGS TOTALS

952-6 dec.	Sri Lanka v India at Colombo (RPS)	1997-98
903-7 dec.	England v Australia at The Oval	1938
849	England v West Indies at Kingston	1929-30
790-3 dec.	West Indies v Pakistan at Kingston	1957-58
758-8 dec.	Australia v West Indies at Kingston	1954-55
729-6 dec.	Australia v England at Lord's	1930
708	Pakistan v England at The Oval	1987
701	Australia v England at The Oval	1934
699-5	Pakistan v India at Lahore	1989-90
695	Australia v England at The Oval	1930
692-8 dec.	West Indies v England at The Oval	1995
687-8 dec.	West Indies v England at The Oval	1976
681-8 dec.	West Indies v England at Port-of-Spain	1953-54
676-7	India v Sri Lanka at Kanpur	1986-87
674-6	Pakistan v India at Faisalabad	1984-85
674	Australia v India at Adelaide	1947-48
671-4	New Zealand v Sri Lanka at Wellington	1990-91
668	Australia v West Indies at Bridgetown	1954-55
660-5 dec.	West Indies v New Zealand at Wellington	1994-95

The highest innings for the countries not mentioned above are:

622-9 dec.	South Africa v Australia at Durban	1969-70
544-4 dec.	Zimbabwe v Pakistan at Harare	1994-95

HIGHEST FOURTH-INNINGS TOTALS

To win

406-4	India (needing 403) v West Indies at Port-of-Spain	1975-76
404-3	Australia (needing 404) v England at Leeds.	1948
362-7	Australia (needing 359) v West Indies at Georgetown	1977-78
348-5	West Indies (needing 345) v New Zealand at Auckland	1968-69
344-1	West Indies (needing 342) v England at Lord's	1984

Note: Australia scored 369-6 (needing 369) to beat Pakistan at Hobart in 1999-2000, after the deadline for this section.

To tie

347	India v Australia at Madras	1986-87

To draw

654-5	England (needing 696 to win) v South Africa at Durban	1938-39
429-8	India (needing 438 to win) v England at The Oval	1979
423-7	South Africa (needing 451 to win) v England at The Oval	1947
408-5	West Indies (needing 836 to win) v England at Kingston	1929-30

To lose

445	India (lost by 47 runs) v Australia at Adelaide	1977-78
440	New Zealand (lost by 38 runs) v England at Nottingham	1973
417	England (lost by 45 runs) v Australia at Melbourne	1976-77
411	England (lost by 193 runs) v Australia at Sydney	1924-25
402	Australia (lost by 103 runs) v England at Manchester.	1981

MOST RUNS IN A DAY (BOTH SIDES)

588	England (398-6), India (190-0) at Manchester (2nd day)	1936
522	England (503-2), South Africa (19-0) at Lord's (2nd day)	1924
508	England (221-2), South Africa (287-6) at The Oval (3rd day)	1935

MOST RUNS IN A DAY (ONE SIDE)

503	England (503-2) v South Africa at Lord's (2nd day).	1924
494	Australia (494-6) v South Africa at Sydney (1st day)	1910-11
475	Australia (475-2) v England at The Oval (1st day)	1934
471	England (471-8) v India at The Oval (1st day)	1936
458	Australia (458-3) v England at Leeds (1st day)	1930
455	Australia (455-1) v England at Leeds (2nd day)	1934

MOST WICKETS IN A DAY

27	England (18-3 to 53 all out and 62) v Australia (60) at Lord's (2nd day)	1888
25	Australia (112 and 48-5) v England (61) at Melbourne (1st day)	1901-02

HIGHEST MATCH AGGREGATES

Runs	Wkts			Days played
1,981	35	South Africa v England at Durban	1938-39	10†
1,815	34	West Indies v England at Kingston	1929-30	9‡
1,764	39	Australia v West Indies at Adelaide	1968-69	5
1,753	40	Australia v England at Adelaide	1920-21	6
1,723	31	England v Australia at Leeds.	1948	5
1,661	36	West Indies v Australia at Bridgetown	1954-55	6

† *No play on one day.*   ‡ *No play on two days.*

SUMMARY OF ALL TEST MATCHES

To September 8, 1999

	Opponents	Tests	E	A	SA	WI	NZ	I	P	SL	Z	Tied	Drawn
England	Australia	296	93	117	–	–	–	–	–	–	–	–	86
	South Africa	115	49	–	21	–	–	–	–	–	–	–	45
	West Indies	121	28	–	–	51	–	–	–	–	–	–	42
	New Zealand	82	37	–	–	–	6	–	–	–	–	–	39
	India	84	32	–	–	–	–	14	–	–	–	–	38
	Pakistan	55	14	–	–	–	–	–	9	–	–	–	32
	Sri Lanka	6	3	–	–	–	–	–	–	2	–	–	1
	Zimbabwe	2	0	–	–	–	–	–	–	–	0	–	2
Australia	South Africa	65	–	34	14	–	–	–	–	–	–	–	17
	West Indies	90	–	37	–	31	–	–	–	–	–	1	21
	New Zealand	35	–	15	–	–	7	–	–	–	–	–	13
	India	54	–	25	–	–	–	11	–	–	–	1	17
	Pakistan	43	–	15	–	–	–	–	11	–	–	–	17
	Sri Lanka	10	–	7	–	–	–	–	–	0	–	–	3
South Africa	West Indies	6	–	–	5	1	–	–	–	–	–	–	0
	New Zealand	24	–	–	13	–	3	–	–	–	–	–	8
	India	10	–	–	4	–	–	2	–	–	–	–	4
	Pakistan	7	–	–	3	–	–	–	1	–	–	–	3
	Sri Lanka	5	–	–	3	–	–	–	–	0	–	–	2
	Zimbabwe	1	–	–	1	–	–	–	–	–	0	–	0
West Indies	New Zealand	28	–	–	–	10	4	–	–	–	–	–	14
	India	70	–	–	–	28	–	7	–	–	–	–	35
	Pakistan	34	–	–	–	12	–	–	10	–	–	–	12
	Sri Lanka	3	–	–	–	1	–	–	–	0	–	–	2
New Zealand	India	37	–	–	–	–	7	13	–	–	–	–	17
	Pakistan	39	–	–	–	–	5	–	18	–	–	–	16
	Sri Lanka	18	–	–	–	–	7	–	–	4	–	–	7
	Zimbabwe	8	–	–	–	–	3	–	–	–	0	–	5
India	Pakistan	47	–	–	–	–	–	5	9	–	–	–	33
	Sri Lanka	20	–	–	–	–	–	7	–	1	–	–	12
	Zimbabwe	3	–	–	–	–	–	1	–	–	1	–	1
Pakistan	Sri Lanka	21	–	–	–	–	–	–	10	3	–	–	8
	Zimbabwe	12	–	–	–	–	–	–	6	–	2	–	4
Sri Lanka	Zimbabwe	7	–	–	–	–	–	–	–	4	0	–	3
		1,458	256	250	64	134	42	60	74	14	3	2	559

	Tests	Won	Lost	Drawn	Tied	Toss Won
England	761	256	220	285	–	371
Australia	593	250	167	174	2	300
South Africa	233	64	90	79	–	111
West Indies	352	134	91	126	1	182
New Zealand	271	42	110	119	–	137
India	325	60	107	157	1	168
Pakistan	258	74	59	125	–	125
Sri Lanka	90	14	38	38	–	44
Zimbabwe	33	3	15	15	–	20

ENGLAND v AUSTRALIA

Season	England	Australia	T	E	A	D
1876-77	James Lillywhite	D. W. Gregory	2	1	1	0
1878-79	Lord Harris	D. W. Gregory	1	0	1	0
1880	Lord Harris	W. L. Murdoch	1	1	0	0
1881-82	A. Shaw	W. L. Murdoch	4	0	2	2
1882	A. N. Hornby	W. L. Murdoch	1	0	1	0

THE ASHES

Season	England	Australia	T	E	A	D	Held by
1882-83	Hon. Ivo Bligh	W. L. Murdoch	4*	2	2	0	E
1884	Lord Harris[1]	W. L. Murdoch	3	1	0	2	E
1884-85	A. Shrewsbury	T. P. Horan[2]	5	3	2	0	E
1886	A. G. Steel	H. J. H. Scott	3	3	0	0	E
1886-87	A. Shrewsbury	P. S. McDonnell	2	2	0	0	E
1887-88	W. W. Read	P. S. McDonnell	1	1	0	0	E
1888	W. G. Grace[3]	P. S. McDonnell	3	2	1	0	E
1890†	W. G. Grace	W. L. Murdoch	2	2	0	0	E
1891-92	W. G. Grace	J. McC. Blackham	3	1	2	0	A
1893	W. G. Grace[4]	J. McC. Blackham	3	1	0	2	E
1894-95	A. E. Stoddart	G. Giffen[5]	5	3	2	0	E
1896	W. G. Grace	G. H. S. Trott	3	2	1	0	E
1897-98	A. E. Stoddart[6]	G. H. S. Trott	5	1	4	0	A
1899	A. C. MacLaren[7]	J. Darling	5	0	1	4	A
1901-02	A. C. MacLaren	J. Darling[8]	5	1	4	0	A
1902	A. C. MacLaren	J. Darling	5	1	2	2	A
1903-04	P. F. Warner	M. A. Noble	5	3	2	0	E
1905	Hon. F. S. Jackson	J. Darling	5	2	0	3	E
1907-08	A. O. Jones[9]	M. A. Noble	5	1	4	0	A
1909	A. C. MacLaren	M. A. Noble	5	1	2	2	A
1911-12	J. W. H. T. Douglas	C. Hill	5	4	1	0	E
1912	C. B. Fry	S. E. Gregory	3	1	0	2	E
1920-21	J. W. H. T. Douglas	W. W. Armstrong	5	0	5	0	A
1921	Hon. L. H. Tennyson[10]	W. W. Armstrong	5	0	3	2	A
1924-25	A. E. R. Gilligan	H. L. Collins	5	1	4	0	A
1926	A. W. Carr[11]	H. L. Collins[12]	5	1	0	4	E
1928-29	A. P. F. Chapman[13]	J. Ryder	5	4	1	0	E
1930	A. P. F. Chapman[14]	W. M. Woodfull	5	1	2	2	A
1932-33	D. R. Jardine	W. M. Woodfull	5	4	1	0	E
1934	R. E. S. Wyatt[15]	W. M. Woodfull	5	1	2	2	A
1936-37	G. O. B. Allen	D. G. Bradman	5	2	3	0	A
1938†	W. R. Hammond	D. G. Bradman	4	1	1	2	A
1946-47	W. R. Hammond[16]	D. G. Bradman	5	0	3	2	A
1948	N. W. D. Yardley	D. G. Bradman	5	0	4	1	A
1950-51	F. R. Brown	A. L. Hassett	5	1	4	0	A
1953	L. Hutton	A. L. Hassett	5	1	0	4	E
1954-55	L. Hutton	I. W. Johnson[17]	5	3	1	1	E
1956	P. B. H. May	I. W. Johnson	5	2	1	2	E
1958-59	P. B. H. May	R. Benaud	5	0	4	1	A
1961	P. B. H. May[18]	R. Benaud[19]	5	1	2	2	A
1962-63	E. R. Dexter	R. Benaud	5	1	1	3	A
1964	E. R. Dexter	R. B. Simpson	5	0	1	4	A
1965-66	M. J. K. Smith	R. B. Simpson[20]	5	1	1	3	A
1968	M. C. Cowdrey[21]	W. M. Lawry[22]	5	1	1	3	A
1970-71†	R. Illingworth	W. M. Lawry[23]	6	2	0	4	E
1972	R. Illingworth	I. M. Chappell	5	2	2	1	E
1974-75	M. H. Denness[24]	I. M. Chappell	6	1	4	1	A
1975	A. W. Greig[25]	I. M. Chappell	4	0	1	3	A
1976-77‡	A. W. Greig	G. S. Chappell	1	0	1	0	—
1977	J. M. Brearley	G. S. Chappell	5	3	0	2	E
1978-79	J. M. Brearley	G. N. Yallop	6	5	1	0	E
1979-80‡	J. M. Brearley	G. S. Chappell	3	0	3	0	—
1980‡	I. T. Botham	G. S. Chappell	1	0	0	1	—
1981	J. M. Brearley[26]	K. J. Hughes	6	3	1	2	E

11-228 (6-130, 5-98)†	M. W. Tate, Sydney.	1924-25
11-88 (5-58, 6-30)	F. S. Trueman, Leeds	1961
11-93 (7-66, 4-27)	P. C. R. Tufnell, The Oval	1997
10-130 (4-45, 6-85)	F. H. Tyson, Sydney	1954-55
10-82 (4-37, 6-45)	D. L. Underwood, Leeds	1972
11-215 (7-113, 4-102)	D. L. Underwood, Adelaide	1974-75
15-104 (7-61, 8-43)	H. Verity, Lord's	1934
10-57 (6-41, 4-16)	W. Voce, Brisbane	1936-37
13-256 (5-130, 8-126)	J. C. White, Adelaide	1928-29
10-49 (5-29, 5-20)	F. E. Woolley, The Oval.	1912

For Australia (40)

	T. M. Alderman, Leeds	1989
10-151 (5-107, 5-44)	L. O'B. Fleetwood-Smith, Adelaide	1936-37
10-239 (4-129, 6-110)	G. Giffen, Sydney.	1891-92
10-160 (4-88, 6-72)	C. V. Grimmett, Sydney.	1924-25
11-82 (5-45, 6-37)†	C. V. Grimmett, Nottingham	1930
10-201 (5-107, 5-94)	R. M. Hogg, Perth	1978-79
10-122 (5-65, 5-57)	R. M. Hogg, Melbourne.	1978-79
10-66 (5-30, 5-36)	H. V. Hordern, Sydney.	1911-12
12-175 (5-85, 7-90)†	H. V. Hordern, Sydney.	1911-12
10-161 (5-95, 5-66)	E. Jones, Lord's	1899
10-164 (7-88, 3-76)	G. F. Lawson, Brisbane	1982-83
11-134 (6-47, 5-87)	D. K. Lillee, The Oval	1972
10-181 (5-58, 5-123)	D. K. Lillee, Melbourne.	1976-77
11-165 (6-26, 5-139)	D. K. Lillee, Melbourne.	1979-80
11-138 (6-60, 5-78)	D. K. Lillee, The Oval	1981
11-159 (7-89, 4-70)	C. G. Macartney, Leeds	1909
11-85 (7-58, 4-27)	C. J. McDermott, Perth	1990-91
11-157 (8-97, 3-60)	S. C. G. MacGill, Sydney	1998-99
12-107 (5-57, 7-50)	A. A. Mailey, Adelaide	1920-21
10-302 (5-160, 5-142)	A. A. Mailey, Melbourne.	1920-21
13-236 (4-115, 9-121)	R. A. L. Massie, Lord's	1972
16-137 (8-84, 8-53)†	K. R. Miller, Lord's	1956
10-152 (5-72, 5-80)	M. A. Noble, Melbourne.	1901-02
13-77 (7-17, 6-60)	M. A. Noble, Sheffield.	1902
11-103 (5-51, 6-52)	W. J. O'Reilly, Melbourne	1932-33
10-129 (5-63, 5-66)	W. J. O'Reilly, Nottingham	1934
11-129 (4-75, 7-54)	W. J. O'Reilly, Leeds	1938
10-122 (5-66, 5-56)	G. E. Palmer, Sydney	1881-82
11-165 (7-68, 4-97)	G. E. Palmer, Melbourne.	1882-83
10-126 (7-65, 3-61)	B. A. Reid, Melbourne	1990-91
13-148 (6-97, 7-51)	F. R. Spofforth, Melbourne.	1878-79
13-110 (6-48, 7-62)	F. R. Spofforth, The Oval	1882
14-90 (7-46, 7-44)	F. R. Spofforth, Sydney	1882-83
11-117 (4-73, 7-44)	F. R. Spofforth, Sydney	1884-85
10-144 (4-54, 6-90)	H. Trumble, The Oval	1896
12-89 (6-59, 6-30)	H. Trumble, Manchester.	1902
10-128 (4-75, 6-53)	H. Trumble, The Oval	1902
12-173 (8-65, 4-108)	C. T. B. Turner, Sydney	1887-88
12-87 (5-44, 7-43)	C. T. B. Turner, Lord's	1888
10-63 (5-27, 5-36)	S. K. Warne, Brisbane	1994-95
11-110 (3-39, 8-71)		

† *Signifies ten wickets or more on first appearance in England–Australia Tests.*

Note: J. Briggs, J. C. Laker, T. Richardson in 1896, R. M. Hogg, A. A. Mailey, H. Trumble and
C. T. B. Turner took ten wickets or more in successive Tests. J. Briggs was omitted, however
from the England team for the first Test match in 1893.

MOST WICKETS IN A SERIES

England in England	46 (average 9.60)	J. C. Laker	1956
England in Australia	38 (average 23.18)	M. W. Tate	1924-25
Australia in England	42 (average 21.26)	T. M. Alderman (6 Tests) .	1981
Australia in Australia	41 (average 12.85)	R. M. Hogg (6 Tests)	1978-79

WICKET-KEEPING – MOST DISMISSALS

	M	Ct	St	Total
†R. W. Marsh (Australia)	42	141	7	148
I. A. Healy (Australia)	33	123	12	135
A. P. E. Knott (England)	34	97	8	105
†W. A. Oldfield (Australia)	38	59	31	90
A. A. Lilley (England)	32	65	19	84
A. T. W. Grout (Australia)	22	69	7	76
T. G. Evans (England)	31	64	12	76

† The number of catches by R. W. Marsh (141) and stumpings by W. A. Oldfield (31) are respective records in England–Australia Tests.

SCORERS OF OVER 2,000 RUNS

	T	I	NO	R	HS	Avge
D. G. Bradman	37	63	7	5,028	334	89.78
J. B. Hobbs	41	71	4	3,636	187	54.26
A. R. Border	47	82	19	3,548	200*	56.31
D. I. Gower	42	77	4	3,269	215	44.78
G. Boycott	38	71	9	2,945	191	47.50
W. R. Hammond	33	58	3	2,852	251	51.85
H. Sutcliffe	27	46	5	2,741	194	66.85
C. Hill	41	76	1	2,660	188	35.46
J. H. Edrich	32	57	3	2,644	175	48.96
G. A. Gooch	42	79	0	2,632	196	33.31
G. S. Chappell	35	65	8	2,619	144	45.94
S. R. Waugh	37	60	16	2,574	177*	58.50
M. A. Taylor	33	61	2	2,496	219	42.30
M. C. Cowdrey	43	75	4	2,433	113	34.26
L. Hutton	27	49	6	2,428	364	56.46
R. N. Harvey	37	68	5	2,416	167	38.34
V. T. Trumper	40	74	5	2,263	185*	32.79
D. C. Boon	31	57	8	2,237	184	45.65
W. M. Lawry	29	51	5	2,233	166	48.54
S. E. Gregory	52	92	7	2,193	201	25.80
W. W. Armstrong	42	71	9	2,172	158	35.03
I. M. Chappell	30	56	4	2,138	192	41.11
K. F. Barrington	23	39	6	2,111	256	63.96
A. R. Morris	24	43	2	2,080	206	50.73

For South Africa (72)

E. J. Barlow (1)
138   Cape Town. .   1964-65
K. C. Bland (2)
144*   Johannesburg   1964-65
127   The Oval . . .   1965
M. V. Boucher (1)
108   Durban   1999-00
R. H. Catterall (3)
120   Birmingham .   1924
120   Lord's   1924
119   Durban   1927-28
W. J. Cronje (1)
126   Nottingham .   1998
D. J. Cullinan (2)
108   Johannesburg   1999-00
120   Cape Town. .   1999-00
E. L. Dalton (2)
117   The Oval . . .   1935
102   Johannesburg   1938-39
W. R. Endean (1)
116*   Leeds   1955
G. A. Faulkner (1)
123   Johannesburg   1909-10
T. L. Goddard (1)
112   Johannesburg   1964-65
C. M. H. Hathorn (1)
102   Johannesburg   1905-06
J. H. Kallis (2)
132   Manchester. .   1998
105   Cape Town. .   1999-00
G. Kirsten (3)
110   Johannesburg   1995-96
210   Manchester. .   1998
275   Durban   1999-00
P. N. Kirsten (1)
104   Leeds   1994

L. Klusener (1)
174   Port Elizabeth   1999-00
D. J. McGlew (2)
104*   Manchester. .   1955
133   Leeds   1955
R. A. McLean (3)
142   Lord's   1955
100   Durban   1956-57
109   Manchester. .   1960
B. M. McMillan (1)
100*   Johannesburg   1995-96
A. Melville (4)
103   Durban   1938-39
189 }   Nottingham .   1947
104* }
117   Lord's   1947
B. Mitchell (7)
123   Cape Town. .   1930-31
164*   Lord's   1935
128   The Oval . . .   1935
109   Durban   1938-39
120 }
189 }   The Oval . . .   1947
120   Cape Town. .   1948-49
A. D. Nourse (7)
120   Cape Town. .   1938-39
103   Durban   1938-39
149   Nottingham .   1947
115   Manchester. .   1947
112   Cape Town. .   1948-49
129*   Johannesburg   1948-49
208   Nottingham .   1951
H. G. Owen-Smith (1)
129   Leeds   1929
A. J. Pithey (1)
154   Cape Town. .   1964-65
R. G. Pollock (2)
137   Port Elizabeth   1964-65

125   Nottingham .   1965
J. N. Rhodes (1)
117   Lord's   1998
E. A. B. Rowan (2)
156*   Johannesburg   1948-49
236   Leeds   1951
P. W. Sherwell (1)
115   Lord's   1907
I. J. Siedle (1)
141   Cape Town. .   1930-31
J. H. Sinclair (1)
106   Cape Town. .   1898-99
H. W. Taylor (7)
109   Durban   1913-14
176   Johannesburg   1922-23
101   Johannesburg   1922-23
102   Durban   1922-23
101   Johannesburg   1927-28
121   The Oval . . .   1929
117   Cape Town. .   1930-31
P. G. V. van der Bijl (1)
125   Durban   1938-39
K. G. Viljoen (1)
124   Manchester. .   1935
W. W. Wade (1)
125   Port Elizabeth   1948-49
J. H. B. Waite (1)
113   Manchester. .   1955
K. C. Wessels (1)
105†   Lord's   1994
G. C. White (2)
147   Johannesburg   1905-06
118   Durban   1909-10
P. L. Winslow (1)
108   Manchester. .   1955

† Signifies hundred on first appearance in England–South Africa Tests. K. C. Wessels had earlier scored 162 on his Test debut for Australia against England at Brisbane in 1982-83.

‡ P. F. Warner carried his bat through the second innings.

Notes: A. Melville's four hundreds were made in successive Test innings.

     H. Wood scored the only hundred of his career in a Test match.

RECORD PARTNERSHIPS FOR EACH WICKET

For England

359	for 1st†	L. Hutton and C. Washbrook at Johannesburg	1948-49
280	for 2nd	P. A. Gibb and W. J. Edrich at Durban	1938-39
370	for 3rd†	W. J. Edrich and D. C. S. Compton at Lord's	1947
197	for 4th	W. R. Hammond and L. E. G. Ames at Cape Town	1938-39
237	for 5th	D. C. S. Compton and N. W. D. Yardley at Nottingham	1947
206*	for 6th	K. F. Barrington and J. M. Parks at Durban	1964-65
115	for 7th	J. W. H. T. Douglas and M. C. Bird at Durban	1913-14
154	for 8th	C. W. Wright and H. R. Bromley-Davenport at Johannesburg	1895-96
71	for 9th	H. Wood and J. T. Hearne at Cape Town	1891-92
92	for 10th	A. C. Russell and A. E. R. Gilligan at Durban	1922-23

For South Africa

260	for 1st†	B. Mitchell and I. J. Siedle at Cape Town	1930-31
238	for 2nd	G. Kirsten and J. H. Kallis at Manchester	1998
319	for 3rd	A. Melville and A. D. Nourse at Nottingham	1947
214	for 4th†	H. W. Taylor and H. G. Deane at The Oval	1929
192	for 5th†	G. Kirsten and M. V. Boucher at Durban	1999-00
171	for 6th	J. H. B. Waite and P. L. Winslow at Manchester	1955
123	for 7th	H. G. Deane and E. P. Nupen at Durban	1927-28
119	for 8th	L. Klusener and M. V. Boucher at Port Elizabeth	1999-00
137	for 9th	E. L. Dalton and A. B. C. Langton at The Oval	1935
103	for 10th†	H. G. Owen-Smith and A. J. Bell at Leeds	1929

† *Denotes record partnership against all countries.*

MOST RUNS IN A SERIES

England in England	753 (average 94.12)	D. C. S. Compton . . .	1947
England in South Africa	653 (average 81.62)	E. Paynter	1938-39
South Africa in England	621 (average 69.00)	A. D. Nourse	1947
South Africa in South Africa . . .	582 (average 64.66)	H. W. Taylor	1922-23

TEN WICKETS OR MORE IN A MATCH

For England (25)

11-110 (5-25, 6-85)†	S. F. Barnes, Lord's	1912
10-115 (6-52, 4-63)	S. F. Barnes, Leeds	1912
13-57 (5-28, 8-29)	S. F. Barnes, The Oval	1912
10-105 (5-57, 5-48)	S. F. Barnes, Durban	1913-14
17-159 (8-56, 9-103)	S. F. Barnes, Johannesburg	1913-14
14-144 (7-56, 7-88)	S. F. Barnes, Durban	1913-14
12-112 (7-58, 5-54)	A. V. Bedser, Manchester	1951
11-118 (6-68, 5-50)	C. Blythe, Cape Town	1905-06
15-99 (8-59, 7-40)	C. Blythe, Leeds	1907
10-104 (7-46, 3-58)	C. Blythe, Cape Town	1909-10
15-28 (7-17, 8-11)	J. Briggs, Cape Town	1888-89
13-91 (6-54, 7-37)†	J. J. Ferris, Cape Town	1891-92
10-122 (5-60, 5-62)	A. R. C. Fraser, Nottingham	1998
10-207 (7-115, 3-92)	A. P. Freeman, Leeds	1929
12-171 (7-71, 5-100)	A. P. Freeman, Manchester	1929
12-130 (7-70, 5-60)	G. Geary, Johannesburg	1927-28
11-90 (6-7, 5-83)	A. E. R. Gilligan, Birmingham	1924
10-119 (4-64, 6-55)	J. C. Laker, The Oval	1951
15-45 (7-38, 8-7)†	G. A. Lohmann, Port Elizabeth	1895-96
12-71 (9-28, 3-43)	G. A. Lohmann, Johannesburg	1895-96
10-138 (1-81, 9-57)	D. E. Malcolm, The Oval	1994
11-97 (6-63, 5-34)	J. B. Statham, Lord's	1960
12-101 (7-52, 5-49)	R. Tattersall, Lord's	1951
12-89 (5-53, 7-36)	J. H. Wardle, Cape Town	1956-57
10-175 (5-95, 5-80)	D. V. P. Wright, Lord's	1947

For South Africa (7)

11-127 (6-53, 5-74)	A. A. Donald, Johannesburg	1999-00
11-112 (4-49, 7-63)†	A. E. Hall, Cape Town	1922-23
11-150 (5-63, 6-87)	E. P. Nupen, Johannesburg	1930-31
10-87 (5-53, 5-34)	P. M. Pollock, Nottingham	1965

R. Illingworth (1)
113   Lord's   1969
D. R. Jardine (1)
127   Manchester. .   1933
A. P. E. Knott (1)
116   Leeds   1976
A. J. Lamb (6)
110   Lord's   1984
100   Leeds   1984
100*   Manchester .   1984
113   Lord's   1988
132   Kingston . . .   1989-90
119   Bridgetown .   1989-90
P. B. H. May (3)
135   Port-of-Spain   1953-54
285*   Birmingham .   1957
104   Nottingham . .   1957
C. Milburn (1)
126*   Lord's   1966
J. T. Murray (1)
112†   The Oval . . .   1966

J. M. Parks (1)
101*†   Port-of-Spain   1959-60
W. Place (1)
107   Kingston . . .   1947-48
M. R. Ramprakash (1)
154   Bridgetown .   1997-98
P. E. Richardson (2)
126   Nottingham . .   1957
107   The Oval . . .   1957
J. D. Robertson (1)
133   Port-of-Spain   1947-48
A. Sandham (2)
152†   Bridgetown .   1929-30
325   Kingston . . .   1929-30
M. J. K. Smith (1)
108   Port-of-Spain   1959-60
R. A. Smith (3)
148*   Lord's   1991
109   The Oval . . .   1991
175   St John's . . .   1993-94

D. S. Steele (1)
106†   Nottingham .   1976
A. J. Stewart (2)
118 ⎫
143 ⎭   Bridgetown .   1993-94
R. Subba Row (1)
100†   Georgetown .   1959-60
G. P. Thorpe (1)
103   Bridgetown .   1997-98
E. Tyldesley (1)
122†   Kingston . . .   1928
C. Washbrook (2)
114†   Lord's   1950
102   Nottingham . .   1950
W. Watson (1)
116†   Kingston . . .   1953-54
P. Willey (2)
100*·   The Oval . . .   1980
102*   St John's . . .   1980-81

For West Indies (110)

J. C. Adams (1)
137   Georgetown .   1993-94
K. L. T. Arthurton (1)
126   Kingston . . .   1993-94
I. Barrow (1)
105   Manchester. .   1933
C. A. Best (1)
164   Bridgetown .   1989-90
B. F. Butcher (2)
133   Lord's   1963
209*   Nottingham .   1966
G. M. Carew (1)
107   Port-of-Spain   1947-48
S. Chanderpaul (1)
118   Georgetown .   1997-98
C. A. Davis (1)
103   Lord's   1969
P. J. L. Dujon (1)
101   Manchester. .   1984
R. C. Fredericks (3)
150   Birmingham .   1973
138   Lord's   1976
109   Leeds   1976
A. G. Ganteaume (1)
112†   Port-of-Spain   1947-48
H. A. Gomes (2)
143   Birmingham .   1984
104*   Leeds   1984
C. G. Greenidge (7)
134 ⎫
101 ⎭   Manchester. .   1976
115   Leeds   1976
214*   Lord's   1984
223   Manchester. .   1984
103   Lord's   1988
149   St John's . . .   1989-90

D. L. Haynes (5)
184   Lord's   1980
125   The Oval . . .   1984
131   St John's . . .   1985-86
109   Bridgetown .   1989-90
167   St John's . . .   1989-90
G. A. Headley (8)
176†   Bridgetown .   1929-30
114 ⎫
112 ⎭   Georgetown .   1929-30
223   Kingston . . .   1929-30
169*   Manchester . .   1933
270*   Kingston . . .   1934-35
106 ⎫
107 ⎭   Lord's   1939
D. A. J. Holford (1)
105*   Lord's   1966
J. K. Holt (1)
166   Bridgetown .   1953-54
C. L. Hooper (3)
111   Lord's   1991
127   The Oval . . .   1995
108*   St John's . . .   1997-98
C. C. Hunte (3)
182   Manchester. .   1963
108*   The Oval . . .   1963
135   Manchester. .   1966
B. D. Julien (1)
121   Lord's   1973
A. I. Kallicharran (2)
158   Port-of-Spain   1973-74
119   Bridgetown .   1973-74
R. B. Kanhai (5)
110   Port-of-Spain   1959-60
104   The Oval . . .   1966
153   Port-of-Spain   1967-68

150   Georgetown .   1967-68
157   Lord's   1973
C. B. Lambert (1)
104   St John's . . .   1997-98
B. C. Lara (5)
167   Georgetown .   1993-94
375   St John's . . .   1993-94
145   Manchester. .   1995
152   Nottingham .   1995
179   The Oval . . .   1995
C. H. Lloyd (5)
118†   Port-of-Spain   1967-68
113*   Bridgetown .   1967-68
132   The Oval . . .   1973
101   Manchester. .   1980
100   Bridgetown .   1980-81
S. M. Nurse (2)
137   Leeds   1966
136   Port-of-Spain   1967-68
A. F. Rae (2)
106   Lord's   1950
109   The Oval . . .   1950
I. V. A. Richards (8)
232†   Nottingham .   1976
135   Manchester. .   1976
291   The Oval . . .   1976
145   Lord's   1980
182*   Bridgetown .   1980-81
114   St John's . . .   1980-81
117   Birmingham .   1984
110*   St John's . . .   1985-86
R. B. Richardson (4)
102   Port-of-Spain   1985-86
160   Bridgetown .   1985-86
104   Birmingham .   1991
121   The Oval . . .   1991

C. A. Roach (2)						E. D. Weekes (3)		
122	Bridgetown	1929-30	145	Georgetown	1959-60	141	Kingston	1947-48
209	Georgetown	1929-30	102	Leeds	1963	129	Nottingham	1950
L. G. Rowe (3)			161	Manchester	1966	206	Port-of-Spain	1953-54
120	Kingston	1973-74	163*	Lord's	1966	**K. H. Weekes** (1)		
302	Bridgetown	1973-74	174	Leeds	1966	137	The Oval	1939
123	Port-of-Spain	1973-74	113*	Kingston	1967-68	**F. M. M. Worrell** (6)		
O. G. Smith (2)			152	Georgetown	1967-68	131*	Georgetown	1947-48
161†	Birmingham	1957	150*	Lord's	1973	261	Nottingham	1950
168	Nottingham	1957	**C. L. Walcott** (4)			138	The Oval	1950
G. S. Sobers (10)			220	Bridgetown	1953-54	167	Port-of-Spain	1953-54
226	Bridgetown	1959-60	124	Port-of-Spain	1953-54	191*‡	Nottingham	1957
147	Kingston	1959-60	116	Kingston	1953-54	197*	Bridgetown	1959-60

† *Signifies hundred on first appearance in England–West Indies Tests. S. C. Griffith provides the only instance for England of a player hitting his maiden century in first-class cricket in his first Test.*

‡ *Carried his bat.*

RECORD PARTNERSHIPS FOR EACH WICKET

For England

212	for 1st	C. Washbrook and R. T. Simpson at Nottingham	1950
266	for 2nd	P. E. Richardson and T. W. Graveney at Nottingham	1957
303	for 3rd	M. A. Atherton and R. A. Smith at St John's	1993-94
411	for 4th†	P. B. H. May and M. C. Cowdrey at Birmingham	1957
150	for 5th	A. J. Stewart and G. P. Thorpe at Bridgetown	1993-94
205	for 6th	M. R. Ramprakash and G. P. Thorpe at Bridgetown	1997-98
197	for 7th†	M. J. K. Smith and J. M. Parks at Port-of-Spain	1959-60
217	for 8th	T. W. Graveney and J. T. Murray at The Oval	1966
109	for 9th	G. A. R. Lock and P. I. Pocock at Georgetown	1967-68
128	for 10th	K. Higgs and J. A. Snow at The Oval	1966

For West Indies

298	for 1st†	C. G. Greenidge and D. L. Haynes at St John's	1989-90
287*	for 2nd	C. G. Greenidge and H. A. Gomes at Lord's	1984
338	for 3rd†	E. D. Weekes and F. M. M. Worrell at Port-of-Spain	1953-54
399	for 4th†	G. S. Sobers and F. M. M. Worrell at Bridgetown	1959-60
265	for 5th	S. M. Nurse and G. S. Sobers at Leeds	1966
274*	for 6th†	G. S. Sobers and D. A. J. Holford at Lord's	1966
155*	for 7th‡	G. S. Sobers and B. D. Julien at Lord's	1973
99	for 8th	C. A. McWatt and J. K. Holt at Georgetown	1953-54
150	for 9th	E. A. E. Baptiste and M. A. Holding at Birmingham	1984
70	for 10th	I. R. Bishop and D. Ramnarine at Georgetown	1997-98

† *Denotes record partnership against all countries.*

‡ *231 runs were added for this wicket in two separate partnerships: G. S. Sobers retired ill and was replaced by K. D. Boyce when 155 had been added.*

TEN WICKETS OR MORE IN A MATCH

For England (12)

11-98 (7-44, 4-54)	T. E. Bailey, Lord's	1957
11-110 (8-53, 3-57)	A. R. C. Fraser, Port-of-Spain	1997-98
10-93 (5-54, 5-39)	A. P. Freeman, Manchester	1928
13-156 (8-86, 5-70)	A. W. Greig, Port-of-Spain	1973-74

11-48 (5-28, 6-20)	G. A. R. Lock, The Oval	1957
10-137 (4-60, 6-77)	D. E. Malcolm, Port-of-Spain	1989-90
11-96 (5-37, 6-59)†	C. S. Marriott, The Oval	1933
10-142 (4-82, 6-60)	J. A. Snow, Georgetown	1967-68
10-195 (5-105, 5-90)†	G. T. S. Stevens, Bridgetown	1929-30
11-152 (5-100, 5-52)	F. S. Trueman, Lord's	1963
12-119 (5-75, 7-44)	F. S. Trueman, Birmingham	1963
11-149 (4-79, 7-70)	W. Voce, Port-of-Spain	1929-30

For West Indies (14)

10-127 (2-82, 8-45)	C. E. L. Ambrose, Bridgetown	1989-90
11-84 (5-60, 6-24)	C. E. L. Ambrose, Port-of-Spain	1993-94
10-174 (5-105, 5-69)	K. C. G. Benjamin, Nottingham	1995
11-147 (5-70, 6-77)†	K. D. Boyce, The Oval	1973
11-229 (5-137, 6-92)	W. Ferguson, Port-of-Spain	1947-48
11-157 (5-59, 6-98)†	L. R. Gibbs, Manchester	1963
10-106 (5-37, 5-69)	L. R. Gibbs, Manchester	1966
14-149 (8-92, 6-57)	M. A. Holding, The Oval	1976
10-96 (5-41, 5-55)†	H. H. H. Johnson, Kingston	1947-48
10-92 (6-32, 4-60)	M. D. Marshall, Lord's	1988
11-152 (5-66, 6-86)	S. Ramadhin, Lord's	1950
10-123 (5-60, 5-63)	A. M. E. Roberts, Lord's	1976
11-204 (8-104, 3-100)†	A. L. Valentine, Manchester	1950
10-160 (4-121, 6-39)	A. L. Valentine, The Oval	1950

† *Signifies ten wickets or more on first appearance in England–West Indies Tests.*

Note: F. S. Trueman took ten wickets or more in successive matches.

ENGLAND v NEW ZEALAND

Captains

Season	England	New Zealand	T	E	NZ	D
1929-30	A. H. H. Gilligan	T. C. Lowry	4	1	0	3
1931	D. R. Jardine	T. C. Lowry	3	1	0	2
1932-33	D. R. Jardine[1]	M. L. Page	2	0	0	2
1937	R. W. V. Robins	M. L. Page	3	1	0	2
1946-47	W. R. Hammond	W. A. Hadlee	1	0	0	1
1949	F. G. Mann[2]	W. A. Hadlee	4	0	0	4
1950-51	F. R. Brown	W. A. Hadlee	2	1	0	1
1954-55	L. Hutton	G. O. Rabone	2	2	0	0
1958	P. B. H. May	J. R. Reid	5	4	0	1
1958-59	P. B. H. May	J. R. Reid	2	1	0	1
1962-63	E. R. Dexter	J. R. Reid	3	3	0	0
1965	M. J. K. Smith	J. R. Reid	3	3	0	0
1965-66	M. J. K. Smith	B. W. Sinclair[3]	3	0	0	3
1969	R. Illingworth	G. T. Dowling	3	2	0	1
1970-71	R. Illingworth	G. T. Dowling	2	1	0	1
1973	R. Illingworth	B. E. Congdon	3	2	0	1
1974-75	M. H. Denness	B. E. Congdon	2	1	0	1
1977-78	G. Boycott	M. G. Burgess	3	1	1	1
1978	J. M. Brearley	M. G. Burgess	3	3	0	0
1983	R. G. D. Willis	G. P. Howarth	4	3	1	0
1983-84	R. G. D. Willis	G. P. Howarth	3	0	1	2
1986	M. W. Gatting	J. V. Coney	3	0	1	2
1987-88	M. W. Gatting	J. J. Crowe[4]	3	0	0	3
1990	G. A. Gooch	J. G. Wright	3	1	0	2

Season	England	New Zealand	T	E	NZ	D
1991-92	G. A. Gooch	M. D. Crowe	3	2	0	1
1994	M. A. Atherton	K. R. Rutherford	3	1	0	2
1996-97	M. A. Atherton	L. K. Germon[5]	3	2	0	1
1999	N. Hussain[6]	S. P. Fleming	4	1	2	1
	In New Zealand		38	15	2	21
	In England		44	22	4	18
	Totals		82	37	6	39

Notes: the following deputised for the official touring captain or were appointed by the home authority for only a minor proportion of the series:

[1]R. E. S. Wyatt (Second). [2]F. R. Brown (Third and Fourth). [3]M. E. Chapple (First). [4]J. G. Wright (Third). [5]S. P. Fleming (Third). [6]M. A. Butcher (Third).

HIGHEST INNINGS TOTALS

For England in England: 567-8 dec. at Nottingham 1994
in New Zealand: 593-6 dec. at Auckland 1974-75

For New Zealand in England: 551-9 dec. at Lord's 1973
in New Zealand: 537 at Wellington. 1983-84

LOWEST INNINGS TOTALS

For England in England: 126 at Birmingham 1999
in New Zealand: 64 at Wellington. 1977-78

For New Zealand in England: 47 at Lord's 1958
in New Zealand: 26 at Auckland 1954-55

INDIVIDUAL HUNDREDS

For England (83)

G. O. B. Allen (1)
122† Lord's 1931
L. E. G. Ames (2)
137† Lord's 1931
103 Christchurch . 1932-33
D. L. Amiss (2)
138*† Nottingham . 1973
164* Christchurch . 1974-75
M. A. Atherton (4)
151† Nottingham . 1990
101 Nottingham . 1994
111 Manchester. . 1994
118 Christchurch . 1996-97

T. E. Bailey (1)
134* Christchurch . 1950-51
K. F. Barrington (3)
126† Auckland. . . 1962-63
137 Birmingham . 1965
163 Leeds 1965
I. T. Botham (3)
103 Christchurch . 1977-78
103 Nottingham . 1983
138 Wellington . . 1983-84
E. H. Bowley (1)
109 Auckland. . . 1929-30

G. Boycott (2)
115 Leeds 1973
131 Nottingham . 1978
B. C. Broad (1)
114† Christchurch . 1987-88
D. C. S. Compton (2)
114 Leeds 1949
116 Lord's 1949
M. C. Cowdrey (2)
128* Wellington . . 1962-63
119 Lord's 1965
M. H. Denness (1)
181 Auckland. . . 1974-75

ENGLAND v INDIA

Captains

Season	England	India	T	E	I	D
1932	D. R. Jardine	C. K. Nayudu	1	1	0	0
1933-34	D. R. Jardine	C. K. Nayudu	3	2	0	1
1936	G. O. B. Allen	Maharaj of Vizianagram	3	2	0	1
1946	W. R. Hammond	Nawab of Pataudi sen.	3	1	0	2
1951-52	N. D. Howard[1]	V. S. Hazare	5	1	1	3
1952	L. Hutton	V. S. Hazare	4	3	0	1
1959	P. B. H. May[2]	D. K. Gaekwad[3]	5	5	0	0
1961-62	E. R. Dexter	N. J. Contractor	5	0	2	3
1963-64	M. J. K. Smith	Nawab of Pataudi jun.	5	0	0	5
1967	D. B. Close	Nawab of Pataudi jun.	3	3	0	0
1971	R. Illingworth	A. L. Wadekar	3	0	1	2
1972-73	A. R. Lewis	A. L. Wadekar	5	1	2	2
1974	M. H. Denness	A. L. Wadekar	3	3	0	0
1976-77	A. W. Greig	B. S. Bedi	5	3	1	1
1979	J. M. Brearley	S. Venkataraghavan	4	1	0	3
1979-80	J. M. Brearley	G. R. Viswanath	1	1	0	0
1981-82	K. W. R. Fletcher	S. M. Gavaskar	6	0	1	5
1982	R. G. D. Willis	S. M. Gavaskar	3	1	0	2
1984-85	D. I. Gower	S. M. Gavaskar	5	2	1	2
1986	M. W. Gatting[4]	Kapil Dev	3	0	2	1
1990	G. A. Gooch	M. Azharuddin	3	1	0	2
1992-93	G. A. Gooch[5]	M. Azharuddin	3	0	3	0
1996	M. A. Atherton	M. Azharuddin	3	1	0	2
	In England		41	22	3	16
	In India		43	10	11	22
	Totals.		84	32	14	38

Notes: the 1932 Indian touring team was captained by the Maharaj of Porbandar but he did not play in the Test match.

The following deputised for the official touring captain or were appointed by the home authority for only a minor proportion of the series:

[1]D. B. Carr (Fifth). [2]M. C. Cowdrey (Fourth and Fifth). [3]Pankaj Roy (Second). [4]D. I. Gower (First). [5]A. J. Stewart (Second).

HIGHEST INNINGS TOTALS

For England in England: 653-4 dec. at Lord's.	1990
in India: 652-7 dec. at Madras	1984-85
For India in England: 606-9 dec. at The Oval.	1990
in India: 591 at Bombay	1992-93

LOWEST INNINGS TOTALS

For England in England: 101 at The Oval	1971
in India: 102 at Bombay	1981-82
For India in England: 42 at Lord's	1974
in India: 83 at Madras	1976-77

INDIVIDUAL HUNDREDS

For England (76)

D. L. Amiss (2)
188	Lord's	1974
179	Delhi	1976-77

M. A. Atherton (2)
131	Manchester. .	1990
160	Manchester. .	1996

K. F. Barrington (3)
151*	Bombay. . . .	1961-62
172	Kanpur	1961-62
113*	Delhi	1961-62

I. T. Botham (5)
137	Leeds	1979
114	Bombay. . . .	1979-80
142	Kanpur	1981-82
128	Manchester. .	1982
208	The Oval . . .	1982

G. Boycott (4)
246*†	Leeds	1967
155	Birmingham .	1979
125	The Oval . . .	1979
105	Delhi	1981-82

M. C. Cowdrey (3)
160	Leeds	1959
107	Calcutta. . . .	1963-64
151	Delhi	1963-64

M. H. Denness (2)
118	Lord's	1974
100	Birmingham .	1974

E. R. Dexter (1)
126*	Kanpur	1961-62

B. L. D'Oliveira (1)
109†	Leeds	1967

J. H. Edrich (1)
100*	Manchester. .	1974

T. G. Evans (1)
104	Lord's	1952

K. W. R. Fletcher (2)
113	Bombay. . . .	1972-73
123*	Manchester. .	1974

G. Fowler (1)
201	Madras	1984-85

M. W. Gatting (3)
136	Bombay. . . .	1984-85
207	Madras	1984-85
183*	Birmingham .	1986

G. A. Gooch (5)
127	Madras	1981-82
114	Lord's	1986
333 } 123 }	Lord's	1990
116	Manchester. .	1990

D. I. Gower (2)
200*†	Birmingham .	1979
157*	The Oval . . .	1990

T. W. Graveney (2)
175†	Bombay. . . .	1951-52
151	Lord's	1967

A. W. Greig (3)
148	Bombay. . . .	1972-73
106	Lord's	1974
103	Calcutta. . . .	1976-77

W. R. Hammond (2)
167	Manchester. .	1936
217	The Oval . . .	1936

J. Hardstaff jun. (1)
205*	Lord's	1946

G. A. Hick (1)
178	Bombay. . . .	1992-93

N. Hussain (2)
128†	Birmingham .	1996
107*	Nottingham .	1996

L. Hutton (2)
150	Lord's	1952
104	Manchester. .	1952

R. Illingworth (1)
107	Manchester. .	1971

B. R. Knight (1)
127	Kanpur	1963-64

A. J. Lamb (3)
107	The Oval . . .	1982

139	Lord's	1990
109	Manchester. .	1990

A. R. Lewis (1)
125	Kanpur	1972-73

C. C. Lewis (1)
117	Madras	1992-93

D. Lloyd (1)
214*	Birmingham .	1974

B. W. Luckhurst (1)
101	Manchester. .	1971

P. B. H. May (1)
106	Nottingham .	1959

P. H. Parfitt (1)
121	Kanpur	1963-64

G. Pullar (2)
131	Manchester. .	1959
119	Kanpur	1961-62

D. W. Randall (1)
126	Lord's	1982

R. T. Robinson (1)
160	Delhi	1984-85

R. C. Russell (1)
124	Lord's	1996

D. S. Sheppard (1)
119	The Oval . . .	1952

M. J. K. Smith (1)
100†	Manchester. .	1959

R. A. Smith (2)
100*†	Lord's	1990
121*	Manchester. .	1990

C. J. Tavaré (1)
149	Delhi	1981-82

B. H. Valentine (1)
136†	Bombay. . . .	1933-34

C. F. Walters (1)
102	Madras	1933-34

A. J. Watkins (1)
137*†	Delhi	1951-52

T. S. Worthington (1)
128	The Oval . . .	1936

For India (64)

L. Amarnath (1)
118†	Bombay. . . .	1933-34

M. Azharuddin (6)
110†	Calcutta. . . .	1984-85
105	Madras	1984-85
122	Kanpur	1984-85
121	Lord's	1990
179	Manchester. .	1990
182	Calcutta. . . .	1992-93

A. A. Baig (1)
112†	Manchester. .	1959

F. M. Engineer (1)
121	Bombay. . . .	1972-73

S. C. Ganguly (2)
131†	Lord's	1996
136	Nottingham .	1996

S. M. Gavaskar (4)
101	Manchester. .	1974
108	Bombay. . . .	1976-77
221	The Oval . . .	1979
172	Bangalore . .	1981-82

Hanumant Singh (1)
105†	Delhi	1963-64

V. S. Hazare (2)
164*	Delhi	1951-52
155	Bombay. . . .	1951-52

M. L. Jaisimha (2)
127	Delhi	1961-62
129	Calcutta. . . .	1963-64

V. G. Kambli (1)
224	Bombay. . . .	1992-93

Kapil Dev (2)
116	Kanpur	1981-82
110	The Oval . . .	1990

S. M. H. Kirmani (1)
102	Bombay. . . .	1984-85

B. K. Kunderan (2)
192	Madras	1963-64
100	Delhi	1963-64

ENGLAND v SRI LANKA

	Captains					
Season	*England*	*Sri Lanka*	*T*	*E*	*SL*	*D*
1981-82	K. W. R. Fletcher	B. Warnapura	1	1	0	0
1984	D. I. Gower	L. R. D. Mendis	1	0	0	1
1988	G. A. Gooch	R. S. Madugalle	1	1	0	0
1991	G. A. Gooch	P. A. de Silva	1	1	0	0
1992-93	A. J. Stewart	A. Ranatunga	1	0	1	0
1998	A. J. Stewart	A. Ranatunga	1	0	1	0
	In England		4	2	1	1
	In Sri Lanka		2	1	1	0
	Totals.		6	3	2	1

HIGHEST INNINGS TOTALS

For England in England: 445 at The Oval 1998
           in Sri Lanka: 380 at Colombo (SSC) 1992-93

For Sri Lanka in England: 591 at The Oval 1998
            in Sri Lanka: 469 at Colombo (SSC). 1992-93

LOWEST INNINGS TOTALS

For England in England: 181 at The Oval 1998
           in Sri Lanka: 223 at Colombo (PSS) 1981-82

For Sri Lanka in England: 194 at Lord's 1988
            in Sri Lanka: 175 at Colombo (PSS) 1981-82

INDIVIDUAL HUNDREDS

For England (6)

J. P. Crawley (1)	**G. A. Hick** (1)	**R. A. Smith** (1)
156*† The Oval. . . 1998	107 The Oval. . . 1998	128 Colombo (SSC) 1992-93
G. A. Gooch (1)	**A. J. Lamb** (1)	**A. J. Stewart** (1)
174 Lord's. 1991	107† Lord's. 1984	113*† Lord's. 1991

For Sri Lanka (5)

P. A. de Silva (1)	**L. R. D. Mendis** (1)	**S. Wettimuny** (1)
152 The Oval. . . 1998	111 Lord's. 1984	190 Lord's. 1984
S. T. Jayasuriya (1)	**S. A. R. Silva** (1)	
213 The Oval. . . 1998	102*† Lord's. 1984	

† *Signifies hundred on first appearance in England–Sri Lanka Tests.*

RECORD PARTNERSHIPS FOR EACH WICKET

For England

78 for 1st	G. A. Gooch and H. Morris at Lord's	1991
139 for 2nd	G. A. Gooch and A. J. Stewart at Lord's	1991
112 for 3rd	R. A. Smith and G. A. Hick at Colombo (SSC)	1992-93
128 for 4th	G. A. Hick and M. R. Ramprakash at The Oval	1998
40 for 5th	A. J. Stewart and I. T. Botham at Lord's	1991
87 for 6th	A. J. Lamb and R. M. Ellison at Lord's	1984
63 for 7th	A. J. Stewart and R. C. Russell at Lord's	1991

20 for 8th	J. E. Emburey and P. W. Jarvis at Colombo (SSC)	1992-93
37 for 9th	P. J. Newport and N. A. Foster at Lord's	1988
89 for 10th	J. P. Crawley and A. R. C. Fraser at The Oval	1998

For Sri Lanka

99 for 1st	R. S. Mahanama and U. C. Hathurusinghe at Colombo (SSC)	1992-93
83 for 2nd	B. Warnapura and R. L. Dias at Colombo (PSS)	1981-82
243 for 3rd†	S. T. Jayasuriya and P. A. de Silva at The Oval	1998
148 for 4th	S. Wettimuny and A. Ranatunga at Lord's	1984
150 for 5th†	S. Wettimuny and L. R. D. Mendis at Lord's	1984
138 for 6th	S. A. R. Silva and L. R. D. Mendis at Lord's	1984
74 for 7th	U. C. Hathurusinghe and R. J. Ratnayake at Lord's	1991
29 for 8th	R. J. Ratnayake and C. P. H. Ramanayake at Lord's	1991
83 for 9th†	H. P. Tillekeratne and M. Muralitharan at Colombo (SSC)	1992-93
64 for 10th	J. R. Ratnayeke and G. F. Labrooy at Lord's	1988

† *Denotes record partnership against all countries.*

TEN WICKETS OR MORE IN A MATCH

For Sri Lanka (1)

| 16-220 (7-155, 9-65) | M. Muralitharan at The Oval | 1998 |

Note: the best match figures by an England bowler are 8-95 (5-28, 3-67) by D. L. Underwood at Colombo (PSS), 1981-82.

ENGLAND v ZIMBABWE

		Captains				
Season	England	Zimbabwe	T	E	Z	D
1996-97	M. A. Atherton	A. D. R. Campbell	2	0	0	2

HIGHEST INNINGS TOTALS

For England: 406 at Bulawayo 1996-97

For Zimbabwe: 376 at Bulawayo 1996-97

INDIVIDUAL HUNDREDS

For England (3)

| **J. P. Crawley** (1) | **N. Hussain** (1) | **A. J. Stewart** (1) |
| 112† Bulawayo. . . 1996-97 | 113† Bulawayo. . . 1996-97 | 101* Harare. . . . . 1996-97 |

For Zimbabwe (1)

A. Flower (1)
112† Bulawayo. . . 1996-97

† *Signifies hundred on first appearance in England–Zimbabwe Tests.*

HUNDRED PARTNERSHIPS

For England

137 for 2nd	N. V. Knight and A. J. Stewart at Bulawayo	1996-97
106* for 4th	A. J. Stewart and G. P. Thorpe at Harare	1996-97
148 for 5th	N. Hussain and J. P. Crawley at Bulawayo	1996-97

For Zimbabwe

| 127 for 2nd | G. W. Flower and A. D. R. Campbell at Bulawayo | 1996-97 |

BEST MATCH BOWLING ANALYSES

For England

6-137 (2-76, 4-61)†   P. C. R. Tufnell, Bulawayo   1996-97

For Zimbabwe

7-186 (5-123, 2-63)†   P. A. Strang, Bulawayo   1996-97

† *Signifies on first appearance in England–Zimbabwe Tests.*

AUSTRALIA v SOUTH AFRICA

	Captains					
Season	*Australia*	*South Africa*	*T*	*A*	*SA*	*D*
1902-03S	J. Darling	H. M. Taberer[1]	3	2	0	1
1910-11A	C. Hill	P. W. Sherwell	5	4	1	0
1912E	S. E. Gregory	F. Mitchell[2]	3	2	0	1
1921-22S	H. L. Collins	H. W. Taylor	3	1	0	2
1931-32A	W. M. Woodfull	H. B. Cameron	5	5	0	0
1935-36S	V. Y. Richardson	H. F. Wade	5	4	0	1
1949-50S	A. L. Hassett	A. D. Nourse	5	4	0	1
1952-53A	A. L. Hassett	J. E. Cheetham	5	2	2	1
1957-58S	I. D. Craig	C. B. van Ryneveld[3]	5	3	0	2
1963-64A	R. B. Simpson[4]	T. L. Goddard	5	1	1	3
1966-67S	R. B. Simpson	P. L. van der Merwe	5	1	3	1
1969-70S	W. M. Lawry	A. Bacher	4	0	4	0
1993-94A	A. R. Border	K. C. Wessels[5]	3	1	1	1
1993-94S	A. R. Border	K. C. Wessels	3	1	1	1
1996-97S	M. A. Taylor	W. J. Cronje	3	2	1	0
1997-98A	M. A. Taylor	W. J. Cronje	3	1	0	2
	In South Africa		36	18	9	9
	In Australia		26	14	5	7
	In England		3	2	0	1
	Totals		65	34	14	17

S Played in South Africa.   A Played in Australia.   E Played in England.

Notes: the following deputised for the official touring captain or were appointed by the home authority for only a minor proportion of the series:
[1]J. H. Anderson (Second), E. A. Halliwell (Third). [2]L. J. Tancred (Third). [3]D. J. McGlew (First). [4]R. Benaud (First). [5]W. J. Cronje (Third).

HIGHEST INNINGS TOTALS

For Australia in Australia: 578 at Melbourne   1910-11
            in South Africa: 628-8 dec. at Johannesburg   1996-97

For South Africa in Australia: 595 at Adelaide   1963-64
            in South Africa: 622-9 dec. at Durban   1969-70

LOWEST INNINGS TOTALS

For Australia in Australia: 111 at Sydney   1993-94
            in South Africa: 75 at Durban   1949-50

For South Africa in Australia: 36† at Melbourne   1931-32
            in South Africa: 85‡ at Johannesburg   1902-03
                    85‡ at Cape Town   1902-03

† *Scored 45 in the second innings giving the smallest aggregate of 81 (12 extras) in Test cricket.*
‡ *In successive innings.*

INDIVIDUAL HUNDREDS

For Australia (65)

W. W. Armstrong (2)
159*‡ Johannesburg 1902-03
132 Melbourne . . 1910-11
W. Bardsley (3)
132† Sydney 1910-11
121 Manchester. . 1912
164 Lord's 1912
R. Benaud (2)
122 Johannesburg 1957-58
100 Johannesburg 1957-58
G. S. Blewett (1)
214‡ Johannesburg 1996-97
B. C. Booth (2)
169† Brisbane . . . 1963-64
102* Sydney 1963-64
D. G. Bradman (4)
226† Brisbane . . . 1931-32
112 Sydney 1931-32
167 Melbourne . . 1931-32
299* Adelaide . . . 1931-32
W. A. Brown (1)
121 Cape Town. . 1935-36
J. W. Burke (1)
189 Cape Town. . 1957-58
A. G. Chipperfield (1)
109† Durban 1935-36
H. L. Collins (1)
203 Johannesburg 1921-22
J. H. Fingleton (3)
112 Cape Town. . 1935-36
108 Johannesburg 1935-36
118 Durban 1935-36

J. M. Gregory (1)
119 Johannesburg 1921-22
R. N. Harvey (8)
178 Cape Town. . 1949-50
151* Durban 1949-50
100 Johannesburg 1949-50
116 Port Elizabeth 1949-50
109 Brisbane . . . 1952-53
190 Sydney 1952-53
116 Adelaide . . . 1952-53
205 Melbourne . . 1952-53
A. L. Hassett (3)
112† Johannesburg 1949-50
167 Port Elizabeth 1949-50
163 Adelaide . . . 1952-53
C. Hill (3)
142† Johannesburg 1902-03
191 Sydney 1910-11
100 Melbourne . . 1910-11
C. Kelleway (2)
114 Manchester. . 1912
102 Lord's 1912
W. M. Lawry (1)
157 Melbourne . . 1963-64
S. J. E. Loxton (1)
101† Johannesburg 1949-50
C. G. Macartney (2)
137 Sydney 1910-11
116 Durban 1921-22
S. J. McCabe (2)
149 Durban 1935-36
189* Johannesburg 1935-36
C. C. McDonald (1)
154 Adelaide . . . 1952-53

J. Moroney (2)
118 } Johannesburg 1949-50
101*}
A. R. Morris (2)
111 Johannesburg 1949-50
157 Port Elizabeth 1949-50
R. T. Ponting (1)
105† Melbourne . . 1997-98
K. E. Rigg (1)
127† Sydney 1931-32
J. Ryder (1)
142 Cape Town. . 1921-22
R. B. Simpson (1)
153 Cape Town. . 1966-67
K. R. Stackpole (1)
134 Cape Town. . 1966-67
M. A. Taylor (2)
170 Melbourne . . 1993-94
169*‡ Adelaide . . . 1997-98
V. T. Trumper (2)
159 Melbourne . . 1910-11
214* Adelaide . . . 1910-11
M. E. Waugh (4)
113* Durban 1993-94
116 Port Elizabeth 1996-97
100 Sydney 1997-98
115* Adelaide . . . 1997-98
S. R. Waugh (2)
164† Adelaide . . . 1993-94
160 Johannesburg 1996-97
W. M. Woodfull (1)
161 Melbourne . . 1931-32

For South Africa (40)

E. J. Barlow (5)
114† Brisbane . . . 1963-64
109 Melbourne . . 1963-64
201 Adelaide . . . 1963-64
127 Cape Town. . 1969-70
110 Johannesburg 1969-70
K. C. Bland (1)
126 Sydney 1963-64
W. J. Cronje (1)
122 Johannesburg 1993-94
W. R. Endean (1)
162* Melbourne . . 1952-53
G. A. Faulkner (3)
204 Melbourne . . 1910-11
115 Adelaide . . . 1910-11
122* Manchester. . 1912

C. N. Frank (1)
152 Johannesburg 1921-22
A. C. Hudson (1)
102 Cape Town. . 1993-94
B. L. Irvine (1)
102 Port Elizabeth 1969-70
J. H. Kallis (1)
101 Melbourne . . 1997-98
G. Kirsten (1)
108* Adelaide . . . 1997-98
D. T. Lindsay (3)
182 Johannesburg 1966-67
137 Durban 1966-67
131 Johannesburg 1966-67
D. J. McGlew (2)
108 Johannesburg 1957-58

105 Durban 1957-58
A. D. Nourse (2)
231 Johannesburg 1935-36
114 Cape Town. . 1949-50
A. W. Nourse (1)
111 Johannesburg 1921-22
R. G. Pollock (5)
122 Sydney 1963-64
175 Adelaide . . . 1963-64
209 Cape Town. . 1966-67
105 Port Elizabeth 1966-67
274 Durban 1969-70
B. A. Richards (2)
140 Durban 1969-70
126 Port Elizabeth 1969-70

For West Indies

250*	for 1st	C. G. Greenidge and D. L. Haynes at Georgetown	1983-84
297	for 2nd	D. L. Haynes and R. B. Richardson at Georgetown	1990-91
308	for 3rd	R. B. Richardson and I. V. A. Richards at St John's	1983-84
198	for 4th	L. G. Rowe and A. I. Kallicharran at Brisbane	1975-76
322	for 5th†‡	B. C. Lara and J. C. Adams at Kingston	1998-99
165	for 6th	R. B. Kanhai and D. L. Murray at Bridgetown	1972-73
347	for 7th†	D. St E. Atkinson and C. C. Depeiza at Bridgetown	1954-55
87	for 8th	P. J. L. Dujon and C. E. L. Ambrose at Port-of-Spain	1990-91
122	for 9th	D. A. J. Holford and J. L. Hendriks at Adelaide	1968-69
56	for 10th	J. Garner and C. E. H. Croft at Brisbane	1979-80

† *Denotes record partnership against all countries.*

‡ *344 runs were added between the fall of the 4th and 5th wickets: P. T. Collins retired hurt when he and Lara had added 22 runs.*

TEN WICKETS OR MORE IN A MATCH

For Australia (13)

10-113 (4-31, 6-82)	M. G. Bevan, Adelaide	1996-97
11-96 (7-46, 4-50)	A. R. Border, Sydney	1988-89
11-222 (5-135, 6-87)†	A. K. Davidson, Brisbane	1960-61
11-183 (7-87, 4-96)†	C. V. Grimmett, Adelaide	1930-31
10-115 (6-72, 4-43)	N. J. N. Hawke, Georgetown	1964-65
10-144 (6-54, 4-90)	R. G. Holland, Sydney	1984-85
13-217 (5-130, 8-87)	M. G. Hughes, Perth	1988-89
11-79 (7-23, 4-56)	H. Ironmonger, Melbourne	1930-31
11-181 (8-112, 3-69)	G. F. Lawson, Adelaide	1984-85
10-127 (7-83, 3-44)	D. K. Lillee, Melbourne	1981-82
10-78 (5-50, 5-28)	G. D. McGrath, Port-of-Spain	1998-99
10-159 (8-71, 2-88)	G. D. McKenzie, Melbourne	1968-69
10-185 (3-87, 7-98)	B. Yardley, Sydney	1981-82

For West Indies (4)

10-120 (6-74, 4-46)	C. E. L. Ambrose, Adelaide	1992-93
10-113 (7-55, 3-58)	G. E. Gomez, Sydney	1951-52
11-107 (5-45, 6-62)	M. A. Holding, Melbourne	1981-82
10-107 (5-69, 5-38)	M. D. Marshall, Adelaide	1984-85

† *Signifies ten wickets or more on first appearance in Australia–West Indies Tests.*

AUSTRALIA v NEW ZEALAND

		Captains				
Season	Australia		New Zealand	T	A	NZ	D
1945-46N	W. A. Brown		W. A. Hadlee	1	1	0	0
1973-74A	I. M. Chappell		B. E. Congdon	3	2	0	1
1973-74N	I. M. Chappell		B. E. Congdon	3	1	1	1
1976-77N	G. S. Chappell		G. M. Turner	2	1	0	1
1980-81A	G. S. Chappell		G. P. Howarth¹	3	2	0	1
1981-82N	G. S. Chappell		G. P. Howarth	3	1	1	1

TRANS-TASMAN TROPHY

	Captains						
Season	*Australia*	*New Zealand*	*T*	*A*	*NZ*	*D*	*Held by*
1985-86*A*	A. R. Border	J. V. Coney	3	1	2	0	NZ
1985-86*N*	A. R. Border	J. V. Coney	3	0	1	2	NZ
1987-88*A*	A. R. Border	J. J. Crowe	3	1	0	2	A
1989-90*A*	A. R. Border	J. G. Wright	1	0	0	1	A
1989-90*N*	A. R. Border	J. G. Wright	1	0	1	0	NZ
1992-93*N*	A. R. Border	M. D. Crowe	3	1	1	1	NZ
1993-94*A*	A. R. Border	M. D. Crowe[2]	3	2	0	1	A
1997-98*A*	M. A. Taylor	S. P. Fleming	3	2	0	1	A
	In Australia		19	10	2	7	
	In New Zealand		16	5	5	6	
	Totals		35	15	7	13	

A Played in Australia.   N Played in New Zealand.

Note: the following deputised for the official touring captain: [1]M. G. Burgess (Second). [2]K. R. Rutherford (Second and Third).

HIGHEST INNINGS TOTALS

For Australia in Australia: 607-6 dec. at Brisbane 1993-94
         in New Zealand: 552 at Christchurch 1976-77

For New Zealand in Australia: 553-7 dec. at Brisbane 1985-86
         in New Zealand: 484 at Wellington 1973-74

LOWEST INNINGS TOTALS

For Australia in Australia: 162 at Sydney..................... 1973-74
         in New Zealand: 103 at Auckland 1985-86

For New Zealand in Australia: 121 at Perth 1980-81
         in New Zealand: 42 at Wellington 1945-46

INDIVIDUAL HUNDREDS

For Australia (32)

D. C. Boon (3)
143   Brisbane . . . 1987-88
200   Perth. 1989-90
106   Hobart 1993-94
A. R. Border (5)
152* Brisbane . . 1985-86
140 } Christchurch . 1985-86
114*
205   Adelaide . . . 1987-88
105   Brisbane . . . 1993-94
G. S. Chappell (3)
247* } Wellington . . 1973-74
133 }
176   Christchurch . 1981-82
I. M. Chappell (2)
145 } Wellington . . 1973-74
121 }

M. T. G. Elliott (1)
114   Hobart. 1997-98
G. J. Gilmour (1)
101   Christchurch . 1976-77
I. A. Healy (1)
113* Perth 1993-94
G. R. Marsh (1)
118   Auckland . . . 1985-86
R. W. Marsh (1)
132   Adelaide . . . 1973-74
G. R. J. Matthews (2)
115† Brisbane . . 1985-86
130   Wellington . . 1985-86
I. R. Redpath (1)
159*‡ Auckland . . . 1973-74
M. J. Slater (1)
168   Hobart 1993-94

K. R. Stackpole (1)
122† Melbourne . . 1973-74
M. A. Taylor (2)
142* Perth 1993-94
112   Brisbane . . . 1997-98
K. D. Walters (3)
104* Auckland . . . 1973-74
250   Christchurch . 1976-77
107   Melbourne . . 1980-81
M. E. Waugh (1)
111   Hobart 1993-94
S. R. Waugh (1)
147* Brisbane . . . 1993-94
G. M. Wood (2)
111† Brisbane . . . 1980-81
100   Auckland . . . 1981-82

INDIVIDUAL HUNDREDS

For Australia (53)

S. G. Barnes (1)
112	Adelaide . . .	1947-48

D. C. Boon (6)
123†	Adelaide . . .	1985-86
131	Sydney	1985-86
122	Madras	1986-87
129*	Sydney	1991-92
135	Adelaide . . .	1991-92
107	Perth.	1991-92

A. R. Border (4)
162†	Madras	1979-80
124	Melbourne . .	1980-81
163	Melbourne . .	1985-86
106	Madras	1986-87

D. G. Bradman (4)
185†	Brisbane . . .	1947-48
132 }	Melbourne . .	1947-48
127* }		
201	Adelaide . . .	1947-48

J. W. Burke (1)
161	Bombay. . . .	1956-57

G. S. Chappell (1)
204†	Sydney	1980-81

I. M. Chappell (2)
151	Melbourne . .	1967-68
138	Delhi	1969-70

R. M. Cowper (2)
108	Adelaide . . .	1967-68
165	Sydney	1967-68

L. E. Favell (1)
101	Madras	1959-60

R. N. Harvey (4)
153	Melbourne . .	1947-48
140	Bombay. . . .	1956-57
114	Delhi	1959-60
102	Bombay. . . .	1959-60

A. L. Hassett (1)
198*	Adelaide . . .	1947-48

K. J. Hughes (2)
100	Madras	1979-80
213	Adelaide . . .	1980-81

D. M. Jones (2)
210†	Madras	1986-87
150*	Perth.	1991-92

W. M. Lawry (1)
100	Melbourne . .	1967-68

A. L. Mann (1)
105	Perth.	1977-78

G. R. Marsh (1)
101	Bombay. . . .	1986-87

G. R. J. Matthews (1)
100*	Melbourne . .	1985-86

T. M. Moody (1)
101†	Perth.	1991-92

A. R. Morris (1)
100*	Melbourne . .	1947-48

N. C. O'Neill (2)
163	Bombay. . . .	1959-60
113	Calcutta. . . .	1959-60

G. M. Ritchie (1)
128†	Adelaide . . .	1985-86

A. P. Sheahan (1)
114	Kanpur	1969-70

R. B. Simpson (4)
103	Adelaide . . .	1967-68
109	Melbourne . .	1967-68
176	Perth.	1977-78
100	Adelaide . . .	1977-78

K. R. Stackpole (1)
103†	Bombay. . . .	1969-70

M. A. Taylor (2)
100	Adelaide . . .	1991-92
102*	Bangalore . .	1997-98

K. D. Walters (1)
102	Madras	1969-70

M. E. Waugh (1)
153*	Bangalore . .	1997-98

G. M. Wood (1)
125	Adelaide . . .	1980-81

G. N. Yallop (2)
121†	Adelaide . . .	1977-78
167	Calcutta. . . .	1979-80

For India (39)

M. Amarnath (2)
100	Perth.	1977-78
138	Sydney	1985-86

M. Azharuddin (2)
106	Adelaide . . .	1991-92
163*	Calcutta. . . .	1997-98

N. J. Contractor (1)
108	Bombay. . . .	1959-60

S. M. Gavaskar (8)
113†	Brisbane . . .	1977-78
127	Perth.	1977-78
118	Melbourne . .	1977-78
115	Delhi	1979-80
123	Bombay. . . .	1979-80
166*	Adelaide . . .	1985-86
172	Sydney	1985-86
103	Bombay. . . .	1986-87

V. S. Hazare (2)
116 }	Adelaide . . .	1947-48
145 }		

M. L. Jaisimha (1)
101	Brisbane . . .	1967-68

Kapil Dev (1)
119	Madras	1986-87

S. M. H. Kirmani (1)
101*	Bombay. . . .	1979-80

V. Mankad (2)
116	Melbourne . .	1947-48
111	Melbourne . .	1947-48

N. R. Mongia (1)
152†	Delhi	1996-97

Nawab of Pataudi jun. (1)
128*†	Madras	1964-65

S. M. Patil (1)
174	Adelaide . . .	1980-81

D. G. Phadkar (1)
123	Adelaide . . .	1947-48

G. S. Ramchand (1)
109	Bombay. . . .	1956-57

R. J. Shastri (2)
121*	Bombay. . . .	1986-87
206	Sydney	1991-92

K. Srikkanth (1)
116	Sydney	1985-86

S. R. Tendulkar (4)
148*	Sydney	1991-92
114	Perth.	1991-92
155*	Chennai. . . .	1997-98
177	Bangalore . .	1997-98

D. B. Vengsarkar (2)
112	Bangalore . .	1979-80
164*	Bombay. . . .	1986-87

G. R. Viswanath (4)
137†	Kanpur	1969-70
161*	Bangalore . .	1979-80
131	Delhi	1979-80
114	Melbourne . .	1980-81

Yashpal Sharma (1)
100*	Delhi	1979-80

† *Signifies hundred on first appearance in Australia–India Tests.*

RECORD PARTNERSHIPS FOR EACH WICKET

For Australia

217	for 1st	D. C. Boon and G. R. Marsh at Sydney	. . . .	1985-86
236	for 2nd	S. G. Barnes and D. G. Bradman at Adelaide	. . . .	1947-48
222	for 3rd	A. R. Border and K. J. Hughes at Madras	. . . .	1979-80
178	for 4th	D. M. Jones and A. R. Border at Madras	. . . .	1986-87
223*	for 5th	A. R. Morris and D. G. Bradman at Melbourne	. . . .	1947-48
151	for 6th	T. R. Veivers and B. N. Jarman at Bombay	. . . .	1964-65
66	for 7th	G. R. J. Matthews and R. J. Bright at Melbourne	. . . .	1985-86
73	for 8th	T. R. Veivers and G. D. McKenzie at Madras	. . . .	1964-65
96	for 9th	I. A. Healy and G. R. Robertson at Chennai	. . . .	1997-98
77	for 10th	A. R. Border and D. R. Gilbert at Melbourne	. . . .	1985-86

For India

192	for 1st	S. M. Gavaskar and C. P. S. Chauhan at Bombay	. . . .	1979-80
224	for 2nd	S. M. Gavaskar and M. Amarnath at Sydney	. . . .	1985-86
159	for 3rd	S. M. Gavaskar and G. R. Viswanath at Delhi	. . . .	1979-80
159	for 4th	D. B. Vengsarkar and G. R. Viswanath at Bangalore	. . . .	1979-80
196	for 5th	R. J. Shastri and S. R. Tendulkar at Sydney	. . . .	1991-92
298*	for 6th†	D. B. Vengsarkar and R. J. Shastri at Bombay	. . . .	1986-87
132	for 7th	V. S. Hazare and H. R. Adhikari at Adelaide	. . . .	1947-48
127	for 8th	S. M. H. Kirmani and K. D. Ghavri at Bombay	. . . .	1979-80
81	for 9th	S. R. Tendulkar and K. S. More at Perth	. . . .	1991-92
94	for 10th	S. M. Gavaskar and N. S. Yadav at Adelaide	. . . .	1985-86

† *Denotes record partnership against all countries.*

TEN WICKETS OR MORE IN A MATCH

For Australia (11)

11-105 (6-52, 5-53)	R. Benaud, Calcutta	1956-57
12-124 (5-31, 7-93)	A. K. Davidson, Kanpur.	1959-60
12-166 (5-99, 7-67)	G. Dymock, Kanpur	1979-80
10-168 (5-76, 5-92)	C. J. McDermott, Adelaide	1991-92
10-91 (6-58, 4-33)†	G. D. McKenzie, Madras	1964-65
10-151 (7-66, 3-85)	G. D. McKenzie, Melbourne	1967-68
10-144 (5-91, 5-53)	A. A. Mallett, Madras	1969-70
10-249 (5-103, 5-146)	G. R. J. Matthews, Madras	1986-87
12-126 (6-66, 6-60)	B. A. Reid, Melbourne	1991-92
11-31 (5-2, 6-29)†	E. R. H. Toshack, Brisbane.	1947-48
11-95 (4-68, 7-27)	M. R. Whitney, Perth.	1991-92

For India (6)

10-194 (5-89, 5-105)	B. S. Bedi, Perth	1977-78
12-104 (6-52, 6-52)	B. S. Chandrasekhar, Melbourne	1977-78
10-130 (7-49, 3-81)	Ghulam Ahmed, Calcutta	1956-57
11-122 (5-31, 6-91)	R. G. Nadkarni, Madras.	1964-65
14-124 (9-69, 5-55)	J. M. Patel, Kanpur.	1959-60
10-174 (4-100, 6-74)	E. A. S. Prasanna, Madras	1969-70

† *Signifies ten wickets or more on first appearance in Australia–India Tests.*

AUSTRALIA v PAKISTAN

	Captains					
Season	*Australia*	*Pakistan*	*T*	*A*	*P*	*D*
1956-57*P*	I. W. Johnson	A. H. Kardar	1	0	1	0
1959-60*P*	R. Benaud	Fazal Mahmood[1]	3	2	0	1
1964-65*P*	R. B. Simpson	Hanif Mohammad	1	0	0	1
1964-65*A*	R. B. Simpson	Hanif Mohammad	1	0	0	1
1972-73*A*	I. M. Chappell	Intikhab Alam	3	3	0	0
1976-77*A*	G. S. Chappell	Mushtaq Mohammad	3	1	1	1
1978-79*A*	G. N. Yallop[2]	Mushtaq Mohammad	2	1	1	0
1979-80*P*	G. S. Chappell	Javed Miandad	3	0	1	2
1981-82*A*	G. S. Chappell	Javed Miandad	3	2	1	0
1982-83*P*	K. J. Hughes	Imran Khan	3	0	3	0
1983-84*A*	K. J. Hughes	Imran Khan[3]	5	2	0	3
1988-89*P*	A. R. Border	Javed Miandad	3	0	1	2
1989-90*A*	A. R. Border	Imran Khan	3	1	0	2
1994-95*P*	M. A. Taylor	Salim Malik	3	0	1	2
1995-96*A*	M. A. Taylor	Wasim Akram	3	2	1	0
1998-99*P*	M. A. Taylor	Aamir Sohail	3	1	0	2
	In Pakistan		20	3	7	10
	In Australia		23	12	4	7
	Totals		43	15	11	17

A Played in Australia. P Played in Pakistan.

Notes: the following deputised for the official touring captain or were appointed by the home authority for only a minor proportion of the series:
[1]Imtiaz Ahmed (Second). [2]K. J. Hughes (Second). [3]Zaheer Abbas (First, Second and Third).

HIGHEST INNINGS TOTALS

For Australia in Australia: 585 at Adelaide 1972-73
in Pakistan: 617 at Faisalabad 1979-80

For Pakistan in Australia: 624 at Adelaide 1983-84
in Pakistan: 580-9 dec. at Peshawar. 1998-99

LOWEST INNINGS TOTALS

For Australia in Australia: 125 at Melbourne 1981-82
in Pakistan: 80 at Karachi. 1956-57

For Pakistan in Australia: 62 at Perth 1981-82
in Pakistan: 134 at Dacca 1959-60

INDIVIDUAL HUNDREDS

For Australia (47)

J. Benaud (1)
142   Melbourne . . 1972-73
D. C. Boon (1)
114* Karachi 1994-95
A. R. Border (6)
105† Melbourne . . 1978-79
150* } Lahore 1979-80
153   }
118   Brisbane . . . 1983-84
117* Adelaide . . . 1983-84
113* Faisalabad . . 1988-89
G. S. Chappell (6)
116* Melbourne . . 1972-73
121   Melbourne . . 1976-77
235   Faisalabad . . 1979-80
201   Brisbane . . . 1981-82
150* Brisbane . . . 1983-84
182   Sydney 1983-84
I. M. Chappell (1)
196   Adelaide . . . 1972-73
G. J. Cosier (1)
168   Melbourne . . 1976-77
I. C. Davis (1)
105† Adelaide . . . 1976-77

K. J. Hughes (2)
106   Perth 1981-82
106   Adelaide . . . 1983-84
D. M. Jones (2)
116 } Adelaide . . . 1989-90
121* }
J. L. Langer (1)
116   Peshawar . . . 1998-99
R. B. McCosker (1)
105   Melbourne . . 1976-77
R. W. Marsh (1)
118† Adelaide . . . 1972-73
N. C. O'Neill (1)
134   Lahore 1959-60
W. B. Phillips (1)
159† Perth 1983-84
I. R. Redpath (1)
135   Melbourne . . 1972-73
G. M. Ritchie (1)
106* Faisalabad . . 1982-83
A. P. Sheahan (1)
127   Melbourne . . 1972-73
R. B. Simpson (2)
153 }†Karachi 1964-65
115 }

M. J. Slater (2)
110   Rawalpindi . . 1994-95
108   Rawalpindi . . 1998-99
M. A. Taylor (4)
101† Melbourne . . 1989-90
101* Sydney 1989-90
123   Hobart 1995-96
334* Peshawar . . . 1998-99
K. D. Walters (1)
107   Adelaide . . . 1976-77
M. E. Waugh (2)
116   Sydney 1995-96
117   Karachi 1998-99
S. R. Waugh (2)
112* Brisbane . . . 1995-96
157   Rawalpindi . . 1998-99
K. C. Wessels (1)
179   Adelaide . . . 1983-84
G. M. Wood (1)
100   Melbourne . . 1981-82
G. N. Yallop (3)
172   Faisalabad . . 1979-80
141   Perth 1983-84
268   Melbourne . . 1983-84

For Pakistan (41)

Aamir Sohail (2)
105   Lahore 1994-95
133   Karachi 1998-99
Asif Iqbal (3)
152* Adelaide . . . 1976-77
120   Sydney 1976-77
134* Perth 1978-79
Hanif Mohammad (2)
101* Karachi 1959-60
104   Melbourne . . 1964-65
Ijaz Ahmed, sen. (5)
122   Faisalabad . . 1988-89
121   Melbourne . . 1989-90
137   Sydney 1995-96
155   Peshawar . . . 1998-99
120* Karachi 1998-99
Imran Khan (1)
136   Adelaide . . . 1989-90
Javed Miandad (6)
129* Perth 1978-79
106* Faisalabad . . 1979-80

138   Lahore 1982-83
131   Adelaide . . . 1983-84
211   Karachi 1988-89
107   Faisalabad . . 1988-89
Khalid Ibadulla (1)
166† Karachi 1964-65
Majid Khan (3)
158   Melbourne . . 1972-73
108   Melbourne . . 1978-79
110* Lahore 1979-80
Mansoor Akhtar (1)
111   Faisalabad . . 1982-83
Mohsin Khan (3)
135   Lahore 1982-83
149   Adelaide . . . 1983-84
152   Melbourne . . 1983-84
Moin Khan (1)
115*† Lahore 1994-95
Mushtaq Mohammad (1)
121   Sydney 1972-73

Qasim Omar (1)
113   Adelaide . . . 1983-84
Sadiq Mohammad (2)
137   Melbourne . . 1972-73
105   Melbourne . . 1976-77
Saeed Ahmed (1)
166   Lahore 1959-60
Saeed Anwar (2)
145   Rawalpindi . . 1998-99
126   Peshawar . . . 1998-99
Salim Malik (2)
237   Rawalpindi . . 1994-95
143   Lahore 1994-95
Taslim Arif (1)
210* Faisalabad . . 1979-80
Wasim Akram (1)
123   Adelaide . . . 1989-90
Zaheer Abbas (2)
101   Adelaide . . . 1976-77
126   Faisalabad . . 1982-83

† *Signifies hundred on first appearance in Australia–Pakistan Tests.*

RECORD PARTNERSHIPS FOR EACH WICKET

For Australia

176 for 1st	M. A. Taylor and M. J. Slater at Rawalpindi	1994-95
279 for 2nd	M. A. Taylor and J. L. Langer at Peshawar	1998-99
203 for 3rd	G. N. Yallop and K. J. Hughes at Melbourne	1983-84
217 for 4th	G. S. Chappell and G. N. Yallop at Faisalabad	1979-80
171 for 5th	{ G. S. Chappell and G. J. Cosier at Melbourne	1976-77
	{ A. R. Border and G. S. Chappell at Brisbane	1983-84
139 for 6th	R. M. Cowper and T. R. Veivers at Melbourne	1964-65
185 for 7th	G. N. Yallop and G. R. J. Matthews at Melbourne.	1983-84
117 for 8th	G. J. Cosier and K. J. O'Keeffe at Melbourne	1976-77
83 for 9th	J. R. Watkins and R. A. L. Massie at Sydney	1972-73
52 for 10th	{ D. K. Lillee and M. H. N. Walker at Sydney	1976-77
	{ G. F. Lawson and T. M. Alderman at Lahore	1982-83

For Pakistan

249 for 1st	Khalid Ibadulla and Abdul Kadir at Karachi.	1964-65
233 for 2nd	Mohsin Khan and Qasim Omar at Adelaide	1983-84
223* for 3rd	Taslim Arif and Javed Miandad at Faisalabad	1979-80
155 for 4th	Mansoor Akhtar and Zaheer Abbas at Faisalabad	1982-83
186 for 5th	Javed Miandad and Salim Malik at Adelaide	1983-84
196 for 6th	Salim Malik and Aamir Sohail at Lahore.	1994-95
104 for 7th	Intikhab Alam and Wasim Bari at Adelaide	1972-73
111 for 8th	Majid Khan and Imran Khan at Lahore.	1979-80
120 for 9th	Saeed Anwar and Mushtaq Ahmed at Rawalpindi	1998-99
87 for 10th	Asif Iqbal and Iqbal Qasim at Adelaide.	1976-77

TEN WICKETS OR MORE IN A MATCH

For Australia (4)

10-111 (7-87, 3-24)†	R. J. Bright, Karachi	1979-80
10-135 (6-82, 4-53)	D. K. Lillee, Melbourne.	1976-77
11-118 (5-32, 6-86)†	C. G. Rackemann, Perth	1983-84
11-77 (7-23, 4-54)	S. K. Warne, Brisbane	1995-96

For Pakistan (6)

11-218 (4-76, 7-142)	Abdul Qadir, Faisalabad.	1982-83
13-114 (6-34, 7-80)†	Fazal Mahmood, Karachi	1956-57
12-165 (6-102, 6-63)	Imran Khan, Sydney	1976-77
11-118 (4-69, 7-49)	Iqbal Qasim, Karachi.	1979-80
11-125 (2-39, 9-86)	Sarfraz Nawaz, Melbourne	1978-79
11-160 (6-62, 5-98)†	Wasim Akram, Melbourne	1989-90

† *Signifies ten wickets or more on first appearance in Australia–Pakistan Tests.*

AUSTRALIA v SRI LANKA

Season	Australia	Sri Lanka	*T*	*A*	*SL*	*D*
		Captains				
1982-83S	G. S. Chappell	L. R. D. Mendis	1	1	0	0
1987-88A	A. R. Border	R. S. Madugalle	1	1	0	0
1989-90A	A. R. Border	A. Ranatunga	2	1	0	1
1992-93S	A. R. Border	A. Ranatunga	3	1	0	2
1995-96A	M. A. Taylor	A. Ranatunga¹	3	3	0	0
	In Australia................		6	5	0	1
	In Sri Lanka		4	2	0	2
	Totals.....................		10	7	0	3

A Played in Australia. S Played in Sri Lanka.

Note: the following deputised for the official touring captain:
¹P. A. de Silva (Third).

HIGHEST INNINGS TOTALS

For Australia in Australia: 617-5 dec. at Perth........................... 1995-96
in Sri Lanka: 514-4 dec. at Kandy 1982-83

For Sri Lanka in Australia: 418 in Brisbane 1989-90
in Sri Lanka: 547-8 dec. at Colombo (SSC) 1992-93

LOWEST INNINGS TOTALS

For Australia in Australia: 224 at Hobart 1989-90
in Sri Lanka: 247 at Colombo (KS) 1992-93

For Sri Lanka in Australia: 153 at Perth 1987-88
in Sri Lanka: 164 at Colombo (SSC)..................... 1992-93

INDIVIDUAL HUNDREDS

For Australia (15)

D. C. Boon (1)
110 Melbourne . . 1995-96
A. R. Border (1)
106 Moratuwa . . 1992-93
D. W. Hookes (1)
143*† Kandy..... 1982-83
D. M. Jones (3)
102† Perth...... 1987-88
118* Hobart..... 1989-90

100* Colombo (KS) 1992-93
T. M. Moody (1)
106† Brisbane . . . 1989-90
M. J. Slater (1)
219† Perth...... 1995-96
M. A. Taylor (2)
164† Brisbane . . . 1989-90
108 Hobart..... 1989-90

M. E. Waugh (1)
111 Perth...... 1995-96
S. R. Waugh (3)
134* Hobart..... 1989-90
131* Melbourne . . 1995-96
170 Adelaide . . . 1995-96
K. C. Wessels (1)
141† Kandy..... 1982-83

For Sri Lanka (7)

P. A. de Silva (1)
167 Brisbane . . . 1989-90
A. P. Gurusinha (2)
137 Colombo (SSC) 1992-93
143 Melbourne . . 1995-96

S. T. Jayasuriya (1)
112 Adelaide . . . 1995-96
R. S. Kaluwitharana (1)
132*† Colombo (SSC) 1992-93

A. Ranatunga (1)
127 Colombo (SSC) 1992-93
H. P. Tillekeratne (1)
119 Perth...... 1995-96

† *Signifies hundred on first appearance in Australia–Sri Lanka Tests.*

RECORD PARTNERSHIPS FOR EACH WICKET

For Australia

228	for 1st	M. J. Slater and M. A. Taylor at Perth	1995-96
170	for 2nd	K. C. Wessels and G. N. Yallop at Kandy	1982-83
158	for 3rd	T. M. Moody and A. R. Border at Brisbane	1989-90
163	for 4th	M. A. Taylor and A. R. Border at Hobart	1989-90
155*	for 5th	D. W. Hookes and A. R. Border at Kandy	1982-83
260*	for 6th	D. M. Jones and S. R. Waugh at Hobart	1989-90
129	for 7th	G. R. J. Matthews and I. A. Healy at Moratuwa	1992-93
56	for 8th	G. R. J. Matthews and C. J. McDermott at Colombo (SSC)	1992-93
45	for 9th	I. A. Healy and S. K. Warne at Colombo (SSC)	1992-93
49	for 10th	I. A. Healy and M. R. Whitney at Colombo (SSC)	1992-93

For Sri Lanka

110	for 1st	R. S. Mahanama and U. C. Hathurusinghe at Colombo (KS).	1992-93
92	for 2nd	R. S. Mahanama and A. P. Gurusinha at Colombo (SSC)	1992-93
125	for 3rd	S. T. Jayasuriya and S. Ranatunga at Adelaide	1995-96
230	for 4th	A. P. Gurusinha and A. Ranatunga at Colombo (SSC)	1992-93
116	for 5th	H. P. Tillekeratne and A. Ranatunga at Moratuwa	1992-93
96	for 6th	A. P. Gurusinha and R. S. Kaluwitharana at Colombo (SSC).	1992-93
144	for 7th†	P. A. de Silva and J. R. Ratnayeke at Brisbane	1989-90
33	for 8th	A. Ranatunga and C. P. H. Ramanayake at Perth	1987-88
46	for 9th	H. D. P. K. Dharmasena and G. P. Wickremasinghe at Perth	1995-96
27	for 10th	P. A. de Silva and C. P. H. Ramanayake at Brisbane	1989-90

    † *Denotes record partnership against all countries.*

BEST MATCH BOWLING ANALYSES

For Australia

8-156 (3-68, 5-88)	M. G. Hughes, Hobart	1989-90

For Sri Lanka

8-157 (5-82, 3-75)	C. P. H. Ramanayake, Moratuwa	1992-93

SOUTH AFRICA v WEST INDIES

Season	South Africa	*Captains* West Indies	T	SA	WI	D
1991-92*W*	K. C. Wessels	R. B. Richardson	1	0	1	0
1998-99*S*	W. J. Cronje	B. C. Lara	5	5	0	0
	In South Africa		5	5	0	0
	In West Indies		1	0	1	0
	Totals		6	5	1	0

S Played in South Africa.   W Played in West Indies.

HIGHEST INNINGS TOTALS

For South Africa in South Africa: 406-8 dec. at Cape Town   1998-99
      in West Indies: 345 at Bridgetown.   1991-92

For West Indies in South Africa: 271 at Cape Town.   1998-99
      in West Indies: 283 at Bridgetown   1991-92

LOWEST INNINGS TOTALS

For South Africa in South Africa: 195 at Port Elizabeth   1998-99
      in West Indies: 148 at Bridgetown.   1991-92

For West Indies in South Africa: 121 at Port Elizabeth   1998-99
      in West Indies: 262 at Bridgetown   1991-92

INDIVIDUAL HUNDREDS

For South Africa (6)

M. V. Boucher (1)	**A. C. Hudson** (1)	**G. Kirsten** (1)
100 Centurion. . . 1998-99	163† Bridgetown . 1991-92	134 Centurion . . 1998-99
D. J. Cullinan (1)	**J. H. Kallis** (1)	**J. N. Rhodes** (1)
168 Cape Town. . 1998-99	110 Cape Town. . 1998-99	103* Centurion . . 1998-99

Highest score for West Indies: 86 at Cape Town 1998-99 by C. L. Hooper.

† *Signifies hundred on first appearance in South Africa–West Indies Tests.*

RECORD PARTNERSHIPS FOR EACH WICKET

For South Africa

97 for 1st	G. Kirsten and H. H. Gibbs at Durban	1998-99
125 for 2nd	A. C. Hudson and K. C. Wessels at Bridgetown	1991-92
235 for 3rd	J. H. Kallis and D. J. Cullinan at Cape Town.	1998-99
107 for 4th	G. Kirsten and W. J. Cronje at Centurion	1998-99
115 for 5th	G. Kirsten and J. N. Rhodes at Centurion	1998-99
92 for 6th	J. N. Rhodes and S. M. Pollock at Port Elizabeth	1998-99
92 for 7th	J. H. Kallis and M. V. Boucher at Centurion	1998-99
55 for 8th	M. V. Boucher and L. Klusener at Centurion	1998-99
66 for 9th	P. L. Symcox and A. A. Donald at Port Elizabeth	1998-99
25 for 10th	P. L. Symcox and D. J. Terbrugge at Johannesburg	1998-99

For West Indies

99 for 1st	D. L. Haynes and P. V. Simmons at Bridgetown	1991-92
56 for 2nd	D. L. Haynes and B. C. Lara at Bridgetown.	1991-92
160 for 3rd	S. Chanderpaul and B. C. Lara at Durban	1998-99
91 for 4th	S. Chanderpaul and C. L. Hooper at Johannesburg	1998-99
74 for 5th	C. L. Hooper and D. Ganga at Cape Town	1998-99
68 for 6th	R. D. Jacobs and C. L. Hooper at Johannesburg	1998-99
81 for 7th	R. D. Jacobs and N. A. M. McLean at Centurion	1998-99
65 for 8th	R. D. Jacobs and N. A. M. McLean at Cape Town	1998-99
34 for 9th	R. D. Jacobs and C. E. L. Ambrose at Cape Town	1998-99
64 for 10th	R. D. Jacobs and M. Dillon at Cape Town.	1998-99

BEST MATCH BOWLING ANALYSES

For South Africa

9-103 (5-54, 4-49)   S. M. Pollock, Johannesburg   1998-99

For West Indies

8-79 (2-28, 6-51)   C. E. L. Ambrose, Port Elizabeth   1998-99

SOUTH AFRICA v NEW ZEALAND

	Captains					
Season	South Africa	New Zealand	T	SA	NZ	D
1931-32N	H. B. Cameron	M. L. Page	2	2	0	0
1952-53N	J. E. Cheetham	W. M. Wallace	2	1	0	1
1953-54S	J. E. Cheetham	G. O. Rabone[1]	5	4	0	1
1961-62S	D. J. McGlew	J. R. Reid	5	2	2	1
1963-64N	T. L. Goddard	J. R. Reid	3	0	0	3
1994-95S	W. J. Cronje	K. R. Rutherford	3	2	1	0
1994-95N	W. J. Cronje	K. R. Rutherford	1	1	0	0
1998-99N	W. J. Cronje	D. J. Nash	3	1	0	2
	In New Zealand		11	5	0	6
	In South Africa		13	8	3	2
	Totals		24	13	3	8

N Played in New Zealand.   S Played in South Africa.

Note: the following deputised for the official touring captain:
[1]B. Sutcliffe (Fourth and Fifth).

HIGHEST INNINGS TOTALS

For South Africa in South Africa: 464 at Johannesburg   1961-62
in New Zealand: 621-5 dec. at Auckland   1998-99

For New Zealand in South Africa: 505 at Cape Town   1953-54
in New Zealand: 364 at Wellington   1931-32

LOWEST INNINGS TOTALS

For South Africa in South Africa: 148 at Johannesburg   1953-54
in New Zealand: 223 at Dunedin   1963-64

For New Zealand in South Africa: 79 at Johannesburg   1953-54
in New Zealand: 138 at Dunedin   1963-64

INDIVIDUAL HUNDREDS

For South Africa (20)

X. C. Balaskas (1)
122* Wellington . . 1931-32
J. A. J. Christy (1)
103† Christchurch . 1931-32
W. J. Cronje (2)
112 Cape Town . . 1994-95
101 Auckland. . . 1994-95
D. J. Cullinan (2)
275* Auckland. . . 1998-99
152 Wellington . . 1998-99
W. R. Endean (1)
116 Auckland. . . 1952-53

H. H. Gibbs (2)
211* Christchurch . 1998-99
120 Wellington . . 1998-99
J. H. Kallis (1)
148* Christchurch . 1998-99
G. Kirsten (1)
128 Auckland. . . 1998-99
D. J. McGlew (3)
255*† Wellington . . 1952-53
127*‡ Durban 1961-62
120 Johannesburg 1961-62

R. A. McLean (2)
101 Durban 1953-54
113 Cape Town. . 1961-62
B. Mitchell (1)
113† Christchurch . 1931-32
A. R. A. Murray (1)
109† Wellington . . 1952-53
D. J. Richardson (1)
109 Cape Town . . 1994-95
J. H. B. Waite (1)
101 Johannesburg 1961-62

For New Zealand (7)

P. T. Barton (1)
109 Port Elizabeth 1961-62
P. G. Z. Harris (1)
101 Cape Town. . 1961-62

G. O. Rabone (1)
107 Durban 1953-54
J. R. Reid (2)
135 Cape Town . . 1953-54
142 Johannesburg 1961-62

B. W. Sinclair (1)
138 Auckland. . . 1963-64
H. G. Vivian (1)
100† Wellington . . 1931-32

† *Signifies hundred on first appearance in South Africa–New Zealand Tests.*
‡ *Carried his bat.*

RECORD PARTNERSHIPS FOR EACH WICKET

For South Africa

196	for 1st	J. A. J. Christy and B. Mitchell at Christchurch	1931-32
315	for 2nd†	H. H. Gibbs and J. H. Kallis at Christchurch	1998-99
183	for 3rd	G. Kirsten and D. J. Cullinan at Auckland.	1998-99
145	for 4th	D. J. Cullinan and W. J. Cronje at Wellington	1998-99
141	for 5th	D. J. Cullinan and J. N. Rhodes at Auckland	1998-99
126*	for 6th	D. J. Cullinan and S. M. Pollock at Auckland	1998-99
246	for 7th†	D. J. McGlew and A. R. A. Murray at Wellington	1952-53
95	for 8th	J. E. Cheetham and H. J. Tayfield at Cape Town	1953-54
60	for 9th	P. M. Pollock and N. A. T. Adcock at Port Elizabeth.	1961-62
47	for 10th	D. J. McGlew and H. D. Bromfield at Port Elizabeth	1961-62

For New Zealand

126	for 1st	G. O. Rabone and M. E. Chapple at Cape Town.	1953-54
90	for 2nd	M. J. Horne and N. J. Astle at Auckland.	1998-99
94	for 3rd	M. B. Poore and B. Sutcliffe at Cape Town	1953-54
171	for 4th	B. W. Sinclair and S. N. McGregor at Auckland	1963-64
174	for 5th	J. R. Reid and J. E. F. Beck at Cape Town	1953-54
100	for 6th	H. G. Vivian and F. T. Badcock at Wellington	1931-32
84	for 7th	J. R. Reid and G. A. Bartlett at Johannesburg	1961-62
74	for 8th	S. A. Thomson and D. J. Nash at Johannesburg	1994-95
69	for 9th	C. F. W. Allcott and I. B. Cromb at Wellington	1931-32
57	for 10th	S. B. Doull and R. P. de Groen at Johannesburg.	1994-95

† *Denotes record partnership against all countries.*

TEN WICKETS OR MORE IN A MATCH

For South Africa (1)

11-196 (6-128, 5-68)†   S. F. Burke, Cape Town.......................   1961-62

  † *Signifies ten wickets or more on first appearance in South Africa–New Zealand Tests.*

Note: the best match figures by a New Zealand bowler are 8-134 (3-57, 5-77), M. N. Hart at Johannesburg, 1994-95.

SOUTH AFRICA v INDIA

		Captains					
Season	*South Africa*	*India*		*T*	*SA*	*I*	*D*
1992-93*S*	K. C. Wessels	M. Azharuddin		4	1	0	3
1996-97*I*	W. J. Cronje	S. R. Tendulkar		3	1	2	0
1996-97*S*	W. J. Cronje	S. R. Tendulkar		3	2	0	1
	In South Africa			7	3	0	4
	In India			3	1	2	0
	Totals......................			10	4	2	4

S Played in South Africa.   I Played in India.

HIGHEST INNINGS TOTALS

For South Africa in South Africa: 529-7 dec. at Cape Town   1996-97
                in India: 428 at Calcutta   1996-97

For India in South Africa: 410 at Johannesburg......................   1996-97
            in India: 400-7 dec. at Kanpur   1996-97

LOWEST INNINGS TOTALS

For South Africa in South Africa: 235 at Durban   1996-97
                in India: 105 at Ahmedabad........................   1996-97

For India in South Africa: 66 at Durban   1996-97
            in India: 137 at Calcutta   1996-97

INDIVIDUAL HUNDREDS

For South Africa (10)

W. J. Cronje (1)
135   Port Elizabeth 1992-93

D. J. Cullinan (2)
153*   Calcutta.... 1996-97
122*   Johannesburg 1996-97

A. C. Hudson (1)
146   Calcutta.... 1996-97

G. Kirsten (3)
102   ⎫
133   ⎬ Calcutta.... 1996-97
103   ⎭ Cape Town.. 1996-97

L. Klusener (1)
102*   Cape Town.. 1996-97

B. M. McMillan (1)
103*   Cape Town.. 1996-97

K. C. Wessels (1)
118†   Durban 1992-93

For India (8)

P. K. Amre (1)			163*	Kanpur 1996-97	**Kapil Dev** (1)	
103†	Durban 1992-93	115	Cape Town. . 1996-97	129	Port Elizabeth 1992-93	
M. Azharuddin (3)		**R. Dravid** (1)		**S. R. Tendulkar** (2)		
109	Calcutta. . . . 1996-97	148	Johannesburg 1996-97	111	Johannesburg 1992-93	
				169	Cape Town. . 1996-97	

† *Signifies hundred on first appearance in South Africa–India Tests.*

RECORD PARTNERSHIPS FOR EACH WICKET

For South Africa

236	for 1st	A. C. Hudson and G. Kirsten at Calcutta	1996-97
212	for 2nd	G. Kirsten and D. J. Cullinan at Calcutta	1996-97
114	for 3rd	G. Kirsten and D. J. Cullinan at Cape Town	1996-97
94	for 4th	A. C. Hudson and D. J. Cullinan at Cape Town	1996-97
99	for 5th	D. J. Cullinan and J. N. Rhodes at Cape Town	1992-93
112	for 6th	B. M. McMillan and S. M. Pollock at Johannesburg	1996-97
101*	for 7th	B. M. McMillan and S. M. Pollock at Cape Town.	1996-97
147*	for 8th†	B. M. McMillan and L. Klusener at Cape Town	1996-97
60	for 9th	P. S. de Villiers and A. A. Donald at Ahmedabad	1996-97
74	for 10th	B. M. McMillan and A. A. Donald at Durban	1996-97

For India

90	for 1st	V. Rathore and N. R. Mongia at Johannesburg	1996-97
85	for 2nd	M. Prabhakar and S. V. Manjrekar at Cape Town	1992-93
54	for 3rd	R. Dravid and S. R. Tendulkar at Johannesburg	1996-97
145	for 4th	R. Dravid and S. C. Ganguly at Johannesburg	1996-97
87	for 5th	M. Azharuddin and P. K. Amre at Durban	1992-93
222	for 6th	S. R. Tendulkar and M. Azharuddin at Cape Town	1996-97
76	for 7th	R. Dravid and J. Srinath at Johannesburg	1996-97
161	for 8th†	M. Azharuddin and A. Kumble at Calcutta	1996-97
77	for 9th	Kapil Dev and A. Kumble at Port Elizabeth	1992-93
19	for 10th	S. R. Tendulkar and D. Ganesh at Cape Town	1996-97

† *Denotes record partnership against all countries.*

TEN WICKETS OR MORE IN A MATCH

For South Africa (1)

12-139 (5-55, 7-84)	A. A. Donald, Port Elizabeth	1992-93

For India (1)

10-153 (5-60, 5-93)	B. K. V. Prasad, Durban	1996-97

SOUTH AFRICA v PAKISTAN

Season	South Africa	*Captains*	Pakistan	T	SA	P	D
1994-95S	W. J. Cronje		Salim Malik	1	1	0	0
1997-98P	W. J. Cronje		Saeed Anwar	3	1	0	2
1997-98S	W. J. Cronje[1]		Rashid Latif[2]	3	1	1	1
	In South Africa			4	2	1	1
	In Pakistan			3	1	0	2
	Totals......................			7	3	1	3

S Played in South Africa.   P Played in Pakistan.

Notes: the following deputised for the official touring captain or were appointed by the home authority for only a minor proportion of the series:
[1]G. Kirsten (First). [2]Aamir Sohail (First and Second).

HIGHEST INNINGS TOTALS

For South Africa: 460 at Johannesburg 1994-95

For Pakistan: 456 at Rawalpindi............................... 1997-98

LOWEST INNINGS TOTALS

For South Africa: 214 at Faisalabad 1997-98

For Pakistan: 92 at Faisalabad................................ 1997-98

INDIVIDUAL HUNDREDS

For South Africa (3)

G. Kirsten (1)	**B. M. McMillan** (1)	**P. L. Symcox** (1)
100*‡ Faisalabad .. 1997-98	113† Johannesburg 1994-95	108 Johannesburg 1997-98

For Pakistan (5)

Ali Naqvi (1)	**Azhar Mahmood** (3)	**Saeed Anwar** (1)
115† Rawalpindi.. 1997-98	128*† Rawalpindi.. 1997-98	118 Durban 1997-98
	136 Johannesburg 1997-98	
	132 Durban 1997-98	

† *Signifies hundred on first appearance in South Africa–Pakistan Tests.*
‡ *Carried his bat.*

RECORD PARTNERSHIPS FOR EACH WICKET

For South Africa

135 for 1st	G. Kirsten and A. M. Bacher at Sheikhupura	1997-98
114 for 2nd	G. Kirsten and J. H. Kallis at Rawalpindi	1997-98
83 for 3rd	J. H. Kallis and H. D. Ackerman at Durban	1997-98
79 for 4th	G. Kirsten and W. J. Cronje at Johannesburg	1994-95
43 for 5th	P. L. Symcox and W. J. Cronje at Faisalabad	1997-98
157 for 6th	J. N. Rhodes and B. M. McMillan at Johannesburg	1994-95
106 for 7th	S. M. Pollock and D. J. Richardson at Rawalpindi	1997-98
124 for 8th	G. Kirsten and P. L. Symcox at Faisalabad	1997-98
195 for 9th†	M. V. Boucher and P. L. Symcox at Johannesburg	1997-98
71 for 10th	P. S. de Villiers and A. A. Donald at Johannesburg	1994-95

For Pakistan

101 for 1st	Saeed Anwar and Aamir Sohail at Durban	1997-98
69 for 2nd	Ali Naqvi and Mohammad Ramzan at Rawalpindi	1997-98
72 for 3rd	Ijaz Ahmed, sen. and Mohammad Wasim at Johannesburg	1997-98
93 for 4th	Asif Mujtaba and Inzamam-ul-Haq at Johannesburg	1994-95
44 for 5th	Ali Naqvi and Mohammad Wasim at Rawalpindi	1997-98
144 for 6th	Inzamam-ul-Haq and Moin Khan at Faisalabad	1997-98
35 for 7th	Salim Malik and Wasim Akram at Johannesburg	1994-95
40 for 8th	Inzamam-ul-Haq and Kabir Khan at Johannesburg	1994-95
80 for 9th	Azhar Mahmood and Shoaib Akhtar at Durban	1997-98
151 for 10th†	Azhar Mahmood and Mushtaq Ahmed at Rawalpindi	1997-98

† *Denotes record partnership against all countries.*

TEN WICKETS OR MORE IN A MATCH

For South Africa (1)

10-108 (6-81, 4-27)†	P. S. de Villiers, Johannesburg	1994-95

For Pakistan (1)

10-133 (6-78, 4-55)	Waqar Younis, Port Elizabeth	1997-98

† *Signifies ten wickets or more on first appearance in South Africa–Pakistan Tests.*

SOUTH AFRICA v SRI LANKA

	Captains					
Season	South Africa	Sri Lanka	T	SA	SL	D
1993-94*SL*	K. C. Wessels	A. Ranatunga	3	1	0	2
1997-98*SA*	W. J. Cronje	A. Ranatunga	2	2	0	0
	In South Africa		2	2	0	0
	In Sri Lanka		3	1	0	2
	Totals		5	3	0	2

SA Played in South Africa.   SL Played in Sri Lanka.

HIGHEST INNINGS TOTALS

For South Africa: 495 at Colombo (SSC).   1993-94

For Sri Lanka: 331 at Moratuwa.   1993-94

LOWEST INNINGS TOTALS

For South Africa: 200 at Centurion.   1997-98

For Sri Lanka: 119 at Colombo (SSC).   1993-94

INDIVIDUAL HUNDREDS

For South Africa (5)

W. J. Cronje (1)	**D. J. Cullinan** (3)		**J. N. Rhodes** (1)
122 Colombo (SSC) 1993-94	102	Colombo (PSS) 1993-94	101*† Moratuwa . . 1993-94
	113	Cape Town. . 1997-98	
	103	Centurion. . . 1997-98	

For Sri Lanka (1)

A. Ranatunga (1)
131†   Moratuwa . .   1993-94

† *Signifies hundred on first appearance in South Africa–Sri Lanka Tests.*

HUNDRED PARTNERSHIPS

For South Africa

137 for 1st	K. C. Wessels and A. C. Hudson at Colombo (SSC)	1993-94
104 for 1st	K. C. Wessels and A. C. Hudson at Moratuwa	1993-94
116 for 3rd	J. H. Kallis and D. J. Cullinan at Cape Town.	1997-98
105 for 3rd	W. J. Cronje and D. J. Cullinan at Colombo (SSC)	1993-94
116 for 4th	G. Kirsten and W. J. Cronje at Centurion	1997-98
122 for 6th	D. J. Cullinan and D. J. Richardson at Colombo (PSS)	1993-94

For Sri Lanka

129 for 3rd	M. S. Atapattu and P. A. de Silva at Cape Town.	1997-98
118 for 4th	R. S. Mahanama and A. Ranatunga at Centurion.	1997-98
101 for 4th	P. A. de Silva and A. Ranatunga at Colombo (PSS).	1993-94
121 for 5th	P. A. de Silva and A. Ranatunga at Moratuwa	1993-94
103 for 6th	A. Ranatunga and H. P. Tillekeratne at Moratuwa	1993-94

BEST MATCH BOWLING ANALYSES

For South Africa

9-106 (5-48, 4-58)   B. N. Schultz, Colombo (SSC).   1993-94

For Sri Lanka

8-157 (5-63, 3-94)   M. Muralitharan, Centurion   1997-98

SOUTH AFRICA v ZIMBABWE

		Captains				
Season	*South Africa*	*Zimbabwe*	*T*	*SA*	*Z*	*D*
1995-96Z	W. J. Cronje	A. Flower	1	1	0	0

Z Played in Zimbabwe.

HIGHEST INNINGS TOTALS

For South Africa: 346 at Harare   1995-96

For Zimbabwe: 283 at Harare   1995-96

INDIVIDUAL HUNDREDS

For South Africa (1)

A. C. Hudson (1)
135†   Harare   1995-96

Highest score for Zimbabwe: 63 by A. Flower at Harare 1995-96.

† *Signifies hundred on first appearance in South Africa–Zimbabwe Tests.*

HUNDRED PARTNERSHIP

For South Africa

101 for 6th   A. C. Hudson and B. M. McMillan at Harare.   1995-96

Note: the highest partnership for Zimbabwe is 97 for the 5th wicket between A. Flower and G. J. Whittall at Harare, 1995-96.

For India (59)

H. R. Adhikari (1)		120	Delhi	1978-79	150 Bridgetown . 1970-71
114*† Delhi	1948-49	147*	Georgetown .	1982-83	**R. J. Shastri** (2)
M. Amarnath (3)		121	Delhi	1983-84	102 St John's . . . 1982-83
101* Kanpur	1978-79	236*	Madras	1983-84	107 Bridgetown 1988-89
117 Port-of-Spain	1982-83	**V. S. Hazare** (2)			**N. S. Sidhu** (3)
116 St John's . . .	1982-83	134*	Bombay. . . .	1948-49	116 Kingston . . . 1988-89
M. L. Apte (1)		122	Bombay. . . .	1948-49	107 Nagpur 1994-95
163* Port-of-Spain	1952-53	**Kapil Dev** (4)			201 Port-of-Spain 1996-97
C. G. Borde (3)		126*	Delhi	1978-79	**E. D. Solkar** (1)
109 Delhi	1958-59	100*	Port-of-Spain	1982-83	102 Bombay. . . . 1974-75
121 Bombay. . . .	1966-67	109	Madras	1987-88	**S. R. Tendulkar** (1)
125 Madras	1966-67	**S. V. Manjrekar** (1)			179 Nagpur 1994-95
S. A. Durani (1)		108	Bridgetown .	1988-89	**P. R. Umrigar** (3)
104 Port-of-Spain	1961-62	**V. L. Manjrekar** (1)			130 Port-of-Spain 1952-53
F. M. Engineer (1)		118	Kingston . . .	1952-53	117 Kingston . . . 1952-53
109 Madras	1966-67	**R. S. Modi** (1)			172* Port-of-Spain 1961-62
A. D. Gaekwad (1)		112	Bombay. . . .	1948-49	**D. B. Vengsarkar** (6)
102 Kanpur	1978-79	**Mushtaq Ali** (1)			157* Calcutta. . . . 1978-79
S. M. Gavaskar (13)		106†	Calcutta. . . .	1948-49	109 Delhi 1978-79
116 Georgetown .	1970-71	**B. P. Patel** (1)			159 Delhi 1983-84
117* Bridgetown .	1970-71	115*	Port-of-Spain	1975-76	100 Bombay. . . . 1983-84
124 } Port-of-Spain 220 }	1970-71	**M. Prabhakar** (1)			102 Delhi 1987-88
		120	Mohali	1994-95	102* Calcutta. . . . 1987-88
156 Port-of-Spain	1975-76	**Pankaj Roy** (1)			**G. R. Viswanath** (4)
102 Port-of-Spain	1975-76	150	Kingston . . .	1952-53	139 Calcutta. . . . 1974-75
205 Bombay. . . .	1978-79	**D. N. Sardesai** (3)			112 Port-of-Spain 1975-76
107 } Calcutta. . . . 182* }	1978-79	212	Kingston . . .	1970-71	124 Madras 1978-79
		112	Port-of-Spain	1970-71	179 Kanpur 1978-79

† *Signifies hundred on first appearance in West Indies–India Tests.*

RECORD PARTNERSHIPS FOR EACH WICKET

For West Indies

296	for 1st	C. G. Greenidge and D. L. Haynes at St John's	1982-83
255	for 2nd	E. D. A. McMorris and R. B. Kanhai at Kingston	1961-62
220	for 3rd	I. V. A. Richards and A. I. Kallicharran at Bridgetown	1975-76
267	for 4th	C. L. Walcott and G. E. Gomez at Delhi	1948-49
219	for 5th	E. D. Weekes and B. H. Pairaudeau at Port-of-Spain	1952-53
250	for 6th	C. H. Lloyd and D. L. Murray at Bombay	1974-75
130	for 7th	C. G. Greenidge and M. D. Marshall at Kanpur	1983-84
124	for 8th†	I. V. A. Richards and K. D. Boyce at Delhi	1974-75
161	for 9th†	C. H. Lloyd and A. M. E. Roberts at Calcutta	1983-84
98*	for 10th	F. M. M. Worrell and W. W. Hall at Port-of-Spain.	1961-62

For India

153	for 1st	S. M. Gavaskar and C. P. S. Chauhan at Bombay	1978-79
344*	for 2nd†	S. M. Gavaskar and D. B. Vengsarkar at Calcutta	1978-79
177	for 3rd	N. S. Sidhu and S. R. Tendulkar at Nagpur	1994-95
172	for 4th	G. R. Viswanath and A. D. Gaekwad at Kanpur	1978-79
204	for 5th	S. M. Gavaskar and B. P. Patel at Port-of-Spain	1975-76
170	for 6th	S. M. Gavaskar and R. J. Shastri at Madras	1983-84
186	for 7th	D. N. Sardesai and E. D. Solkar at Bridgetown	1970-71
107	for 8th	Yashpal Sharma and B. S. Sandhu at Kingston	1982-83
143*	for 9th	S. M. Gavaskar and S. M. H. Kirmani at Madras	1983-84
64	for 10th	J. Srinath and S. L. V. Raju at Mohali	1994-95

† *Denotes record partnership against all countries.*

TEN WICKETS OR MORE IN A MATCH

For West Indies (4)

11-126 (6-50, 5-76)	W. W. Hall, Kanpur	1958-59
11-89 (5-34, 6-55)	M. D. Marshall, Port-of-Spain.	1988-89
12-121 (7-64, 5-57)	A. M. E. Roberts, Madras	1974-75
10-101 (6-62, 4-39)	C. A. Walsh, Kingston	1988-89

For India (4)

11-235 (7-157, 4-78)†	B. S. Chandrasekhar, Bombay	1966-67
10-223 (9-102, 1-121)	S. P. Gupte, Kanpur	1958-59
16-136 (8-61, 8-75)†	N. D. Hirwani, Madras	1987-88
10-135 (1-52, 9-83)	Kapil Dev, Ahmedabad	1983-84

† *Signifies ten wickets or more on first appearance in West Indies–India Tests.*

WEST INDIES v PAKISTAN

Captains

Season	West Indies	Pakistan	T	WI	P	D
1957-58W	F. C. M. Alexander	A. H. Kardar	5	3	1	1
1958-59P	F. C. M. Alexander	Fazal Mahmood	3	1	2	0
1974-75P	C. H. Lloyd	Intikhab Alam	2	0	0	2
1976-77W	C. H. Lloyd	Mushtaq Mohammad	5	2	1	2
1980-81P	C. H. Lloyd	Javed Miandad	4	1	0	3
1986-87P	I. V. A. Richards	Imran Khan	3	1	1	1
1987-88W	I. V. A. Richards[1]	Imran Khan	3	1	1	1
1990-91P	D. L. Haynes	Imran Khan	3	1	1	1
1992-93W	R. B. Richardson	Wasim Akram	3	2	0	1
1997-98P	C. A. Walsh	Wasim Akram	3	0	3	0
	In West Indies		16	8	3	5
	In Pakistan		18	4	7	7
	Totals.		34	12	10	12

P Played in Pakistan.   W Played in West Indies.

Note: the following was appointed by the home authority for only a minor proportion of the series:
[1]C. G. Greenidge (First).

HIGHEST INNINGS TOTALS

For West Indies in West Indies: 790-3 dec. at Kingston	1957-58
in Pakistan: 493 at Karachi	1974-75
For Pakistan in West Indies: 657-8 dec. at Bridgetown	1957-58
in Pakistan: 471 at Rawalpindi	1997-98

LOWEST INNINGS TOTALS

For West Indies in West Indies: 127 at Port-of-Spain	1992-93
in Pakistan: 53 at Faisalabad	1986-87
For Pakistan in West Indies: 106 at Bridgetown.	1957-58
in Pakistan: 77 at Lahore.	1986-87

INDIVIDUAL HUNDREDS

For West Indies (25)

L. Baichan (1)			**I. V. A. Richards** (2)		
105*†	Lahore	1974-75	120*	Multan	1980-81
P. J. L. Dujon (1)			123	Port-of-Spain	1987-88
106*	Port-of-Spain	1987-88	**I. T. Shillingford** (1)		
R. C. Fredericks (1)			120	Georgetown .	1976-77
120	Port-of-Spain	1976-77	**G. S. Sobers** (3)		
C. G. Greenidge (1)			365*	Kingston . . .	1957-58
100	Kingston . . .	1976-77	125 }	Georgetown .	1957-58
D. L. Haynes (3)			109* }		
117	Karachi	1990-91	**C. L. Walcott** (1)		
143*‡	Port-of-Spain	1992-93	145	Georgetown .	1957-58
125	Bridgetown .	1992-93	**E. D. Weekes** (1)		
C. L. Hooper (3)			197†	Bridgetown .	1957-58
134	Lahore	1990-91			

178*	St John's . . .	1992-93
106	Karachi	1997-98
C. C. Hunte (3)		
142†	Bridgetown .	1957-58
260	Kingston . . .	1957-58
114	Georgetown .	1957-58
B. D. Julien (1)		
101	Karachi	1974-75
A. I. Kallicharran (1)		
115	Karachi	1974-75
R. B. Kanhai (1)		
217	Lahore	1958-59
C. H. Lloyd (1)		
157	Bridgetown .	1976-77

For Pakistan (22)

Aamir Sohail (2)			**Imran Khan** (1)		
160	Rawalpindi . .	1997-98	123	Lahore	1980-81
160	Karachi	1997-98	**Inzamam-ul-Haq** (2)		
Asif Iqbal (1)			123	St John's . . .	1992-93
135	Kingston . . .	1976-77	177	Rawalpindi . .	1997-98
Hanif Mohammad (2)			**Javed Miandad** (2)		
337†	Bridgetown .	1957-58	114	Georgetown .	1987-88
103	Karachi	1958-59	102	Port-of-Spain	1987-88
Ijaz Ahmed, sen. (1)			**Majid Khan** (2)		
151	Karachi	1997-98	100	Karachi	1974-75
Imtiaz Ahmed (1)			167	Georgetown .	1976-77
122	Kingston . . .	1957-58	**Mushtaq Mohammad** (2)		
			123	Lahore	1974-75

121	Port-of-Spain	1976-77
Saeed Ahmed (1)		
150	Georgetown .	1957-58
Salim Malik (1)		
102	Karachi	1990-91
Wasim Raja (2)		
107*	Karachi	1974-75
117*	Bridgetown .	1976-77
Wazir Mohammad (2)		
106	Kingston . . .	1957-58
189	Port-of-Spain	1957-58

† *Signifies hundred on first appearance in West Indies–Pakistan Tests.*
‡ *Carried his bat.*

RECORD PARTNERSHIPS FOR EACH WICKET

For West Indies

182	for 1st	R. C. Fredericks and C. G. Greenidge at Kingston	1976-77
446	for 2nd†	C. C. Hunte and G. S. Sobers at Kingston.	1957-58
169	for 3rd	D. L. Haynes and B. C. Lara at Port-of-Spain	1992-93
188*	for 4th	G. S. Sobers and C. L. Walcott at Kingston.	1957-58
185	for 5th	E. D. Weekes and O. G. Smith at Bridgetown	1957-58
151	for 6th	C. H. Lloyd and D. L. Murray at Bridgetown	1976-77
70	for 7th	C. H. Lloyd and J. Garner at Bridgetown	1976-77
60	for 8th	C. L. Hooper and A. C. Cummins at St John's	1992-93
61*	for 9th	P. J. L. Dujon and W. K. M. Benjamin at Bridgetown	1987-88
106	for 10th†	C. L. Hooper and C. A. Walsh at St John's	1992-93

For Pakistan

298	for 1st†	Aamir Sohail and Ijaz Ahmed, sen. at Karachi	1997-98
178	for 2nd	Hanif Mohammad and Saeed Ahmed at Karachi	1958-59
323	for 3rd	Aamir Sohail and Inzamam-ul-Haq at Rawalpindi	1997-98
174	for 4th	Shoaib Mohammad and Salim Malik at Karachi	1990-91

88	for 5th	Basit Ali and Inzamam-ul-Haq at St John's		1992-93
166	for 6th	Wazir Mohammad and A. H. Kardar at Kingston		1957-58
128	for 7th[1]	Wasim Raja and Wasim Bari at Karachi		1974-75
94	for 8th	Salim Malik and Salim Yousuf at Port-of-Spain		1987-88
96	for 9th	Inzamam-ul-Haq and Nadeem Khan at St John's		1992-93
133	for 10th	Wasim Raja and Wasim Bari at Bridgetown		1976-77

† *Denotes record partnership against all countries.*

[1]*Although the seventh wicket added 168 runs against West Indies at Lahore in 1980-81, this comprised two partnerships with Imran Khan adding 72* with Abdul Qadir (retired hurt) and a further 96 with Sarfraz Nawaz.*

TEN WICKETS OR MORE IN A MATCH

For Pakistan (3)

12-100 (6-34, 6-66)	Fazal Mahmood, Dacca	1958-59
11-121 (7-80, 4-41)	Imran Khan, Georgetown	1987-88
10-106 (5-35, 5-71)	Mushtaq Ahmed, Peshawar	1997-98

Note: the best match figures for West Indies are 9-95 (8-29, 1-66) by C. E. H. Croft at Port-of-Spain, 1976-77.

WEST INDIES v SRI LANKA

	Captains					
Season	West Indies	Sri Lanka	T	WI	SL	D
1993-94S	R. B. Richardson	A. Ranatunga	1	0	0	1
1996-97W	C. A. Walsh	A. Ranatunga	2	1	0	1
	In West Indies		2	1	0	1
	In Sri Lanka		1	0	0	1
	Totals		3	1	0	2

W Played in West Indies.   S Played in Sri Lanka.

HIGHEST INNINGS TOTALS

For West Indies: 343 at St Vincent 1996-97
For Sri Lanka: 233-8 at St Vincent 1996-97

LOWEST INNINGS TOTALS

For West Indies: 147 at St Vincent 1996-97
For Sri Lanka: 152 at St John's 1996-97

INDIVIDUAL HUNDREDS

For West Indies (1)

B. C. Lara (1)
115   St Vincent . . 1996-97

Highest score for Sri Lanka: 90 by S. T. Jayasuriya at St Vincent.   1996-97

HUNDRED PARTNERSHIPS

For West Indies

160 for 1st   S. L. Campbell and S. C. Williams at St John's   1996-97

For Sri Lanka

110 for 4th   S. T. Jayasuriya and A. Ranatunga at St John's.   1996-97

BEST MATCH BOWLING ANALYSES

For West Indies

8-78 (5-37, 3-41)   C. E. L. Ambrose, St John's   1996-97

For Sri Lanka

8-106 (5-34, 3-72)   M. Muralitharan, St John's   1996-97

NEW ZEALAND v INDIA

Captains

Season	New Zealand	India	T	NZ	I	D
1955-56*I*	H. B. Cave	P. R. Umrigar[1]	5	0	2	3
1964-65*I*	J. R. Reid	Nawab of Pataudi jun.	4	0	1	3
1967-68*N*	G. T. Dowling[2]	Nawab of Pataudi jun.	4	1	3	0
1969-70*I*	G. T. Dowling	Nawab of Pataudi jun.	3	1	1	1
1975-76*N*	G. M. Turner	B. S. Bedi[3]	3	1	1	1
1976-77*I*	G. M. Turner	B. S. Bedi	3	0	2	1
1980-81*N*	G. P. Howarth	S. M. Gavaskar	3	1	0	2
1988-89*I*	J. G. Wright	D. B. Vengsarkar	3	1	2	0
1989-90*N*	J. G. Wright	M. Azharuddin	3	1	0	2
1993-94*N*	K. R. Rutherford	M. Azharuddin	1	0	0	1
1995-96*I*	L. K. Germon	M. Azharuddin	3	0	1	2
1998-99*N*†	S. P. Fleming	M. Azharuddin	2	1	0	1
	In India		21	2	9	10
	In New Zealand		16	5	4	7
	Totals.		37	7	13	17

I Played in India.   N Played in New Zealand.

    † *The First Test at Dunedin was abandoned without a ball being bowled and is excluded.*

Notes: the following deputised for the official touring captain or were appointed by the home authority for a minor proportion of the series:
[1]Ghulam Ahmed (First). [2]B. W. Sinclair (First). [3]S. M. Gavaskar (First).

HIGHEST INNINGS TOTALS

For New Zealand in New Zealand: 502 at Christchurch 1967-68
in India: 462-9 dec. at Calcutta 1964-65

For India in New Zealand: 482 at Auckland 1989-90
in India: 537-3 dec. at Madras 1955-56

LOWEST INNINGS TOTALS

For New Zealand in New Zealand: 100 at Wellington 1980-81
in India: 124 at Hyderabad 1988-89

For India in New Zealand: 81 at Wellington 1975-76
in India: 88 at Bombay 1964-65

INDIVIDUAL HUNDREDS

For New Zealand (22)

C. L. Cairns (1)
126   Hamilton . . .   1998-99
M. D. Crowe (1)
113   Auckland . . .   1989-90
G. T. Dowling (3)
129   Bombay . . .   1964-65
143   Dunedin . . .   1967-68
239   Christchurch .   1967-68
J. W. Guy (1)
102†   Hyderabad . .   1955-56
G. P. Howarth (1)
137*   Wellington . .   1980-81

A. H. Jones (1)
170*   Auckland . . .   1989-90
J. M. Parker (1)
104   Bombay . . .   1976-77
J. F. Reid (1)
123*   Christchurch .   1980-81
J. R. Reid (2)
119*   Delhi   1955-56
120   Calcutta   1955-56
I. D. S. Smith (1)
173   Auckland . . .   1989-90

B. Sutcliffe (3)
137*†   Hyderabad . .   1955-56
230*   Delhi   1955-56
151*   Calcutta   1964-65
B. R. Taylor (1)
105†   Calcutta   1964-65
G. M. Turner (2)
117   Christchurch .   1975-76
113   Kanpur   1976-77
J. G. Wright (3)
110   Auckland . . .   1980-81
185   Christchurch .   1989-90
113*   Napier   1989-90

For India (27)

S. Amarnath (1)
124†   Auckland . . .   1975-76
M. Azharuddin (2)
192   Auckland . . .   1989-90
103*   Wellington . .   1998-99
C. G. Borde (1)
109   Bombay   1964-65
R. Dravid (2)
190 }   Hamilton . . .   1998-99
103* }
S. C. Ganguly (1)
101†   Hamilton . . .   1998-99
S. M. Gavaskar (2)
116†   Auckland . . .   1975-76
119   Bombay   1976-77

A. G. Kripal Singh (1)
100*†   Hyderabad . .   1955-56
V. L. Manjrekar (3)
118†   Hyderabad . .   1955-56
177   Delhi   1955-56
102*   Madras   1964-65
V. Mankad (2)
223   Bombay   1955-56
231   Madras   1955-56
Nawab of Pataudi jun. (2)
153   Calcutta   1964-65
113   Delhi   1964-65
G. S. Ramchand (1)
106*   Calcutta   1955-56

Pankaj Roy (2)
100   Calcutta   1955-56
173   Madras   1955-56
D. N. Sardesai (2)
200*   Bombay   1964-65
106   Delhi   1964-65
N. S. Sidhu (1)
116†   Bangalore . .   1988-89
S. R. Tendulkar (1)
113   Wellington . .   1998-99
P. R. Umrigar (1)
223†   Hyderabad . .   1955-56
G. R. Viswanath (1)
103*   Kanpur   1976-77
A. L. Wadekar (1)
143   Wellington . .   1967-68

† *Signifies hundred on first appearance in New Zealand–India Tests. B. R. Taylor provides the only instance for New Zealand of a player scoring his maiden hundred in first-class cricket in his first Test.*

INDIVIDUAL HUNDREDS

For New Zealand (13)

J. J. Crowe (1)
120* Colombo (CCC) 1986-87
M. D. Crowe (2)
299 Wellington . . 1990-91
107 Colombo (SSC) 1992-93
S. P. Fleming (1)
174* Colombo (RPS) 1997-98
R. J. Hadlee (1)
151* Colombo (CCC) 1986-87

A. H. Jones (3)
186 Wellington . . 1990-91
122 } Hamilton . . . 1990-91
100* }
C. D. McMillan (1)
142† Colombo (RPS) 1997-98
J. F. Reid (1)
180 Colombo (CCC) 1983-84

K. R. Rutherford (1)
105 Moratuwa . . 1992-93
J. G. Wright (1)
101 Hamilton . . . 1990-91
B. A. Young (1)
267* Dunedin . . . 1996-97

For Sri Lanka (12)

P. A. de Silva (2)
267† Wellington . . 1990-91
123 Auckland . . . 1990-91
R. L. Dias (1)
108† Colombo (SSC) 1983-84
A. P. Gurusinha (3)
119 } Hamilton . . . 1990-91
102 }

127 Dunedin . . . 1994-95
D. P. M. D. Jayawardene (1)
167 Galle 1997-98
R. S. Kaluwitharana (1)
103† Dunedin . . . 1996-97
D. S. B. P. Kuruppu (1)
201*† Colombo (CCC) 1986-87

R. S. Mahanama (2)
153 Moratuwa . . 1992-93
109 Colombo (SSC) 1992-93
H. P. Tillekeratne (1)
108 Dunedin . . . 1994-95

† *Signifies hundred on first appearance in New Zealand–Sri Lanka Tests.*

Note: A. P. Gurusinha and A. H. Jones at Hamilton in 1990-91 provided the second instance of a player on each side hitting two separate hundreds in a Test match.

RECORD PARTNERSHIPS FOR EACH WICKET

For New Zealand

161	for 1st	T. J. Franklin and J. G. Wright at Hamilton	1990-91
140	for 2nd	B. A. Young and M. J. Horne at Dunedin	1996-97
467	for 3rd†‡	A. H. Jones and M. D. Crowe at Wellington	1990-91
240	for 4th	S. P. Fleming and C. D. McMillan at Colombo (RPS)	1997-98
151	for 5th	K. R. Rutherford and C. Z. Harris at Moratuwa	1992-93
246*	for 6th	J. J. Crowe and R. J. Hadlee at Colombo (CCC).	1986-87
47	for 7th	D. N. Patel and M. L. Su'a at Dunedin	1994-95
79	for 8th	J. V. Coney and W. K. Lees at Christchurch	1982-83
43	for 9th	A. C. Parore and P. J. Wiseman at Galle	1997-98
52	for 10th	W. K. Lees and E. J. Chatfield at Christchurch	1982-83

For Sri Lanka

102	for 1st	R. S. Mahanama and U. C. Hathurusinghe at Colombo (SSC)	1992-93
138	for 2nd	R. S. Mahanama and A. P. Gurusinha at Moratuwa	1992-93
159*	for 3rd[1]	S. Wettimuny and R. L. Dias at Colombo (SSC)	1983-84
192	for 4th	A. P. Gurusinha and H. P. Tillekeratne at Dunedin	1994-95
130	for 5th	R. S. Madugalle and D. S. de Silva at Wellington	1982-83
109*	for 6th[2]	R. S. Madugalle and A. Ranatunga at Colombo (CCC).	1983-84
137	for 7th	R. S. Kaluwitharana and W. P. U. J. C. Vaas at Dunedin	1996-97
73	for 8th	H. P. Tillekeratne and G. P. Wickremasinghe at Dunedin	1996-97
31	for 9th	{ G. F. Labrooy and R. J. Ratnayake at Auckland	1990-91
		{ S. T. Jayasuriya and R. J. Ratnayake at Auckland	1990-91
71	for 10th	R. S. Kaluwitharana and M. Muralitharan at Colombo (SSC)	1997-98

† *Denotes record partnership against all countries.*

‡ *Record third-wicket partnership in first-class cricket.*

[1] *163 runs were added for this wicket in two separate partnerships: S. Wettimuny retired hurt and was replaced by J. R. Ratnayeke when 159 had been added.*

[2] *119 runs were added for this wicket in two separate partnerships: R. S. Madugalle retired hurt and was replaced by D. S. de Silva when 109 had been added.*

TEN WICKETS OR MORE IN A MATCH

For New Zealand (1)

10-102 (5-73, 5-29)   R. J. Hadlee, Colombo (CCC).   1983-84

For Sri Lanka (1)

10-90 (5-47, 5-43)†   W. P. U. J. C. Vaas, Napier.   1994-95

† *Signifies ten wickets or more on first appearance in New Zealand–Sri Lanka Tests.*

NEW ZEALAND v ZIMBABWE

		Captains				
Season	*New Zealand*	*Zimbabwe*	*T*	*NZ*	*Z*	*D*
1992-93Z	M. D. Crowe	D. L. Houghton	2	1	0	1
1995-96N	L. K. Germon	A. Flower	2	0	0	2
1997-98Z	S. P. Fleming	A. D. R. Campbell	2	0	0	2
1997-98N	S. P. Fleming	A. D. R. Campbell	2	2	0	0
	In New Zealand		4	2	0	2
	In Zimbabwe		4	1	0	3
	Totals		8	3	0	5

N Played in New Zealand.   Z Played in Zimbabwe.

HIGHEST INNINGS TOTALS

For New Zealand in New Zealand: 460 at Auckland   1997-98
in Zimbabwe: 403 at Bulawayo   1997-98

For Zimbabwe in New Zealand: 326 at Auckland   1995-96
in Zimbabwe: 461 at Bulawayo   1997-98

LOWEST INNINGS TOTALS

For New Zealand in New Zealand: 251 at Auckland   1995-96
in Zimbabwe: 207 at Harare   1997-98

For Zimbabwe in New Zealand: 170 at Auckland   1997-98
in Zimbabwe: 137 at Harare   1992-93

INDIVIDUAL HUNDREDS

For New Zealand (7)

N. J. Astle (1)
114   Auckland . . .   1997-98
C. L. Cairns (1)
120   Auckland . . .   1995-96
M. D. Crowe (1)
140   Harare   1992-93
M. J. Horne (1)
157   Auckland . . .   1997-98
R. T. Latham (1)
119†   Bulawayo. . .   1992-93
C. D. McMillan (1)
139†   Wellington . .   1997-98
C. M. Spearman (1)
112   Auckland . . .   1995-96

For Zimbabwe (5)

K. J. Arnott (1)
101*†   Bulawayo. . .   1992-93
G. W. Flower (2)
104 }   Harare   1997-98
151 }
D. L. Houghton (1)
104*   Auckland . . .   1995-96
G. J. Whittall (1)
203*   Bulawayo. . .   1997-98

† *Signifies hundred on first appearance in New Zealand–Zimbabwe Tests.*

MOST APPEARANCES
(200 or more)

	Total	E	A	SA	WI	NZ	I	P	SL	Z	Ass
M. Azharuddin (I)	323	24	43	27	43	39	–	61	53	22	11
Salim Malik (P)	283	26	26	16	46	43	52	–	53	13	8
Wasim Akram (P)	275	27	34	17	56	28	41	–	43	20	9
A. R. Border (A)	273	43	–	15	61	52	38	34	23	5	2
A. Ranatunga (SL)	269	18	33	16	22	35	56	67	–	15	7
S. R. Waugh (A).	268	27	–	37	47	50	41	33	21	8	4
P. A. de Silva (SL)	259	13	30	16	25	31	54	67	–	15	8
D. L. Haynes (WI)	238	35	64	8	–	13	36	65	14	3	–
Ijaz Ahmed, sen. (P) . . .	235	19	28	18	38	25	49	–	38	13	7
Javed Miandad (P)	233	27	35	3	64	24	35	–	35	6	4
Kapil Dev (I)	225	23	41	13	42	29	–	32	34	9	2
R. B. Richardson (WI). .	224	35	51	9	–	11	32	61	21	3	1
S. R. Tendulkar (I)	218	14	22	28	24	25	–	36	39	20	10
R. S. Mahanama (SL) . .	213	11	26	15	22	22	45	52	–	14	6

Most appearances for other Test-playing countries:

	Total	E	A	SA	WI	NZ	I	P	SL	Z	Ass
J. G. Wright (NZ)	149	30	42	–	11	–	21	18	24	2	1
W. J. Cronje (SA)	168	18	39	–	17	20	26	21	15	8	4
G. A. Gooch (E).	125	–	32	1	32	16	17	16	7	3	1
A. J. Stewart (E).	125	–	20	14	22	19	14	15	12	6	3
A. Flower (Z).	113	7	8	8	3	16	21	20	16	–	14

CAPTAINCY

LIMITED-OVERS INTERNATIONAL CAPTAINS

England (301 matches; 21 captains)

G. A. Gooch 50; M. A. Atherton 43; M. W. Gatting 37; A. J. Stewart 30; R. G. D. Willis 29; J. M. Brearley 25; D. I. Gower 24; A. J. Hollioake 14; M. H. Denness 12; I. T. Botham 9; K. W. R. Fletcher 5; J. E. Emburey 4; A. J. Lamb 4; D. B. Close 3; R. Illingworth 3; G. Boycott 2; N. Gifford 2; A. W. Greig 2; J. H. Edrich 1; N. Hussain 1; A. P. E. Knott 1.

Australia (435 matches; 14 captains)

A. R. Border 178; M. A. Taylor 67; G. S. Chappell 49; K. J. Hughes 49; S. R. Waugh 49; I. M. Chappell 11; S. K. Warne 11; I. A. Healy 8; G. R. Marsh 4; G. N. Yallop 4; R. B. Simpson 2; R. J. Bright 1; D. W. Hookes 1; W. M. Lawry 1.

South Africa (173 matches; 3 captains)

W. J. Cronje 118; K. C. Wessels 52; C. E. B. Rice 3.

West Indies (372 matches; 14 captains)

I. V. A. Richards 108; R. B. Richardson 87; C. H. Lloyd 81; C. A. Walsh 43; B. C. Lara 23; C. G. Greenidge 8; D. L. Haynes 7; C. L. Hooper 4; J. C. Adams 3; M. A. Holding 2; R. B. Kanhai 2; D. L. Murray 2; P. J. L. Dujon 1; A. I. Kallicharran 1.

New Zealand (332 matches; 14 captains)

G. P. Howarth 60; S. P. Fleming 49; M. D. Crowe 44; K. R. Rutherford 37; L. K. Germon 36; J. G. Wright 31; J. V. Coney 25; J. J. Crowe 16; M. G. Burgess 8; G. M. Turner 8; D. J. Nash 7; B. E. Congdon 6; G. R. Larsen 3; A. H. Jones 2.

India (405 matches; 14 captains)

M. Azharuddin 174; Kapil Dev 74; S. R. Tendulkar 54; S. M. Gavaskar 37; D. B. Vengsarkar 18; K. Srikkanth 13; R. J. Shastri 11; A. Jadeja 8; S. Venkataraghavan 7; B. S. Bedi 4; A. L. Wadekar 2; M. Amarnath 1; S. M. H. Kirmani 1; G. R. Viswanath 1.

Pakistan (435 matches; 18 captains)

Imran Khan 139; Wasim Akram 93; Javed Miandad 62; Salim Malik 34; Aamir Sohail 22; Ramiz Raja 22; Rashid Latif 13; Zaheer Abbas 13; Saeed Anwar 8; Asif Iqbal 6; Abdul Qadir 5; Wasim Bari 5; Mushtaq Mohammad 4; Intikhab Alam 3; Majid Khan 2; Moin Khan 2; Sarfraz Nawaz 1; Waqar Younis 1.

Sri Lanka (302 matches; 10 captains)

A. Ranatunga 193; L. R. D. Mendis 61; P. A. de Silva 18; R. S. Madugalle 13; B. Warnapura 8; A. P. B. Tennekoon 4; R. S. Mahanama 2; D. S. de Silva 1; S. T. Jayasuriya 1; J. R. Ratnayeke 1.

Zimbabwe (125 matches; 5 captains)

A. D. R. Campbell 68; A. Flower 28; D. L. Houghton 17; D. A. G. Fletcher 6; A. J. Traicos 6.

Associate Members (88 matches; 12 captains)

A. Y. Karim (Kenya) 21; Akram Khan (Bangladesh) 15; Aminul Islam (Bangladesh) 11; M. O. Odumbe (Kenya) 9; Gazi Ashraf (Bangladesh) 7; Sultan M. Zarawani (UAE) 7; G. Salmond (Scotland) 5; S. W. Lubbers (Holland) 4; B. M. Mauricette (Canada) 3; Harilal R. Shah (East Africa) 3; Minhaz-ul-Abedin (Bangladesh) 2; R. P. Lefebvre (Holland) 1.

WORLD CUP RECORDS 1975–1999

WORLD CUP FINALS

1975	WEST INDIES (291-8) beat Australia (274) by 17 runs	Lord's
1979	WEST INDIES (286-9) beat England (194) by 92 runs	Lord's
1983	INDIA (183) beat West Indies (140) by 43 runs	Lord's
1987-88	AUSTRALIA (253-5) beat England (246-8) by seven runs	Calcutta
1991-92	PAKISTAN (249-6) beat England (227) by 22 runs	Melbourne
1995-96	SRI LANKA (245-3) beat Australia (241-7) by seven wickets	Lahore
1999	AUSTRALIA (133-2) beat Pakistan (132) by eight wickets	Lord's

[*Patrick Eagar*

You never doubted us, did you? Steve Waugh and the Australian team with the World Cup.

The overall quality of the Australian team meant that no one – not even an Englishman – could begrudge their right to the trophy. But Pakistan and South Africa would have been worthy winners too. The class of these three teams (one might add India's batting as well) gave the tournament enough lustre to make the whole thing seem like a triumph. Five months later, the rugby World Cup, also held in Britain, was much nearer a flop.

Yet the success came against a background of travail almost as great as Australia's. England's main objective in staging the World Cup was to reinvigorate the nation's love of the game, which had been flagging after so many years of failure by the national team. For the organisers, the worst-case scenario was that England would go out quickly.

By the time they had completed no-nonsense wins over Sri Lanka, Kenya and Zimbabwe, that fear had receded to vanishing point. Some newspapers claimed that England were already through to the Super Six stage. For them to fail, Zimbabwe had to beat South Africa, which in advance seemed improbable bordering on impossible, and then England had to lose to India very badly. It all happened. Only 16 days into the tournament, with a further 21 to go, England were gone. It was an outcome wholly in keeping with many of the farcical organisational aspects of the whole competition. The hosts were reduced to just that: handing round the cucumber sandwiches at their own tea party.

The fact that the tournament maintained public interest, even in England, in spite of this disaster, represented its greatest achievement. The fact that it got into such a pickle in the first place was its biggest failure. In previous World Cups, this situation could not have arisen. The system used

IT'S THE END OF THE WORLD

"There are honourable defeats, unfortunate defeats and then ignominious defeats. The manner by which England's interest in the cricket World Cup ended yesterday rests, unfortunately, in the final category."

Leader, *The Times*

"Let's get things fully in proportion – this was only the most catastrophic day ever for English cricket."

John Etheridge, *The Sun*

" 'We weren't quite up to it,' said Alec Stewart, world-renowned understater and wicket-keeper. Never mind up. They weren't even in the reclining position. They were flat-out rotten."

Sue Mott, *Daily Telegraph*

"We have been found wanting when it really mattered."

David Lloyd, England coach

"Flippin' Useless"

Headline, *Daily Express*

"The carnival lives on."

Tim Lamb, ECB chief executive

---

in Australasia in 1992, when all played all in a round robin with the top four going into the semi-finals, was widely admired and enjoyed. But this became impossible once it was decided to admit the top three non-Test countries, making 12 teams in all. In 1996, a ludicrous format was employed whereby everyone meandered around the subcontinent for three weeks simply to reduce nine serious contenders to eight. Then the competition proper, in effect, was staged as a straight knockout over a week.

For 1999, Terry Blake, the ECB marketing director, introduced a novel method. The 12 entrants were split into two groups, and the top three in each group went into the Super Six, carrying with them the points they had earned against the two teams who had also qualified from their group. They then played the qualifying teams from the other group, creating a final all-played-all league table, with the top four going into the semi-finals.

It took a while for people to cotton on. Then a perception grew that this was all rather elegant. Finally, the flaws became obvious. Notionally, ties on points were to be resolved by the result between the teams involved. Unfortunately, there were three-way ties in both qualifying groups; and New Zealand and Zimbabwe, fourth and fifth in the Super Six, had shared the one washed-out game of the entire tournament. The next determinant was "net run-rate", familiar for many years from one-day cricket's triangulars and quadrangulars, but little understood, and impossible for the casual spectator to work out.

This vile technicality decided the whole tournament, since the tied semi-final was resolved by the teams' positions in the Super Six, and net run-rate

ENGLAND v KENYA

At Canterbury, May 18. England won by nine wickets. Toss: England.

The first international fixture on the St Lawrence Ground proved low-key, to England's relief. Their only hiccup on the way to an unruffled victory was a 100-run stand between Shah and Tikolo, who enhanced his reputation by thumping eight fours in his 71. But Gough returned to find Shah's inside edge, then castled Odumbe for his 100th one-day wicket. He was the third player to reach the mark for England, following Ian Botham and Phil DeFreitas. The only Kenyan to make any impression after that was Odoyo, already dubbed "the African Botham", who hit one cracking six in his 34 not out, before bowling Stewart with a ball that held its line. The atmosphere was muted by filthy weather: rain delayed the start, brought the players off after 20 overs of England's innings, and would have forced a reserve day if the Kenyans had not agreed to resume in thinner drizzle at 6.40 p.m. The finish would have been earlier had the umpires correctly interpreted the regulations allowing them to cut the interval. The remaining 106 runs took Hussain and Hick only 19 overs.

Man of the Match: S. O. Tikolo.   *Attendance:* 9,643.

Kenya

†K. O. Otieno c Thorpe b Austin	0	Mohammad Sheikh b Gough	7
R. D. Shah c Stewart b Gough	46	M. A. Suji run out	0
S. O. Tikolo c Gough b Ealham	71	B 1, l-b 5, w 6, n-b 3	15
M. O. Odumbe b Gough	6		
H. S. Modi run out	5	1/7 (1) 2/107 (2) 3/115 (4) (49.4 overs) 203
A. V. Vadher b Croft	6	4/130 (5) 5/142 (6)
T. M. Odoyo not out	34	6/150 (3) 7/181 (8)
*A. Y. Karim b Ealham	9	8/186 (9) 9/202 (10)
A. O. Suji b Gough	4	10/203 (11) Score at 15 overs: 44-1

Bowling: Gough 10–1–34–4; Austin 9.4–0–41–1; Mullally 10–0–41–0; Ealham 10–0–49–2; Croft 10–1–32–1.

England

N. Hussain not out	88
*†A. J. Stewart b Odoyo	23
G. A. Hick not out	61
B 5, l-b 6, w 13, n-b 8	32
1/45 (2) (1 wkt, 39 overs) 204	
Score at 15 overs: 73-1	

G. P. Thorpe, N. H. Fairbrother, A. Flintoff, M. A. Ealham, R. D. B. Croft, I. D. Austin, D. Gough and A. D. Mullally did not bat.

Bowling: M. A. Suji 9–0–46–0; A. O. Suji 3–0–6–0; Odoyo 10–0–65–1; Karim 8–0–39–0; Odumbe 6–1–23–0; Mohammad Sheikh 3–0–14–0.

Umpires: K. T. Francis and R. E. Koertzen.   Referee: Talat Ali.

INDIA v ZIMBABWE

At Leicester, May 19. Zimbabwe won by three runs. Toss: India.

A tumultuous crowd witnessed the closest match of the tournament so far. India needed only nine from two overs when Olonga returned to the attack. His previous three overs had cost 17, as he lost his run-up and bowled some spectacular wides and a beamer. But this time Singh was caught at cover off his second ball, Srinath yorked with his fifth, and Prasad lbw to the last. Zimbabwe had played two, won two; India played two, lost two. Zimbabwe made slow progress with the bat, except when Andy Flower and Campbell were together, but haywire bowling donated 51 extras, a fifth of the total. The resulting over-rate was so slow that India's reply was docked a crucial four overs. Not that Zimbabwe were misers, either: there were 90 extras in the match, a World Cup record, but one which lasted only 24 hours. India started well enough, bringing up 44 in the seventh over before Dravid fell. Ramesh, replacing Tendulkar who had flown back to Mumbai to attend his father's funeral, and Jadeja added 99 before Ramesh holed out to mid-on. The middle order rattled along and, when Srinath lofted two huge sixes, India seemed home and dry until Olonga's over. Mongia made five dismissals to equal the one-day international record.

Man of the Match: G. W. Flower.   *Attendance:* 4,005.

Zimbabwe

N. C. Johnson c Mongia b Srinath	7	E. A. Brandes c Mongia b Prasad	2
G. W. Flower c Mongia b Jadeja	45	H. K. Olonga not out	1
P. A. Strang b Agarkar	18	L-b 14, w 21, n-b 16	51
M. W. Goodwin c Singh b Ganguly	17		
†A. Flower not out	68	1/12 (1) 2/45 (3) (9 wkts, 50 overs)	252
*A. D. R. Campbell st Mongia b Kumble	24	3/87 (4) 4/143 (2)	
G. J. Whittall b Kumble	4	5/203 (6) 6/211 (7)	
S. V. Carlisle b Srinath	1	7/214 (8) 8/243 (9)	
H. H. Streak c Mongia b Prasad	14	9/250 (10) Score at 15 overs: 64-2	

Bowling: Srinath 10–1–35–2; Prasad 10–1–37–2; Agarkar 9–0–70–1; Ganguly 5–0–22–1; Singh 2–0–11–0; Kumble 10–0–41–2; Jadeja 4–0–22–1.

India

S. C. Ganguly c Brandes b Johnson	9	A. Kumble not out	1
S. Ramesh c Goodwin b G. W. Flower	55	B. K. V. Prasad lbw b Olonga	0
R. Dravid c G. W. Flower b Streak	13	B 1, l-b 4, w 24, n-b 10	39
*M. Azharuddin c Campbell b Streak	7		
A. Jadeja lbw b Streak	43	1/13 (1) 2/44 (3) 3/56 (4) (45 overs)	249
R. R. Singh c Campbell b Olonga	35	4/155 (2) 5/174 (5)	
A. B. Agarkar run out	1	6/175 (7) 7/219 (8)	
†N. R. Mongia b Whittall	28	8/246 (6) 9/249 (9)	
J. Srinath b Olonga	18	10/249 (11) Score at 13 overs: 80-3	

Bowling: Brandes 3–0–27–0; Johnson 7–0–51–1; Streak 9–0–36–3; Olonga 4–0–22–3; Whittall 4–0–26–1; Strang 8–0–49–0; G. W. Flower 10–0–33–1.

Umpires: D. L. Orchard and P. Willey.   Referee: C. W. Smith.

SOUTH AFRICA v SRI LANKA

At Northampton, May 19. South Africa won by 89 runs. Toss: Sri Lanka.

The South Africans showed their resilience with a brilliant victory after a start that would probably have floored any other team in the world. Put in, South Africa collapsed, with two of the wickets falling to contentious decisions from the third umpire Ken Palmer. First, he ruled that Pollock was caught when the ball ricocheted off Ranatunga's shin to the bowler; everyone else who saw the replay thought it had bounced first. Palmer then gave out Cullinan, caught by Vaas, who got rid of the ball just before he toppled over the boundary. This seemed justifiable under Law 32: Vaas retained "complete control over the further disposal of the ball" before touching the rope. Few South Africans took this view. Cullinan's dismissal made South Africa 122 for eight. They got to 199 thanks to a blast from Klusener, who hit an unbeaten 52 off 45 deliveries, including 22 in the last over off Vaas. South Africa took the field fired up. Kallis achieved swing at a fierce pace, removed Sri Lanka's top three in nine balls, and had a slip catch dropped. The sight of Donald coming on second change and Klusener next was far too much for the remaining batsmen.

Man of the Match: L. Klusener.   *Attendance:* 7,326.

South Africa

G. Kirsten b Vaas	14	L. Klusener not out 52
H. H. Gibbs c Kaluwitharana b Vaas ...	5	S. Elworthy c Kaluwitharana b Vaas ... 23
†M. V. Boucher b Wickremasinghe	1	A. A. Donald not out 3
J. H. Kallis c Mahanama		L-b 2, w 7, n-b 4 13
b Wickremasinghe ..	12	
D. J. Cullinan c Vaas b Muralitharan ...	49	1/22 (1) 2/24 (2) (9 wkts, 50 overs) 199
*W. J. Cronje run out	8	3/24 (3) 4/53 (4)
J. N. Rhodes c Jayasuriya		5/69 (6) 6/103 (7)
b Muralitharan .	17	7/115 (8) 8/122 (5)
S. M. Pollock c and b Muralitharan....	2	9/166 (10)
		Score at 15 overs: 54-4

Bowling: Wickremasinghe 10-1-45-2; Vaas 10-0-46-3; Jayawardene 10-0-46-0; Muralitharan 10-1-25-3; Chandana 7-0-26-0; Jayasuriya 3-1-9-0.

Sri Lanka

S. T. Jayasuriya b Kallis	5	W. P. U. J. C. Vaas c Pollock
†R. S. Kaluwitharana c Cullinan		b Klusener . 1
b Kallis .	5	G. P. Wickremasinghe b Klusener 6
M. S. Atapattu c Boucher b Kallis.....	1	M. Muralitharan not out 0
P. A. de Silva lbw b Pollock	1	L-b 5, w 10, n-b 2......... 17
R. S. Mahanama lbw b Pollock.......	36	
*A. Ranatunga c Boucher b Donald....	7	1/12 (2) 2/13 (1) 3/14 (3) (35.2 overs) 110
D. P. M. D. Jayawardene c Kallis		4/14 (4) 5/31 (6)
b Elworthy .	22	6/66 (7) 7/86 (8)
U. D. U. Chandana c Cullinan		8/98 (9) 9/110 (5)
b Klusener .	9	10/110 (10) Score at 15 overs: 37-5

Bowling: Pollock 8-3-10-2; Kallis 8-0-26-3; Elworthy 8-1-23-1; Donald 6-1-25-1; Klusener 5.2-1-21-3.

Umpires: S. A. Bucknor and R. S. Dunne.   Referee: J. R. Reid.

ENGLAND v SOUTH AFRICA

At The Oval, May 22. South Africa won by 122 runs. Toss: England.

England's comfortable passage thus far was put in stark perspective by the South African steamroller. The attack was reshaped, with Fraser replacing Austin. This achieved little as Kirsten and Gibbs started with a century stand at five an over. But Ealham wobbled the ball around to good effect, and three wickets tumbled for one run. Gough then took two wickets in successive balls before Klusener's inimitable clean hitting swelled the total: he clubbed an undefeated 48 in 40 balls, and took 12 off Ealham's last over. The target was still modest but England struggled from the start. Stewart and Hussain may have been unlucky with their decisions, but there was no excuse for the middle order's performance. Donald trapped Thorpe in his first over, and removed Flintoff for a duck in his third. In between, the battle of Zimbabwe's expatriates was won by Elworthy, who had Hick caught at mid-wicket. An inspired parry and grab by Rhodes at point accounted for Croft, and England just limped into three figures. Failure to reach a respectable total damaged their net run-rate; little noticed at the time, this was to prove fatal.

Man of the Match: L. Klusener.   *Attendance:* 18,665.

South Africa

G. Kirsten c Stewart b Ealham	45	S. M. Pollock b Gough	0
H. H. Gibbs c Hick b Ealham	60	†M. V. Boucher not out	16
J. H. Kallis b Mullally	0	L-b 7, w 5	12
D. J. Cullinan c Fraser b Mullally	10		
*W. J. Cronje c Stewart b Flintoff	16	1/111 (2) 2/112 (1)	(7 wkts, 50 overs) 225
J. N. Rhodes c sub (N. V. Knight)		3/112 (3) 4/127 (4)	
b Gough	18	5/146 (5) 6/168 (6)	
L. Klusener not out	48	7/168 (8)	Score at 15 overs: 73-0

S. Elworthy and A. A. Donald did not bat.

Bowling: Gough 10–1–33–2; Fraser 10–0–54–0; Mullally 10–1–28–2; Croft 2–0–13–0; Ealham 10–2–48–2; Flintoff 8–0–42–1.

England

N. Hussain c Boucher b Kallis	2	A. R. C. Fraser c Kirsten b Pollock	3
*†A. J. Stewart lbw b Kallis	0	A. D. Mullally not out	1
G. A. Hick c Gibbs b Elworthy	21	L-b 4, w 9, n-b 1	14
G. P. Thorpe lbw b Donald	14		
N. H. Fairbrother lbw b Donald	21	1/2 (2) 2/6 (1) 3/39 (4)	(41 overs) 103
A. Flintoff c Rhodes b Donald	0	4/44 (3) 5/45 (6)	
M. A. Ealham c Cullinan b Donald	5	6/60 (7) 7/78 (8)	
R. D. B. Croft c Rhodes b Klusener	12	8/97 (9) 9/99 (5)	
D. Gough c Cronje b Elworthy	10	10/103 (10)	Score at 15 overs: 42-3

Bowling: Kallis 8–0–29–2; Pollock 9–3–13–1; Elworthy 10–3–24–2; Donald 8–1–17–4; Klusener 6–0–16–1.

Umpires: R. S. Dunne and S. Venkataraghavan.   Referee: C. W. Smith.

SRI LANKA v ZIMBABWE

At Worcester, May 22. Sri Lanka won by four wickets. Toss: Sri Lanka.

Sri Lanka's flimsy hopes of defending their title were kept alive for a few days longer after Zimbabwe turned in their most error-strewn performance to date. They lost two batsmen to unnecessary run-outs and two more (Andy Flower and Streak) to catches off reverse sweeps. Sri Lanka responded to gifts like these by bowling and fielding with more zest than at any time in this competition. Though Brandes and Olonga took 17 off the last over, from Vaas, Zimbabwe lost any hope of advantage with another flurry of wides, 21 in all, taking their total to 70 in three games. Though Jayasuriya and de Silva – the fallen idols – failed once again, Sri Lanka were put on the way to victory by Mahanama and Atapattu, and were not seriously troubled. Zimbabwe's coach, Dave Houghton, ascribed the wides to nerves: "I think the guys are nervous because we're doing so well."

Man of the Match: M. S. Atapattu.   *Attendance:* 5,107.

Zimbabwe

N. C. Johnson c Wickremasinghe b Upashantha .	8	S. V. Carlisle run out	27
G. W. Flower c Kaluwitharana b Wickremasinghe .	42	H. H. Streak c Atapattu b Muralitharan .	10
		E. A. Brandes not out	19
P. A. Strang b Wickremasinghe	5	H. K. Olonga not out	5
M. W. Goodwin run out	21	L-b 3, w 6	9
†A. Flower c Kaluwitharana b Jayasuriya	41		
*A. D. R. Campbell c Kaluwitharana b Wickremasinghe .	6	1/21 (1) 2/34 (3) (9 wkts, 50 overs) 197	
		3/78 (4) 4/81 (2)	
G. J. Whittall c Ranatunga b Muralitharan .	4	5/89 (6) 6/94 (7)	
		7/162 (8) 8/162 (5)	
		9/176 (9) Score at 15 overs: 53-2	

Bowling: Vaas 10–1–47–0; Upashantha 10–1–43–1; Wickremasinghe 10–1–30–3; Jayawardene 1–0–8–0; Muralitharan 10–2–29–2; Jayasuriya 7–0–28–1; de Silva 2–0–9–0.

Sri Lanka

S. T. Jayasuriya c Goodwin b Johnson . .	6	†R. S. Kaluwitharana not out	18
R. S. Mahanama b G. J. Whittall	31	W. P. U. J. C. Vaas not out	17
M. S. Atapattu c Campbell b Streak. . . .	54	L-b 6, w 21, n-b 5	32
P. A. de Silva c sub (A. R. Whittall) b G. J. Whittall .	6		
		1/13 (1) 2/75 (2) (6 wkts, 46 overs) 198	
*A. Ranatunga c and b G. J. Whittall. . .	3	3/93 (4) 4/108 (5)	
D. P. M. D. Jayawardene lbw b Streak . .	31	5/150 (3) 6/157 (6) Score at 15 overs: 54-1	

K. E. A. Upashantha, G. P. Wickremasinghe and M. Muralitharan did not bat.

Bowling: Brandes 8–0–28–0; Johnson 7–1–29–1; Streak 8–1–30–2; G. J. Whittall 10–1–35–3; Olonga 9–0–50–0; G. W. Flower 2–0–10–0; Strang 2–0–10–0.

Umpires: S. A. Bucknor and D. R. Shepherd.   Referee: Talat Ali.

INDIA v KENYA

At Bristol, May 23. India won by 94 runs. Toss: Kenya.

A passionate, awe-inspiring display by Tendulkar kept India in the hunt for the Super Six. He had returned from his father's funeral in India the day before. And, when he came in at 92 for two, Bristol heard a roar from the crowd that probably startled the lions in the zoo. Tendulkar started carefully, but accelerated after each landmark: 50 came off 54 balls, 100 in 84. He flicked the last ball of the innings over mid-wicket for six – his third, in addition to 16 fours – to finish on 140 from 101 balls. It was his 22nd one-day international century, but the first when he was not opening. The stand of 237 in 29 overs with Dravid, who was in lovely touch while scoring a century (almost ignored), was the highest in World Cup history – until India's next match. It beat the 207, also against Kenya, by the Waughs in 1996. Kenya's batsmen were so stunned that they failed to hit the boundary until the tenth over. But Tikolo guided them to respectability in a partnership of 118 with Otieno. In the absence of the injured Kumble and Prasad, Mohanty, swinging the ball both ways, was the pick of the bowlers. But the day belonged to Tendulkar, who dedicated his highest World Cup score to his father's memory.

Man of the Match: S. R. Tendulkar.   *Attendance:* 8,508.

India

S. Ramesh run out	44
S. C. Ganguly lbw b Suji	13
R. Dravid not out	104
S. R. Tendulkar not out	140
L-b 5, w 20, n-b 3	28

1/50 (2) 2/92 (1)   (2 wkts, 50 overs) 329
Score at 15 overs: 63-1

*M. Azharuddin, A. Jadeja, †N. R. Mongia, A. B. Agarkar, J. Srinath, N. Chopra and D. S. Mohanty did not bat.

Bowling: Suji 10–2–26–1; Angara 7–0–66–0; Odoyo 9–0–59–0; Tikolo 9–1–62–0; Karim 7–0–52–0; Odumbe 8–0–59–0.

Kenya

†K. O. Otieno c Agarkar b Chopra	56	A. V. Vadher not out	6
R. D. Shah c sub (R. R. Singh) b Mohanty	9	M. A. Suji not out	1
S. K. Gupta lbw b Mohanty	0		
S. O. Tikolo lbw b Mohanty	58	L-b 10, w 31, n-b 3	44
M. O. Odumbe c sub (R. R. Singh) b Mohanty	14	1/29 (2) 2/29 (3) (7 wkts, 50 overs) 235	
T. M. Odoyo b Agarkar	39	3/147 (1) 4/165 (4)	
*A. Y. Karim b Srinath	8	5/193 (5) 6/209 (7)	
		7/233 (6) Score at 15 overs: 51-2	

H. S. Modi and J. O. Angara did not bat.

Bowling: Srinath 10–3–31–1; Agarkar 10–0–35–1; Mohanty 10–0–56–4; Ganguly 9–0–47–0; Chopra 10–2–33–1; Tendulkar 1–0–23–0.

Umpires: D. B. Cowie and I. D. Robinson.   Referee: P. J. Burge.

ENGLAND v ZIMBABWE

At Nottingham, May 25. England won by seven wickets. Toss: England.

In their first match against England in England, Zimbabwe played like the novices they had never resembled when facing them elsewhere. On a cool morning, their batsmen failed to warm to the task. Strang gave a new twist to pinch-hitting: you had to pinch yourself if he hit the ball. His duck stretched over 17 deliveries. England's six-pack of seamers were fizzing: Fraser was his old immaculate self, and even held a running catch in the deep. Zimbabwe gave themselves a chance by surviving 50 overs and taking two early wickets, but the sun came out, the swing evaporated and Hussain and Thorpe coolly compiled 123 in 22 overs – their first century one-day partnership. England's determination to make certain was again to prove disastrous in retrospect. Fairbrother scored seven in 23 balls at the end without worrying about net run-rate.

Man of the Match: A. D. Mullally.　　　　*Attendance:* 14,191.

Zimbabwe

N. C. Johnson b Gough	6	H. H. Streak not out	11
G. W. Flower c Thorpe b Ealham	35	H. K. Olonga not out	1
P. A. Strang c Hick b Mullally	0	L-b 16, w 17, n-b 1	34
M. W. Goodwin c Thorpe b Mullally	4		
†A. Flower run out	10	1/21 (1) 2/29 (3)　(8 wkts, 50 overs)	167
*A. D. R. Campbell c Stewart b Fraser	24	3/47 (4) 4/79 (5)	
G. J. Whittall lbw b Ealham	28	5/86 (2) 6/124 (6)	
S. V. Carlisle c Stewart b Gough	14	7/141 (7) 8/159 (8)　Score at 15 overs: 39-2	

M. Mbangwa did not bat.

Bowling: Gough 10–2–24–2; Fraser 10–0–27–1; Mullally 10–4–16–2; Ealham 10–1–35–2; Flintoff 3–0–14–0; Hollioake 7–0–35–0.

England

N. Hussain not out	57
*†A. J. Stewart c Goodwin b Johnson	12
G. A. Hick c A. Flower b Mbangwa	4
G. P. Thorpe c Campbell b Mbangwa	62
N. H. Fairbrother not out	7
L-b 3, w 16, n-b 7	26
1/21 (2) 2/36 (3)　(3 wkts, 38.3 overs)	168
3/159 (4)　Score at 15 overs: 54-2	

A. Flintoff, A. J. Hollioake, M. A. Ealham, D. Gough, A. R. C. Fraser and A. D. Mullally did not bat.

Bowling: Johnson 7–2–20–1; Streak 8–0–37–0; Mbangwa 7–1–28–2; Whittall 4–0–23–0; Olonga 3–0–27–0; Strang 9.3–1–30–0.

Umpires: S. A. Bucknor and D. B. Hair.　Referee: Talat Ali.

INDIA v SRI LANKA

At Taunton, May 26. India won by 157 runs. Toss: Sri Lanka.

Undisciplined Sri Lankan bowling, a pitch of even bounce, short boundaries and batting which ranged from the classical to the brutal set a welter of one-day international records. Ganguly and Dravid's partnership of 318 in 45 overs was the highest in any limited-overs international, surpassing the previous record of 275 set by Azharuddin and Jadeja against Zimbabwe in 1997-98. Ganguly made 183 in 158 balls, with 16 fours and seven sixes, the fourth-highest one-day international score, and the second in World Cup history behind Gary Kirsten's 188 not out against the United Arab Emirates in 1996. India's 373 for six was the second highest total in limited-overs internationals after Sri Lanka's 398 for five against Kenya in the 1996 World Cup, and thus the highest against Test opposition. Ranatunga's decision to bowl seemed justified when Vaas cut the ball back sharply to hit Ramesh's off stump. However, Dravid, aggressively, and Ganguly, elegantly, soon gained complete dominance, with even Muralitharan unable to stem the flow of runs. Dravid established himself as the pacemaker, reaching his second successive hundred at almost a run a ball. But Ganguly made his own century, from 119 deliveries, then began to hit over the top, racing to 183 in another 39 balls. Sri Lanka restored Kaluwitharana to open the innings but, once he and Jayasuriya were out within five overs, the game was all but finished. Likewise Sri Lanka's defence of their crown.

Man of the Match: S. C. Ganguly.   *Attendance:* 6,778.

India

S. Ramesh b Vaas	5	*M. Azharuddin not out	12
S. C. Ganguly c sub (U. D. U. Chandana) b Wickremasinghe	183	J. Srinath not out	0
†R. Dravid run out	145	L-b 3, w 12, n-b 6	21
S. R. Tendulkar b Jayasuriya	2		
A. Jadeja c and b Wickremasinghe	5	1/6 (1) 2/324 (3)	(6 wkts, 50 overs) 373
R. R. Singh c de Silva b Wickremasinghe	0	3/344 (4) 4/349 (5)	
		5/349 (6) 6/372 (2)	Score at 15 overs: 94-1

A. Kumble, B. K. V. Prasad and D. S. Mohanty did not bat.

Bowling: Vaas 10–0–84–1; Upashantha 10–0–80–0; Wickremasinghe 10–0–65–3; Muralitharan 10–0–60–0; Jayawardene 3–0–21–0; Jayasuriya 3–0–37–1; de Silva 4–0–23–0.

Sri Lanka

S. T. Jayasuriya run out	3	G. P. Wickremasinghe not out	2
†R. S. Kaluwitharana lbw b Srinath	7	M. Muralitharan c Tendulkar b Singh	4
M. S. Atapattu lbw b Mohanty	29		
P. A. de Silva lbw b Singh	56	B 4, l-b 12, w 8, n-b 7	31
D. P. M. D. Jayawardene lbw b Kumble	4		
*A. Ranatunga b Singh	42	1/5 (1) 2/23 (2) 3/74 (3)	(42.3 overs) 216
R. S. Mahanama run out	32	4/79 (5) 5/147 (4)	
W. P. U. J. C. Vaas c Ramesh b Singh	1	6/181 (6) 7/187 (8)	
K. E. A. Upashantha c Azharuddin b Singh	5	8/203 (9) 9/204 (7)	
		10/216 (11)	Score at 15 overs: 78-3

Bowling: Srinath 7–0–33–1; Prasad 8–0–41–0; Mohanty 5–0–31–1; Kumble 8–0–27–1; Ganguly 5–0–37–0; Singh 9.3–0–31–5.

Umpires: R. S. Dunne and D. R. Shepherd.   Referee: C. W. Smith.

KENYA v SOUTH AFRICA

At Amstelveen, May 26. South Africa won by seven wickets. Toss: South Africa.

The World Cup crossed to the Continent as the Netherlands staged its first official one-day international. Amstelveen, a southern suburb of Amsterdam, provided a picturesque ground, and a genuine grass pitch, provoking plenty of cannabis jokes. The first hour hinted that Kenya could pull off a surprise, as their openers galloped to 66 by the 16th over; Shah showed no fear of Donald and his colleagues. But, once Elworthy made the breakthrough, the South Africans got a grip on the game, and Klusener took five wickets to claim his third consecutive match award. For once, he was not required to bat as well. A target of 153 hardly extended South Africa, though they used up a leisurely 41 overs; Gibbs hit a run-a-ball 38, and then Kallis, who almost missed the match after forgetting to bring his passport, and Cullinan completed the job.

Man of the Match: L. Klusener.   *Attendance:* 4,260.

Kenya

†K. O. Otieno lbw b Elworthy	26	M. A. Suji not out	6
R. D. Shah c Boucher b Donald	50	J. O. Angara b Klusener	6
S. K. Gupta b Elworthy	1	L-b 5, w 7, n-b 2	14
S. O. Tikolo c Cronje b Klusener	10		
M. O. Odumbe b Donald	7	1/66 (1) 2/80 (3) 3/82 (2) (44.3 overs) 152	
A. V. Vadher c and b Klusener	2	4/91 (5) 5/104 (4)	
T. M. Odoyo lbw b Klusener	0	6/104 (7) 7/107 (6)	
*A. Y. Karim lbw b Cronje	22	8/138 (8) 9/140 (9)	
Mohammad Sheikh b Klusener	8	10/152 (11) Score at 15 overs: 64-0	

Bowling: Pollock 8–1–22–0; Kallis 8–0–37–0; Donald 8–1–42–2; Elworthy 10–2–20–2; Klusener 8.3–3–21–5; Cronje 2–0–5–1.

South Africa

G. Kirsten b Odumbe	27	D. J. Cullinan not out	35
H. H. Gibbs lbw b Odoyo	38	B 4, w 1, n-b 1	6
†M. V. Boucher c Mohammad Sheikh b Angara	3	1/55 (2) 2/58 (3) (3 wkts, 41 overs) 153	
J. H. Kallis not out	44	3/86 (1) Score at 15 overs: 63-2	

*W. J. Cronje, J. N. Rhodes, L. Klusener, S. M. Pollock, S. Elworthy and A. A. Donald did not bat.

Bowling: Suji 6–0–18–0; Karim 7–0–43–0; Angara 8–1–34–1; Odoyo 9–3–18–1; Mohammad Sheikh 4–0–21–0; Odumbe 7–1–15–1.

Umpires: D. B. Cowie and P. Willey.   Referee: R. Subba Row.

SOUTH AFRICA v ZIMBABWE

At Chelmsford, May 29. Zimbabwe won by 48 runs. Toss: Zimbabwe.

The upset of the cup to date was a disaster for both England and, ultimately, South Africa, whose elimination in the semi-final could be backdated to losing this match. Zimbabwe got off to a flyer. Johnson – who had played for South Africa A before defecting back in September 1998 – and Grant Flower flailed at loose stuff from Kallis and Pollock, racing to 65 in 14 overs. It did not quite last. After hitting ten fours in his fifty, Johnson failed to manage another, and Donald grabbed three wickets; Campbell was his 200th victim in 117 one-day internationals. No one thought 233 would be enough, but a rainstorm at lunch did funny things. Johnson's opening delivery reared up at Kirsten, and Andy Whittall took the first of three great catches. Gibbs was run out by Huckle, Boucher was caught off a Streak no-ball only to be trapped in the same over, and Kallis went fourth ball. Then Cronje was yorked by Johnson, and Rhodes snared by the inspired Streak. South Africa were in disarray and 40 for six; Zimbabwe's fielding was electric. Pollock scored a fine fifty, but when he was caught on the long-off boundary it was virtually over. Not even Klusener, who went to his fifty with a swept six, could save them. Zimbabwe were probably more stunned than South Africa; it was their first win over their neighbours at any level, and meant that they started the Super Six stage joint leaders with Pakistan.

Man of the Match: N. C. Johnson.   *Attendance:* 4,696.

Zimbabwe

N. C. Johnson c Pollock b Donald	76	H. H. Streak not out		9
G. W. Flower c Cullinan b Elworthy	19			
M. W. Goodwin c Kirsten b Klusener	34	B 1, l-b 15, w 8, n-b 4		28
†A. Flower run out	29			—
*A. D. R. Campbell lbw b Donald	0	1/65 (2) 2/131 (3)	(6 wkts, 50 overs)	233
G. J. Whittall c Cullinan b Donald	20	3/170 (1) 4/175 (5)		
S. V. Carlisle not out	18	5/186 (4) 6/214 (6)	Score at 15 overs: 66-1	

A. R. Whittall, A. G. Huckle and H. K. Olonga did not bat.

Bowling: Pollock 10–1–39–0; Kallis 6–0–36–0; Donald 10–1–41–3; Elworthy 6–0–32–1; Klusener 9–0–36–1; Cronje 9–0–33–0.

South Africa

G. Kirsten c A. R. Whittall b Johnson	0	S. Elworthy c A. R. Whittall b Streak		1
H. H. Gibbs run out	9	A. A. Donald c Streak b Olonga		7
†M. V. Boucher lbw b Streak	8	B 2, l-b 1, w 8, n-b 7		18
J. H. Kallis c A. Flower b Johnson	0			—
D. J. Cullinan c and b A. R. Whittall	29	1/0 (1) 2/24 (2) 3/25 (3)	(47.2 overs)	185
*W. J. Cronje b Johnson	4	4/25 (4) 5/34 (6)		
J. N. Rhodes lbw b Streak	5	6/40 (7) 7/106 (5)		
S. M. Pollock c Olonga b A. R. Whittall	52	8/149 (8) 9/150 (10)		
L. Klusener not out	52	10/185 (11)	Score at 15 overs: 53-6	

Bowling: Johnson 8–1–27–3; Streak 9–1–35–3; G. J. Whittall 4–0–20–0; Olonga 4.2–0–17–1; Huckle 10–1–35–0; A. R. Whittall 10–0–41–2; G. W. Flower 2–0–7–0.

Umpires: D. R. Shepherd and S. Venkataraghavan.   Referee: R. Subba Row.

KENYA v SRI LANKA

At Southampton, May 30. Sri Lanka won by 45 runs. Toss: Kenya.

The last time these teams met in the World Cup, at Kandy in March 1996, Sri Lanka piled up 398 for five, still the highest total in a one-day international, as they surged irresistibly towards the capture of the trophy. This was a much quieter affair, on a grey and drizzly day, between two teams with nothing to play for. A more modest 275 was still comfortably Sri Lanka's highest score of the competition. The openers managed 72 in 15 overs before Odoyo snatched three quick wickets, but Sri Lanka owed most to a stand of 64 in seven between Jayawardene and Vaas – though by then the ball was so wet the Kenyans had trouble gripping it. Their reply slumped to 52 for five, before Odumbe and Vadher brought Kenya's campaign to a dignified conclusion by adding 161, a record for the sixth wicket in any limited-overs international.

Man of the Match: M. O. Odumbe.   *Attendance:* 4,670.

Sri Lanka

S. T. Jayasuriya lbw b Odoyo	39	W. P. U. J. C. Vaas not out			29
R. S. Mahanama b Odoyo	21	G. P. Wickremasinghe not out			0
M. S. Atapattu c Otieno b Angara	52				
P. A. de Silva c Suji b Odoyo	10	L-b 7, w 16, n-b 3			26
*A. Ranatunga run out	50				
U. D. U. Chandana c Otieno b Kamande	0	1/72 (1) 2/74 (2)	(8 wkts, 50 overs)		275
D. P. M. D. Jayawardene c Shah b Suji	45	3/87 (4) 4/191 (5)			
†R. S. Kaluwitharana c Chudasama		5/191 (6) 6/199 (3)			
b Angara	3	7/209 (8) 8/273 (7)	Score at 15 overs: 72-1		

M. Muralitharan did not bat.

Bowling: Suji 9–1–58–1; Angara 10–0–50–2; Odoyo 10–2–56–3; Karim 10–0–35–0; Kamande 9–0–51–1; Odumbe 2–0–18–0.

Kenya

†K. O. Otieno lbw b Vaas	0	A. V. Vadher not out			73
R. D. Shah c Muralitharan		T. M. Odoyo not out			16
b Jayawardene	12	B 4, l-b 8, w 8, n-b 1			21
D. N. Chudasama b Vaas	3				
S. O. Tikolo lbw b Wickremasinghe	19	1/0 (1) 2/10 (3)	(6 wkts, 50 overs)		230
*A. Y. Karim lbw b Jayawardene	4	3/33 (4) 4/36 (2)			
M. O. Odumbe b Jayasuriya	82	5/52 (5) 6/213 (6)	Score at 15 overs: 37-4		

M. A. Suji, J. O. Angara and J. K. Kamande did not bat.

Bowling: Vaas 7–1–26–2; Wickremasinghe 9–1–27–1; Jayawardene 10–0–56–2; Muralitharan 3–0–11–0; Chandana 1–0–13–0; Jayasuriya 10–1–39–1; de Silva 10–0–46–0.

Umpires: D. L. Orchard and P. Willey.   Referee: Talat Ali.

GROUP B

AUSTRALIA v SCOTLAND

At Worcester, May 16. Australia won by six wickets. Toss: Australia. International debuts: Scotland (all).

Australia recorded the expected victory, but it was a sluggish performance: Steve Waugh called his team's fielding "atrocious". Three chances went down – and the bowling was almost as uninspired. Salmond twice skipped down the pitch to McGrath during his perky 31. The first ball of Scotland's first official international was crashed through the covers for four by Patterson, an Ayr estate agent, but they managed only one more run before the end of the fifth over, struggling under overcast skies. Late impetus came from Hamilton, the Yorkshire all-rounder born near Edinburgh, who unfurled some booming cover drives. Australia used up all but five overs of their innings to win. Gilchrist perished early, snaffled at leg slip off Asim Butt, the Lahore-born seamer, but they passed 100 without further loss. Then Ponting was wonderfully caught by Allingham, running full tilt and diving at mid-wicket, and Lehmann dragged one on from off-spinner Dyer. Mark Waugh scored the game's only fifty, and his brother Steve struck seven fours to see them past their modest target. Steve was jostled by pitch invaders as he left the field, a less alarming experience than the rioting he had recently survived in the Caribbean, but enough for him to demand better security. The atmosphere – boozy but cheery – was typified by a spectator wearing an Australian team shirt and a kilt.

Man of the Match: M. E. Waugh.   *Attendance:* 5,086.

Scotland

B. M. W. Patterson c Gilchrist b Fleming	10	J. A. R. Blain not out	3
I. L. Philip c S. R. Waugh b McGrath . .	17		
M. J. D. Allingham st Gilchrist b Warne .	3	L-b 9, w 22, n-b 8	39
M. J. Smith c Bevan b Lee	13		
*G. Salmond c Gilchrist b S. R. Waugh .	31	1/19 (1) 2/37 (3) (7 wkts, 50 overs) 181	
G. M. Hamilton b Warne	34	3/52 (2) 4/87 (4)	
J. E. Brinkley c Dale b Warne	23	5/105 (5) 6/167 (7)	
†A. G. Davies not out	8	7/169 (6) Score at 15 overs: 29-1	

Asim Butt and N. R. Dyer did not bat.

Bowling: Fleming 9–2–19–1; Dale 10–2–35–0; McGrath 9–0–32–1; Warne 10–0–39–3; Lee 6–1–25–1; S. R. Waugh 6–0–22–1.

Australia

†A. C. Gilchrist c Philip b Asim Butt . .	6	M. G. Bevan not out	11
M. E. Waugh c and b Dyer	67	L-b 3, w 5, n-b 8	16
R. T. Ponting c Allingham b Blain	33		
D. S. Lehmann b Dyer	0	1/17 (1) 2/101 (3) (4 wkts, 44.5 overs) 182	
*S. R. Waugh not out	49	3/101 (4) 4/141 (2) Score at 15 overs: 48-1	

S. Lee, S. K. Warne, D. W. Fleming, A. C. Dale and G. D. McGrath did not bat.

Bowling: Blain 8–0–35–1; Asim Butt 10–3–21–1; Brinkley 8–0–43–0; Hamilton 8.5–0–37–0; Dyer 10–1–43–2.

Umpires: R. S. Dunne and P. Willey.   Referee: R. S. Madugalle.

PAKISTAN v WEST INDIES

At Bristol, May 16. Pakistan won by 27 runs. Toss: Pakistan. International debut: R. L. Powell.

In front of a vociferous crowd – mostly their own supporters – Pakistan overcame a grim start thanks to their superior depth in batting and bowling. At 42 for four in the 19th over, Wasim Akram's decision to bat under leaden skies looked questionable. But Lara, a bowler short to beef up the batting, persisted too long with his three strike bowlers. Ijaz Ahmed saw off the immediate danger, and allowed Wasim and Azhar Mahmood to feast on part-timers. Lara was hampered by an ankle injury to Arthurton, and ended up giving the 47th over to the debutant Powell, with disastrous results: all but four of the last 15 overs came from second-string bowlers, enabling Pakistan to crash 80 from the last 48 balls. West Indies began with a bemused Campbell edging an intended pull off Shoaib Akhtar's first ball for six over the slips. Shoaib gained revenge in his next over when Campbell missed a straight, extremely fast, delivery. None of the top order prospered against an unrelenting attack, and it fell to Chanderpaul to fight back single-handedly.

Man of the Match: Azhar Mahmood.　　　　　*Attendance:* 8,629.

Pakistan

Saeed Anwar c Lara b Walsh	10	†Moin Khan not out 11
Shahid Afridi c Jacobs b Walsh	11	Saqlain Mushtaq not out 2
Abdur Razzaq b Dillon	7	
Ijaz Ahmed, sen. lbw b Dillon	36	B 1, l-b 12, w 23, n-b 2 38
Inzamam-ul-Haq c Jacobs b Dillon	0	
Yousuf Youhana c and b Simmons	34	1/22 (2) 2/23 (1)　(8 wkts, 50 overs) 229
Azhar Mahmood c sub (N. O. Perry)		3/42 (3) 4/42 (5)
b Ambrose	37	5/102 (4) 6/135 (6)
*Wasim Akram b Walsh	43	7/209 (7) 8/217 (8)　Score at 15 overs: 38-2

Shoaib Akhtar did not bat.

Bowling: Ambrose 10–2–36–1; Walsh 10–3–28–3; Dillon 10–1–29–3; Simmons 10–0–40–1; Arthurton 1–0–10–0; Adams 8–0–57–0; Powell 1–0–16–0.

West Indies

S. L. Campbell b Shoaib Akhtar	9	C. E. L. Ambrose c Moin Khan
†R. D. Jacobs c Inzamam-ul-Haq		b Abdur Razzaq . 1
b Abdur Razzaq .	25	K. L. T. Arthurton c Saeed Anwar
J. C. Adams c Inzamam-ul-Haq		b Azhar Mahmood . 6
b Azhar Mahmood .	23	M. Dillon run out 6
*B. C. Lara c sub (Mushtaq Ahmed)		C. A. Walsh not out 0
b Abdur Razzaq .	11	B 1, l-b 8, w 20, n-b 6 35
S. Chanderpaul c Yousuf Youhana		
b Shoaib Akhtar .	77	1/14 (1) 2/72 (3) 3/84 (4)　(48.5 overs) 202
R. L. Powell c Yousuf Youhana		4/101 (2) 5/121 (6)
b Saqlain Mushtaq .	4	6/141 (7) 7/142 (8)
P. V. Simmons c Moin Khan		8/161 (9) 9/195 (10)
b Azhar Mahmood .	5	10/202 (5)　Score at 15 overs: 66-1

Bowling: Wasim Akram 10–3–37–0; Shoaib Akhtar 9.5–1–54–2; Saqlain Mushtaq 9–0–22–1; Azhar Mahmood 10–0–48–3; Abdur Razzaq 10–3–32–3.

Umpires: D. B. Hair and D. L. Orchard.　Referee: R. Subba Row.

BANGLADESH v NEW ZEALAND

At Chelmsford, May 17. New Zealand won by six wickets. Toss: New Zealand.

On the field, Bangladesh's first World Cup outing proved a rather low-key affair, though you would never have known it from their fanatical support. Several thousand travelled from London to Chelmsford, and their carefree celebrations betrayed no sign of New Zealand's dominance. Bangladesh began feebly, losing the toss, and their first wicket to the third ball of the day. At 51 for seven in the 21st over, they were in danger of going under by lunchtime against New Zealand's customary tight bowling, with Larsen meanest of all. But the tailenders produced some effective slogs, and then rearranged themselves into an even more effective bowling attack. Hasibul Hussain and Manjurul Islam gave New Zealand's batsmen a thorough examination, and they were fortunate to lose only four wickets as they inched to their target of 117.

Man of the Match: G. R. Larsen.   *Attendance:* 4,402.

Bangladesh

Shahriar Hossain lbw b Allott	0	Hasibul Hussain c Horne b Allott	16
Mehrab Hossain lbw b Allott	2	Manjurul Islam not out	6
Akram Khan c and b Larsen	16	L-b 4, w 5, n-b 8	17
*Aminul Islam b Cairns	15		
†Khaled Masud b Larsen	4	1/0 (1) 2/7 (2) 3/38 (4) (37.4 overs)	116
Naimur Rahman lbw b Larsen	18	4/38 (3) 5/46 (5)	
Khaled Mahmud c Twose b Cairns	3	6/49 (7) 7/51 (8)	
Mohammad Rafiq lbw b Cairns	0	8/85 (6) 9/96 (9)	
Enamul Haque b Harris	19	10/116 (10) Score at 15 overs: 42-4	

Bowling: Allott 8.4–0–30–3; Nash 10–1–30–0; Cairns 7–1–19–3; Larsen 10–0–19–3; Harris 2–0–14–1.

New Zealand

M. J. Horne lbw b Naimur Rahman	35	R. G. Twose not out	30
N. J. Astle c Aminul Islam b Manjurul Islam	4	C. L. Cairns not out	7
C. D. McMillan c Naimur Rahman b Hasibul Hussain	20	L-b 1, w 4	5
*S. P. Fleming c Khaled Masud b Mohammad Rafiq	16	1/5 (2) 2/33 (3) (4 wkts, 33 overs)	117
		3/78 (4) 4/105 (1) Score at 15 overs: 44-2	

†A. C. Parore, C. Z. Harris, D. J. Nash, G. R. Larsen and G. I. Allott did not bat.

Bowling: Hasibul Hussain 10–2–33–1; Manjurul Islam 8–3–23–1; Khaled Mahmud 7–2–12–0; Enamul Haque 3–0–21–0; Mohammad Rafiq 3–0–22–1; Naimur Rahman 2–0–5–1.

Umpires: I. D. Robinson and S. Venkataraghavan.   Referee: P. J. Burge.

[*Craig Prentis, Allsport*

It's a chill wind: Clive Lloyd makes a statement about the Irish weather.

BANGLADESH v WEST INDIES

At Castle Avenue, Dublin, May 21. West Indies won by seven wickets. Toss: Bangladesh.

West Indies won the first official one-day international played on Irish soil comfortably enough, despite some deplorable fielding. A bitter wind and squally showers were scant excuse for four dropped catches, three by Simmons. And, just as they did against Pakistan, West Indies failed to exploit early successes: Mehrab Hossain and Naimur Rahman added a confident 85 after coming together at 55 for four. Ambrose was nursing a sore shoulder, but Walsh compensated, and picked up four victims at little cost. Bangladesh's attack caused few worries, and all three West Indian wickets fell to unforced errors. Campbell hoisted a full toss to deep square leg; Jacobs was undone by athletic fielding by Shahriar Hossain; and Lara, after briefly entertaining the crowd with four fours, patted the ball tamely to cover. For West Indies, though, haunted by their defeat by Kenya in the 1996 World Cup, the manner of victory was of secondary importance. In conditions not unusual for an Irish May, the drinks cart dispensed hot soup, while West Indian manager Clive Lloyd watched swathed in blankets.

Man of the Match: C. A. Walsh.   *Attendance:* 3,339.

Bangladesh

Shahriar Hossain c Campbell b Walsh	2	Hasibul Hussain b Bryan	1
Mehrab Hossain c Chanderpaul b Simmons	64	Manjurul Islam not out	0
Akram Khan c Lara b Dillon	4	L-b 8, w 25, n-b 5	38
*Aminul Islam c Jacobs b King	2		
Minhazul Abedin c Jacobs b King	5	1/8 (1) 2/29 (3) 3/39 (4) (49.2 overs) 182	
Naimur Rahman lbw b Walsh	45	4/55 (5) 5/140 (2)	
Khaled Mahmud c Bryan b Walsh	13	6/159 (6) 7/167 (8)	
†Khaled Masud b King	4	8/180 (7) 9/182 (9)	
Enamul Haque c Lara b Walsh	4	10/182 (10) Score at 15 overs: 37-2	

Bowling: Walsh 10–0–25–4; Dillon 10–0–43–1; Bryan 9.2–0–30–1; King 10–1–30–3; Simmons 10–0–46–1.

West Indies

S. L. Campbell c Manjurul Islam b Khaled Mahmud	36	S. Chanderpaul not out	11
†R. D. Jacobs run out	51	L-b 2, w 5	7
J. C. Adams not out	53		
*B. C. Lara c Hasibul Hussain b Minhazul Abedin	25	1/67 (1) 2/115 (2) (3 wkts, 46.3 overs) 183	
		3/150 (4) Score at 15 overs: 51-0	

S. C. Williams, P. V. Simmons, H. R. Bryan, M. Dillon, R. D. King and C. A. Walsh did not bat.

Bowling: Hasibul Hussain 7–1–28–0; Manjurul Islam 7–1–15–0; Khaled Mahmud 8–0–36–1; Enamul Haque 8–1–31–0; Naimur Rahman 9.3–0–43–0; Minhazul Abedin 7–0–28–1.

Umpires: K. T. Francis and D. B. Hair. Referee: R. S. Madugalle.

AUSTRALIA v PAKISTAN

At Leeds, May 23. Pakistan won by ten runs. Toss: Australia.

A memorable struggle tilted Pakistan's way when Shoaib Akhtar, bowling at terrifying speed in murky conditions, hurled an in-swinger into Steve Waugh's stumps. That left Australia 238 for six, chasing 276. Though the contest went to the last over, Wasim Akram then clean-bowled Martyn and McGrath to seal a ten-run win – and pass Imran Khan's record of 34 World Cup wickets. The match award went to Inzamam-ul-Haq for his 81, the centrepiece of Pakistan's innings, although this rather overlooked the damage inflicted by his idiosyncratic running. Three times he found himself at the same end as his partner, and twice it cost a wicket. Still, Inzamam's patient stand of 118 with Abdur Razzaq paved the way for a volcanic eruption in the last ten overs, which yielded 108 runs. Moin Khan lashed an unbeaten 31 from a mere 12 balls. Australia's pursuit started confidently enough, but two wickets in three balls from Saqlain Mushtaq stalled them at 101 for four. A 113-run stand between Steve Waugh and Bevan kept the game alive, until Pakistan's quicks returned to close it out in fading light. After the finish, 21 minutes late, Waugh asked why slow over-rate penalties should apply only to teams who bowl first.

Man of the Match: Inzamam-ul-Haq. *Attendance:* 15,474.

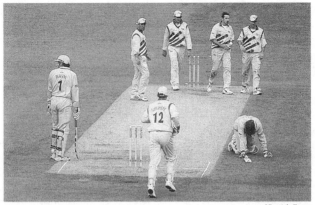

[*Patrick Eagar*

Another fine mess: Inzamam-ul-Haq is run out after one of his characteristic mix-ups.

Pakistan

Wajahatullah Wasti c S. R. Waugh		
b McGrath .	9	
Saeed Anwar c Gilchrist b Reiffel	25	
Abdur Razzaq c Fleming b Warne	60	
Ijaz Ahmed, sen. lbw b Fleming	0	
Inzamam-ul-Haq run out	81	
Yousuf Youhana run out	29	
*Wasim Akram c Gilchrist b Fleming . .	13	
†Moin Khan not out	31	

Azhar Mahmood run out   1
Saqlain Mushtaq not out   0

B 1, l-b 5, w 15, n-b 5   26
                                    ——
1/32 (2) 2/44 (1)   (8 wkts, 50 overs) 275
3/46 (4) 4/164 (3)
5/216 (6) 6/230 (5)
7/262 (7) 8/265 (9)   Score at 15 overs: 58-3

Shoaib Akhtar did not bat.

Bowling: Fleming 10–3–37–2; Reiffel 10–1–49–1; McGrath 10–1–54–1; Warne 10–0–50–1; S. R. Waugh 6–0–37–0; Martyn 2–0–25–0; Lehmann 2–0–17–0.

Australia

†A. C. Gilchrist b Wasim Akram	0	
M. E. Waugh c Moin Khan		
b Abdur Razzaq .	41	
R. T. Ponting c Saeed Anwar		
b Saqlain Mushtaq .	47	
D. S. Lehmann c Moin Khan		
b Saqlain Mushtaq .	5	
*S. R. Waugh b Shoaib Akhtar	49	
M. G. Bevan c Ijaz Ahmed		
b Wasim Akram .	61	
D. R. Martyn b Wasim Akram	18	
S. K. Warne run out	1	

P. R. Reiffel c Wasim Akram
                    b Saqlain Mushtaq .   1
D. W. Fleming not out   4
G. D. McGrath b Wasim Akram   0

B 7, l-b 10, w 14, n-b 7   38
                                    ——
1/0 (1) 2/91 (2) 3/100 (3)   (49.5 overs) 265
4/101 (4) 5/214 (6)
6/238 (5) 7/248 (8)
8/251 (9) 9/265 (7)
10/265 (11)   Score at 15 overs: 76-1

Bowling: Wasim Akram 9.5–1–40–4; Shoaib Akhtar 10–0–46–1; Azhar Mahmood 10–0–61–0; Saqlain Mushtaq 10–1–51–3; Abdur Razzaq 10–0–50–1.

Umpires: R. E. Koertzen and P. Willey.   Referee: R. Subba Row.

NEW ZEALAND v WEST INDIES

At Southampton, May 24. West Indies won by seven wickets. Toss: West Indies.

Seam bowling of relentless hostility proved far too good for New Zealand, who had been in confident mood after defeating Australia. Yet again, the toss was vital: under the grey skies that characterised the early stages of the competition, Lara leapt at the chance to bowl. On a pitch tailor-made for them, Walsh, Ambrose and company found lift and movement, keeping New Zealand literally and figuratively on the back foot. McMillan coped better than most: between the third over, when Horne scored two, and the 19th, when Cairns got off the mark, he hit all 21 runs from the bat. The first boundary came in the 21st over. The ball kept on bouncing, swinging and seaming and, for the first time ever in a World Cup match, all ten wickets fell to catches. Jacobs held five, and so equalled the record for dismissals in a limited-overs international. He then steered West Indies to their modest target with an undefeated 80, his highest international score. Lara batted entertainingly, and struck an effortless straight six off Larsen, but for the third time in three games was out to a soft dismissal when he gave a steepling catch to mid-on.

Man of the Match: R. D. Jacobs.   *Attendance:* 4,638.

New Zealand

M. J. Horne c Lara b Walsh	2	G. R. Larsen c Jacobs b Simmons	14
N. J. Astle c Jacobs b Ambrose	2	G. I. Allott not out	0
C. D. McMillan c Jacobs b Simmons	32	L-b 6, w 17, n-b 6	29
*S. P. Fleming c Jacobs b King	0		
R. G. Twose c Williams b King	0	1/2 (2) 2/13 (1) 3/22 (4) (48.1 overs) 156	
C. L. Cairns c Lara b Dillon	23	4/31 (5) 5/59 (3)	
†A. C. Parore c Jacobs b Dillon	23	6/75 (6) 7/125 (7)	
C. Z. Harris c Campbell b Dillon	30	8/130 (9) 9/155 (10)	
D. J. Nash c Williams b Dillon	1	10/156 (8) Score at 15 overs: 28-3	

Bowling: Walsh 10–1–23–1; Ambrose 10–0–19–1; King 10–1–29–2; Simmons 9–2–33–2; Dillon 9.1–0–46–4.

West Indies

S. L. Campbell lbw b Nash	8
†R. D. Jacobs not out	80
J. C. Adams c Parore b Allott	3
*B. C. Lara c Nash b Harris	36
S. C. Williams not out	14
L-b 4, w 5, n-b 8	17

1/29 (1) 2/49 (3)   (3 wkts, 44.2 overs) 158
3/121 (4)   Score at 15 overs: 36-1

S. Chanderpaul, P. V. Simmons, C. E. L. Ambrose, M. Dillon, C. A. Walsh and R. D. King did not bat.

Bowling: Allott 10–2–39–1; Nash 10–2–25–1; Cairns 9.2–1–42–0; Larsen 7–1–29–0; Harris 8–2–19–1.

Umpires: Javed Akhtar and S. Venkataraghavan.   Referee: R. S. Madugalle.

SCOTLAND v WEST INDIES

At Leicester, May 27. West Indies won by eight wickets. Toss: Scotland. International debut: J. G. Williamson.

At just on three hours, this was the shortest limited-overs international ever played to a result. History will suggest that Salmond, facing a team including Ambrose and Walsh, was misguided in choosing to bat on a surface that encouraged seam, swing and bounce. But he felt it was unlikely to improve and that his team was happier setting a target: "I thought if we got a few on the board, we could give them a game," he explained afterwards. At 18 for one after 14 overs, and barely a shot off the middle of the bat, Salmond's optimism was already floundering. Eight overs later, at 29 for seven, his priority was to better the 43 made by Pakistan against West Indies at Cape Town in 1992-93, the lowest one-day international total. Hamilton, playing with a confidence alien to his team-mates, averted that catastrophe, but ran out of partners. Between them, Walsh and Ambrose bowled 17 overs for 15 runs. Determined to up their net run-rate, West Indies stormed out of the blocks and won with 239 balls to spare, a record for 50-over internationals.

Man of the Match: C. A. Walsh.   *Attendance:* 3,936.

Scotland

M. J. Smith c Jacobs b Simmons	.....	1
M. J. D. Allingham c Jacobs b Ambrose	..	6
I. M. Stanger c Jacobs b Walsh	......	7
*G. Salmond c Jacobs b Ambrose	.....	1
G. M. Hamilton not out	....	24
J. G. Williamson c Williams b Bryan	..	1
J. E. Brinkley c Simmons b Walsh	....	2
†A. G. Davies lbw b Bryan	....	0
J. A. R. Blain lbw b Bryan	....	3

Asim Butt c Williams b King 11
N. R. Dyer c Williams b King 0
        W 9, n-b 3 12
                                          —
1/6 (1) 2/18 (2) 3/20 (3)   (31.3 overs) 68
4/20 (4) 5/25 (6)
6/29 (7) 7/29 (8)
8/47 (9) 9/67 (10)
10/68 (11)   Score at 15 overs: 20-2

Bowling: Ambrose 10–4–8–2; Simmons 7–1–15–1; Walsh 7–1–7–3; Bryan 6–0–29–2; King 1.3–0–9–2.

West Indies

P. V. Simmons c Stanger b Blain	......	7
S. Chanderpaul not out	....	30
S. C. Williams lbw b Blain	....	0
*B. C. Lara not out	....	25
L-b 2, w 4, n-b 2	....	8

1/21 (1) 2/22 (3)   (2 wkts, 10.1 overs) 70

S. L. Campbell, †R. D. Jacobs, J. C. Adams, H. R. Bryan, R. D. King, C. E. L. Ambrose and C. A. Walsh did not bat.

Bowling: Blain 5.1–0–36–2; Asim Butt 4–1–15–0; Hamilton 1–0–17–0.

Umpires: Javed Akhtar and I. D. Robinson.   Referee: P. J. Burge.

NEW ZEALAND v PAKISTAN

At Derby, May 28. Pakistan won by 62 runs. Toss: New Zealand.

Pakistan completed their fourth win out of four without difficulty, ensuring that they would head Group B. Asked to bat, their openers whipped 23 runs off the first two overs. More sedate batting from Abdur Razzaq and Ijaz Ahmed reached a comfortable 127 for two, and then Inzamam-ul-Haq powered to an unbeaten 73 from 61 balls. His notoriously unreliable running saw off Ijaz, but he also showed his value as he hit Cairns's final over for 14. Shoaib Akhtar then beheaded New Zealand, having both Astle and Horne caught behind for a combined total of one run. His team-mates closed in on the middle order, and in the 20th over successive deliveries from Azhar Mahmood had both Cairns and Parore leg-before for ducks. There was little their captain, Fleming, could do after that, except to nurse his side's net run-rate in anticipation of a tie-breaker.

Man of the Match: Inzamam-ul-Haq.   *Attendance:* 3,074.

Pakistan

Saeed Anwar b Allott	28	Azhar Mahmood c Twose b Allott	14
Shahid Afridi c Parore b Allott	17	Saqlain Mushtaq not out	0
Abdur Razzaq run out	33	B 4, l-b 10, w 8, n-b 3	25
Ijaz Ahmed, sen. run out	51		
Inzamam-ul-Haq not out	73	1/40 (2) 2/51 (1) (8 wkts, 50 overs) 269
Salim Malik b Allott	8	3/127 (3) 4/163 (4)	
†Moin Khan c McMillan b Astle	19	5/180 (6) 6/221 (7)	
*Wasim Akram lbw b Cairns	1	7/226 (8) 8/255 (9) Score at 15 overs: 63-2

Shoaib Akhtar did not bat.

Bowling: Nash 10–1–36–0; Allott 10–0–64–4; Larsen 10–0–35–0; Cairns 7–0–46–1; Harris 8–0–47–0; Astle 5–0–27–1.

New Zealand

M. J. Horne c Moin Khan b Shoaib Akhtar	1	†A. C. Parore lbw b Azhar Mahmood	0
N. J. Astle c Moin Khan b Shoaib Akhtar	0	C. Z. Harris c Abdur Razzaq b Saqlain Mushtaq	42
C. D. McMillan c Salim Malik b Wasim Akram	20	D. J. Nash not out	21
*S. P. Fleming c Wasim Akram b Azhar Mahmood	69	G. R. Larsen not out	3
R. G. Twose c Inzamam-ul-Haq b Saqlain Mushtaq	13	L-b 15, w 13, n-b 10	38
C. L. Cairns lbw b Azhar Mahmood	0	1/2 (2) 2/12 (1) (8 wkts, 50 overs) 207

1/2 (2) 2/12 (1)   (8 wkts, 50 overs) 207
3/34 (3) 4/69 (5)
5/70 (6) 6/70 (7)
7/152 (4) 8/200 (8)   Score at 15 overs: 50-3

G. I. Allott did not bat.

Bowling: Wasim Akram 9–0–27–1; Shoaib Akhtar 7–1–31–2; Azhar Mahmood 10–0–38–3; Saqlain Mushtaq 10–1–34–2; Shahid Afridi 6–1–26–0; Abdur Razzaq 8–0–36–0.

Umpires: K. T. Francis and R. E. Koertzen.   Referee: R. S. Madugalle.

[*Patrick Eagar*

Prize scalp: Glenn McGrath bowls Brian Lara.

AUSTRALIA v WEST INDIES

At Manchester, May 30. Australia won by six wickets. Toss: Australia.

A game that in advance looked one of the most relishable of the tournament dawdled to a close amid booing, slow hand-clapping and spectators walking out. Needing only 111, Australia slowed their chase to a crawl, doing just enough to ensure they would enter the Super Six on net run-rate, while enabling West Indies to improve their own side of the equation against New Zealand. The Australians openly admitted their intention. Under tournament rules, they would retain points won against fellow-qualifiers. Against New Zealand, that meant nought; against West Indies, two. Lara angrily denied collusion; there was no need for it – the captains understood the tactics, even if spectators did not. There had been some action for the crowd earlier in the day. McGrath got into his stride at last, collecting three wickets in 13 balls to finish with five for 14 – the fourth-best analysis in World Cup history and the best by an Australian in any limited-overs international against West Indies. Only Jacobs, the first man to carry his bat through a World Cup innings, got the score to 110. Beginning Australia's reply after a rain-extended break, Gilchrist batted brightly, and there was even a hint of a twist when Ambrose struck three times. But once Steve Waugh and Bevan were certain they could not lose, run-scoring became secondary to run-rate manipulation. Their final 19 runs were dragged out across 13 overs, and the victory came from a no-ball.

Man of the Match: G. D. McGrath.   *Attendance:* 21,238.

West Indies

S. L. Campbell c M. E. Waugh b McGrath .	2	R. D. King lbw b Warne	1	
†R. D. Jacobs not out	49	C. A. Walsh b McGrath	6	
J. C. Adams lbw b McGrath	0			
*B. C. Lara b McGrath	9	L-b 3, w 18, n-b 1	22	
S. Chanderpaul b Warne	16			
S. C. Williams c M. E. Waugh b Moody	3	1/7 (1) 2/7 (3) 3/20 (4) (46.4 overs) 110		
P. V. Simmons b Fleming	1	4/64 (5) 5/67 (6)		
C. E. L. Ambrose lbw b Warne.	1	6/69 (7) 7/70 (8)		
M. Dillon lbw b McGrath	0	8/71 (9) 9/88 (10)		
		10/110 (11) Score at 15 overs: 42-3		

Bowling: McGrath 8.4–3–14–5; Fleming 7–1–12–1; Moody 7–0–16–1; Julian 7–1–36–0; Warne 10–4–11–3; Bevan 7–0–18–0.

Australia

†A. C. Gilchrist b Ambrose	21	M. G. Bevan not out.	20	
M. E. Waugh c Jacobs b Ambrose	3	L-b 4, w 7, n-b 8	19	
R. T. Ponting c Chanderpaul b King . . .	20			
D. S. Lehmann c Adams b Ambrose . . .	9	1/10 (2) 2/43 (1) (4 wkts, 40.4 overs) 111		
*S. R. Waugh not out	19	3/53 (4) 4/62 (3) Score at 15 overs: 53-2		

T. M. Moody, B. P. Julian, S. K. Warne, D. W. Fleming and G. D. McGrath did not bat.

Bowling: Ambrose 10–0–31–3; Walsh 10-3–25–0; Dillon 7.4–1–22–0; King 10–2–27–1; Simmons 3–2–2–0.

Umpires: R. S. Dunne and K. T. Francis.   Referee: J. R. Reid.

BANGLADESH v PAKISTAN

At Northampton, May 31. Bangladesh won by 62 runs. Toss: Pakistan.

At the last possible moment, a non-Test team felled a giant. Bangladesh had never even come close to beating a major power – while Pakistan were unbeaten in this competition. Since this was a completely dead match, accusations of Pakistani match-fixing grew louder again. English bookmakers had rated Pakistan 33 to 1 on, and there were no reports of unusual betting, but inevitably there were rumours about the subcontinent's illegal bookmakers. Nothing diminished the Bangladeshi fans' euphoria. It was the greatest day in their cricketing history, and perhaps no event since independence had united the country with such delight. Both captains spoke of Bangladesh earning Test cricket soon; with Pakistan unaffected, the only person with reason not to enjoy the result was Gordon Greenidge, sacked as Bangladesh coach just before this game, who quietly left at lunchtime. Put in, the Bangladeshi openers advanced confidently to 69 in 16 overs, before Saqlain Mushtaq, the only Pakistani on song, intervened. Khaled Mahmud dashed to 27 in 34 balls. But a target of 224 hardly looked a problem – until Pakistan's top order folded. Five men were out by the 13th over, three to Mahmud. Azhar Mahmood and Wasim Akram pushed towards three figures, but it was far too late. With nine wickets down, the umpires called for a TV verdict on whether Saqlain had been run out. He was, but the jubilant Bangladeshi fans were already pouring on to the field. The County Ground had never seen anything like it – at least not since the old footballing days there, when Northampton Town knocked Arsenal out of the FA Cup in 1958. The build-up was just as frenzied: Northamptonshire could have sold three times the available tickets.

Man of the Match: Khaled Mahmud.   *Attendance:* 7,203.

THE NEW ZEALAND TOURING PARTY

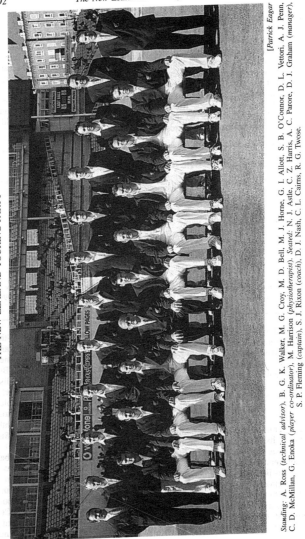

[*Patrick Eagar*

Standing: A. Ross (*technical advisor*), B. G. K. Walker, M. G. Croy, M. D. Bell, M. J. Horne, G. I. Allott, S. B. O'Connor, D. L. Vettori, A. J. Penn, C. D. McMillan, G. Enoka (*player co-ordinator*), M. Harrison (*physiotherapist*). *Seated:* N. J. Astle, C. Z. Harris, A. C. Parore, D. J. Graham (*manager*), S. P. Fleming (*captain*), S. J. Rixon (*coach*), D. J. Nash, C. L. Cairns, R. G. Twose.

1986, the last time they lost a series to New Zealand. Instead, England made do with Graham Gooch, who supervised nets and fielding practices, and manager David Graveney. Lloyd's wholehearted moral support was badly missed, as was the layer of insulation he provided between team and management.

Yes, Lloyd was eccentric, impulsive, and sometimes plain wrong-headed. But he had never got into anything like this muddle. The worst confusion surrounded the selection of captains – captains plural, because England were led by four different men during the summer, just as they were during the notorious 1988 series against West Indies. Alec Stewart oversaw the World Cup campaign, and paid the price for failure, despite two creditable Test series in charge. The baton then passed to Hussain, Stewart's heir apparent for the previous year. But there was no obvious deputy to Hussain. Murphy's Law applied and, when he broke a finger at Lord's, the policy of not appointing a vice-captain for home Test series was exposed.

On his way to the ambulance, Hussain asked Graham Thorpe, his best friend in the team, to take over. With New Zealand already piling up a weighty advantage, this was what you might call a hospital pass. Sure enough, Thorpe went into his shell, England went down by nine wickets, and the selection committee (Mike Gatting, Gooch and chairman Graveney) went looking for other options. When Hussain failed to recover in time for Old Trafford, they decided that Mark Butcher should lead the team – a big ask, in the professionals' idiom, for a man who was neither a county captain nor a Test fixture.

In the event, England were almost as rudderless as they had been at Lord's. Butcher scored five and nine and, if he felt lonely in the field as New Zealand steamed to 496 for nine declared, it must have been worse still when he was sent down after the game to face the media. Even experienced captains are usually accompanied by a coach or manager, but this time the only support came from Brian Murgatroyd, England's media relations officer. Fortunately, Butcher is one of the most thoughtful, articulate cricketers in the country: he genially accepted that England's performance had been substandard, and said that his place was in danger. He was right on both counts. When Hussain returned for The Oval, Butcher had to sling his hook.

So did two of the selectors. Before Old Trafford, Gooch and Gatting had successfully argued that Graeme Hick should represent England for the eighth summer out of nine, a decision described by the *Daily Telegraph* cricket correspondent as "buttock-clenchingly grim". Hick's performance was inconclusive – his one innings yielded 12 runs and a hopeless lbw decision – but his two leading supporters drew flak for being preoccupied with their old chums from the county circuit. They were quietly asked to step down, leaving the bulletproof Graveney to pick the Oval squad with advice from Hussain and England's incoming coach Duncan Fletcher, who was not due to take over officially until the South African tour.

Gooch was characteristically tight-lipped about the affair, except to say: "In my experience, the best sides in any sport are a balance between experience and youth." And to be fair, there was no shortage of fresh blood running through England's veins. Four players made their Test debuts during the summer, starting at Edgbaston with Read, Nottinghamshire's wicket-

[*Laurence Griffiths, Allsport*

Falling for it: Read ducks beneath a slower ball from Cairns and is bowled for nought.

keeper, and Aftab Habib, the Leicestershire batsman. They brought the average age of the side down to 28, two years lower than it was for the opening World Cup game against Sri Lanka. But Habib was dropped like a hot potato after Lord's, having failed three times, and Read predictably gave way to Stewart when the chips were down at The Oval. Just as predictably, once he had taken back the gloves, Stewart gave away his wicket for scores of 11 and 12.

Still, Read had shown enough grit to suggest he could yet become a pearl. And he wasn't the only youngster to shine. Surrey's 21-year-old fast bowler Alex Tudor made a positive impression on the Ashes tour, but that was as nothing compared to his fearless *tour de force* at Edgbaston. After bowling wastefully, Tudor went in as night-watchman, with England chasing 208 to win, and turned the game upside down. Flailing his heavy bat at anything wide, and clipping off his toes like an overgrown Gavaskar, he acted the senior partner in vital stands with Butcher and Hussain, and was only stranded one run short of a maiden first-class hundred by Thorpe's thoughtlessness. It was a thunderous innings, but, in such a summer, even England's silver linings seemed to fade back into the clouds. Tudor withdrew from the Second

Test when a scan revealed a "hot spot" in his knee that threatened to become a stress fracture. He would not appear again in the series. The England camp were furious, as Surrey had arranged the medical appointment without telling them – another damaging outbreak of county-versus-country strife.

Apart from Tudor, Caddick was the only England player who genuinely enhanced his reputation. Absent from the team for 15 months, he bowled with stamina, accuracy, jarring bounce and elusive swing, and finished with 20 wickets at 20.60. His comment that "it was just like playing for Somerset" reflected well on Hussain, who felt that his predecessors had been guilty of ostracising complex or awkward characters rather than making them feel part of the team. Caddick also finished a worthy sixth in the batting averages, despite an infuriating habit of running himself out. The irony was that he might have been playing for the opposition if Cairns had not kept him out of New Zealand's age-group sides.

Although the rest of England's bowling was unexceptional, the team's real problem was a lack of runs. The top score for England over the four Tests was Tudor's 99 not out – the first time since the 19th century (discounting the handful of Testless seasons and the one-off against India in 1932) that England had gone through a domestic summer without a home-made Test hundred. Mike Atherton, called up after the Lord's débâcle, showed all his old stickability in scoring 11 in 136 minutes at Old Trafford, but only he, Hussain and Stewart averaged more than 30. At the end of the season, the selectors responded by ditching Mark Ramprakash, England's most consistent batsman on the last two winter tours. Thorpe had already announced that he would rather stay at home with his family than go to South Africa. His leadership credentials had been dismissed, for England as they had been for Surrey. It was unclear what impact this made on his decision.

While Ramprakash drew criticism for not imposing himself on the game, England generally erred in the other direction: when runs dried up, they lost patience too quickly. New Zealand forced the issue by maintaining an impeccable off-stump line throughout the last three Tests. As Stephen Fleming said, denial was a form of attack. Cairns was supported superbly by Dion Nash, now fully recovered from a horrendous back injury and an unhappy year at Middlesex, while the studentish 20-year-old Daniel Vettori looked more threatening than Tufnell, his slow left-arm rival. With those three bowlers also contributing resourceful runs, New Zealand's batting order resembled Doctor Dolittle's two-headed pushmi-pullyu. At Old Trafford, every man in the side had made a first-class century.

Tail-end runs were often needed, because New Zealand's top order was even worse than England's. Over the series, their first six wickets averaged 147 to England's 149, and Matt Horne was the only specialist batsman to play a decisive innings. His opening partner for the last three Tests, Matthew Bell, finished top of the averages, compensating for his limited palette with unlimited doggedness. Craig McMillan and Nathan Astle each notched up a fiery hundred at Old Trafford, but otherwise struggled on a series of suspect pitches.

Spectators were thin on the ground, thanks to a combination of factors: unglamorous opposition, England's ineptitude, the hangover from the World

Bowling: *First Innings*—Pushpakumara 12–0–87–1; Gallage 13–3–51–0; Perera 13.5–2–73–7; Boteju 10–0–45–1; Herath 6–0–30–0; Arnold 3–0–19–0. *Second Innings*—Pushpakumara 18–1–91–1; Perera 5–1–20–0; Herath 21–5–69–1; Gallage 19–2–69–2; Boteju 17–3–49–2; Arnold 2–0–8–0.

Sri Lanka A

*R. P. Arnold c Innes b Logan	24	– c Sales b Innes	14
D. A. Gunawardene c Innes b Sutcliffe	0	– c A. J. Swann b Sutcliffe	4
T. M. Dilshan lbw b Logan	11	– lbw b Logan	115
S. Kalawithigoda c Ripley b Innes	5	– b Davies	63
S. I. de Saram lbw b Sales	12	– c Sales b Innes	61
†H. P. W. Jayawardene c Ripley b Sales	0	– lbw b A. J. Swann	27
H. Boteju c Ripley b Innes	15	– b Sutcliffe	5
A. S. A. Perera b Innes	12	– b Innes	27
R. Herath c Ripley b Sales	4	– c Warren b Innes	10
I. S. Gallage lbw b Innes	1	– not out	32
K. R. Pushpakumara not out	1	– lbw b Sales	8
L-b 1	1	B 2, l-b 16, w 1	19

1/4 2/35 3/36 4/53 5/53   86 1/4 2/55 3/197 4/222 5/285 385
6/53 7/65 8/79 9/85   6/303 7/316 8/338 9/366

Bowling: *First Innings*—Logan 8–2–24–2; Sutcliffe 8–3–13–1; Innes 6.4–2–23–3; Sales 6–2–25–4. *Second Innings*—Logan 22–3–77–1; Sutcliffe 26–7–88–2; Innes 25–4–85–4; G. P. Swann 4–0–20–0; Sales 4–1–15–1; Davies 18–3–63–1; A. J. Swann 3–0–19–1.

Umpires: D. J. Constant and G. Sharp.

---

†At Cheltenham, July 19. Sri Lanka A won by five wickets. Toss: Gloucestershire. Gloucestershire 189 for nine (50 overs) (D. R. Hewson 64, M. C. J. Ball 51; I. S. Gallage three for 42); Sri Lanka A 193 for five (43 overs) (S. Kalawithigoda 31, S. I. de Saram 75, L. P. C. Silva 38 not out).

ESSEX v SRI LANKA

At Chelmsford, July 21, 22, 23, 24. Drawn. Toss: Essex. First-class debuts: A. C. McGarry, T. J. Phillips.

After their terrible collapse at Northampton, Sri Lanka A were intent on occupying the crease; resuming on the final day 107 ahead with seven wickets left, they batted until ten minutes before the scheduled close. The loss of Pushpakumara, unable to bowl because of a leg strain, was also a factor, but their refusal to make a game of it earned slow handclaps from disgruntled spectators. On the first day, Tim Phillips, an 18-year-old left-arm spinner, took four for 42 on his first-class debut, while two 17-year-old fast bowlers, Andrew McGarry and Justin Bishop, also looked promising. Dilshan was dropped three times in making 86. Essex then set up a 78-run lead, thanks to centuries from Grayson, who batted five hours, and Irani, whose career-best 153, with 24 fours, took nearly six. In contrast, seven Sri Lankans passed 50 during the match, but none reached three figures.

Close of play: First day, Sri Lanka A 364; Second day, Essex 261-3 (Irani 88*, Hyam 5*); Third day, Sri Lanka A 185-3 (Kalawithigoda 16*, Silva 34*).

Sri Lanka A

*R. P. Arnold c Grayson b Phillips	70	– c Hyam b Bishop	22
D. A. Gunawardene lbw b McGarry	26	– c Hyam b McGarry	72
T. M. Dilshan c Napier b Phillips	86	– lbw b McGarry	11
S. Kalawithigoda c Peters b Phillips	48	– c Grayson b Phillips	73
L. P. C. Silva c Hyam b Law	27	– b Such	80
†H. P. W. Jayawardene b McGarry	12	– c Napier b Bishop	89
N. R. G. Perera b Phillips	40	– c Grayson b Flanagan	49
A. S. A. Perera c Hyam b Bishop	9	– not out	71
P. P. Wickremasinghe c Irani b Grayson	12	– not out	11
M. S. Villavarayen lbw b Grayson	9		
K. R. Pushpakumara not out	0		
B 1, l-b 8, w 6, n-b 10	25	B 12, l-b 14, w 7, n-b 14	47

1/37 2/133 3/215 4/252 5/280   364   1/60 2/113 3/119   (7 wkts dec.) 525
6/292 7/305 8/345 9/364   4/276 5/298
                                    6/428 7/448

Bowling: *First Innings*—Law 18–3–94–1; Bishop 17–3–58–1; McGarry 20–2–72–2; Napier 3–0–20–0; Such 18–5–40–0; Phillips 17–7–42–4; Grayson 10.3–6–29–2. *Second Innings*—Bishop 19–3–89–2; Law 22–1–119–0; Such 31–6–73–1; McGarry 20–3–77–2; Phillips 20–5–83–1; Flanagan 14.3–4–50–1; Hyam 2–0–8–0.

Essex

I. N. Flanagan c Jayawardene b Villavarayen	29	T. J. Phillips c Kalawithigoda b Arnold	16
A. P. Grayson c Jayawardene b A. S. A. Perera	125	G. R. Napier b N. R. G. Perera	27
		D. R. Law c Silva b Arnold	24
S. D. Peters c Jayawardene b A. S. A. Perera	0	P. M. Such lbw b Villavarayen	20
		J. E. Bishop b N. R. G. Perera	17
*R. C. Irani c Jayawardene b N. R. G. Perera	153	A. C. McGarry not out	0
†B. J. Hyam c N. R. G. Perera b A. S. A. Perera	7	L-b 4, w 1, n-b 19	24

1/89 2/102 3/229 4/265 5/329   442
6/369 7/388 8/408 9/438

Bowling: Pushpakumara 16–3–57–0; A. S. A. Perera 29–4–103–3; Villavarayen 26.5–3–96–2; Wickremasinghe 23–5–72–0; Arnold 22–6–61–2; N. R. G. Perera 16–4–49–3.

Umpires: J. H. Evans and A. A. Jones.

---

†At Chester-le-Street, July 26. Durham won by 82 runs. Toss: Sri Lanka A. Durham 290 for six (50 overs) (J. A. Daley 81, N. J. Speak 34, J. J. B. Lewis 57, M. P. Speight 54; I. S. Gallage three for 46); Sri Lanka A 208 (37.4 overs) (D. A. Gunawardene 32, L. P. C. Silva 71; N. Killeen three for 37).

Durham scored 121 in their last ten overs.

---

†At Chester-le-Street, July 28. First-Class Counties Select XI won by 25 runs. Toss: Sri Lanka A. First-Class Counties Select XI 276 for six (50 overs) (D. I. Stevens 30, D. L. Maddy 110, V. S. Solanki 53); Sri Lanka A 251 for nine (50 overs) (D. A. Gunawardene 62, H. P. W. Jayawardene 31, A. S. A. Perera 75).

1864 Surrey; 1865 Nottinghamshire; 1866 Middlesex; 1867 Yorkshire; 1868 Nottinghamshire; 1869 Nottinghamshire and Yorkshire; 1870 Yorkshire; 1871 Nottinghamshire; 1872 Nottinghamshire; 1873 Gloucestershire and Nottinghamshire; 1874 Gloucestershire; 1875 Nottinghamshire; 1876 Gloucestershire; 1877 Gloucestershire; 1878 undecided; 1879 Lancashire and Nottinghamshire; 1880 Nottinghamshire; 1881 Lancashire; 1882 Lancashire and Nottinghamshire; 1883 Nottinghamshire; 1884 Nottinghamshire; 1885 Nottinghamshire; 1886 Nottinghamshire; 1887 Surrey; 1888 Surrey; 1889 Lancashire, Nottinghamshire and Surrey.

Official champions					
1890	Surrey	1928	Lancashire	1967	Yorkshire
1891	Surrey	1929	Nottinghamshire	1968	Yorkshire
1892	Surrey	1930	Lancashire	1969	Glamorgan
1893	Yorkshire	1931	Yorkshire	1970	Kent
1894	Surrey	1932	Yorkshire	1971	Surrey
1895	Surrey	1933	Yorkshire	1972	Warwickshire
1896	Yorkshire	1934	Lancashire	1973	Hampshire
1897	Lancashire	1935	Yorkshire	1974	Worcestershire
1898	Yorkshire	1936	Derbyshire	1975	Leicestershire
1899	Surrey	1937	Yorkshire	1976	Middlesex
1900	Yorkshire	1938	Yorkshire	1977 {	Middlesex
1901	Yorkshire	1939	Yorkshire		Kent
1902	Yorkshire	1946	Yorkshire	1978	Kent
1903	Middlesex	1947	Middlesex	1979	Essex
1904	Lancashire	1948	Glamorgan	1980	Middlesex
1905	Yorkshire	1949 {	Middlesex	1981	Nottinghamshire
1906	Kent		Yorkshire	1982	Middlesex
1907	Nottinghamshire	1950 {	Lancashire	1983	Essex
1908	Yorkshire		Surrey	1984	Essex
1909	Kent	1951	Warwickshire	1985	Middlesex
1910	Kent	1952	Surrey	1986	Essex
1911	Warwickshire	1953	Surrey	1987	Nottinghamshire
1912	Yorkshire	1954	Surrey	1988	Worcestershire
1913	Kent	1955	Surrey	1989	Worcestershire
1914	Surrey	1956	Surrey	1990	Middlesex
1919	Yorkshire	1957	Surrey	1991	Essex
1920	Middlesex	1958	Surrey	1992	Essex
1921	Middlesex	1959	Yorkshire	1993	Middlesex
1922	Yorkshire	1960	Yorkshire	1994	Warwickshire
1923	Yorkshire	1961	Hampshire	1995	Warwickshire
1924	Yorkshire	1962	Yorkshire	1996	Leicestershire
1925	Yorkshire	1963	Yorkshire	1997	Glamorgan
1926	Lancashire	1964	Worcestershire	1998	Leicestershire
1927	Lancashire	1965	Worcestershire	1999	Surrey
		1966	Yorkshire		

Notes: since the championship was constituted in 1890 it has been won outright as follows: Yorkshire 29 times, Surrey 16, Middlesex 10, Lancashire 7, Essex and Kent 6, Warwickshire and Worcestershire 5, Nottinghamshire 4, Glamorgan and Leicestershire 3, Hampshire 2, Derbyshire 1.

The title has been shared three times since 1890, involving Middlesex twice, Kent, Lancashire, Surrey and Yorkshire.

Wooden Spoons: Since the major expansion of the Championship from nine teams to 14 in 1895, the counties have finished outright bottom as follows: Derbyshire, Northamptonshire and Somerset 11; Glamorgan 9; Nottinghamshire 8; Gloucestershire, Leicestershire and Sussex 7; Worcestershire 6; Hampshire 5; Durham and Warwickshire 3; Essex and Kent 2; Yorkshire 1. Lancashire, Middlesex and Surrey have never finished bottom. Leicestershire have also shared bottom place twice, once with Hampshire and once with Somerset.

From 1977 to 1983 the Championship was sponsored by Schweppes, from 1984 to 1998 by Britannic Assurance, and from 1999 by PPP Healthcare.

COUNTY CHAMPIONSHIP – FINAL POSITIONS, 1890-1999

	Derbyshire	Essex	Glamorgan	Gloucestershire	Hampshire	Kent	Lancashire	Leicestershire	Middlesex	Northamptonshire	Nottinghamshire	Somerset	Surrey	Sussex	Warwickshire	Worcestershire	Yorkshire
1890	—	—	—	6	—	3	2	—	7	—	5	—	1	8	—	—	3
1891	—	—	—	9	—	5	2	—	3	—	4	5	1	7	—	—	8
1892	—	—	—	7	—	7	4	—	5	—	2	3	1	9	—	—	6
1893	—	—	—	9	—	4	2	—	3	—	6	8	5	7	—	—	1
1894	—	—	—	9	—	4	4	—	3	—	7	6	1	8	—	—	2
1895	5	9	—	4	10	14	2	12	6	—	12	8	1	11	6	—	3
1896	7	5	—	10	8	9	2	13	3	—	6	11	4	14	12	—	1
1897	14	3	—	5	9	12	1	13	8	—	10	11	2	6	7	—	4
1898	9	5	—	3	12	7	6	13	2	—	8	13	4	9	9	—	1
1899	15	6	—	9	10	8	4	13	2	—	10	13	1	5	7	12	3
1900	13	10	—	7	15	3	2	14	7	—	5	11	7	3	6	12	1
1901	15	10	—	14	7	7	3	12	2	—	9	12	6	4	5	11	1
1902	10	13	—	14	15	7	5	11	12	—	3	7	4	2	6	9	1
1903	12	8	—	13	14	8	4	14	1	—	5	10	11	2	7	6	3
1904	10	14	—	9	15	3	1	7	4	—	5	12	11	6	7	13	2
1905	14	12	—	8	16	6	2	5	11	13	10	15	4	3	7	8	1
1906	16	7	—	9	8	1	4	15	11	11	5	11	3	10	6	14	2
1907	16	7	—	10	12	8	6	11	5	15	1	14	4	13	9	2	2
1908	14	11	—	10	9	2	7	13	4	15	8	16	3	5	12	6	1
1909	15	14	—	16	8	1	2	13	6	7	10	11	5	4	12	8	3
1910	15	11	—	12	6	1	4	10	3	9	5	16	2	7	14	13	8
1911	14	6	—	12	11	2	4	15	3	10	8	16	5	13	1	9	7
1912	12	15	—	11	6	3	4	13	5	2	8	14	7	10	9	16	1
1913	13	15	—	9	10	1	8	14	6	4	5	16	3	7	11	12	2
1914	12	8	—	16	5	3	11	13	2	9	10	15	1	6	7	14	4
1919	9	14	—	8	7	2	5	9	13	12	3	5	4	11	15	—	1
1920	16	9	—	8	11	5	2	13	1	14	7	10	3	6	12	15	4
1921	12	15	17	7	6	4	5	11	1	13	8	10	2	9	16	14	3
1922	11	8	16	13	6	4	5	14	7	15	2	10	3	9	12	17	1
1923	10	13	16	11	7	5	3	14	8	17	2	9	4	6	12	15	1
1924	17	15	13	6	12	5	4	11	2	16	6	8	3	10	9	14	1
1925	14	7	17	10	9	5	3	12	6	11	4	15	2	13	8	16	1
1926	11	9	8	15	7	3	1	13	6	16	4	14	5	10	12	17	2
1927	5	8	15	12	13	4	1	7	9	16	2	14	6	10	11	17	3
1928	10	16	15	5	12	2	1	9	8	13	3	14	6	7	11	17	4
1929	7	12	17	4	11	8	2	9	6	13	1	15	10	4	14	16	2
1930	9	6	11	2	13	5	1	12	16	17	4	13	8	7	15	10	3
1931	7	10	15	2	12	3	6	16	11	17	5	13	8	4	9	14	1
1932	10	14	15	13	8	3	6	12	10	16	4	7	5	2	9	17	1
1933	6	4	16	10	14	3	5	17	12	13	8	11	9	2	7	15	1
1934	3	8	13	7	14	5	1	12	10	17	9	15	11	2	4	16	5
1935	2	9	13	15	16	10	4	6	3	17	5	14	11	7	8	12	1
1936	1	9	16	4	10	8	11	15	2	17	5	7	6	14	13	12	3
1937	3	6	7	4	14	12	9	16	2	17	10	13	8	5	11	15	1
1938	5	6	16	10	14	9	4	15	2	17	12	7	3	8	13	11	1
1939	9	4	13	3	15	5	6	17	2	16	12	14	8	10	11	7	1
1946	15	8	6	5	10	6	3	11	2	16	13	4	11	17	14	8	1
1947	5	11	9	2	16	4	3	14	1	17	11	11	6	9	15	7	7

	Derbyshire	Durham	Essex	Glamorgan	Gloucestershire	Hampshire	Kent	Lancashire	Leicestershire	Middlesex	Northamptonshire	Nottinghamshire	Somerset	Surrey	Sussex	Warwickshire	Worcestershire	Yorkshire
1948	6	—	13	1	8	9	15	5	11	3	17	14	12	2	16	7	10	4
1949	15	—	9	8	7	16	13	11	17	1	6	11	9	5	13	4	3	1
1950	5	—	17	11	7	12	9	1	16	14	10	15	7	1	13	4	6	3
1951	11	—	8	5	12	9	16	3	15	7	13	17	14	6	10	1	4	2
1952	4	—	10	7	9	12	15	3	6	5	8	16	17	1	13	10	14	2
1953	6	—	12	10	6	14	16	3	3	5	11	8	17	1	2	9	15	12
1954	3	—	15	4	13	14	11	10	16	7	7	5	17	1	9	6	11	2
1955	8	—	14	16	12	3	13	9	6	5	7	11	17	1	4	9	15	2
1956	12	—	11	13	3	6	16	2	17	5	4	8	15	1	9	14	9	7
1957	4	—	5	9	12	13	14	6	17	7	2	15	8	1	9	11	16	3
1958	5	—	6	15	14	2	8	7	12	10	4	17	3	1	13	16	9	11
1959	7	—	9	6	2	8	13	5	16	10	11	17	12	3	15	4	14	1
1960	5	—	6	11	8	12	10	2	17	3	9	16	14	7	4	15	13	1
1961	7	—	6	14	5	1	11	13	9	3	16	17	10	15	8	12	4	2
1962	7	—	9	14	4	10	11	16	17	13	8	15	6	5	12	3	2	1
1963	17	—	12	2	8	10	13	15	16	6	7	9	3	11	4	4	14	5
1964	12	—	10	11	17	12	7	14	16	6	3	2	8	4	9	2	1	5
1965	9	—	15	3	10	12	5	13	14	6	2	17	7	8	16	11	1	4
1966	9	—	16	14	15	11	4	12	8	12	5	17	3	7	10	6	2	1
1967	6	—	15	14	17	12	2	11	2	7	9	15	8	4	13	10	5	1
1968	8	—	14	3	16	5	2	6	9	10	13	4	12	15	17	11	7	1
1969	16	—	6	1	2	5	10	15	14	11	9	8	17	3	7	4	12	13
1970	7	—	12	2	17	10	1	3	15	16	14	11	13	5	9	7	6	4
1971	17	—	10	16	8	9	4	3	5	6	14	12	7	1	11	2	15	13
1972	17	—	5	13	3	9	2	15	6	8	4	14	11	12	16	1	7	10
1973	16	—	8	11	5	1	4	12	9	13	3	17	10	2	15	7	6	14
1974	17	—	12	16	14	2	10	8	4	6	3	15	5	7	13	9	1	11
1975	15	—	7	9	16	3	5	4	1	11	8	13	12	6	17	14	10	2
1976	15	—	6	17	3	12	14	16	4	1	2	13	7	9	10	5	11	8
1977	7	—	6	14	3	11	1	16	5	1	9	17	4	14	8	10	13	12
1978	14	—	2	13	10	8	1	12	6	3	17	7	5	16	9	11	15	4
1979	16	—	1	17	10	12	5	13	6	14	11	9	8	3	4	15	2	7
1980	9	—	8	13	7	17	16	15	10	1	12	3	5	2	4	14	11	6
1981	12	—	5	14	13	7	9	16	8	4	15	1	3	6	2	17	11	10
1982	11	—	7	16	15	3	13	12	2	1	9	4	6	5	8	17	14	10
1983	9	—	1	15	12	3	7	12	4	2	6	14	10	8	11	5	16	17
1984	12	—	1	13	17	15	5	16	4	3	11	2	7	8	6	9	10	14
1985	13	—	4	12	3	2	9	14	16	1	10	8	17	6	7	15	5	11
1986	11	—	1	17	2	6	8	15	7	12	9	4	16	3	14	12	5	10
1987	6	—	12	13	10	5	14	2	3	16	7	1	11	4	17	15	9	8
1988	14	—	3	17	10	15	2	9	8	7	12	5	11	4	16	6	1	13
1989	6	—	2	17	9	6	15	4	13	3	5	11	14	12	10	8	1	16
1990	12	—	2	8	13	3	16	6	7	1	11	13	15	9	17	5	4	10
1991	3	—	1	12	13	9	6	8	16	15	10	4	17	5	11	2	6	14
1992	5	18	1	14	10	15	2	12	8	11	3	4	9	13	7	6	17	16
1993	15	18	11	3	17	13	8	13	9	1	4	7	5	6	10	16	2	12
1994	17	16	6	18	12	13	9	10	2	4	5	3	11	7	8	1	15	13
1995	14	17	5	16	6	13	18	4	7	2	3	11	9	12	15	1	10	8
1996	2	18	5	10	13	14	4	15	1	9	16	17	11	3	12	8	7	6
1997	16	17	8	1	7	14	2	11	10	4	15	13	12	8	18	4	3	6
1998	10	14	18	12	4	6	11	2	1	17	15	16	9	5	7	8	13	3
1999	9	8	12	14	18	7	5	2	3	16	13	17	4	1	11	10	15	6

MATCH RESULTS, 1864-1999

County	Years of Play	Played	Won	Lost	Tied	Drawn
Derbyshire	1871-87; 1895-1999	2,275	569	833	1	872
Durham	1992-1999	140	23	79	0	38
Essex	1895-1999	2,237	646	656	5	930
Glamorgan	1921-1999	1,772	393	604	0	775
Gloucestershire . . .	1870-1999	2,511	745	932	2	832
Hampshire	1864-85; 1895-1999	2,346	611	807	4	924
Kent	1864-1999	2,635	953	793	5	884
Lancashire	1865-1999	2,712	1,009	567	3	1,133
Leicestershire	1895-1999	2,204	502	801	1	900
Middlesex	1864-1999	2,414	900	612	5	897
Northamptonshire .	1905-1999	1,972	484	688	3	797
Nottinghamshire . .	1864-1999	2,544	768	686	1	1,089
Somerset	1882-85; 1891-1999	2,245	534	899	3	809
Surrey	1864-1999	2,792	1,108	620	4	1,060
Sussex	1864-1999	2,684	747	930	6	1,001
Warwickshire	1895-1999	2,217	607	647	1	962
Worcestershire . . .	1899-1999	2,159	541	747	2	869
Yorkshire	1864-1999	2,812	1,249	488	2	1,073
Cambridgeshire	1864-69; 1871	19	8	8	0	3
		20,345	12,397	12,397	24	7,924

Notes: Matches abandoned without a ball bowled are wholly excluded.

Counties participated in the years shown, except that there were no matches in the years 1915-18 and 1940-45; Hampshire did not play inter-county matches in 1868-69, 1871-74 and 1879; Worcestershire did not take part in the Championship in 1919.

SUMMARY OF RESULTS, 1999

	Derbyshire	Durham	Essex	Glamorgan	Gloucestershire	Hampshire	Kent	Lancashire	Leicestershire	Middlesex	Northamptonshire	Nottinghamshire	Somerset	Surrey	Sussex	Warwickshire	Worcestershire	Yorkshire
Derbyshire	—	L	L	D	W	L	W	L	W	W	W	W	L	L	L	L	W	D
Durham	W	—	D	L	W	L	L	L	D	D	W	W	D	L	L	W	D	L
Essex	W	D	—	W	D	D	L	L	L	W	L	W	D	L	L	W	D	L
Glamorgan	D	W	L	—	W	L	D	L	D	L	D	W	L	L	W	D	L	W
Gloucestershire	L	L	D	L	—	D	D	D	L	L	D	W	W	D	L	L	L	L
Hampshire	W	W	D	W	D	—	D	L	D	W	L	L	D	L	D	D	W	L
Kent	L	W	W	D	D	D	—	L	D	D	W	W	D	L	D	W	W	L
Lancashire	W	W	W	W	D	W	W	—	L	A	L	W	D	L	W	L	D	W
Leicestershire	L	D	W	D	W	D	D	W	—	D	L	D	L	D	W	D	D	W
Middlesex	L	D	L	W	W	L	D	A	D	—	W	L	D	D	W	D	D	W
Northamptonshire	L	L	W	D	D	W	L	W	W	L	—	D	L	L	D	D	L	D
Nottinghamshire	L	L	L	L	L	W	L	L	D	W	D	—	W	L	L	L	W	L
Somerset	W	D	D	W	L	D	D	D	W	D	W	L	—	W	D	L	D	W
Surrey	W	W	W	W	D	W	W	W	D	D	W	W	W	—	W	W	D	D
Sussex	W	W	W	L	W	D	D	L	D	L	D	W	L	L	—	L	D	W
Warwickshire	W	L	L	D	W	D	L	W	D	D	D	W	D	L	W	—	W	L
Worcestershire	L	D	D	W	W	L	L	D	D	D	D	W	L	W	D	D	—	L
Yorkshire	D	W	W	L	W	W	W	L	L	L	D	W	L	D	L	W	W	—

Home games in bold, away games in italics. W = Won, L = Lost, D = Drawn, A = Abandoned.

COUNTY CHAMPIONSHIP STATISTICS FOR 1999

County	For Runs	For Wickets	For Avge	Against Runs	Against Wickets	Against Avge
Derbyshire	6,986	263	26.56	7,397	277	26.70
Durham	7,293	269	27.11	7,342	278	26.41
Essex	8,039	264	30.45	7,778	260	29.91
Glamorgan	6,699	241	27.79	7,059	232	30.42
Gloucestershire . . .	7,024	272	25.82	8,251	257	32.10
Hampshire	7,636	245	31.16	8,498	264	32.18
Kent	7,355	256	28.73	7,628	258	29.56
Lancashire	6,975	219	31.84	6,810	250	27.24
Leicestershire	7,954	245	32.46	7,117	243	29.28
Middlesex	7,602	250	30.40	7,111	218	32.61
Northamptonshire .	7,304	233	31.34	7,440	250	29.76
Nottinghamshire . .	7,259	300	24.19	7,644	249	30.69
Somerset	8,390	227	36.96	8,187	263	31.12
Surrey	7,725	219	35.27	6,840	304	22.50
Sussex	7,553	277	27.26	7,622	260	29.31
Warwickshire	6,284	256	24.54	6,080	237	25.65
Worcestershire . . .	7,402	281	26.34	7,358	243	30.27
Yorkshire	7,445	293	25.40	6,763	267	25.32
	132,925	4,610	28.83	132,925	4,610	28.83

OVERS BOWLED AND RUNS SCORED IN THE COUNTY CHAMPIONSHIP, 1999

County	Over-rate per hour	Run-rate/ 100 balls
*Derbyshire (9).	15.85	54.29
*Durham (8).	15.64	49.09
*Essex (12)	15.78	49.75
Glamorgan (14).	16.06	50.94
Gloucestershire (18)	16.01	49.42
*Hampshire (7).	15.59	51.53
*Kent (5).	15.57	50.26
Lancashire (2).	16.49	55.37
*Leicestershire (3).	15.93	53.32
*Middlesex (16)	15.77	48.94
Northamptonshire (13)	16.50	56.12
†Nottinghamshire (17)	15.26	53.46
*Somerset (4).	15.69	52.07
*Surrey (1).	15.61	57.33
*Sussex (11).	15.58	50.45
Warwickshire (10)	16.05	50.45
†Worcestershire (15)	15.44	48.31
†Yorkshire (6).	15.44	48.14
1999 average rate	15.79	51.49

1999 Championship positions are shown in brackets.
* £4,000 fine.   † £6,000 fine.

ECB COUNTY PITCHES TABLE OF MERIT

First-Class Matches and Under-19 Tests

		Points	Matches	Average in 1999	Average in 1998
1	Somerset (2)	97	9	5.39	5.18
2	Leicestershire (3)	92	9	5.11	5.11
3	Surrey (7)	109	11	4.95	4.78
4	Essex (9=)	117	12	4.88	4.65
5	Hampshire (1)	87	9	4.83	5.25
6	Kent (18)	86	9	4.78	4.05
7	Sussex (11)	76	8	4.75	4.60
7	Cambridge University (6)	57	6	4.75	4.80
9	Glamorgan (19)	85	9	4.72	3.94
10	Middlesex (13)	94	10	4.70	4.45
11	Derbyshire (9=)	75	8	4.69	4.65
12	Gloucestershire (4)	84	9	4.67	5.05
12	Oxford University (5)	56	6	4.67	4.83
14	Worcestershire (14)	82	9	4.56	4.41
15	Northamptonshire (20)	89	10	4.45	3.81
16	Yorkshire (17)	67	8	4.19	4.18
17	Warwickshire (15)	92	11	4.18	4.39
18	Durham (12)	82	10	4.10	4.56
19	Lancashire (16)	89	11	4.05	4.22
20	Nottinghamshire (8)	69	9	3.83	4.70

One-Day Matches

		Points	Matches	Average in 1999	Average in 1998
1	Somerset (11)	105	10	5.25	4.45
2	Middlesex (12)	113	11	5.14	4.39
3	Sussex (14=)	91	9	5.06	4.27
4	Hampshire (5)	101	10	5.05	4.88
5	Derbyshire (16)	89	9	4.94	4.20
6	Nottinghamshire (6)	87	9	4.83	4.75
7	Leicestershire (8)	76	8	4.75	4.53
7	Northamptonshire (17)	95	10	4.75	4.13
9	Essex (3)	82	9	4.56	5.00
9	Warwickshire (10)	82	9	4.56	4.46
11	Glamorgan (13)	90	10	4.50	4.36
12	Durham (14=)	97	11	4.41	4.27
13	Gloucestershire (2)	112	13	4.31	5.25
14	Surrey (4)	60	7	4.29	4.90
15	Worcestershire (9)	68	8	4.25	4.50
16	Kent (7)	73	9	4.06	4.73
17	Cambridge University (–)	8	1	4.00	–
18	Yorkshire (18)	77	10	3.85	3.88
19	Lancashire (19)	76	11	3.45	3.77
	Oxford University (1)	–	–	–	5.33

In both tables 1998 positions are shown in brackets. Each umpire in a game marks the pitch on the following scale of merit: 6 – very good; 5 – good; 4 – above average; 3 – below average; 2 – poor; 1 – unfit.

The tables, provided by the ECB, cover all major matches, including Tests, Under-19 internationals and women's internationals, played on grounds under the club's jurisdiction. Middlesex pitches at Lord's are the responsibility of MCC.

The ECB points out that the tables of merit are not a direct assessment of the groundsmen's ability. Marks may be affected by many factors including weather, soil conditions and the resources available.

DERBYSHIRE

President: H. L. Jackson

Chairman: G. T. Bowring

Secretary/General Manager: J. Smedley

Chairman, Cricket Committee: L. C. Elliott

Captain: D. G. Cork

Cricket Manager: C. M. Wells

Head Groundsman: B. Marsh

Scorer: S. W. Tacey

Paul Aldred

Derbyshire, playing to their traditional strength, seam bowling, finished in the top half of the Championship – though only by virtue of having one more victory than Warwickshire, who were level on points. Still, had they scored another three runs in the contentious final match against Hampshire, Derbyshire would have been fourth rather than ninth. For an essentially unbalanced team, a place in the first division was a considerable achievement, reflecting credit not only on the players but on Dominic Cork's leadership and the support of Colin Wells, appointed as cricket manager before the season.

Nothing at the County Ground is ever straightforward, however, and at the end of the season Derbyshire lost five players they would prefer to have kept. Phillip DeFreitas and Adrian Rollins asked to be released from their contracts, Ian Blackwell, Andrew Harris and Robin Weston rejected the offer of further engagements. The county started to rebuild by taking on two former Test players, Rob Bailey, the former Northamptonshire captain, and Tim Munton from Warwickshire, plus Mathew Dowman from Nottinghamshire and Luke Sutton, a reserve wicket-keeper from Somerset.

Kim Barnett had already departed after overseeing his last political battle in the winter, when a dispute about the extent of Cork's powers – while he was touring Australia – had split the membership. It culminated in an extraordinary general meeting at Pride Park Stadium, Derby County's home, in March, when a vote of no confidence in the committee was carried by 501 votes to 348. The committee resigned, but four of them, including chairman Trevor Bowring, regained seats in the June elections. The weakness of the campaign was that there was no alternative structure to put in place. Former committee members were among the fiercest critics of the regime, while making it clear that they had no intention of returning, though David Griffin, who organised the campaign, was elected. Barnett accepted a settlement of his contract and joined Gloucestershire.

The administrative hiatus did not affect the team. There were two impressive early Championship victories, over Kent at Canterbury and Northamptonshire at Derby, the only home win of the summer. The final table showed Derbyshire's erratic nature: only Surrey, Lancashire and Yorkshire had more than their seven victories; only Nottinghamshire and

Gloucestershire more than their eight defeats. Draws were not in Derbyshire's vocabulary, except when caused by bad weather. They could play with bristling purpose, never better than in the defeat of Leicestershire, when they were confronting the follow-on until DeFreitas, batting at No. 9, scored a glorious century. They could also be inept, especially when spinners of the quality of Muttiah Muralitharan and Saqlain Mushtaq set them impenetrable problems. Derbyshire's worst spell was in July, when they lost to Somerset, Durham and Sussex, but they retained an optimistic faith and won four of the next six.

Even before the departure of Barnett, the most prolific scorer in the county's history, the batting was uncertain. Steve Titchard, released by Lancashire, did an honest job without recapturing the authority of his century against Northamptonshire. Michael Slater scored 171 in the same innings but again fell short of expectations and was to be replaced by fellow-Australian Michael Di Venuto in 2000. Slater's lack of runs in two summers was hard to explain, especially as he scored five hundreds for Australia in 1998-99, and sad too, because he was an exemplary overseas player in every other way. Weston blossomed with centuries in three successive games. Not surprisingly, he was unable to maintain this. Rollins, who ended the season in commanding form, was nearest to 1,000 runs. There was a gap at No. 5; Matthew Cassar never reached 50 despite two National League centuries, and the damage caused by a brittle top order could not always be repaired. Cork and DeFreitas played some good innings, Blackwell and Ben Spendlove glittered occasionally and Karl Krikken, whose wicket-keeping standards seldom wavered, was as determined as ever.

Heroics were needed from the bowlers and, despite injuries that resulted in the use of 25 players, they responded magnificently. At the age of 30, Paul Aldred was a revelation. Having taken 47 wickets in four seasons, he added 50 in 12 matches and was capped while returning his best match figures against Lancashire. From a man struggling to earn a new contract, he became at ease with himself, enjoying life in the front line. Kevin Dean, Derbyshire's leading bowler in 1998, suffered back trouble, played only three Championship games and ended the season facing surgery. Harris fought back from a similar problem and regained rhythm until he had a thumb fractured while batting as a night-watchman at Trent Bridge. He is not a lucky cricketer.

DeFreitas, who had seldom bowled better, took his 1,000th wicket in the victory over Nottinghamshire and displayed craftsmanship of a high order. Cork, apparently well out of the England picture, retained his capacity to make things happen; not the least of his virtues is that he leads from the front. After a frustrating absence caused by sore shins, Trevor Smith, with his strong, high action, confirmed his valuable knack of taking important wickets, including ten to beat Leicestershire. Derbyshire had four seam bowlers in the top 30 of the averages, a rating beyond any of their batsmen.

Derbyshire's one-day performances, including a swift exit from the NatWest Trophy, were consistently poor. In the later stages of the National League, they frequently rested players ahead of more important Championship engagements. The Second Eleven, coached by Andrew Brown, made a strong bid for the title to strengthen an air of cautious optimism. – GERALD MORTIMER.

DERBYSHIRE 1999

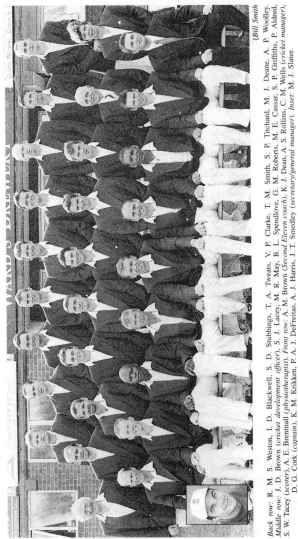

[Bill Smith]

Back row: R. M. S. Weston, I. D. Blackwell, S. D. Stubbings, T. A. Tweats, V. P. Clarke, T. M. Smith, S. P. Titchard, M. J. Deane, A. P. Woolley. Middle row: J. D. Brown (cricket development officer), S. J. Lacey, M. R. May, B. L. Spendlove, G. M. Roberts, M. E. Cassar, S. P. Griffiths, P. Aldred, S. W. Tacey (scorer), A. E. Brentnall (physiotherapist). Front row: A. M. Brown (Second Eleven coach), K. J. Dean, A. S. Rollins, C. M. Wells (cricket manager), D. G. Cork (captain), K. M. Krikken, P. A. J. DeFreitas, A. J. Harris, J. T. Smedley (secretary/general manager). Inset: M. J. Slater.

DERBYSHIRE RESULTS

All first-class matches – Played 17: Won 7, Lost 8, Drawn 2.

County Championship matches – Played 17: Won 7, Lost 8, Drawn 2.

Competition placings – PPP Healthcare County Championship, 9th;
NatWest Trophy, 4th round; CGU National League, 8th in Division 2.

COUNTY CHAMPIONSHIP AVERAGES

BATTING

Cap		M	I	NO	R	HS	100s	50s	Avge	Ct/St
1995	A. S. Rollins	15	28	3	965	113	2	5	38.60	9
	R. M. S. Weston . . .	15	26	2	838	156	3	2	34.91	9
1998	M. J. Slater§.	10	18	1	540	171	1	2	31.76	9
	S. P. Titchard	17	31	4	752	136	1	2	27.85	2
1993	D. G. Cork.	14	22	2	535	82	0	4	26.75	18
1994	P. A. J. DeFreitas. . .	13	18	1	441	105	1	2	25.94	7
	S. J. Lacey.	6	8	2	154	42	0	0	25.66	5/1
	I. D. Blackwell† . . .	10	16	2	347	62*	0	2	24.78	6
1992	K. M. Krikken	12	19	3	389	88	0	3	24.31	30/1
	B. L. Spendlove†. . .	7	13	0	279	63.	0	2	21.46	2
	S. D. Stubbings. . . .	5	10	0	213	45	0	0	21.30	3
	M. E. Cassar.	14	24	3	393	42	0	0	18.71	5
	S. P. Griffiths	5	7	1	108	35	0	0	18.00	16/1
	T. M. Smith†	8	9	6	52	20*	0	0	17.33	2
1996	A. J. Harris	7	11	7	48	8*	0	0	12.00	4
1999	P. Aldred†	12	17	2	122	29*	0	0	8.13	4
	J. P. Pyemont	3	6	1	23	13	0	0	4.60	3
	T. A. Tweats.	4	7	0	21	10	0	0	3.00	2

Also batted: S. J. Base (1 match) 17, 8*; K. J. Dean† (cap 1998) (3 matches) 5, 10* (1 ct);
M. J. Deane† (2 matches) 1, 0, 10 (1 ct); R. L. Eagleson (1 match) 0 (1 ct); M. Newell (1 match)
25, 7 (1 ct); P. A. Thomas (1 match) 1, 0; A. P. Woolley† (1 match) 8, 1.

* Signifies not out.   † Born in Derbyshire.   § Overseas player.

BOWLING

	O	M	R	W	BB	5W/i	Avge
K. J. Dean	66.4	14	198	12	4-34	0	16.50
T. M. Smith	183.4	34	646	31	5-63	3	20.83
P. Aldred	362.4	85	1,063	50	7-101	5	21.26
P. A. J. DeFreitas	477.2	121	1,284	59	6-41	4	21.76
D. G. Cork.	427.3	91	1,229	55	6-113	4	22.34
A. J. Harris	229.3	44	752	26	5-63	2	28.92
M. E. Cassar	164	34	562	19	5-51	1	29.57
I. D. Blackwell	250.1	69	595	12	3-30	0	49.58

Also bowled: S. J. Base 10–3–34–0; M. J. Deane 31.4–8–112–2; R. L. Eagleson 10.5–2–34–1;
K. M. Krikken 9.2–1–54–1; S. J. Lacey 81–15–238–3; M. J. Slater 4–0–23–0; S. D. Stubbings
5–0–41–0; P. A. Thomas 16–1–74–2; S. P. Titchard 8–3–19–0; R. M. S. Weston 6–1–23–1;
A. P. Woolley 11–1–61–0.

COUNTY RECORDS

Highest score for:	274	G. Davidson v Lancashire at Manchester	1896
Highest score against:	343*	P. A. Perrin (Essex) at Chesterfield	1904
Best bowling for:	10-40	W. Bestwick v Glamorgan at Cardiff.	1921
Best bowling against:	10-45	R. L. Johnson (Middlesex) at Derby	1994
Highest total for:	645	v Hampshire at Derby	1898
Highest total against:	662	by Yorkshire at Chesterfield	1898
Lowest total for:	16	v Nottinghamshire at Nottingham	1879
Lowest total against:	23	by Hampshire at Burton upon Trent	1958

DERBYSHIRE v GLAMORGAN

At Derby, April 20, 21, 22, 23. Drawn. Derbyshire 4 pts, Glamorgan 5 pts. Toss: Glamorgan. First-class debut: D. S. Harrison. County debuts: S. P. Titchard; K. Newell.

Play was possible only on the third day, and even then cramped by the weather to less than 70 overs. Glamorgan began encouragingly and, with Watkin predictably mean, Derbyshire slid to 54 for four. Rollins, who missed much of the 1998 season with disc trouble, and Cork ensured there were no further inroads with an unbroken partnership of 114. Cork, who had been omitted from the England World Cup squad, demonstrated his determination to add restrained and significant runs to his wickets by scoring only four in 14 overs before tea, though he could not resist hitting Croft – who was among the chosen ones – for a four and two sixes in one over. Glamorgan's 17-year-old debutant all-rounder, David Harrison, was barred from using the gym and swimming pool at the team hotel without supervision because he was under age.

Close of play: First day, No play; Second day, No play; Third day, Derbyshire 168-4 (Rollins 79*, Cork 45*).

Derbyshire

M. J. Slater c Watkin b Thomas	5	*D. G. Cork not out	45
A. S. Rollins not out	79		
R. M. S. Weston c Dale b Watkin	3	B 6, l-b 1, n-b 10	17
S. P. Titchard c James b Jones	14		
M. E. Cassar c Shaw b Dale	5	1/5 2/15 3/41 4/54 (4 wkts)	168

P. A. J. DeFreitas, †K. M. Krikken, P. Aldred, T. M. Smith and K. J. Dean did not bat.

Bonus point – Glamorgan 1.

Bowling: Watkin 15–6–16–1; Thomas 15–4–36–1; Harrison 10–2–33–0; Dale 11.5–5–23–1; Jones 9–2–18–1; Croft 9–2–35–0.

Glamorgan

S. P. James, A. W. Evans, A. Dale, *M. P. Maynard, K. Newell, R. D. B. Croft, †A. D. Shaw, D. S. Harrison, S. D. Thomas, S. P. Jones and S. L. Watkin.

Umpires: N. T. Plews and A. G. T. Whitehead.

At Canterbury, April 28, 29, 30. DERBYSHIRE beat KENT by ten wickets.

At Derby, May 8. DERBYSHIRE v PAKISTANIS. No result (See Other Matches).

At Derby, May 9. DERBYSHIRE beat ZIMBABWEANS by five wickets (See Other Matches).

At Birmingham, May 14, 15, 16, 17. DERBYSHIRE lost to WARWICKSHIRE by 84 runs.

DERBYSHIRE v NORTHAMPTONSHIRE

At Derby, May 19, 20, 21. Derbyshire won by eight wickets. Derbyshire 20 pts, Northamptonshire 6 pts. Toss: Derbyshire.

Derbyshire convincingly ended a run of seven consecutive Championship defeats by Northamptonshire, whose batting slumped quickly after DeFreitas, bowling beautifully to end with five for 48, made the initial breakthrough. Penberthy gave the innings some substance. But before the end of the first day, Northamptonshire dropped Titchard twice, and he and Slater made them pay in an aggressive stand of 296, Derbyshire's highest against this opposition for any wicket. Both made their first Championship century for Derbyshire: Slater in his 28th innings as their overseas player, Titchard in his fifth after signing from Lancashire. Slater went on to a blistering 171 from 226 balls, though he seldom outpaced his partner. Hayden responded with his third century of the summer, but a good spell of left-arm spin from Blackwell hastened the end. Derbyshire claimed the extra eight overs, and won with nine balls and a day to spare.

Close of play: First day, Derbyshire 90-1 (Slater 44*, Titchard 32*); Second day, Northamptonshire 54-2 (Hayden 36*, Taylor 0*).

Northamptonshire

R. J. Bailey c Griffiths b Smith	30	– lbw b Cork	5
*M. L. Hayden lbw b DeFreitas	13	– c Griffiths b DeFreitas	111
M. B. Loye b Harris	0	– lbw b Cork	6
R. J. Warren b DeFreitas	33	– (5) c Slater b Blackwell	40
D. J. Sales lbw b DeFreitas	18	– (6) c and b Blackwell	20
A. L. Penberthy lbw b Smith	98	– (7) c Griffiths b DeFreitas	20
G. P. Swann lbw b Cork	24	– (8) c Harris b Blackwell	4
†D. Ripley c Griffiths b Cork	5	– (9) c Griffiths b Harris	35
J. P. Taylor c Cork b DeFreitas	26	– (4) run out	0
D. Follett b DeFreitas	0	– c sub b DeFreitas	0
D. E. Malcolm not out	10	– not out	5
B 5, l-b 9, w 6	20	B 6, l-b 7, n-b 4	17
	270		**261**

1/28 2/29 3/79 4/79 5/99 6/162 7/190 8/236 9/247 270
1/26 2/52 3/54 4/124 5/194 6/200 7/207 8/233 9/233 261

Bonus points – Northamptonshire 2, Derbyshire 4.

Bowling: *First Innings*—Cork 21-4-75-2; DeFreitas 21.1-5-48-5; Harris 17-1-47-1; Smith 21-5-85-2; Blackwell 1-0-1-0. *Second Innings*—Cork 16-2-41-2; DeFreitas 30-6-100-3; Smith 7-3-19-0; Harris 5.5-1-24-1; Blackwell 25-4-64-3.

Derbyshire

M. J. Slater b Malcolm	171	– (2) c Sales b Taylor	30
A. S. Rollins c Ripley b Malcolm	11	– (1) c Hayden b Taylor	3
S. P. Titchard b Hayden	136	– not out	19
M. E. Cassar c Ripley b Swann	22	– not out	8
B. L. Spendlove c Ripley b Malcolm	20		
I. D. Blackwell c Malcolm b Bailey	28		
P. A. J. DeFreitas lbw b Follett	7		
*D. G. Cork c Bailey b Penberthy	21		
†S. P. Griffiths c Warren b Taylor	13		
A. J. Harris b Swann	4		
T. M. Smith not out	7		
B 14, l-b 8, n-b 4	26	L-b 4, w 2	6
	466	(2 wkts)	**66**

1/25 2/321 3/352 4/379 5/384 6/409 7/429 8/440 9/445 466
1/13 2/50 (2 wkts) 66

Bonus points – Derbyshire 4, Northamptonshire 4.

Bowling: *First Innings*—Malcolm 24-2-139-3; Taylor 19-3-84-1; Follett 15-4-61-1; Swann 19-0-98-2; Penberthy 15-5-39-1; Hayden 6-0-19-1; Bailey 3-1-4-1. *Second Innings*—Malcolm 5-0-28-0; Taylor 7.3-1-27-2; Follett 3-0-7-0.

Umpires: R. Julian and J. F. Steele.

Bowling: *First Innings*—Harris 36–9–101–5; Aldred 33.4–8–74–5; Blackwell 40–14–69–0; Deane 7–2–30–0; Lacey 22–5–63–0. *Second Innings*—Harris 15–2–51–1; Aldred 13–1–39–0; Blackwell 24–8–50–0; Lacey 7–2–22–1; Titchard 6–1–19–0.

Umpires: D. J. Constant and T. E. Jesty.

At Chester-le-Street, July 15, 16. DERBYSHIRE lost to DURHAM by seven wickets.

DERBYSHIRE v SUSSEX

At Derby, July 21, 22, 23. Sussex won by 85 runs. Sussex 18 pts, Derbyshire 5 pts. Toss: Derbyshire. First-class debut: B. V. Taylor.

In their last two Championship matches, Derbyshire had suffered both defeat and the indignity of a century from a former player. This time, they narrowly averted a hat-trick of hundreds – Adams fell eight short – but could not avoid losing again. Even so, Adams more than made his point to his former employers, scoring an astonishing 92 on a green pitch, facing only 68 balls and hitting two sixes and 18 fours – 91 per cent of his runs. There were five stoppages on a blustery first day and, despite Cork taking six wickets, Sussex were allowed to score too freely. They gained a lead of 45 after Robinson and Lewry ran through Derbyshire, with Extras easily making top score. On the third morning, Sussex collapsed against DeFreitas, back in the team after injury. Needing 222, and with ample time, Derbyshire had every chance but showed alarming lack of technique against swing. Lewry consistently put the ball in the right place and became the fourth bowler in the game to take six or more in an innings; his seven for 38 was a career-best analysis. Khan recorded a king pair.

Close of play: First day, Derbyshire 95-3 (Spendlove 16*, Krikken 3*); Second day, Sussex 147-4 (Peirce 55*, Cottey 8*).

Sussex

R. R. Montgomerie lbw b Cork	42	– c Cork b DeFreitas	40
M. T. E. Peirce c Krikken b Cork	10	– run out	55
W. G. Khan lbw b Cork	0	– lbw b DeFreitas	0
M. J. Di Venuto c Krikken b Cork	24	– c Cork b Aldred	13
*C. J. Adams c Weston b Aldred	92	– c Spendlove b Cork	16
P. A. Cottey b Cork	22	– b Cork	11
J. J. Bates c Cork b DeFreitas	4	– c Cork b DeFreitas	15
†N. J. Wilton b Harris	39	– lbw b DeFreitas	0
B. V. Taylor c Rollins b Cork	14	– lbw b DeFreitas	0
J. D. Lewry b Harris	3	– not out	10
M. A. Robinson not out	1	– b DeFreitas	0
B 4, l-b 2, n-b 14	20	B 1, l-b 11, w 4	16
	271		**176**

1/21 2/21 3/92 4/101 5/153   271
6/174 7/226 8/250 9/270

1/74 2/74 3/89 4/133 5/147   176
6/156 7/157 8/157 9/176

Bonus points – Sussex 2, Derbyshire 4.

Bowling: *First Innings*—Cork 24–2–113–6; Harris 12.5–1–51–2; DeFreitas 14–0–61–1; Aldred 12–4–40–1. *Second Innings*—Cork 20–6–44–2; Harris 15–2–51–0; DeFreitas 17.3–3–41–6; Aldred 12–4–28–1.

Derbyshire

	First Innings		Second Innings	
A. S. Rollins c Cottey b Lewry	29	– b Lewry	0
S. P. Titchard lbw b Robinson	17	– (3) lbw b Lewry	8
R. M. S. Weston lbw b Lewry	7	– (4) lbw b Lewry	0
B. L. Spendlove c Taylor b Robinson	29	– (5) c Wilton b Lewry	8
†K. M. Krikken c Adams b Robinson	3	– (6) c Montgomerie b Robinson	15
M. J. Slater c Di Venuto b Lewry	18	– (2) lbw b Lewry	23
I. D. Blackwell c Adams b Robinson	14	– c Di Venuto b Lewry	1
P. A. J. DeFreitas c Adams b Robinson	25	– (9) c Bates b Robinson	3
*D. G. Cork lbw b Taylor	4	– (8) c Wilton b Lewry	37
P. Aldred not out	29	– c Wilton b Taylor	0
A. J. Harris c Adams b Robinson	4	– not out	6
B 2, l-b 7, w 8, n-b 30	47	B 7, l-b 2, w 16, n-b 10	35

1/41 2/52 3/81 4/100 5/133   226   1/0 2/8 3/8 4/34 5/47   136
6/152 7/153 8/168 9/214   6/53 7/98 8/106 9/107

Bonus points – Derbyshire 1, Sussex 4.

Bowling: *First Innings*—Lewry 18–2–75–3; Taylor 15–3–54–1; Robinson 21.5–4–88–6. *Second Innings*—Lewry 12.1–3–38–7; Taylor 10–1–54–1; Robinson 15–4–35–2.

Umpires: J. W. Lloyds and A. G. T. Whitehead.

At Derby, July 28. DERBYSHIRE lost to NEW ZEALANDERS by 130 runs (See New Zealand tour section).

At Nottingham, July 30, 31, August 1. DERBYSHIRE beat NOTTINGHAMSHIRE by six wickets.

DERBYSHIRE v LANCASHIRE

At Derby, August 4, 5, 6. Lancashire won by 192 runs. Lancashire 17 pts, Derbyshire 4 pts. Toss: Lancashire. Championship debut: R. L. Eagleson.

Muralitharan's short Championship season ended as it had begun – with a succession of bamboozled batsmen. Strangely, he was not the leading bowler in the match: his 11 were surpassed by 13 from Aldred, who improved his career-best figures twice, and was capped. However, Muralitharan transfixed Derbyshire, claiming the last seven wickets of the game, and taking his total to 66 from 12 innings at an average of 11.77. On another grassy pitch, Lancashire slid to 71 for six before the score was doubled by Hegg and Chapple, whose 83 was his highest authentic score – he was paid a 27-ball hundred by Glamorgan in 1993. Martin then bowled with customary good sense, and Muralitharan started his work to give Lancashire a lead of 92. However, their top order was just as awful at the next attempt, and this time Hegg had to help Lloyd redeem the situation. Derbyshire's attack suffered yet more injuries: Cork could bowl only six overs after jarring his back and Ryan Eagleson, from Northern Ireland, marked his debut by breaking his finger. Though Aldred shone again, he was soon upstaged by Muralitharan, and Derbyshire were beaten heavily. Lancashire twelfth man Smethurst had to abandon three bacon and egg rolls by the boundary when he was summoned to replace Crawley.

Close of play: First day, Derbyshire 24-2 (Rollins 8*, Titchard 0*); Second day, Lancashire 91-5 (Lloyd 25*, Hegg 29*).

At Bristol, September 8, 9, 10. DERBYSHIRE beat GLOUCESTERSHIRE by six wickets.

DERBYSHIRE v HAMPSHIRE

At Derby, September 15, 16, 17, 18. Hampshire won by two runs. Hampshire 20 pts, Derbyshire 5 pts. Toss: Derbyshire.

A controversial match reached a dramatic climax when a skin-of-their-teeth victory ensured that Hampshire joined Derbyshire in the first division in 2000. Such were the complex permutations surrounding the last round of matches that both could have finished in the lower half: realistically, Hampshire needed a win, while Derbyshire had slightly more leeway. The result squeezed Warwickshire out of the top division, and they complained to the ECB about the collusion between the captains. By the third morning, Warwickshire had already won, which left Derbyshire needing two batting points to be safe. They were 231 for eight, still 19 short, when Udal – in charge while Smith was off the field – brought on White, a very occasional leg-spinner. Runs, and safety for Derbyshire, quickly followed. Cork and Smith maintained that discussions began at lunchtime, *after* Derbyshire had been guaranteed a top-half finish, but some smelled a rat. After rubbish was bowled to speed a third declaration, Smith offered a target, conditioned by an adverse weather forecast, of 285 in four sessions. Members protested at the shenanigans, but the upshot was an enthralling run-chase. Derbyshire recovered from losing three wickets in the sixties, with Cork and DeFreitas, dropped by Hartley on 34, batting well. As a home victory neared, Lacey had his right hand broken by McLean. He battled on and, when he had added 104 with DeFreitas, fourth place – and thus £15,000 – were 18 runs away. Then two wickets fell, leaving the last pair to get six. Hartley made amends, juggling a return catch from Lacey. The ECB later ruled that the captains were trying to win, leaving Warwickshire as the game's only losers.

Close of play: First day, Hampshire 246-5 (Aymes 40*, Mascarenhas 19*); Second day, Derbyshire 143-3 (Titchard 28*, Cassar 26*); Third day, Derbyshire 109-4 (Weston 30*, Cork 14*).

Hampshire

J. S. Laney st Krikken b Aldred	67	– b Smith	8
D. A. Kenway b Aldred	21	– c Lacey b Weston	44
W. S. Kendall c Krikken b Smith	8	– c Lacey b Smith	0
*R. A. Smith c Krikken b Smith	64		
G. W. White c Krikken b Smith	0	– (4) lbw b Aldred	27
†A. N. Aymes c and b DeFreitas	86	– (5) not out	39
A. D. Mascarenhas b DeFreitas	51	– (6) st Lacey b Krikken	45
S. D. Udal c Cork b DeFreitas	3	– (7) not out	19
N. A. M. McLean not out	24		
B 6, l-b 21, w 2, n-b 9	38	B 8, l-b 3, w 6	17

1/37 2/58 3/172 4/178 (8 wkts. dec.) 362
5/180 6/307 7/313 8/362

1/13 2/13 3/80 (5 wkts. dec.) 199
4/80 5/164

P. J. Hartley and S. J. Renshaw did not bat.

Bonus points – Hampshire 4, Derbyshire 3.

Bowling: *First Innings*—Cork 23–10–60–0; DeFreitas 26–4–88–3; Aldred 27–4–86–2; Smith 22–5–78–3; Cassar 6–2–23–0. *Second Innings*—Aldred 8.2–1–37–1; Smith 3–1–6–2; Cassar 4–0–35–0; Weston 5–1–15–1; Krikken 9.2–1–54–1; Stubbings 5–0–41–0.

Friday, June 16

Gloucester   Glos v Zimbabweans

Sunday, June 18

†CGU National League, Division One
(1 day)

Northampton   Northants v Somerset
Leeds   Yorks v Kent

†CGU National League, Division Two
(1 day)

Basingstoke   Hants v Durham
Lord's   Middx v Derbys
Leicester   †Leics v New Zealand A (1 day)
Oxford   †Oxford U. v Cambridge U.

Monday, June 19

The Oval   †Surrey v New Zealand A (1 day)

Wednesday, June 21

Cambridge   British Universities v Zimbabweans (3 days)
Chelmsford   West Indians v New Zealand A

†NatWest Trophy – Third Round (1 day)
(see page 1592)

Friday, June 23

†CGU National League, Division One
(1 day)

Manchester   Lancs v Northants (day/night)
Hove   Sussex v Kent (day/night)

†CGU National League, Division Two
(1 day)

Birmingham   Warwicks v Surrey (day/night)

Saturday, June 24

†CGU National League, Division One
(1 day)

Bristol   Glos v Yorks
Taunton   Somerset v Worcs

†CGU National League, Division Two
(1 day)

Cardiff   Glam v Hants
Nottingham   Notts v Essex

Sunday, June 25

†CGU National League, Division One
(1 day)

Leicester   Leics v Glos
Leeds   Yorks v Northants

†CGU National League, Division Two
(1 day)

Chester-le-Street   Durham v Middx
Birmingham   Warwicks v Essex

Southampton   †Hants v West Indians (1 day)
Taunton   †Somerset v Zimbabweans (1 day)

Monday, June 26

†CGU National League, Division Two
(1 day)

Derby   Derbys v Notts (day/night)

Worcester   †Worcs v New Zealand A (1 day)

Tuesday, June 27

†CGU National League, Division One
(1 day)

Manchester   Lancs v Yorks (day/night)

†CGU National League, Division Two
(1 day)

Southampton   Hants v Surrey

Chester-le-Street   †Durham v Zimbabweans (1 day)

Wednesday, June 28

PPP County Championship, Division One

Darlington   Durham v Derbys
Maidstone   Kent v Somerset

PPP County Championship, Division Two

Chelmsford   Essex v Middx
Swansea   Glam v Worcs
Birmingham   Warwicks v Glos

Hove   Sussex v New Zealand A

Thursday, June 29

Lord's   ENGLAND v WEST INDIES (2nd Cornhill Test, 5 days)

PPP County Championship, Division One

Southampton	Hants v Surrey
Manchester	Lancs v Yorks
Nottingham	†Notts v Zimbabweans (1 day)

Saturday, July 1

Northampton	†Northants v Zimbabweans (1 day)

Sunday, July 2

†CGU National League, Division One
(1 day)

Maidstone	Kent v Somerset
Northampton	Northants v Sussex
Worcester	Worcs v Leics

†CGU National League, Division Two
(1 day)

Darlington	Durham v Derbys
Chelmsford	Essex v Middx
Swansea	Glam v Warwicks

Monday, July 3

Bristol	†Zimbabweans v New Zealand A (1 day, day/night)

Tuesday, July 4

Bristol	†West Indians v New Zealand A (1 day, day/night)
North Wales	†Triple Crown Tournament (3 days)

Wednesday, July 5

†NatWest Trophy – Fourth Round (1 day)
(see page 1592)

Thursday, July 6

Bristol	†WEST INDIES v ZIMBABWE (1-day Triangular Tournament, day/night)

Friday, July 7

PPP County Championship, Division One

Derby	Derbys v Lancs
Oakham School	Leics v Surrey
Taunton	Somerset v Hants
Leeds	Yorks v Durham

PPP County Championship, Division Two

Southgate	Middx v Worcs
Northampton	Northants v Glam

Nottingham	Notts v Essex
Birmingham	Warwicks v Sussex
Milton Keynes	First-Class Counties Select XI v New Zealand A

Saturday, July 8

The Oval	†ENGLAND v ZIMBABWE (1-day Triangular Tournament)

Sunday, July 9

Lord's	†ENGLAND v WEST INDIES (1-day Triangular Tournament)

Tuesday, July 11

Canterbury	†WEST INDIES v ZIMBABWE (1-day Triangular Tournament)
Lord's	Oxford U. v Cambridge U.

Wednesday, July 12

PPP County Championship, Division One

Derby	Derbys v Kent
Leicester	Leics v Durham
Taunton	Somerset v Lancs
The Oval	Surrey v Yorks

PPP County Championship, Division Two

Cheltenham	Glos v Northants
Southgate	Middx v Glam
Arundel	Sussex v Essex
Worcester	Worcs v Notts
Portsmouth	Hants v New Zealand A

Thursday, July 13

Manchester	†ENGLAND v ZIMBABWE (1-day Triangular Tournament, day/night)

Saturday, July 15

Chester-le-Street	†ENGLAND v WEST INDIES (1-day Triangular Tournament)

Sunday, July 16

Chester-le-Street	†WEST INDIES v ZIMBABWE (1-day Triangular Tournament)

†CGU National League, Division One
(1 day)

Cheltenham	Glos v Worcs
Leicester	Leics v Northants
Taunton	Somerset v Lancs
Arundel	Sussex v Yorks

†CGU National League, Division Two
(1 day)

Derby	Derbys v Warwicks
Southgate	Middx v Durham
The Oval	Surrey v Glam

Monday, July 17

Cheltenham	†Glos v New Zealand A (1 day)

Tuesday, July 18

Birmingham	†ENGLAND v ZIMBABWE (1-day Triangular Tournament, day/night)
Oxford	MCC v New Zealand A

Wednesday, July 19

PPP County Championship, Division One

Portsmouth	Hants v Kent
Manchester	Lancs v Durham
Guildford	Surrey v Leics
Scarborough	Yorks v Somerset

PPP County Championship, Division Two

Chelmsford	Essex v Worcs
Cardiff	Glam v Northants
Cheltenham	Glos v Warwicks
Hove	Sussex v Notts

Thursday, July 20

Nottingham	†ENGLAND v WEST INDIES (1-day Triangular Tournament)

Friday, July 21

Scotland	†European Championship (7 days)

Saturday, July 22

Lord's	†TRIANGULAR TOURNAMENT FINAL (1 day)

Sunday, July 23

†CGU National League, Division One
(1 day)

Cheltenham	Glos v Kent

Leicester	Leics v Lancs
Scarborough	Yorks v Somerset

†CGU National League, Division Two
(1 day)

Chelmsford	Essex v Derbys
Portsmouth	Hants v Middx
Guildford	Surrey v Notts
Birmingham	Warwicks v Durham

Monday, July 24

Northampton or Leeds	Northants or Yorks v West Indians (3 days)

Subject to involvement in NatWest quarter-finals.

Tuesday, July 25

NatWest Trophy – Quarter-finals (1 day)

Wednesday, July 26

NatWest Trophy – Quarter-finals (1 day)

Friday, July 28

PPP County Championship, Division One

Chester-le-Street	Durham v Somerset
Canterbury	Kent v Derbys
Leeds	Yorks v Lancs

PPP County Championship, Division Two

Southgate	Middx v Sussex
Birmingham	Warwicks v Northants
Worcester	Worcs v Glos
Leicester	Leics v West Indians (3 days)
Cardiff	†England Under-19 v Sri Lanka Under-19 (1st 1-day)

Saturday, July 29

Cardiff	†England Under-19 v Sri Lanka Under-19 (2nd 1-day)

Sunday, July 30

†CGU National League, Division Two
(1 day)

Southampton	Hants v Essex

Monday, July 31

Hove	†England Under-19 v Sri Lanka Under-19 (3rd 1-day, day/night)

Tuesday, August 1
†CGU National League, Division Two
(1 day)

Nottingham　　　Notts v Warwicks
　　　　　　　　(day/night)

Wednesday, August 2
PPP County Championship, Division One

Derby　　　　　Derbys v Hants
Canterbury　　　Kent v Leics
Taunton　　　　Somerset v Yorks
The Oval　　　　Surrey v Lancs

PPP County Championship, Division Two

Bristol　　　　　Glos v Glam
Lord's　　　　　Middx v Essex

†CGU National League, Division One
(1 day)

Northampton　　Northants v Worcs
　　　　　　　　(day/night)

Thursday, August 3

Manchester　　　ENGLAND v WEST
　　　　　　　　INDIES (3rd
　　　　　　　　Cornhill Test, 5 days)

PPP County Championship, Division Two

Nottingham　　　Notts v Warwicks

Friday, August 4
PPP County Championship, Division Two

Northampton　　Northants v Worcs

Sunday, August 6
†CGU National League, Division One
(1 day)

Canterbury　　　Kent v Leics
Taunton　　　　Somerset v Yorks

†CGU National League, Division Two
(1 day)

Derby　　　　　Derbys v Hants
Cardiff　　　　　Glam v Durham
Lord's　　　　　Middx v Surrey

Monday, August 7
†CGU National League, Division One
(1 day)

Hove　　　　　Sussex v Lancs
　　　　　　　　(day/night)

†AON Trophy Semi-finals (1 day)

Tuesday, August 8

Exmouth　　　　†Minor Counties v
　　　　　　　　MCC (1 day)

Wednesday, August 9
PPP County Championship, Division One

Chester-le-Street　Durham v Kent
Southampton　　Hants v Leics

PPP County Championship, Division Two

Northampton　　Northants v Sussex
Nottingham　　　Notts v Middx
Kidderminster　　Worcs v Essex

Derby　　　　　Derbys v West Indians
　　　　　　　　(3 days)

†CGU National League, Division One
(1 day)

Bristol　　　　　Glos v Somerset
　　　　　　　　(day/night)
Leeds　　　　　Yorks v Lancs
　　　　　　　　(day/night)

†CGU National League, Division Two
(1 day)

Whitgift School　Surrey v Warwicks

Thursday, August 10

Lord's　　　　　†Under-15 World Cup
　　　　　　　　Final (1 day)

Saturday, August 12
†NatWest Trophy – 1st Semi-final (1 day)

Sunday, August 13
†NatWest Trophy – 2nd Semi-final (1 day)

†CGU National League, Division One
(1 day)

Manchester　　　Lancs v Glos
Northampton　　Northants v Leics
Worcester　　　Worcs v Sussex

†CGU National League, Division Two
(1 day)

Derby　　　　　Derbys v Essex
Chester-le-Street　Durham v Warwicks
Southampton　　Hants v Glam
Nottingham　　　Notts v Middx

Titwood, Glasgow　†Scotland v West
　　　　　　　　Indians (1 day)
Oakham School　†England Board XI v
　　　　　　　　Sri Lankan Under-19
　　　　　　　　(1 day)

Tuesday, August 15

†CGU National League, Division One
(1 day)

Manchester	Lancs v Kent (day/night)
Nottingham	†England Under-19 v Sri Lanka Under-19 (1st Test, 4 days)
Lord's	†MCC v Scotland (2 days)

Wednesday, August 16

PPP County Championship, Division One

Leicester	Leics v Yorks
Taunton	Somerset v Durham
The Oval	Surrey v Derbys

PPP County Championship, Division Two

Colchester	Essex v Glos
Cardiff	Glam v Notts
Eastbourne	Sussex v Northants

†CGU National League, Division Two
(1 day)

Birmingham	Warwicks v Middx (day/night)

Thursday, August 17

Leeds	ENGLAND v WEST INDIES (4th Cornhill Test, 5 days)
Lord's	†MCC v Minor Counties (1 day)

PPP County Championship, Division One

Manchester	Lancs v Kent

PPP County Championship, Division Two

Birmingham	Warwicks v Middx

Saturday, August 19

Ayr	Scotland v Ireland

Sunday, August 20

†CGU National League, Division One
(1 day)

Leicester	Leics v Yorks
Eastbourne	Sussex v Northants
Worcester	Worcs v Somerset

†CGU National League, Division Two
(1 day)

Colchester	Essex v Hants

Colwyn Bay	Glam v Notts
The Oval	Surrey v Derbys

Monday, August 21

Northampton	†England Under-19 v Sri Lanka Under-19 (2nd Test, 4 days)

Tuesday, August 22

PPP County Championship, Division One

Derby	Derbys v Durham
Canterbury	Kent v Hants
Leicester	Leics v Lancs

PPP County Championship, Division Two

Colwyn Bay	Glam v Sussex
Bristol	Glos v Middx
Worcester	Worcs v Warwicks

Wednesday, August 23

Taunton or Nottingham	Somerset or Notts v West Indians

Subject to involvement in NatWest Trophy final.

†CGU National League, Division Two
(1 day)

Colchester	Essex v Surrey (day/night)

Saturday, August 26

Lord's	†NATWEST TROPHY FINAL (1 day)

Sunday, August 27

†CGU National League, Division One
(1 day)

Canterbury	Kent v Worcs

†CGU National League, Division Two
(1 day)

Derby	Derbys v Glam
Chester-le-Street	Durham v Essex

Monday, August 28

†CGU National League, Division One
(1 day)

Bristol	Glos v Leics (day/night)
Northampton	Northants v Yorks
Hove	Sussex v Somerset (day/night)

†CGU National League, Division Two
(1 day)

Richmond   Middx v Notts

Tuesday, August 29
†CGU National League, Division Two
(1 day)

Chester-le-Street   Durham v Hants
(day/night)

Worcester   †England Under-19 v
Sri Lanka Under-19
(3rd Test, 4 days)

Wednesday, August 30
PPP County Championship, Division One

Scarborough   Yorks v Surrey

PPP County Championship, Division Two

Southend   Essex v Glam
Northampton   Northants v Glos
Nottingham   Notts v Sussex
Birmingham   Warwicks v Worcs

†CGU National League, Division One
(1 day)

Taunton   Somerset v Leics
(day/night)

Lord's   †ECB 38-County Final

Thursday, August 31

The Oval   ENGLAND v WEST
INDIES (5th
Cornhill Test, 5 days)

PPP County Championship, Division One

Chester-le-Street   Durham v Hants

Friday, September 1
PPP County Championship, Division One

Taunton   Somerset v Leics

Lord's   †National Club
Championship Final
(1 day)

Sunday, September 3
†CGU National League, Division One
(1 day)

Northampton   Northants v Kent
Worcester   Worcs v Lancs
Scarborough   Yorks v Sussex

†CGU National League, Division Two
(1 day)

Southend   Essex v Glam
Nottingham   Notts v Surrey
Birmingham   Warwicks v Derbys

Lord's   †National Village
Championship Final
(1 day)

Monday, September 4
†AON Trophy Final (1 day)

Tuesday, September 5
PPP County Championship, Division Two

Lord's   Middx v Warwicks

†CGU National League, Division One
(1 day)

Canterbury   Kent v Yorks
(day/night)
Hove   Sussex v Glos
(day/night)

Wednesday, September 6
PPP County Championship, Division One

Southampton   Hants v Derbys
The Oval   Surrey v Durham

PPP County Championship, Division Two

Northampton   Northants v Essex
Nottingham   Notts v Glam

†CGU National League, Division One
(1 day)

Manchester   Lancs v Somerset
(day/night)

Thursday, September 7
PPP County Championship, Division One

Canterbury   Kent v Yorks

PPP County Championship, Division Two

Hove   Sussex v Glos

Friday, September 8
PPP County Championship, Division One

Manchester   Lancs v Somerset

†CGU National League, Division One
(1 day)

Leicester   Leics v Worcs
(day/night)

Saturday, September 9

†CGU National League, Division Two
(1 day)

Lord's	Middx v Warwicks

Sunday, September 10

†CGU National League, Division Two
(1 day)

Southampton	Hants v Derbys
Nottingham	Notts v Glam
The Oval	Surrey v Durham

†Minor Counties Final (3 days)

Wednesday, September 13

PPP County Championship, Division One

Derby	Derbys v Somerset
Southampton	Hants v Yorks
Manchester	Lancs v Surrey
Leicester	Leics v Kent

PPP County Championship, Division Two

Chelmsford	Essex v Warwicks
Cardiff	Glam v Middx
Bristol	Glos v Notts
Worcester	Worcs v Northants

Sunday, September 17

†CGU National League, Division One
(1 day)

Bristol	Glos v Northants
Manchester	Lancs v Sussex
Leicester	Leics v Somerset
Worcester	Worcs v Kent

†CGU National League, Division Two
(1 day)

Derby	Derbys v Durham
Chelmsford	Essex v Warwicks
Cardiff	Glam v Middx
Southampton	Hants v Notts

†NATWEST TROPHY, 2000

All matches are of one day's duration.

First Round – Tuesday, May 2

1	Colwall	Herefordshire v Sussex Board XI
2	Northampton	Northants Board XI v Northumberland
3	Hertford	Herts v Cambs
4	Boughton Hall, Chester	Cheshire v Lincs
5	Castle Avenue, Dublin	Ireland v Salop
6	Kidderminster	Worcs Board XI v Kent Board XI
7	Walsall	Staffs v Somerset Board XI
8	South Wilts	Wilts v Scotland
9	Pontarddulais	Wales v Bucks
10	Cheltenham	Glos Board XI v Notts Board XI
11	Gateshead Fell	Durham Board XI v Leics Board XI
12	Mildenhall	Suffolk v Lancs Board XI
13	Truro	Cornwall v Norfolk
14	Cove	Hants Board XI v Hunts

Second Round – Tuesday, May 16

15	Colwall or Hastings	Match 1 winner v Berks
16	Northampton or Jesmond	Match 2 winner v Beds
17	Hertford or March Town	Match 3 winner v Cumberland
18	Boughton Hall, Chester or Grantham	Match 4 winner v Holland
19	Lurgan or Shifnal	Match 5 winner v Surrey Board XI
20	Stratford-upon-Avon	Warwicks Board XI v Match 6 winner
21	Torquay	Devon v Match 7 winner
22	Southgate	Middx Board XI v Match 8 winner
23	Cardiff or Dinton	Match 9 winner v Oxon
24	Heanor Town	Derbys Board XI v Match 10 winner
25	Hartlepool or Hinckley Town	Match 11 winner v Denmark
26	Chelmsford	Essex Board XI v Match 12 winner
27	Bournemouth	Dorset v Match 13 winner
28	Cove or Godmanchester	Match 14 winner v Yorks Board XI

Third Round – Wednesday, June 21

29	Kington or Hove or Finchampstead	Match 15 winner v Durham
30	Northampton or Jesmond or Wardown Park	Match 16 winner v Leics
31	Hertford or March Town or Carlisle	Match 17 winner v Kent
32	Bowdon or Cleethorpes or Amstelveen	Match 18 winner v Lancs
33	Waringstown or Telford or Cheam	Match 19 winner v Somerset
34	Kidderminster or Canterbury or Edgbaston	Match 20 winner v Hants
35	Leek or Taunton or Exmouth	Match 21 winner v Surrey
36	South Wilts or Edinburgh or Southgate	Match 22 winner v Sussex
37	Swansea or Milton Keynes or Banbury	Match 23 winner v Essex
38	Bristol (provisional) or Boots Ground, Nottingham or Derby	Match 24 winner v Derbys
39	Durham or Oakham or Tring*	Match 25 winner v Northants
40	Mildenhall or Middleton or Billericay	Match 26 winner v Warwicks
41	Truro or Lakenham or Bournemouth	Match 27 winner v Glam
42	Southampton or Godmanchester or Harrogate	Match 28 winner v Yorks
43	Worcester	Worcs v Glos
44	Lord's	Middx v Notts

* If Denmark qualify, they will play away.

Fourth Round – Wednesday, July 5

45	Match 29 winner v Match 34 winner	49	Match 44 winner v Match 33 winner
46	Match 39 winner v Match 42 winner	50	Match 31 winner v Match 41 winner
47	Match 40 winner v Match 38 winner	51	Match 30 winner v Match 43 winner
48	Match 32 winner v Match 37 winner	52	Match 35 winner v Match 36 winner

Quarter-finals to be played on Tuesday, July 25, and Wednesday, July 26.

1st Semi-final to be played on Saturday, August 12;
2nd Semi-final to be played on Sunday, August 13.

Final to be played on Saturday, August 26, at Lord's.

†MINOR COUNTIES CHAMPIONSHIP, 2000

Unless otherwise indicated, all matches are of two days' duration.

MAY

21–Berks v Wales (Hungerford); Cumberland v Herts (Barrow); Herefordshire v Dorset (Colwall); Lincs v Staffs (Bourne); Salop v Oxon (Shrewsbury).

23–Cheshire v Oxon (Alderley Edge); Northumberland v Herts (Jesmond).

28–Berks v Herefordshire (Finchampstead); Devon v Dorset (Torquay); Lincs v Beds (Sleaford); Wilts v Wales (Westbury).

31–Lincs v Northumberland (Sleaford).

JUNE

4–Beds v Northumberland (Flitwick); Salop v Wilts (Wellington).

5–Cumberland v Norfolk (Netherfield).

6–Cambs v Northumberland (Wisbech).

7–Staffs v Norfolk (Stone).

11–Beds v Cumberland (Bedford); Dorset v Salop (Weymouth); Oxon v Wales (Banbury CC); Wilts v Berks (Warminster).

12–Cornwall v Cheshire (Truro).

13–Staffs v Bucks (Cannock).

14–Cambs v Suffolk (Saffron Walden); Devon v Cheshire (Bovey Tracey).

25–Herefordshire v Devon (Kington).

28–Cambs v Staffs (March).

JULY

2–Berks v Cornwall (Hurst CC); Bucks v Norfolk (Beaconsfield); Herts v Suffolk (Long Marston); Lincs v Cumberland (Lincoln Lindum); Wales v Salop (Colwyn Bay).

4–Cambs v Cumberland (Cambridge); Oxon v Cornwall (Oxford).

9–Northumberland v Staffs (S. Northumberland).

11–Cumberland v Staffs (Askam).

12–Cambs v Bucks (Cambridge).

16–Cheshire v Herefordshire (Cheadle Hulme); Cornwall v Dorset (Penzance); Herts v Bucks (Bishop's Stortford); Lincs v Cambs (Grantham); Suffolk v Beds (Ipswich School); Wilts v Oxon (Marlborough).

23–Bucks v Beds (Marlow); Dorset v Berks (Bournemouth); Norfolk v Lincs (Lakenham); Oxon v Devon (Christ Church, Oxford); Salop v Herefordshire (Whitchurch); Suffolk v Northumberland (Ransomes, Ipswich); Wales v Cornwall (Neath); Wilts v Cheshire (South Wilts CC).

24–Staffs v Herts (Brewood).

25–Berks v Devon (Falkland CC); Dorset v

Cheshire (Bournemouth); Herefordshire v Cornwall (Dales, Leominster); Norfolk v Northumberland (Lakenham); Suffolk v Lincs (Ransomes, Ipswich).

30–Beds v Herts (Dunstable); Cheshire v Wales (Oxton); Devon v Salop (Budleigh Salterton); Dorset v Oxon (Bournemouth); Herefordshire v Wilts (Luctonians).

31–Cumberland v Suffolk (Millom); Norfolk v Cambridgeshire (Lakenham).

AUGUST

1–Cornwall v Salop (Cambourne).

2–Norfolk v Herts (Lakenham); Staffs v Suffolk (Leek).

6–Beds v Norfolk (Wardown Park); Bucks v Suffolk (Milton Keynes); Devon v Wilts (Exmouth); Herts v Wilts (Radlett); Oxon v Herefordshire (Thame); Wales v Dorset (Ynysygerwn).

13–Beds v Cambs (Southill Park); Cheshire v Berks (Neston); Cornwall v Wilts (Falmouth); Northumberland v Bucks (Jesmond); Wales v Devon (Pontarddulais).

15–Cumberland v Bucks (Carlisle); Salop v Berks (Bridgnorth).

20–Berks v Oxon (Reading CC); Bucks v Lincs (High Wycombe); Cheshire v Salop (Bowdon); Cornwall v Devon (St Austell); Herefordshire v Wales (Brockhampton); Herts v Cambs (Stevenage); Northumberland v Cumberland (Jesmond); Staffs v Beds (Walsall); Suffolk v Norfolk (Bury St Edmunds); Wilts v Dorset (Corsham).

SEPTEMBER

10–Final (3 days).

†ECB 38-COUNTY COMPETITION

All matches are of one day's duration.

Teams are County Board XIs and do not include first-class counties.

MAY

14–Salop v Herefordshire (St Georges); Somerset v Wilts (Bristol Optimists); Suffolk v Hunts (Mildenhall).

21–Cheshire v Derbys (New Brighton); Norfolk v Beds (Lakenham).

25–Yorks v Lancs (Elland CC).

28–Salop v Worcs (Oswestry); Somerset v Cornwall (North Perrott); Staffs v Notts (Porthill Park).

30–Cumberland v Lancs (Keswick).

JUNE

4—Berks v Sussex (Thatcham); Bucks v Kent (Wormsley); Derbys v Notts (Heanor Town); Devon v Somerset (Sidmouth); Middx v Herts (Finchley); Warwicks v Wales (Knowle & Dorridge).

7—Surrey v Oxon (Imber Court).

11—Cambs v Norfolk (Wisbech); Cornwall v Devon (St Just); Derbys v Staffs (Heanor Town); Essex v Hunts (Chelmsford); Herts v Suffolk (Hertford); Northants v Leics (Raunds); Northumberland v Yorks (Jesmond); Notts v Lincs (Boots Ground, Nottingham); Worcs v Herefordshire (Halesowen).

15—Cumberland v Yorks (Penrith); Middx v Essex (Richmond).

18—Cambs v Beds (March); Durham v Northumberland (Stockton); Glos v Cornwall (Bristol University); Hants v Dorset (Burridge); Herefordshire v Wales (Luctonians); Leics v Norfolk (Oakham School); Staffs v Lincs (Longton); Sussex v Berks (Horsham); Warwicks v Salop (Stratford-upon-Avon); Wilts v Devon (Corsham).

25—Beds v Leics (Bedford Town); Berks v Dorset (Finchampstead); Herts v Essex (Hertford); Kent v Surrey (Ashford); Lincs v Cheshire (Grimsby Town); Norfolk v Northants (Lakenham); Northumberland v Cumberland (Tynemouth); Oxon v Bucks (Christ Church, Oxford); Suffolk v Middx (Copdock); Sussex v Hants (Stirlands); Wales v Worcs (Ynysygerwn); Wilts v Glos (Swindon).

26—Lancs v Durham (Haslingden).

27—Yorks v Durham (Stamford Bridge).

28—Surrey v Bucks (Banstead).

JULY

2—Cheshire v Staffs (Nantwich); Dorset v Hants (Bournemouth); Glos v Somerset (Bristol University); Hunts v Middx (Kimbolton School); Lancs v Northumberland (Ormskirk); Northants v Cambs (Raunds); Oxon v Kent (Challow & Childrey).

4—Worcs v Warwicks (Kidderminster).

9—Beds v Northants (Dunstable); Bucks v Surrey (Aylesbury); Cornwall v Wilts (Helston); Devon v Glos (Instow); Dorset v Sussex (Weymouth); Durham v Cumberland (Ropery Lane, Chester-le-Street); Essex v Suffolk (Chelmsford); Hants v Berks (Liphook); Herefordshire v Warwicks (Brockhampton); Hunts v Herts (Godmanchester); Leics v Cambs (Ratcliffe College); Lincs v Derbys (Cleethorpes); Notts v Cheshire (Boots Ground, Nottingham); Wales v Salop (St Fagans).

11—Kent v Oxon (The Mote).

Quarter-finals to be played on July 19.

Semi-finals to be played on August 10.

Final to be played on August 30 at Lord's.

Some venues were subject to confirmation when Wisden *went to press.*

†SECOND ELEVEN CHAMPIONSHIP, 2000

Unless otherwise stated, all matches are of three days' duration

APRIL

19—Kent v Lancs (Ashford); Northants v Notts (Milton Keynes).

25—Glam v Glos (Cardiff; 4 days); Lancs v Worcs (Manchester; 4 days).

26—Durham v Yorks (Chester-le-Street); Northants v Middx (Northampton); Surrey v Notts (The Oval); Sussex v Derbys (Hove).

MAY

2—Notts v Durham (Nottingham; 4 days); Somerset v Kent (Taunton; 4 days); Warwicks v Hants (Moseley; 4 days).

3—Derbys v Northants (Derby); Sussex v Yorks (Horsham); Worcs v Glam (Worcester).

9—Glos v Somerset (Bristol; 4 days); Lancs v Yorks (Crosby; 4 days).

10–Notts v Derbys (Worksop); Sussex v Worcs (Stirlands).

15–Kent v Leics (Canterbury; 4 days).

16–Middx v Notts (Ealing; 4 days); Northants v Warwicks (Northampton; 4 days); Yorks v Durham (Scarborough; 4 days).

17–Essex v Glos (Saffron Walden); Hants v Lancs (Southampton).

22–Durham v Derbys (Darlington; 4 days).

23–Sussex v Somerset (Hove; 4 days); Warwicks v Yorks (Studley CC; 4 days); Worcs v Hants (Kidderminster; 4 days).

24–Kent v Glam (Ashford); Lancs v Middx (Blackpool); Leics v Essex (Hinckley); Surrey v Northants (Cheam).

29–Glos v Worcs (Bristol).

30–Derbys v Lancs (Dunstall; 4 days); Glam v Middx (Ammanford); Kent v Hants (Maidstone; 4 days); Northants v Durham (Northampton; 4 days).

31–Somerset v Yorks (Taunton).

JUNE

6–Hants v Sussex (West End, Southampton; 4 days); Leics v Glos (Leicester; 4 days); Surrey v Middx (The Oval; 4 days).

7–Derbys v Somerset (Cheadle); Essex v Lancs (Coggeshall); Glam v Durham (Pontarddulais); Worcs v Notts (Worcester).

12–Yorks v Leics (Harrogate).

13–Derbys v Warwicks (Derby); Durham v Worcs (Chester-le-Street; 4 days); Essex v Kent (Chelmsford; 4 days); Hants v Surrey (Finchampstead); Notts v Glos (Nottingham; 4 days); Somerset v Glam (Taunton; 4 days).

20–Glos v Lancs (Bristol; 4 days); Hants v Glam (West End, Southampton; 4 days); Kent v Notts (Canterbury; 4 days); Middx v Essex (Harrow; 4 days); Yorks v Northants (Todmorden; 4 days).

21–Leics v Worcs (Hinckley); Surrey v Durham (The Oval); Warwicks v Sussex (Knowle & Dorridge).

JULY

11–Essex v Surrey (Chelmsford; 4 days).

12–Glam v Derbys (Cardiff) ; Northants v Glos (Stowe School); Notts v Warwicks (Nottingham HS).

18–Leics v Lancs (Hinckley); Middx v Derbys (Vine Lane, Uxbridge; 4 days); Northants v Hants (Northampton; 4 days).

19–Durham v Sussex (Stockton); Glos v Warwicks (Bristol); Kent v Yorks (Canterbury); Somerset v Notts (Taunton); Worcs v Essex (Worcester).

24–Leics v Sussex (Oakham School; 4 days).

25–Derbys v Essex (Heanor Town; 4 days); Kent v Northants (Maidstone; 4 days); Middx v Yorks (Vine Lane, Uxbridge; 4 days); Warwicks v Worcs (Stratford-upon-Avon; 4 days).

26–Glam v Surrey (Panteg); Lancs v Somerset (Middleton); Notts v Hants (Worksop College).

31–Essex v Yorks (Chelmsford; 4 days); Leics v Derbys (Hinckley; 4 days).

AUGUST

1–Durham v Kent (Chester-le-Street); Glam v Warwicks (Usk; 4 days); Notts v Surrey (Unity Casuals, Nottingham; 4 days); Worcs v Northants (Barnt Green; 4 days).

2–Glos v Sussex (Bristol); Somerset v Hants (Clevedon).

9–Essex v Hants (Halstead); Lancs v Glam (Southport); Middx v Worcs (Harrow); Somerset v Northants (Taunton); Surrey v Leics (Wimbledon CC); Warwicks v Kent (Walmley CC); Yorks v Derbys (Rotherham).

14–Notts v Leics (Caythorpe; 4 days).

15–Durham v Lancs (Chester-le-Street; 4 days); Glos v Middx (Bristol; 4 days); Sussex v Kent (Hastings; 4 days); Worcs v Somerset (Kidderminster; 4 days).

16–Northants v Essex (Dunstable); Warwicks v Surrey (Leamington).

22–Derbys v Notts (Heanor Town; 4 days); Hants v Glos (West End, Southampton; 4 days); Lancs v Warwicks (Manchester; 4 days); Middx v Kent (Ealing); Somerset v Surrey (North Perrott; 4 days).

23–Durham v Essex (Gateshead Fell); Northants v Leics (Milton Keynes); Yorks v Glam (Harrogate).

29–Glam v Leics (Cardiff; 4 days); Surrey v Sussex (Oxted; 4 days); Warwicks v Essex (Kenilworth Wardens; 4 days); Yorks v Notts (Middlesbrough; 4 days).

30–Glos v Durham (Bristol); Hants v Derbys (Bournemouth); Lancs v Northants (Lytham).

SEPTEMBER

6–Derbys v Glos (Derby); Essex v Somerset (Wickford); Kent v Worcs (Ashford); Lancs v Surrey (Blackpool); Middx v Warwicks (Southgate); Notts v Northants (Boots Ground, Nottingham); Yorks v Hants (Leeds).

12–Surrey v Glam (The Oval; 4 days); Sussex v Middx (Hove; 4 days).

Some venues were subject to confirmation when Wisden *went to press.*

†AON TROPHY, 2000

All matches are of one day's duration.

MAY

8–Derbys v Northants (Duffield).

11–Minor Counties v Glam (Swindon).

15–Hants v Somerset (Southampton).

19–Minor Counties v Leics (Dunstable).

22–Worcs v Yorks (Worcester).

25–Minor Counties v Notts (Sleaford).

26–Notts v Minor Counties (Farnsfield).

30–Warwicks v Yorks (Leamington).

JUNE

1–Warwicks v Worcs (West Bromwich Dartmouth).

2–Glam v Minor Counties (Cardiff).

5–Leics v Glos (Leicester); Northants v Derbys (Stowe School).

12–Essex v Kent (Chelmsford); Hants v MCC Young Cricketers (Southampton); Middx v Northants (Ealing); Notts v Glos (Worksop College).

19–Middx v Essex (Harrow); Somerset v MCC Young Cricketers (Taunton).

26–Essex v Northants (Billericay); Glos v Glam (Bristol); Leics v Notts (Hinckley); Surrey v Somerset (The Oval); Sussex v Hants (Middleton).

27–Kent v Northants (Canterbury); Notts v Leics (Welbeck Colliery); Yorks v Worcs (York).

28–Durham v Warwicks (Sunderland); Lancs v Yorks (Nelson); Leics v Glam (Hinckley); Surrey v Hants (The Oval).

29–Derbys v Middx (Derby); Lancs v Durham (Bolton); Minor Counties v Glos (Banbury); Northants v Kent (Northampton); Notts v Glam (Collingham).

30–Derbys v Kent (Derby); Leics v Minor Counties (Hinckley); Northants v Middx (Isham); Somerset v Hants (Taunton); Worcs v Warwicks (Worcester); Yorks v Durham (Bingley).

JULY

3–Glam v Glos (Cardiff); Hants v Sussex (West End, Southampton); Middx v Kent (Richmond); Northants v Essex (Northampton); Somerset v Surrey (Taunton); Warwicks v Durham (Birmingham); Worcs v Lancs (Worcester).

4–Glam v Notts (Newport); Lancs v Warwicks (Manchester University); Somerset v Sussex (Taunton); Worcs v Durham (Ombersley).

5–Glos v Notts (Bristol University); Hants v Surrey (Southampton); Kent v Derbys (Folkestone).

6–Durham v Yorks (Hartlepool); Glos v Leics (Bristol University); Kent v Essex (Folkestone); MCC Young Cricketers v Somerset (Uxbridge CC); Middx v Derbys (Finchley); Sussex v Surrey (Hove); Warwicks v Lancs (Coventry & North Warwicks).

7–Durham v Worcs (South Shields); Essex v Derbys (Saffron Walden); Glam v Leics (Ebbw Vale); MCC Young Cricketers v Surrey (Uxbridge CC); Sussex v Somerset (Hove).

10–Durham v Lancs (Seaton Carew); Essex v Middx (Old Brentwoods); MCC Young Cricketers v Hants (Uxbridge CC); Surrey v Sussex (Sutton); Yorks v Warwicks (Harrogate).

11–MCC Young Cricketers v Sussex (Uxbridge CC); Yorks v Lancs (Castleford).

13–Kent v Middx (Canterbury); Lancs v Worcs (Radcliffe).

14–Sussex v MCC Young Cricketers (Hastings).

17–Surrey v MCC Young Cricketers (The Oval).

24–Derbys v Essex (Repton School).

28–Glos v Minor Counties (Bristol).

Semi-finals to be played on August 7 (reserve day August 8).

Final to be played on September 4 (reserve day September 5).

Some venues were subject to confirmation when Wisden *went to press.*

†WOMEN'S CRICKET, 2000

JUNE

20	Chelmsford	ENGLAND v SOUTH AFRICA (1st one-day international)
22	Nottingham	ENGLAND v SOUTH AFRICA (2nd one-day international)
25	Canterbury	ENGLAND v SOUTH AFRICA (3rd one-day international)
28	Taunton	ENGLAND v SOUTH AFRICA (4th one-day international)

JULY

1	Worcester	ENGLAND v SOUTH AFRICA (5th one-day international)
29	Cambridge	County Championship (5 days)

AUGUST

13	Colwall	Cricket Week (6 days)

SEPTEMBER

2	Milton Keynes	Premier League final
9	Sheffield	National Club Knockout/Plate finals

INTERNATIONAL SCHEDULES

ENGLAND'S INTERNATIONAL SCHEDULE

Home

2001	Tests and one-day internationals v Australia and Pakistan
2002	Tests and one-day internationals v India and Sri Lanka
2003	Tests and one-day internationals v South Africa and New Zealand
2004	Tests and one-day internationals v Pakistan and Zimbabwe
2005	Tests and one-day internationals v Australia

Away

2000-01	Tests and one-day internationals in Pakistan and Sri Lanka
2001-02	Tests and one-day internationals in India and New Zealand
2002-03	Tests and one-day internationals in Australia
	WORLD CUP in South Africa
2003-04	Tests and one-day internationals in the West Indies
2004-05	Tests and one-day internationals in South Africa

All tours subject to confirmation.

INTERNATIONAL SCHEDULE, 2000-01

The following tours were arranged as at November 1999.

2000

August	South Africans to Sri Lanka
October	New Zealanders to Zimbabwe
October–November	Australians to Pakistan
October–December	England to Pakistan
November	Zimbabweans to India
November–December	New Zealanders to South Africa
November–January 2001	West Indians to Australia
December–January 2001	Pakistanis to South Africa
December–January 2001	Sri Lankans to Australia
December–January 2001	Zimbabweans to Australia

2001

January	Sri Lankans to New Zealand
January–February	Indians to Pakistan
January–March	England to Sri Lanka
February–March	Australians to India
February–March	Pakistanis to New Zealand
February–April	South Africans to West Indies
May–August	Australians to England

All tours subject to confirmation.